To be ignorant of what happened before you were born is to be ever a child. For what is man's lifetime unless the memory of past events is woven with those of earlier times?

Cicero

It is the true office of history to represent the events themselves, together with the counsels, and to leave the observations and conclusions thereupon to the liberty and faculty of every man's judgment.

Francis Bacon

If men could learn from history, what lessons it might teach us!

Samuel Taylor Coleridge

History, by apprising [people] of the past, will enable them to judge of the future; it will avail them of the experience of other times and other nations.

Thomas Jefferson

History with its flickering lamp stumbles along the trail of the past, trying to reconstruct its scenes, to revive its echoes, and kindle . . . the passion of former days . . . .

Winston Churchill

History is all those things—waves, tides and currents—and like the sea, no matter how tranquil the surface, it is never still. A sequence of events is like a series of waves . . . and the trick . . . is to tell which crest is a surge of the tide and which a mere accident of the wind.

Theodore H. White

PEOPLE AND OUR WORLD

A Study of World History

ALLAN O. KOWNSLAR
Professor of History
Trinity University

TERRY L. SMART
Professor of History
Trinity University

HOLT, RINEHART AND WINSTON, PUBLISHERS
New York • Toronto • Mexico City • London • Sydney • Tokyo

ALLAN O. KOWNSLAR is Professor of History at Trinity University in San Antonio, Texas. He was formerly a Research Historian at Carnegie-Mellon University, where he received his doctorate in history. Dr. Kownslar has also taught social studies on the junior and senior high school levels in San Antonio, Texas, Amherst, Massachusetts, and Pittsburgh, Pennsylvania. He has worked as a consultant in social studies teaching and curriculum development with teachers throughout the nation. Dr. Kownslar has written several books and numerous articles in professional journals. In 1974, Dr. Kownslar served as editor of *Teaching American History: The Quest for Relevancy,* the 44th Yearbook of the National Council for the Social Studies, and in 1979 wrote *Teaching about Social Issues in American History* for the Social Science Education Consortium. He has worked as a consultant in social studies teaching and curriculum development with teachers throughout the nation.

TERRY L. SMART is Professor of History and Chairman of the Department of History at Trinity University in San Antonio, Texas. He was formerly a world history teacher and social studies curriculum writer in the Houston, Texas, schools. Dr. Smart, who is a specialist in Asian and European History, received his doctorate in history from the University of Kansas. He has served as a consultant in social studies curriculum development to numerous private schools and public school systems.

Art and photo credits begin on page 728.
Acknowledgments for previously copyrighted matter appear with the materials used.

Any material on evolution presented in this textbook is presented as theory rather than fact.

ISBN 0-03-063714-7
456 039 9876543

Consultants

Joseph K. Adjaye
University of Illinois at Urbana-Champaign

Joseph D. Baca
New Mexico Department of Education

Theodore S. Hamerow
University of Wisconsin at Madison

Stephen L. Lamy
University of Denver

Douglas R. McManis
Geographical Review

Gordon D. Newby
North Carolina State University

Jane Giegengack White
Hunter College

Table of Contents

unit 2 The World of the Ancient Far East

unit 3 The World of Ancient Greece and Rome 110

unit 4 The World of West Europe

unit 5 The World of East Europe and Islam

234

unit 7 The New World

unit 9 The World of Nationalism 432

unit 10 Your World

Maps

Building Your Geography Skills

Geography is mainly the study of particular places on the surface of the earth. In their studies, **geographers** attempt to find out all the characteristics that make one place different from other places. Most importantly, geographers try to learn how these characteristics are related.

For example, imagine that you are a geographer studying modern Iraq, a country in the Middle East. Where would you begin your study? First, you might want to look at the area's physical environment. Physical environment includes the formation of the land: the mountains, valleys, plateaus, and so on. You would also look at the climate. Is the area under study a desert area? Second, you would want to know something about the cultural characteristics of the area. Some of the questions to investigate here would include: Where do the people live? What kinds of jobs do they work at? What do they eat? What do they believe in? What kinds of things are important to them? Finally, and most important, you would find out how all the physical and cultural characteristics of the area are related to each other. How do they influence one another? How do they come together to make this area different from other areas in the world?

When you study geography in relation to world history, you will be concerned mainly with studying how people in history have used, shaped, and lived in their physical environment. For example, you will study the physical environment of the valleys of the Tigris and Euphrates, the Nile, the Indus, and the Yellow rivers. You will find out how each of the peoples living in these areas worked to build a civilization. And you may consider questions like these: How did they use the available resources to improve their lives? How did these peoples learn to live in their surroundings? How did they change the environment so they could live in it without constant concern for survival?

RELATING GEOGRAPHY TO A STUDY OF WORLD HISTORY

In studying the geography of a particular place in relation to world history, try to keep the following ideas or concepts in mind. You will find it helpful to form your questions about geography around the following topics:

1. The earth is divided into many different regions. A region is an area of any size that has physical and cultural characteristics in common.

2. Physical characteristics of a region include the climate, land forms, and resources.

xvi

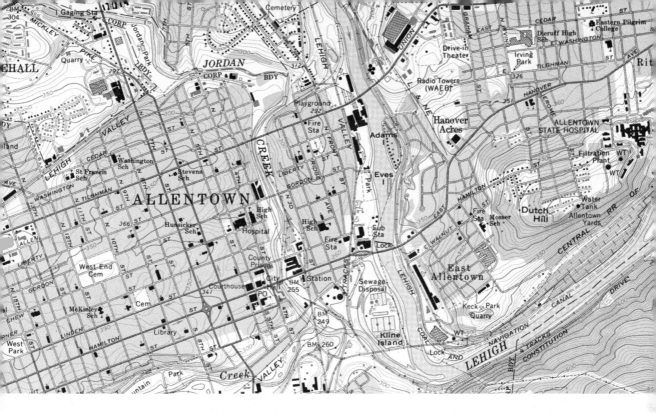

How is this map of Allentown, Pennsylvania, similar to maps of your community?

3. Cultural characteristics of a region include the number of people living there, their religious beliefs, technical skills, types of food, and quality of life.
4. A region's physical and cultural characteristics are related to one another. These physical and cultural characteristics influence each other.
5. People in regions interact with each other and are interdependent. Interdependence means the exchange of ideas, goods, or services by two or more groups of people so that the needs of everyone are satisfied.
6. Political and economic relations between areas are always undergoing change. Your study of world history will view relations between countries and people in given regions and how these have strengthened or weakened over the years. For example, the pres-

ent-day countries of the Middle East were once under the political and economic control of the industrialized nations of Europe. Today, the now independent Middle Eastern countries strongly influence the economies of those same European nations through their control of the world's oil supply.

METHODS OF STUDYING GEOGRAPHY

Geographers use many of the methods used by other social scientists in studying and identifying regions on the earth. Geographers, like historians, archaeologists, and sociologists, gather information, classify it, measure it, then form a hypothesis, or guess, about the information.

xvii

The process of gathering information is carried out in a variety of ways. One way is by actually traveling to a place and observing its physical and cultural characteristics. This is called field observation. For example, geographers might study the rise and fall of a river's water level to compare it with some observation made by another geographer years and maybe centuries before. Geographers would also compare the location and appearance of a present-day city with those of the same city as it existed in the past. To make these comparisons geographers, like historians, use written records, descriptions, drawings, paintings, photographs, and maps from the past.

Once this kind of information is gathered, some geographers feed it into a computer to be analyzed. This is called statistical analysis. By doing such an analysis, a geographer can get results or answers that are mathematically exact. Finally, one of the most common but important tools used by geographers to collect information on a place is the study of maps or the making of a map.

Using Maps and Globes We can best learn about the geography of the earth by observing it from a distance, from the outer regions of space. Pictures taken of the earth from spacecraft cameras have provided geographers with valuable information about the changing character of the earth's surface. An example of such a picture is found on page 7. Then this information is transferred to maps and globes. These maps and globes are the tools most often used by geographers.

The Globe A globe is a scaled down model of the earth in miniature. If you

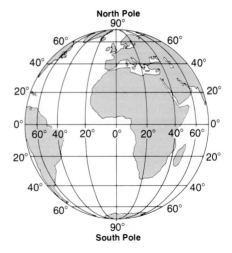

Globe with Full Grid

look at a globe, you will notice the variety of information shown: oceans, continents, rivers, islands, mountains, deserts, cities, and so on. You will also notice the network of lines covering the globe. Of course, the earth itself has no such series of lines. But on the globe, these lines serve a special purpose. They were devised by geographers and map makers to help you locate places on the earth's surface and to help in the construction of maps.

Latitude and Longitude Lines drawn on the globe from the North Pole to the South Pole are called **meridians.** All meridians are of equal length and converge at the poles. The prime meridian is used as a starting line for measuring **meridians of longitude**—distances east and west of the prime meridian. The **prime meridian** is marked 0° and runs through Greenwich (GREN-ich), England, a suburb of the city of London. (Refer to the maps on page xix as you read.)

Distances east and west of the prime meridian are called east and west longitude. Longitude is measured

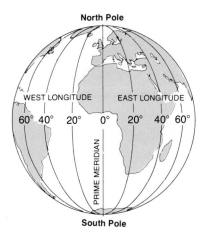

Meridians of Longitude

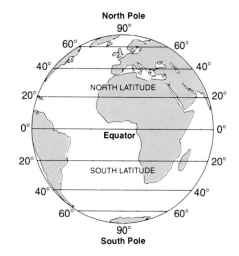

Parallels of Latitude

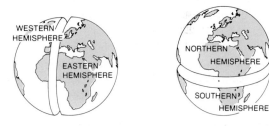

The Hemispheres

in degrees (°), minutes ('), and seconds ("). There are 180° of east longitude and 180° of west longitude. Any place in the world 10 degrees east of the prime meridian is said to be 10 degrees east longitude (10°E). Any place that is 20° degrees west of the prime meridian is said to be 20 degrees west longitude (20°W).

The lines drawn east to west parallel to the equator are called **parallels of latitude.** All parallels of latitude circle the earth although their circumferences (distances around the earth) become smaller toward the poles. The **equator** is the largest circle and is used as a starting line for measuring parallels of latitude—distances north and south of the equator. The equator is marked 0°. The distances north and south of the equator are north and south latitude. Latitude is also measured in degrees (°), minutes ('), and seconds ("). From the equator to either the North or South Pole is 90 degrees. The North Pole is 90 degrees north latitude. Any place in the world 10 degrees north of the equator is 10 degrees north latitude (10°N). Any place in the world 30 degrees south of the equator is 30 degrees south latitude (30°S).

All parallels of latitude and meridians of longitude intersect at right angles except at the poles. By using the intersections of latitude and longitude, you can locate any place on the earth. New York City, for example, is 41°N latitude and 74°W longitude.

The earth may be divided into hemispheres or halves along any meridian of longitude. The only parallel of latitude that cuts the earth in half is the equator. (See the diagrams above.)

MAPS

Globes are the most realistic representation of the earth available to us. They show correct distance, correct direction, correct shape, and correct area.

But there are some disadvantages to using globes. For instance, they take up a lot of space. Can you imagine carrying a globe around with you in order to find directions to wherever you wanted to go? Also, the size of the globe would have to be increased in order to show all the information you would need.

Maps were developed as a convenient way to show information about the earth. They are also capable of showing the entire surface of the earth at one time. Maps, unlike globes, are easy to carry and store. You probably have more maps than you realize. You may find four or five in the glove compartment of your family car. You probably have a map showing bus and train routes in your city or town.

For all their convenience, maps have some serious drawbacks. Geographers and map makers tried to transfer the information on a globe to a flat surface. But there were real problems in doing this. The curved surface of the earth cannot be transferred to a flat piece of paper. Imagine cutting an orange in half and removing the inside. You can't make the skin of the orange lie down flat without cutting it again. In order to show one type of information accurately on a flat surface, other types of information have to be distorted. For example, in showing direction correctly on a map, map makers could not show distance correctly. The solution they arrived at was to make up maps for different uses.

Map Projections   Imagine a glass globe with a lightbulb inside it. Map makers project the outlines of land areas, parallels, and meridians from the globe onto a cylinder-shaped piece of paper. Then they cut the cylinder and roll it out flat. The lines of longi-

tude and latitude of the earth are now on paper. Map makers are ready to plot locations and make a map of the earth. This method of flattening a globe onto a piece of paper is called a projection. Using a glass globe is only one way of making a map projection and there are many different kinds of projections. Some of the different projections are described and illustrated in the following pages. How many of these projections do you recognize? How many are new to you?

Mercator Projection   The Mercator projection is a modification of a cylindrical projection. The shapes of the land areas are accurate closest to the equator. Near the Poles, however, the land areas become distorted. For example, although South America is in reality ten times larger than Greenland, on a Mercator map, Greenland seems larger. Despite distortions in land size, this projection shows all directions correctly. The Mercator projection was often used by ship's navigators in the sixteenth century because no other projection shows directions as accurately.

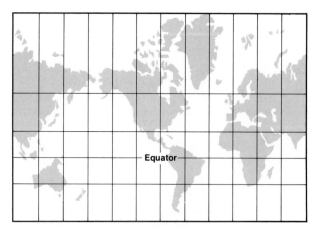

Mercator Projection

Azimuthal Equidistant Projection or Polar Projection   Lines of latitude and longitude are projected from the Poles on this type of map. The relationships of the land area around the North Pole are accurately shown. Land areas away from the Poles are increasingly distorted. Polar projections are used extensively by airplane pilots. The straight lines that radiate from the center of the map are called great circle routes. Distances for air travel can be easily measured because all great circles are straight lines on this projection.

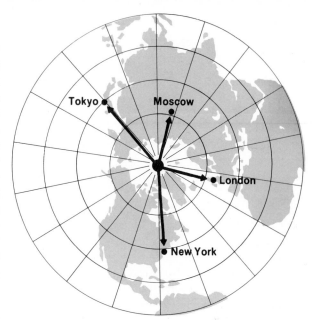

Polar Airline Routes imposed on a Polar Projection

Conic Projections   A conic projection is made by placing a paper cone over the globe. Lines of longitude are lines radiating down from the peak of the cone. Lines of latitude are circles. The projection shown here is a modified conic projection with one standard parallel, the one where the cone touches the globe. This is the area of least distortion. Conic projections are good for showing areas the size of the United States, the Soviet Union, or Europe.

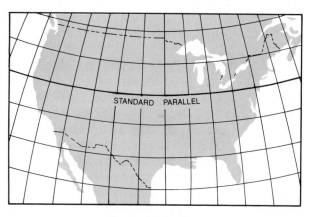

Conic Projection

Interrupted Projection   There is a central meridian for each continent in this projection. The concept used here is that of taking the skin of an orange and cutting sections of it away so it can be flattened out. The interruptions, or cuts, in this map have been made in the oceans in order to keep the shape and size of the land areas as accurate as possible.

Because there are distortions in every map projection, always refer to a globe as a way of correcting these distortions.

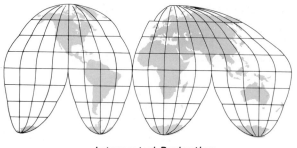

Interrupted Projection

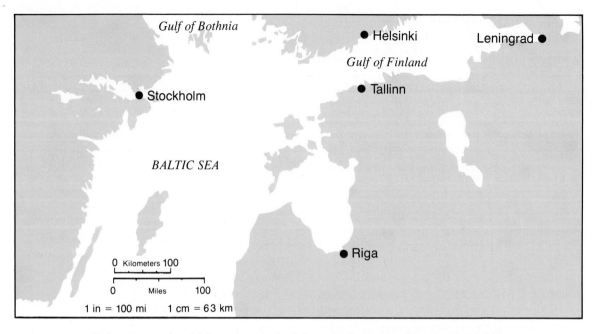

Using the scale of kilometers (miles), how far is it from Riga to Helsinki?

Scale on Maps and Globes   Scale on a map or globe tells us what distance on the earth is represented by a certain distance on the map or globe. The scale of kilometers or miles may be a graph or it may state in words that one centimeter or inch equals a certain number of kilometers or miles. In an atlas, a world map may show a scale of 1:350,000,000 centimeters (140,000,000 miles). This means that one centimeter represents 350 million centimeters or one inch represents 140 million inches on the actual surface of the earth. On a 30 centimeter (12 inch) globe, the scale is usually 1:104,544,000 or 1,056 kilometers to the centimeter (1:41,817,600 or about 660 miles to the inch).

Symbols on Maps   Symbols represent certain information on a map. For the sake of saving space, it is best to devise a picture or symbol that stands for the information you want to convey on the map. While there are no standard symbols for all maps, there are some that are used very often. In order to be sure that people reading a map know what they are looking at, map makers include a legend as part of the map. A legend is a sectioned-off piece of the map that shows the symbols used and explains what each stands for. Examples of some symbols are included here. How many do you recognize? What conclusions can you draw about Allentown from the map on page xvii? Look through the other maps in the book. What symbols are used for battle sites, invasions, trade routes, gold fields, and other important historical sites and routes?

MAP SYMBOLS

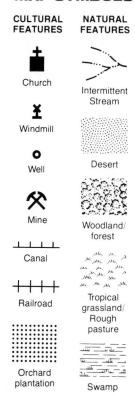

CULTURAL FEATURES

Church

Windmill

Well

Mine

Canal

Railroad

Orchard plantation

NATURAL FEATURES

Intermittent Stream

Desert

Woodland/ forest

Tropical grassland/ Rough pasture

Swamp

SECTION REVIEW

1. In your own words, briefly identify geographers, meridians, prime meridian, parallels of latitude, equator.
2. Why is it important to study the geography of an area along with its history?
3. Using the Atlas, locate by means of latitude and longitude coordinates each of the following: Dallas, Texas; Adelaide, Australia; Quito, Ecuador; Calcutta, India; Munich, West Germany; Astrakhan, U.S.S.R.; Nairobi, Kenya.
4. Using the Atlas, find the distance in kilometers and miles between each of the following cities: Atlanta, Georgia and Toronto, Canada; Recife, Brazil and Lima, Peru; Oslo, Norway and Copenhagen, Denmark.
5. Using the elevation guide below, list the highest and lowest elevations shown. Then turn to the Atlas map that shows the area in which you live and list its elevation.

Color in Maps   The maps in the Atlas that follows use color to indicate the various elevations on the earth. Areas near sea level may be green, plains areas may be yellow, and mountains may be reddish brown. Color is also used to show the different kinds of vegetation found on the earth. On a political map, the choice of color is left up to the individual map maker. The map maker explains in a legend what information is indicated by certain colors on the map. In this book, colors are sometimes used to show the extent of empires, kingdoms, colonies, and other political units.

ELEVATION

Meters		Feet
Above 4,000		Above 13,120
2,000-4,000		6560-13,120
500-2,000		1640-6560
200-500		656-1640
0-200		0-656

xxiii

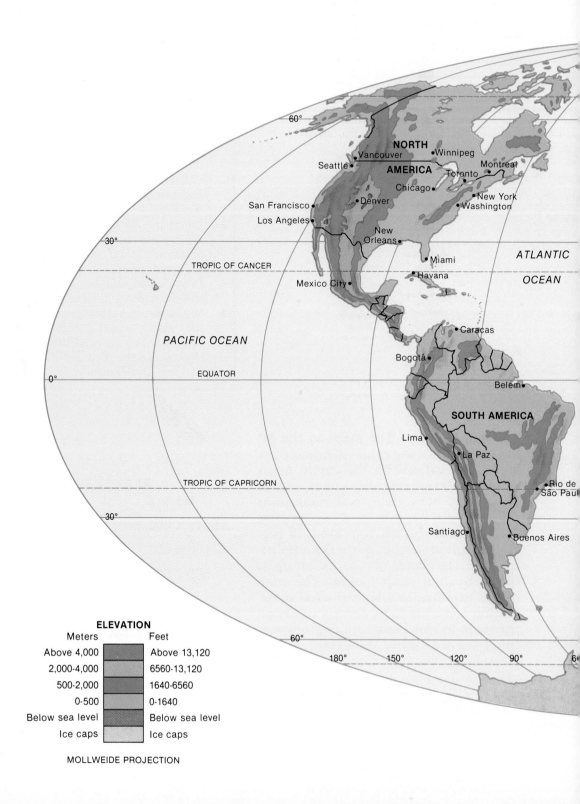

60°

NORTH
AMERICA

Vancouver •Winnipeg
Seattle • •Montreal
Toronto
Chicago•
Denver
San Francisco• •New York
•Washington
Los Angeles•

New
Orleans•

30°

TROPIC OF CANCER

•Miami

Mexico City•
•Havana

ATLANTIC

OCEAN

•Caracas

Bogotá•

PACIFIC OCEAN

•Belém

EQUATOR
0°

SOUTH AMERICA

Lima•

•La Paz

TROPIC OF CAPRICORN

•Rio de
São Pau

30°

Santiago•
•Buenos Aires

60°

180°   150°   120°   90°   6

ELEVATION

Meters		Feet
Above 4,000		Above 13,120
2,000-4,000		6560-13,120
500-2,000		1640-6560
0-500		0-1640
Below sea level		Below sea level
Ice caps		Ice caps

MOLLWEIDE PROJECTION

The World

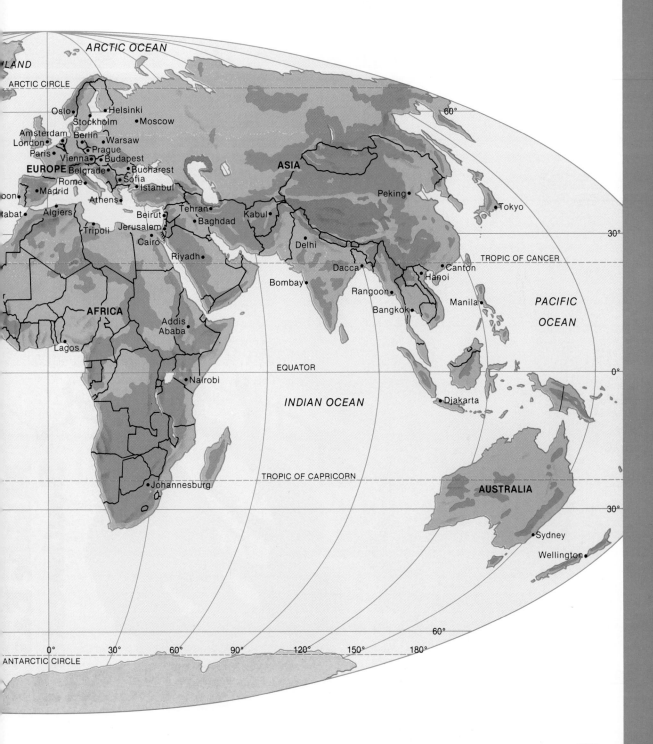

ARCTIC OCEAN

LAND

ARCTIC CIRCLE

Oslo • • Helsinki
Stockholm • • Moscow
Amsterdam Berlin
London • • • Warsaw
Paris • Prague
Vienna • • Budapest
EUROPE Belgrade Bucharest
Rome • Sofia
• Madrid Istanbul
oon • Athens •
abat • Algiers Tehran •
Tripoli Beirut • Baghdad
Jerusalem •
Cairo
Riyadh •

AFRICA
Addis
Ababa
Lagos •

ASIA

Peking •

Tokyo •

60°

30°

TROPIC OF CANCER

Delhi •
Bombay •
Dacca •
Canton •
Hanoi
Rangoon •
Bangkok •
Manila •

Kabul •

PACIFIC
OCEAN

Nairobi •

EQUATOR

INDIAN OCEAN

Djakarta •

0°

TROPIC OF CAPRICORN

AUSTRALIA

• Johannesburg

30°

Sydney •

Wellington •

0° 30° 60° 90° 120° 150° 180°

60°

ANTARCTIC CIRCLE

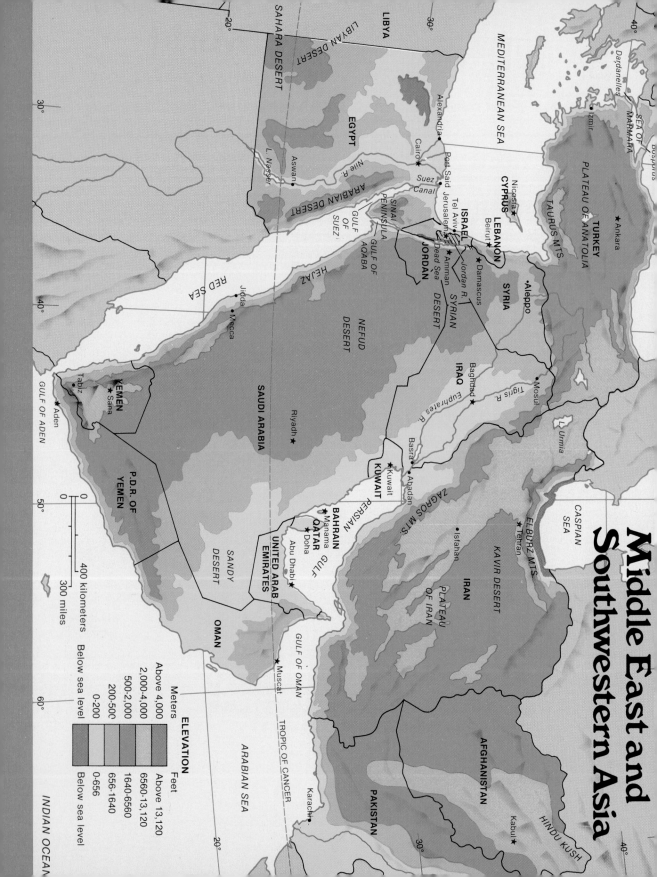

Middle East and Southwestern Asia

ELEVATION

Meters	Feet
Above 4,000	Above 13,120
2,000-4,000	6560-13,120
500-2,000	1640-6560
200-500	656-1640
0-200	0-656
Below sea level	Below sea level

0 400 kilometers
0 300 miles

INDIAN OCEAN

SAHARA DESERT

LIBYA

LIBYAN DESERT

EGYPT

MEDITERRANEAN SEA

SEA OF MARMARA

Dardanelles

Bosporus

Izmir

TURKEY

PLATEAU OF ANATOLIA

Ankara

TAURUS MTS.

CYPRUS

Nicosia

LEBANON

Beirut

Aleppo

SYRIA

Damascus

Alexandria

Cairo

Port Said

Suez Canal

Nile R.

ARABIAN DESERT

SINAI PENINSULA

GULF OF SUEZ

ISRAEL

Tel Aviv

Jerusalem

JORDAN

Amman

Jordan R.

Dead Sea

GULF OF AQABA

L. Nasser

Aswan

RED SEA

HEJAZ

Jidda

Mecca

NEFUD DESERT

SYRIAN DESERT

IRAQ

Baghdad

Mosul

L. Urmia

Tabriz

Euphrates R.

Tigris R.

SAUDI ARABIA

Riyadh

Basra

Abadan

KUWAIT

Kuwait

ZAGROS MTS.

CASPIAN SEA

Tehran

ELBURZ MTS.

Isfahan

KAVIR DESERT

IRAN

PLATEAU OF IRAN

BAHRAIN

Manama

QATAR

Doha

PERSIAN GULF

Abu Dhabi

UNITED ARAB EMIRATES

SANDY DESERT

OMAN

GULF OF OMAN

Muscat

AFGHANISTAN

Kabul

HINDU KUSH

PAKISTAN

Karachi

YEMEN

Sana

P.D.R. OF YEMEN

Aden

GULF OF ADEN

ARABIAN SEA

TROPIC OF CANCER

Middle East and Southwestern Asia

20°

30°

40°

30°

40°

50°

60°

20°

30°

40°

20°

Far East

PACIFIC OCEAN

HOKKAIDO

SEA OF JAPAN

JAPAN
HONSHU
Tokyo
Yokohama
Osaka
Kyoto
SHIKOKU
Nagasaki
KYUSHU
RYUKYU ISLANDS

TROPIC OF CANCER

Harbin
MANCHURIA
Shenyang
GREAT KHINGA

NORTH KOREA
Pyongyang
SOUTH KOREA
Seoul
YELLOW SEA

Peking
Tientsin
INNER MONGOLIA

Nanking

Shanghai
EAST CHINA SEA

Taipei
TAIWAN
Formosa Strait

Canton
HONG KONG (G. B.)
MACAO (Port.)

Ulan Bator
PLATEAU OF MONGOLIA
MONGOLIA
GOBI DESERT

Yellow R.
Si R.

Wuhan
Yangtze R.

CHINA

HAINAN

PHILIPPINES
LUZON
Manila

MINDANAO

CELEBES SEA

CELEBES

PACIFIC OCEAN

PAPUA NEW GUINEA

IRIAN JAYA

MOLUCCAS

ARAFURA SEA

EQUATOR

TIMOR

ALTAI MTS.
PLATEAU OF MONGOLIA

SINKIANG
KUNLUN MTS.
PLATEAU OF TIBET
TIBET
Lhasa

Mekong R.
Mandalay
Irrawaddy R.
BURMA
Rangoon

Hanoi
VIETNAM
LAOS
Vientiane

THAILAND
Bangkok

KAMPUCHEA
Phnom Penh
GULF OF THAILAND

Ho Chi Minh City (Saigon)

SOUTH CHINA SEA

BRUNEI (G. B.)
BORNEO

INDONESIA

JAVA SEA
Jakarta
JAVA
BALI

TIEN SHAN
PAMIR PLATEAU
HINDU KUSH
AFGHANISTAN
Kabul
Islamabad
PAKISTAN
Karachi

HIMALAYAS MTS.
NEPAL
Kathmandu
BHUTAN
Thimphu
Brahmaputra R.
Dacca
Calcutta
BANGLADESH

New Delhi
Agra
Ganges R.
Indus R.
THAR DESERT

Bombay
INDIA
DECCAN PLATEAU
EASTERN GHATS
WESTERN GHATS
Madras

MALAYSIA
Kuala Lumpur
SINGAPORE
Strait of Malacca
SUMATRA

ARABIAN SEA

LACCADIVE ISLANDS

MALDIVES
Malé

SRI LANKA
Colombo

BAY OF BENGAL

ANDAMAN ISLANDS

NICOBAR ISLANDS

INDIAN OCEAN

600 kilometers
500 miles

ELEVATION

Feet	Meters
Above 13,120	Above 4,000
6560-13,120	2,000-4,000
1640-6560	500-2,000
656-1640	200-500
0-656	0-200

LAMBERT'S PROJECTION

Europe

ICELAND
★ Reykjavik

ARCTIC CIRCLE

Faeroe Is. (Den.)

Shetland Is. (G. B.)

Hebrides (G. B.)   Orkney Is. (G. B.)

NARVIK

NORTH CAPE

KJØLEN MTS.

NORWAY
• Bergen
Oslo ★

SWEDEN
L. Vänern
Stockholm ★
Göteborg
L. Vättern

FINLAND
Helsinki ★

GULF OF BOTHNIA

GULF OF FINLAND

BALTIC SEA

SCOTLAND
SCOTTISH HIGHLANDS
BRITISH ISLES
Glasgow • Firth of Forth
• Edinburgh

NORTHERN IRELAND
Belfast ★
Dublin •

IRELAND
IRISH SEA

GREAT BRITAIN
• Liverpool

WALES
Cardiff •
London •
Thames R.

ENGLAND

NORTH SEA

SKAGERRAK

JUTLAND PENINSULA

DENMARK
Copenhagen •

Frisian Is.
Hamburg •

EAST GERMANY
Berlin ★

POLAND
Warsaw ★
Vistula R.

Amsterdam ★
The Hague • Rotterdam
IJSSELMEER

Antwerp •
Brussels ★

Cologne •
Bonn •

Elbe R.
Neisse R.
Oder R.

Krakow •

ATLANTIC OCEAN

ENGLISH CHANNEL

PLATEAU OF BRITTANY

Seine R.
Paris •

LUXEMBOURG
Frankfurt •

WEST GERMANY
VOSGES MTS.
Rhine R.
BLACK FOREST
Munich •

Prague •

CZECHOSLOVAKIA
Brno •

CARPATHIAN MTS.

Loire R.

FRANCE

SWITZERLAND
L. Geneva • Bern
Geneva •

LIECHTENSTEIN

AUSTRIA
Vienna ★

Budapest •

HUNGARY

ROMANIA
• Ploesti

BAY OF BISCAY

Garonne R.
Bordeaux •

CENTRAL MASSIF

Lyon •

Rhone R.

ALPS

ALPS

Turin •

Milan •

Trieste •
Venice •
Po R.

Drava R.

Zagreb •

Sava R.

Belgrade •

Bucharest ★

Danube R.

Marseilles •

MONACO

Genoa •

SAN MARINO

Florence •

DINARIC ALPS

YUGOSLAVIA

BULGARIA
Sofia ★

RHODOPE MTS.

CANTABRIAN MTS.
Oporto •
Douro R.
PYRENEES
ANDORRA
GUADARRAMA MTS.
Barcelona •

Tiber R.
Rome •
Vatican City •
APENNINES

ITALY

ADRIATIC SEA

Dubrovnik •

Tirana •

ALBANIA

GREECE

• Salonika

PORTUGAL
Lisbon •
Madrid ★
Tagus R.
SPAIN
MESETA
SIERRA MORENA
Guadalquivir R.

CORSICA (Fr.)

SARDINIA (Ital.)

TYRRHENIAN SEA

BALEARIC IS. (Sp.)

Cagliari •

IONIAN SEA

Athens ★

AEGEAN SEA

STRAIT OF GIBRALTAR
Gibraltar (G. B.) •

• Palermo
SICILY (Ital.)

Valletta ★
MALTA

MEDITERRANEAN SEA

CRETE (Gr.)

ELEVATION

Meters	Feet
Above 4,000	Above 13,120
2,000-4,000	6560-13,120
500-2,000	1640-6560
200-500	656-1640
0-200	0-656
Below sea level	Below sea level

CONIC PROJECTION

0   600 kilometers

0   500 miles

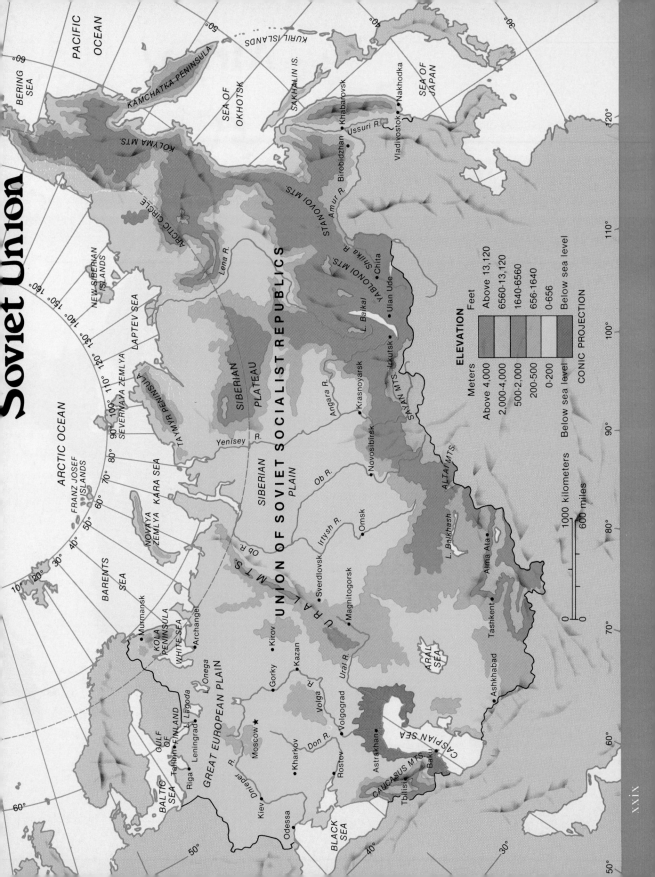

Soviet Union

PACIFIC OCEAN

BERING SEA

KAMCHATKA PENINSULA

SEA OF OKHOTSK

KURIL ISLANDS

SAKHALIN IS.

SEA OF JAPAN

KOLYMA MTS.

ARCTIC CIRCLE

NEW SIBERIAN ISLANDS

LAPTEV SEA

Khabarovsk
Birobidzhan
Amur R.
Ussuri R.
Vladivostok
Nakhodka

STANOVOI MTS

YABLONOI MTS

Chita
Ulan Ude
Irkutsk
L. Baikal

Lena R.

SIBERIAN PLATEAU

Shilka R.
Argun R.

ARCTIC OCEAN

FRANZ JOSEF ISLANDS

SEVERNAYA ZEMLYA

TAYMYR PENINSULA

Yenisey R.

SIBERIAN PLAIN

WEST SIBERIAN PLAIN

Ob R.

Angara R.
Krasnoyarsk
Novosibirsk
Omsk

SAYAN MTS.

ALTAI MTS.

UNION OF SOVIET SOCIALIST REPUBLICS

NOVAYA ZEMLYA

KARA SEA

BARENTS SEA

Irtysh R.
Ob R.
Sverdlovsk
Magnitogorsk

U R A L   M T S.

L. Balkhash
Alma Ata
Tashkent

Murmansk

KOLA PENINSULA

WHITE SEA

Archangel

L. Onega

L. Ladoga

FINLAND

GULF OF FINLAND

BALTIC SEA

Tallinn
Riga
Leningrad

Kirov
Kazan
Gorky

Volga R.

Ural R.

Ashkhabad

ARAL SEA

GREAT EUROPEAN PLAIN

Moscow ★

Kharkov
Kiev
Odessa

Dnieper R.

Don R.
Rostov
Volgograd
Astrakhan

CAUCASUS MTS.

Tbilisi
Baku

CASPIAN SEA

BLACK SEA

ELEVATION

Meters	Feet
Above 4,000	Above 13,120
2,000-4,000	6560-13,120
500-2,000	1640-6560
200-500	656-1640
0-200	0-656
Below sea level	Below sea level

CONIC PROJECTION

1000 kilometers
600 miles

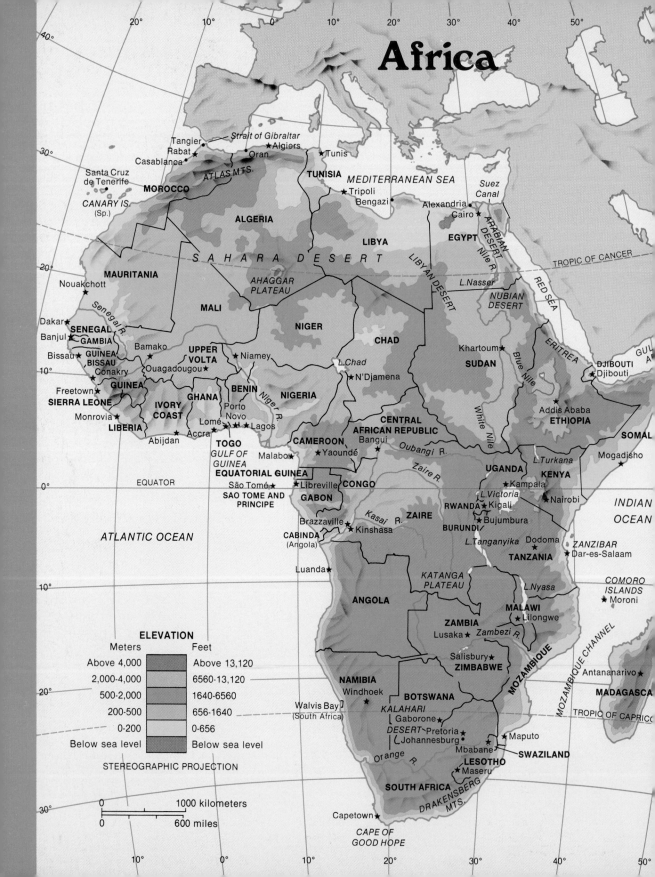

Africa

Strait of Gibraltar
Tangier •
Rabat • • Algiers
Casablanca • • Oran • Tunis
ATLAS MTS.
MOROCCO
Santa Cruz
de Tenerife •
CANARY IS.
(Sp.)

TUNISIA
MEDITERRANEAN SEA
★ Tripoli
Bengazi • *Suez Canal*
Alexandria • *ARABIAN DESERT*
Cairo ★
EGYPT

ALGERIA
LIBYA

S A H A R A   D E S E R T

LIBYAN DESERT

TROPIC OF CANCER

MAURITANIA
Nouakchott •
AHAGGAR PLATEAU
L.Nasser
NUBIAN DESERT
RED SEA

MALI
NIGER
CHAD
Khartoum ★
Blue Nile
ERITREA
DJIBOUTI
Djibouti •

Dakar • *Senegal R.*
SENEGAL
Banjul •
GAMBIA
Bissau • **GUINEA BISSAU**
Bamako •
★ Niamey
Ouagadougou •
UPPER VOLTA
L.Chad
SUDAN
White Nile
Addis Ababa •
ETHIOPIA
SOMAL

Conakry ★
GUINEA
Freetown ★
SIERRA LEONE
Monrovia ★
LIBERIA
IVORY COAST
GHANA
Porto Novo
Lomé ★ ★
Accra ★
Abidjan •
BENIN
NIGERIA
Niger R.
• N'Djamena
CENTRAL AFRICAN REPUBLIC
Bangui ★
Oubangi R.
Mogadisho •

★ Lagos
TOGO
GULF OF GUINEA
Malabo •
CAMEROON
★ Yaoundé
UGANDA
L.Turkana
KENYA
Kampala •
Nairobi ★

São Tomé ★ ★ Libreville
CONGO
EQUATORIAL GUINEA
SAO TOME AND PRINCIPE
GABON
Zaire R.
RWANDA
Kigali ★
L.Victoria

EQUATOR

ATLANTIC OCEAN
Brazzaville ★ ★ Kinshasa
CABINDA
(Angola)
Kasai R.
ZAIRE
Bujumbura ★
BURUNDI
L.Tanganyika
Dodoma •
TANZANIA
Dar-es-Salaam •
ZANZIBAR

INDIAN OCEAN

Luanda ★
KATANGA PLATEAU
L.Nyasa
COMORO ISLANDS
• Moroni

ANGOLA
ZAMBIA
MALAWI
Lilongwe ★
Lusaka ★ *Zambezi R.*
Salisbury ★
ZIMBABWE
MOZAMBIQUE
Antananarivo •
MADAGASCA

NAMIBIA
Windhoek •
BOTSWANA
KALAHARI DESERT
Gaborone ★
Pretoria ★
Johannesburg •
Mbabane •
Maputo •
SWAZILAND
MOZAMBIQUE CHANNEL
TROPIC OF CAPRICO

Walvis Bay
(South Africa)
Orange R.
LESOTHO
Maseru ★

SOUTH AFRICA
DRAKENSBERG MTS.
Capetown •
CAPE OF GOOD HOPE

ELEVATION

Meters	Feet
Above 4,000	Above 13,120
2,000-4,000	6560-13,120
500-2,000	1640-6560
200-500	656-1640
0-200	0-656
Below sea level	Below sea level

STEREOGRAPHIC PROJECTION

0   1000 kilometers
0   600 miles

North America

NORTH POLE

ARCTIC OCEAN

BERING SEA

BERING STRAIT

180° 170° 160° 150° 140° 130° 120° 110° 100° 90° 80° 70° 60°

PRUDHOE BAY

BROOKS RANGE

ALASKA

Fairbanks

Anchorage

KODIAK IS.

GREENLAND (Den.)

VICTORIA IS.

Great Bear Lake

Yukon R.

Mackenzie R.

ARCTIC CIRCLE

DAVIS STRAIT

BAFFIN IS.

Juneau

Great Slave Lake

SOUTHAMPTON IS.

60°

50°

PACIFIC OCEAN

CANADA

CANADIAN SHIELD

HUDSON BAY

VANCOUVER IS.

Vancouver

Seattle

Portland

Calgary

Saskatchewan R.

Nelson R.

L. Winnipeg

COAST MTS.

ROCKY

NEWFOUNDLAND IS.

GULF OF ST. LAWRENCE

CAPE BRETON IS.

FRASER R.

RANGE

COLUMBIA PLATEAU

Columbia R.

Snake R.

Winnipeg

L. of the Woods

L. Nipigon

St. Lawrence R.

Quebec

Montreal

Halifax

CASCADE RANGE

Missouri R.

L. Superior

Ottawa

Great Salt Lake

Salt Lake City

Minneapolis

L. Huron

L. Michigan

Toronto

L. Ontario

Hudson R.

Boston

40°

San Francisco

SIERRA NEVADA

COAST RANGES

GREAT BASIN

Platte R.

Chicago

Detroit

Cleveland

L. Erie

Pittsburgh

New York

Philadelphia

ATLANTIC OCEAN

Los Angeles

San Diego

Colorado R.

Denver

COLORADO PLATEAU

GREAT PLAINS

St. Louis

Ohio R.

CENTRAL PLAINS

APPALACHIAN MTS.

PIEDMONT

Washington

UNITED STATES

Phoenix

Red R.

Tennessee R.

Atlanta

ATLANTIC COASTAL PLAIN

BERMUDA (G. B.)

30°

El Paso

Dallas

Mississippi R.

Charleston

BAJA CALIFORNIA

GULF OF CALIFORNIA

WESTERN SIERRA MADRE

CENTRAL PLATEAU

EASTERN SIERRA MADRE

Rio Grande

GULF COASTAL PLAIN

Houston

New Orleans

Miami

Nassau

TROPIC OF CANCER

OAHU

Honolulu

HAWAII

HAWAII

Monterrey

GULF OF MEXICO

BAHAMAS

20°

Tampico

MEXICO

Mexico City

Vera Cruz

YUCATAN PENINSULA

Acapulco

CARIBBEAN SEA

10°

ELEVATION

Meters	Feet
Above 4,000	Above 13,120
2,000-4,000	6560-13,120
500-2,000	1640-6560
200-500	656-1640
0-200	0-656
Below sea level	Below sea level
Ice caps	Ice caps

AZIMUTHAL PROJECTION

110° 100° 90° 80° 70°

0   800 kilometers
0   600 miles

Latin America

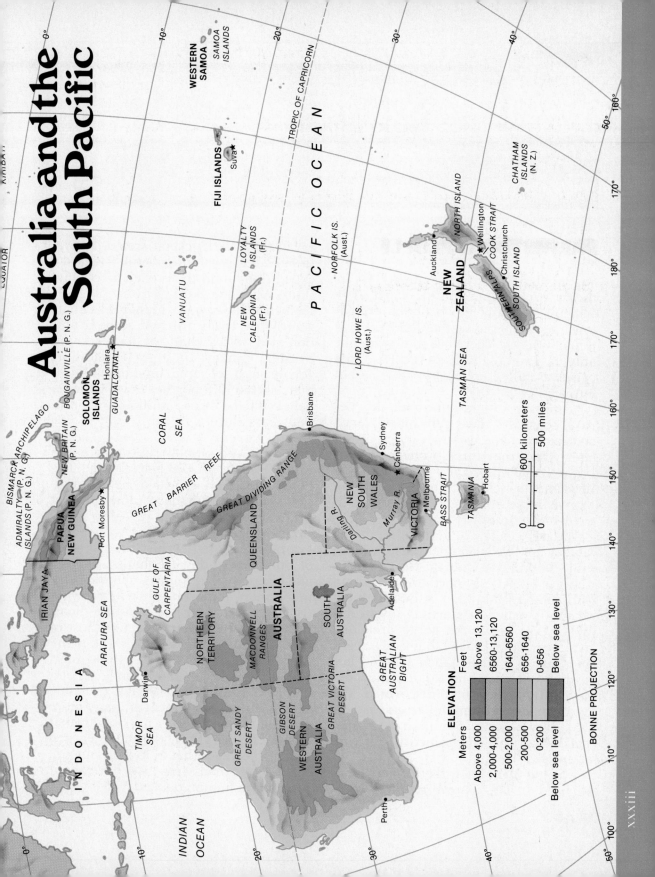

Australia and the South Pacific

PACIFIC OCEAN

INDIAN OCEAN

EQUATOR

TROPIC OF CAPRICORN

WESTERN SAMOA

SAMOA ISLANDS

KIRIBATI

FIJI ISLANDS
Suva ★

LOYALTY ISLANDS (Fr.)

NEW CALEDONIA (Fr.)

VANUATU

SOLOMON ISLANDS
Honiara ★
GUADALCANAL
BOUGAINVILLE (P. N. G.)

NEW BRITAIN (P. N. G.)

BISMARCK ARCHIPELAGO (P. N. G.)

ADMIRALTY ISLANDS (P. N. G.)

PAPUA NEW GUINEA
Port Moresby ★

IRIAN JAYA

I N D O N E S I A

TIMOR SEA

ARAFURA SEA

CORAL SEA

GREAT BARRIER REEF

NORFOLK IS. (Aust.)

LORD HOWE IS. (Aust.)

TASMAN SEA

NEW ZEALAND
Auckland ●
Wellington ★
COOK STRAIT
Christchurch ●
SOUTHERN ALPS
NORTH ISLAND
SOUTH ISLAND

CHATHAM ISLANDS (N. Z.)

• Brisbane

GULF OF CARPENTARIA

NORTHERN TERRITORY

QUEENSLAND

GREAT DIVIDING RANGE

Darwin ●

GREAT SANDY DESERT

GIBSON DESERT

GREAT VICTORIA DESERT

MACDONNELL RANGES

AUSTRALIA

WESTERN AUSTRALIA

SOUTH AUSTRALIA

GREAT AUSTRALIAN BIGHT

Perth ●

Adelaide ●

NEW SOUTH WALES

Darling R.

Murray R.

Sydney ●
Canberra ★
VICTORIA
Melbourne ●

BASS STRAIT

TASMANIA
Hobart ●

ELEVATION

Meters	Feet
Above 4,000	Above 13,120
2,000-4,000	6560-13,120
500-2,000	1640-6560
200-500	656-1640
0-200	0-656
Below sea level	Below sea level

0   600 kilometers
0   500 miles

BONNE PROJECTION

0°   10°   20°   30°   40°   50°   60°   70°   80°   90°   100°   110°   120°   130°   140°   150°   160°   170°   180°

Introduction

PREHISTORIC PEOPLE

People have always wondered about the first inhabitants on the earth. It is difficult to know much about **prehistoric** people because they had no system of writing. Therefore they were not able to leave any written records. This period is called *prehistory*—a time before written history.

In order to find out about this period, scientists must rely on evidence such as tools and weapons found at the sites where they think prehistoric people may have lived. By studying such implements, scientists have been able to give us possible theories about life in prehistoric times.

Mary Leakey and the late Louis Leakey are two such scientists. In 1959, after working at Olduvai Gorge (OLE-duh-vie GORJ) in northern Tanzania (tan-zuh-NEE-uh) for almost thirty years, they made a startling discovery. While digging in the gorge area one morning, Mary Leakey found two teeth and part of a skull. When she and her husband studied the fossils, they believed that they had discovered the fragments of a human-like individual who lived about 1.75 million years ago. This discovery soon gained worldwide attention.

Some years later, the Leakeys' son, Richard, began his own research project in the Lake Turkana area of Kenya. In 1972, a Kenyan member of Richard's expedition found the broken pieces of a skull. When the skull was assembled, it seemed to have many human-like characteristics. It also proved to be a million years older than the fossils found by Mary Leakey. In 1974, Donald Carl Johanson discovered an almost complete skeleton in northeastern Ethiopia believed to be from 3 million to 3.5 million years old.

In November 1975, Mary Leakey discovered fossils 40 kilometers (25 miles) south of Olduvai Gorge. The bones she found appear to be 3.75 million years old. Further examination of those same fossil beds revealed many things. There, Mary Leakey was able to examine the long extinct predecessors of our present-day elephants, hyenas, and hares. Yet she found something else much more important. It was *hominid* (HOM-uh-nud), or human-like, footprints that were very much like those of modern people. Mary Leakey and many of her colleagues believe these footprints are at least 3.5 million years old.

As the search goes on, it is probable that scientists will unearth many more remains. New findings may contradict or support everything they have learned so far. The pages that follow summarize the theories many scientists have about prehistoric human beings.

THE OLD STONE AGE

Scientists divide prehistory into periods according to the kinds of tools that people used. The earliest phase is called the **Old Stone Age,** or **Paleolithic** (pay-lee-oe-LITH-ik), Age. The word *Paleolithic* comes from the Greek word *palaios* (PAY-lee-oes), meaning old, and *lithos*, meaning stone. The era is so named because people made tools from stone. Most scholars think that the Old Stone Age may have lasted until about 10,000 B.C.

Archaeologists (ahr-kee-AHL-uh-justs), scientists who study the remains of ancient peoples, do not know much about the people of the Old Stone Age. They think these people were **nomads** (NOE-mads) or wanderers who lived by hunting animals and gathering wild plants. The study of ancient campsites shows that Stone Age hunters usually lived in small groups. A group of hunters remained in one area for a short time. During their stay, they hunted for food. Sometimes they hunted for days but caught nothing. When they had eaten as many plants and animals as they could find, they moved on. The hunt began again in a different place.

Archaeologists believe there were several kinds of early people. They think one type of early people lived between 1,200,000 and 500,000 years ago. Their remains have been found in Java (JAH-vuh), in Indonesia (in-doe-NEE-shuh), and near Peking (PEE-king) in China (CHIE-nuh).

Scientists think the early people who lived on Java used spoken language. They had larger brains than the people found in other parts of the world. Some scientists believed the prehistoric people in China used fire and such advanced stone tools as the hand ax. But no complete skeletons of these people have been found by archaeologists.

Remains from another group of early people come from the Neanderthal (nee-AN-dur-thal) Valley in Germany (JURM-uh-nee). These people are believed to have lived about 120,000–75,000 years ago. Scholars call them **Neanderthal people,** after the place in which their remains were found.

We think Neanderthal men and women were stocky and heavy. They probably stood about 150 centimeters (five feet) tall and had short arms and legs. Scientists think that Neanderthal people believed in an afterlife, because

Cave paintings such as this have been discovered in France, the Sahara, and other parts of the world. How can scientists use this evidence to help them learn more about the life of early peoples?

they buried their dead with tools and other materials. They also think that the Neanderthal people may have practiced some form of religion, since a belief in an afterlife is a common factor in many religions.

Remains of another prehistoric people were found in southern France. These people are believed to have lived about 35,000 years ago. Scientists call them **Cro-Magnon** (kroe-MAG-nun) people. They were probably taller than the Neanderthals. Cro-Magnon people made more complex weapons than did their predecessors. They were probably the first to use the fishhook, harpoon, and, eventually, the bow and arrow.

The most outstanding contribution of Cro-Magnon people was their cave paintings. They were probably the first people to draw pictures of their daily lives. Scientists think that Cro-Magnon people developed several forms of art as early as 30,000 years ago.

THE NEW STONE AGE

During long periods of the earth's history, its climate was much colder than it is today. Glaciers, or ice sheets, covered large areas of the world. Scientists call these periods ice ages. They believe the most recent Ice Age began more than 1.5 million years ago. During this era, prehistoric peoples hunted the hardy animals that thrived in the rugged climate. By our standards, the life of prehistoric hunters was difficult since they depended entirely upon the availability of game for their survival.

About 10,000 years ago, the earth's climate began to grow warmer. The large animals people had been using for food began to die out. Smaller animals that were easier to hunt increased in number. Instead of hunting big game, people gradually began to use these smaller animals, as well as fish and shellfish. They began to eat more vegetation, such as wild grains, nuts, and fruits, which were able to grow in the warmer weather. As the climate changed, people began to alter their style of living. The need to search for big game decreased. Some people became less nomadic. They learned to grow their own food. Once they began to farm, people needed better implements. They soon began to improve their stone tools. This era, in which people began to farm and improve their tools, is called the **New Stone Age,** or the **Neolithic** (nee-uh-LITH-ik) **Age.**

The development of agriculture in the New Stone Age was a slow process. People at first gathered only what they needed each year. Once the wild plants in an area became exhausted, people moved on in search of new plants. This became more and more difficult, however, as the years passed. People had to go farther and farther to find enough plant life to support them. Then an important development took place. People slowly discovered how to grow their own plants. This meant taking a seed, planting it, and watching it grow. Scientists think that experimenting with farming could have begun 18,500 years ago in southern Egypt, and that by 5000 B.C. farming had spread to Eastern Europe and by 3000 B.C. to Great Britain. Farming might also have been independently discovered in the Americas (uh-MER-uh-kuz).

As farming began to develop, people began to invent better tools. The art of making stone tools was perfected toward the end of the New Stone Age. The new tools were made by polishing rather than by chipping the cutting edges. Polished axes were much better for chopping wood. They were stronger than the chipped tools and could cut deeper into the wood surface. People also invented the wheel during this time. The newer stone tools are called *neoliths*, from which the Neolithic, or New Stone Age, gets its name.

People began to **domesticate** animals during the New Stone Age. They gradually learned to tame sheep, goats, cows, horses, and pigs. These animals became more useful to people as agriculture developed.

Scholars do not know exactly how people learned to tame animals. Perhaps a few wild dogs strayed near human camping areas to look for food. People may have noticed that the animals could warn them of approaching danger. Perhaps the dogs went along with some of the hunters. The hunters may have noticed that the animals could help them spot game. If so, they probably decided to take the dogs with them when they realized they could hunt more efficiently with dogs. In return for their services. the dogs were fed. People may have decided to tame other animals because of their success with the dog.

Remains found at Neolithic sites show that the art of making pottery was known during much of the New Stone Age. The development of this skill shows that technology was advancing even before people knew how to write. Pottery is not easy to make. Early people had to make several discoveries before they could become good potters. They had to learn to use special clay that could be softened with water in order for it to be molded. Other material, such as sand, often needed to be added to give the clay body so it would hold its shape. Neolithic people invented the process of firing, or baking, to make the pottery hard and durable. Several of the processes they invented are still in use today.

Neolithic people also knew how to weave. They could make baskets, mats, and nets. Remains of primitive looms have been found in places where archaeologists think people lived during the New Stone Age. Tools for making pottery and weaving could not be carried easily. The heavy implements would hinder the mobility of people who hunted to survive. Since scientists have found remains of heavy tools at Neolithic campsites, they believe that people began to form more settled communities out of necessity during the New Stone Age. The development of agriculture and the establishment of permanent communities were two of the most important advances toward civilization as we know it today.

CULTURE GROWS AND DEVELOPS

The **culture** of a society includes such things as science, art, economic activity, religious beliefs, and government. Societies develop their cultures over a period of many years. They develop them by passing on, and thus preserving, certain aspects of their way of life from one generation to the next.

Human culture grew more complex when people began to live in cities and towns. The growth of cities was first made possible by the new developments in agriculture. More people were needed in one place to perform the many duties involved in farming. By 7000 B.C., agriculture was spreading throughout the Middle East and Mediterranean (med-uh-tuh-RAY-nee-un) areas. A steady supply of food in these areas enabled people to settle permanently instead of moving constantly to hunt migrating animals. Once settled, people established villages near their fields and chose leaders. Thus the first government probably began in primitive farming communities.

As people had more to eat and began to live longer, the population began to increase. Farmers learned more about their crops and improved their farming methods. Gradually, they were able to produce surplus crops. Since there was a surplus of food, people no longer had to spend most of their time working only at agriculture. They had more free time to try new things. They were able to create and develop crafts and trades. People also made many new and important inventions.

As technology advanced, individuals began to specialize in one particular craft. For example, one family may have made the tools used by several farmers. The textile industry, one of the first industries to develop, began with the basic weaving techniques of Neolithic peoples. Skilled workers employed in these crafts were called *artisans*. As towns grew larger, the artisans became an important element in society.

The division of labor among several artisans gave rise to the need for trade. The services of traders and merchants were necessary for the smooth flow of goods between the artisans and their customers. The growth of a merchant group within the community gave rise to the need for accountants to help tradespeople keep records of their transactions. Many scholars think that writing may have been invented so that people could keep permanent records of what was bought and sold.

OUR KNOWLEDGE OF PREHISTORIC PEOPLE

Despite all the digging and searching done by archaeologists, we still do not have a full picture of prehistoric people. One reason for our limited knowledge is that prehistoric people lived and died out in the open. Exposed to the weather, their bodies decayed. Their bones were chewed by animals and bleached by the sun. Our information is limited for other reasons. Prehistoric people did not write their language. We have no written records to examine to find out how they lived. We have to "read" their story in bones, tools, and the other remains of their lives. With this evidence, we can piece together parts of their story. But we have to make guesses about the rest.

THE BEGINNING OF THE HISTORIC PERIOD

Writing was invented about 3000 B.C. Scholars believe that this invention marks the beginning of the **historic** period. The period is called historic because once people began to write, they could keep a record, or history, of what happened in their daily lives. After the invention of writing, people could record events, their ideas, their beliefs, their values, and their attitudes.

Historians use written materials to learn how people of the past lived. By deciphering and analyzing ancient written materials, historians try to form a picture of life in the past. The materials from which they get their information are called "historical evidence." Figuring out what these materials mean is called "interpreting historical evidence."

To the Student

As you begin your study of world history in *People and Our World*, we would like you to keep several things in mind—about the study of history in general and the study of this book in particular.

The first thing to remember is that much of what happened in the past was never recorded. Only a fragment of what took place was written down. One reason for this is that people of the past did not recall everything that happened around them, any more than you can recall everything that has happened in your life. There is another reason too. People of the past, like people today, noticed and recorded only what they thought was important.

Sometimes, however, people in the same society had different ideas about what was important. This influenced the way they recorded events. For instance, two observers of the same event might emphasize different aspects of it. Or the event might seem important to them for different reasons. As a result, historians often find differing, and even conflicting, records of what happened in the past. When writing about the past, historians weigh all the records before forming their own conclusions about what happened.

Historians use primary source materials (or documents), written in the period they are researching, when writing about the past. When using source materials, they usually have one or more questions in mind that help them focus on a specific topic. For example, a historian examining a collection of letters written by ancient Chinese men and women might focus his or her attention on a question such as: What do these letters reveal about ancient Chinese family life? When you examine the primary sources in the "Book of Readings" at the back of the book, you too will keep some questions in mind. These questions will help you focus your study of the sources.

As you read the book, you will notice that some questions are set off by a symbol ◗ . This symbol has been used to show you that questions have a special purpose: to encourage you to consider how a study of world history could relate to your own life. Some of them will show you that questions historians ask about the past could also be asked about the present.

The information and questions you will encounter in *People and Our World* have a common purpose: to help you acquire knowledge and skills that will enable you to assume the responsibilities of citizenship. How you and your contemporaries exercise your responsibilities as citizens will be one of the most important things future historians will study about your generation.

ALLAN O. KOWNSLAR

TERRY L. SMART

The World of the Ancient Middle East

"Who's buried in Grant's Tomb?" is an old joke that fools few people today. In ancient Sumer, someone might have asked you, "Who's buried in Queen So-and-so's tomb?" But it would have been no joke. And you'd have been hard pressed to say.

In Queen Shub–ad's tomb, for instance, archaeologists found the remains of nearly 100 bodies—servants, court officials, soldiers, musicians, animals, and their keepers. They also found wooden chariots covered with gold and lapis lazuli. In front of the chariots lay the crushed skeletons of the animals and drivers that had pulled them into the tomb. Near the chariots were tools and weapons made of gold, many vessels of silver, copper, marble, glass, and precious stones, two large lions' heads made of silver, and a richly inlaid board on which games were played. Only a few of the people found in the tomb were dead when they arrived there. Most walked into the grave alive. In the grave, a ceremony was held. Musicians played. A sleeping potion was brewed in a huge copper pot. Everyone dipped a cup into the potion, drank it, lay down on the floor, and fell into a deep sleep. Someone came down and killed the animals. Then bricks and earth were flung into the tomb from above. The unconscious men and women soon died of suffocation.

The grave was then filled in gradually, layer by layer. As each layer was finished, the earth was tramped down to make a hard floor. Offerings to the dead were spread on the floor, and a human victim was sacrificed. This procedure was repeated several times. Finally, a funeral chapel was built on the finished tomb to mark it as a holy spot.

The tomb of Shub-ad and the things found there were full of clues about the world of the ancient Middle East. The instruments people played while waiting for death and the cups from which they sipped the fatal potion are all evidence about the earliest days of this area. In this part of the world, scholars have also found the first written records of human life. A royal seal, made of stone and covered with writing, told archaeologists the name of the king whose queen lay buried in a tomb. On the map on page 5, ancient Sumer (SOO-mur), where Queen Shub-ad's tomb is located, can be found.

Historians are interested in where something happened, as well as what happened. So the map on page 5 also provides information about the geography of the ancient Middle East. It shows the major land forms—mountains, rivers, and plains—of the area, and the leading cities. Because history is concerned not only with the past but also with its relationship to the present, the boundaries of nations of the present-day Middle East are shown on the map as well. Additional information about the geography of the Middle East is provided on the map of the Middle East in the Atlas.

Unit Goals

1. To know how the geography of the Middle East affected the way of life there.
2. To identify the major contributions to ancient Middle Eastern and to present-day life made by the ancient Sumerians, Amorites, Hittites, Assyrians, Chaldeans, Persians, Phoenicians, Hebrews, and Egyptians during the period 4000 B.C.–300 B.C.
3. To know the importance of a system of writing, a code of laws, and a system of trade in the ancient Middle East.
4. To identify the major developments in ancient Egyptian life during the period 2850 B.C.–1090 B.C.
5. To compare and contrast the religions and governments of the peoples of the ancient Middle East.
6. To identify some ways in which future historians will be able to know about your life.

Middle East

ARAL SEA

Danube R.

BLACK SEA

CAUCASUS MTS.

CASPIAN SEA

• Troy

• Hattusas

ASIA   MINOR

• Sardis

TAURUS MTS.

Tigris R.

MESOPOTAMIA

• Nineveh

ASSYRIA

ELBURZ MTS.

Knossos
CRETE

CYPRUS

PHOENICIA

SYRIA

Euphrates R.

MEDITERRANEAN SEA

• Damascus

• Tyre

BABYLONIA

Babylon •

MEDIA

ISRAEL

• Jerusalem

JUDAH

• Susa

ZAGROS MTS.

NILE DELTA

Isthmus
of Suez

Ur •

SUMER

• Persepolis

Memphis •

Sinai
Peninsula

SYRIAN

PERSIA

LOWER EGYPT

▲ Mt. Sinai

DESERT

SAHARA

Nile R.

PERSIAN GULF

DESERT

• Thebes

UPPER EGYPT

RED SEA

ARABIA

1st cataract

TROPIC OF CANCER

2nd cataract

3rd cataract

4th cataract

5th cataract

NUBIA

6th cataract

ARABIAN SEA

CONIC PROJECTION

	Fertile Crescent
- - - -	Modern political boundaries

0   300   600 kilometers

0   200   400 miles

30°   40°   50°   60°

40°

30°

20°

10°

Early Peoples of the Ancient Middle East

THE SUMERIANS

In the region that is now Iraq (ih-RAHK), the Tigris (TIE-gris) and Euphrates (yew-FRAY-teez) rivers flow side by side for more than 1,600 kilometers (1,000 miles). Between these two great rivers lies a fertile valley. The ancient Greeks called this valley **Mesopotamia** (mes-oe-poe-TAY-mee-uh), which means "land between the rivers." This rich valley forms the eastern part of the **Fertile Crescent.** The Fertile Crescent is a strip of rich, well-watered land that extends in a great arch from the coast of the Mediterranean (med-uh-tuh-RAY-nee-un) Sea to to the Persian (PUR-zhun) Gulf. (See the map on page 5.) Many of the ideas of Western civilization began in this region, and many of the plants and animals we have today were first domesticated there.

People began to move into Mesopotamia at a very early time. They settled at the lower end of the valley where the rivers empty into the Persian Gulf. They called their land Sumer. The *Sumerians* (soo-MER-ee-unz), the people of Sumer, were among the first people to leave a written record.

By about 4000 B.C., the Sumerians were living in large villages, with buildings made of sun-dried mud brick.

By about 3000 B.C., they had become prosperous enough to develop cities. These cities included Uruk (UHR-uk), Nippur (NIP-poor), Ur (OOHR), and Lagash (LAH-gash). (See the map on page 13.)

Taming the Rivers   The Tigris is the deeper of the two rivers of the Fertile Crescent and carries a larger amount of water. The Euphrates, however, is faster and carries large amounts of soil along with its waters. This soil gradually sinks to the bottom of the river and makes it shallower. For this reason, the Euphrates often overflows its banks and floods the valley. This can be dangerous because it is not always possible to tell when the floods will take place. It is also difficult to know how much water will cover the land.

Historians believe that the Tigris and Euphrates rivers had an important part in the development of the great Sumerian cities. After the early settlers arrived in the valley, they began to work at controlling the floodwaters of the rivers. They built a large irrigation system with a network of canals and dikes. The canals led water from the rivers to the fields. The dikes kept the rivers from flooding the land and washing away crops and homes.

This irrigation system finally grew so large that many people were needed to take care of it. Each year, large numbers of people had to clean the irrigation channels and repair the dikes. Work done on such a large scale had to be organized so that it could be done efficiently. Some historians believe that this need to plan and supervise large work projects helped the Sumerians develop the skills that enabled them to form a complex society.

The irrigated fields produced much larger crops than fields that used only rainfall. Also, the rich soil carried by the rivers helped keep the land fertile. Thus the Sumerians could support their population on the same land year after year, even though the number of people continued to increase.

Sumerian Society   As the food supply became more plentiful, not everyone was needed to work in the fields. Larger numbers of people were free to work at other jobs. They became carpenters, potters, metalworkers, stone carvers, and religious leaders. Gradually, they developed new and more specialized skills. During the height of the Sumerian civilization, there were boat builders, scribes who kept written records, jewelers, and people who made tools and weapons of bronze. There were also many traders. Some Sumerian merchants traveled from city to city, or had agents in distant places.

The Sumerian cities were like large states. In fact, historians often call

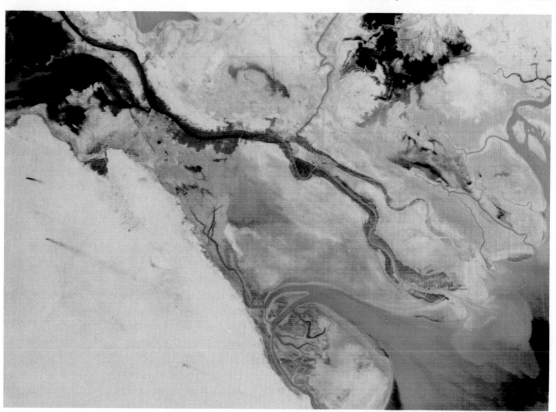

This picture of the Fertile Crescent was taken by a NASA satellite. The red areas are croplands. Why do you think people first settled here?

7

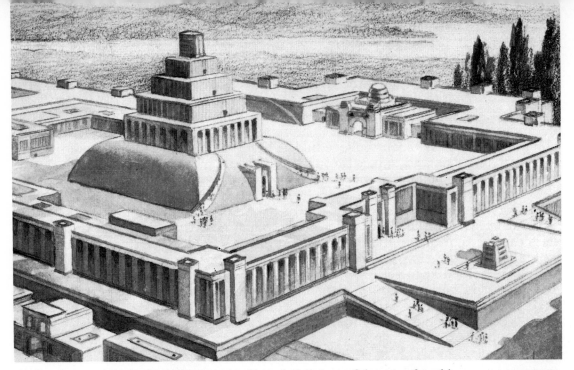

This drawing of a ziggurat is based on descriptions of the ruins found by archaeologists. Based on this drawing, what kind of civilization do you think the Sumerians must have had?

cities such as those in Sumer **city-states.** These cities had control over much of the land around them and competed with each other for leadership. From a study of Sumerian writings, historians believe that the cities were ruled at first by groups of adult free men. Only in time of danger did the citizens choose a king to lead them. Later, when cities had grown to great size, the kings became permanent rulers. The Sumerians, however, considered the king to be only the representative on earth of the true king—the god of the city—who owned the city and everything in it.

Sumerian Inventions At its height, Sumerian society was very complex, wealthy, and powerful. Among the greatest works of the Sumerians were their huge temples and the invention of a system of writing. The Sumerian temples were called **ziggurats** (ZIG-uh-ratz). They were built of sun-dried mud brick. The ziggurats had several stories. The top story was set aside for the worship of an important god or goddess. Ziggurats, probably representing mountains, often were 45 or more meters (150 feet) high. They towered over the countryside and could be seen for kilometers. Some were so large that their bases covered 45,000 square meters (500,000 square feet). Located around the ziggurats were storehouses. These held sacks of grain, precious gems, metals, and fine textiles. In addition to its religious importance, the temple was the center of economic and commercial activity.

Sumerian Religion The religion of the Sumerians was a complex one. In it, the gods owned all the land. The king was their main servant. Priests ran the temples but were not above the king except in certain carefully defined situations. The kings selected the high priests. In some smaller communities, where no king existed, a high priest could also serve as the main ruler. Kings usually communicated with the many gods by use of dreams. The king, for example, would visit a temple, offer a sacrifice, pray, and fall asleep. While he was dreaming, the gods supposedly would give orders to him. This allowed the king to be above all other people in the land. Orders were then passed down to the lowest order of citizens. Everyone was supposed to help build temples, roads, and irrigation projects. The belief in the Sumerian gods, therefore, played an important role in Sumerian society.

A Writing System The writing system invented by the Sumerians is called **cuneiform** (kyoo-NEE-uh-form) writing. It was probably the greatest creation of the Sumerians. The writing was developed so that temple priests could keep track of the goods entering and leaving the storehouses. Wedge-shaped marks were made with a sharp reed on a wet clay tablet. When the tablet dried, it became very hard. The marks made on it were then a permanent record. A different mark was used for each item. At first, cuneiform began as a kind of picture writing. This system worked well while the storehouses were small. But as the cities grew, the types of things recorded became more varied and numerous. New marks had to be invented to record them all. Soon it became impossible to use this system.

Instead, the Sumerians began to

DEVELOPMENT OF CUNEIFORM

MEANING	Earth	Man	Woman	Water In	To Drink	Fish
EARLY CUNEIFORM						
PICTOGRAPH IN POSITION OF LATER CUNEIFORM						
ORIGINAL PICTOGRAPH						
CLASSIC ASSYRIAN						

use existing or new signs to stand for separate sounds. In this way the name of a person or thing was represented by a combination of signs. The picture writing was gradually made simpler so it would be easier to draw. From this simpler style, cuneiform developed. There were about 600 cuneiform signs. They stood for ideas, objects, syllables, or single sounds. (See the chart on page 9.) The Sumerians were able to write whole sentences with these signs.

The Contributions of the Sumerians

The Sumerians wrote down more than lists of goods. They left a rich literature. It included poetry about the deeds of their gods and myths about their own creation. The Sumerians also wrote

A Closer Look

THE EPIC OF GILGAMESH

Among the best-known tales in Mesopotamian literature is the ancient Epic of Gilgamesh (GILL-guh-mesh). In the story, Enkidu (en-KID-yew), the best friend of Gilgamesh, the hero, dies suddenly, and Gilgamesh becomes very distressed.

"Enkidu, my friend, my younger brother—who with me . . . hunted . . . panther in the plains; who with me could do all, who climbed the crags . . . Now—what sleep is this that seized you? . . ."
He did not raise his eyes.
Gilgamesh touched his heart, it was not beating . . .
Again and then again he turned toward his friend, tearing his hair and scattering the tufts, stripping and flinging down the finery off his body.

Refusing to accept his friend's death, Gilgamesh sets out to discover the secret of immortality. In the end, however, he is defeated. The advice Gilgamesh receives on his difficult quest is described below.

Life, which you look for, you will never find.
For when the gods created man, they let death be his share, and life withheld in their own hands.
Gilgamesh, fill your belly . . . dance and make music day and night.
And wear fresh clothes, and wash your head and bathe.
Look at the child that is holding your hand . . .
These things alone are the concern of men.

Adapted from: H. and H. A. Frankfort, John A. Wilson, Thorkild Jacobean. *The Intellectual Adventure of Ancient Man.* Chicago: University of Chicago Press, 1946, pp. 209–211.

1. How does Gilgamesh feel about his friend's death?
2. What does the advice Gilgamesh receives tell us about people and society in Mesopotamia at the time?
3. What tales do we have that might reveal our view of life to future historians? List and discuss them.

down prayers to the gods, fables that were designed to teach proper behavior, scientific writings, and a great deal of history. They also left legal documents written in cuneiform.

Education was also highly valued by the Sumerians. But it was available only to boys of the upper classes. Lessons were given in the temples and were conducted by the priests. Students learned reading, writing, history, mathematics, foreign languages, and map-making. Some also studied law and medicine.

The Sumerians developed many new ideas that are now part of our daily lives. They created some of the rules of algebra, and they invented a calendar based on the movements of the moon. They divided a circle into 360 degrees. Each degree had 60 minutes, and each minute had 60 seconds. If you look at a clock, you will see that this is the same system we use today.

Sumerians and the Bronze Age   The Sumerians were among the first known people to use bronze. They learned to make bronze about 3500 B.C. Bronze began to replace stone and soft copper as the main material for making implements. For this reason, historians call this new period the **Bronze Age.**

Bronze is a mixture of copper and tin. As much as one fourth of bronze can be tin. It is a very strong metal. Other materials can also be combined with bronze to make it more useful. Phosphorus, for example, helps strengthen bronze, especially in the making of tools and weapons. Lead lowers the melting point of bronze so that it can be poured into molds.

The Sumerians used bronze to make cups, vases, battle axes, helmets, knives, shields, spear points, swords, various ornaments, and even cooking stoves. The Sumerians, as well as many other ancient peoples, continued to use bronze on a large scale until about 1200–1000 B.C. At that time, iron, a much stronger substance, replaced bronze in the making of weapons and tools. The Iron Age will be discussed in greater detail when you study about the Hittites and the Assyrians.

The Decline of the Sumerians   In spite of their great civilization, the Sumerians were not very strong politically. By 2500 B.C., their government had begun to weaken. And their decline was so rapid that within 400 years the Sumerian language was no longer spoken. Other regions became more powerful and began to take over Sumer.

SECTION REVIEW

1. Mapping: Using the map on page 5, describe the relationship and the relative location of: Mesopotamia, the Tigris and Euphrates rivers, the Persian Gulf, Sumer.

2. In your own words, briefly identify: Mesopotamia, Fertile Crescent, cuneiform writing, city-state, ziggurat.

3. Briefly describe the physical geography of Mesopotamia. How do you think it might have affected life in Sumer?

4. What was the role of the king in the Sumerian religion? How did this role affect Sumerian society?

5. How was the history of ancient Sumer recorded?

◗ How are historical events recorded today? List the different methods. Which method do you think would be the most useful to future historians in describing life today? Explain.

THE AMORITES

Throughout the history of the ancient Middle East, cities and high civilizations were conquered by desert nomads. As the population of the nomads increased and their needs became greater, they began to press closer and closer to the borders of the city-states, threatening invasion.

The nomads who replaced the Sumerians as a political power in Mesopotamia were the *Amorites* (AM-ur-ritez). These people were nomads who lived in the Syrian (SIR-ee-un) Desert. As Sumer began to decline, the Amorites swept in from the deserts. They managed to overcome the Sumerians and take over the village of Babylon (BAB-uh-lun) about 1900 B.C. (See the map on page 13.) Babylon was made the capital of the whole region. Later Amorite rulers used Babylon as a base for building a large empire called Babylonia (bab-uh-LOE-nyuh).

Code of Hammurabi Hammurabi (ham-uh-RAHB-ee) is the most famous of the Amorite kings of Babylon. He united the city-states of Mesopotamia about 1750 B.C. and governed them well. During his rule, laws were set down in a uniform way. Organizing and writing down the laws of a society is called **codification** (KOD-uh-fuh-KAY-shun). The laws of Hammurabi are called the **Code of Hammurabi.**

Human societies have always had rules to guide people's actions. In early times, laws were usually passed down by word of mouth. Younger members of a society would learn the rules from the older members. A group of people would often be given the job of remembering all the laws and deciding if they had been broken. Under this system, justice depended on the opinion of a small group of people, or even on only one person. There was no list of laws to which anyone could go for guidance.

The codification of laws under Hammurabi was one of the first times that laws were collected, classified, and listed by a society. From this time on, judges could decide someone's guilt or innocence by looking at the written law instead of deciding for themselves what judgment should be passed.

The Code of Hammurabi has told historians much about life in ancient Mesopotamia. Women held a high position in society, and foreigners were treated well. There were many laws that regulated industry and trade, so these must have been important activities. The Code also indicates that land was owned privately. But peasants who rented land could not be put off the land until their leases ran out.

Marriage was a legal contract, and both husband and wife had definite rights. Even though a wife was thought to be the property of her husband, she could return to her family if her husband mistreated her. A divorced woman was allowed to keep her children. Also, women were allowed to conduct business and had the same rights in business as did men.

People who falsely accused others of crimes received the punishment that the accused would have received. If a city was not able to catch a thief, that city had to pay the victim of the robbery. Members of society had special duties toward their neighbors. For example, a farmer who did not keep his dikes in good repair had to pay for any flood damage to the fields of his neighbors. If he could not pay, the farmer

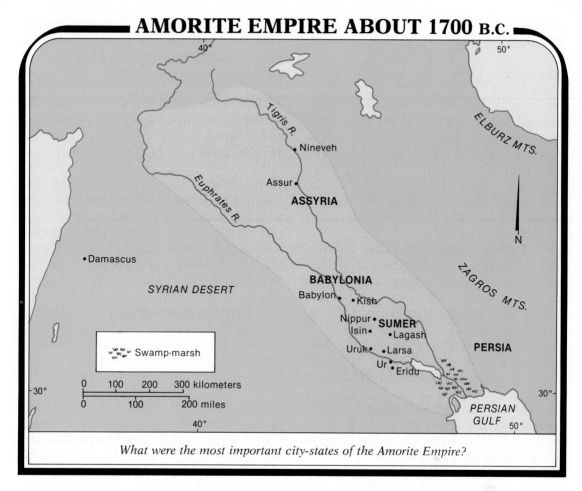

AMORITE EMPIRE ABOUT 1700 B.C.

Swamp-marsh

0   100   200   300 kilometers
0   100   200 miles

What were the most important city-states of the Amorite Empire?

could be sold into slavery. Doctors' fees were regulated by the Code. A doctor could be punished for injuring a patient or for failing to do what he had promised to do.

Justice in Babylon did not apply equally to everyone, however. Crimes committed against nobles were punished more severely than those against ordinary people, farmers or slaves. But nobles also received severe punishment for their crimes. Merchants were punished for dishonesty more severely than their employees. And punishment by death was not uncommon.

SECTION REVIEW

1. Mapping: Using the map on page 5, locate by means of latitude and longitude coordinates the cities of Babylon, Nineveh, and Ur.
2. In your own words, briefly identify: Hammurabi, the Code of Hammurabi.
3. What does the Code of Hammurabi tell us about life in ancient Babylon?
◗ Do you live by any code or set of laws? What are they? Pick one and tell how you think future historians would use it to tell about your life.

THE HITTITES AND THE ASSYRIANS

The *Hittites* (HIH-tites) were probably nomadic herders in the grasslands north of the Black and Caspian (KAS-pee-un) seas. About 1650 B.C., they moved south through the Caucasus (KAW-kuh-sus) Mountains and into the area that is now modern Turkey. (See the map on page 15.) By 1600 B.C., the Hittites had formed a confederation of states with its capital at Hattusas (HAT-too-shus).

The Hittite Empire The Hittites had a strong army, and their confederation was ruled by a king. One Hittite king, Suppiluliumas (soo-pee-loo-lee-UHM-us) I, who ruled from 1375 to 1335 B.C., extended his rule almost to the borders of Egypt (EE-jupt). One scholar thinks that at that time an Egyptian delegation went to the king to propose that one of his sons marry the widow of **Tutankhamun** (too-tang-KAHM-un), the now famous boy-king of ancient Egypt. But when the son of Suppiluliumas was murdered on the way to Egypt, the alliance fell apart.

For many years thereafter, the Hittites and Egyptians often clashed. A treaty of peace was finally arranged after a battle between the Hittite king, Muwatallis (MOO-wah-tahl-is) and **Rameses** (RAM-seez) **II** of Egypt. The date of the treaty was 1296 B.C. Peace then reigned for about seventy years. By the end of that time, the Hittite Empire had lost much of its power. About 1200 B.C., the Hittites were overcome by another nomadic people. But before their fall, the Hittites made important additions to the civilization of the ancient Middle East.

Hittite Religion Most of the religion of the Hittites was based on that of nearby peoples, especially the Sumerians. The Hittite kings were for the most part selected by nobles and warriors. A king was also a chief priest. This made him responsible to their sun goddess, called *Arinna* (AH-ri-na). She was one of the most important gods in the Hittite religion.

Hittite Law The Hittite system of laws was less severe than the Code of Hammurabi. Punishment by death was limited to serious crimes, such as treason. Payment of fines was a more usual punishment than cruel revenge. In addition, persons accused of crimes were allowed to question their accusers and to defend themselves during their trials.

The Hittites' Ironworking Although bronze was in wide use in the ancient Middle East by 2000 B.C., the Hittites were the first people to make useful tools and weapons out of iron. Earlier peoples had known of iron. Some peoples in the Middle East had made a few tools by hammering iron from fallen meteors. But such supplies of iron ore were very limited, and the use of them was very expensive.

Around 1400 B.C., the Hittites developed a new method of ironworking. They invented a furnace that could produce enough heat to purify the iron ore by separating it from other elements. This was done by forcing air through the furnace to make the fire burn hotter. The new process produced strong, rust-resistant iron tools and weapons. These tools and weapons gave the Hittites a great advantage over their neighbors.

The eventual spread of iron production throughout the ancient Middle East after 1000 B.C. brought important changes to farming as well as to warfare. Iron plows and sickles helped

HITTITE AND ASSYRIAN EMPIRES

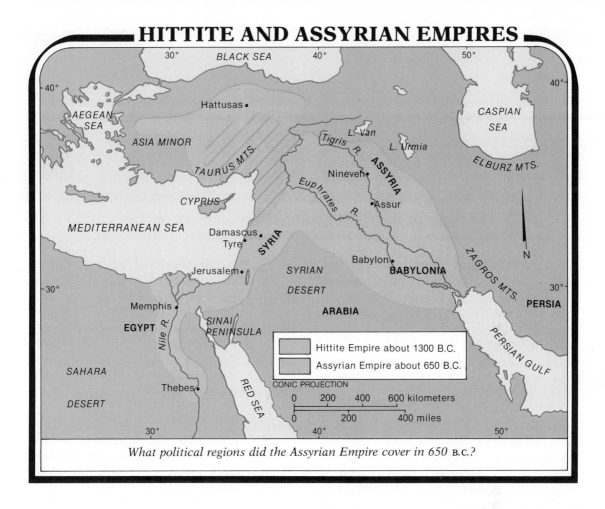

BLACK SEA

AEGEAN SEA

ASIA MINOR

Hattusas •

TAURUS MTS.

CYPRUS

MEDITERRANEAN SEA

Damascus •
Tyre •

SYRIA

Jerusalem •

Memphis •

EGYPT

SINAI PENINSULA

SAHARA

Thebes •

DESERT

RED SEA

Nile R.

SYRIAN DESERT

ARABIA

Tigris R.

L. Van

L. Urmia

Nineveh •

ASSYRIA

Euphrates R.

• Assur

Babylon •

BABYLONIA

CASPIAN SEA

ELBURZ MTS.

ZAGROS MTS.

PERSIA

PERSIAN GULF

N

Hittite Empire about 1300 B.C.

Assyrian Empire about 650 B.C.

CONIC PROJECTION

0   200   400   600 kilometers

0   200   400 miles

What political regions did the Assyrian Empire cover in 650 B.C.?

farmers clear more fields and to increase food production. Farmers now had to have specialists to make their iron tools. So they had to depend on people in the towns. Thus, iron working brought about a closer relationship between the countryside and the towns.

For a long time, the Hittites kept their method of making iron a secret. They would not trade iron goods with other people because they were afraid their methods of iron production would be discovered. However, about 1200 B.C. when the Hittite Empire fell, the metalworkers moved to other parts of the Middle East. They took their knowl-edge of ironworking with them. As a result, the use of iron tools and weapons spread throughout the region. Historians mark this time as the end of the Bronze Age and the beginning of the **Iron Age** in the ancient Middle East.

The Assyrian Empire   About 900 B.C., the *Assyrians* (uh-SIR-ee-uns) moved into the northern part of Mesopotamia and built city-states. They were the first people to use iron widely. They built their vast empire by warfare, using iron weapons, chariots, and mounted cavalry. Especially useful was an iron battering ram that could be used to break through city walls.

15

This stone relief was found in the Assyrian city of Nineveh. What does it tell a historian about the role of the chariot in this ancient empire?

The Assyrians could be brutal. They killed or deported conquered people who resisted their rule. But the Assyrians were efficient soldiers and governors. They united a large area by building roads to link all parts of the empire. They also created a messenger service to carry news of important events to the capital.

Nineveh (NIN-uh-vuh), the Assyrian capital, was a large and prosperous city. It had a continual supply of fresh water that was brought in from mountain streams. It also had the world's largest cuneiform library. It contained thousands of clay tablets from all over Mesopotamia. The library was built on the orders of Assurbanipal (ah-shoor-BAHN-ih-pahl), an Assyrian king. From these preserved records, scholars have been able to trace how this once peaceful people became a warrior society. The tablets have also provided information about the Assyrian religion. It seems that many of the Assyrian religious beliefs were borrowed from the Sumerians.

The Assyrians had a highly efficient military organization. But this was not enough to preserve their empire. There were often revolts by the people they had conquered. Also, the continual warfare used up more and more soldiers. Soldiers had to be drafted from among defeated enemies in order to keep the army at its full strength. These foreign soldiers did not fight as willingly as the Assyrian troops. Because of this, the Assyrian Empire was weakened. It finally fell about 612 B.C.

SECTION REVIEW

1. Mapping: Using the map on page 15, describe the relative location of: the Hittite Empire, the Black Sea, the Syrian Desert, Egypt, Hattusas.
2. In your own words, briefly identify: the Hittites, the Assyrians.
3. How did the Hittites and the Egyptians get along with each other?
4. What did the Hittites have to do with ironworking?
5. List two contributions made by the Assyrians to life in the ancient Middle East.
6. What did the remains of iron goods made by the Hittites tell historians about life in the ancient Middle East?
◗ Do you own any things made of metal? Pick three of these things and describe what historians might be able to tell about your life by examining these items.

THE CHALDEANS AND THE PERSIANS

The Assyrian Empire was defeated by three groups of people who fought together. These were the *Medes* (MEEDZ) who came from a plateau area in the east called Media (MEED-ee-uh); the *Scythians* (SITH-ee-unz) who came from the area north of the Caspian Sea and Aral (AR-ul) Sea; and the *Chaldeans* (kal-DEE-unz) who came from Babylon. (See the map on page 18.) After the defeat of the Assyrians, the Medes and Scythians returned to their homelands.

The Chaldean Empire The Chaldeans combined the remains of the Assyrian Empire with their own kingdom to form a new empire. This new empire was ruled by a strong leader called **Nebuchadnezzar** (neb-uh-kud-NEZ-ur). At its height, the empire covered most of the Fertile Crescent. (See the map on page 18.)

About 600 B.C., during the rule of Nebuchadnezzar, Babylon was rebuilt. It was surrounded by a wall more than 20 kilometers (13 miles) long. Beautiful buildings were built inside the wall. Among the greatest of these were the ziggurat and the palace of the king. The palace had hanging gardens of tropical plants. These hanging gardens of Babylon were considered to be one of the wonders of the ancient world. The ziggurat is believed to be the largest one ever built.

Babylon was a rich and important city. The arts and commerce were highly developed. In the schools, scientists made maps of the heavens. They also worked out a system for recording the length of the year that is very much like the system used today.

The Medes While the Chaldean Empire was at its height, the Medes were also growing in power. The Medes gradually extended their empire westward toward Babylon. (See the map on page 18.) As the Medes added to their territory, they conquered the *Persians* (PUR-zhuns). In time, the Persians rebelled against the Medes. A Persian prince named **Cyrus** (SIE-rus) united both of these groups under one rule. Together, the Medes and the Persians were a powerful force. As they continued to expand westward into the Fertile Crescent, they became a threat to the Chaldean Empire.

Cyrus the Great Cyrus was the greatest conquerer in the history of the ancient Middle East. In only eleven years, between 550 and 539 B.C., he invaded lands from the heart of India in the east to Babylonia in the west. The armies of Cyrus entered Babylon in 539 B.C. According to Cyrus' records, the city surrendered to his army without a battle. This event marked the end of political organization of the older civilizations of Mesopotamia. From this time onward, the cities of the river valleys were united politically with the plateau region of present-day Iran. Thus the Chaldean Empire was added to Cyrus' other lands and became part of the Persian Empire.

The Persian Empire The Persian Empire was larger than either the Assyrian Empire or the Chaldean Empire. It stretched as far east as India and as far west as the Aegean (ih-JEE-un) Sea. (The map on page 18 indicates the great size of the Persian Empire at its height under the rule of Darius I.) The empire was well organized and well governed. It was divided into provinces with capitals that included the cities of Babylon, Persepolis (pur-SEP-uh-lus), and

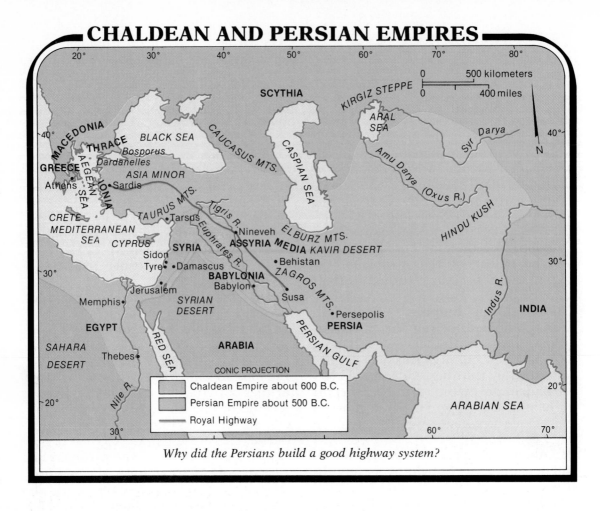

CHALDEAN AND PERSIAN EMPIRES

SCYTHIA

KIRGIZ STEPPE

500 kilometers

400 miles

MACEDONIA
THRACE
BLACK SEA
Bosporus
Dardanelles
GREECE
ASIA MINOR
Athens • Sardis
CRETE
MEDITERRANEAN
SEA
CYPRUS
Sidon
Tyre • Damascus
Jerusalem
Memphis •
SYRIAN
DESERT
EGYPT
SAHARA
DESERT
Thebes •

CAUCASUS MTS.

ARAL
SEA
Darya
Syr

Amu Darya (Oxus R.)

HINDU KUSH

CASPIAN SEA

ELBURZ MTS.

TAURUS MTS.
Tarsus •
Tigris R.
• Nineveh
ASSYRIA
MEDIA
KAVIR DESERT
SYRIA
• Behistan
Euphrates R.
BABYLONIA
ZAGROS MTS.
Babylon •
• Susa
• Persepolis
PERSIA
Indus R.
INDIA

ARABIA

PERSIAN GULF

CONIC PROJECTION

RED SEA

Nile R.

ARABIAN SEA

Chaldean Empire about 600 B.C.
Persian Empire about 500 B.C.
Royal Highway

Why did the Persians build a good highway system?

Susa (SOO-zuh). Each province was under the control of a government official called a **satrap** (SAY-trap). These officials were responsible for governing the provinces and for supplying soldiers in time of war. The officials, in turn, were checked by people sent by the king and could be dismissed if they did not rule properly. The satraps could also be dismissed if they were found to be disloyal to the emperor, or for crimes such as taking bribes.

The major cities of the empire were connected by a network of highways built by slaves. Along these highways, messengers went to and from Susa, the capital city. The excellent system of roads also aided trade.

The Persians did not try to change the customs of the people they conquered. Those who did not try to rebel against Persian rule were allowed religious freedom and some local government. Many of the conquered people joined the Persian army or became traders on Persian ships. But native Persians were given special rights within the empire. For example, they were usually taxed less than other peoples and received the best posts in the imperial government.

Persian Religion   At the height of

18

Persian power, a new religion, **Zoroastrianism** (zore-uh-WASS-tree-uh-niz-um), became popular among many people in Persia and Mesopotamia. Its founder was a prophet named Zoroaster (ZORE-uh-was-tur) or Zarathustra (zar-uh-THOO-struh). He probably lived during the seventh century B.C. Zoroaster undoubtedly borrowed many of his ideas from earlier times. According to Zoroaster, *Ahura-Mazda* (ah-HOOR-ah-MAHZ-duh), the god of light and goodness, had created the world. He was in a never-ending battle with *Ahriman* (ah-REE-MAHN), the god of darkness or wickedness. People had an obligation to help Ahura-Mazda in his struggle against Ahriman. Zoroaster also preached a definite belief in a future life after physical death. Life after death was another new idea for many of the people of that area of the world.

The Persian Empire lasted for more than 200 years. It was eventually defeated about 330 B.C. by the armies of Alexander the Great. This will be discussed further in Unit 3.

SECTION REVIEW

1. Mapping: Using the map on page 18, describe the location of the homelands of the Medes, the Scythians, the Chaldeans, and the Persians.
2. In your own words, briefly identify: the Medes, the Persians, the Chaldeans, the Scythians, Nebuchadnezzar, Cyrus, Alexander the Great.
3. How did the highway system built by the Persians contribute to life in ancient Mesopotamia?
4. What was Zoroastrianism?
◗ What do you regard as one important contribution made by your town? Describe how that contribution might affect future generations.

THE PHOENICIANS

Phoenicia (fih-NISH-ee-uh) is the ancient Greek name for a narrow strip of land about 19 kilometers (12 miles) wide and 320 kilometers (200 miles) long, located on the eastern coast of the Mediterranean Sea. This land is in the region of present-day Syria and Lebanon (LEB-uh-nun). (See the map on page 22.) It was made up of a group of loosely united city-states. These states usually paid tribute to other, more powerful states in the area.

Phoenicia was a hilly land with poor soil. Large-scale agriculture was impossible. So the *Phoenicians* (fih-NISH-ee-unz) turned to the sea for their living. They were skilled sailors and became the most successful traders of the ancient world. They founded colonies throughout the Mediterranean region and in northwest Africa. Phoenicia reached the height of its power from about 1000 B.C. to 774 B.C.

Phoenician Traders The Phoenicians carried on active trade with the people of the region that is present-day Spain. They sailed as far as the British Isles for tin. It is possible that at the beginning of the seventh century, a Phoenician fleet sailed completely around the African continent.

About 800 B.C., the Phoenicians began to develop their trading posts into colonies. One of the most important of these colonies was Carthage (KAHR-thij) in North Africa. In time, Carthage became independent and spread its influence throughout the Mediterranean area. Carthage was especially important because of its strategic location on the northern coastline of Africa. It was also a stopover point for Phoenician merchants and sailors on their longer voyages westward.

The Phoenicians were also skilled craftsmen. They brought raw materials from other lands and used them to make objects of gold, silver, copper, and bronze. They also made beautiful glass and textiles. One of their most valuable products was cloth that was dyed a rich purple. The dye was made from a shellfish that is found along the Mediterranean coast.

The Phoenician Alphabet The most important invention of the Phoenicians was their **alphabet.** It was not actually their own creation, but something they took over from another people and improved upon. As you know, the Sumerians developed a form of writing called cuneiform. But they did not use an alphabet. Cuneiform was made up of signs that stood for things or syllables. An alphabet is a set of signs, each standing for a single sound.

The first alphabet was invented some time between 1700 B.C. and 1500 B.C. by the *Aramaeans* (AR-uh-MAY-uns). The Aramaeans lived in the area of the Sinai Peninsula (SIE-nie) and northern Syria. These people used fewer than thirty signs to represent all the sounds of their speech. They used only consonants, no vowels. The Phoenicians adopted this system and developed their own alphabet with twenty-two consonants.

The alphabet we use today is based upon the Phoenician alphabet, which was adopted and improved upon by the Greeks. The Greeks added signs to stand for vowel sounds. The alphabet used today is a further development of the one used by the Greeks. The chart below shows how the alphabet developed in several steps from the earliest system to the one in use today.

DEVELOPMENT OF THE ALPHABET

PHOENICIAN	≮	ᐈ	∧	◁	∃	Y		⊟	⇌	⅄	(	ᙢ	५	○	⟩	Φ	⟨	ⱳ	✕					
GREEK	A	B	Γ	Δ	E			H	I	K	Λ	M	N	O	Π		P	Σ		Y	X			Ω
LATIN	A	B	C	D	E	F	G	H	I (J)	K	L	M	N	O	P	Q	R	S	T	V	X	Y	Z	

SECTION REVIEW

1. Mapping: Using the map on page 22, describe the relative location of: the Mediterranean Sea, Phoenicia, Israel, and the Lebanon Mountains.
2. In your own words, briefly define an alphabet.
3. Describe the physical geography of Phoenicia.
4. Why do you think the Phoenician alphabet is considered to be such an important contribution to the ancient world?

▷ The Phoenicians borrowed the alphabet from the Aramaeans. Make a list of items we have borrowed from other cultures. Why would future historians be interested in things in your daily life that have been borrowed from other cultures?

THE HEBREWS

The *Hebrews* (HEE-brooz) were a nomadic people who lived by herding sheep. About 1800 B.C., they moved with their flocks from the Sumerian city of Ur to the region presently occupied by Israel (IZ-ree-ul) and Jordan (JORD-'n). This area was called Canaan (KAY-nun), home of the *Canaanites*. Canaan was part of the ancient Middle East between the Jordan River and the Mediterranean Sea. (See the map on page 22.)

The Hebrews were led into Canaan first by Abraham and then by his son Isaac and his grandson, Jacob. Years later, when Jacob was an old man, famine struck his people. The Hebrews were forced to move south into Egypt where grain was available.

The Hebrews remained in Egypt for many years. Then, about 1275 B.C., when a pharaoh began to make slaves of the Hebrews, they left Egypt. Moses, the leader of the Hebrews, led them back toward Canaan. But he died before they reached their goal. It is said that the journey back to Canaan took the Hebrews forty years.

The Hebrew Kingdoms   When they first moved back into Canaan, the Hebrews were organized into twelve tribes. The tribes cooperated with each other when necessary. Common problems were settled by judges who were chosen for their holiness.

The Hebrews' neighbors, the Canaanites, were farmers. As the Hebrews increased in number, they began to take over the Canaanites' fields as grazing land for their sheep. This caused conflicts and finally led to war. When war broke out with the Canaanites, the Hebrews needed some form of central organization. Samuel, the last of the judges, gathered all the tribes together. He then chose from among them an especially strong and able young man named **Saul** (SAWL) to be their king.

Saul led the Hebrews from about 1020 to 1004 B.C. Finally he was killed in a battle with the Canaanites. **David,** his son-in-law, then became king. David defeated the Canaanites and took their city of Jerusalem. He made Jerusalem (jeh-ROO-suh-lum) the capital of the Hebrew kingdom. (See the map on page 22.)

By the time David became ruler of the Hebrews, they were no longer simple nomads. From their neighbors they had learned horse breeding, chariot warfare, ironworking, and other skills. David's reign, from 1004 B.C. to 965 B.C., was quite peaceful. The Hebrews had good relations with neighboring kingdoms, and trade developed. Under the rule of David's son, **Solomon** (SAHL-uh-mun), the Hebrew kingdom reached

PHOENICIA AND THE HEBREW KINGDOMS

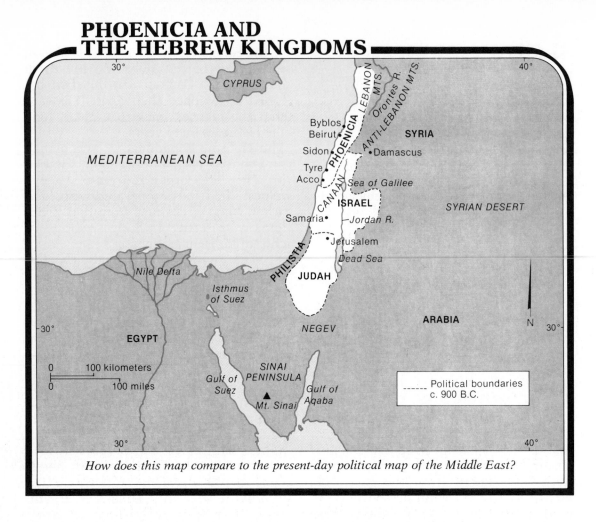

How does this map compare to the present-day political map of the Middle East?

a new level of peace, wealth, and cultural development during the years 965–933 B.C. The kingdom was well organized. Beautiful buildings were constructed in Jerusalem. Among these was the great temple, which was later destroyed by the Chaldeans. Commerce and trade increased, and learning and the arts were encouraged.

Solomon was known for his great wisdom. But he spent great amounts of money to encourage the arts and construct huge buildings. People were heavily taxed, and some had to work without pay. This led to much unrest and bad feelings in the kingdom.

The Fall of Israel and Judah

Solomon's rule ended in 933 B.C. After his death, the kingdom was split in two by revolution. The northern kingdom was called Israel and was ruled from the city of Samaria (suh-MER-ee-uh). The southern kingdom was called Judah (JOO-duh). (See the map above.) It was ruled from Jerusalem. For nearly 200 years, the kingdoms fought with each other from time to time. The conflicts weakened the two kingdoms internally so that they could not resist outside attacks.

In 721 B.C., the kingdom of Israel fell to the Assyrians. In 586 B.C., Judah was conquered by the Chaldeans from the east. Nebuchadnezzar, the king of the Chaldeans, destroyed the temple at Jerusalem and exiled to Babylon many of those living in Judah. Thereafter, the term Jew was used to describe the Hebrews. In modern times, the Jews living in Israel came to be known as Israelis.

After the Persians conquered the Chaldeans, many Hebrews were allowed to return to their homeland. But the Hebrews remained subjects of the Persians until about 165 B.C.

Early Hebrew Religion Before the Hebrews went to Egypt, they had been a nomadic desert people. As one grazing area was used up, they moved to another with their flocks. The rules of conduct they followed were based on this nomadic way of life. During the long stay in Egypt, however, the Hebrews gave up their old ways and settled in one place. They gradually forgot the rules that had governed them when they were nomads.

Once the Hebrews had returned to their lives as nomadic herders in Canaan, however, Moses realized that they needed rules to govern their daily actions. Knowledge of the old rules of conduct had been lost and new ones had to be created to replace them. The old rules had been passed from generation to generation by word of mouth. But Moses believed that the new ones should be written down. Then they would not be forgotten if the Hebrews were ever forced to move to a foreign land again.

Mosaic Law According to the Hebrews, who believed in an afterlife, Moses received the rules from their God on Mount Sinai, a desert mountain between Egypt and Canaan. These rules are called the *Ten Commandments*.

They governed the actions of the Hebrews in their religious, family, and community life. These commandments today are observed by Christians as well as by the descendants of the ancient Hebrews.

This is a segment of one of the Dead Sea Scrolls found in a cave in 1947 near the Dead Sea. These scrolls contain both religious and secular materials from the first century B.C. to the eighth century A.D. Why are historians interested in the writings of people from the past?

The Ten Commandments were the foundation of Hebrew law. Gradually, other rules developed around them. Because Moses was the first lawgiver of the ancient Hebrews, they are known as **Mosaic** (moe-ZAY-ik) **law.** Most of the rules that make up the Mosaic law are believed to have been created much earlier, at the time of the judges. These laws are often compared with the Code of Hammurabi. Under the Mosaic law, for example, punishment for certain crimes involved the cutting off of a limb or blinding. However, the Mosaic law set a higher value on human life than did the Code of Hammurabi. It accepted slavery, which was not considered evil in the ancient world. But it insisted on kindness to slaves, as well as to strangers and to the poor.

The Writings of the Prophets The Hebrews worshiped only one God, who they referred to as **Yahweh** (YAH-way). Today, many Jews use the word "Adonai," meaning "My Lord," in place of Yahweh, which is considered by some to be too sacred to pronounce.

When the Hebrews returned to Canaan, however, they came into contact with the fertility gods worshiped by the Canaanite farmers. The Canaanites believed that their fertility gods ensured rich harvests and prosperity. Soon, many of the Hebrews began to worship not only Yahweh but the fertility gods as well.

Some of the Hebrews still held to their belief in one God. Among them were the **prophets** (PRAHF-uts). A Hebrew prophet was a great religious thinker and teacher. The prophets said that it was wrong to worship any god other than Yahweh. They also said that Yahweh would punish the Hebrews for worshiping the fertility gods. The words of the prophets were written down. They became part of the Hebrew holy writings because the prophets were believed to speak for their God. The Hebrew people studied the holy writings to find out how their God wished them to behave. Besides being a source of religious wisdom and a guide to proper conduct, the writings of the prophets contain some of the world's most beautiful poetry.

Ethical Monotheism Most of the peoples in the ancient Middle East worshiped a number of gods. According to their religions, these gods carried on their own activities with little concern for the people who worshiped them. The Hebrew religion was different. First of all, the Hebrews worshiped only one God, Yahweh. The worship of one God is called **monotheism** (MAHN-uh-thee-iz-um). In addition, the religion of the Hebrews focused on the daily lives of the people. It encouraged good behavior in individuals—both in their own personal lives and toward others. This proper conduct is called **ethics** (ETH-iks). The Hebrew religion is the first example in recorded history of **ethical monotheism.** It encourages worship of one God and teaches that this God requires proper conduct on the part of the people.

The Synagogue While they were in exile in Babylon, the Hebrews developed a new form of worship. It centered on the **synagogue** (SIN-ih-gahg). The synagogue was a meeting place where the Hebrews could come together each week to read and learn about the holy writings. Every person could not be an expert in these writings, so in time each synagogue had one person who was specially trained in explaining them. It was the duty of this teacher, called a **rabbi** (RAB-ie), to interpret the holy writings for the others.

The creation of the synagogue was an important step in the development of religion. For the first time, a god could be worshiped anywhere, as long as there were enough people gathered together. Before this, people believed that gods or goddesses could be worshiped only in specific sacred places. They believed that a special ritual had to be performed by a priest or priestess. After the synagogue was created, people could worship wherever they could gather together. Their religion was no longer tied to a certain location. Synagogues could be found in many places.

The existence of a synagogue was important because it could be set up wherever the Hebrews lived. It helped them to keep their identity as a separate people. Hebrews were allowed to read the holy writings of their religion together. They strengthened one another's faith, even though they were in a foreign land. This was an important development because in most other religions only the priest or priestess could read and explain the holy writings. These religious leaders decided what the gods or goddesses wanted the people to do. They had great power over the people, and this power was often abused.

The Bible Many of the sacred writings of the ancient Hebrews are included in the books of the Bible. They contain the rules of conduct that form Hebrew law, the writings of the proph-

ets, and books of poetry. They also contain a detailed record of Hebrew history. The Hebrews recorded major events of their history because they believed that Yahweh's will was involved in those events. As a result, we have a more extensive written record of history of the Hebrews than of any other people in the ancient Middle East.

One of the best-known writings in the Bible is the Hebrew account of the creation. It appears in the Book of Genesis: Chapter 1, verses 1–21, and Chapter 2, verses 1–3. In this account, the Hebrews wrote how they believed God created the heavens, the earth, light, darkness, water, land, plants, animals, and human beings.

SECTION REVIEW

1. Mapping: Using the map on page 22, describe the relative location of: Canaan, Egypt, Israel, Judah, Jerusalem, Mount Sinai.
2. In your own words, briefly identify: ethical monotheism, the prophets, synagogue, rabbi.
3. List the major events in Hebrew history from the time of Abraham to the return of the Hebrews from exile in Babylon.
4. What was different about the religious ideas of the Hebrews? Explain briefly.
▶ How have the religious ideas of the Hebrews affected your own life? Give a specific example.

The Egyptians

THE EARLY EGYPTIANS

In Chapter 1, you read about some of the peoples of the ancient Middle East who lived in the Tigris-Euphrates Valley and along the eastern coast of the Mediterranean Sea. In this chapter, another group, the ancient *Egyptians,* will be discussed. The Egyptians developed a great civilization along the banks of

Why was irrigation such an important innovation in agriculture?

the Nile River in the northeastern part of Africa. (See the map on page 29.)

The Nile River   The Nile River begins in Lake Victoria (vik-TORE-ee-uh) and flows northward for about 6,400 kilometers (4,000 miles) until it reaches the Mediterranean Sea. The Nile is an important source of water for vast stretches of land where there is little rainfall. Egypt has been called the gift of the Nile because when the river floods every spring, it deposits rich black soil on the land.

From very early times, the Nile farmers relied heavily on the yearly spring floods. They harvested their crops before the flood. Then they waited for the great river to overflow its banks and deposit the rich black soil carried by its waters. After that, they planted their next crop. Farmers were able to plant as many as three crops a year on this very rich soil. Each new generation was able to reuse the same plot of land, because the soil was renewed each year by the floods.

The Egyptian farmers watered their land by building networks of dikes and canals, much as was done in ancient Mesopotamia. They built dikes all around a field and used canals to lead the water from the Nile. Then they opened the dikes in such a way that the water irrigated one field at a time.

The Nile River gave the Egyptians another advantage as well. It was easy to travel by boat along the Nile. This encouraged the development of an active river trade. It also made it possible to unite the region under one rule.

The Nile Delta At the northern end of the Nile is the Nile Delta (DEL-tuh). This is a broad, fan-shaped plain of fertile soil deposited by the river as it empties into the Mediterranean Sea. At the delta, the Nile branches into many smaller rivers. Some people have said that this network of rivers makes the delta look like the back of a leaf, with its many veins. The Nile Delta is a rich agricultural area. For this reason, it has been heavily populated throughout its history.

The Nile Valley The Nile Valley differs from the broad, well-watered delta area. The climate of the valley is hotter and drier. The valley itself is about 19 kilometers (12 miles) wide and several hundred kilometers long. It is bordered on both sides by high rock walls. Beyond these walls on either side is the desert. The rock walls and the desert formed a barrier that helped protect the people of the Nile Valley from raids by desert nomads.

The Isthmus of Suez The Isthmus of Suez (soo-EZ) is a narrow neck of land that connects the northeastern part of Africa with Asia. It is bordered on the north by the Mediterranean Sea and on the south by the Red Sea. (See the map on page 29.) The Isthmus of Suez is the only break in the natural barriers formed by the rock walls of the Nile Valley. It linked Egypt with the rest of the ancient Middle East and provided a route to and from Egypt for both travelers and invaders. This is the route the Hebrews used when they traveled to Egypt.

In this Egyptian tomb painting, the pharaoh is shown to be larger than all other people and animals. How does this reflect Egyptian beliefs about the pharaohs?

Natural Resources of Ancient Egypt Ancient Egypt was a prosperous land because of its rich natural resources. A wide variety of crops were grown in the fertile soil of the delta and on the farm lands bordering the river. There were pasture lands for cattle, goats, and sheep. Fish were plentiful, and birds were hunted in the tall reeds that grew along the river banks. The reeds themselves provided material for baskets, mats, sandals, and boats. Most important of all, the Egyptians invented a method of splitting and pressing the river reeds together to make a substance similar to present-day writing paper. This material was called papyrus (puh-PIE-rus).

The fine river mud was used for making bricks and clay pots, jars, and other containers. Blocks of limestone and sandstone were cut from the rock walls bordering the Nile. These were used in building the great pyramids and temples of ancient Egypt. Copper was mined in the eastern desert and the Sinai Peninsula. Gold came from the nearby desert and a region to the south. In addition, there was the Nile itself. This great river could be called the Egyptians' greatest natural resource.

Prehistoric Egypt   Historians have been able to learn much about prehistoric Egypt from the work of archaeologists and from the myths, traditions, and customs that were passed down through the ages. Archaeologists found the oldest remains of prehistoric Egypt in the cliffs that border the Nile Valley and in the desert beyond. There scientists found the bones of ancient animals. They also found stone tools used by the hunters who lived there nearly 12,000 years ago. During the period when hunters roamed the northern part of Africa, it was covered with broad, rolling grasslands and many rivers. Wild animals were abundant and were used as a food supply for the hunters and their families.

Gradually, the climate became drier, however, and the region became a desert. People were forced to move to places with a greater water supply. Some of them moved to the banks of the Nile. They settled in the low desert that bordered the swamps of the Nile Valley. Ancient houses and cemeteries have been found in that area. They indicate that gradually, over a period of 4,000 years, the swamps were cleared and settled.

As the swamps were cleared, people began to farm the fertile land. Historians think that the first crop was planted about 7,000 years ago. The pre-

historic Egyptians learned to domesticate wild animals. They grew *flax* and wove the fibers into linen for clothing. They made tools from wood and stone. They made pottery on a rotating wheel and made glass and worked with copper. Some people traded things such as copper, ivory, and materials used in perfumes.

These early farmers formed villages along the Nile. They built their homes of reeds and mud from the banks of the river. Remains of their cemeteries show that the Nile farmers buried their dead in shallow graves. The bodies were laid on their sides. The hot, dry sands of the desert often preserved the bodies for thousands of years. Some pots, weapons, and food were usually placed beside the dead person. This practice suggests that the prehistoric Egyptians believed in a life after death.

SECTION REVIEW

1. Mapping: Using the map on page 29, describe the relative location of: the Mediterranean Sea, the Nile Delta, the Nile River, the Isthmus of Suez, the Red Sea.

2. In your own words, briefly identify: flax, delta, papyrus, Nile Valley.

3. List the chief natural resources of ancient Egypt. Why do you think natural resources are such an important feature of this area?

4. Where have the oldest remains of prehistoric Egypt been found? What do these remains tell archaeologists about prehistoric Egyptian life?

▷ Where would future archaeologists find the remains of the earliest days of your community? What might these remains be? What would they indicate about the earliest life of your community?

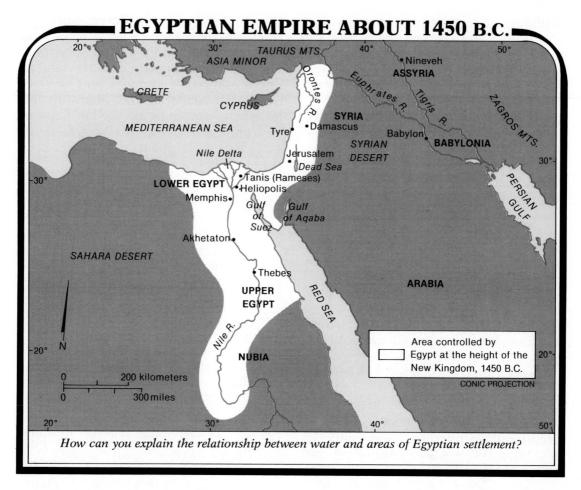

EGYPTIAN EMPIRE ABOUT 1450 B.C.

TAURUS MTS.
ASIA MINOR
Nineveh
ASSYRIA
CRETE
CYPRUS
MEDITERRANEAN SEA
Orontes R.
Euphrates R.
Tigris R.
ZAGROS MTS.
SYRIA
Tyre
Damascus
Babylon
BABYLONIA
Nile Delta
Jerusalem
SYRIAN DESERT
Dead Sea
LOWER EGYPT
Tanis (Rameses)
Heliopolis
Memphis
Gulf of Suez
Gulf of Aqaba
PERSIAN GULF
Akhetaton
SAHARA DESERT
Thebes
UPPER EGYPT
RED SEA
ARABIA
Nile R.
N
NUBIA

Area controlled by Egypt at the height of the New Kingdom, 1450 B.C.

CONIC PROJECTION

0 — 200 kilometers
0 — 300 miles

How can you explain the relationship between water and areas of Egyptian settlement?

THE OLD KINGDOM

Historians divide Egyptian history into three main periods. These periods are known as the **Old Kingdom** (2850–2200 B.C.), the **Middle Kingdom** (2050–1792 B.C.), and the **New Kingdom** (1570–1090 B.C.). These dates sometimes vary because of the kinds of records the Egyptians kept. Historians do not have enough information to say exactly when each period began or how long it lasted.

The Uniting of Egypt   Before the beginning of the Old Kingdom, Egypt was divided into two parts. The northern part was called Lower Egypt because that is the region where the Nile, as it flows north, ends its long course. It is also the area where the Nile forms a delta on its way to the Mediterranean. The southern part was called Upper Egypt because it is the source of the Nile where the river begins its long course. (The map above shows the location of Upper and Lower Egypt.)

About 2850 B.C., a prince of Upper Egypt named *Menes* (MEE-neez) conquered Lower Egypt and united the two parts into one kingdom. He founded his capital city at Memphis (MEM-fus), located near modern Cairo

29

(KIE-roe). (See the map on page 29.) This unification marked the beginning of the Old Kingdom. During this time, Egypt remained united politically. Power passed smoothly from one member of Menes' family to another.

Menes and his successors were what is called a **dynasty** (DIE-nuh-stee), or a family of rulers. In a dynasty, power to rule passes from one generation to the next within a family. It ends only when a family dies out or is overthrown. The Egyptians dated their histories by reigns of various rulers. They referred to an event as having occurred during a certain reign rather than in a certain year. This is why historians are not always sure about the exact date that an event took place.

The Pharaohs Egyptian rulers were religious leaders as well as political leaders. A ruler was thought to be a god and was called a **pharaoh** (FEHR-oe). This is the Egyptian word meaning "great house." The power of the pharaoh was linked to the power of the main Egyptian gods. It was thought that the ruler was the son or daughter of the gods. As a god, the pharaoh was thought to have special powers that made it possible for him or her to rule Egypt with perfect judgment and complete power. The pharaoh was believed to control not only men and women, but also the natural world. Therefore, in Egyptian art the pharaoh is always shown as larger than other humans or animals. The Egyptians also believed that the pharaoh's powers were responsible for the flooding of the Nile. If the river rose too much or too little, it was believed to be the pharaoh's fault.

As a god, and the son or daughter of gods, the pharaoh was supreme ruler of all Egypt. He or she was the giver of all law and the judge of all the people.

Government officials never spoke or acted on their own. They always said they were speaking for the pharaoh. The pharaoh also owned all the land in Egypt and received goods and services from the farmers. The pharaohs allowed the people to use the land and to buy and sell it. But the pharaohs always had the right to take any part of the land they wished.

SECTION REVIEW

1. Mapping: Using the map and the text on page 29, describe the location of: Upper Egypt, Lower Egypt, Memphis.
2. In your own words, briefly identify: Menes, the Old Kindgom, pharaoh, dynasty.
3. What are the dates for the Old Kingdom? What was significant about the Old Kingdom? List one thing.
4. How was the power of the pharaoh related to Egyptian religious beliefs?
▷ Do you think that people in the United States today relate the power of their leaders to their religious beliefs in any way? Explain briefly.

EGYPT DURING THE OLD KINGDOM

Egyptian civilization reached its height during the Old Kingdom. The uniting of Upper and Lower Egypt brought peace and prosperity. New farming methods improved the crops, and some farmers raised cattle. The animals spent the dry months of the year grazing along the Nile. When the rains came, the animals were rounded up, fenced in, and fed by hand. Once a year the herd would be looked over by its owner. At that time, some of the cattle were set aside for the pharaoh. They were the tax paid by the farmer to the pharaoh. A part of the harvest was also given to the pharaoh.

Egyptian Scribes Many farmers hired **scribes.** Their job was to keep detailed records of the farmers' business dealings. The scribes wrote on papyrus with a brush dipped into black or red ink. A message written in cuneiform on a clay tablet weighed as much as 45 kilograms (10 pounds) and was hard to carry around. But a roll of papyrus with 50 times the writing surface could be carried easily. The convenience of writing in ink helped spread Egyptian writing to Phoenicia and later led to the development of the alphabet.

The Egyptians had two kinds of writing. The earliest Egyptian writing is called **hieroglyphic** (hie-ruh-GLIF-ik) writing. It dates back to at least 3000 B.C. There were more than 600 signs, which were used mainly by priests for religious purposes. These signs were carved into stone monuments. The Egyptians did not develop a true alphabet as the Phoenicians did. But they gradually made hieroglyphic writing more simple. One of these simpler writing systems was a kind of handwriting called **hieratic** (hie-RAT-ik). This was the system used by the scribes. It was used mostly for legal papers and record keeping. While hieroglyphics were carved on stone, hieratic was used for more temporary records. It was written in ink on papyrus.

Scribes were among the most important members of Egyptian society. They attended a special school. Anyone who studied at this school learned to read and write and was taught the lit-erature and history of Egypt. Scribes also had to know mathematics, bookkeeping, mechanics, surveying, and law.

Egyptian Art Artists also had an important place in Egyptian society during the Old Kingdom. Sculpture was a highly developed art form. Works ranged from huge stone statues to beautifully worked small figures of people and animals in copper, bronze, stone, and wood. Buildings were decorated with detailed paintings showing scenes of daily life. Historians have been able to learn much about the daily life and history of the Old Kingdom by studying Egyptian art.

The Pyramids The Egyptians of the Old Kingdom made important advances in building with stone. They learned to move huge blocks of stone weighing several tons from one place to another. They cut the stones into the right shapes with copper saws and then fitted them tightly into place. This method was used in building temples, palaces, and pyramids.

The Egyptians used a special unit of measure called the *royal cubit* (KYOO-but). One cubit measured about 53 centimeters (21 inches), or about the length of an Egyptian's arm from fingertips to elbow. They also used the width of a hand (without the thumb) and the width of one finger as units of measure. With this simple measuring system, the Egyptians were able to build pyramids having bases the size of eleven football fields!

The first pyramid was begun about 2600 B.C. It was built for the pharaoh **Zoser** (ZOE-sir). The pyramid was built in steps or layers of stone. It was surrounded by beautiful white limestone temples and other buildings used for worshiping the dead pharaoh.

The building of a pyramid was a huge public work project, taking many years. Construction took place during the seasons when little work was needed on the Egyptian farms. Thousands of Egyptians worked under the direction of architects and overseers. One historian recorded that the building of a great pyramid for one of the pharaohs required the labor of 100,000 people for twenty years.

Scholars are not exactly certain why the pyramids were built. Perhaps the pyramid shape represented a change in the old Egyptian sun religion. It might also have represented some belief in life after death. Many scholars now think the pyramids were a type of funeral temple built to house the remains of the dead pharaohs.

As the Egyptians became more skilled, they built other kinds of monuments. An obelisk was erected for Thutmose III (thoot-MOE-seh), who began his rule in 1480 B.C. An *obelisk* (AHB-uh-lisk) is a tall, pointed stone column that is shaped like a huge needle. Originally built at Heliopolis (hee-lee-AHP-uh-lus), this monument now stands in Central Park in New York City. Temples, such as the one at Karnak (KAHR-nak), were decorated with sculptured stone sphinxes (SFINGKS-us). A *sphinx* is a figure having the body of a lion and the head of a human being, ram, or hawk. One of the most well known of the Egyptian sphinxes is one found at Giza (GEE-suh). It has the head of a man and the body of a lion.

While such stone monuments were being built, towns grew up nearby that supplied the needs of everyone working on the project. Later, these towns were used by the priests who held religious services for the dead king. The pyramids were surrounded by groups of buildings. They included temples for worshiping the dead and tombs for the pharaoh's family, nobles, high government officals, and servants. It was believed the pharaoh would need his or her relatives, friends, and servants in the next world. Personal things, such as furniture, clothing, and jewels, were buried with the pharaoh. It was believed that he or she would also need these items in the next world.

The pharaoh was thought to be the son or daughter of *Re* (RAY), the sun god. Re was believed to sail through the sky in a boat during the day. At night, Re sailed through the underworld and battled with the forces of darkness. Boats have been found buried near the tombs of the pharaohs. Archaeologists believe that these boats were intended to be used by the pharaoh to accompany Re on the journeys through the sky and the underworld.

Burying the Pharaoh   The Egyptians believed that the soul of the pharaoh would return to the body it had occupied during life. For this reason it was important to preserve the body as carefully as possible. Otherwise, the soul would not be able to recognize the body, and there would be no afterlife for the pharaoh. The body of the pharaoh was prepared for burial by a process called *mummification* (mum-ih-fuh-KAY-shun). The whole process took about seventy days. The brain was drawn out of the skull through the nose. The heart was left in the body because it was thought to be the center of a person's will and intelligence. But other organs were removed. They were preserved in jars, which were placed in the tomb near the mummy. Chemicals were put inside the stomach area to keep the body from decaying. Finally, the body was very carefully wrapped in

This is an Egyptian step pyramid. How do the tombs of important people in your community differ from the pyramid tombs of Egypt?

hundreds of strips of linen. The mummy of the pharaoh was then placed in the pyramid. Workers let huge stone blocks crash down to seal the entrance to discourage thieves from trying to enter the tomb. The only openings left were two secret air holes. These were to allow the pharaoh's spirit to enter and leave the tomb.

In spite of these careful preparations, most mummified bodies were damaged or destroyed by later plundering. The bodies of poor people, which were buried in the hot, dry desert sand, often remained in better condition.

Egyptian Beliefs about Death   The Egyptians believed that after they were buried, their spirits went to a great hall, where their sins were judged. There they pleaded for eternal life be-fore forty-two gods. The dead had to declare virtue. They also had to know the secret names of the gods. And they had to be able to cast magic spells that would drive off dangerous snakes and crocodiles. Spells were also necessary to survive the dangers of a journey across a lake of fire, and to keep the dead from forgetting their own names. If a dead person forgot his or her name, that person would die again. If, after all these trials, the dead arrived at a place called the "Field of Rushes," their lives would remain pleasant forever. The Egyptian beliefs about death and eternal life were written down in a book called the **Book of the Dead.** It is a large collection of spells and information about Egyptian beliefs. Many of those beliefs were probably thousands of

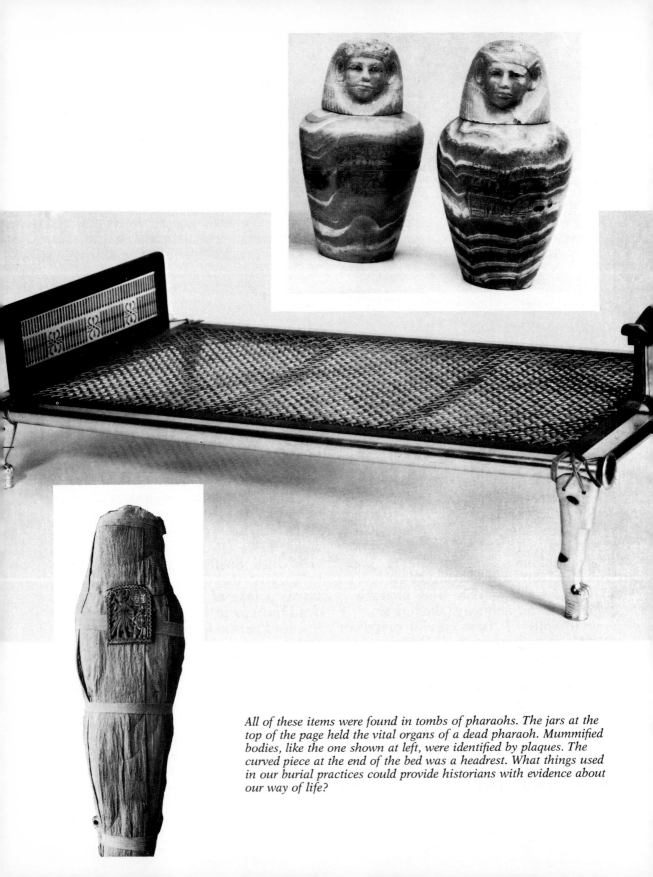

All of these items were found in tombs of pharaohs. The jars at the top of the page held the vital organs of a dead pharaoh. Mummified bodies, like the one shown at left, were identified by plaques. The curved piece at the end of the bed was a headrest. What things used in our burial practices could provide historians with evidence about our way of life?

years old before becoming part of the Book of The Dead. Historians have learned much about the ancient Egyptians by interpreting this important written document.

SECTION REVIEW

1. Mapping: Using the map on page 29, describe in which region of Egypt the cities of Thebes, Tanis, and Heliopolis were located.
2. In your own words, briefly identify: scribes, hieroglyphic writing, hieratic writing, pyramid, mummification, royal cubit, obelisk, sphinx.
3. Look at the picture on page 39 and describe the way hieroglyphic writing differs from the writing you use today.
4. What were some Egyptian advances in stonebuilding?
5. What might the Egyptian pyramids have represented?
6. Why could the Book of the Dead be used as a source of information about early Egyptian beliefs? Give an example.
▷ How could your beliefs about death and burial be used as a source of information about your life? Explain.

THE MIDDLE KINGDOM AND THE NEW KINGDOM

Between 2200 B.C. and 2050 B.C., a great struggle for power took place in Egypt. The priests and local nobles fought among themselves for leadership. The pharaoh's position was weakened, and Egypt became a divided country. It was divided because the central government had collapsed. For the most part, local nobles became the real rulers. Yet even with the breakdown of a central government, records show that the common people did not rebel or attempt to gain a share of the government. The common people did seem to miss the security of a supreme ruler of the land, however. During these troubled times, the pharaohs still existed but did not really rule.

The Middle Kingdom   Around 2050 B.C., a prince from the city of Thebes (THEEBZ) began to restore the power of the pharaoh. He united the country. Thus began the period known as the Middle Kingdom. This period lasted from 2050 B.C. to 1792 B.C.

The work of uniting Egypt was completed by a new pharaoh, Amenemhet I (ah-men-em-HET). During his rule, and during the next two dynasties, the role of the pharaoh changed. As before, the pharaohs were considered to be gods. But they no longer had absolute power. Now they had to share their power and wealth with the nobles and priests. In addition, the people no longer feared the pharaohs. Rather, they considered them to be protectors. The pharaohs themselves seemed more concerned with the welfare of the people than they had been before.

The Middle Kingdom was a time of peace and prosperity. Trade with other nations grew. All classes of people were thought to be equal in the next world. And even the poor received fine funerals. One of the most important changes was in the role of the priests. They had more religious duties and acted as intermediary between the people and the gods. They also were healers and took part in the government. Gradually the position of priest was passed from father to son. The priests formed a large and wealthy class whose power rivaled that of the pharaohs.

The strengthening of the priests' influence and the weakening of the pharaoh's created many problems. One of the worst results was that the kingdom became less powerful. When local nobles refused to submit to the pharaoh's authority, the kingdom was divided and wars began once again.

The Hyksos Invade Egypt   About 1730 B.C., a new disaster struck Egypt.

A battle between the pharaoh Rameses (the larger figure) and a Hyksos soldier is shown in this stone relief. The Hyksos conquered and ruled the Egyptians for nearly 150 years. What impression, however, does this picture give?

A people called the *Hyksos* (HIK-soes) swept over the Isthmus of Suez and conquered the Nile Delta. The Hyksos, using chariots drawn by horses, quickly defeated the Egyptians. They ruled Egypt for nearly 150 years. The Hyksos leaders became pharaohs. They tried to force their ideas and customs on the Egyptians. But the Egyptians hated these foreigners and resisted their ways. The Egyptians were able to drive the Hyksos out of their country about 1570 B.C. Unfortunately for later scholars, the Egyptians managed to destroy most of the records of Hyksos rule.

The New Kingdom   After the Hyksos were driven out, Egypt entered another period of unity and peace. This period is called the New Kingdom. It lasted from about 1570 B.C. to 1090 B.C. During this time, Egypt was ruled from Thebes by a series of strong pharaohs. The pharaohs of the New Kingdom were absolute rulers, like those of the Old Kingdom. They took some power away from the priests and the nobles, and kept a close control over the entire government.

After the Hyksos invasion, the Egyptians realized that their land could be invaded and occupied. They knew that they must be strong enough to protect it. Building an army was one step in that direction. The Egyptians felt that they would be safe only if they controlled the areas all around them, thereby keeping this territory out of the hands of rival powers. The Egyptian army of the New Kingdom was much larger than it had been in the Old and Middle Kingdoms. It was modeled on the Hyksos army. It used horses, chariots, and bronze weapons. The light, two-wheeled war chariot was introduced into the ancient Middle East about 1700 B.C.

The Egyptian Empire   Just as the Hittites had used the chariot to create their huge empire, so did the Egyptians use it to expand their territory. The pharaoh had a full-time army, ready to fight at a moment's notice. Many of the soldiers in the Egyptian army had been prisoners of war. They gained their freedom by serving in the Egyptian army. With this new and stronger army, the Egyptians conquered the whole Mediterranean area as far north as the Taurus (TAW-rus) Mountains. Then they moved south into the region that is now the Sudan (soo-DAN). (See the map on page 29.)

The mixture of peoples and ideas that resulted from this empire building did much to change the cultures of the ancient Middle East. The Egyptians took more and more land, and the empire grew rapidly. But the pharaohs soon found that it was sometimes easier to conquer a land than to rule it. During the reign of weak pharaohs, parts of the empire revolted and tried to break away. Only strong pharaohs managed to hold the early empire together.

Two Pharaohs of the New Kingdom   Among the ablest and most powerful pharaohs of the Egyptian Empire were **Hatshepsut** (hat-SHEP-soot) and her step-son **Thutmose III.** Hatshepsut was a wise and strong pharaoh who ruled jointly with Thutmose III from about 1500 B.C. to 1480 B.C. She was more interested in building a secure and prosperous Egyptian society than in extending the empire. During Hatshepsut's rule, Egyptian women enjoyed a better position than women in the ancient world. They had full legal rights and could inherit and sell property without asking their husbands.

Hatshepsut restored the temples that had been ruined during the Hyksos occupation. Paintings and carvings on the walls of these temples show important events that took place during her rule. Hatshepsut also completed huge building projects.

After Hatshepsut's death, Thutmose III ruled Egypt by himself from 1480 to 1448 B.C. While Hatshepsut governed Egypt, Thutmose had been jealous of her great power. Not long after her death, he and his followers destroyed paintings, sculptures, and buildings created during her rule. They even destroyed the tombs of her most faithful servants.

Thutmose III was a very active pharaoh. But most of his energy was reserved for war. He extended the borders of the empire as far as the Euphrates River. (See the map on page 29.) He also improved the Egyptian army and set up military posts in all parts of the empire. These were designed to put down revolts. The military posts were a constant reminder of Egyptian power and ensured that the conquered people did not fail to pay their tribute to the pharaoh.

Thutmose took the children of conquered princes back to Egypt with him and educated them there. The children were taught that the pharaohs were powerful enough both to protect conquered peoples and to punish any of them who tried to revolt. Therefore, when the children grew up and became rulers of their own lands, they would not often oppose the pharaoh.

Thutmose was a very able ruler. He devoted much time to the ruling of his empire, and personally judged legal cases. He also rebuilt and decorated temples, using the labor of war prisoners. Men and women who had been taken prisoner by the Egyptians in a war became slaves. They usually worked as laborers. But some reached a very high place in Egyptian society. They became military commanders, scribes, and even priests.

Thutmose was also a skilled artist. He designed many of the sacred vessels used in the temples that he had restored. Trade contacts with other countries also increased during the rule of Thutmose. Wall paintings from about 1500 B.C. show foreign sailors bringing the products of their lands to exchange for Egyptian goods.

The Common People Lose Their Rights
The military victories of Thutmose and other pharaohs of the New Kingdom made Egypt rich and powerful. The pharaohs and the nobles became wealthy because of the tribute they collected from the conquered peoples. But the benefits of the whole empire did not filter down to the common people. While the rulers grew rich, most of the Egyptian people were still as poor as ever. Also, as the pharaohs became more powerful, the common people had less and less freedom. They had no political rights of their own and came to depend entirely on the will of the pharaohs for justice.

Egypt was thought to be the property of the pharaohs because they were gods. But until the New Kingdom, the pharaohs had allowed the people to use the land as if it were their own. The pharaohs of the New Kingdom, however, took large amounts of land. They treated it as their private property and forced the peasants to work the land for them. They also rounded up the peasants from time to time and put them to work on huge building projects. This caused great discontent among the Egyptian people.

SECTION REVIEW

1. Mapping: Using the map on page 29, describe the locations of: the Taurus Mountains, the Euphrates River, the Syrian Desert.
2. In your own words, briefly identify: Amenemhet I, the Hyksos, Hatshepsut, Thutmose III.
3. What is an empire?
4. What were the dates of the Middle Kingdom? Briefly describe a few of the main features of Egyptian life during the Middle Kingdom.
5. What were the dates of the New Kingdom? Briefly describe a few of the main features of Egyptian life during the New Kingdom.
6. What rights did Egyptian women have during Hatshepsut's reign? What happened to the rights of the Egyptian peasants during the New Kingdom?
◗ What are some of the rights you have? Make a list of five or more. Pick one right from your list and tell how your life would be different if you didn't have that right.

THE DECLINE OF THE NEW KINGDOM

The New Kingdom reached its greatest heights during the rule of Amenhotep III (ahm-un-HOE-tep). During his long reign, the priests and nobles enjoyed many years of prosperity. Great buildings were constructed, including two huge temples. Amenhotep personally gave valuable gifts to important visitors to Egypt.

A New Egyptian Religion   The new pharaoh, Amenhotep IV, was not a strong ruler and had little interest in saving the empire. Instead he became famous because of the new religion he created in Egypt around 1375 B.C.

In the Egyptian religion, one of the most important gods was *Aton* (AH-ton), the sun god. Amenhotep IV believed that Aton was the only true god—not just the most important. To show that this sun god was different, Amenhotep changed his own name to **Akhenaton** (ah-keh-NAH-ton). The name means "he who serves the Aton." During this period, the Aton was shown in Egyptian art as the sun holding its outstretched hands over the land of Egypt. The pharaoh also built a new capital city, which was named Akhenaton, "the place of the glory of the Aton."

The new capital city built by Akhenaton was located on the site of the present-day town of Tell el-Amarna (TELL el-uh-MARN-uh). There scholars have discovered pictures of the pharaoh, his wife, Queen Nefertiti (neh-fer-TEE-tee), and their children. The royal family is shown in a new naturalistic art style. They are depicted in various aspects of everyday life. The art style is called the *Amarna* (uh-MARN-uh) *style* or *period* after the town where the pictures were found.

This stone relief of Akhenaton's family was found in Tell el-Amarna. How is this artist's style different from those of artists who did the other tomb paintings shown in this chapter?

The priests of the older religion, whose main god was *Amen* (AH-men) not Aton, had grown very powerful over the years. But now that the center for worship had been moved to another city and the nature of the god had been changed, the priests lost much power. The pharaoh believed he was the son of Aton and allowed Aton to be worshiped only through himself—not through the priests. In this way, the priests lost much of their power to the pharaoh. They also lost much of the wealth they had received in the form of gifts from the worshipers of Amen.

The priests of the older religion became angry at Akhenaton's power over the Egyptian people. To make matters worse, Akhenaton placed his followers in high positions that, in the past, had been filled by the priests. And the wealth that used to go to the priests of Amen and for building temples to the old gods went instead to the pharaoh's new temples for the Aton.

The Empire Falls Apart While Akhenaton and Queen Nefertiti were focusing their attention on the new religion, the Egyptian Empire continued to decline. Foreign princes were challenging the pharaoh's strength in the empire and tried to gain control over their land. Rebellions against Egyptian rule had already succeeded in Canaan. Even the Egyptian people were unhappy about the pharaoh's new religion. It promised them nothing. The new religion offered little hope of a life in the next world for common people.

Tutankhamun Succeeds Akhenaton The priests of Amen and the other gods had a strong hold over the people. The priests continually stirred up discontent over the new religion. Finally, when Akhenaton died, the priests became strong once more. In 1361 B.C.,

Tutankhamun (too-tang-KAHM-un), the young prince who succeeded Akhenaton, became pharaoh. Under pressure from the priests, he restored the old Egyptian religion and its gods. He also moved the capital back to Thebes.

Rameses II Meanwhile, Tutankhamun was not able to stop the decline of the empire. Egypt continued to fall into disorder. The situation improved a bit under an army general who succeeded Tutankhamun after his early death. But the following dynasty saw the final stages of the Egyptian Empire.

The most famous pharaoh of this dynasty was **Rameses II** (RAM-seez). He ruled from 1279 B.C. to 1212 B.C. He collected enough taxes from the remains of the empire to construct huge buildings. He also built a new capital at Tanis (TAY-nus) in the Nile Delta. (See the map on page 29.) This city was called Rameses. One of his battles, with the Hittites, was concluded by the first recorded peace treaty in history. This battle was followed by years of peace. But nomadic tribes continued to challenge Egypt's rule in Canaan.

Egypt Is Defeated Rameses II was the last pharaoh to win a major victory over Egypt's rivals. After this, Egypt was no longer able to fight off invaders. Disorder spread rapidly, and Egypt was invaded and conquered continually. The *Ethiopians* (ee-thee-OE-pee-unz) invaded Egypt from the south. The Assyrians invaded it from the northeast in 670 B.C. They conquered the entire country but were themselves defeated by the Persians around 525 B.C. The Persians ruled Egypt until they in turn were defeated by Alexander the Great in 332 B.C. Later, falling under the domination of Romans, Turks, French, and British, Egypt did not become independent again until the twentieth century.

Tutankhamun

The rather short and uneventful reign of Tutankhamun would hardly have received any mention in most history books except for one thing—the discovery of his tomb. Tutankhamun ruled as pharaoh in ancient Egypt from about 1361 B.C. to 1352 B.C. He was a child of eight or nine when he became pharaoh and reigned because of his childhood marriage with a daughter of the pharaoh Akhenaton. Tutankhamun died when he was only nineteen years old and was buried in a small four-room tomb. His burial place was in the Valley of the Kings.

Tutankhamun's tomb was the first ancient royal Egyptian tomb to be examined that was somewhat intact from the day of his burial. Previously, all known tombs of royalty in the Valley of the Kings had been thoroughly plundered by robbers. While Tutankhamun's tomb had been entered on several occasions after his death, much of the tomb's contents remained intact.

The search for his tomb began with two Englishmen, Lord Carnarvon and Howard Carter. In 1907, they started their archaeological digging and continued for many years. World War I interrupted the digs from 1914 to 1917.

The debris left from other excavations in the valley complicated the search for the tomb. As other tombs had been dug into by earlier archaeologists, they had piled rubble upon rubble outside. By some good fortune, it was some of that very rubble that actually saved Tutankhamun's tomb from later plunderers. Debris from a nearby tomb had been dumped over the entrance, and the tomb had been overlooked. Carter was removing some of the waste material when, on November 4, 1922, he discovered a stone step leading downward. He uncovered fifteen other steps. Carter next found a blocked-up doorway.

Carter sent for Carnarvon, then in England. Upon Carnarvon's arrival on November 24, the two began to make their way into what proved to be one of the most important archaeological discoveries of the twentieth century. As Carter slowly worked his way into the tomb, he recalled: "My eyes grew accustomed to the light, details of the room within emerged slowly, and gold—everywhere the glint of gold. For the moment—an eternity it must have seemed to the others standing by—I was struck dumb with amazement, and when Lord Carnarvon, unable to stand the suspense any longer, enquired anxiously, 'Can you see anything?' it was all I could do to get out the words, 'Yes, wonderful things!'" Included among the treasures were the three coffins of the king and an effigy of the young ruler made of gold, colored stones, and glass—all undisturbed for more than 3,000 years! Many of the items from the tomb were sent by Egypt on a tour of the United States in the late 1970's so that Americans could share the experience of what Carter had called "wonderful things."

1. What had Howard Carter found in 1922?
2. Why was his discovery important?

3. Do you think important evidence about our way of life could ever get "buried"? Explain.

SECTION REVIEW

1. Mapping: Using the maps on pages 29 and xxx, locate by means of latitude and longitude coordinates: Akhetaton, Thebes, Tanis. Describe the location of Ethiopia in relation to Egypt.
2. In your own words, briefly identify: Akhenaton, Nefertiti, the Aton, Tutankhamun, Rameses II.
3. Briefly list the major events that led to the collapse of the Egyptian Empire in 332 B.C.
4. Describe the new religion started by Akhenaton. Why did the common people dislike it?
◗ What could your religious beliefs tell a future historian about your life? Give two examples.

DAILY LIFE IN ANCIENT EGYPT

By studying the remains of ancient Egyptian culture, historians have been able to form quite a complete picture of daily life in ancient Egypt.

The Egyptian Family   Family life in Egypt was a favorite subject of painters and sculptors. From this art work, historians have learned much about family relationships. The Egyptian family is shown as a very close and happy one. Women were in charge of running the household. In wealthy families, they usually directed a large staff of servants. Women could carry on business and own and inherit property. But most women were not taught to read or write. And as far as we know, none held office in the government except for three women who were pharaohs.

Children were important members of the family. They also had important duties—to love and honor their parents and to help them in their old age. Sons of wealthy families were responsible for tending the tombs of their parents after they died.

Families usually had several pets. Paintings show men with their hunting dogs. The family cat is often shown hunting birds in the marshes. Small dogs, cats, and monkeys are depicted sitting under the chairs of their owners. Another favorite pet was the Nile Goose. It may have been used to guard the house, just as we would use a watchdog.

Wealthy families had many servants. The butler, the nurse, and the husband's aide held important positions. Slaves performed many kinds of work. Some slaves were freed by their owners or adopted by them. Slaves could also own property and rent land. But not all slaves were well treated. Many records refer to runaway slaves and the harsh punishment they were given.

Egyptian Houses   Models of houses placed in tombs have given historians some idea of what ancient Egyptian houses looked like. The houses usually had several rooms and were made of mud bricks. They had a courtyard inside the entrance gate. The front of the house was covered by a porch. A staircase outside the house led to the flat roof. On the roof were a storage place for grain, an oven for baking bread, and places for sleeping on hot summer nights. The houses of the wealthy usually had beautiful gardens surrounding them. Most houses also had their own wells for drinking water.

Egyptian houses had little furniture. The wealthy people sat on stools or chairs. But the poor sat on the floor. Beds were also a luxury of the wealthy. Other people slept on the gound on a mat or a pile of linen, or on a raised brick platform at one end of the room. Instead of pillows, the Egyptians used curved headrests of wood, pottery, or stone.

Clothes were stored in chests or baskets. Tables were rare. Instead, small stands might be placed near guests at a meal. The stands held wine jugs, water pots, or pitchers and basins for washing hands between the courses of a meal.

Egyptian Clothing   Egyptian clothes were usually made of linen. Men wore a kind of shirt made of a piece of cloth wrapped around their hips and tucked into a belt. This garment could be knee-length or long enough to reach the ankles. Women wore long dresses. These were either white or brightly colored. Both men and women wore jewelry. Men covered their chests with wide necklaces. And women wore heavy necklaces and bracelets. Men and women cut their hair short or shaved their heads and wore wigs. Sandals were worn only on special occasions. Otherwise, people went barefoot.

Egyptian Food   From tomb paintings, we know much about how Egyptian food was grown and prepared. The food of Egyptian peasants was very simple. They ate bread, beans, and salads of onions and lettuce. Wealthier people ate a wide variety of fruits and vegetables, many different kinds of meat and fish, milk and milk products, bread, and cakes.

At mealtimes, the adults sat alone or in pairs at small tables. The children sat on cushions on the floor. Knives, forks, and spoons were not used. People ate with their hands.

Transportation   in   Ancient   Egypt Wheeled carts drawn by oxen were sometimes used for transportation. But

This model of an Egyptian granary was found in a pharaoh's tomb. How do such models as this provide historians with evidence about the Egyptian way of life?

the donkey was the most widely used beast of burden. Goods were carried in large baskets slung over the donkey's back. Heavy loads such as blocks of stone were dragged along the ground on sleds to the river and floated on barges to the building site.

Reed boats that could be carried from place to place on a person's back were used when the Egyptians went fishing. Larger reed boats had a mast and sail and could carry several people. Heavy cargoes were transported in wooden boats, which were powered by sails or oars.

Trade in Ancient Egypt   The Egyptians traded with many parts of the ancient world. Their ships brought timber from Phoenicia, finely worked objects from Sumer, and carved ivories and weapons from Syria. They also brought olive oil, honey, copper, wine, tin, lead, and iron from other countries of the ancient Middle East. Caravans brought back ebony, ivory, animal skins, and gold, as well as slaves, from the lands south of Egypt. There is some evidence that Egyptian ships sailed as far as the Aegean Sea, the Persian Gulf, and the coast of India to trade.

Money was not used in ancient Egypt. All trade was done by bartering. To **barter** is to exchange one type of thing, such as timber, for another of equal value, such as ivory. Historians believe that Egyptian trade was well organized. But little is known of Egyptian business methods such as banking and contracts. A few commercial records on papyrus have been found. But the Egyptian records are not as complete as the cuneiform tablets historians have analyzed from other ancient Middle Eastern peoples.

Egyptian Science The Egyptians were expert in astronomy and geometry. They developed an accurate calendar so that they could predict the time of the flooding of the Nile River. They also measured the angle of the sun's rays at various times. This was done in order to arrange the construction of the temples in such a way that the rays of the sun would fall on certain important places during special rituals.

The Egyptians based the length of their year on the time that passed between the appearances of the star we call Sirius (SIR-ee-us), or the Dog Star. This period of time was 365 days. The 365 days were then divided into twelve months of thirty days each. At the end

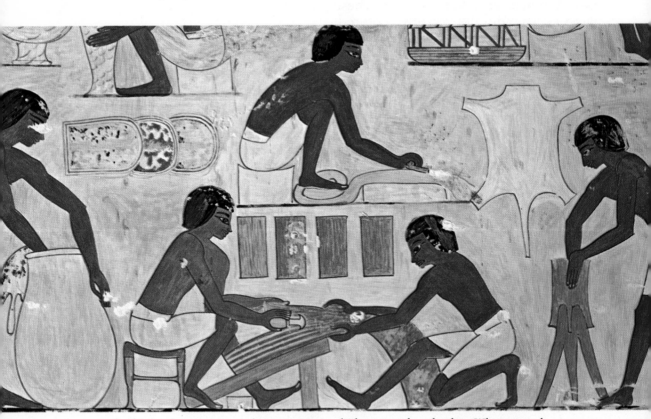

In this tomb painting, workers are tanning hides to produce leather. Why are such paintings as this invaluable resources to historians?

of each year, there were five days left over. These days were used as holidays.

The ancient Egyptians numbered the years by the rule of the pharaohs. They spoke of an event as occuring in the tenth year of the rule of Hatshepsut, for example. Using this sytem of dating, historians have been able to trace Egyptian history back to about 2700 B.C.

Egyptian geometry was developed for very practical reasons. In a land where the borders of fields might be wiped out by the yearly floods, exact measurement to restore these borders was necessary. Geometry was also used to lay out the system of dikes and canals used to water the fields. The pyramids and other great monuments were planned and built according to complex geometrical formulas. In contrast to their extensive knowledge of geometry, the Egyptians had a simple numbering system. There were signs for ones, tens, hundreds, thousands, and so on, up to one million. Numbers were written by using these few signs. For example, the number 22 would be written $10 + 10 + 1 + 1$. At least twenty-seven separate signs were needed to write 999. The Egyptians multiplied by doubling numbers until they reached the multiple they were looking for. They used the same process in reverse when dividing numbers. Fractions were used, but no fraction could be written unless it contained the number one. Thus the fraction ¾ would be written ½ + ¼. Although this system was a limiting one, the Egyptians were able to use it to solve most of their practical problems.

Egyptian Medicine   Medical writings on papyrus provide much information about Egyptian medicine. The writings list important cases that were treated. They also tell how a patient was examined, what treatment was prescribed, and how the doctor thought the case would turn out. Sometimes possible causes of a disease were listed. Drawings show that the doctors knew a great deal about human anatomy. It is believed that they gained this knowledge while preparing bodies for burial.

Egyptian medicine was valued throughout the ancient world. Egyptian doctors were sent to distant lands to treat rulers and nobles. Most of the large temples had medical libraries and medical schools for training doctors. Foreign doctors often wrote about the drugs and methods of treating disease they learned while studying in the Egyptian temple schools.

Egyptian Agriculture   The first people who lived in the Nile Valley caught fish and game and gathered wild fruits and vegetables. Later, barley and wheat were brought into Egypt from lands to the east. Barley and wheat grew easily in the fertile Nile Delta and the Nile Valley. They were two important staple crops of ancient Egypt. A **staple crop** is one that is used widely and continually. For this reason, it is usually grown in large amounts. Staple crops were grown on large estates. They were produced by men and women using wooden plows and hoes. The Egyptian farm lands were so fertile that as many as three crops could be grown in a year.

At harvest time, everyone helped to bring in the crops. The ripe grain was cut with sickles and collected in baskets or nets. Then it was threshed. This separated the grain from the chaff, or unusable part of the plant. The peasants kept only a small part of the crop. The rest belonged to the pharaoh or the noble who owned the estate. Flax and

In the top part of this picture, Egyptians are measuring a field of grain. In the bottom part, the grain is being delivered to the storehouse where scribes record the amount of the harvest. Where could you find a similar pictorial record of the business activities of your society?

cotton were also grown as staple crops. The fibers were spun and woven into linen and cotton cloth.

Fruits and vegetables needed large amounts of water, so orchards and gardens were crisscrossed with small canals. Grape growing was an important activity in the delta area. There were many large vineyards owned by the pharaoh and by the temples. Some were privately owned as well. The juice of the grapes was made into wine. Other crops included figs, dates, and a kind of cherry.

Egyptian Government   The pharaoh was the supreme ruler of Egypt. Next to the pharaoh, the most important person was the **vizier** (vuh-ZIR). Almost every part of Egyptian government was run by the vizier's office, and official records were kept there. These included royal commands, private wills, and contracts. The reports of local officials to the pharaoh came to the vizier first. He looked them over and passed them on to the pharaoh. Then he sent the pharaoh's commands back to the local officials.

The vizier acted as a judge. He tried cases and heard appeals. He also appointed judges in the local courts. The vizier had many other duties as well. He controlled irrigation and agriculture. He was also responsible for collecting taxes, receiving the tribute of foreign rulers, and entertaining important visitors from other lands. The vizier also was responsible for keeping the roads and buildings in good repair, and for running the police force and the army.

Other important officials included the high priest, the chief architect, the royal treasurer, the royal official who looked after the pharaoh's household, the army generals, and the teachers of the royal children.

Egyptian Law   Documents such as wills, contracts, deeds, and marriage agreements show that the ancient Egyptians liked to keep a record of their legal dealings. Although no codified set of laws from Egypt has been found, such as those known from Hammurabi and the Amorites, informal laws covered day-to-day events. Writings also show that disputes were sometimes settled very simply. A local wise man or woman would be asked for advice. Or a god's statue would be asked to decide between the two sides in a case. The statue was thought to give its opinion by moving to one side or the other.

Egyptian Religion   The Egyptians had many gods. Throughout Egypt, each of the main gods had his or her own temple. The temple was staffed by priests, who acted as servants of the god. The office of priest was passed from father to son. Within the temple, the priests ranked from the lowest temple servants to the high priest and his assistants. The most important priests were usually men of great wealth and power. Local temples usually had between twenty to fifty priests. Huge national temples had thousands of priests.

Religion in ancient Egypt was complex. The religion often followed political developments. Each local area had its own gods and goddesses. And as these areas were united with the rest of Egypt, their gods and goddesses were accepted by the whole region. The leading god or goddess of Egypt was often the one that belonged to the place where the ruler came from. There were many Egyptian gods and goddesses, and their positions changed through the years. For this reason, it is difficult to understand their place in Egyptian religion. We do know, however, that two of the main gods were *Horus*, (HAW-rus) the falcon, and Re, the sun god. Egyptians believed that the pharaoh was descended from Horus and Re.

The Egyptian people did not take part in the daily activities of the temple. Nor were they allowed to take part in the temple services. Important people could bring offerings to the outer court of the temple. But only the priests were allowed inside, and only the highest priests could go into the holiest parts of the temple. During yearly festivals, however, the god's statue would be carried into the streets on the shoulders of the priests. There would be special feasts and celebrations at these times. The whole population of a city turned out to join in the celebrations.

SECTION REVIEW

1. Mapping: Using the maps on pages 5 and 29, describe the location in relation to Egypt of: Phoenicia, Sumer, and Syria.

2. In your own words, briefly identify: staple crop, vizier.

3. Briefly describe *two* of the following aspects of daily life in ancient Egypt: the Egyptian family; Egyptian houses, food, and clothing; Egyptian transportation and trade; Egyptian science; Egyptian agriculture; Egyptian government; Egyptian religion.

◗ What sources of information will future historians have about daily life in your community? List them. Which of these sources of information do you think will be the most useful in writing a history of your life? Why?

Reviewing the Unit

Unit Summary

After you have read the selection below, answer the questions that follow.

We owe a great debt to many of the early peoples of the ancient Middle East. The Sumerians were among the first to leave a written record, in cuneiform, of their lives. The Amorites developed one of the earliest known written codes of law about 1750 B.C. on the orders of Hammurabi, an Amorite king. A new method of iron working was introduced by the Hittites about 1400 B.C. The Assyrians, however, were the first people to use iron widely. They also were among the earliest known people to maintain a large library of cuneiform tablets. Their civilization reached its peak about 800 B.C..

While the Assyrians gained power, the Phoenicians built a great sea-trading civilization that reached its height from about 1000 B.C. to 774 B.C. The most important contribution of the Phoenicians was, however, the development of an alphabet. It provided the basis for the one we use today.

The Hebrews began to organize under the leadership of certain men including Moses. The Hebrews contributed ideas such as those expressed in the Ten Commandments. Their downfall came in 586 B.C. when the Chaldeans conquered the Hebrews.

Culture continued to develop in the ancient Middle East even after the decline of these civilizations. The Chaldeans, for example, by 600 B.C. had rebuilt Babylon into a beautiful capital city. The Persians created a well-organized empire that lasted from about 500 B.C. to 330 B.C.

Farther to the west, the ancient Egyptians were using the waters of the Nile River to develop their land. Egyptian rulers, called pharaohs, were religious as well as political leaders. Historians know a great deal about the early Egyptians because of the system of hieroglyphic writing they developed. Their mathematical and stonebuilding skills are also evident from the many monuments they constructed.

Developing Your Reading Skills

1. Which *one* of the following do you think is the main point of this reading? Explain why. The early peoples of the ancient Middle East and northeastern Africa
   a. had many wars.
   b. developed many new ideas.
   c. were very well read.
   d. were usually uncivilized.

2. What do you think is the main idea in this reading about *each* of the following:
   a. Sumerians
   b. Amorites
   c. Hittites
   d. Assyrians
   e. Hebrews
   f. Chaldeans
   g. Persians
   h. Egyptians

Developing a Sense of Time

Examine the time line below and answer the questions that follow it.

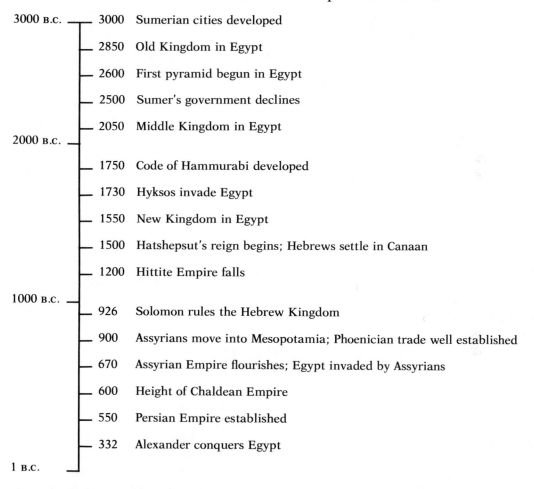

3000 B.C.	3000	Sumerian cities developed
	2850	Old Kingdom in Egypt
	2600	First pyramid begun in Egypt
	2500	Sumer's government declines
	2050	Middle Kingdom in Egypt
2000 B.C.		
	1750	Code of Hammurabi developed
	1730	Hyksos invade Egypt
	1550	New Kingdom in Egypt
	1500	Hatshepsut's reign begins; Hebrews settle in Canaan
	1200	Hittite Empire falls
1000 B.C.		
	926	Solomon rules the Hebrew Kingdom
	900	Assyrians move into Mesopotamia; Phoenician trade well established
	670	Assyrian Empire flourishes; Egypt invaded by Assyrians
	600	Height of Chaldean Empire
	550	Persian Empire established
	332	Alexander conquers Egypt
1 B.C.		

1. Which emerged first: the development of Sumerian cities or the Old Kingdom in Egypt?
2. What period of Egyptian history occurred shortly after the development of the Code of Hammurabi?
3. When was Phoenician trade well established?
4. What key events from Unit 1 can you add to this time line? Name three such events or developments; give a reason for selecting each.

Recalling the Facts

1. What contributions did the Sumerians make to ancient life?
2. Who were the Amorites? What was one noteworthy act by one of their kings?
3. What special uses did the Hittites and the Assyrians make of iron?
4. Why were Assyrian libraries important for the time they were in use, and for recent times?
5. What were four significant developments of the Persian Empire?
6. What did the Phoenicians contribute to us?
7. Briefly summarize the main developments in ancient Egypt during the Old Kingdom, the Middle Kingdom, and the New Kingdom.
8. What was distinctive about the religions of the ancient Egyptians?
9. What was distinctive about the religion of the Hebrews? Compare it to the religion of the Egyptians.

Using Your Vocabulary

1. Why is an archaeologist's work necessary in order to learn about ancient peoples?
2. What is the difference between cuneiform and hieroglyphic writing?
3. What does the meaning of *codification* have to do with laws?
4. How are the terms *pharaoh* and *dynasty* related to one another?
5. In your own words, define the terms *religion* and *government*.
6. Using your definition of *religion*, briefly describe the religion of each of the following.
   a. Sumerians   c. Hebrews
   b. Zoroaster   d. Egyptians
7. Using your definition of *government*, briefly describe the government of each of the following.
   a. Sumerians   c. Persians
   b. Amorites   d. Egyptians
8. Why do you think the terms *religion* or *government* can have different meanings for different peoples?

Using Your Geography Skills

1. Describe the physical geography of the Fertile Crescent during ancient times.
2. Referring to the map on page 5 and the text on page 6, describe how the geographic features of the Fertile Crescent could have led to the development of Sumer.
3. Using the maps in this unit, describe the geographical location of each of the following civilizations: Amorites, Assyrian, Hittite, Chaldean, and Hebrew.
4. How did the Phoenicians make use of the physical geography around them?
5. Using the map on page 22 and the descriptions on page 27, describe how the Nile River and Delta areas helped the ancient Egyptians to develop a civilization based on agriculture.
6. In general, do you think the physical environment of an area can significantly affect the way a people live? Explain, using an example.

Developing Your Writing Skills

In this unit you have examined the major cultures of the ancient Middle East as well as the culture of Egyptian society. You studied about developments within the cultures of the Sumerians, Amorites, Hittites, Assyrians, Phoenicians, Hebrews, Chaldeans, Persians, and Egyptians.

FORMING AN OPINION

1. What do you think are the most lasting contributions of those ancient cultures to our modern society? List them.

2. Of that list, which *three* have affected you the most? How have they affected you?

SUPPORTING AN OPINION

3. Write a paragraph or essay that gives your opinion of the importance of the contributions to us made by the people you studied in Unit 1. Support your opinion with facts from the unit. Begin by completing the following topic sentence: The ancient peoples of the Middle East _____

Why Study the Past?

The introduction and use of iron by the Hittites and Assyrians was a major innovation. It provided them with better and stronger weapons and tools and contributed to their advanced technology. Name one recent innovation that has improved our technology. How will it improve our lives?

Your History Bookshelf

Aldred, Cyril. *Egypt to the End of the Old Kingdom.* New York: McGraw Hill, 1965.

Casson, Lionel. *Ancient Egypt.* New York: Time-Life Books, Inc., 1965.

———. *Daily Life in Ancient Egypt.* New York: American Heritage, 1975.

Cottrell, Leonard. *Five Queens of Egypt.* Indianapolis: Bobbs-Merrill Co., Inc., 1969.

Davidson, Marshall B., ed. *The Horizon Book of Lost Worlds.* New York: American Heritage, 1962.

Easton, Steward C. *The Heritage of the Ancient World.* New York: Holt, Rinehart, and Winston, 1970.

Gray, John. *Near Eastern Mythology: Mesopotamia, Syria, Palestine.* New York: Hamlyn, 1969.

Jons, Veronica. *Egypt Mythology.* New York: Crown, 1972.

Klagsbrun, Francine. *The Story of Moses.* New York: Franklin Watts, 1968.

National Geographic Society. *Ancient Egypt.* Washington D.C.: National Geographic, 1978.

The World of the
Ancient Far East

Many years ago, a Dutch trader on a visit to China was invited to the home of a local merchant. The Chinese merchant had prepared a wonderful feast for his European guest. And the trader thoroughly enjoyed every morsel of the food his host offered. Indeed, each new course was better than the last. The trader was particularly impressed by a special sauce the Chinese merchant suggested he try on the roast goose and other dishes. The trader inquired if this was one of the merchant's own special blends. The merchant said it was not. The special sauce was quite common in the area. He told the trader that it was called *ke-tsiap*. In Chinese, this means "the brine of pickled fish." However, the trader was told that *ke-tsiap* contained many ingredients, including the juices of mushrooms and walnuts.

The Dutch trader grew more interested in this tasty sauce. He thought the people of the Netherlands might like to try it. So he and the Chinese merchant agreed to ship several casks of the sauce to the trader's homeland. The product was an enormous success there. In fact, when the Dutch came to America, they brought some of their special sauce with them.

Over the years, the recipe for this delicious seasoning underwent some changes, as did the name of the sauce itself. Because the Dutch found the Chinese word difficult to pronounce, they called the sauce *ketjap*. The Americans found it just as difficult to say *ketjap* as *ke-tsiap*. So they began calling it ketchup or catsup.

The peoples of the ancient Middle Eastern and Mediterranean (med-uh-tuh-RAY-nee-un) lands were separated from the peoples of the Far East not only by great distances, but by geographic barriers as well. For centuries, barriers such as vast deserts and high mountain ranges limited overland contacts between these parts of the ancient world. They also isolated many Asian peoples from one another. The huge subcontinent of India (IN-dee-uh), for example, was cut off from its neighbors by the great Himalaya (HIM-uh-LAY-uh) range. The sea was a geographic barrier as was the land area called Indochina (IN-doe-CHIE-nuh). Indochina is a large land mass that juts southward into the sea. Its location made the voyage from India to China or other places in the Far East a long and dangerous one in ancient times, since ships had to sail a great distance to get around it.

Despite these barriers, the lands of the ancient Far East maintained contact with each other. Occasionally, these ancient empires and kingdoms received visits from non-Asians. And Asians (AY-zhunz) traveled to other parts of the world from time to time. The cultures of China and India influenced nearly all the cultures of the world.

In this unit, you will be studying three major cultures of the Far East in detail—India, China, and Japan (juh-PAN).

Unit Goals

1. To know the geographical features of India, China, and Japan.
2. To know how the lands of the ancient and early Far East were cut off from contact with other parts of the world by geographical barriers.
3. To know the main contributions to world civilization made by the peoples of the ancient and early Far East.
4. To compare and contrast the ways of life of ancient and early India, China, and Japan.
5. To know the religious beliefs of ancient and early India, China, and Japan.
6. To identify and compare obstacles to the development of stable, centralized governments in ancient and early India, China, and Japan.

Far East

50°

140°

HOKKAIDO

40°

ALTAI MTS.

MONGOLIA

MANCHURIA

HONSHU

GOBI DESERT

JAPAN

Tokyo ★

30°

TARIM BASIN

Yellow R. Peking ★

KOREA

Kyoto •
Nara •

SHIKOKU

*YELLOW
SEA*

• Nagasaki
KYUSHU

SH

ER PASS

C H I N A

Wei R.

Nanking •

*EAST
CHINA
SEA*

PLATEAU OF TIBET

Hangchow •

a •

Delhi ★

HIMALAYA MTS.

Mt. Everest ▲

Yangtze R.

TAIWAN

PACIFIC OCEAN

aro •

Agra •

SERT

TROPIC OF CANCER

20°

Ganges R.

PLAIN OF HINDUSTAN

Si R. Canton •

INDIA

DECCAN PLATEAU

Irrawaddy R.

130°

EASTERN GHATS

ERN GHATS

*BAY OF
BENGAL*

Mekong R.

SOUTH CHINA SEA

10°

CEYLON

INDIAN OCEAN

0°

- - - Modern political boundaries

EQUATOR

0   800 kilometers

0   500 miles

80°   90°   100°   110°   120°

3

The Early Indians

EARLY CIVILIZATION IN INDIA

Today much is known about the early civilizations that appeared in the Middle Eastern world. But scholars know less about the history of ancient India. We know there was a highly developed culture in India as early as 2500 B.C. This civilization flourished at the same time the first pyramids were begun in Egypt (EE-jupt), and at the same time as the decline of ancient Sumerian government. But we do not know who the people of this culture in India were, where they came from, or what finally became of them.

Ancient Cities of the Indus Valley We do know something about the life of these ancient Indian people, however. About fifty years ago, archaeologists discovered the ruins of ancient cities in the valley of the Indus (IN-dus) River. (See the map on page 58.)

Two of the cities of ancient India, Mohenjo-Daro (moe-HEN-joe-DAH-roe) and Harappa (huh-RAP-uh), were large, well-planned communities. They had wide, straight streets with lampposts. The houses were built of brick, and many were several stories high. Most houses had conveniences such as bathrooms and tanks to store fresh water.

Archaeologists have also unearthed many small statues of humans and an-imals, as well as decorated toys, jewelry, razors, pottery, mirrors, fishhooks, and woven cloth. These artifacts tell us that the artisans of Mohenjo-Daro and Harappa were skilled in many crafts.

Archaeologists have also found objects that they believe were not made in Mohenjo-Daro or Harappa. The people of these two cities probably acquired such objects through trade. The objects show that Mohenjo-Daro and Harappa were in contact not only with other parts of India but also with places as distant as Sumer (SOOH-mer) and Egypt. Beads, rings, and bracelets made of turquoise have been found. Since turquoise comes from Persia (PUR-zhuh), we can conclude that the people of the Indus Valley traded with Persia. Copper bowls indicate that the people traded with copper-rich Afghanistan (af-GAN-uh-stan).

We do not know what became of the cultures of Mohenjo-Daro and Harappa. The fate of these cities remains a mystery. They might have been destroyed by a series of floods of the Indus River. A plague might have wiped out the population. Or an enemy might have invaded and destroyed the cities. Whatever happened, Mohenjo-Daro and Harappa had been abandoned by 1500 B.C. The once-flourishing Indus River Valley became a desolate place.

The excavated remains of Mohenjo-Daro give us a glimpse into the civilization of the early Indus Valley. The streets were wide and straight and were built so as to meet at right angles. How could such streets have been an advantage for a trading city?

The Aryans Invade India   Around 1500 B.C., warlike newcomers migrated into India. The newcomers were the *Aryans* (AR-ee-uhnz), a nomadic people who herded livestock. They may have come to India from an area east of the Caspian Sea. (See the Atlas, page xxix.)

Aryans lived a nomadic life. They never settled in one place but traveled about with their herds of livestock. For nearly 1,000 years, tribe after tribe of Aryans migrated to India. They came through the mountain passes in the northwest. (See the map on page 58.) Aryan warrior-bowmen, led by soldiers in horse-drawn chariots, conquered all of northern India. Only the people in the south remained independent. These people were known as the *Dravidians* (druh-VID-ee-uhnz).

The earliest Aryans had no interest in cities or trading. They destroyed the cities they entered and left the ruins to decay. These conquerors were not builders. In fact, the Aryans had no word for "brick" in their language. During and after their conquest of India, the nomadic Aryans looked down on the settled way of life of the Indians. The Aryans had no respect for the Indian culture and treated the natives as slaves. However, as the Aryans became more settled between 1000 B.C., and 500 B.C., conflicts between the two cultures decreased. They intermarried and adopted one another's customs.

The Aryans eventually settled down and established small kingdoms. Each was ruled by a king and a council of warriors. Within the Aryan kingdoms were many villages. These villages were so independent that they were like smaller states within the kingdoms. Each one was governed by the heads of the village families. But because the kingdoms were not united under a central authority, they often warred with each other.

The settled Aryans farmed the plain between the Indus and Ganges

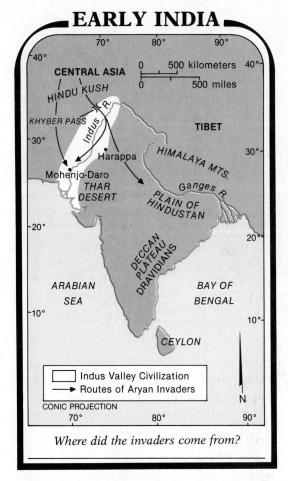

EARLY INDIA

Where did the invaders come from?

Map legend:
- Indus Valley Civilization
- Routes of Aryan Invaders

CONIC PROJECTION

During times of war the Kshatriyas became more important than the Brahmins. But during peaceful periods the Brahmins ranked higher. Next in rank were the *Vaisyas* (VISHE-yuhz) who tended to be farmers, merchants, and craftspeople. *Sudras* (SOO-druhz), or laborers, comprised the lowest caste. People who performed undesirable jobs did not belong to a caste. They were considered *pariahs* (puh-RIE-uhz) or *untouchables.* Members of the castes wanted nothing to do with pariahs.

A person was born into his or her parents' caste and rarely left it. Each caste observed rules regulating such things as occupations, marriages, and dress. For example, marriage between castes was usually forbidden. A member of one caste rarely performed the work assigned to another caste. It was very difficult, but not impossible, to change castes. No one really knows precisely how the **caste system** began.

The Vedas   The earliest written information about the Aryans comes from their religious books. These books are called the **Vedas** (VAY-duhz). The word *veda* means knowledge. The Aryans had no written language when the Vedas were first composed. So these books were memorized and handed down by word of mouth. Centuries later, they were recorded in the Aryan written language called **Sanskrit.**

The *Rig-Veda* (RIG-VAY-duh) contains hymns of praise to the gods. The *Sama-Veda* (SAH-muh-VAH-duh) are songs and chants. Formulas for conducting sacrifices comprise the *Yajur-Veda* (YUJ-oor-VAY-duh), and the *Atharva-Veda* (ah-TAHR-vuh-VAY-duh) contains charms and magic spells. All of these Vedas show that the Aryans, like the Egyptians, worshiped more than one god.

rivers. (See the map above.) It is one of the most fertile areas in the world. Their main crop was barley. Land was divided among the families of a village, but they all worked together to keep the land irrigated. Only men could inherit land and land could not be sold to strangers.

The Caste System   Based on legend, Aryan society was divided into four groups or *castes*. Each caste became identified with an occupation. *Brahmins* (BRAHM-unz), many of whom were priests and scholars, made up the highest ranking caste. Below them were the *Kshatriyas* (kshat-REE-uhz), among whom were rulers and warriors.

After the Vedas were completed, a collection of prose and poetry was written commenting on the meaning of the Vedas. This collection is known as the *Upanishads* (oo-PAN-ee-shads). The word *upanishads* means a meeting or a lesson with a teacher. The Upanishads deal with the nature of the universe and the meaning of life for humans. This collection of writings remained the core of Aryan religious beliefs.

Early Epic Literature   Between 400 B.C. and 200 A.D., the two greatest epics of Indian literature began to take their final form. One of these epics, the *Mahabharata* (muh-HAH-BAH-ruh-tuh) is one of the longest poems in literature. It tells the story of an eighteen-day battle between the armies of two rival families for the throne of a kingdom in northern India. Some scholars believe that the *Mahabharata* may describe an actual struggle that took place around 1400 B.C.

The most famous section of the *Mahabharata* is called the *Bhagavad-Gita* (BUHG-uh-vud-GEE-tuh). This is a dialogue between a warrior and his chariot driver, who actually is an Aryan god in disguise. The theme of the *Bhagavad-Gita* is that death is not to be feared because the soul cannot be destroyed.

The second of India's two great epics is the *Ramayana* (rah-MAH-yuh-nuh). This poem relates the wanderings of a heroic prince Rama (RAH-muh) and the adventures he faces in returning home to his wife, Sita (SEE-tuh). The main characters represent the Indian concepts of the ideal man and woman.

From these pieces of early literature, scholars have learned much about life in ancient India. The Aryans erected no temples and made no images to worship. Worship consisted mainly of offering sacrifices to the gods. These sacrifices were performed to obtain favors. As centuries passed, the rituals associated with these sacrifices became more complex. The number of gods increased and beliefs slowly changed.

Hinduism   Eventually the old Aryan religion evolved into the religion called **Hinduism** (HIN-doo-iz-um). The Upanishads became the core of Hindu religious thought. Among the basic teachings of Hinduism was a belief that the human soul never dies but is reborn, time after time, in different bodies. This belief in rebirth is known as **reincarnation** (REE-in-kahr-NAY-shun). The soul of someone who has lived a good life is reborn in the body of a more fortunate person, perhaps someone of a higher social position or of a higher caste. On the other hand, a wicked person might suffer rebirth as someone less fortunate, or of a lower caste, or even as an animal. Thus, Hinduism taught that a person's status at any time depended entirely upon what had taken place during a previous life.

The goal of a Hindu was to live life in such a way that he or she would merit a better existence in the next life. To accomplish this a believer might offer prayers or sacrifices to the gods. There were complex rites and ceremonies to be performed, usually under the direction of a priest. Or a person might observe numerous daily acts that were thought to bring benefits to a believer. These acts included reading aloud from sacred writings, bathing, and avoiding forbidden foods.

Hinduism gave approval to the existing caste system and linked caste to reincarnation. An individual's caste was an indication of how far that individual had progressed in perfecting his

This colorful facade depicts Shiva, a god who had many roles in the Hindu religion. What could you conclude about the Hindu religion from viewing this Indian temple?

or her soul. Any person of the Brahmin caste was believed to have lived better previous lives than any member of lower castes. Brahmins also were thought to be closer to attaining moksha (MOE-kshah). *Moksha* was a release from the process of endless reincarnation. An individual's soul that had obtained moksha then was absorbed by Brahma or the "World Soul" and did not return to the earth.

Hinduism involved the worship of many gods who were believed to be the different aspects of Brahma, the "World Soul." Three of these gods came to be regarded as the most impor-

tant. *Brahma* (BRAH-muh) was the source and creator of all life. *Vishnu* (VISH-noo) was the protector of living things. The third major god was *Shiva* (SHEE-vuh), the god of death and destruction. Vishnu and Shiva were the most popular of all the Hindu gods. Vishnu's followers believed that the god constantly watched over the world's welfare and had on numerous occasions come to the earth to save it from disaster. Shiva, on the other hand, was revered for his great powers of destruction. This god often was depicted with a terrible appearance, sometimes having several arms and faces that represented his various powers and attributes.

Buddhism   Around 500 B.C., another major religion appeared in India. Its founder was Prince Siddhartha Gautama (sid-AHR-thuh gaw-TAH-muh). The religion he founded became known as **Buddhism** (BOOD-izm).

Gautama's father ruled a small kingdom at the foot of the Himalayas in northern India. The prince grew up surrounded by wealth and luxury. But he was troubled by the misery and poverty of his father's subjects. He felt pity for the unfortunate people he believed were destined to be reborn time after time in such a life. At the age of twenty-nine, the prince decided to give up his luxurious life. He left his wife and young son and set out in search of the cause and cure of human suffering. Years of wandering and study followed. He sought out Hindu scholars to tutor him in the Vedas and Upanishads. He lived alone. He almost died from fasting, but he found no answer to the problem that troubled him. Then one day, six or seven years after leaving his home, while meditating beneath a tree, he felt that the truth had come to him.

At least he believed he understood the cause of human suffering and how to end it. From that time, he was known as the "Enlightened One," or the *Buddha* (BOOD-uh).

Instead of returning home to enjoy the peace of mind he had acquired, Buddha spent the rest of his life—almost forty years—wandering through the Ganges River Valley and instructing followers. Legends tell that he always wore a yellow robe and relied on the goodness of others for his needs. He went from village to village, where crowds flocked to hear him preach. He shunned the company of the wealthy and powerful. He preferred to be in the company of common peasant farmers.

Buddhism was not entirely a new religion. The Buddha clung to the belief in reincarnation. And like the Hindus, he taught that all life was sacred. Many Hindus and Buddhists refused to kill an animal because they believed that all living beings possessed a soul. Hindus and Buddhists shared a belief that the world was filled with evil and life was filled with misery.

However, unlike the Hindus, the Buddha taught his followers that human suffering was the result of desires for such things as wealth and power, health and long life, and pleasures. The longing for these desires produced suffering because none of them could give permanent satisfaction to the person who acquired them. Thus, the Buddha taught, the only way to escape from suffering was to do away with all desires. The individual who rejected desire for any sort of permanent satisfaction, even for life itself, would be free from suffering. Such an individual would enter a state of peacefulness that Buddhists called *Nirvana* (nir-VAHN-uh). The Buddha created rules for living that, he claimed, would enable his followers to reach the goal of Nirvana. In this way, the soul would escape reincarnation by being absorbed by the "World Soul."

The Buddha's religion had no place for the Hindu priests. Nor was there room for their complex religious rituals. He taught that neither sacrifices nor prayers would help a soul escape reincarnation. Everything, he said, depended on a believer's conduct and thinking. To reach Nirvana, his followers had to observe a strict moral code. In addition, the Buddha left his followers a set of moral rules that forbade stealing, killing, lying, and drinking intoxicating liquors.

The Buddha rejected the many Hindu gods. He denounced Hindu acts of devotion as superstition. Before his death, he called for an end to castes. He told his followers that all castes should be united in the new religion.

After the Buddha's death, many of his followers banded together under special rules he had laid down for them. They made him a god. They hoped to devote their lives to following the Buddha's teachings. They lived together in places known as monasteries, and they became known as monks. Their monasteries developed into important centers of learning. Meanwhile, the new religion spread rapidly over central and northern India and Buddhism became a rival of Hinduism.

The Spread of Buddhism Buddhism spread rapidly for a variety of reasons. Some people turned to the new religion out of dissatisfaction with the powers of the Brahmins and the complex, elaborate rites of Hinduism. Others were unhappy with the caste system of which Hinduism approved. And many Indians probably accepted the new religion simply because it seemed very similar to Hinduism.

Buddhism spread from India to Burma (BUR-muh), Thailand (TIE-land), and southeastern Asia. It entered Tibet (tuh-BET) and China from India's northeast and was carried from there to Korea (kuh-REE-uh) and Japan (juh-PAN). As the new religion spread, it was interpreted in different ways. A variety of Buddhist sects sprang up, each having its own doctrine. In general, however, two branches of Buddhism evolved. These were the *Therevada* (THER-uh-vah-duh) and the *Mahayana* (MAH-huh-yah-nuh) Therevada was the form of Buddhism that spread to southeastern Asia. Therevada remained close to the original teachings of Buddha. The Mahayanas, however, placed more emphasis on worship of the Buddha as a god who had come to save humans from the unending cycle of reincarnation. Mahayana spread to the northern parts of Asia, such as central Asia, China, Korea, and Japan.

SECTION REVIEW

1. Mapping: Using the map on page 55, describe the location of the ruins of Harappa and Mohenjo-Daro and the location of India in relation to the rest of Asia.
2. In your own words, briefly define and identify: the Aryans, the Dravidians, the Vedas, Sanskrit, reincarnation, Prince Siddhartha Gautama.
3. Describe the caste system and how it worked in ancient India.
4. Compare and contrast Buddhism and Hinduism.
   ◗ Are any groups of individuals in your community considered better or worse than others? Why do you think this situation exists?

THE AGE OF EMPIRES

The Aryans were not the last invaders to enter India through the mountain passes in the northwest. Time after time, the peoples of early India were threatened by foreign conquerors.

The Maurya Empire During one such period of struggle, an Indian general named Chandragupta Maurya (chahn-druh-GOOP-tuh MOW-ree-uh) established a kingdom of his own with his capital at Pataliputra (pah-tuh-lih-POO-truh). He drove foreign invaders from India and then turned against the native rulers of northern India. By about 322 B.C., Chandragupta had founded his own dynasty. The **Maurya** (MOW-ree-uh) **Empire** he created was the first in Indian history and lasted almost 150 years.

The greatest ruler of the Maurya Dynasty was Chandragupta's grandson, King Asoka (uh-SOKE-uh), whose reign lasted almost forty years (270–232 B.C.). He brought under his control all of India except the southern tip. (See the map on page 63). But Asoka tired of war and became a devout Buddhist. He did all he could to spread the new religion throughout India. Then he dispatched missionaries, including his own son, to carry Buddhism to foreign lands.

Meanwhile, King Asoka provided his own people with a just and efficient government. His officials were sent throughout the empire to determine the needs of his subjects. Asoka reformed the harsh system of punishments in India and tried to set a personal example by governing in accordance with the religious principles of Buddhism.

The Decline of the Maurya Empire The government Asoka established did

MAURYA AND KUSHAN EMPIRES

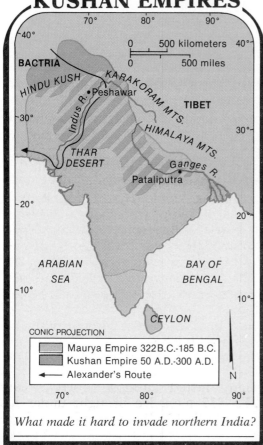

What made it hard to invade northern India?

not survive long after his death. His successors lacked his wisdom and ability. The last Maurya ruler was assassinated about 185 B.C. and the empire fell apart. When it collapsed, India was again divided into many rival kingdoms. For nearly 500 years, kings quarreled with each other, and foreign armies invaded the land. Much of India suffered chaos and violence until about 300 A.D.

During the Maurya Dynasty, parts of India came under the control of foreign rulers. Among the first were the Greeks from the Mediterranean area. Under an outstanding military ruler, Alexander the Great, the Greeks had

conquered much of the Middle East earlier. Alexander's armies invaded India and reached the Indus River in 326 B.C. The Greek kingdom of Bactria (BACK-tree-uh), which bordered India's northwest, was formed around 200 B.C. Bactria brought most of northern India from the Ganges River to the northwest frontier under Greek control.

The Greeks influenced India by introducing new forms of medicine, science, drama, and art. Within Bactria, Greek and Indian languages and cultures intermingled.

The Kushan Empire   About 30 B.C., Bactria was conquered by nomad invaders from central Asia. By 50 A.D., one of these invaders, the *Kushans* (kuh-SHAHNZ), had pushed into India and seized most Greek-held territory for their own empire. Greek cities were destroyed and most traces of Greek culture in India were wiped out.

The Kushans, India's new conquerors, encouraged Indian art and science and adopted the religion of their subjects. The Kushan conquest was a very important period in the history of Buddhism. The greatest Kushan ruler, Kanishka (kuh-NISH-kuh), came to power about 100 A.D. He established his capital at Peshawar (peh-SHAH-wir). Kanishka called together a great council of Buddhist monks. This meeting set forth the doctrines of the Mahayana, one of the two major branches of Buddhism. The Mahayana at this time also began to spread eastward, following trade routes to Tibet and China, and from there to Korea and Japan.

Buddhism in India was tolerant of foreigners like the Greeks and Kushans. And foreign rulers like Kanishka favored Buddhism rather than Hinduism. As a result, many Indians came to associate Buddhism with foreigners.

63

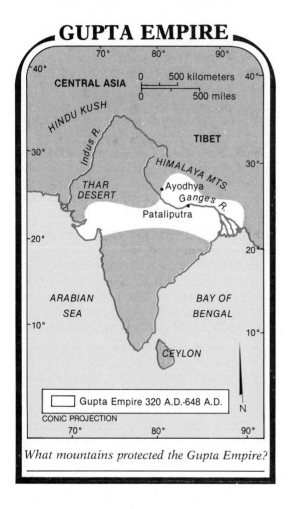

GUPTA EMPIRE

CENTRAL ASIA

HINDU KUSH

TIBET

Indus R.

THAR DESERT

HIMALAYA MTS.

Ayodhya

Ganges R.

Pataliputra

ARABIAN SEA

BAY OF BENGAL

CEYLON

☐ Gupta Empire 320 A.D.-648 A.D.

CONIC PROJECTION

N

What mountains protected the Gupta Empire?

Hinduism, on the other hand, came to be regarded as the native religion of India. Eventually, the support of India's foreign rulers may be one reason Buddhism gradually declined in popularity and disappeared from the land of its origin.

The Deccan   During the period of Greek and Kushan rule in northern India, the *Deccan,* or the southern part of India excluding its southern tip, was experiencing political disunity. Political unity was difficult to achieve due to the rugged terrain of the area.

While Buddhism was popular in the north, Hinduism was strong in most of the Deccan and especially strong among Dravidian peoples in the southern tip of India. Rulers of the south were tolerant of all religions and were friendly toward foreigners. This attitude made cultural exchanges with peoples of other lands possible.

Although the Kushans in the north traded with faraway lands, the bulk of India's trade left from southern ports. The east and west coasts were dotted with seaports and the Dravidians were a seagoing people. By the first century A.D., Indian ships were carrying cargoes of pearls, silks, spices, muslins, and works of art as far away as Egypt and the Mediterranean area. Even in the ruins of ancient cities in Italy, archaeologists have discovered Indian works of art.

The Gupta Empire   About 320 A.D., northern India once again was united by a royal family, the Guptas (GOOP-tuhz). The **Gupta Empire** reached its height under the rule of Vikramaditya (VIK-rah-mah-dit-yah), which lasted from 375 to 415 A.D. At that time, cities were growing and there was widespread prosperity. Foreign visitors to India noted that roads were well maintained, taxes were not too heavy, and there seemed to be little crime. Hinduism had become extremely popular, and Buddhist and Hindu believers lived alongside one another in a spirit of religious toleration.

The Gupta Empire was not as large as the Maurya Empire. At most, it included only half the land area of India. (See the map above.) The Gupta rulers had to be on guard almost constantly against invaders. The kingdoms of central and southern India were enemies of the Gupta. And to the north of India were the *Huns* (HUHNZ), a nomadic people of central Asia.

The Reign of Harsha The Guptas defended India against the Huns, but the struggle was too much for them. By the sixth century A.D., the Gupta power was broken and the Huns had established their empire across northern India. But the empire of the conquering Huns was short-lived.

As the Huns declined in power, an able government was restored by Harsha (HUR-shuh), a native king who ruled from 606 to 648 A.D. He was one of India's most famous rulers. Harsha was a military leader with a huge, efficient army that reunited most of northern India. He also was a capable ruler who promoted art, literature, and religion. In his early years, Harsha chose to worship some of the Hindu gods. Therefore, Hinduism began a revival during Harsha's reign that continued long after his death.

King Harsha's death in 648 A.D. left the empire in chaos. Once again there was political disunion throughout India along with a constant threat of foreign invasion. This went on for about 400 years. Eventually, around 1,000 A.D., foreign invaders pushed into India who worked to restore order and unity.

The Muslims Conquer India Around 1000 A.D., *Turks* (TURKS) and *Afghans* (AF-ganz), new invaders from northern central Asia, migrated to the northwest frontier of India. In the eleventh century, they began to annex and settle territories in India. Slowly they pushed into India. The rulers of India were disunited and were not a military match for these invaders. By the early thirteenth century, invading generals set up a strong empire that reunited most of northern India. They made their capital at Delhi (DELL-ee) and took the title of **sultan** (SULL-t'n). This empire was the Delhi Sultanate.

These new conquerors of India were loyal to a religious faith known as **Islam** (ISS-lahm). (You will learn more about the origins and beliefs of Islam in Unit 5.) Followers of Islam are called **Muslims** (MUZ-lums). The Muslim conquerors considered themselves superior to the Indians and looked down on Hinduism. Unlike the Hindus, the Muslims believed strictly in one God. Because Muslims were intolerant of other religions, they believed it their duty to stamp out the Hindu faith. They forced many Hindus to choose between death or converting to the Muslim faith. Previous invaders had adopted Indian dress, customs, and ways of life, but not the Muslims. They kept themselves apart from their Indian subjects.

Although the Delhi Sultanate persecuted Hindus, it restored political unity to India during the 1200's and 1300's. The sultans pushed their authority southward and brought most of southern India under their control. The unity of all India did not last long. Rival sultans seized territory and set up their own states. Once again, central government in India broke down. At about this time, another invader appeared on the northwestern frontier.

The Mongols Invade India In 1398, the *Mongols* (MAHNG-guls) invaded India, led by Timur (TEE-moor) the Lame, later known as Tamerlane (TAM-uhr-layn). The Mongols already had conquered Persia and Mesopotamia (MESS-uh-puh-tay-mee-uh). They were a fierce, warlike invader that neither the Muslims nor the Hindus could defeat. For nearly a year, Tamerlane ravaged across northern India. Delhi was looted and 100,000 of Tamerlane's prisoners were murdered. Then the Mongols departed westward, leaving behind political chaos in India.

The Taj Mahal was built by a seventeenth-century emperor, Shah Jahan, to serve as a tomb for his favorite wife, Mumtaz Mahal. How does this tomb compare to the tombs the Egyptians built for their pharaohs?

The Mogul Empire   A century later, a descendant of Tamerlane, Babur (BAHB-ur), attacked India's northwest frontier with his army. Babur's army was Muslim. They swept into India, conquered Muslim and Hindu rulers, and established Babur as the new sultan in 1526. Babur's empire is known as the **Mogul** (MOE-gul) **Empire.** The name *Mogul* may have come from Mongol, a name dreaded in India for its association with Tamerlane.

Babur's grandson, Akbar (AK-bar), was the most famous of the Mogul rulers. He reigned from 1556 until 1605. The empire was extended southward to include most of the Deccan and also eastward and northward. Akbar provided stable, efficient government. Historians have said that by 1600 the Mogul government was probably the best organized in the world. What distinguished Akbar from other Mogul sultans was his belief in religious freedom. He hoped his Muslim and Hindu subjects could learn to live side-by-side in peace. He wished that Muslim and Hindu cultures might learn from each other. Mogul culture flourished under Akbar and his successors. The Moguls supported the arts, especially architecture. Mogul architecture reached a high point under Akbar's grandson, Shah Jahan (SHAH juh-HAHN). One of the most magnificant works of Mogul art and architecture is the Taj Mahal (TAZH muh-hal). It was built between 1632 and 1653 in the city of Agra (AH-gruh) as a tomb for Shah Jahan's wife.

Unlike Akbar, Shah Jahan and his son, Aurangzeb (AW-rung-zeb) were intolerant of any religion other than Islam. As a result, Hindus were cruelly persecuted. Hindu temples were destroyed and the Hindu religion was prohibited. These measures of religious intolerance stimulated uprisings and weakened the power of the Mogul rulers. Through the 1600's, their power gradually declined. By the 1700's, they faced opposition from their own subjects and foreign powers. You will learn more about the collapse of the Mogul Empire in Unit 9.

SECTION REVIEW

1. Mapping: Using the maps on page 63 and 64, describe the locations of the Maurya and Gupta empires.
2. In your own words, define or identify: Chandragupta Maurya, Asoka, the Guptas, Harsha, Delhi, Islam, Muslims, Tamerlane, Akbar.
3. Why was southern India important?
4. What did the Muslim conquerors of India think of the Indians? Why did they feel this way?
 ◗ List four ways foreign cultures have affected the American way of life.

LIFE IN EARLY INDIA

The majority of people living in ancient India were farmers. They lived in small villages. They plowed their fields with teams of oxen. In these fields they raised crops of wheat, rice, barley, sugar cane, and vegetables. Very early, Indian farmers discovered that the same crop could not be planted year after year without ruining the soil. So they learned to rotate crops each season or to let a field remain unplanted for a time to replenish the soil.

In most of India, there was little rainfall from October until May. Fields were irrigated by canals and ditches that carried water from streams and rivers. By the end of April, however, the land had grown dry. Temperatures soared and hot winds blew. Crops ceased to grow and animals died from lack of water. For Indian farmers, work was reduced to a minimum. But in June began the *monsoon* (mahn-SOON) or torrential rains. For a few months, heavy rains fell at intervals making outdoor activity difficult. The monsoon, however, restored the land each year for another season of planting and growing crops.

Most farmers raised livestock for milk products, not meat. Wealth in early times was measured by the number of cattle a person owned, and to kill or steal a cow was a serious crime in early India. Offenders were dealt with severely.

Village Government Each village was governed by a council of the oldest inhabitants, the elders. Religious rules were the main rules of the village. Early Indians believed that the rules set down for everyday actions were the most important rules of life. Public holidays were also religious holidays.

Trade in Early India Merchants were an important group in early India. The Indian coast was dotted with ports from which cargoes were sent to distant lands. Indian ports traded with east Africa (AF-rih-kuh), the kingdoms of the Persian Gulf, China, and southeast Asia. (See the Atlas.) Ivory, precious stones, perfumes, and spices from India were in great demand. Persian, Arab, and Chinese ships regularly visited Indian ports. Cargoes such as silk, pottery, porcelain, textiles, glassware, and slaves were unloaded and transported overland by caravans to the rest of India and as far away as northern Asia.

India exported more things than it imported. Some scholars believe the Indians were the first to learn how to produce many goods like cotton, cashmere, and chintz. In other parts of the world, these goods were in great demand. India also exported a variety of luxury items such as precious stones and silks. One of its chief imports was black African slaves. Indians bought these slaves from Arab traders. Slaves belonged to no caste. If freed by their masters, they were treated as untouchables.

Indian Education During the Gupta Empire, India developed important centers of education. They attracted scholars from all over Asia. Many students received scholarships from the government. They studied religion, philosophy, science, medicine, art, architecture, and farming. Education of children was limited to the children of the upper classes. Other children were taught only crafts and trades that would become their life's work.

Indian Contributions to World Culture One of the main contributions India made to world culture was Buddhism. It began to decline between 400 and 700 A.D. and eventually disappeared in India, but not before it quickly spread to China, Japan, and other parts of Asia where it still remains a major religion. Today, there are more than 300 million Buddhists.

India also made lasting contributions to science and mathematics. The arabic numerals as well as the decimal system we use today originated in India. Indian scholars contributed a great deal to our knowledge of geometry and even more to our knowledge of algebra. Indians also were skilled astronomers. They could predict eclipses and determine the size of heavenly bodies. They also believed the earth was round and rotated on an axis. Indian scientists worked on the theory of gravity too, but they never proved their theories.

Indian art had a great influence on the cultures of Asia. After 100 A.D., many Indians began to move into southeast Asia. As a result, Indian art influenced the cultures of Asia. The temples of Cambodia (kam-BOE-dee-uh), Burma (BUR-muh), and Indonesia (in duh-NEE-zhuh) reflect the Indian style of building. Particularly Indian was the *stupa* (STOOP-uh). This was a large mound of earth, covered by brick and surrounded by a fence with elaborate stone gates. Originally, it was a shrine or holy place. Some stupas marked the birthplace of a religious leader. As Buddhism spread, so did the building of stupas. The Chinese imitated the Indian stupa and changed it gradually to the type of building known as the pagoda (puh-GOE-duh).

A Golden Age in India Indian culture reached a high point during the Gupta Empire. During this period, the arts flourished. Rulers supported poets, storytellers, and playwrights. India's two great epic poems, the *Mahabharata*

The great stupa of Sanchi was built between the third and first centuries B.C. The elaborate carvings on the gates depict events in the life of the Buddha. How does the decoration on this gate compare with the Hindu temple facade on page 60?

and the *Ramayana*, were written down. Drama and poetry had an important place under the Guptas. And Indian painting developed a unique style.

During the age of the Guptas, the Indians began to write down their literature. As a result, a whole class of scribes developed. As you recall, not all Vedas survived because they were not written down when they were first composed. However, most of the works composed in the Gupta period have come down to this day because there were professional scribes to write them down. Many Indian stories—especially fables and fairy tales—became popular in other parts of the world. The story of Sinbad the Sailor, for instance, came to us from India.

SECTION REVIEW

1. Mapping: Using the map on page 55, and the information on page 68, describe the possible trade routes in and out of early India.
2. In your own words define: monsoon, stupa.
3. List and describe the main contributions of early India to world culture.
4. In your own words describe the life of a farmer in early India.
5. Why do you think the Gupta Empire has been called India's "Golden Age"?
▷ What do you think future historians will regard as America's chief contributions to world culture?

The Early Chinese

THE FOUNDATIONS OF ANCIENT CHINA

In a cave near the city of Peking (PEE-KING), human remains were discovered that scholars believe may be hundreds of thousands of years old. These are some of the oldest traces of ancient people in the Far East.

Elsewhere in China, archaeologists have found evidence that civilization may have developed in China as early as 2000 B.C.

In 1979, new discoveries were reported. The remains of more than a dozen villages were discovered in central China. Some of these villages may be 4,000 to 5,000 years old. Pottery, axes, and arrowheads found in these villages may provide scholars with new evidence about the origins of the Chinese.

Early Chinese Civilization and Geography As in Mesopotamia, China's early civilization developed near great rivers—the Yellow and the Yangtze (YANG-SEE) rivers. These two rivers were sources of irrigation and transportation to the people who lived in the surrounding valleys. The Yellow and the Yangtze river valleys are separated by a range of mountains running east-west. Other great mountain ranges can be found in the west, northwest, and southwest of China. (See the map on page 55.)

To some extent, China's geography protected it from outside forces. The Pacific Ocean on the east, high mountains in the west, and the Gobi (GOE-bee) Desert in the northwest all acted as natural barriers.

Although China's geography was considerably protective, it limited the amount of contact and influence of foreigners on China. High mountains also limited overland trade to or from China. As a result, early Chinese culture developed relatively free from foreign influence.

Some scholars believe civilization in China first appeared in northern China along the Yellow River. (See the map on page 55.) Despite bitter cold winters, this area of China was suitable for farming. The land was free of forests and the soil was fertile. Rainfall was light, but rivers and streams provided the water needed to raise crops. And each year the flooding of the Yellow River replenished farmlands with deposits of new soil.

The Yellow River has been a mixed blessing to China through the ages. The name describes the river's muddy color, which is caused by the soil it carries from the mountains and highlands to the plains. The Yellow River has also

What does this Chinese painting tell you about transportation in ancient China?

been referred to as "China's Sorrow." The very floods that replenished the soil each year also caused great suffering among the people who lived in the river valley. The sediment deposited in the river's bed slowly forced the water level higher and higher. To hold back the waters, the Chinese began building dikes thousands of years ago. But the job of controlling the waters of the mighty river became increasingly more difficult. The dikes caused the river bed and the water level to rise more quickly. As a result, the dikes had to be built higher and higher and living in the river valley became more and more dangerous.

The Chinese have many legends about their origins and earliest times. These legends mention wise rulers who supposedly founded Chinese culture. For instance, Fu Hsi (FOO-SHEE) is said to have taught the Chinese to hunt. Another ruler, Shen Nung (SHUN-NOONG), is supposed to have developed farming. We also learn from legends that the first *dynasty*, or ruling family, that governed China was known as the Hsia (SHYAH) Dynasty. Historians do not know for certain whether there was a **Hsia Dynasty.** The legends claim it ruled the region from approximately 2200 to 1500 B.C. However, it is known that during this period of Chinese history, a family-centered society developed. In very ancient times, a family name came from the name of a *clan*, or a group of families. Then, as today in China, the family name always came before the name given an individual by his or her parents.

During this early period, the people who lived in the river valleys of China regarded their land as the center of civilization. However, they probably were not acquainted with far away civilizations like that of early India. Consequently, they called China "the central country" or "the Middle Kingdom." **The Shang Dynasty**   For centuries,

SHANG KINGDOM

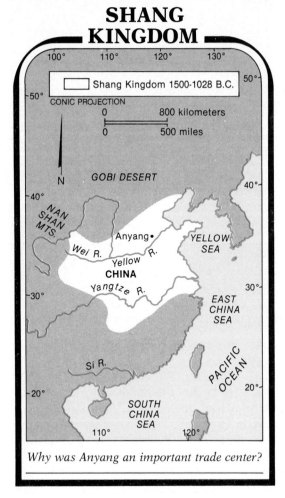

Shang Kingdom 1500-1028 B.C.

CONIC PROJECTION

0   800 kilometers
0   500 miles

N

GOBI DESERT

NAN SHAN MTS.

Anyang•

Wei R.
Yellow R.

YELLOW SEA

CHINA

Yangtze R.

EAST CHINA SEA

Si R.

PACIFIC OCEAN

SOUTH CHINA SEA

Why was Anyang an important trade center?

scholars thought that all the legends and other stories about early China were myths. But in the late 1800's and early 1900's, they began to change their minds. Archaeologists began making discoveries that proved some stories were based on fact. Near the city of Anyang (AHN-YAHNG), they dug up the remains of one of the dynasties mentioned in the stories—the **Shang** (SHAHNG) **Dynasty.** The Shang is the first dynasty for which we possess real historical evidence. It ruled China from about 1500 to 1028 B.C. (See the map above.)

Shang Art and Architecture   The archaeological evidence found at Anyang shows that Shang architecture was quite advanced. The upper class lived in magnificent houses of wood and stone. There were huge palaces, government buildings, and ancestral shrines. The Shang people knew a great deal about building. Scholars have found many architectural terms in the earliest writings. Shang tombs were as magnificently built and furnished as palaces. In them, archaeologists found the remains of many people, horses, and dogs. The furnishings included beautiful ornaments of stone, jade, and bone, as well as bronze vessels and weapons, and chariots of wood. The finest tombs were probably built for members of the royal family.

There were many fine artisans who produced early Chinese artwork. Some were responsible for making the beautiful artifacts found in the tombs of the royal family. Others learned to use *kaolin* (KAY-uh-lin), a fine white clay for making pottery. Potters developed many unique shapes and glazes for their pottery. Artisans also developed a unique style for the bronzes they made.

The remains of Shang culture are numerous. Scholars found city walls, foundations of houses and buildings, tombs, and pottery factories. They unearthed many artifacts as well. These included pottery, objects made of bronze, bone, stone, shell, ivory, jade, and gold, and stamps for pressing designs on things made of clay. They also found pieces of ox bone and tortoise shell with writing cut into them. Scholars believe that this might be the first Chinese writing.

Shang Oracle Bones   Some of the writing on bones shows that the Shang consulted oracles (OR-uh-k'lz). An *oracle* is someone thought to have the power to predict the future and give wise answers to questions. For example, a man or woman would bring a question to the oracle: "How will this year's rice crop turn out?" The oracle would then heat a bone over a fire until it cracked. From the shape of the crack, the oracle would decide the answer to the question. Both the question and the answer were then written on the bone. At times, the oracle would sign and date the bone as well. Nearly 200,000 oracle bones have been found. Some 17,000 were found in one spot alone!

Shang Government   Anyang was the capital of the Shang dynasty. (See the map on page 72.) From this city, the royal family ruled the Shang Kingdom. The king governed with the help of the leading nobles. Wealth came mostly from tribute, or payments to the Shang from peoples they had defeated in war. The king sacrificed animals and food to both his ancestors and the gods and asked for their advice.

Shang Farming   Most of the people of Shang China were farmers. They planted *millet* (a form of cereal), wheat, and some rice. Many practiced *sericulture* (SER-uh-kul-chur), or the cultivation of silkworms for the production of silk. Tools such as hoes and spades made of stone or shell were their main tools. They also had a plow that was pushed with the foot. Farmers domesticated and raised cattle, horses, goats, pigs, and fowl, as well as crops. Irrigation was used on many fields.

To help farmers know when to plant and harvest, the Shang developed a calendar. One year was measured as 360 days. It was divided into months of thirty days each. Sometimes, however, a thirteenth month was added. This month was usually added at the end of the year. Because measuring time was important to this agricultural civiliza-

Scholars have learned about many aspects of ancient Chinese life through the examination of oracle bones. Why have people always wanted to know about the future? What means do people use today to predict the future?

tion, astrologers had an important place at the royal court. An *astrologer* is one who predicts events by studying the positions of the stars and planets.

Shang Trade   Shang China traded widely. The Shang imported shells from southeast Asia. Tin, lead, and copper came from southern China. Cowrie (KOW-ree) shells, used as money, came from islands in the Pacific Ocean. And salt was brought from the shores of the Yellow Sea. Shang merchants exported silk to many parts of the ancient world.

The Chinese System of Writing Writing in China may have begun as it did in ancient Egypt. First, pictures were used to represent words. By Shang times, however, the Chinese writing system had developed beyond pictures. The Shang people used 2,000 different symbols in place of pictures. Each symbol was known as a character. Today, there are more than 50,000 characters in the Chinese language.

Writing usually ran from the top of a page to the bottom. Some characters or symbols, called *pictographs*, resembled the word they stood for. For example, the characters for sun, moon, and tree looked like drawings of those objects. Other characters stood for sounds or ideas. The character for the number three was simply three straight lines drawn one above another.

Chinese writing was extremely difficult to master. At least 2,000–3,000 characters had to be memorized before a person could read the most simple writing. Individuals who could read and write were always respected.

Writing was done with a brush. Rules dictated how many brush strokes were used in forming a particular character. Some characters were very complex and required twenty-five strokes to draw. As a result, *calligraphy*, or handwriting, emerged as an art form.

SECTION REVIEW

1. Mapping: Using the map on page 55 and textbook pages 70–71, describe the location of China in relation to the rest of the ancient world of the Far East. Locate the main geographic features of China and describe how they affected early China.

2. In your words, briefly define or identify: "China's sorrow," Fu Hsi, Shen Nung, sericulture, calligraphy, Hsia Dynasty.

3. What evidence about the Shang Dynasty led scholars to change their minds about the meaning of ancient Chinese legends?

4. What are "oracle bones" and how were they used by the people of the Shang Dynasty?

D Did the culture of the Shang Dynasty share any characteristics with your own culture? Explain.

THE DEVELOPMENT OF A CHINESE EMPIRE

The Chou Dynasty   About 1028 B.C., the last Shang king was overthrown. Previously, the Shang had conquered the *Chou* (JOE), a people from the Wei (WAY) River Valley. As the Shang leaders became weaker and weaker, the Chou formed an alliance with several other Chinese peoples and gradually overwhelmed the Shang. They destroyed the city of Anyang. Most of its inhabitants were slaughtered. But some escaped and carried Shang culture to other parts of the Far East. Some traces of Shang culture have even been found in Korea.

The **Chou Dynasty** was the longest dynasty in China's history. It lasted from about 1028 to 256 B.C.—almost 800 years. The Chou Dynasty established a new capital at Hao (HOW) near the modern city of Sian (SHEEAN). (See the map on page 75). They brought most of northern China under their control. Northern China was a vast plain. The lack of efficient communication and transportation made it impossible for the Chou to unite all the lands they had conquered. As a result, Chou rulers parceled out most of their land to their allies who had helped them overthrow the Shang. Those who received land were known as **vassals.** In return for land, vassals agreed to provide soldiers for the Chou kings in time of war. This system of exchanging land for military aid was called **feudalism.**

Chou Government   The Chou rulers had a difficult time governing their vast territories. To keep in touch with every part, they traveled constantly. While traveling, the ruler depended on his vassals for food and shelter. The vassals also traveled to the capital city and

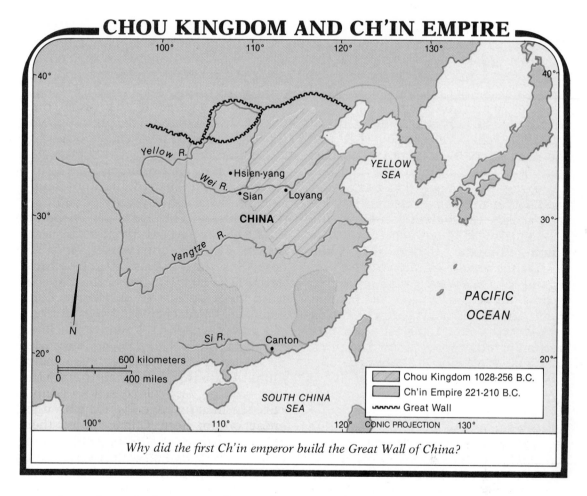

CHOU KINGDOM AND CH'IN EMPIRE

Chou Kingdom 1028-256 B.C.
Ch'in Empire 221-210 B.C.
Great Wall

CONIC PROJECTION

Why did the first Ch'in emperor build the Great Wall of China?

stayed at the ruler's court. If vassals tried to rebel, the ruler's army crushed the revolt quickly.

The vassals of the Chou lived in walled towns and ruled the surrounding countryside. The areas under their control were known as city-states. Vassals had small courts of their own. They too had officials to help them govern. If a vassal controlled several large areas, he had a governor for each one. There was also an official to watch over forests and farmlands. Another official supervised roads and bridges. Others regulated trade, acted as judges, ran prisons, or hunted criminals.

The position of vassals became *hereditary*, that is, it was passed from a father to his son. Vassal rulers eventually became all-powerful in their own territories. They ruled as if they were kings. Gradually, the domains and power of the Chou vassals grew so great that these feudal nobles threatened the power of the Chou ruler.

In 771 B.C., a group of Chou vassals attacked the capital and murdered the Chou ruler. Part of the royal family escaped safely to eastern China. They set up a new capital at Lo-yang (LWAH-YAHNG). There the Chou Dynasty continued for about another 500 years. The resettled royal family became known as the Eastern Chou Dynasty.

Chou rulers never recovered the power they once held. As both royal power and territory diminished, vassal states in eastern China grew stronger. Larger vassal city-states conquered weaker neighbors. Between 403 and 256 B.C., there was almost constant warfare in eastern China and the Chou ruler was no longer effective. After about 300 B.C., many vassal rulers began to call themselves kings, a title used only by the Chou rulers until then.

China Prospers Under the Chou
Despite the breakdown in royal authority and frequent wars, China prospered during the Chou period of history. Trade and industry grew. People flocked to the cities to invest in the production of silk, copper, iron, and other products. As a result, cities became centers of wealth and luxury. In one city, it was said that merchants covered their carriages with gold and jewels.

Culture Under the Chou   Education grew as rapidly as industry. People were trained in various occupations such as judges, diplomats, doctors, lawyers, priests, scribes, artists, poets, scientists, and historians. There was also an interest in scientific farming and gardening. Canals were dug as a means of improving transportation and communication. The use of the horse also was introduced and became important in military power.

These cultural advances under the Chou developed a sense of pride among the Chinese. They considered themselves part of a superior civilization. They looked down on foreigners and referred to them as "barbarians," or people without culture.

Most of the leading thinkers, or philosphers, of the time were interested in the problems of their society. One of the main problems was that of government. The philosophers saw the central government breaking down and the country dividing into warring states. They tried to find a new order that would save society. The philosophers' writings reflected what they felt this order should be.

The Teaching of Confucius   During the times of great trouble and confusion of the Chou Dynasty, *Confucius* (kun-FYOO-shuss) was the leading Chou philosopher. He is also the best-known Chinese philosopher. In Chinese, his name was K'ung Fu-tzu (KUN-FOO-DZUH). *Tzu* is the Chinese word meaning master or scholar. Confucius was a teacher. He traveled from place to place with his pupils, teaching his philosophy. Near the end of his life, he returned to his home in northern China. There he spent his time teaching and writing. After his death, Confucius' teachings were collected and written down in books. These books are called the *Classics*. The way of life they describe is called **Confucianism** (kun-FYOO-shu-niz-um).

Confucius believed that Chinese society would be better if people followed a code of conduct. He particularly stressed the teaching of morals. Confucius believed that educated people should provide a good example and moral leadership for the country. He taught that three virtues were important: wisdom, love, and courage. These virtues included others, such as respect for elders, generosity, sincerity, humility, self-respect, loyalty, friendliness, and eagerness to learn. Confucius believed that a noble man or woman was one who practiced these virtues. Simply being a virtuous person was not enough however.

Goodness, Confucius believed, should serve society. The good person must help others become virtuous. According to Confucius, society should have five things in order to be perfect. These are (1) love between parents and children, (2) fairness between ruler and ruled, (3) a clear division of duties and responsibilities between husband and wife, (4) respect between elders and the young, and (5) good relations between friends.

According to Confucius, every person was born to play a particular role in society. Society would be more stable if every individual was content to do whatever he or she was born to do, instead of trying to become something better. Confucius said, "Let the ruler be a ruler, and the subject a subject; let the father be a father, and the son a son."

Confucius did not challenge the authority of government. But he did not believe a ruler was free to do whatever he or she wanted. Instead, Confucius insisted that rulers had an obligation to set a proper example for all their subjects. A good ruler was a virtuous individual. Thus, the goal for a ruler should be to promote virtue, not power.

Confucius' most famous follower was Meng-tzu (MUNG-DZUH), or *Mencius* (MEN-chuss), a philosopher who made important contributions of his own to Confucianism. Mencius taught that if a ruler was moral, he or she would enjoy the respect and support of subjects. This, Mencius said, was because heaven expressed its approval of a ruler through the ruler's subjects. Thus a good ruler was thought to possess the *Mandate of Heaven*, or a divine right to govern. But if a ruler governed badly or was not moral, the people would rise in revolt and overthrow the ruler. This meant the Mandate of Heaven had been withdrawn and the ruler no longer had the divine right to govern.

Confucius, the Chinese philosopher, is shown here in a print by a T'ang artist. What connection did Confucius make between morals and governing a society? Do such ideas influence contemporary governments?

Mencius did not originate the Mandate of Heaven. It was used by the Chou as their excuse for overthrowing the Shang Dynasty. Since Mencius' time, the Chinese have believed in the Mandate of Heaven.

Throughout Chinese history, when there were famines, floods, or foreign invasions, rebels claimed these disasters were signs that the Mandate of Heaven had been lost by the government in power. This provided them with a justification for revolution.

During the Chou period, there were a number of other philosophers besides Confucius. Next to Confucianism, the most important school of philosophy was **Taoism** (DOW-iz-um). Its founder was Lao-tzu (LAO-DZUH) who is believed to have lived from 604 to 531 B.C.

Taoism seems to have developed as a protest against Confucian rules. Confucianism taught a code of conduct for all society to follow. But Taoism favored individualism. It taught its followers to scorn the values set by society. Instead, each individual was to seek his or her own way to live in harmony with nature. The word *tao* meant a road or path to follow. For a Taoist, this meant a life of simplicity.

Taoists believed the world ran smoothly according to the laws of nature. People, however, were always trying to improve the world or change society. This, the Taoists taught, often ran contrary to the laws of nature. Thus, the best life to live, they believed, was a spontaneous one, "flowing like water." Even knowledge, Taoists thought, could corrupt men and women because it created desires for things that were not essential. Taoism taught individuals to live a more simple, primitive life, in order for society to return to a more simple way of living.

The End of the Chou Dynasty   During the years 480–256 B.C., the power of the Chou greatly declined. Vassal states had become powerful kingdoms. One of them, the kingdom of the Ch'in (CHIN), destroyed the Chou Dynasty in 256 B.C. and then went on to conquer all its rivals. By 256 B.C., the *Ch'in* had united the various kingdoms and territories of China and established the first Chinese **empire.** Thus, the king of Ch'in became China's first emperor. And it was from the Ch'in that China derived its name.

The Ch'in Dynasty   Shih-huang-ti (SHUH-HUAHNG-DEE) was the title of the first Ch'in emperor. He extended his borders as far south as the Si(SHEE) River. (See the map on page 75.) He realized that his empire would not last unless China could be protected from its northern enemies. These enemies were the nomadic tribes who lived on the plains northwest of China.

The Great Wall of China   To defend China against these nomads, the emperor decided to connect existing sections of walls to form a huge wall. The wall, known as the *Great Wall of China,* extended across some 2,240 kilometers (1,400 miles) of northern China and still stands today. Roughly one third of all able Chinese men were forced to help build the wall. Someone has estimated that if the materials used on the wall were shipped to the equator, they would make a wall 240 centimeters (eight feet) high and 90 centimeters (three feet) thick circling the whole globe! From the watchtowers and the road along the top of the Great Wall, soldiers could protect China against its enemies. The wall served other purposes besides that of security. It kept Chinese soldiers who were unhappy with the government from leaving and

The Great Wall of China was built by the first Ch'in emperor and later extended under the reign of other dynasties. What means do modern nations use to secure their boundaries?

joining the enemy. And by establishing garrisons on the wall, it kept most of the huge Chinese army out of the mainstream of Chinese life. The emperor wanted to keep the army busy because soldiers often were the first to overthrow a dynasty.

The Ch'in emperor did not distribute land among his supporters as the Chou rulers had done. Instead, he destroyed the power of the nobles who in the past had so often warred among each other. Nobles of the old ruling class were forced to move to the capital, Hsien-Yang (SHYEN-YAHNG), where they could be controlled. The country then was divided into thirty-six provinces. Over each province, the

emperor placed a governor, a military commander, and other officials. They were responsible to the emperor. All subjects, except the emperor's soldiers, were ordered to turn over all their weapons to the government. It was thought that this procedure would help prevent rebellions. The emperor's goal was to unify his far-flung empire and keep it under the control of one central government. Almost all Chinese rulers for a thousand years afterwards followed this goal held by the first emperor, Shih-huang-ti.

To unify China, roads were built to improve communications. One system of weights and measures was introduced. Coins used as money were standardized. A single code of laws replaced local laws. Farmers' crops were taxed by the central government. The central government even ordered the width of wagons to be the same so all vehicles would be able to use the new royal roads.

Around 213 B.C., Shih-huang-ti ordered the burning of certain books. All books considered hostile to the government were destroyed. Philosophers were especially persecuted. This was because they usually praised good rulers of the past and criticized mistakes of Shih-huang-ti's government. Scholars who spoke out against the government were imprisoned or killed.

When Shih-huang-ti died in 210 B.C., generals fought one another for power. Finally, one general, Liu Pang (LYOO-BAHNG), emerged victorious and established a new dynasty—the *Han* (HAHN).

The Han Dynasty   The Han ruled China from 202 B.C. until 220 A.D. During its long life the **Han Dynasty** tried to preserve the system of government begun under the Ch'in Empire. New territories were conquered. The Han eventually controlled an empire as large, as wealthy, and as powerful as any that had appeared in the ancient world. (See the map on page 81.)

Han emperors ruled this huge empire through a great number of officials who were paid salaries for their services. These officials were known as the *bureaucracy* (byoo-ROK-ruh-see). The bureaucracy became so large that by the first century A.D., there was one *bureaucrat*, or official, for every 500 Chinese.

Trade During the Han Dynasty   Han officials and merchants traveled widely selling Chinese goods, plants such as medicinal herbs, and animals. The Mediterranean peoples valued Chinese silk highly. Silk was in constant demand in parts of ancient Europe such as Italy, Spain, France, and Britain. They also bought Chinese goods of bronze, jade, and lacquered wood.

The Achievements under the Han   Paper was invented during the Han Dynasty. It replaced wood and bamboo writing materials. The first large Chinese dictionary was published, and important medical discoveries were made. Scholars began writing histories. At this time, Buddhism began to enter China from India.

The greatest of the Han emperors was Wu Ti (WOO-DEE) He ruled from 140 B.C. until 87 B.C., He enlarged the empire by conquering lands to the south of China. But Wu Ti's greatest wars were fought along China's northern borders. Army after army was sent against a nomadic people known as the Huns (HUNZ). One expedition consisted of more than 100,000 Chinese soldiers. The Huns were a fierce opponent. Chinese armies suffered terrible losses. But eventually the Huns weakened. By 119 B.C., they were pushed back to the Gobi Desert. By 52 B.C., about half of the Hun tribes had given up the struggle. Those who refused to live under Chinese rule migrated westward.

The long struggle against the Huns brought vast territories into the Chinese empire. The Great Wall was extended westward to Yu-men (YOO-MUN) and thousands of colonists were sent to settle the new lands. Wu Ti also sent armies toward the northeast. Parts of Manchuria (man-CHOOR-ee-uh) and Korea (ko-REE-uh) were conquered.

As the Han Empire grew in size, the cost of governing it increased. To cover this cost, the government raised taxes. Most of the tax burden fell on the

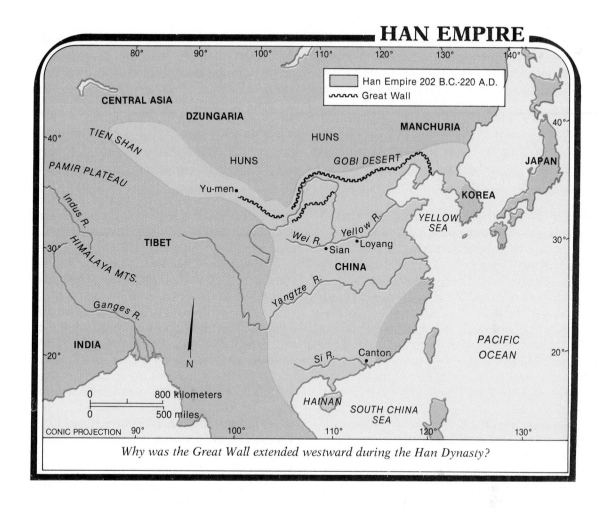

HAN EMPIRE

Han Empire 202 B.C.-220 A.D.
Great Wall

CENTRAL ASIA
DZUNGARIA
TIEN SHAN
PAMIR PLATEAU
HUNS
HUNS
MANCHURIA
GOBI DESERT
Yu-men
JAPAN
KOREA
YELLOW SEA
Indus R.
HIMALAYA MTS.
TIBET
Wei R.
Yellow R.
Sian
Loyang
Ganges R.
CHINA
Yangtze R.
INDIA
N
PACIFIC OCEAN
Si R.
Canton
800 kilometers
500 miles
HAINAN
SOUTH CHINA SEA
CONIC PROJECTION

Why was the Great Wall extended westward during the Han Dynasty?

peasants. Eventually the burden became so great that the peasants rebelled. Imperial armies had to be dispatched to put down these revolts. But this only increased the government's expenses and caused more tax increases. In 8 A.D., the Han Dynasty was overthrown during one of these revolts. However, in 25 A.D., the Han successfully regained control of their empire and ruled again until 220 A.D.

Later Han rulers never possessed the power of early Han emperors. In the provinces, military leaders known as *warlords* rose to power during peasant revolts. When the revolts were put down, the warlords refused to give up their power. Han rulers could not bring these warlords under control.

The Six Dynasties   Following the final fall of the Han Dynasty, China was torn apart by civil wars and invasions. From about 220 to 589 A.D., six dynasties rose and fell in quick succession. And during this time, the Huns seized parts of northern China.

The Sui Dynasty   The invading Huns were finally overthrown by Yang Chien (YAHNG-JEN) a Chinese government official. He founded the **Sui**

81

(SWAY) **Dynasty** in 589 A.D. and reunited northern and southern China. He also built the Grand Canal that linked the Yellow River to the Yangtze River and northern China to southern China. In this way, the agricultural Yangtze Valley could be connected to the strategic and highly-populated northern area. Since the Yellow and Yangtze rivers ran east-west, transportation by water north-south was impossible before the building of the Grand Canal. (See the map on page 84.)

But the success of the Sui Dynasty was short-lived. Unsuccessful attempts to conquer southern Manchuria and northern Korea by this dynasty were costly. And the decline of the Sui Dynasty was aided by invading Turks from the northwest.

The T'ang Dynasty   In 618 A.D., China finally was reunited under the rule of Li Yüan (LEE-YOOAHN) who established the strong **T'ang** (TAHNG) **Dynasty.** The T'ang rulers were as powerful and important as the Han. They restored a strong central government and expanded the size of the empire by defeating the invading Turks and extending the Chinese frontier farther west than during any previous dynasty. (See the map on page 84.) One of the rulers of this empire was a woman named Wu (WOO). In 690 A.D., she took the title of Emperor. She was the first woman ruler in Chinese history. **Empress Wu** proved to be a strong and able ruler.

Extending the T'ang Empire   The T'ang made Korea a protectorate of China. This meant that, in exchange for their independence, the Koreans promised to do as the T'ang rulers wished. The Chinese, in turn, promised to protect Korea. They also gave Koreans special trading rights with China.

The T'ang capital, Changan (CHAHNG-AHN), became a cultural center where people from many different lands lived together. Chinese teachers spread Buddhism and other Chinese religions to Japan and Korea.

The greatest T'ang ruler was T'ai Tsung (TIE-DZUNG), who reigned from 626 to 649 A.D. He was famous as a soldier. His armies warred against nomads along China's northwest frontier. He extended his control as far as the Pamir (puh-MIR) Mountains. (See the map on page 84.) He also pushed his empire southward to include northern Vietnam (vee-et-NAHM). (See the map on page 84.)

Tibet (tuh-BET) lay to the southwest of China. It too was made part of the empire. Chinese officials in Tibet crossed the mountains into India. But travel across the mountain barrier was difficult, so contacts with India were few. (See the map on page 84.)

These non-Chinese territories added to T'ai Tsung's empire were permitted to keep their native rulers. However, the Chinese emperor had to be acknowledged as their master. In this way, native rulers eventually became vassals of the T'ang emperors.

Culture during the T'ang Dynasty
T'ang China was wealthy and powerful. It is considered a golden age in Chinese history. The arts flourished. Chinese painting developed free of foreign influences. Sculptors borrowed ideas from India for their work but tried to develop a unique Chinese style of sculpture. Scholars compiled encyclopedias and the writings of history were greatly increased.

During the T'ang period of history, great value was placed on literary skills. Every educated person was expected to be able to read and write

Empress Wu

Wu Chao (WOO-JOW) was twenty-four years old when her first emperor-husband died. She was then sent away to a Buddhist convent, as was customary when an empress's husband died. There the former empress and other widows shaved their heads and were expected to live the rest of their lives in quiet seclusion.

One day, she was visited at the convent by the new T'ang emperor, Kao-tsung (GAH-OE-DZOONG). Kao-tsung had long admired Wu Chao's beauty and was charmed by her wit, knowledge, and courage. The new emperor broke tradition and brought Wu Chao back to court and made her his empress. Emperor Kao-tsung suffered a long illness and, therefore, allowed the control of affairs to pass into the hands of his talented empress during the thirty-four years of his reign.

Empress Wu gained the support of Chinese scholars from whom she commissioned works. She encouraged agriculture and silk production. She reduced taxes and reduced the amount of labor that peasants were forced to contribute to the government.

By 675 A.D., Empress Wu's armies had won a war of conquest in Korea and she announced a policy of peace. She disbanded a large number of troops. Empress Wu then moved the capital of the empire from Changan to Lo-yang.

Emperor Kao-tsung died in 683 A.D., and in 690 Wu assumed the imperial title of emperor herself. She was sixty-two years old and the only Chinese woman to become emperor.

During her rule, government was well-administered and the kingdom was at peace. But many court officials resented being ruled by a woman because it was a Chinese tradition that women should play no role in public life. Others resented Wu because she did not come from a wealthy high-ranking family. Wu aroused much disapproval when she established examinations for government posts for women.

As she grew old, Empress Wu fell under the influence of a group of corrupt court officials. By 705, Wu was ill and weak and had to rely upon others to govern the empire for her. As a result, a group of plotters successfully seized control of the government. They executed some of Wu's corrupt officials and sent others into exile. They forced Empress Wu to turn her throne over to one of her sons. She died ten months later in 705.

(Adapted from: Hilda Hookham, **A Short History of China.** New York: St. Martin's Press, 1970, pp. 93–94.)

1. How did Wu rise to power as emperor of China?
2. What were her accomplishments?
3. Why did court officials resent being ruled by a woman?
4. How did Wu fall into disfavor?

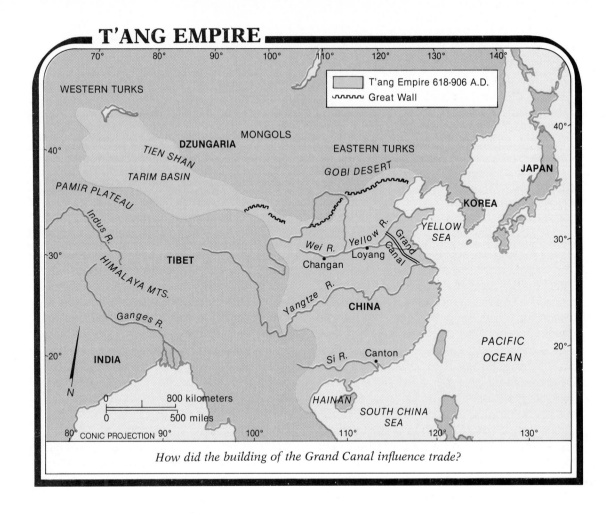

How did the building of the Grand Canal influence trade?

Chinese. The ability to compose poetry was especially prized. The works of more than 2,000 T'ang poets have been preserved.

The most famous of China's poets lived at this time. He was Li Po (LEE-BOE), who lived from 701 to 762 A.D. Li Po at one time had been a Taoist priest. His poems reflect a love of nature. They also show his deep concern and sympathy for the problems of ordinary people in the society of his own day. Poets like Li Po were imitated by Chinese writers for centuries after the end of the T'ang dynasty.

The Invention of Printing   One of the most important contributions made during the T'ang period was the development of printing. The Chinese were the first people to invent printing. (The method they used is shown on page 94.) Printing was an extremely important invention. Previously, books had to be copied by hand. Printing made it possible to reproduce books faster and in larger quantities. Thus knowledge spread more widely than had been possible before.

Under the T'ang, there was a gradual decline of the warlike spirit among the Chinese. Previously, all dynasties had had a military spirit. Even the early T'ang rulers had been great warriors. But by the fall of the T'ang Dynasty in 906 A.D., most Chinese held an anti-military outlook. There was contempt for warriors. Instead, the scholar replaced the warrior in Chinese esteem.

Buddhism Becomes a Part of Chinese Life   Buddhism was introduced to China under the Han Dynasty. After 200 A.D., Buddhism began to make great gains and became as popular as Confucianism. By the close of the T'ang period, however, Buddhism had reached a peak in China and had begun to decline. The upper classes reemphasized Confucianism because it stressed duty and responsibility. Confucianism was the major philosophy by the late T'ang period and has remained so until modern times.

The old nobles of China had been destroyed by the Ch'in and Han dynasties. Under the T'ang a new ruling class emerged. It was known as the *gentry* (JEN-tree). It was made up of wealthy landowners who could afford to give their children a good education. Thus the children of the gentry became the scholars of China. From these scholars, Chinese government selected its officials. Therefore, the gentry became the new leaders of China.

Decline of the T'ang   Like all dynasties before it, the T'ang eventually went into a decline. In the ninth century, governors of the provinces became military leaders. The emperors were ineffective. Eventually, the provinces declared themselves independent states. The central government had no means of preventing this, and China once again became disunited. In 906 A.D., the T'ang Dynasty came to an end.

SECTION REVIEW

1. Mapping: Using the maps on pages 75, 81, and 84, (a) describe the extent of the kingdom ruled by the Chou, (b) describe and compare the empires of the Ch'in, Han, and T'ang dynasties, and (c) describe the location of the Pamir Mountains and the Great Wall. Using the map on page 55, describe the relative geographic locations of Korea, Manchuria, and Tibet to China.
2. In your own words, define or identify: vassals, feudalism, Confucius, barbarians, the Great Wall of China, the Huns, warlords, Sui Dynasty, Li Po.
3. In what ways did Shih-huang-ti secure the Ch'in Empire in China?
4. In your own words, compare and contrast Confucianism and Taoism.
5. What were the cultural achievements during the T'ang Dynasty?
6. How might the Mandate of Heaven have been used to justify the overthrow of a dynasty?
◗ How do new government administrations or the election of a new political leader in your area affect your life?

CHINA UNDER NATIVE AND FOREIGN RULE

The Sung Dynasty   Another period of turmoil followed the end of T'ang rule. There was a complete political breakup of China. In a period of fifty-three years, five dynasties rose and fell in northern China. In the south, ten kingdoms were established and lasted through most of this period. "Barbarian" peoples overran the northwestern parts of the former T'ang Empire.

Chao K'uang-yin (JOW-KWAHNG-YIN), one of the generals whose army was defending northern China from "barbarian" invaders, decided to seize the throne for himself. He founded the **Sung** (SOONG) **Dynasty,** which lasted from 960 to 1279. The city of Kaifeng (KIE-FUHNG) became his capital. (See the map on page 88.)

After making northern China safe from "barbarian" attacks, the new Sung emperor began a conquest of the south. By 979, almost all China had been reunited by force.

The Sung are thought to have brought China into the modern age. Great cities were built. They were among the most modern in the world at that time. There were wide, main streets with streetlights and regular street cleaning. A fire department served each city. Restaurants and places of amusement enlivened city life. Fairs and markets were frequent. There were orphanages, homes for the aged, schools, and first-aid stations.

Chinese civilization advanced in other areas too. Chinese scientists developed a smallpox vaccine. A new and more accurate clock was invented. Cotton was introduced to China from India. New kinds of rice that were more productive were introduced into China from Vietnam, doubling China's rice production. Algebra was developed and the sciences made progress in such fields as zoology (the study of animals), botany (the study of plants), and chemistry. By the twelfth century, the Chinese had produced gunpowder. At first, it was used for fireworks. Later, it was used in warfare in hand grenades and explosive mines. Mapmaking also developed during this period. And by the end of the 1100's, the Chinese were using the magnetic compass.

Chinese art, especially painting, made progress. Landscape and nature paintings produced by Sung artists are considered to be outstanding examples of Chinese art from this period. During the Sung Dynasty, Chinese artists perfected the skill of painting on silk.

The Chinese Civil Service System

Sung government has been called modern. A *civil service system* was set up to bring talented people into government. Formerly, government jobs were given only to supporters of powerful officials. Now, applicants for a position took examinations. These tests measured the applicants' qualifications. Those who scored highest on the exams received the jobs. The examination system had originated earlier under the T'ang Dynasty. It was more fully developed under the Sung and it continued with few changes until the twentieth century.

Many Chinese took the examinations for government jobs time after time, yet they never passed. Individuals are known to have failed as many as fifteen times. The government often grew worried about older men who failed to pass. It feared that disappointment might turn these individuals against the dynasty. To prevent discontent, some of those persons who repeatedly failed were given jobs through special exams they were able to pass.

Under the Sung, trade increased with other parts of the world. The ports of southern China at Hangchow (HANG-CHOW) and Canton (KAN-TAHN) grew in importance. Caravan trade brought goods such as incense, ivory, coral, rock crystal, steel, and amber from central Asia and India. The Sung Dynasty may have been richer than any previous dynasty.

Despite great wealth, the emperors faced difficult problems. They lacked

The scroll shown here may have been the work of an emperor of the Northern Sung Dynasty named Hui Tsung. "Ladies Preparing Newly Woven Silk" depicts the production of silk cloth: the women beat silk fibers with flails, drew out the threads, and then ironed the completed bolt of cloth. How do fabric production methods differ today?

the military power of the Han or the T'ang. For this reason, parts of the former Chinese empire never were recovered. Territories in Vietnam and the deserts of the northwest were lost. Nomadic peoples to the north of China were always threatening to invade the empire. To prevent this, the Sung offered bribes to the "barbarians" in order to keep peace. Although the country was prospering, the government found it difficult to collect enough taxes to meet its needs. Many wealthy landowners found means to escape paying taxes altogether. This meant the tax paid by peasants had to be increased. Increased taxes usually created discontent and led to uprisings.

Eventually most of northern China slipped from the hands of the Sung. Non-Chinese invaders called the *Jurchens* set up their own foreign dynasty there called the Chin Dynasty. The Sung royal family moved to the south. They made Hangchow their new capital and continued to rule the south-ern part of their former empire until 1279 A.D.

The Mongol Dynasty   The first foreign peoples to invade and conquer China were the Mongols. The Mongols were a nomadic people from central Asia. In the early 1200's, the Mongols were united under a strong warrior-leader, **Genghis Khan** (GENG-guh-SKAHN). Under his leadership, the Mongols became one of the finest fighting forces in the world. The Mongol army consisted only of cavalry, which fought with bow and arrow. From 1206 till 1234, these horsemen carried out the conquest of the Chin Dynasty of the Jurchens in the north.

Genghis Khan died in 1227. But his son began the slow process of conquering the Sung Dynasty rooted in the south. Despite a heroic defense, the Sung lands of southern China were overrun and the dynasty collapsed.

In 1271, **Kublai Khan** (koo-blie-KAHN), Genghis Khan's grandson, founded the **Mongol Dynasty** in China.

SUNG AND MONGOL EMPIRES

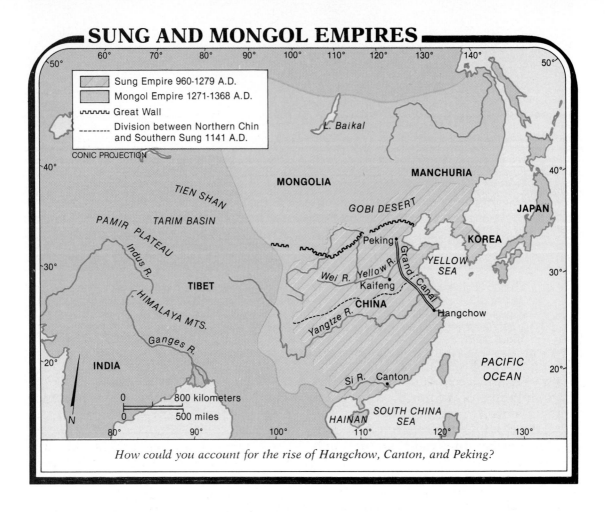

Legend:
- Sung Empire 960-1279 A.D.
- Mongol Empire 1271-1368 A.D.
- ∿∿∿ Great Wall
- ------- Division between Northern Chin and Southern Sung 1141 A.D.

CONIC PROJECTION

How could you account for the rise of Hangchow, Canton, and Peking?

He gave it a Chinese name, the **Yüan** (YOOAHN) **Dynasty.** The Mongols ruled the Yüan Dynasty in China until 1368. (See the map above.)

During Kublai Khan's reign, Peking was rebuilt and became the Mongol capital. It became one of the most magnificent cities, not only of China, but of the world. Peking was described in the *Travels of Marco Polo.* Marco Polo (MAHR-koe POE-loe) was an Italian merchant who visited China while Kublai Khan was on the throne. The stories of China he carried back to Italy gave Europeans their first glimpse of Chinese life.

Under Kublai Khan, China advanced in many areas. He believed the Mongols should give up "barbarian" ways. He claimed they had much to learn from the Chinese civilization. The Mongol conquerors did not change the structure of government they found in China. The Chinese continued to serve as officials. However, key positions were filled only by Mongols. Government business still was conducted in the Chinese language. The Mongol language was used only for matters concerning the royal family. The Mongols continued to select officials through the traditional civil service system.

The Arts in China Flourished Drama had been introduced earlier under the T'ang. During Mongol rule it became popular. Opera also developed during this period. It was a combination of singing, acting, and dancing, performed to musical accompaniment. In the 1300's, China's first novel appeared. The novel quickly developed as a new form of literature.

When Kublai Khan died in 1294, eight Mongol emperors followed him but all were too weak to rule the empire effectively. Slowly, they permitted Mongol military power to decline. Eventually, they no longer could even defend the coasts against pirate raids. Famines and floods plagued the country. Many Chinese became convinced the Mongols had lost the Mandate of Heaven. These problems helped inspire revolts. In the 1350's, China fell into turmoil again. Rebellions against Mongol rule broke out. One of these was led by a Buddhist monk named Chu Yüanchang (JOO-YOOAHN-JAHNG). He led an army across China and captured Peking. The Mongol Dynasty was destroyed and Chu became the founder of the Ming (MING) Dynasty.

The Ming Dynasty The **Ming Dynasty** was the last native dynasty to

A Closer Look

LAW CODES OF THE MONGOL DYNASTY IN CHINA

Law codes are usually a reflection of the society or culture from which they arise. Keeping this in mind, read these Chinese law codes and then answer the questions that follow them.

A man shall be punished if he refuses to take into his home a member of his family who has been widowed, orphaned, or is aged, crippled, or ill and cannot support himself or herself.

A wife who is deserted by her husband may return to her parents and may remarry. Her first husband has lost all his legal rights by his act of desertion and the marriage is ended.

A government official who is so harsh in collecting taxes as to force parents to enslave their children shall be punished by law.

A man will receive eighty-seven blows by a wooden stick if he marries during the period of mourning for the death of one of his parents [this period of mourning lasted three years]. His marriage is declared invalid and his wife is free to leave him.

A man who falsely accuses another person of wrongdoing will receive ninety-seven blows of a wooden stick. His wife is free to leave him.

Adapted from: Dan J. Li, ed. *The Essence of Chinese Civilization.* New York: D. Van Nostrand Co., 1967, pp. 402–407, and 412.

1. What were some of the duties of a Chinese citizen according to the laws of this time?
2. How did these laws try to protect and preserve the Chinese family?
3. Do you think any of these would make good laws for your society today?

rule China. They reigned from 1368 to 1644—nearly 300 years. Nanking (NAHN-KING) was their capital. Under their rule, prosperity returned. But most of the Ming emperors were weak rulers. They could not restore China's military power. Nor could they recover the territories that formerly had been part of China's empire under earlier dynasties. Lacking military strength, the Ming had to live in peace with neighbors they considered "barbarians."

The Tribute System The Ming developed a system for carrying on peaceful relations with foreign "barbarian" countries. It was known as the *tribute system.* Until the late 1800's, it was the basis for Chinese foreign policy. The tribute system was built on the Chinese belief that China and its ruler were superior to all other countries. The Chinese assumed other rulers had much to gain from trading with China and learning about its civilization. If foreign kings were willing to become vassals of the emperor, China would trade with them and there would be peace between them.

To become a *vassal state,* a foreign ruler sent a representative to the Chinese court bearing gifts or tribute. This tribute was presented to the emperor in a ceremony during which diplomats kneeled and bowed low, touching their forehead to the ground. This act was known as the *kowtow* (kowtow). In Chinese eyes, this was acknowledgement that their own emperor was chief among all world rulers.

Vassal states had much to gain from becoming part of China's tribute system—increased trade and the promise of Chinese military protection against enemies. In the 1360's and 1370's, a number of states including Korea, Vietnam, and Japan sent tribute. Most of southeast Asia joined the system as well as small states on the coast of India.

In the mid-1400's, educated Chinese began to look backward for inspiration to the Han, T'ang, and Sung dynasties. These were thought to have been great ages for China. Anything that happened in the past was imitated. This attitude influenced even the Ming emperors. They became more concerned with the past than the present. Instead of seeking new ways to progress, they imitated the old ways of doing things. They wanted no change. They refused to learn from other foreign peoples. They increased their sense of cultural superiority. For example, a map of the world drawn by Chinese mapmakers in the 1500's showed China as the center of a flat world with other nations represented as islands on the map's edges.

In the 1500's and early 1600's, the empire rapidly lost strength. Peasant uprisings became numerous due to high taxes and corruption in the government. Bandits could not be controlled. Law and order broke down.

Dynastic Rule Ends with Manchus Around 1644, bandit hordes swarmed into the city of Peking. The Chinese found it hard to drive them out. Finally, a general asked the *Manchus* (man-CHOOZ), a people from Manchuria, a land north of China, for help. He opened the passes of the Great Wall and let the Manchus enter China. With their help, the bandits were driven out. But the Manchus seized Peking. For nearly thirty years, they warred with the Ming and their armies. By 1674, the Manchus had gained control of all China and established a new dynasty called the **Manchu** or **Ch'ing** (CHING) **Dynasty.** (See map on page 91.)

MING AND MANCHU EMPIRES

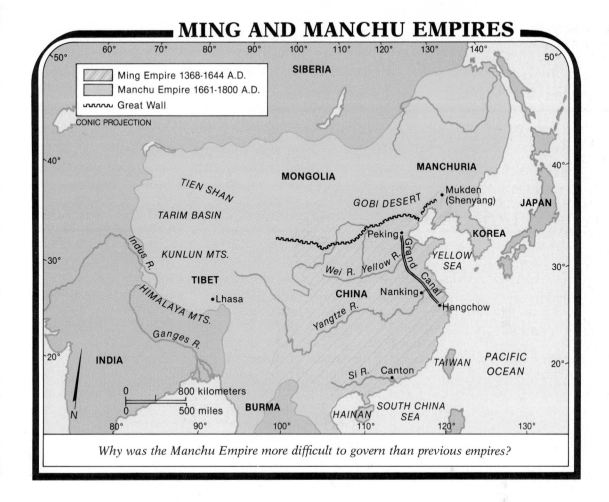

Ming Empire 1368-1644 A.D.
Manchu Empire 1661-1800 A.D.
Great Wall
CONIC PROJECTION

SIBERIA

MONGOLIA

MANCHURIA

TIEN SHAN

TARIM BASIN

GOBI DESERT

Mukden (Shenyang)

JAPAN

KUNLUN MTS.

Peking

KOREA

TIBET

Wei R. Yellow R.

Grand Canal

YELLOW SEA

Indus R.

HIMALAYA MTS.

Lhasa

CHINA

Nanking

Ganges R.

Yangtze R.

Hangchow

INDIA

0   800 kilometers
0   500 miles

N

BURMA

Si R.   Canton

TAIWAN

PACIFIC OCEAN

HAINAN

SOUTH CHINA SEA

Why was the Manchu Empire more difficult to govern than previous empires?

Under the rule of the second Manchu emperor, K'ang-hsi (KAHNG-SHEE), from 1661 to 1722, China was governed carefully and wisely. Foreign powers had seized parts of China during the Ming Dynasty. K'ang-hsi strictly controlled these foreign powers or drove them out. European scholars who spoke Chinese fluently and who adopted Chinese customs were welcome visitors to China during K'ang-hsi's reign. Though few in number, these scholars introduced the Chinese court to European learning. They acted as interpreters between the Chinese and other Europeans.

Weak and Harsh Emperors Rule China   The Manchu rulers who followed K'ang-hsi were weak. Some were also harsh rulers. The last years of the Manchu Dynasty were disastrous for China. There were many wars with foreign powers, and the Chinese lost most of them. The last ruler was an empress named Tzu Hsi (dzoo-SHEE). When she died, leaving an infant on the throne, revolution broke out. In 1912, the last Chinese emperor was dethroned.

A Pattern in Chinese History   The story of the rise and fall of dynasties reveals a pattern throughout Chinese history. Whenever a dynasty fell, China was plunged into a time of disorder. It lasted until some powerful leader established a new dynasty. The country was then reunited under a central authority. The new dynasty ruled for a century or sometimes several centuries. Often the new dynasty introduced reforms. Sooner or later, though, the dynasty began to decline. When weak rulers came to the throne, they gradually lost control of the country. And finally they were overthrown by rebels. When the dynasty did collapse, China was plunged once more into chaos. During the disorder that followed rebellion, rivals struggled against each other to establish a new dynasty. Sometimes foreigners invaded China and established themselves as a new dynasty. But no matter who the new rulers were, the pattern was usually repeated. This pattern continued until the end of imperial rule in the twentieth century.

SECTION REVIEW

1. Mapping: Using the maps on pages 88 and 91, describe the extent of the empires of the Sung, Ming, and Manchus. Describe the location of central Asia and the Yangtze River. Give the latitude and longitude coordinates for the cities of Hangchow and Peking.
2. In your own words define or identify: Kublai Khan, Marco Polo, tribute system, vassal state, Manchus.
3. What were the main achievements of the Sung, Mongol, Ming, and Manchu dynasties?
4. In this section, which dynasties were foreign? Using evidence from the text, explain the Chinese attitude toward foreigners.
5. What pattern is revealed by the rise and fall of Chinese dynasties?
D List the different taxes in this country? What purposes do they serve?

LIFE IN EARLY CHINA

Early China was a land of peasant farmers living in small villages. Many owned their small farms. But large numbers were landless and worked for wages. They grew rice, wheat, other grains, and vegetables. Rice, the most important crop, was grown chiefly in southern China. Chinese farmers also raised cattle, sheep, and pigs. Many peasants, especially the women, practiced sericulture, or the keeping of silkworms for the production of silk. Usually all members of a family, including the children, worked in the fields.

The Chinese Family   Family ties were strong in China. Loyalty to relatives, for example, was valued more than loyalty to the emperor or to the country. It was not uncommon for three generations of one family to live under the same roof. When a young Chinese couple married, they did not set up their own home. They moved into the home of the husband's parents. The duty of the head of the family was to see that his family's basic needs were met and that they lived together harmoniously. He also was expected to maintain peace with his neighbors.

Chinese Religion   Like many of the peoples you have already studied, the Chinese believed in many gods. They believed the world was inhabited by spirits. The spirits lived in places such as mountains, trees, and other natural objects. After death, the human soul was thought to live on as a part of the spirit world. The Chinese believed the living had an obligation to revere the spirits of deceased relatives. Therefore, a part of the house often was set aside as a shrine to their ancestors. And at certain times of the year, animal and food sacrifices were offered to the spirits of the dead. Chinese practices such as these are called ancestor worship.

The Importance of Land   Because China was an agricultural country, land was the chief source of wealth. The goal of peasants was to own a farm of their own. Poor peasants often moved to the city where they worked for many years. They saved their money until they had enough to return home and purchase land of their own.

The Role of Confucianism   The way of life in thousands of villages was reinforced by the teachings of Confucius. Every educated Chinese learned to read in order to study the *Classics* and he or she memorized long portions of them. The educated person was expected to apply the teachings of Confucius to daily life. A Chinese scholar, therefore, was usually someone who had learned not only to read and write the language, but also to cite an appropriate passage from the *Classics* as the solution to a problem.

Few peasants had the means to obtain the education necessary to become a scholar. Schooling on the higher levels took many years and was expensive. As a result, scholars usually came from the upper class.

Chinese Writing   In addition to Confucianism, the Chinese made other enduring contributions to world culture. The Chinese were among the first people in the Far East to develop a system of writing. (See page 73.) Chinese writing was borrowed by other Asian peoples. They adapted it to their own languages. For example, between written Chinese and written Japanese and Korean, there are many similarities. (See the chart on page 99.)

Although its written language was difficult to learn, China produced more written literature than any other ancient culture. Chinese literature was rich in philosophy, poetry, novels, folklore, drama, and history. The first historians in the Far East were Chinese. Because the Chinese thought it important to record history, others who admired Chinese civilization thought they, too, should record their histories. Consequently, we can thank China for much of our knowledge about the history of the ancient Far East.

The Chinese Invent Printing   The invention of printing around 700 A.D. was one of China's most important contributions to the world. It was made possible by two earlier Chinese inventions—paper and ink. The process of printing a book was simple. First, a page from the book was written on a sheet of thin paper, using a brush and ink. Next a block of soft wood was covered with paste and the page was laid on this, inked side down. The printer then rubbed the paper with a rounded pad so the ink would stain the wood beneath. The paper was then removed. With an engraving knife, the surface of the wood block was carved away. This raised the Chinese characters. The printer then coated the raised characters with a special ink. Next, a sheet of paper, intended as a page of a book, was placed over the raised characters. A dry brush was run lightly across the page, and the writing was thus transferred from the block to the page. The page was then peeled off the wood block and set aside to dry. When all pages of a book had been printed, they were sewn together as a book. (The pictures on page 94 show the steps of the printing process.)

Chinese Sculpture   The art of early China is famous throughout the world. It is one of China's outstanding contributions to world civilization. Pieces of

Printing in Early China

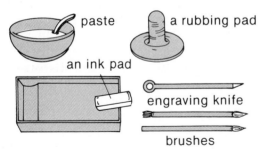
paste   a rubbing pad

an ink pad

engraving knife

brushes

1. A Chinese printer's tools

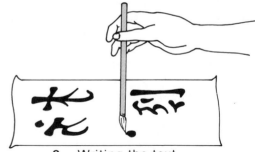

2. Writing the text

3. Applying paste and paper

4. Staining the wood

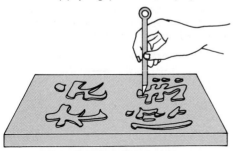

5. Carving the block

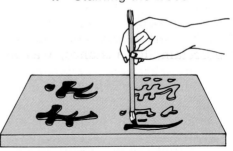

6. Inking the raised surfaces

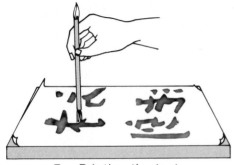

7. Printing the text

8. Removing the page

sculpture made of bronze, jade, stone, and ivory are among the most beautiful forms of Chinese art. Bronze sculpture is perhaps the best-known form.

The Chinese have been making bronze pieces for more than 3,500 years. Bronzes could serve many practical purposes. There were bronze food containers, wine goblets, and vessels that looked like teapots but were made for mixing wine and water.

Many of the bronzes of early China were used for ancestor worship. The ancestor was often named in the inscription on a bronze. These bronzes frequently depict important events in the ancestor's life. Their inscriptions, therefore, can be used as evidence about life in early China. Sometimes such bronzes were meant to be passed down from one generation to the next.

The Chinese were distinguished for their porcelain. *Porcelain* is a ceramic from which bowls, plates, cups, and other vessels—as well as sculptured figures—are made. It is very delicate and light, but very strong too. Sung Dynasty porcelain, for instance, was as thin as an egg-shell. The Chinese were so renowned for their porcelain that the word "china" has come to mean porcelain of the highest quality.

Chinese Painting   Chinese painting today is valued as one of the major art forms of the world. In the West, people tend to value a painting done by a famous artist. The painting itself is worth hundreds of thousands of dollars because it is considered unique. Copies of the painting can be made. But the original work is always considered to have the greatest value.

This was not so in China. There the practice of making copies was encouraged. One of an artist's duties was to copy the works of fine painters who had lived and worked in earlier periods. In this way, it was felt, the best art would be preserved. Future generations would be able to admire the work of the finest artists. As a result, scholars cannot tell who painted many pictures. If an artist's name is found on a picture, it does not mean that artist painted it. It usually means that it is a copy of that artist's work by someone else.

Chinese painting differed from Western painting in another important respect. Much of Western painting portrays things as they actually appear, whereas Chinese painting expresses what the artist considers an ideal form. For instance, the portrait of a man would aim at showing how he embodied the ideal of the Confucian scholar. Birds, flowers, and fish would usually be shown as moving and growing to stress that they are part of the movement of nature. When they painted pic-

How does this portrayal of a Chinese leader differ from portrayals of presidents and other leaders by Western artists? How do Chinese portraits differ from Western portraits?

95

tures of the Buddha, artists tried to show perfect shape and proportion. They did this to show not what the Buddha looked like but what a godlike form should be.

Chinese Literature   There were five main categories of Chinese literature. These included the *Classics* of Confucian philosophy, historical writings, philosophical writings, the collected works of one writer, and poetry. Historical writings included biographies, travel books, and geographies. The collected works of a writer included all the poems, letters, and essays by a single man or woman. However, they did not include a writer's novels or plays.

More men than women became well-known writers in ancient China. This was because many women did not get the opportunity to be as well-educated as men and because their social activities were more limited. A woman, for example, could not hold a professional position. She could not advance in the world through her work. However, women writers were not unknown. Pan Chao (BANN-JOW), an historian, wrote a history of the Han Dynasty with her brother. Li Chingchao (LEE-CHING-JOW), a poet of the Sung Dynasty, is famous for her songs. Ts'ai Yen (DZIE-YEN) wrote a long poem about her captivity by a nomadic tribe during the Han Dynasty. Scholars believe that many anonymous poems of early China were written by women.

Chinese Architecture   The Chinese were excellent architects and builders. As you know, when Buddhism entered China from India, it brought the Indian stupa with it. The Chinese modified the stupa, developing the structure known as the *pagoda* (puh-GOE-duh). Like a stupa, the pagoda was used originally as a shrine. Each pagoda had the same

Do any architectural forms in Western society have a symbolic interpretation similar to that of the pagoda?

basic design. There were many floors, but all floors were not the same size. The largest was the bottom floor. The others grew smaller as they mounted upward. Furthermore, each floor of the pagoda had its own roof, with long corners curving upward.

SECTION REVIEW

1. Mapping: Examine the map of China on page 55 very carefully. Which geographic features contributed to the success of Chinese agriculture?
2. In your own words, briefly define or identify: Ts'ai Yen, ancestor worship, porcelain, pagoda.
3. List four contributions to world culture made by the early Chinese. Why is each important?
▷ List and explain the kinds of contributions you now think are the most important ones any nation can make to world culture.

chapter 5

The Early Japanese

EARLY JAPAN

Geography of Japan   Japan is an **archipelago** (ahr-kuh-PEL-uh-goe), or a group of islands. The Japanese archipelago stretches in the shape of an arch more than 2,400 kilometers (1,500 miles) from the island of Hokkaido (HOE-KIE-DOE) in the north to the island of Kyushu (KYOO-SHOO) in the south. Hokkaido and Kyushu are two of four main islands. The other two are Shikoku (SHEE-KOE-KOO), the smallest of the four islands, and Honshu (HAHN-SHOO), the largest of the four. In addition to these, there are hundreds of smaller islands in the Japanese archipelago. (See the map on page 55.)

Resources of Japan   The islands of Japan have a climate with four distinct seasons. There is abundant rainfall and a long growing season. Though the climate is good for farming, farmland is scarce. Most of Japan is very hilly and mountainous. Much of it is forest. Crops can be grown on no more than about 15 percent of the land. The Japanese cultivate this land carefully, however. They make the most of their limited farmlands. A crop is planted wherever the land permits. Even steep hills and small mountains are terraced and cultivated. The main crops of Japan are barley, soybeans, wheat, fruit, vegetables, and, of course, rice. The Japanese farm today just as they did in the past. Only sericulture, the cultivation of silk worms, is no longer widely practiced in Japan.

Mineral resources in Japan are as scarce as farmland. However, dense forests provide timber. And water is an important resource. Japan has always had one very important resource—the sea. Fishing has been a major economic activity since very early times. The Japanese cultivate the sea in other ways, too. For centuries, they have extracted pearls from oysters for export to other areas of the world.

The First Japanese Histories   The first Japanese histories—the *Kojiki* (KOE-JEE-KEE), meaning the Record of Ancient Things, and the *Nihon-shoki* (NYEE-HAHN SHOE-KEE), meaning the Chronicles of Japan—were not written until 712 A.D. and 720 A.D. respectively. Scholars believe that these writings were originally legends that were transformed into historical chronicles. However, when we combine the information they contain with evidence from archaeology, myths, and accounts of early travelers, a picture of the earliest days of Japan emerges.

The Origins of the Japanese   The first inhabitants of the Japanese archipelago seem to have been a people called the *Ainu* (IE-noo). At first, they occupied all four main islands. As other peoples arrived, however, the Ainu

97

Rice was one of the most important crops grown in the ancient Far East. It was used not only for food, but for other things as well—making paper, for example. Rice was grown on hills and small mountains, as well as in flat fields. How does the method of rice cultivation pictured here show people adapting to their environment?

were pushed farther and farther north. They eventually settled on Hokkaido, the northernmost island where their descendants still live today. The next people to arrive in Japan after the Ainu are believed to be the ancestors of the modern Japanese. Some migrated east from the mainland of Asia. Others came from the Philippines (FILL-uh-peenz) and the islands of the South Pacific.

Early Japanese Society   The earliest Japanese were a polytheistic people who worshiped different aspects of nature as gods. Animal sacrifices had to be offered to these gods to keep them happy. The most important deity was the sun goddess. In fact, the Japanese called their land *Nippon* (NIP-AHN) or *Nihon* (NEE-HAWN), which means "source of the sun."

Early Japanese society was divided into clans, or groups of related families. These clans may have varied in size from 1,000 to 70,000 families. Some were so large that early Chinese visitors to Japan called the clans "countries." Each clan had its own ruler. Some were governed by kings, others by queens.

Japan Under the Yamato   The island of Honshu seems to have been the center of early Japanese life. Near Kyoto (KEE-OTE-OE), the Yamato (YAH-MAH-TOE) clan was established. It conquered its neighbors and brought lands as far away as modern Tokyo (TOE-KYOE) under its control. The government created around 400 to 500 A.D. has been called the **Yamato State.** Yamato rulers considered themselves superior to the other clans. They took the title of emperor or empress.

Members of each clan worshiped a particular god or goddess. The deity was thought to have been the founder of the clan. As clans grew, branches within the clan developed. They broke away from the main clan and moved to another place. But the clan branches always worshiped the same deity as the main clan. The Yamato clan worshiped the sun goddess, *Amaterasu* (AH-MAH-TEH-RAH-SOO). Eventually, Amaterasu became the most important of the deities in Japan. The imperial family claimed to be descended from the sun goddess.

Myths about the creation of Japan tell us the sun goddess sent her grandson, *Ninigi* (NEE-NEE-GEE), to the island of Kyushu. Legends also tell us that *Jimmu* (JIM-MOO), the great grandson of Ninigi, conquered all the other gods on the islands of Japan and established the Yamato State. Jimmu is supposed to have been the earthly founder of the royal family that still occupies the Japanese throne. As a result, the Japanese believed in the divinity of their rulers until the twentieth century.

In Chapter 4 you learned that Chinese history is filled with the rise and fall of dynasties. The Mandate of Heaven was justification for overthrowing a dynasty in China. In Japan, however, the royal family was never overthrown because the royal family was thought to be divine. Thus, the only political struggles were those between rival clans who hoped to gain power and influence over the royal family.

The great clans of early Japan constantly vied with each other for power. They also threatened the power of the imperial family. When an emperor or empress died, there was no rule of succession to the throne. As a result, clans sponsored rival members of the imperial family for the position. Many Yamato emperors and empresses reigned but did not always rule. The power behind their throne often was a relative or member of a related clan.

Between 600 and 900 A.D., Japan came into contact with Chinese civilization. At this time, China was experiencing a golden age under the T'ang Dynasty. Chinese influence was especially strong in Korea, Japan's closest neighbor on the mainland of Asia.

Chinese Influence on Japan During this period, the Japanese tried to imitate the Chinese. Buddhism, which originated in India, was introduced into Japan through China. The government tried to carry out reforms based on the Chinese government. Taxes were collected as they were in China. Chinese styles of art influenced Japanese artists. And the Japanese borrowed the Chinese method of writing and later formed their own writing system based on the Chinese system.

In the 700's, Japan adopted the Chinese system of writing and began to keep written records. By learning and adopting the Chinese language, the Japanese learned about Chinese advances in medicine, astronomy, and other sciences. They also adopted the Chinese calendar. Their philosophy was influenced by Confucianism.

CHINESE				
加	多	奴	保	利

JAPANESE				
力	夕	又	木	リ

KOREAN				
가	다	노	보	리

One of the most important Chinese influences on Japan concerned government. The Japanese adopted the Chinese style of government. An imperial capital was established in 794 A.D. at Kyoto. The imperial court remained there for 1,000 years and resembled the Chinese court in the way it conducted business and ceremonies. Even the Japanese palaces resembled those of the Chinese.

During the period 592–770, half the rulers of Japan were empresses. Since then, however, only two women have held the throne. This sudden change in practice may have come about as a result of Chinese influence since in early China men usually held the imperial throne.

Part of the Japanese ruler's duties were to perform at religious ceremonies, such as offering sacrifices to the gods. But in political matters, the emperor or empress was only a figurehead. That is, imperial rulers and the members of their court paid less attention to the business of governing and more to the pursuit of pleasures.

The Period of the Fujiwara   By the 800's, real power slipped into the hands of a noble clan at court, the **Fujiwara** (FOO-JEE-WAH-RAH). The Fujiwara were distant relatives of the royal family. They were able to gain control over the emperor and use his power to obtain what they wanted. They accomplished this by securing ties to the royal family and by marrying Fujiwara daughters to the emperors. The Fujiwara controlled the court. Several Fujiwara served as regents. A *regent* is an individual who governs in the name of the ruler in case the ruler is ill, or too young to act on his or her own. The Fujiwara were the power behind Japan's throne from about 800 to 1100.

Feudalism Under the Fujiwara   As you know, the system in which a noble gives land to his or her supporters in return for their help in times of war is called feudalism. This sytem developed in China during the Chou Dynasty. (See page 74.) Feudalism had fully developed by 1100 in Japan.

Japanese nobles gradually accumulated huge tracts of land. Because they paid no taxes on this land, they grew very wealthy. With their wealth, they acquired great power. Eventually, these nobles became powerful enough to rule their lands without the approval of the imperial court at Kyoto.

The nobles organized bands of warriors known as **samurai** (SAM-UH-RIE). In exchange for land and peasants to work the land, these warriors swore total allegiance to the nobles. They promised to support the nobles in times of crisis. The crops raised by peasants on samurai lands were taxed heavily. The peasants paid taxes to the samurai and these taxes were the samurai's only means of support. Often one samurai would parcel out his land to other samurai. They would promise to support him as he had promised to support his superior. In this way, some samurai became leaders of their own bands of warriors.

The samurai eventually grew so numerous that they became a separate class in Japanese society. All samurai were expected to fight in times of war. But because their military duties were few during times of peace, many became government officials and scholars.

In addition to the upper class samurai, there were three other classes in early Japanese society. In rank order, they were the artisans, peasants, and merchants. There also were outcasts, known as *eta* (AY-TUH). Classes in early Japan, like those in early India, largely corresponded to occupations. A Japanese, however, was able to move from one class to another without great difficulty.

SECTION REVIEW

1. Mapping: Using the map on page 55, and information on page 97 of the text, identify the four main islands of Japan.
2. In your own words, define or identify: archipelago, Ainu, Yamato, Amaterasu, Kyoto, Fujiwara, feudalism, samurai.
3. What political roles did the clans play in early Japan?
4. Summarize the main Chinese influences on early Japanese civilization.
5. List the four main classes of Japanese society and describe their occupations. How did the class structure of early Japan basically differ from that of early India?
◗ Are there different classes in your society? What are they? Is a person able to move from one class to another? How?

THE RISE OF THE SHOGUNS

The period of the Fujiwara came to an end in the 1100's. The Fujiwara quarreled among themselves and faced opposition from other families. The court at Kyoto divided into groups that struggled with each other for power. Great nobles at the capital called on their samurai throughout the countryside to support them. A long series of civil wars broke out, lasting from about 1156 until 1185.

Japan Under the Minamoto The civils wars ended in a victory for Minamoto Yoritomo (MEE-NAH-MOE-TOE

The first Japanese shogun is pictured here in his formal robes. Notice the sword in its sheath and the forceful look on the shogun's face. Why are leaders portrayed in this fashion?

YOE-REE-TOE-MOE), a samurai general. Yoritomo, who was the leader of the Minamoto clan, established a new form of government. It was a military government. From the emperor, Yoritomo received the title **shogun** (SHOE-GUN), which meant chief general. Thus Yoritomo's government was called a **shogunate** (SHOE-gun-ate). The imperial capital at Kyoto was left undisturbed. But Yoritomo set up his own capital at Kamakura (KAH-MAH-KOO-RAH). He appointed his own set of officials. They replaced the emperor's officials in governing the country so Japan had really two governments. But real power was exercised by the Kamakura shogunate under Yoritomo. Eventually, the position of shogun became hereditary. It was passed from father to son.

Developments in Japan offer an interesting contrast to what took place in China. In China, military leaders were held in low regard. Scholars had great prestige. And civilian rulers controlled the military leaders. But in Japan, military power dominated civilian authority and warriors were respected more than scholars were. All the country was united under a single military leader who ruled but did not seize the throne from the emperor.

The period under the Minamoto was important in the history of Buddhism in Japan. The Mahayana branch of Buddhism spread and became popular among the common people. It also was popular among philosophers. A variety of Buddhist sects grew, each interpreting Buddhism in its own way.

Only twice in its history has Japan faced the threat of invasion. The first took place during the period of Minamoto in the thirteenth century when the Mongol ruler of China, Kublai Khan, tried to invade and conquer Japan. Both his attempts in 1274 and 1281 were repulsed. The Japanese were not threatened from outside forces again until the twentieth century.

The Decline of the Minamoto Eventually, the Minamoto declined in power. Like the emperors, the shoguns became only figureheads in their own court. Important nobles now dominated the shogunate. These nobles came to be known as *daimyo* (DIE-MYOE). As the central government of the shogunate broke down, a new line of shoguns seized power in 1338. These were the weak *Ashikaga* (AH-SHEE-KAH-GAH) shoguns who took control of various parts of Japan for over 200 years. They moved the shogun's capital from Kamakura to Kyoto, the imperial capital. Meanwhile, the daimyo became all-powerful in their own territories. They warred against each other with bands of samurai warriors. Neither emperors nor shoguns could stop

From this depiction of a Japanese samurai and the shogun pictured earlier, how would you describe the different functions of the samurai and the shogun in feudal Japan?

the civil wars that plagued Japan from about 1330 until 1573.

This period of Japanese history was the age of the samurai who were horsemen. They wore light armor and used the bow and arrow. They were expected to be skilled swordsmen.

The samurai gradually developed their own code of conduct, called *Bushido* (BOO-SHEE-DOE). This code stressed loyalty to superiors, even if it meant death. The code stressed pride in one's family and name.

A samurai was expected to be polite, patient, and able to endure suffering. He was also expected to be willing to commit *seppuku* (SEH-POO-KOO) to save his honor or the honor of his family. Seppuku, also known as *harakiri* (HAH-RAH-KEE-REE), was a form of ritual suicide. This form of public suicide developed rules of its own that had to be observed. The kneeling warrior stabbed himself in the stomach with a special dagger. A fellow samurai then beheaded him with his sword. Suicide not only wiped away disgrace, it was also a way to prove complete devotion to one's superior.

The Reunification of Japan under the Tokugawa   The long period of civil war following the fall of the Minamoto was filled with political chaos and decentralization. In 1603, a leading military figure, Tokugawa Ieyasu (TOE-KUH-GAH-WAH EE-YEH-YAH-SUH), founded a new line of shoguns who governed Japan until the 1800's. The **Tokugawa** reunited all the country and restored stability to its government. The emperor and his court remained at Kyoto. Meanwhile, Ieyasu established his capital at Edo (EH-DOE), now modern Tokyo, and brought the warring daimyo under control.

The great nobles who had been Ieyasu's enemies were forced to move to Edo. They were kept under close watch. Every other year they were permitted to return to their lands. But to prevent them from raising warriors against him, Ieyasu forced the daimyo to leave close relatives in Edo as hostages.

The daimyo who had supported Ieyasu were rewarded with lands for themselves and their samurai. The daimyo had to remain loyal to stay in possession of land, which they needed to support themselves.

Tokugawa shoguns also sent their representatives to keep watch over the imperial court at Kyoto. It seems the emperor's court was firmly under the shogun's control. As a result, more than a dozen emperors were compelled to give up the throne between 1603 and 1867, the period of Tokugawa rule.

Foreign Contact with Japan   Foreigners, including Europeans, had arrived in Japan during the civil wars. Shoguns and European merchants, eager for trade, brought many Europeans to Japan. Among them were missionaries who spread Christianity to Japan and won large numbers of converts. But the policy of the Tokugawa shoguns was to shut Japan off from all foreign influences. By 1639, foreigners were permitted to visit only the city of Nagasaki (NAH-GAH-SAH-KEE). There was a growing distrust of Christianity, which was considered a foreign influence that denied the divinity of the emperor. The shoguns tried to stamp out the new religion. Thousands of Japanese Christians were killed. Those who remained Christian were forced to practice their religion secretly.

For 200 years, Japan was cut off from contact with the rest of the world. During this period of isolation, the Japanese looked to their leaders for guidance and obeyed their authority. Important changes took place during this period. Around the castles of the great nobles, villages were established. Gradually these villages grew into market towns and cities. As Japan's population increased, many people were forced to move to towns to make a living. The land could not support the additional population by farming alone.

As towns and cities grew, trade within Japan increased. The merchant class became wealthy. Gradually they rivaled the great nobles in wealth. Many samurai were forced to borrow from the merchants. Many samurai were reduced to poverty. They took as their income a share of the crops raised on their lands by peasant-farmers. The size of the crop was determined by the amount of land each samurai possessed. As prices rose, samurai needed larger incomes. But there was no way for them to add land to their possessions. As a result of this, many became impoverished.

Although none of these changes was sudden, over a period of 200 years they caused discontent and suffering. By the 1800's, many were searching for ways to change Japan.

SECTION REVIEW

1. Mapping: Using the map on page 55, describe the geographical relationship of Japan to Korea and China. Locate the following cities by means of longitude and latitude coordinates: Kyoto, Tokyo, Nagasaki.
2. In your own words, define or identify: Minamoto Yoritomo, shogun, shogunate, daimyo, Bushido, seppuku, Tokugawa Ieyasu.
3. Summarize the main characteristics of a samurai warrior.
4. Describe the structure of government in Japan under the shoguns.
5. How did Tokugawa shoguns maintain a strong central government?
   ◗ In our nation today, what do you consider the central government to be? What is local government? Which do you think is more powerful? Why?

THE ACCOMPLISHMENTS OF THE EARLY JAPANESE

Early in their history, the Japanese began to collect and preserve legends about the creation of the world, the lives of their emperors, the deeds of heroes, and other important events. Combined, these stories became the basis of a native Japanese religion called *Shinto* (SHIN-TOE).

Religion in Japan It is not known when Shinto first developed, but its beliefs had been written down by 700 A.D. The Shinto religion taught that Japan had been created by the gods known as *kami* (KAH-MEE). They were believed to have inhabited all parts of nature. For this reason, the Japanese regarded mountains, trees, stones, birds, plants, and other objects of nature as aspects of the gods. From Shinto, the Japanese people developed a lasting love and respect for the beauty of nature.

The purpose of religion, the Japanese believed, was to seek the favor of the gods. This was done by performing ceremonies and offering sacrifices of animals and food to show respect. Shrines were erected as homes for the gods and as places where worshipers could pay their respects to the gods. Acts of worship included the clapping of hands, bowing, and offering sacrifices. Gates called *torii* (TOE-RIH-EE) marked the location of these shrines.

Shinto remained the native Japanese religion. It did not spread to other peoples. Unlike many religions, Shinto had no founder, no sacred books, no teachers, and no moral code or philosophy. Later, many Buddhist and Confucian ideas from China were blended with Shinto beliefs. Japanese even practiced other religions while they clung to Shinto. Later, Shinto was revived under the Tokugawa shoguns.

The introduction of Buddhism from China was important because it stimulated the development of religious art in Japan as early as 500 to 600. Many Buddhist temples were built. One, at Nara (NAH-RAH), is believed to be the oldest wooden structure in the world. Buddhism also influenced Japanese sculpture. For example, the great Buddha in the Todaiji (TOE-DIE-JEE) temple near Nara, is the largest bronze statue in the world. It was completed by Japanese sculptors in 749 A.D. and weighs 340 tonnes (380 tons.)

Japanese Architecture Early Japanese architecture stressed harmony between buildings and their natural surroundings. A traditional Japanese house, for example, was surrounded by a garden. The house and the garden were connected as closely as possible, by a narrow platform around the outside of the house on ground level.

For many years, Japanese buildings looked like copies of Chinese models. The Japanese imitated the Chinese use of rich colors and wood, and the use of large posts and beams in building construction. Some time after 800 A.D., however, Japanese architects and builders began to develop their own styles. They began to free themselves from Chinese influences. Later Japanese painters, sculptors, and artisans began to do the same. Finally a distinctive Japanese style was created in the arts.

Japanese Drama Japanese drama never imitated Chinese sources as extensively as did the other arts. As a result, a uniquely Japanese form of drama was highly developed by the thirteenth century. It was called the *No* (NOE) drama. No plays were slow-moving and dignified. There were only two main actors and they were accompanied by one or more narrators and by musicians. The No plays were performed in special theaters. In No plays the actors wore masks instead of makeup to indicate the roles they were playing. Usually the plays were about the Shinto gods or heroes in Japanese history. One unusual form of drama, called *bunraku* (BUN-RAH-KOO), used half life-size dolls instead of live actors. Three puppeteers were needed to control each puppet. *Kabuki* (KAH-BOO-KEE) drama developed in the 1600's. It used songs and dance in its plays and was much livelier than No drama. Kabuki actors often used highly exaggerated gestures and movements to tell the story of the drama.

Japanese Literature At first, Japanese literature was written in the Chinese language. It followed patterns laid down by Chinese writers. After the ninth century, however, Japanese writers developed a literary style of their own. This development was made possible largely by the invention of a simplified method of writing the Japanese language. A good example of early Japanese literary style is *The Tale of Genji* (GEN-JEE), one of Japan's first novels. Written by Lady Murasaki (MUH-RAH-SAH-KEE), a Japanese woman of the upper class, the novel is a long account of the adventures of a Japanese prince, Genji. It depicts life at the imperial court about 1000 A.D. Many women of noble birth were among Japan's most famous writers and poets. After the rise of the samurai as a ruling class, however, tales of war and heroic deeds became popular. Many have survived as classics of Japanese literature.

SECTION REVIEW

1. Mapping: You have learned that Chinese civilization influenced early Japan. Examine the map on page 55. How did the geography of the region aid in bringing Chinese culture to Japan?
2. In your own words, define or identify: Shinto, kami, torii, No drama, bunraku, Kabuki, *The Tale of Genji*.
3. Summarize the major cultural accomplishments of the early Japanese.
   How has the culture of our country been influenced by cultures in other parts of the world? Explain.

Reviewing the Unit

Unit Summary

After you have read the selection below, answer the questions that follow.

Civilization first appeared in both the Middle East and Far East along the major rivers. India's earliest civilization developed in the Indus River Valley, and China's developed along the Yellow River.

Time after time, invaders entered India through mountain passes in the northwest. One of the earliest groups, the Aryans, brought a religion that later developed into Hinduism. They also established a caste system.

Few rulers united early India. One of the Maurya emperors, Asoka, brought most of India under his control. Later, half of India was reunited by the Guptas. Still later, the Muslim conquerors reunited India for a short while. Throughout India's history, political unity was the exception, not the rule. China, on the other hand, was usually united under a single central government by a dynasty. Beginning with the Ch'in, the Chinese conquered neighboring lands and created great em-pires. Stable government did not last long. Chinese history is filled with the rise and fall of dynasties.

India and China were cultural centers of the Far East. Buddhism was founded in India. It spread over most of Asia. India made contributions to science and mathematics. The Arabic numerals used today originated in ancient India. India's art influenced other parts of the Far East—especially southeastern Asia. Chinese art and culture, such as the Chinese system of writing and printing, were imitated throughout Japan and Korea.

Japan's native religion was Shinto. Shinto and Japanese myths about the creation of Japan reinforced beliefs that the rulers of Japan were human descendents of deities. The ruling family was thought to be divine. As a result, it was not overthrown. Instead, emperors were only figureheads and struggles for power usually were between noble families such as the Fujiwara, Minamoto, and Tokugawa who wanted to control the imperial court.

Developing Your Reading Skills

1. Which of the following statements best expresses the main idea of this reading? Explain your choice.
   a. Indian and Chinese cultures influenced the ancient Far East.
   b. Early Indian and China greatly resembled one another.
   c. Ancient India and China conquered most of the Far East.

2. In your own words, state the main idea in this reading about each of the following: a. India, b. China, and c. Japan.

Developing a Sense of Time

Examine the time line below and answer the questions that follow it:

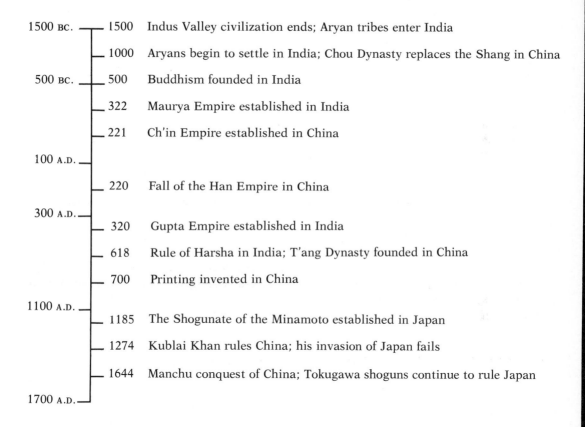

1500 B.C.	1500	Indus Valley civilization ends; Aryan tribes enter India
	1000	Aryans begin to settle in India; Chou Dynasty replaces the Shang in China
500 B.C.	500	Buddhism founded in India
	322	Maurya Empire established in India
	221	Ch'in Empire established in China
100 A.D.		
	220	Fall of the Han Empire in China
300 A.D.		
	320	Gupta Empire established in India
	618	Rule of Harsha in India; T'ang Dynasty founded in China
	700	Printing invented in China
1100 A.D.		
	1185	The Shogunate of the Minamoto established in Japan
	1274	Kublai Khan rules China; his invasion of Japan fails
	1644	Manchu conquest of China; Tokugawa shoguns continue to rule Japan
1700 A.D.		

1. What was happening in India about the time the Chou Dynasty was established in China?
2. Which empire was established first—the Maurya in India or the Ch'in in China?
3. When did the Minamoto establish Japan's first shogunate?
4. List three other events or developments from Unit 2 that can be added to this time line and give a reason for each.

Recalling the Facts

1. What were the four classes in early Indian society?
2. Describe the following early Indian literature: the Vedas, the Mahabharata, the Ramayana.
3. Why did the Muslim conquerors of India consider themselves superior to the Indians?
4. How were Sung government officials selected in China?
5. Name two foreign ruling dynasties established in early China.
6. What was the Mandate of Heaven? Explain its role in the rise and fall of early Chinese dynasties.
7. Compare the position of emperor and empress in early China and Japan.
8. Who were samurai? What role did they perform in early Japan?
9. Briefly describe the Chinese writing system. Why was it adopted in early Japan?
10. List five major achievements of India, China, and Japan.

Using Your Vocabulary

1. What was the caste system?
2. In your own words, define the terms *dynasty* and *empire*.
3. What was Confucianism? Why was it important?
4. In your own words, define Taoism.
5. What was the purpose of the tribute system?
6. How did Buddhism differ from Hinduism? In what ways were they alike?
7. Define the terms *art* and *government* as they apply to your own life, giving examples of each.
8. Would an early Chinese artist have agreed with your definition of art? What examples might he or she have used to illustrate the definition?
9. How do you think a ruler of early China would have defined government? Do you think a Japanese shogun would have offered a similar definition? Explain.
10. Name and describe three types of Japanese drama.

Using Your Geography Skills

1. Near what geographical features in India and China did civilization first appear?
2. As you learned, India was invaded many times from the northwest. Referring to the map on page 58, describe the route followed by the Aryans into India.
3. What part of early India was known as the Deccan?
4. Referring to the map on page 55, and information in your text on page 64, explain why, in ancient times, India's sea-going contacts with southeastern Asia were greater than with China.
5. Use the map on page 55 to explain why there was little contact between India and China in ancient times.
6. Using the maps in this unit, list and describe the extent of the kingdoms

and empires in early India and China.

7. Using the map on page 55, name the four major islands of the Japanese archipelago. Using the Atlas in the front of the book, locate other archipelagoes.

8. How was Japan more geographically secure from foreign invasions than China during ancient times?

9. Using the map on page 55, give the distance in miles and kilometers between each of the following: the northern- and southernmost islands of Japan; the mouth of the Ganges River and the southern tip of India; Peking and the Yangtze River.

Developing Your Writing Skills

In this unit, you learned that civilization in the Far East first appeared in India and China. Indian and Chinese civilizations influenced almost all the other peoples of the Far East.

FORMING AN OPINION

Now consider the following:

1. In your opinion, what is the meaning of the word "civilization"? List as many characteristics of "civilization" as you can.

2. Which three things on your list do you consider most important?

3. Do the civilizations of ancient India, China, and Japan fit your definition of "civilization"? How?

SUPPORTING AN OPINION

Answer these questions in a paragraph or essay. Begin by completing the following topic sentence: The civilizations of the ancient Far East_____

Why Study the Past?

India and China today are two of the world's most populous nations. Modern Japan is one of the world's industrial leaders. How might the knowledge of the history of India, China, and Japan help you to understand the political developments now taking place in these countries? Would this knowledge help you in any way to understand the culture of these countries today? Explain.

Your History Bookshelf

Auboyer, Jeannine. *Daily Life in Ancient India.* New York: Macmillan, 1965.

Cotterell, Arthur, and Morgan, David. *China's Civilization.* New York: Praeger, 1975.

Dilts, Marion M. *Pageant of Japanese History.* New York: David McKay, 1965.

Seegar, Elizabeth. *The Pageant of Chinese History.* New York: David McKay, 1962.

Welty, Paul Thomas. *The Asians.* Philadelphia: Lippincott, 1976.

The World of
Ancient Greece and Rome

When you sit down to dinner, take up the salt shaker and sprinkle a little salt on your food, you probably don't think about what you are doing. Today salt is inexpensive and plentiful. But in ancient times, salt was so scarce that soldiers and officials in Greece and Rome were paid in salt instead of in money. In Rome, the payment was called a salarium.

No one knows when people first became aware of the importance of salt in the human diet. But we do know that, in addition to being very valuable, salt was thought by the ancients to have magical properties. Important people threw salt over their shoulders for good luck. They also sprinkled it on their food as a protection against poison. In time, it became the custom to put a bit of salt on any food that looked doubtful.

Even before this, however, salt was thought to have special powers. Prehistoric Romans usually led their criminals to an altar to be sacrificed as a punishment for their crimes. The priest would place a bit of salt on the head of each guilty person so that he or she would have better luck in the next life.

Salt was so valuable that if any was spilled, it was thought to be bad luck for everyone present. People in many parts of the Western world still believe this is so.

We no longer think that salt can protect us from evil influences, but many of the ideas connected with salt have remained with us. How often have you said "I'll take that with a grain of salt," or "So-and-so is the salt of the earth"? And if you do accidentally spill salt at the dinner table, do you ever feel an urge to pick up a pinch and throw it over your shoulder?

The customs of ancient Greece and Rome have affected nearly all of Western civilization in some way. Indirectly, they have also affected Africa and Asia. Westerners visiting or settling in these places have brought with them many customs that can be traced back thousands of years to Greece and Rome. Africans and Asians, in imitating certain Western ways, have, perhaps unknowingly, imitated ancient Greece and Rome.

Historians study the origins of customs that have come down over great spans of time. They can find evidence about a period or a people in these customs, as well as in written documents, buildings, paintings, and sculpture. In this unit, the customs of ancient Greece and Rome will be considered. Other aspects of these two great cultures, including their forms of government, religious beliefs, daily life, and relations with other peoples, will be discussed. An important facet of this study will be acquiring a knowledge of the geography of Greece and Italy and of the lands that were part of the Grecian and Roman empires at one time or another.

Unit Goals

1. To know the main geographical features of the ancient worlds of Greece and Rome and how geography affected the cultures that developed there.
2. To describe the early cultures of Crete and Mycenae and understand how they affected the culture of classical Greece.
3. To know how the governments of Sparta and Athens worked and how they affected life in these two city-states.
4. To describe the development of the Roman Empire and to explain why it declined.
5. To know the main ideas of early Christianity, its origins, and some of the reasons historians give for its rapid spread throughout the Roman Empire.
6. To identify the ideas the Western world has inherited from the ancient worlds of Greece and Rome.

Ancient Greece and Rome

Legend:
- Roman Empire at its greatest extent, about 117 A.D.
- Grecian City-States
- Grecian Colonies
- Present-day boundaries

0 — 500 Kilometers
0 — 400 Miles

CONIC PROJECTION

ATLANTIC OCEAN

NORTH SEA

BALTIC SEA

BRITAIN
Thames R.

GERMANIA
Rhine R.
Seine R.
Loire R.
Danube R.
GAUL
Garonne R.
Rhône R.
PYRENEES
ALPS
ALPS
Po R.
APENNINES
Tiber R.
Rome
ITALY
Naples
CORSICA
SARDINIA
TYRRHENIAN SEA
SICILY
Syracuse
CARPATHIAN MTS.
ILLYRIA
ADRIATIC SEA
Danube R.
MACEDONIA
THRACE
Byzantium BOSPORUS
BLACK SEA
CAUCASUS MTS.
DARDANELLES
Troy
Pergamum
ASIA MINOR
AEGEAN SEA
GREECE
IONIAN SEA
Corinth
Athens
Olympia
Mycenae
Sparta
TAURUS MTS.
Antioch
SYRIA
Damascus
CYPRUS
CRETE
Knossos
MALTA
MEDITERRANEAN SEA

SPAIN
Douro R.
Tagus R.
Ebro R.
Guadalquivir R.
BALEARIC ISLANDS
ST. OF GIBRALTAR
ATLAS MTS.
Carthage
AFRICA

LIBYA
SAHARA DESERT
LIBYAN DESERT
EGYPT
Alexandria
Nile Delta
Nile R.
GULF OF SUEZ
SINAI PENINSULA
Jerusalem
Dead Sea
SYRIAN DESERT
RED SEA

30° 20° 10° 0° 10° 20° 30° 40° 50°
70° 60° 50° 40° 30°

The Ancient Greeks

EARLY GREEK CIVILIZATION

The civilizations that rose and prospered in the ancient Middle East and Far East after 3000 B.C. were not the only great societies that existed during that time. In the eastern part of the Mediterranean (med-uh-tuh-RAY-nee-un), two early Greek cultures also flourished. One of these developed on the island of Crete (KREET). The other developed on the Greek mainland.

Historians do not know what the ancient people of Crete were called. According to legends, their king was called *Minos* (MIE-nus), so archaeologists have given them the name *Minoans* (muh-NOE-unz). The other great culture on the mainland was centered around an important city called Mycenae (mie-SEE-nee). These people are called *Mycenaeans* (mie-suh-NEE-unz). These two great cultures helped form the basis for what historians call classical Greek civilization. And classical Greece, in many ways, set the foundation for Western civilization.

The Minoans   There are no written histories from the period of the Minoans. All that historians know about these interesting and highly skilled people has come from the work of archaeologists. Scholars know that people were living on the island of Crete by

3000 B.C. (See the map on page 116.) Their remains have been found in the caves that served as their homes and burial places. Some of these people may have come from the areas that are present-day Turkey (TUR-kee), Syria (SIR-ee-uh), Israel, Egypt, and Libya (LIB-ee-uh).

During the 500 years following 3000 B.C., the settlers on Crete prospered. They built large houses and kept oxen, sheep, pigs, and chickens. They also grew corn and grapes and raised olives for oil. The Minoans made tools and weapons of copper and bronze and founded colonies on several neighboring islands.

By 2000 B.C., ships from Crete were trading goods with the Egyptians and the peoples of the eastern coast of the Mediterranean. Crete was strategically located as a trading center. The island lies between the Greek mainland and Egypt and was close to the countries of the ancient Middle East. A large, powerful navy protected Crete and its colonies. (See the map on page 116.)

At about this time, the great Minoan civilization was born. Historians know something about the life of the Minoans from the remains of some of their cities. The most famous of these cities is Knossos (NAHS-uz). There archaeologists have found the remains of well-built houses, which were laid out

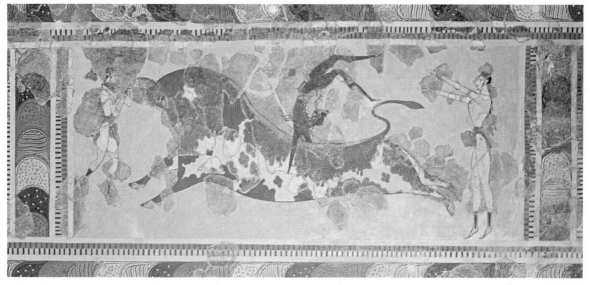

These wall paintings are in the palace of King Minos at Knossos, Crete. Minos' throne stands before the richly colored painting of mythical animals, below. Above, three young men are shown performing the dangerous bull dance. In fact, both young men and young women participated in bull jumping in ancient Crete. In what dangerous or demanding sports do both men and women participate in contemporary society?

MYCENAEAN CIVILIZATION ABOUT 1400 B.C.

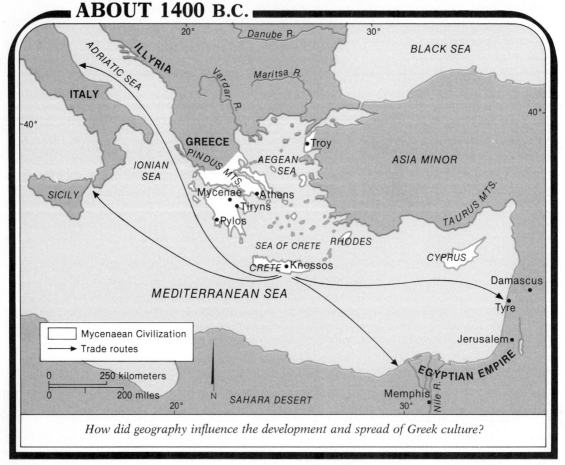

How did geography influence the development and spread of Greek culture?

in rows on terraced hillsides. Paved streets separated the rows of houses. They also found a great palace with large storerooms where the food and the wealth of the city were kept.

The Minoans were famous for their arts and crafts. They were skilled in painting, carving gems, working metal, and making pottery. Minoan pottery was of especially fine quality. It was also an important item for trade throughout the Mediterranean world. At this time, the Minoans also used a form of writing that archaeologists call *Linear A*. So far, however, it has not been deciphered.

The Mycenaeans By about 1400 B.C., the leading cities of Crete were destroyed. Some scholars believe they were ruined during a great earthquake. Others believe they were destroyed by invaders. Historians agree, however, that contact between the Minoans and the Greek mainland became stronger and trade began shortly before this period. Historians now believe that sometime after 1400 B.C., the rulers of Knossos were probably Mycenaeans from the Greek mainland rather than Minoans. (See the map above.)

The physical geography of the mainland of Greece offers many clues

116

about why the Mycenaeans eventually came into contact with the Minoans. Although there was a mild climate in Greece, only about one fifth of all the land was suitable for farming. The fertile river valleys and plains, where most of the farming was done, were closely hemmed in by steep mountains and the sea. In early times, the mountains isolated groups of people from one another. Greece had very little timber and no iron. Only small amounts of gold, silver, copper, zinc, and lead could be found.

With such limited natural resources available, sea trade and navigation became natural occupations for the Mycenaeans. The irregular coast line of the mainland also provided many protected harbors and seaports. So the Mycenaeans, like the Minoans, became great traders and the two probably were in close contact.

The Mycenaeans spread Greek influence and culture as far as Italy and central Europe. The colonies they founded in Europe supplied the Greek mainland with important raw materials. Mycenae took over the trade routes of Crete and became the leading naval power in the region.

After about 1300 B.C., the great influence of the Mycenaeans began to decrease. The kings lived in fortified palaces surrounded by huge stone walls. The people became more warlike and began to raid neighboring lands. The most famous of these attacks was on the fortified city of Troy in Asia Minor about 1200 B.C.

Historians do not know very much about this period in Greek history or about the culture of the Mycenaeans. But two very important pieces of literature about the Trojan (TROE-jun) War, which were written during a later period, have given them some important clues. These epic tales are called the *Iliad* (IL-ee-ud) and the *Odyssey* (AHD-uh-see). They were supposedly written down about 750–700 B.C. by a blind poet named **Homer** (HOE-mur).

The Iliad and the Odyssey   The *Iliad* is a story of the Trojan War, which was fought between the *Trojans* and the Mycenaeans. In the story, Paris, a son of the king of Troy, kidnaps Helen, the wife of King Menelaus (men-uh-LAY-us) of Sparta (SPAHRT-uh). The Mycenaeans sail to Troy to try to bring Helen back. After many battles, the Mycenaeans finally defeat the Trojans through trickery by building a large wooden horse. Mistaking the horse as a gift from the gods, the Trojans bring it into their city. They are defeated when the Mycenaean troops hiding inside sneak out at night and open the gates of the city to the rest of their army.

This ancient Greek relief sculpture depicts the Trojan Horse. How was it used in the Trojan War?

The *Odyssey* is the story of Odysseus (oe-DISS-yoos), a Mycenaean hero and the king of Ithaca (ITH-ih-kuh), who wanders far and wide for ten years after the fall of Troy. After many fantastic adventures, such as a fight with a Cyclops, he finally returns home to Ithaca. There Odysseus kills the many men who have attempted to take his throne by trying to marry his wife, Penelope (puh-NELL-uh-pee).

At one time, scholars did not think the descriptions in the stories of this period of history were very accurate. One scholar, Heinrich Schliemann (HY'N-rick SHLEE-mahn), a retired businessman and noted scholar of languages, admired the *Iliad* so much that he spent his life trying to prove that its account of the Trojan War was true. He found the site of Troy on the northeastern coast of modern-day Turkey and later dug up a fabulous treasure at Mycenae in Greece. The graves he discovered dated back to about 1600 B. C. In the graves were gold masks and other objects, including bronze weapons similar to the ones described in the *Iliad*. The descriptions in the stories were further confirmed when the writing of the Mycenaeans was understood. Clay tablets found at the sites of ancient Mycenaean cities contained inventory lists of clothing, chariots, weapons, and other implements used at the time and described in the *Iliad*.

The Dorian Invasions   The defeat of Troy led to disaster for the people of the Greek mainland. With the fall of Troy, nomads broke into that part of Asia Minor and carried on raids by land and sea. (See the map on page 116.) These raids destroyed the prosperity of the states in the eastern Mediterranean. These states could no longer carry on large-scale trade with the Mycenaeans.

Loss of markets in the area weakened the Mycenaeans greatly.

The weakened Mycenaeans were conquered between 1200 B.C. and 1100 B.C. by a group of nomadic herders from the north called *Dorians* (DORE-ee-unz). In contrast to the Minoans and Mycenaeans, the Dorians had a simple culture. They conquered much of the land that is present-day Greece and destroyed much of the civilization that existed before they arrived. This period is called a "Dark Age." It lasted from about 1100 B.C. to 700 B.C. During this period, trade with other countries stopped and the cities declined. People barely managed to survive in small, isolated communities. They had few possessions and there was a general breakdown of law and order. But the period was not completely dark for this was the time when the great epic poems, the *Iliad* and the *Odyssey*, were written down. It was also the time for important advances in the beginnings of Greek religious thought.

Greek Religion   By about 700 B.C., the Greeks had developed their religious beliefs. These remained mostly unchanged for centuries to come. The Greeks worshiped a large number of gods and goddesses. Some of these had been adopted by the Greeks from earlier peoples. They represented the influences of other civilizations in the ancient Middle East and the Mediterranean region.

The Greeks believed that their gods and goddesses looked like humans, and that they shared the same qualities people had. They also believed that their gods took an active role in daily human affairs. This was quite different from what other people in the ancient Middle East believed about their more distant gods and goddesses.

1. Mapping: Using the map on page 113, list and locate by means of latitude and longitude coordinates the major cities of: Crete, the Greek mainland, Asia Minor.
2. In your own words, briefly identify: the Minoans, the Mycenaeans, the Dorians, the Trojans, the *Iliad*, the *Odyssey*.
3. Describe one way in which Greek religion was different from the way the Egyptians worshiped their gods and goddesses.
4. Why is the rule of the Dorians called a "Dark Age" of Greek history? Was it all "dark" during their rule? Explain.
▷ The *Iliad* and the *Odyssey* were passed down through the years as stories told aloud by storytellers or poets. What kinds of stories do we have that are often told out loud? Why might future historians be suspicious of those stories as evidence about your life?

GREEK CITY STATES: SPARTA AND ATHENS

About 800 B.C., the Greeks began to emerge from the "Dark Age." A new period of Greek history began, marked by the rise of city-states. These city-states were small independent nations. They were made up of a city and the surrounding countryside whose inhabitants obeyed the laws of that city. City-states began when the settlers agreed to obey permanent laws instead of the word of their tribal leaders.

City-states at first probably were just fortresses where a king and his servants and some soldiers lived. Many of those fortresses, which were also places of worship, were built on mounds of limestone found in Greece. They were easy to defend and each soon became known as an **acropolis** (uh-KRAHP-uh-lus) or "high city." When the Mycenaean culture declined, many of the high cities disappeared. Some of those that did not disappear became religious centers. The Greeks believed their gods and goddesses lived there.

As Greek culture began to revive itself, more and more nobles or kings built palaces near an acropolis or *polis* (city). Gradually, new citizens moved nearby and a city-state emerged. It is important to remember that the city-states represented groups of citizens and not areas of territory. In ancient Greece, political boundaries were vague or nonexistent. Instead they were distinguished by allegiance to a noble or king located near a *polis*. By 800 B.C., most of the Greek city-states were ruled by kings and were becoming large urban centers and religious centers. Later, they were ruled by a small group of citizens called an **oligarchy** (AHL-uh-gahr-kee). These early oligarchies were usually made up of wealthy landowners. Some of these landowners were very powerful and became *dictators* or rulers with complete power.

The oligarchs often ruled as they pleased without caring about what most of the people wished or needed. But as the city-states prospered, a middle class of merchants and farmers developed. They were not satisfied with the rule of some of the oligarchs. And by 600 B.C., some city-states had overthrown the oligarchies and created democracies (dih-MAHK-ruh-seez). One of the city-states that became a **democracy** was Athens (ATH-unz). But Sparta followed a different pattern.

Sparta   Sparta did not follow the same path as Athens from kingdom to democracy. This was due partly to Sparta's history and partly to its geography. Sparta was located on a peninsula. It was isolated by mountains in the northeast and in the west. (See the map on page 125.) Sparta did not have good harbors. Without a trading outlet, *Spartans* had to depend upon agriculture for their survival. The natural barriers isolated the Spartans from other peoples. Without a chance to exchange ideas with other parts of the Mediterranean world, the people of Sparta began to ignore the outside world.

Spartan Society   Sparta was made up of three separate groups of people. A small upper class were the descendants of the Dorian conquerors. They were called Spartans. They were only about five or ten percent of the population, but they were the only ones who could be citizens. These people were the rulers, landowners, and soldiers. Most of the rest of the population were called **helots** (HEL-utz). They were descendants of the original settlers of the region who were defeated by the Dorians. The helots were laborers who did most of the work. The Spartans' fear of rebellions against them by the helots turned Sparta into a military state.

The third class of people were called **periocei** (PER-ee-oe-sie) or those who "dwell around." These were the non-Dorian people of neighboring areas that fell under the control of the Spartans. The periocei handled all the economic affairs of the Spartans, especially their dealings with foreigners.

Spartan Government   The government of Sparta was a rather complex one. An Assembly of all male Spartan citizens over the age of thirty elected officials and voted on proposed legislation. All the voting was done out loud and the Assembly was not allowed to debate the issues. A Council of Elders, chosen for life by the Assembly, proposed laws and policies on which the Assembly voted. The Council of Elders was composed of two kings and twenty-eight male members, all over the age of 60. The two kings had power only as army commanders and judges.

Real power was always held, however, by the five **ephors** (EF-urs) or overseers elected by the Assembly. The ephors could scold a king, control the helots, conduct foreign affairs, accept ambassadors, and censor anyone in Sparta. They feared that contact with outside people would weaken Spartans' obedience and discipline. Therefore, they did not permit citizens to travel. Foreign visitors were also discouraged from coming to Sparta.

The Culture of Sparta   Military affairs controlled every part of the daily lives of the Spartans. Between the ages of twenty and sixty, Spartan men had to devote all their time to being citizen-soldiers of the state. But their training began much earlier. Spartan boys were allowed to live with their families only until they were seven years old. Then they went to live in army barracks and learned how to become strong and brave citizen-soldiers.

Spartan boys were forced to undergo all kinds of physical hardships, such as wearing very light clothing in the winter. They were given little to eat and often had to steal food. If they were caught, they were whipped—not for stealing, but for being clumsy enough to get caught. The boys were also whipped each year in public so that they would learn to endure pain in silence. All of this training was given in preparation for battle.

Spartan girls also received hard physical training. The Spartans be-

In the painting on this Greek vessel, a Spartan youth puts on his armor with the help of his parents. The scene symbolizes the importance of bravery, honor, and courage as values in Spartan society. How do parents introduce their children to adulthood in contemporary society?

lieved that women who were physically strong would produce strong children who would grow up to become good citizen-soldiers. Unhealthy or deformed children were often abandoned and left to die. Only the strong and healthy were allowed to live.

Spartans were not allowed to have any kind of luxury or pleasures that might make them soft. Jewelry, fine clothing, and rich food were forbidden. Spartans were also discouraged from having contact with the ideas of foreigners. From the Spartan point of view, a poet or philosopher had little value compared with a well-trained, disciplined soldier.

The military dominance in Spartan society helped it to become the main power in Greece. Sparta became the leader of the **Peloponnesian** (pel-uh-puh-NEE-zhun) **League.** This league was a military alliance of many city-states, including Corinth (KOR-unth). Although Sparta had only one vote when the leaders from each city-state met to decide issues, Sparta's leadership was so strong that few dared to oppose it.

Athens The way of life of the *Athenians* was very different from the way of life of the Spartans. Athens had excellent harbors and a good location for trade. (See the map on page 125.) Athenian ships sailed to cities around the Mediterranean, and its harbors received vessels from many foreign lands. Olive trees grew on the fertile lands surrounding the city. Oil from the olives and wine made from Athenian grapes were major export items. Trade, meetings and discussions in the marketplace, and the acceptance of new ideas became characteristic of life in ancient Athens.

Athenian Government An important feature of Athenian society was its system of government. Several Greek city-states practiced a form of democracy. But in the other city-states, it was usually the wealthy who governed themselves. Athens has become famous as the only Greek city-state in which all male citizens, rich and poor, governed themselves. Women and slaves, however, were not allowed to take part in Athenian democracy.

Early Greek Democracy The movement toward democratic government began in Athens in 594 B.C. Before that time, wealthy landowners had controlled the economic and political life of Athens. As a result, the smaller farmers were unable to make a living and fell into debt. Many lost their land and

121

even became slaves when they could not pay what they owed.

In some of the other city-states, there were open rebellions and even civil wars. To prevent the same thing from happening in Athens, the merchant class joined with the upper class in an effort to reform the government and improve the economy. In 594 B.C., they called upon **Solon** (SOE-lun) to head the Athenian government. He was given full powers to bring about economic and political reforms and ruled until 561 B.C.

Solon's Economic Reforms   Solon was a merchant and a widely traveled man. He also was a poet and had written strong attacks against greed and injustice. Solon quickly realized that he must improve the condition of the Greek economy before he could create political stability. One of the first things Solon did was to stop the practice of punishing people harshly when they could not pay what they owed. He also freed all those who had been enslaved because they could not pay their debts.

Solon helped make agriculture profitable. He discouraged the growing of grain, which was unprofitable, and encouraged the growing of olives and grapes instead. These were the basis of a rich trade in oil and wine throughout the Mediterranean region. And grain could be received from places such as Sicily (SIS-uh-lee) and the coast of the Black Sea under favorable trading arrangements.

Another important act of Solon was the development of industry and trade. He made it the law that every father teach his son a trade. This law served a useful purpose. Poor farmers who did not own any land began to move into the towns and make a living at a trade. Athens soon had a supply of goods made in the towns, which could be sold in neighboring areas and countries in trade for food.

Solon's Political Reforms   Solon gave all citizens a share in the government through the Assembly. Every male citizen of Athens over twenty-one years of age was allowed to sit in the Assembly. It was there that all important matters were debated and voted upon, including the election of heads of state.

In addition to the Assembly, there was the Council. The Council was made up of 500 citizens who were chosen by lot. The chief business of the Council was to prepare legislation for the Athenian Assembly.

Solon also introduced a people's law court so that every citizen could have a part in administering the law. Members of the law court were elected by the people. They heard cases in which decisions made by the official judges were appealed.

Rule by the Tyrants   After Solon's rule, a group of tyrants (TIE-runtz) gained power in Athens. The **tyrants** were rulers whose powers were not controlled by laws or a constitution. Several of the tyrants were dictators ruling with complete power.

After a period of rule by tyrants, a form of democracy was restored. Some nobles rebelled against their tyrant ruler and at first tried to create an oligarchy or rule by a small group of men. But this attempt was resisted by the Athenians. One of the leaders of the nobles who rebelled against the oligarchy was **Cleisthenes** (KLIES-thuh-neez). He supported the rights of all the people, and with his help the oligarchy was defeated.

The Constitution of Cleisthenes Cleisthenes restored democracy in Athens. In 508 B.C., he added to the reforms of Solon and created the first democratic constitution of the Greeks. The constitution, written by Cleisthenes, remained the basis of Athenian independence throughout the whole period of democratic government in Athens.

Through his constitution, Cleisthenes restored the full power of the Assembly, the Council, and the law courts of Solon. But he reformed them to meet new conditions. In addition, either he or his successor formed a board of generals whose main purpose was to take command of the army and navy.

Another development of the Greeks at this time was the practice of **ostracism** (AHS-truh-siz-um). Ostracism was a way of keeping any one person from becoming too powerful. Once a year the Assembly would decide whether any citizen should be sent into exile for ten years. A citizen's name could be written on a piece of broken pottery, called an ostracon (AHS-truh-con), by the voters. If a person received more than 3,000 votes against him, he had to go into exile. In this way the people of Athens hoped to preserve their democratic form of government by getting rid of people who might become tyrants.

Athenian Society   By 510 B.C., democratic government was firmly entrenched in Athens. The chart below shows how the government of Athens was organized. Only citizens could take part in the city's political life. And not all the people of Athens enjoyed the

ATHENIAN DEMOCRACY IN ACTION

ASSEMBLY
The Assembly was made up of all free male citizens 21 years of age or older. It elected the Board of Generals. It also received and considered proposals made by the Council and the Board of Generals. The Assembly discussed and voted on all important matters of state, including declaring war and appropriating money.

COUNCIL
The Council was an executive body that prepared and suggested items to be considered by the Assembly. It also handled most of the routine business of the government. It was made up of ten committees which took turns heading the Assembly. Its 500 members were chosen by lot from all the citizens. Members had to be 30 years of age or older and they served for one year.

BOARD OF GENERALS
The Board of Generals was made up of ten generals who were elected by the Assembly. It advised the Assembly on military matters and led the army and navy in wartime.

BOARD OF OFFICIALS
The Board of Officials was elected to direct public affairs such as the courts of justice.

JURIES
Six thousand people acted as judges and jurors combined. Of these, a minimum of 201 were chosen by lot for each trial. In more important cases the jury would number 501 or more people.

rights of citizenship. To be a citizen, an Athenian had to be a male at least twenty-one years old and the son of free Athenian parents. Only about one third of the people living in Athens were citizens. The other two thirds were women, slaves, and foreigners. Slaves probably made up about one fourth of the entire population.

The women of Athens had an important role in Athenian society but had no part in the government. They were generally not allowed an education nor were they allowed to take part in the intellectual life of the city. Married women of good families sometimes appeared in public, but only after covering their faces with a veil. Some women managed to own property at a later time, but that was unusual in ancient Greece.

Although women in ancient Greece did not take part in politics, they did play an important part in the domestic economy. Women usually stayed at home. The Greek home was a kind of small factory in which cloth was woven, food was processed, and many other necessities of everyday life were produced. All of this activity was supervised by the woman of the house.

Greek Colonies　　An important part of the world of the ancient Greeks was their rich colonies in Asia Minor. These colonies were important sources of wheat to feed the population on the Greek mainland, and the colonies' trade added greatly to the wealth of the Greek city-states. Greek trade extended as far as the Black Sea and to the coasts of what is now the Soviet Union. (See the map on page 125.)

The first Greek colonies, however, were not established for trade purposes. Instead, they were created to satisfy the desire of many Greeks to own land. It was difficult to get ahead in Greece without owning any land and Greek nobles owned most of the land in Greece. Because of this and the Greek policy of enslavement for failure to pay debts, many young Greeks sought a way to make a living elsewhere.

Some of the first colonies were established by wealthy individuals who hoped to benefit later from trade with them. Later, the city-states began to help set up new colonies. However, not all colonies remained under the control of their sponsors. Some even rebelled against mother city-state rule. Others, like Syracuse (SIR-uh-kyoos), became more prosperous and powerful than their sponsoring city. Yet usually wherever one appeared, such Greek colonies succeeded and began a money-making trade or business with some Greek cities as well as their nearby non-Greek neighbors.

The Persian Wars　　While the Greeks prospered, another empire began to emerge in the east. Cyrus (SIE-rus) the Great, who ruled from 559 B.C. to 529 B.C., had emerged as the leader of the Persians (PUR-zhuns). He and two of his successors, Darius (DAH-ree-us) the Great who ruled from 521 B.C. to 485 B.C., and Xerxes (ZURK-seez) who ruled from 485 B.C. to 465 B.C., managed to build an empire that stretched from the borders of India to the Aral (AR-ul) Sea, through Egypt, and to the Aegean (ih-JEE-un) and Black seas. (See the map on page 125.)

In 546 B.C., the Greek colonies in Asia Minor were conquered by Cyrus. The Persians ruled the colonies well. They demanded tribute from the Greeks but did not treat them harshly. The Greeks in Asia Minor valued their independence, however, and in 499 B.C., with the help of Athens, they rebelled

Why did the Persians want to control the Greek colonies in Asia Minor?

against the Persians. This interference from Athens against the Persians led to war between the Greek city-states and the Persian Empire. Faced with this threat from a foreign nation, the Greek city-states united to fight their common enemy.

The main wars between the Greeks and the Persians lasted from 490 B.C. to 479 B.C. During that time some of the Greek city-states accepted Persian rule. But Athens and Sparta refused to surrender, even though the Persians sent a large army and a fleet of ships to attack them. Sparta and Athens fought stubbornly against the powerful Persians.

The first major war between the Persians and the Greeks occurred in 490 B.C. The Persians, then led by Darius, sent word to the Greeks to surrender to their rule. When Athens and Sparta refused, a Persian fleet anchored in the Bay of Marathon (MAR-uh-thahn). This was only a little over 40 kilometers (25 miles) from Athens. The Athenians sent word to Sparta asking for help. Sparta did not send aid immediately because their superstitious religious leaders advised the Spartans not to march until the next full moon.

The Persians, however, were so sure of victory that they did not send all

125

of their troops into battle. The troops that did invade came by land and were soundly defeated at Marathon by the outnumbered Athenians and some troops from Plataea (pluh-TEE-uh). After the Persians were defeated, the Athenians sent a runner to Athens with the news of the victory. This run of over 40 kilometers (25 miles) came to be known as a *marathon*, a term used today for a race of a similar distance.

Once the battle at Marathon ended, the Athenian victors marched to Piraeus (pie-REE-us). They arrived there just as the Persian fleet appeared. The Persians, not wishing another defeat, sailed away.

Ten years later, the Persians mounted another military campaign against the Greeks. This one was led by Xerxes, who had succeeded his father, Darius. Sparta called for help, but little came. Nevertheless, Leonidas (lee-AHN-ud-us), the Spartan king, did take on the Persians in what many historians regarded as the most famous battle of the Greek-Persian wars. This was the battle at a pass between the mountains and the sea called Thermopylae (thur-MAHP-uh-lee). (See the map on page 125.) There a few hundred Spartans died holding the pass against thousands of Persians. It is said that one Spartan soldier was told that the enemy army at Thermopylae was so large that their arrows would hide the sun. He replied, "So much the better. We shall fight in the shade." This kind of heroism was greatly prized by the ancient Greeks.

The army of Xerxes, after defeating the Spartans, moved through the pass and managed to march all the way to Athens. The city was looted and its temples burned. The Athenian-led Greek fleet, however, under the leadership of Themistocles (thu-MIS-tuh-kleez), lured the Persians, now in ships, to the narrows of Salamis (SAL-uh-mus). There the Greek navy won an overwhelming victory. Xerxes then went home and left Mardonias (mahr-DONE-ee-us), his brother-in-law, to continue to do battle. In 479 B.C., Mardonias and his army were finally defeated and killed by a Spartan-led force at Plataea. Thus ended the Persian attempts to control Greece.

The Peloponnesian War   Toward the end of the war with Persia, Athens had gained control of some of the Greek city-states. Sparta became afraid that Athens would next try to take control of one of its closest allies, Corinth. The Gulf of Corinth was the major part of a water route between Athens, the Ionian (ie-OE-nee-un) Sea, and eastern Sicily. So the city-state that controlled Corinth would have control of the trade routes between Greece and Sicily. (See the map on page 125.)

Much of the dispute between the two cities focused on the leagues or alliances each managed to control. Athens had become the leader of the **Delian (DEE-lee-un) League** with its headquarters at Delos (DEE-los). Sparta controlled the Peloponnesian League. Each managed to tax its member city-states in order to remain in power. The height of Athenian power came with the rule of **Pericles** (PER-uh-kleez) during the mid-400's B.C. Pericles was an able statesman and in favor of democracy at home in Athens but was very aggressive in matters of foreign policy. He sought to control the trade of all of Greece.

Sparta and Athens finally went to war to determine which city would control the Mediterranean trade routes as well as the Peloponnesian peninsula, which forms the southern half of Greece. This war is called the Peloponnesian War. The war began in 431 B.C. and lasted for twenty-seven years. Sparta was aided by Persia. With Persian help, plus its own military skill, Sparta defeated Athens by 404 B.C. During the following century, Sparta was the leading power in Greece and the power of Athens declined.

SECTION REVIEW

1. Mapping: Using the scale on the map on page 125, find the distance between: Athens and Sparta, Athens and Marathon, Thermopylae and Sparta, Sparta and Corinth, Athens and Corinth.
2. How did the Greek city-states develop? Explain briefly.
3. In your own words, briefly define or identify: the Spartans, the Athenians, the Persians, oligarchs, helots, periocei, ephors, Solon, tyrants, Cleisthenes, Pericles.
4. Briefly compare the Spartan and the Athenian ways of life.
5. How did physical geography influence the development of Sparta and Athens?
6. Describe the government of Athens. Why do you think the government of Athens could be called democratic?
7. How did the Greek colonies develop? Explain briefly.
8. List and describe the battles of the Persian wars with Greece. What was the final outcome?
9. What were the main causes and the main results of the Peloponnesian War?
▶ What are some of the causes of conflict between countries today and in the recent past? Are any of these the same ones that caused the wars between Sparta and Athens?

GREEK CULTURE

It is difficult to find any part of our lives today that has not been touched by the culture of the ancient Greeks. Public buildings such as those in Washington, D.C., are often modeled after Greek temples; sports such as running, jumping, wrestling, and boxing come from the Greeks; and many of our political and scientific ideas had their origins in ancient Greece.

Two important contributions that the Greeks made to Western civilization have already been discussed: their democratic form of government and the great epic poems, the *Iliad* and the *Odyssey*. In addition to these works about the Trojan War, the Greeks left many other important works of poetry, drama, philosophy, and history.

Greek Religion The one part of Greek culture that affected all other aspects of Greek life was religion. The Greeks worshiped many gods and goddesses. One of the most important of the Greek gods was *Zeus* (ZOOS), the king of the gods and the father of many of the other gods and goddesses. Another favorite was *Apollo* (uh-POL-oe), god of art and music. Two of the most important goddesses were *Aphrodite* (af-ruh-DITE-ee), the goddess of love and beauty, and *Athena* (uh-THEE-nuh), the goddess of wisdom and war.

Beautiful temples were built to honor the gods and goddesses, and athletic games and dramas were held in their honor. In addition, important political activities were accompanied by religious ceremonies and processions. Each Greek city-state also paid special respect to a particular god or goddess who was thought to be its founder. Athena was believed to have founded Athens. The Olympic games that are

This relief sculpture is believed to represent the goddess Athena. Athena, the goddess of wisdom and war, is said to have founded the city of Athens. How did ancient Athenian culture reflect the qualities of the goddess Athena?

honor. From these songs in praise of Dionysus, the Athenians developed their tragic dramas.

At first, the tragedies had a religious form and were sung by a chorus. But in time they began to deal with the personal problems of the people. Although the chorus remained, the individual actors performed special roles. Only a few of the hundreds of tragedies performed in ancient Greece have survived. One favorite subject of these dramas was the tale of a king or queen who, because of their misdeeds and other failings, received terrible punishments from their gods.

Comedies were also performed to honor Dionysus. The comedies were designed to make fun of existing customs or politicians who were not governing properly. They were very important in forming the public opinion of the times.

Greek Theaters and Actors   Greek theaters were huge open-air structures that could hold audiences of as many as 30,000 people. Because the theaters were so big, the audiences had to sit far from the stage. Special costumes, masks, and mechanical devices were used by the actors so that they could be seen and heard at such great distances.

Only men took part in the plays. They played both the male and female roles. Costumes were designed to make it easy for the actors to be seen and identified. Special masks were worn, which were carved or painted to show the various emotions of the players whose faces could not be seen at a distance by the audience. Speaking tubes were used to project the voices of the actors to the audiences.

Greek Poets and Historians   In addition to Greek drama, Greek poetry is famous. Hesiod (HEE-see-ud) was one important poet who wrote soon after

held every four years today began as part of the worship of Zeus at Olympia (oe-LIM-pee-uh) in Greece in 776 B.C.

Greek Drama   An especially important god of the Greeks was *Dionysus* (die-uh-NIE-sus), the god of fertility. Dionysus was a god believed to have originated in a region north of Greece. He was adopted by the Greeks in early times, and songs were written in his

the time of Homer, the author of the *Iliad* and the *Odyssey*. Hesiod wrote a poem called *Works and Days* in which he told how a farmer tried to make a living from the land. In addition to being a poem praising the life of a farmer, *Works and Days* was a kind of agricultural almanac that contained practical advice for farmers. The poetry of Sappho (SAF-oe) has also come down to modern times. She was an outstanding Greek author who wrote love poems.

The Greeks are also famous for their histories. One of the first known Greek historians is *Herodotus* (hih-RAWD-uh-tuz). He began to write an account of the wars between the Greeks and the Persians. But he expanded it to cover a description of all the peoples of the known world. Herodotus traveled to Egypt, Italy, Mesopotamia (mes-uh-puh-TAY-mee-uh), and the lands around the Black Sea. He spoke to people and collected all the information he could about their pasts and their customs. Scholars at first considered Herodotus' histories of early peoples untrue. But as archaeologists continue to discover and study the remains of cities and cultures mentioned by Herodotus, they are finding that much of what he wrote is quite accurate.

Herodotus lived during the middle of the fifth century B.C. About the same time, another famous historian called *Thucydides* (thoo-SID-uh-deez) wrote an account of the Peloponnesian War. The histories of Herodotus and Thucydides differed in some ways. Herodotus wrote about things that had happened before his time and depended a great deal on what people told him. Thucydides had actually lived through the Peloponnesian War and could write about events he had experienced.

The interests of the two historians were also different. Herodotus was concerned with the conflict between the Greeks and the Persians, which he saw as a struggle between the East and the West—between the forces of absolute or complete rule and the forces of freedom. Thucydides was interested in the connection between human behavior and war itself. He hoped people would learn from the past and realize that future wars could be destructive.

The Philosophers   In ancient Greece, scholars did not specialize in just one or two particular areas of study as they do today. Each Greek scholar studied mathematics, physics, logic, music, astronomy, and the use of language in speech and writing. They inquired into the proper ways to govern, the workings of the universe, the relationship

This detail of a Greek vase shows Apollo purifying a man. What relationship existed between the Greeks and their gods?

between mathematics and music, and almost every other concern of an active and imaginative mind. A scholar who studied all these things was called a *Sophist* (SAWF-ust), which means "one who works at being wise."

The Sophists took nothing for granted. They asked: How can anyone really be sure of anything in this world? How can anyone be sure the gods really exist when no one can see, hear, feel, taste, or smell them? And if there are no gods to tell us what is the right thing to do, can we depend on the laws of the people who govern us? Will they be just laws? And for that matter, what kind of people should be allowed to write the laws others have to obey? From these questions it is easy to see why the Sophists were not always popular with the city's leaders or many of its citizens.

Socrates   The most famous of all the philosophers was a short, snub-nosed man called **Socrates** (SAWK-ruh-teez). Socrates lived from 469 B.C. to 399 B.C. He was at the height of his popularity during and immediately following the Peloponnesian War. Unfortunately for Socrates, his popularity was mostly with the young people.

Socrates asked questions about everything, including religion, politics, and the proper behavior of one person toward another. He believed that the only way people could arrive at the truth was by questioning their own opinions. He said they should never place confidence in their traditions or the things they had been told by others. Only by continually questioning their beliefs, forming their own answers, and then discussing those answers with others did Socrates believe people could gain knowledge. This kind of inquiry is called the *Socratic* (suh-KRAT-ik) *method of inquiry.*

None of the writings of Socrates have survived and scholars know about him only through the writings of others. The period in which Socrates lived was one of great unrest and hardship for Athens. The city was struggling against heavy odds in the war with Sparta at that time. And Socrates was encouraging the young people to question the very foundations of the Athenian way of life. Socrates was thought to be very dangerous to the city of Athens because of his influence on the young people. He was considered a threat to Athens' stability during this critical time in his city's history.

Socrates was brought to trial in 399 B.C. for not being loyal to the state. The citizens of Athens charged him with disrespect to the gods and with corrupting the youth of Athens. Socrates was sentenced to die by drinking a cup of hemlock, which is poisonous. It is believed that Socrates preferred death to exile. If a citizen of Athens moved or was exiled to another city, he was considered to be a "foreigner" and was unable to take part in the political life of his new homeland. To Socrates and many other Athenians, exile would have been the same as death. Politics was thought to be one of the most important of human activities.

Plato   Historians know about the teachings of Socrates mainly through the writings of another great philosopher, **Plato** (PLAY-toe). This famous pupil of Socrates wrote about the great philosophical problems that people have faced for centuries. He asked what kind of government would produce the most good, what love was, how a person could behave ethically, and many other questions that have concerned people through the ages. His writings are in the form of *dialogues* (DIE-uh-

130

logs), compositions in which two or more characters have a conversation. Socrates poses questions to a group of his students. The students reply to Socrates and also discuss the answer among themselves. But Socrates never tells them what the answer to the problem is. He answers each question from the students with another question. In this way, the students are forced to continually question themselves and others in an effort to reach the truth.

One of the most famous of Plato's dialogues is the *Republic*. In it, Plato outlines his plan for an ideal society. This ideal society would contain three main groups of people: the scholars; the soldiers; and the farmers, artisans, and merchants. The scholars had the most knowledge and intelligence, according to Plato. So they would be the rulers. The soldiers would defend the country. The class of merchants, artisans, and farmers would produce and distribute goods for the whole community. The group to which a person belonged would be decided by that person's intelligence rather than by birth.

Aristotle   Plato was mostly concerned with the idea of good. He thought there was an ideal virtue and that human good was only a reflection of this ideal. Plato said that people should continually try to improve themselves so that they might come nearer to this ideal good. **Aristotle** (AR-uh-staht-'l), another famous philosopher and a student of Plato, saw the search for truth differently. While Socrates believed in continual questioning and discussion and Plato believed in ideal good as the way to truth, Aristotle approached truth through the study of the natural world around him. He was the first to use modern scientific methods. He classified living things into groups, much as is done in biology today, and then he extended this system into other kinds of inquiry. He classified governments, for example, according to whether they were headed by one man, by a few men, or by many men, and showed how there were good and bad governments.

Aristotle differed from Plato in his idea of the best kind of government. He thought that a society should be ruled by a large middle class and that the government should provide money to help the poor. Aristotle also believed that it was best for people to live moderately and avoid excess in every part of their lives.

Greek Science   Greek science received many ideas from the older Middle Eastern civilizations. Reports about the inventions of Egypt and Mesopotamia were brought home to Greece by traders and travelers. Ideas also passed to the Greek mainland from the colonies in Asia Minor, which were in contact with the civilizations of the Middle East. The great culture of ancient Greece would not have been possible without such things as the ironworking process developed by the Hittites (HIH-tites) or the alphabet of the Phoenicians (fih-NISH-ee-unz). The medical skills and geometry of Egypt and the astronomy of Babylonia (bab-uh-LOE-nyuh) made important contributions to early Greek science.

The Greeks made important changes in scientific thinking that have affected modern science. When the Greeks wondered how things worked, they looked for answers in the natural world around them. Until then, people had depended on myths to explain such events as floods or thunderstorms.

Early Greek Scientists   *Pythagoras* (puh-THAG-uh-rus) was one of the

The Parthenon was built on the Acropolis in Athens and is an example of classical Greek architecture. What buildings in your community show the influence of Greek architecture?

greatest of the ancient Greek mathematicians. Some of the mathematical laws he developed are still used today. He is especially important in the history of modern science because he made one of the earliest attempts to explain the universe in abstract mathematical language. Pythagoras is probably best known for the *Pythagorean* (puh-thag-uh-REE-un) *theorum,* which is one of the most important principles in geometry.

One of the greatest of all the Greek physical scientists was *Archimedes* (ahrk-uh-MEED-eez). He was the first to demonstrate the importance of the lever. To show the power of this simple machine that can move very large loads, he is said to have boasted, "Give me a place to stand, and I will move the world." Today, the usefulness of the lever can be seen in the jack, which even a small child can use to lift an automobile. Archimedes also discovered the principle by which the specific gravity, or weight of a substance compared to water, can be found.

Greek Art   Beautiful works of art were an important part of the life of every citizen of Athens. Temples, gymnasiums, theaters, and other public buildings were all carefully designed and decorated with marble sculptures. Even such household articles as vases and jugs were works of art. They were painted with scenes showing the deeds of the gods and Greek heroes. Some also showed people engaged in daily activities—weaving cloth, attending banquets, or taking part in games and athletic contests.

The Greek building that is perhaps the most famous example of Greek architecture is the *Parthenon* (PAHR-thuh-nahn). It was a temple dedicated to Athena, the patron goddess of Athens. Later, Greek architecture was imitated by many civilizations throughout history. Even today it is not difficult to find examples of the Greek style in the architecture of our own cities.

The design of the Parthenon is an example of the Greeks' concern with simplicity and balance. The columns that surround the outside of the structure were tilted slightly inward so that they would look more solid. Each column was given a slight bulge in the center to adjust for the way a person's eyes distort something seen from a distance.

The columns at both ends of the temple had a triangular slab of marble resting on them. These contained sculptures showing gods and goddesses and battle scenes. Inside the Parthenon was a huge statue of Athena made of ivory and gold. This was ransacked many

When Alexander the Great died in 323 B.C. at the age of thirty-three, he was the ruler of an enormous empire that stretched from Greece to India. What Alexander really wanted to accomplish, however, and how much he would have been able to accomplish had he lived a full lifetime are the subjects of intense debate among present-day historians.

Alexander devised two policies that indicate he was aware of the many problems involved in ruling an empire.

One policy, which Alexander established on his campaigns, was to rule each conquered area according to its own traditions. In Greece, Alexander governed through the officials of the city-states. In Egypt, he assumed the role of a god-king, just like an Egyptian pharaoh. In Persia, he maintained a system of local governors.

Alexander's second policy was to spread Greek culture throughout the empire. He hoped to make Greek culture the common culture of all peoples. Toward this goal, Alexander founded more than seventy cities called Alexandria. Each city was designed to be a center from which knowledge of Greek economic and cultural achievements could flow out into the surrounding area.

Perhaps what intrigues people the most about Alexander, however, was his attempt to fuse the many cultures in his empire together. The Hellenistic Age, which began after the death of Alexander the Great, was characterized by the mixing of ideas of Greek and eastern cultures. This peaceful combination of ideas, many agree, was the fulfillment of what Alexander the Great set out to do.

1. What two policies did Alexander the Great use in governing his empire?
2. Do you think Alexander's plan for his empire would have worked? Why or why not?
3. What makes men or women "great"?

years ago. Although the remains of the Parthenon are now unpainted, the whole building and its statues were once painted in bright colors.

The Spread of Greek Culture The great achievements of Greek culture that have been discussed so far belong to what is called the **Classical Age** of Greece. The culture of ancient Greece reached its height during the fifth century B.C. About a century later, Greek culture had spread from the shores of the Mediterranean all the way to what is now India and Pakistan (pak-ih-STAN). (See the map on page 125.)

Philip of Macedonia (mass-uh-DOE-nee-uh) helped to set the stage for that expansion of Greek culture. He was the third son of a Macedonian king who ruled part of northwest Greece. Philip came to the throne in 359 B.C. During the following twenty-three years, he gained control of every major city-state in Greece except Sparta.

Philip gained great power by having a well-trained and loyal army, by breaking treaties, by using bribery, and, in general, by taking advantage of the weaknesses of and quarrels among the city-states. However, he admired most Greek culture and wanted to have it spread as far as possible. He did not live to see that goal achieved because he was murdered in 336 B.C. in what many historians believe to have been some sort of family fight. Thus, it was left to Alexander, his son, to spread the culture of Greece.

Alexander the Great was only twenty years old when he inherited the kingdom from his father. Yet, within the following twelve years, he had created the largest empire known in the ancient world. After gaining control of all the Greek city-states, including Sparta, Alexander invaded Asia Minor and defeated the Persians. Next he invaded Egypt and defeated it easily. Alexander founded the great port of Alexandria (al-ig-ZAN-dree-uh) on the Nile Delta and built a huge library there. Turning again to the east, Alexander took Assyria (uh-SIR-ee-uh) and Babylonia and pushed onward to what are now Afghanistan (af-GAN-uh-stan) and Pakistan. (See the Atlas of Europe.)

EMPIRE OF ALEXANDER THE GREAT

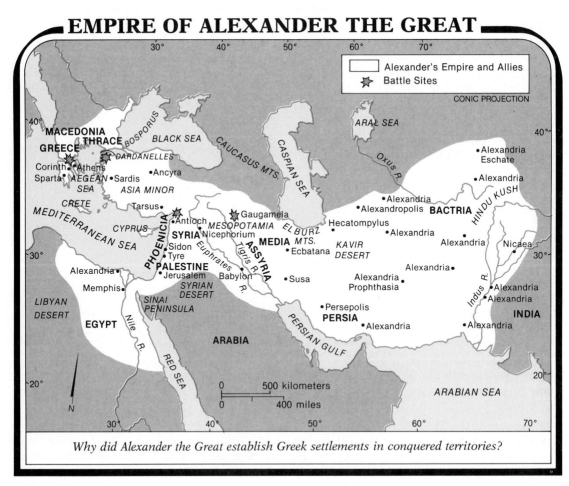

Why did Alexander the Great establish Greek settlements in conquered territories?

134

The eastern limits of his empire reached as far as the Indus (IN-dus) River in India.

Wherever he took lands, Alexander created new armies, built new roads, and founded new towns—each one named Alexandria. And wherever he went, Alexander brought with him the ideas and products of Greek culture. The map on page 134 shows the extent of Alexander the Great's empire. Notice how many of the towns all the way from Central Asia to Egypt are named Alexandria. Each one was planned as an outpost to spread Greek influence. In addition, Alexander arranged for his military leaders to marry into important families of conquered lands.

It is said that Alexander founded seventy Alexandrias. The farthest one was more than 3,680 kilometers (2,300 miles) east of the Mediterranean. Some were only forts, but others were important centers of trade and learning. Alexandria, Egypt, for example, had port facilities that could provide for 1,200 ships at one time (although the ships were much smaller than the ones in use today). Alexandria provided the Greek world with luxury items, such as woolen goods, glass, ivory, linen, and spices, from many parts of the ancient world. It also supplied papyrus (puh-PIE-rus), which was used for written communications throughout the Mediterranean and Middle Eastern worlds.

It is impossible to say what Alexander might have accomplished if he had had the opportunity. In 323 B.C., when he was only thirty-three years old, he died of a fever. Almost immediately, Alexander's generals began to quarrel over parts of the empire. They continually formed and broke alliances and engaged in violence and murder to keep their large territories. Finally, the leaders of the rising Roman Empire began to challenge the successors of Alexander. The Greeks began to lose their lands to Rome, one by one.

Greek ideas influenced the areas conquered by Alexander long after his death. The cultures of these foreign lands also began to influence the culture of Greece. New ideas brought home by Alexander's followers led to a mixing of Greek and eastern cultures. This period of mixing of cultures and the spread of Greek culture is called the **Hellenistic** (hel-uh-NISS-tik) **Age.** It lasted from 323 B.C. until 133 B.C., when Rome began to dominate the eastern Mediterranean.

SECTION REVIEW

1. Mapping: Using the maps on pages 134 and 18, describe the extent of the empires of the Persians and of Alexander the Great. Which of the two covered a larger territory?
2. In your own words, briefly define or identify: Athena, Herodotus, the Sophists, Socrates, Plato, Aristotle, the Parthenon, the Hellenistic Age.
3. Who was Phillip of Macedonia? What did he seek?
4. Who was Alexander the Great? How did he help to spread Greek ideas to the Middle East and Asia?
5. Would you say that much of Greek culture has survived until the present day? Give at least three examples to support your answer.
   Give an example of a modern invention that is being put to use in countries throughout the world. How was this invention introduced to other peoples? List ways in which ideas are spread around the world today.

The Roman Empire

THE FOUNDATIONS OF ANCIENT ROME

At the time classical Greek civilization was at its height, the people of the western Mediterranean region were still living in scattered groups. Not until the rise of the *Etruscans* (ih-TRUS-kunz) and the *Romans* (ROE-munz) did civilization develop in the area that became present-day Italy and central Europe. The Romans gained ideas from the Etruscans and the ancient Greeks. To these they added their own ideas on politics, law, and military organization. Together, these ideas made the Roman Empire one of the greatest civilizations in the world. Many of our own legal and political institutions have come from the Romans.

Early Settlers on the Italian Peninsula People have lived on the Italian peninsula since the early Stone Age. After 2000 B.C., large numbers of people moved into the peninsula from the grasslands north of the Black and Caspian (KAS-pee-un) seas. Among the most important of these were the *Latins*. (LAT-unz). They settled on the western plains of the Italian peninsula in a region called Latium (LAY-sheeum). Some of the Latins built villages along the Tiber (TIE-bur) River. In time, these villages were united into a city-state called Rome.

A second important group of people arrived on the peninsula about 900 B.C. These were the Etruscans. Historians do not know exactly where the Etruscans came from. But most scholars believe they probably came from Asia Minor. The Etruscans settled in an area between the Arno (AHR-noe) and Tiber rivers that extended as far inland as the Apennines (AP-uh-ninez), a mountain range. Later they spread into the Po (POE) Valley. The area settled by the Etruscans is called Etruria (ih-TROOH-ree-uh). (See the map on page 137.)

Most of what is known about the Etruscans comes from the paintings and finely-made metal objects and pottery found in their tombs. They adopted many items of Greek culture, and they also brought with them many elements of the culture of the ancient Middle East. To these influences, the Etruscans added ideas of their own. The result was a highly developed civilization with its own written language. The Etruscans were skilled in architecture and engineering—knowledge of which was passed on to the Romans. By 700 B.C., Etruscan colonies extended from the Po Valley in the north to Naples (NAY-pulz) in southern Italy. (See the map on page 137.)

A third group of people who contributed to Roman civilization were the Greeks. Important colonies were founded by the Greeks in southern Italy and Sicily. (See the map below.) In time they became important city-states. Trade and other contacts with the Greeks had an important effect on the Romans. Roman art, literature, and thought were all based in large part on Greek culture.

The Geography of Italy   The location and topography of the homeland of the Romans had a great influence on the development of the Roman Empire. The Italian peninsula occupies a central position between the eastern and western Mediterranean countries. It extends far out into the Mediterranean Sea and is only 128 kilometers (80 miles) from the coast of North Africa. Thus it forms a kind of bridge between the continents of Europe and Africa.

In contrast to Greece, which was made up of many islands and a mainland divided by a rugged mountainous landscape, Italy's shape made it easier for towns and cities to unite. The solid land mass of the peninsula and the large plains areas made communication easier. This is one of the reasons that the cities of Italy often joined together politically during Roman times, whereas the Greek city-states remained independent and fought each other.

ANCIENT ITALY ABOUT 325 B.C.

How did geography influence where early Italians settled?

The Apennines, a large mountain range which extends down the length of the Italian peninsula, divides Italy into several large plains areas. The great fertile valley of the Po River in the north and the coastal plain in the west were important agricultural regions. This is in contrast with the shortage of fertile land in Greece. Italy also had few good harbors, in spite of its long coastline. These two facts led to different economic developments for the two civilizations. Greece was a great trading and maritime country. Rome tended to be mainly agricultural. But geography alone cannot explain how Rome was able to conquer most of the known world. In order to understand the way Rome developed, it is necessary to go back to its very beginnings.

The Roman Republic According to a legend, Rome was founded in 753 B.C. by two brothers, Romulus (RAHM-yoo-lus) and Remus (REE-mus), who were orphaned and then adopted by a she-wolf. According to history, however, Rome became an important town after a group of Etruscans took over the site and made it their headquarters. By the sixth century B.C., Rome had become one of the leading city-states on the plain of Latium.

In 509 B.C., the people of Rome rebelled against their Etruscan rulers and overthrew the king. They founded a **republic** (ree-PUB-lik)—a government in which power rests with all the citizens who are entitled to vote. The Romans also continued their practice of loosely uniting villages and tribes. These they formed into a federation. In a **federation** (fed-uh-RAY-shun), power is divided between the central and the local governments. The Roman villages and tribes gave up certain powers to the Roman city-states, but they kept a tight hold on the power to manage most of their own affairs.

A similar form of government exists today in the United States. Individual states govern themselves internally, but they have delegated other powers to the federal government. Ancient Rome and the United States are both **federal republics.** One of the great contributions of ancient Rome is the development of the federal republican form of government.

By 287 B.C., the Roman system of government had developed to the form shown in the chart on page 139. With slight changes, its structure remained the same throughout the life of the Roman Empire. Although in theory this system is almost as democratic as the one in existence in the United States in our own time, in Roman times it did not function in a very democratic way.

Roman Society The population of Rome was divided into three classes. The most important group were the **patricians** (puh-TRISH-unz). These were the wealthy nobles whose ancestors had helped to shape Roman history. There were about 300 patrician families. Next came the **plebeians** (plih-BEE-yunz)—farmers, artisans, and merchants. Although some plebeians were wealthy, most of them were poor. The third and largest group were the slaves.

Only male adult patricians and plebeians were allowed to have a voice in the government. Some of the patrician families were more important than others. The heads of some of the important families were members of a council that advised the king. After the Etruscans were overthrown, the heads of these important families became members of the Senate. It was from among these patrician families that the **consuls** (KAHN-sulz) or chief executives of the government were chosen. (Refer to the chart on page 139.)

ROMAN GOVERNMENT IN ACTION

CONSULS
Two consuls served a year's term. They were elected by the Assemblies, and were the chief executives of the government. They also served as commanders of the army.

SENATE
The Senate was the most important governing body. Its 300 members passed laws, elected officials, and determined foreign policy. Members of the Senate were patricians. They were chosen for life. Senators advised the Consuls. This advice could be vetoed by the Assemblies.

ASSEMBLY OF CENTURIES
Voting in this Assembly was controlled by the patricians. The Assembly elected the magistrates, who were the main administrative body of the government.

ASSEMBLY OF TRIBES
This Assembly was controlled by the plebeians. It elected the tribunes and gradually gained the power to make some laws.

MAGISTRATES
The magistrates had supreme administrative authority. They had the right to interpret and execute laws. At first, the magistrates had to be patricians. But later plebeians could also hold this office.

TRIBUNES
Ten tribunes were elected each year by the Assembly of Tribes. They could veto the act of any magistrate.

Many members of the Assembly were from the plebeian class and they took part in electing consuls. And as members of the Assembly, they could veto (VEET-oe) any advice from the senators to the consuls with which they did not agree. An important tool used by the Romans to prevent any person or group from becoming too powerful was the veto. The **veto** is the right of one branch of a government to stop another branch from taking a particular action. In Rome, the Assembly could veto any consul's policy with which they disagreed. Each consul also had veto power over the other, which prevented a consul from becoming a dictator. To prevent power from resting in one branch of the government, the Assembly could veto any senatorial advice it opposed. In this way, each branch of the government was able to control the other branches.

In theory, there was an equal division of power between the plebeian and patrician classes. A closer look at the workings of Roman government, however, shows that this was not the case. Once plebeians secured the right to hold offices in the government, they had to do so without pay. Few plebeians were wealthy enough to stop earning a living in order to serve the people, and all plebeians could be put into prison for failure to pay a debt. No matter which laws the plebeians approved, the senators could use their influence to gain acceptance of their policies.

1. Mapping: Using the map on page 137, locate by means of latitude and longitude coordinates the Greek cities in Italy and the city of Rome.
2. In your own words, briefly define or identify: Etruscans, federation, republic, veto.
3. Why is the government of ancient Rome called a federal republic? In what ways was the political system of Rome the same as the government of the United States?
4. Who were the patricians and the plebeians? What was the position of each in ancient Rome?
   ▶ What arguments can you give that a federal republic is democratic? What arguments can you give that it is not democratic?

BUILDING THE ROMAN EMPIRE

After the overthrow of the Etruscan king, Rome continued its practice of absorbing other city-states into its political network. Soon Rome was extending its territory into the region of the Greek colonies in the south. This led to a series of conflicts between the Romans and the Greeks. When the wars ended, these Greek colonies were part of the Roman federation.

The Carthaginians   Besides the Romans and the Greeks, another powerful people, the *Carthaginians* (kahr-thuh-JIN-ee-unzs), occupied the Mediterranean region. Carthage (KAHR-thij) occupied the island of Sicily as well as much of the coast of North Africa. It was only a matter of time before Rome, which was spreading its influence into southern Italy, would clash with this other great power in the same area. (See the map on page 141.)

The Strait of Messina (muh-SEE-nuh), which separates Sicily from the Italian peninsula, was the boundary between these two strong powers. When the Carthaginians positioned a strong army in Sicily, they had the right to because they were within their own territory. But the Greek colonies considered the Carthaginian presence a threat. They turned to the Romans, with whom they had defense treaties, for help against a common enemy. The result was the first of a series of wars between Rome and Carthage. It marked the beginning of Rome's vast territorial expansion.

Rome Fights Carthage for Control of the Mediterranean   Carthage began as a Phoenician colony on the coast of North Africa. By 265 B.C., Carthage had freed itself from the control of the Phoenicians and had become a great naval and trading power throughout the Mediterranean world. Carthage had colonies on Sicily, Sardinia (sahr-DIN-ee-uh), and Corsica (KOR-sih-kuh), as well as on the coast of North Africa and in Spain. (See the map on page 141.)

Carthage was afraid the Romans would try to expand into Sicily. The Romans were afraid Carthage would use its control of the Strait of Messina to cut off Roman contact with the Adriatic (ay-dree-AT-ik) Sea. Rome was thus only too glad to help the Greek colonies who were alarmed by the military buildup in Sicily. Between 264 and 146 B.C., Carthage and Rome fought three wars. They are called the **Punic** (PYOO-nik) **Wars** because the Latin word for Phoenician is *punicus*.

The First Punic War   The first war between Rome and Carthage lasted for twenty-three years. At first, the Romans, who were not a maritime nation, were unsuccessful in their struggle

ROME AND CARTHAGE AT THE BEGINNING OF THE PUNIC WARS

What was Carthage's advantage over Rome before the Punic Wars?

against the great sea power. Roman soldiers were accustomed to fighting on land. Naval warfare was foreign to them. But to defeat Carthage, the Romans built a fleet of warships. They added a drawbridge to each vessel so that they could draw up close to enemy ships and board them. Then the Roman soldiers fought hand-to-hand battles on the enemy's decks. This development helped turn the tide of the war in favor of the Romans.

The First Roman Provinces After its defeat, Carthage was forced to give Sicily to Rome. Instead of absorbing Sicily into the state, as it had done with other lands, Rome decided to govern Sicily as a province.

In a **province** (PRAHV-untz), people did not become citizens of Rome. They were governed by local officials from their own upper classes. Above the local leaders was a Roman governor chosen by the Senate. He had absolute power over the province. The rule of the Roman governor was backed up by the army.

Later conquests gave Rome control of all of Italy, the islands of Sardinia and Corsica, and the eastern coast of the Adriatic Sea. (See the map on page 143.) These new territories were also

141

governed as provinces. As the empire grew, provinces were created in all the conquered lands. This way of governing conquered peoples became the foundation of the Roman Empire.

The Second Punic War After a series of defeats, Carthage decided to use its colonies in Spain as the base for an attack on Rome. In 218 B.C., a famous general called Hannibal (HAN-uh-bul) launched an invasion of Italy from Spain. Because Rome controlled the seas, he had to travel overland from Spain, across the southern part of Gaul (GAWL), and down the length of the Italian peninsula. The map on page 141 shows the route of Hannibal's march.

Hannibal's most incredible feat was his crossing of the Alps with an army and all their equipment, including elephants. On the march from Spain, Hannibal's soldiers accomplished one of the greatest feats in history. They traveled more than 1,920 kilometers (1,200 miles) through dangerous territory and crossed one of the biggest rivers in Europe, the Po, and two of the highest mountain chains, the Alps and the Pyrennes (PIR-uh-neez). Then, after they had arrived, they threatened the power of Rome on that country's own territory. Yet during the march, half of Hannibal's army was lost. They were attacked by fierce tribes along the way and trapped by heavy snows and landslides. In spite of these hardships, Hannibal finally led his army into the Po Valley of northern Italy.

After several defeats by Hannibal's army, the Romans shut themselves up inside their fortified cities and decided to wait out the war. Hannibal stayed in Italy for fifteen years. But he fought few great battles with the Romans, who stayed mostly within their walls. Finally, Rome brought the war to Carthage by invading Africa. When Carthage, the capital city, was threatened, Hannibal was called home to defend it.

The Third Punic War In 202 B.C., Hannibal and his army were badly beaten by the Romans. Once more, Carthage lost lands to Rome, including its Spanish colonies. It also had to pay a huge sum of money to Rome. Although the city of Carthage remained free, it never again became a political power. But the city quickly began to recover its prosperity. This frightened some of the Roman senators. They wanted Carthage completely destroyed.

During the Third Punic War, which lasted from 149 to 146 B.C., the Romans leveled the city. They took over all the remaining territory of the Carthaginians. The place where Carthage had stood became the Roman province of Africa.

Rome's Eastern Provinces Even before the defeat of Carthage, Rome had been expanding its territory in the eastern Mediterranean. Between 200 and 146 B.C., it took over much of the territory that had belonged to the empire of Alexander the Great. After repeated wars between Rome and Macedonia, the latter finally became a Roman province in 148 B.C. Two years later, in 146 B.C., Rome took over all of Greece. This was the same year that it defeated and destroyed Carthage.

In 133 B.C., the king of Pergamum (PUR-guh-mum) left his state to Rome in his will. With this, Rome's empire expanded into western Asia Minor. By this time, Rome had also gained control of most of Spain.

Problems of the Expanding Empire The rapid expansion of Rome brought a great flow of goods and money from

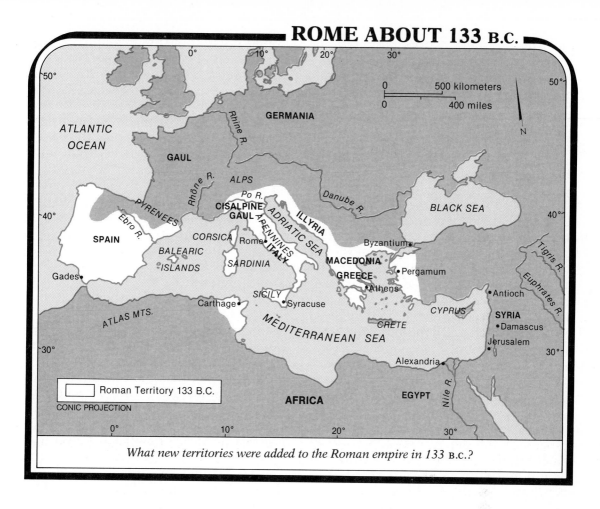

ROME ABOUT 133 B.C.

What new territories were added to the Roman empire in 133 B.C.?

the conquered lands. The upper classes began to accumulate huge estates that required large amounts of cheap labor. Hundreds of thousands of captured people were sent to Italy to work as slaves on the farms of wealthy landowners. The slaves were often chained together in gangs and mistreated. In 176 B.C., when a revolt in Sardinia was crushed by Rome, some 80,000 people were captured or killed. Most of the captives were brought to the slave markets. And in 167 B.C., some 150,000 inhabitants of a Greek city were enslaved. These are only two examples of many such events.

The large landowners eventually forced the small farmers off their lands. The dispossessed farmers flocked to the cities in search of work. But most of the jobs there were held by slaves. Hungry mobs of landless people began to riot in the cities. To keep unrest from spreading, the rulers gave them "bread and circuses." Food was distributed to the hungry mobs. Some slaves were used as contestants in the public arenas to entertain the masses. Slaves fought each other to the death, and some even fought against wild animals. Some slaves were specially trained fighters called *gladiators* who were owned by

143

wealthy Romans. Large amounts of money were bet on such contests.

Through the accident of war, well-educated and skilled people sometimes became slaves. This was especially true of Greeks captured during Rome's conquest of their homeland. Many Greeks served as tutors for the children of the Roman upper classes, thus helping to spread Greek culture in Rome. Skilled slaves were sometimes allowed to earn money of their own and, in time, buy their freedom.

In general, however, most of Rome's slaves were treated horribly. They were often worked to death because there were so many of them that it was easier to replace them than to go to the expense and trouble of treating them decently.

As a result of these social changes, the attitudes of many Romans began to change. The increase in slavery, the forcing of small farmers into poverty, and the presence of mobs in the cities weakened the old ideals of patriotism and self-discipline. Wealth, no matter how it had been gained, replaced character and family position as a way of judging the worth of a person. Standards of behavior declined, and corruption began to spread.

Pompey, Caesar, and Crassus: Three Political Generals   One way to ensure political success in ancient Rome was to be a victorious general. Military leaders who conquered new lands became men of great wealth and power. Often these men tried to take more authority than permitted under the Roman constitution. Pompey (PAHM-pee), Caesar (SEE-zur), and Crassus (KRASS-us) were such men.

Pompey made a reputation for himself by winning victories in Spain. He also put down a serious slave rebellion at home that threatened to destroy the country. Pompey became consul in 70 B.C. and led successful military campaigns in the East. By 64 B.C., he had reorganized all Asia Minor into Roman provinces. He also made Syria into a Roman province in 64 B.C. and took Jerusalem (juh-ROO-suh-lem) that same year. Much new wealth soon flowed into Rome from the conquered lands, and Pompey became rich and powerful.

Crassus, another general, was a member of the patrician class. His power came from his backing by business groups in Rome and from his own wealth in land.

When Pompey returned to Rome, he and Crassus were forced to become political allies of **Julius** (JOOL-yus) **Caesar.** Caesar was a man of great energy and talent from an old aristocratic family. Caesar became consul in 59 B.C. He also was governor of southern Gaul— part of present-day France. Between 58 and 49 B.C., Caesar conquered most of what are now France and Belgium and even fought against Britain. Caesar's armies swept from the Alps to the English Channel. They raided Britain and pushed German tribes beyond the Rhine (RINE) River. These campaigns are known as the **Gallic** (GAL-ik) **Wars.** The effects of these conquests are felt today, since Caesar's successes meant that France, Italy, and Spain would have a language based on Latin.

Caesar, Pompey, and Crassus each wanted to be sole ruler of the Roman Empire but none of them had enough power. Together the three men formed an informal alliance that has become known as the **First Triumvirate** (trie-UM-vahr-it). It lasted from 60 to 43 B.C.

As Caesar became more powerful, a struggle between Caesar, Pompey, and Crassus for leadership of the Roman Empire became unavoidable. Crassus was eliminated when he was slain during a war in 53 B.C. Pompey, then in charge of Rome, made a move to become sole leader of the Roman Empire.

The Death of Caesar After his duties in Gaul were finished, Julius Caesar decided to face Pompey. He was ordered by Pompey not to return to Rome, but in 49 B.C. Caesar disobeyed that order. Caesar fought several successful battles against Pompey in Italy, Greece, and Spain. Pompey was murdered in Egypt by troops of the Egyptian king, at whose court he sought refuge. Egypt had been independent since the breakup of the empire of Alexander the Great. However, through the years, Egypt had come under the influence of Rome. Caesar pursued Pompey to Egypt. While he was in Egypt, Caesar fell in love with Cleopatra (klee-uh-PA-truh), a daughter of the ruling family. He placed her on the throne of Egypt and made Egypt an ally of Rome.

After new victories in Egypt, Africa, and Asia, Caesar returned to Rome in triumph. This was in 45 B.C. Less than a year later, in 44 B.C. on the Ides of March (March 15th), Caesar was stabbed to death on the floor of the Senate by patricians, among them Cassius (KASH-ee-us) and Brutus (BROOT-us) who were afraid Caesar would have attempted to take absolute power.

Although it is possible that Caesar did want to overthrow the republic and become a king, he did a great deal to benefit the people of Rome. He began to stop the importing of slaves because they took work away from free men. He caused many new jobs to be created. He issued the first gold coins. He added citizens other than those from Rome to the Senate. He made many Spaniards

How does this sculpture of Julius Caesar reflect the qualities Romans considered important in their leaders?

and Gauls Roman citizens. He reformed the law courts to make them less corrupt and more efficient. Finally, with help from a Greek astronomer and using the Egyptian calendar as a guide, he created a year with 365 days with

145

every fourth year a leap year. Called the *Julian Calendar*, it is for the most part the one we use today.

The Last of the Republic   After Caesar's death, the struggle for power began all over again. This time it was between Caesar's aid, Mark Antony (AN-tuh-nee), his grandnephew, Octavian (ahk-TAY-vee-un), and Lepidus (LEP-ud-us), another of Caesar's lieutenants. Together they formed the **Second Triumvirate** in 43 B.C. Part of their work involved the defeat of Brutus and Cassius and their forces in 42 B.C., both of whom committed suicide after their defeats by Antony and Octavian. Lepidus by then had been sent to serve in North Africa and was no longer an important political influence.

The empire was finally split into two zones of power. Octavian controlled the entire West, and Antony attempted to gain control of the eastern part. Antony began an alliance with Cleopatra. He and the Queen of Egypt saw themselves as rulers of the entire empire. In a famous battle at Actium (AK-shee-um) off the coast of Greece, Octavian defeated the forces of Antony. When their plans for conquest failed, Antony and Cleopatra committed suicide and Egypt finally fell to Rome. Instead of becoming a Roman province, it became the personal property of Octavian and his successors. Octavian was now the supreme ruler of Rome, and the republic came to an end.

Although he would not let himself be called "dictator," Octavian assumed the title of **Augustus** (aw-GUS-tus), which means "imperial majesty." Augustus brought stability and prosperity to what had now become a great empire. He ruled for 41 years, from 27 B.C. to 14 A.D. During his reign, he extended trade as far east as Arabia (uh-RAY-bee-uh) and India. (See the map on page 147.) For 200 years after the beginning of his reign, serious conflict did not occur within the empire. This period is known as the **pax Romana** (PAKS roe-MAH-nah), the "peace of Rome."

The "peace of Rome" did not just happen. It was mainly due to the careful planning of Augustus. He made himself a *Princeps* (PRIN-seps), or "First Citizen." In reality he became an absolute *monarch* or king, while at the same time he made the Roman Senate feel, at least partly, as if it had some powers and responsibilities.

As supreme leader, Augustus began to reform the Roman Empire through a series of actions. He made the civil service a more honest group of government workers. He allowed many provinces to have some degree of self-government and drew new boundaries so as to provide more efficient administration of the provinces of the Empire. Roman roads were expanded and kept in near perfect condition. Augustus provided a better basis for service in the army. The regular troops were made up of Italians or the most Romanized people of the provinces. One of the ways people of the provinces could attain Roman citizenship was by enlisting in the army.

The armies, when not at war, usually lived in special camps. The soldiers built roads, dug moats, and became skilled artisans. Most were stationed in areas that posed the greatest threat to the Roman Empire.

In Italy, one found few regular troops except for the *Praetorian* (pree-TORE-ee-un) *Guard*. It numbered about 9,000 elite men and had a special camp on the outskirts of Rome.

In the city of Rome, Augustus dealt with the problem of the unemployed

TRADE ROUTES AND PRODUCTS OF THE ROMAN EMPIRE

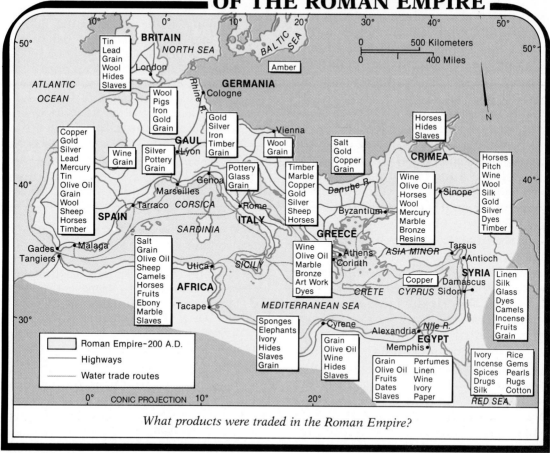

What products were traded in the Roman Empire?

masses. Many were given jobs on public works projects and free or cheap food. Often they were entertained by lavish circuses or combat between gladiators in the Colosseum (kahl-uh-SEE-um). Such contests over the years continued to become more and more brutal in an attempt to satisfy the thirst of the masses for something new.

When Augustus died, his adopted son, Tiberius (tie-BIR-ee-us), replaced him and ruled from 14 A.D. to 37 A.D. Historians usually consider the reign of Tiberius a good one, but it was marked by some unsuccessful attempts on his life and with a Senate growing more

and more unhappy under the rule of an absolute monarch.

After Tiberius's death, a series of rulers followed. Caligula (kuh-LIG-yoo-luh) served from 37 A.D. to 41 A.D. He became insane and was a cruel ruler. After he was murdered by a conspiracy of the Praetorian Guard, Claudius (CLAWD-ee-us) came to power and remained there until 54 A.D. He continued Augustus's attempts at reform of corrupt government until he was killed by his last wife. She in turn had Nero (NEE-roe), her son and a stepson of Claudius, made emperor. During the first five years of his reign (54 A.D.–

147

59 A.D.), two of Nero's advisors actually ruled and ruled well. Then Nero assumed full command. He began to appeal to the masses by giving spectacular games and eventually he spent most of the treasury. All of this upset the upper classes. In 68 A.D., Nero was overthrown in a revolt and murdered when he refused to commit suicide.

For the next year, several people attempted without success to become ruler of the Roman Empire. Finally, Vespasian (veh-SPAY-shun) assumed power in 69 A.D. He managed to restore new dignity to his office and order in the government. In 81 A.D., one of his sons, Domitian (doe-MISH-un), came to power. He was a good administrator but died in a conspiracy in 96 A.D. After his death, the Senate intervened and made Nerva (NUR-vuh) ruler. Nerva, before he died a natural death in 98 A.D., adopted the best Roman general as his son. That man, Trajan (TRAY-jun), upon becoming ruler, began an era known as the "Good Emperors." Trajan ruled from 98 A.D. to 117 A.D. He extended the empire north of the Danube (DAN-yoob) River. Hadrian (HAY-dree-un) assumed power in 117 A.D. and improved the civil service and began new codifications (kod-uh-fuh-KAY-shunz) of Roman law. Antoninus Pius (an-tuh-NIE-us PIE-us), ruling from 138 A.D. to 161 A.D., continued to work on Roman law and had a peaceful reign. Marcus Aurelius (MAR-kus aw-REEL-lee-us), in power from 161 to 180 A.D., was a writer and a good leader but had to spend much of his time defending the empire against enemies at the northern borders. When he died, his son, Commodus (KAHM-uh-dus) began his ineffective reign, 180–193 A.D. It marked the beginning of the decline of the Roman Empire.

SECTION REVIEW

1. Mapping: Using the maps on pages 141 and 147, compare the extent of the territory of Carthage at the beginning of the Punic Wars with the extent of Roman territory by 200 A.D. Which Carthaginian territories did Rome take control of after the war?
2. In your own words, briefly identify each of the following: Hannibal, Pompey, Caesar, Cleopatra, Antony, and Octavian.
3. What were five main achievements of Octavian (Augustus) during his rule from 31 B.C. to 14 A.D.?
4. List and describe the Roman rulers in power during the years 14 A.D.– 193 A.D.
5. How did the tremendous wealth and power that came to Rome as the empire grew affect the lives of its people? Give three examples from the text.
▷ Can you give an example of an individual who has changed the course of history? Why would it be different today if that person had not existed?

ROMAN CIVILIZATION

The Romans owed much to the Greeks and the Etruscans for ideas in the arts and sciences, architecture, and religion. In fact, much of what historians know about these two earlier cultures has come from the Romans. But Rome deserves credit for original and important contributions in law, government, and language.

Roman Law   Much of our legal system is based on that of the Romans. There are three main principles of Roman law. One is that all law must come from one central source. A second is that all people have the same nature and, therefore, laws must be based on the characteristics of all human society. The third idea of Roman law is that laws should be flexible enough to fit special cases.

Roman Religion   The religious life of the Romans was made up of a combination of forms of worship. As the empire spread, the gods and religious ceremonies of conquered lands were added to those of the Romans. The earliest Romans worshiped spirits, which they believed lived in the natural world around them—in the trees, the rivers, and the earth. Then they created a religion based on the worship of household spirits, which they believed governed their everyday lives. Roman households were large. They included parents and unmarried children, married sons and their families, and slaves. The father had complete authority over the household, and he was also the priest in the family worship.

After contact with Greece, the Romans adopted many of the Greek gods and goddesses and gave them Roman names. They also held many festivals in honor of the gods, as did the Greeks. The Romans honored their emperors by considering them to be gods. In addition, the emperors served as high priests in religious ceremonies. Many forms of worship from the eastern parts of the empire became fashionable among the Romans. One of these religions was **Christianity** (kris-chee-AN-uh-tee). For several reasons, it quickly became popular in the empire.

GREEK AND ROMAN GODS

Greek Name	Roman Name	Position
Aphrodite	Venus	Goddess of love
Apollo	Apollo	God of music, poetry, and purity
Ares	Mars	God of war
Artemis	Diana	Goddess of hunting and childbirth
Asclepius	Aesculapius	God of healing
Athena	Minerva	Goddess of crafts, war, and wisdom
Cronus	Saturn	In Greek mythology, ruler of the Titans and father of Zeus; in Roman mythology, also the god of agriculture
Demeter	Ceres	Goddess of growing things
Dionysus	Bacchus	God of wine, fertility, and wild behavior
Eros	Cupid	God of love
Gaea	Terra	Symbol of the earth and mother and wife of Uranus
Hephaestus	Vulcan	Blacksmith for the gods and god of fire and metalworking
Hera	Juno	Protector of marriage and women. In Greek mythology, sister and wife of Zeus; in Roman mythology, wife of Jupiter
Hermes	Mercury	Messenger for the gods; god of commerce and science; and protector of travelers, thieves, and vagabonds
Hestia	Vesta	Goddess of the hearth
Hypnos	Somnus	God of sleep
Hades	Pluto	God of the underworld
Poseidon	Neptune	God of the sea. In Greek mythology, also god of earthquakes and horses
Rhea	Rhea	Wife and sister of Cronus
Uranus	Uranus	Son and husband of Gaea and father of the Titans
Zeus	Jupiter	Ruler of the gods

Roman Literature and Language
The Romans produced many writers whose works have had a lasting effect on the literature of the Western world. They also did much to spread the Latin language. Some Roman writers were inspired by the works of the Greeks. One great writer of comedies was *Plautus* (PLAWT-uz). Characters from his plays reappear time and again in later Western literature—especially that of Shakespeare (SHAKE-spir) and of some Russian (RUSH-un) writers.

Two of Rome's noted poets, *Lucretius* (loo-KREE-shuss) and *Catullus* (kuh-TUL-us), are known for their beautiful language and the emotions created by their poems. In a long poem called "On the Nature of Things," Lucretius says that although the universe is governed by fixed laws, humans, not the gods, control human actions. Catullus wrote beautiful and moving love poems, which some readers consider the finest of all Roman poetry.

Another famous poet was **Vergil** (VUR-jul). He lived from 70 B.C. to 19 B.C. Vergil received his education in Rome and is best known for his epic poem called the *Aeneid* (ih-NEE-id) about the legendary past of Rome. The chief character in Vergil's work was Aeneas (ih-NEE-us), a hero and survivor of the Trojan war, who after many adventures founded the city of Rome. In the *Aeneid*, Vergil stressed the sacred mission of Rome and its destiny to conquer and organize the world.

Rome's greatest writer of prose was *Cicero* (SISS-uh-roe). This famous lawyer and politician carefully prepared his speeches for the law courts and the Senate. He used words in original ways and did much to perfect the use of the Latin language. Cicero also wrote essays on philosophy. These were not original essays but were based on the works of Greek philosophers. The respect Cicero commanded as a spokesman for the Senate aroused such jealousy in Mark Antony that in 43 B.C. he had Cicero put to death.

Two writers of Greek ancestry also became prominent during the Roman period. One was Plutarch (PLOO-tahrk) who was born about 50 A.D. He sought to reveal the secret of greatness by studying about and writing the biographies of famous Romans and Greeks. His *Lives* arranged prominent people in pairs so comparisons could be made. Another noted Greek writer, Lucian (LOO-shahn), was born about 124 A.D. He used dialogues or conversations in his one act plays to seek answers to the proper roles ambition and virtue should assume in peoples' lives.

Among Rome's great historians were *Livy* (LIV-ee) and *Tacitus* (TAS-ut-us). Livy's works told the story of Rome from its beginnings. By writing about the past greatness of Rome, Livy hoped to convince Romans to return to the simple ways of their ancestors. Only 35 of Livy's 142 books have survived. Tactitus lived during the latter part of the Roman Empire. He also wrote a history of the early empire in which he compared the evils of the empire to the glory of Rome's past.

Latin, the language of the Romans, continued in use as the written language of educated people in western Europe long after the end of the Roman Empire. Today, Latin is still in use as a universal language in many fields of study, including medicine and the law. Spoken Latin changed over the years and formed the basis for other European languages including French, Italian, Spanish, Portuguese (POR-chuh-geez), and Rumanian (ru-MAY-nee-un).

THE ROMAN CONQUEST OF FRANCE

Tacitus (TAS-ut-us) was a Roman historian. In the following account, he describes the Roman conquest of the area called Gaul that is now France. In this account, Tacitus tells what a Roman commander probably told the newly conquered people there in 69 A.D. Those same people had earlier been threatened by neighboring warlike Germans and Britons. Under the Romans they had equal rights as citizens of the empire.

Gaul always had its small kingdoms and wars until you submitted to our authority. We, though so often provoked, have used the right of conquest to burden you with nothing except the cost of maintaining peace, for the peace of nations cannot be preserved without armies. Armies cannot exist without pay. Pay cannot be furnished without taxes. From worthy Roman emperors you have equal rights, though you live so far away.

Should the Romans be driven out (which God forbid), what can result but wars between all of you and all of your neighbors, especially the Germans and Britons? Yours will be the worst danger, for you have gold and wealth, and these are the chief reasons for causing other nations to war on you. Give, therefore, your love and respect to the cause of peace and to Rome, in which we, the conquerors and conquered, claim an equal right. Let the lessons of fortune teach you not to prefer rebellion and ruin to submission and safety.

Adapted from: A. J. Church and W. J. Brodribb. *The History of Tacitus.* New York: Macmillan and Co., 1894, p. 184.

1. What arguments does Tacitus use for the Gauls' submission to Roman control?
2. What does this reading tell you about what was important to the Romans? Use examples.
3. Do you think that the rights enjoyed by the Gauls under Roman rule made up for the fact that they were a conquered people? Explain.

English also includes hundreds of words that have Latin origins.
Roman Science and Engineering
"All roads lead to Rome" is a saying that, during the Roman Empire, was certainly true. Geographically, Italy is located at the spot where three continents meet—Africa, Asia, and Europe. Rome was the administrative and commercial center of the huge empire that spanned all three continents. The map on page 147 shows the main highways leading to Rome and the sea routes by which products were brought to the capital from every corner of the empire. Good communication between Rome and the provinces was essential, so the Romans built a useful system of paved highways. Parts of the Roman roads are still being used, 2,000 years later.

The Romans discovered a formula for making concrete. By combining the

The Roman Colosseum pictured here illustrates the use of stone in Roman structures. What building materials are used most often in your community? What interest might a historian have in the answer to this question?

concrete with stones, they were able to make highways, huge *aqueducts* (AK-wuh-duktz) for carrying water to the cities, and buildings of extraordinary size. Perhaps the most famous of all the Roman buildings is the Colosseum. It was the scene of bloody combats between slaves and wild beasts. Animals were kept in cages beneath the wooden floor of the Colosseum. Slaves worked machines similar to elevators that pulled the animal cages up to the level of the arena, which was covered with sand. The sand soaked up the blood of the men and animals that were killed or wounded. Much of the Colosseum still stands in Rome.

The Romans made important advances in medicine. They started the first hospitals and invented a variety of surgical instruments for special opera-tions. However, much superstition existed in the practice of Roman medicine, and it was the Greeks within the Roman Empire who continued to make the most important contributions. In other sciences too, the Romans often depended on the Greeks. A Roman in the first century A.D. made observations of ships approaching the shore and came to the conclusion that the earth was round. But his observations only repeated an idea already stated by a Greek years before.

Roman Art The Romans were among the greatest architects in the world. In Europe, the Middle East, and northern Africa, are temples, arches, baths, and other monuments left by the Romans. In their architecture, the Romans used the Greek column and a rounded arch borrowed from the Etrus-

152

cans. They also improved the new architectural form, the dome. An example of the Roman dome is the one on the Capitol building in Washington, D.C.

Roman buildings and arches were decorated with large sculptures, usually showing battle scenes or victory celebrations. The homes of the wealthy and public buildings often contained beautiful mosaics and wall paintings. The rooms in private homes were small and dark, so paintings of landscapes were used to give the rooms a feeling of space and light.

Daily Life in Rome   The Romans had a wide variety of entertainment.

Wealthy Romans decorated their houses with mosaics and wall paintings like the one shown here. What does this wall decoration reveal about the Romans? What would a historian learn about your society by looking at the walls of your house?

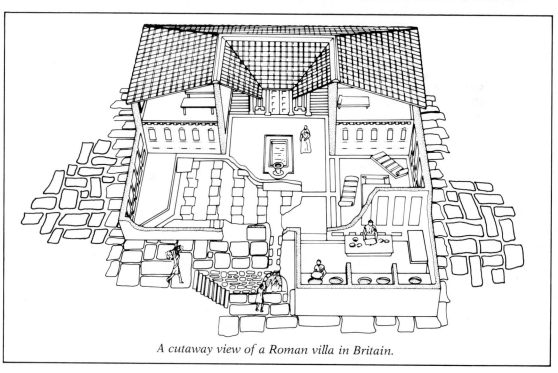

A cutaway view of a Roman villa in Britain.

153

They went to the theater to see comedies, jugglers, dancers, and clowns. They could go to the arenas to watch spectacles and sporting contests. Wealthy men could also visit luxurious public baths and attend fabulous banquets with huge amounts of food from all over the empire. Women were respected. They went about the cities freely and attended public events, but they did not take part in politics.

While the wealthy lived in splendid homes and were attended by slaves, the poor people of the cities often lived in desperate conditions. Large sections of the cities were filled with flimsy, old wooden buildings several stories high. The rickety housing often collapsed, or fires sometimes wiped out whole areas.

SECTION REVIEW

1. Mapping: Using the map on page 113, list and locate by latitude and longitude coordinates the major cities of the Roman Empire.
2. In your own words, identify: Plautus, Lucretius, Catullus, Cicero, Livy, Tacitus, Vergil, Plutarch, Lucian.
3. Describe three ways in which the Greeks influenced the Roman way of life. Were the Greeks the only ones who contributed ideas to ancient Rome?
4. How has the civilization of Rome contributed to life in the United States today? List the contributions in at least three different categories.
   List five kinds of food that are available in your local supermarket that are from other parts of the country. List five others that are from other parts of the world. What do these lists tell you about the kinds of goods traded within your own country and with other parts of the world?

THE BEGINNINGS OF CHRISTIANITY AND THE DECLINE OF ROMAN POWER

Two important developments took place after the republic fell and Augustus took power. Although these developments had no connection with each other, they began about the same time. For this reason, they are usually discussed together. The first was the beginning of a new religion that would soon spread throughout the empire. The other was the beginning of the decline of the power of Rome.

The Life of Jesus During the reign of Augustus, a child, according to Christian belief, was born in Bethlehem to humble Jewish parents, Joseph and Mary. That birth was to affect the lives of future generations for over 2,000 years. This child was **Jesus** (JEE-zus) and the religion he founded is Christianity. Roman histories written during Jesus' lifetime do not refer to him at all. Our knowledge of his life comes mainly from the first four books of the New Testament of the Bible.

Although little is known about the life of Jesus, most historians agree that he was born in Palestine about 4 B.C. and was crucified in Jerusalem about 30 A.D. However, his followers believed that Jesus was the Son of God, arose from the dead, and forty days later ascended into heaven. Jesus was believed to have been a carpenter. He spent much of his adult life, however, traveling through the towns and villages of Palestine teaching people his religious ideas. During this time, Jesus gathered a small group of twelve disciples, or followers, to help him preach. They are called the *Apostles* (uh-PAHS-ulz).

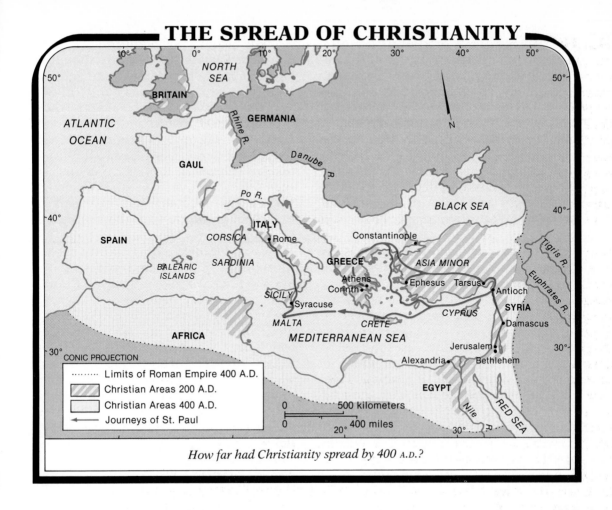

How far had Christianity spread by 400 A.D.?

The teachings of Jesus are based in part on the religious beliefs of the Hebrews (HEE-brooz) or Jews. He taught that the Ten Commandments of the Hebrews were a guide to proper living. Jesus also taught that all people are equal in the eyes of God, that everyone should love God above all else, and that they should treat others the same way they would wish to be treated. The teachings of Jesus, together with those of the Hebrew religion, which formed the foundation of much of his preaching, make up what is called the **Judeo-Christian tradition.**

In his travels with his disciples, Jesus went to Jerusalem. There many people greeted him as their *messiah* (muh-SIE-uh), that is, they thought he was their king and savior as spoken of by their prophets. Others, however, opposed these claims. It seemed to many that Jesus was preaching some kind of revolution and that he planned to overthrow Roman rule. For this reason, Jesus was tried as an enemy of the state and found guilty. He was sentenced to death by crucifixion, which is the way criminals were often put to death in Rome.

The Spread of Christianity After the crucifixion of Jesus, some of his disciples became missionaries. They traveled widely, spreading the teachings of Jesus and his promise to return to earth. One man in particular took the lead in missionary activities, although he was not among the group of followers who had known Jesus during his lifetime. This was a Jew who had converted to Christianity and taken the name *Paul*. Another great missionary, *Peter,* was one of the Apostles of Jesus. Peter, it is believed, traveled to Rome and was put to death there. Paul, too, suffered the same fate as Peter.

By the year 100 A.D., the new faith had spread to many of the eastern territories of Rome and was beginning to take hold in some places in the west as well. Historians believe that many of the early Christians, including Peter and Paul, were put to death for their beliefs because they refused to honor the Roman emperor as a god. They would not make sacrifices to statues of the emperor because they believed it was a sin to have more than one God.

In spite of the persecution, Christianity spread quickly and became a popular religion. Several reasons have been given for this. One is that Christianity appealed to people because it taught that everyone is equal in the sight of God. Some other religions did not allow women to take part in their ceremonies. Others, in which goddesses were worshiped, considered women to be more important than men. Christianity also taught that no matter how terrible life may be on earth, good Christians could look forward to a better life in heaven.

Several great rulers became sympathetic to Christianity. In 313 A.D., one Roman ruler, **Constantine** (KAHN-stun-teen), made Christianity equal to all the other religions of Rome and forbade persecution of Christians. In 394 A.D., the Roman ruler Theodosius (thee-uh-DOE-shuz) commanded his subjects to become Christians. Even though there had been some attempt to restore the older Roman religions, by the fifth century A.D. the Christian church had become too powerful as the official religion of the empire to be overthrown. The map on page 155 shows how quickly Christianity spread throughout Europe and parts of the Middle East. Many elements of Roman civilization were passed down through the early Christian church. For example, the building in which Roman courts met were called *basilicas* (buh-SIL-ih-kuz). The architecture of the basilica was used as a model for churches in all parts of the world. It contained a long, narrow central aisle, side aisles, and a curved enclosure at one end of the building.

The Decline of Rome Augustus has been called the "architect of the Roman Empire" because under his rule the crumbling Roman republic became the great, powerful Roman Empire. He took absolute power and used it to institute many economic, social, and moral reforms. Rome had always depended on two important factors: the ability of the emperor and the loyalty of the army. After the death of Augustus, both of these important elements were missing. Augustus was able to control the army and use it effectively to protect the boundaries of Rome and preserve internal order. But the men who came after him could not do so.

Many reasons are given for the decline of Rome's power. In general, it can be said that the empire grew so large that it was impossible to administer effectively. After a half century of disorder, one emperor named **Diocletian** (die-uh-KLEE-shun) tried to solve the problems of Rome by sharing his power with another emperor. In effect, there were two areas of power: an eastern part of the empire and a western part. Each was ruled by one of the emperors. Diocletian ruled over the eastern part of the empire, which was later to become the more powerful part of Rome's territories.

Another emperor who tried to save the rapidly decaying Roman Empire was Constantine. He is famous in history for several reasons. First, Constantine created a new capital in what is now Turkey. This new capital was called Constantinople (kahn-stant-'n-OE-pul). The second important contribution of Constantine was his legal recognition of the Christian religion. (See page 156.) Constantine had taken absolute power during his rule.

After his death in 337 A.D., there was a return to rule by two emperors. After this, the split between the two parts of the empire became wider. By the year 400 A.D., one could say that there were two Roman Empires: one in the east and one in the west. Power had shifted to the eastern part, where the wealth was. During this period of internal unrest, the empire was under furious attack on all its borders by fierce neighboring tribes. These tribes are usually grouped together under the name *barbarians* (bahr-BER-ee-unz). Especially destructive were the Germanic tribes, who were being pressed forward by the movement into Europe of warlike nomadic peoples from Asia called the Huns (HUNZ).

The collapse of Rome came about gradually. Its military and economic strength was weakened by internal strife and repeated warfare on all the empire's borders. For 200 years, the empire struggled against these forces.

The city of Rome was attacked and looted twice by barbarian armies before the last emperor of Rome resigned in 476 A.D. This brought the western empire to an end. But while it had been declining, the eastern empire had been gaining in wealth and power. The eastern empire lasted for another thousand years, with its capital at Constantinople. Constantinople did not fall until 1453 A.D., when it was defeated by the Ottoman Turks.

SECTION REVIEW

1. Mapping: Look at the map showing the spread of Christianity on page 155. How can you explain the relatively rapid spread of Christianity?
2. In your own words, briefly define or identify each of the following: Jesus, Apostles, Judeo-Christian tradition, Paul, Constantine, basilicas.
3. How did Diocletian try to solve the problem of disorder in the Roman Empire? Were his efforts successful?
4. What reasons are generally given for the decline of Rome's power by 476 A.D.?
5. Did the Roman Empire disappear entirely in 476 A.D.? Explain your answer.

▷ Do you think the power of an important country usually declines for only one reason or could there be several reasons? Explain your answer, giving examples.

Reviewing the Unit

Unit Summary

After you have read the selection below, answer the questions that follow.

Much of the origin of ancient Greek society can be traced to the Minoans (2500 B.C.), the Mycenaeans (1400 B.C.), and the Dorians (1100 B.C.). After the Dorian invasions, Greece entered a "Dark Age." However, during this time the *Iliad* and the *Odyssey* were written.

About 800 B.C. in Greece, city-states emerged. Athens formed a democratic government. Sparta remained a military state. United, the Greeks defeated the Persians in 479 B.C. Later, with the help of the Persians, Sparta defeated Athens in 404 B.C.

Culture flowered in ancient Greece during the period 800 B.C.–300 B.C. Greek religion, with its many gods and goddesses, affected all aspects of life. This influence was reflected in Greek architecture, theatre, and in the Olympics. The Greeks also made notable advances in poetry, philosophy, and the sciences. Greek culture spread during the time of Alexander the Great.

In 509 B.C., a republic was formed in Rome. The patricians and plebians took an active role in the government. The largest group in Rome, the slaves, had no voice in the government.

Between the years 290–146 B.C., Rome took over much of the territory that had been under the rule of Alexander the Great and continued to grow. After the assassination of Caesar in 44 B.C., Octavian won a power struggle over Mark Antony. Octavian then assumed the title of Augustus and brought stability and prosperity to the empire. After his death, a period called the *pax Romana* lasted for over 150 years.

Many of the beginnings of Roman culture can be traced to the Greeks and Etruscans. The Romans did, however, make many original contributions in law, government, and language. Christianity, by the fifth century A.D., had become the official religion of the empire.

By 400 A.D., the decline of the Roman Empire had become inevitable. So great were the empire's troubles that enemy armies forced the resignation of the last emperor of Rome in 476 A.D.

Developing Your Reading Skills

1. What do you think is the main point of this reading?
2. What do you think is the main idea or point in this reading about *each* of the following:
    a. Minoan, Mycenaean, and Dorian cultures
    b. Greek religion
    c. Roman government
    d. Roman contributions
    e. Decline of the Roman Empire
3. Imagine that you had to give this reading a question as a title. What would your question be? Why?

Developing a Sense of Time

Examine the time line below and answer the questions that follow it.

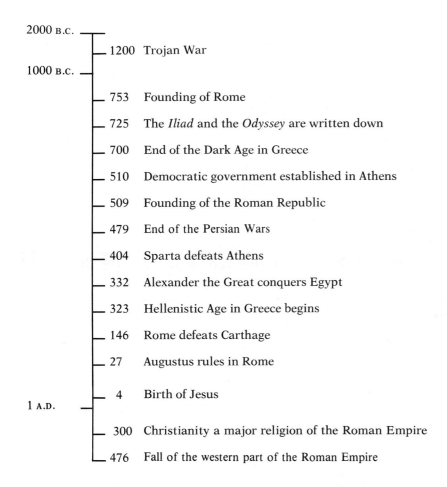

2000 B.C.

1200 Trojan War

1000 B.C.

753 Founding of Rome

725 The *Iliad* and the *Odyssey* are written down

700 End of the Dark Age in Greece

510 Democratic government established in Athens

509 Founding of the Roman Republic

479 End of the Persian Wars

404 Sparta defeats Athens

332 Alexander the Great conquers Egypt

323 Hellenistic Age in Greece begins

146 Rome defeats Carthage

27 Augustus rules in Rome

4 Birth of Jesus

1 A.D.

300 Christianity a major religion of the Roman Empire

476 Fall of the western part of the Roman Empire

1. How many years passed between the founding of Rome and the fall of the Roman Empire?
2. Which came first: The Trojan War or the writing down of the *Iliad* and the *Odyssey*? What is the relationship between the two?
3. Of the events in the time line, which two are the most important in relation to your own life? Why?
4. Why do you think historians are interested in the order of events?

Recalling the Facts

1. How did the early cultures of Crete and Mycenae affect the culture of classical Greece? Which culture had a greater influence?
2. Compare and contrast the governments of Sparta and Athens. Do you think these two forms of government shaped the way of life in the two city-states?
3. What contributions did the Sophists make to Greek life?
4. What was Philip of Macedonia's goal?
5. What did Alexander the Great accomplish?
6. List the main events in the development of the Roman Empire.
7. What reasons are given for the decline of the Roman Empire?
8. What were the main ideas of early Christianity? Why did it spread so rapidly?
9. What ideas has the Western world inherited from ancient Greece and Rome? List them.
10. Which ideas from ancient Greece and Rome have affected your life?

Using Your Vocabulary

1. What was the "Dark Age" in Greek history?
2. Briefly identify or define *acropolis, oligarchy, ostracism.*
3. How did a patrician differ from a plebian in ancient Rome?
4. In your own words define: *slavery, democracy,* and *law.*
5. Define *slavery* as you think a free ancient Greek or Roman would have. Compare this definition to yours. Explain any differences between the two.
6. Define *democracy* as you think a free ancient Greek or Roman would have. Compare this definition to yours. Do the two definitions agree? Explain.
7. Define *law* as you think an ancient Roman would have. Compare the Roman's definition to yours. How can you account for any similarities or differences?.
8. Why are historians interested in how definitions of terms have changed or remained the same over time?

Using Your Geography Skills

1. Using the map on page 113 and the descriptions on page 117, describe the physical geography of ancient Greece.
2. Do you think the physical geography of ancient Greece affected the way of life that developed there? Explain.
3. Using the map on page 134, describe the extent of the empire of Alexander the Great.
4. Using the map on page 113 and the descriptions on page 137, describe the physical geography of Italy.
5. Do you think the physical geography of Italy affected the way of life that developed there? Explain.
6. Using the map on page 113, describe the extent of the Roman Empire at its height.
7. How did the extent of the Roman Empire at its height compare with the empire built by Alexander the Great? Cite examples.

Developing Your Writing Skills

In this unit, you have examined cultures developed by ancient Greeks and Romans. You have studied about the rise and fall of empires created by both groups of people. Now consider the following:

FORMING AN OPINION

1. What do you think were the main strengths of ancient Greek culture? List them.
2. What do you consider to be the main weaknesses of ancient Greek culture? List them.
3. What do you think were the main strengths of ancient Roman culture? List them.
4. What do you consider to be the main weaknesses of ancient Roman culture? List them.

SUPPORTING AN OPINION

5. What can you now conclude about early Greek and Roman cultures? Did their strengths out-rank their weaknesses? Did their weaknesses outrank their strengths? Or were their strengths equal to their weaknesses? Defend your position in a paragraph or essay, beginning with the completion of the following topic sentence:

   Early Greek and Roman cultures had _____

Why Study the Past?

1. List five ways in which your study of the ancient worlds of Greece and Rome can be of value to you today.

Can you think of any ways in which your study of this period might be valuable to you in the future?

Your History Bookshelf

Evslin, Bernard, Dorothy Evslin, and Ned Hopper. *The Greek Gods.* Englewood Cliffs, New Jersey: Scholastic Magazine, 1966.

Gunther, John. *Julius Caesar.* New York: Random House, 1959.

National Geographic Society. *Greece and Rome: Builders of Our World.* Washington, D.C.: National Geographic Society, 1968.

Perowne, Stewart. *Roman Mythology.* New York: Hamlyn, 1969.

Pittenger, W. Norman. *Life of St. Paul.* New York: Franklin Watts, 1968.

Renault, Mary. *Fire from Heaven.* New York: Random House, 1969.

————. *The Persian Boy.* New York: Random House, 1972.

Turlington, Bayly. *Socrates.* New York: Franklin Watts, 1969.

The World of
West Europe

People in every society, at every time in history, have been concerned with "making a good impression."The French men and women of Louis XIV's day were no exception. The numerous books of etiquette published during Louis' reign testify to the interest many French people took in acquiring the right social manner. Here are just a few of the "do's" and "don'ts" an upwardly mobile French man or woman was advised to observe in "polite society."

A woman in mixed company should not pull her skirts up to her knees to warm her legs at the fire, and a man should not be seen in public with any part of his clothing unbuttoned that the tailor meant to be buttoned.

A man should not fidget with his hat, gloves, or stick. He must not yawn, spit, take snuff, or offer his hostess the loan of his handkerchief. In telling your host a story, don't underline your point by hitting him in the stomach.

Never sit down to a meal with your hat on. Furthermore, at dinner you should never wear your sword and your cloak.

Don't tear your meat with your hands like a peasant. Cut it with your knife. Don't eat so much so fast that you give yourself the hiccups.

Don't make noise while you are eating. And remember that to lick your fingers is the height of impoliteness.

During dinner, you should never tell your fellow guests how much you dislike such-and-such a dish. And, finally, at the end of dinner, remember never to stuff your pockets with sweets, fruits, and other leftovers to take home with you.

$\mathbb{B}$ooks of etiquette such as the one from which these excerpts were taken are filled with directions that seem funny, if not ridiculous, today. But no matter how amusing or trivial they may seem to us, the "do's" and "don'ts" you have just read can tell a historian what people wore, what they ate, and even what they thought was important.

Historians must also study the geography of western Europe to understand and interpret the events that took place there throughout its history. For example, the division between eastern and western Europe has never been clearly defined. But most scholars use a dividing line between East and West running southward from the Baltic (BAWL-tik) Sea, along the eastern frontiers of present-day Germany and Austria to the Adriatic (ay-dree-AT-ik) Sea. (See the map on page 165.)

The Pyrenees (PIR-uh-neez) and Alps are the major mountain barriers. Routes through the Pyrenees connect France and Spain. Routes through the Alps connect the Italian peninsula with France and Austria. Therefore, Italy has never been cut off from the rest of Europe. There are many rivers in western Europe used for transportation and commerce.

Since western Europe is bordered by sea on three sides, early contact and communication between the peoples of western Europe were more easily made by sea than by land. As you read this unit, you will find several important events in history that were influenced by the geography of western Europe.

Unit Goals

1. To know why and how the feudal system developed in medieval Europe following the fall of Rome.
2. To know how the Crusades affected the development of medieval European civilization.
3. To know how the monarchies and political events in western Europe shaped the nations of England, France, Spain, Germany, and Italy by the 1500's.
4. To know what the Renaissance was and how it affected European life during the 1600's and 1700's.
5. To know the major religious changes that took place in Europe between 1400 and 1600.
6. To know how the governments of England and France changed during the 1600's and 1700's.

Early Western Europe

20° 10° 0° 10° 20°

Political Boundaries about 1550

CONIC PROJECTION

ATLANTIC OCEAN

SWEDEN

60°

• Bergen
NORWAY

• Stockholm

TEUTONIC
KNIGHTS

SCOTLAND

• Edinburgh

NORTH
SEA

DENMARK
Copenhagen •

BALTIC SEA

PRUSSIA

IRELAND
Dublin •

BRANDENBURG

Elbe R.

POLAND

Amsterdam •

NETHERLANDS

Berlin •

Oder R.

ENGLAND

London •
Thames R.

Cologne •

HOLY

Trier •

ROMAN

Rhine R.

EMPIRE

Mainz •

SAXONY

• Dresden

Prague •

BOHEMIA

50°

Seine R.

Paris •

Danube R.

BAVARIA

Vienna •

AUSTRIA

HUNGARY

Loire R.

FRANCE

BAY OF
BISCAY

Bordeaux •

Garonne R.

Geneva •

Milan •

Po R.

Turin •

Venice •

V E N I C E

Rhône R.

Genoa •

Florence •

PAPAL
STATES

ADRIATIC SEA

OTTOMAN
EMPIRE

Marseilles •

CORSICA
(Genoa)

Rome •

NAPLES
(Sp.)
• Naples

40°

PORTUGAL

Ebro R.

CASTILE

ARAGON

• Barcelona

SARDINIA (Sp.)

Tagus R.

Madrid •

• Toledo

SPAIN

• Lisbon

BALEARIC ISLANDS (Sp.)

MEDITERRANEAN SEA

SICILY (Sp.)

• Seville

AFRICA

0° 10°

0   200   400 Kilometers
0   300 Miles

Western Europe in the Middle Ages

WESTERN EUROPE AFTER THE FALL OF ROME

By 500 A.D., the western parts of the Roman Empire had fallen to Germanic tribes. The Romans considered their Germanic conquerors to be "barbarians" because they had no written language and no system of science, philosophy, and law. The eastern half of the Roman Empire survived for 1,000 years. But almost all of western Europe was divided among the major Germanic tribes. The collapse of the Roman Empire marked the beginning of a period of new developments in western Europe.

This long period, 500–1500 A.D., is sometimes called the **medieval** (meed-ee-EE-vul) period—meaning middle. It is called this because it falls between the ancient period and modern period. For this reason it is also called the Middle Ages.

The Germanic Conquest of Western Europe The Germanic tribes were warlike people occupying most of northern Europe. The Rhine and Danube (DAN-yoob) rivers separated the Germanic tribes from Roman lands. But the Romans had to be on guard against Germanic invaders. As you read in Unit 3, Julius Caesar had defended Gaul (GAWL), or present-day France,

against them. It appears that the Germanic peoples had no plans to conquer the empire. They simply admired the Romans and were attracted by Roman wealth and culture.

Romans looked down on the Germanic peoples. They considered them to be uncivilized. Roman generals, however, admired the fighting qualities of these "barbarians." They permitted limited numbers of Germanic peoples to enter the imperial armies as soldiers. As the empire grew weaker, the Romans were forced to seek more and more of the Germanic peoples for the armed forces. By the end of the fourth century, the bulk of the Roman troops in western Europe were Germanic.

The basic unit of Germanic society was the family. A group of families formed a clan. Larger groups organized themselves as tribes. Each had its own chief. There also was a council in each tribe. All the adult males except slaves belonged to the council. The council discussed the policies of their chief. Eventually, tribes united and their numbers grew so large the Romans considered them to be nations.

In the fourth century A.D., Germanic lands were invaded by the Huns (HUNZ). The Huns were an Asiatic people. The first Germanic peoples to face the Huns were the *Ostrogoths* (AHS-truh-goths), or East Goths. They were

Above is Charlemagne's throne as it stood in his imperial palace at Aachen. The crossed figure in the middle of the writing at the top is Charlemagne's mark. Because the emperor could not write, a scribe wrote on either side of the mark the words "The mark of the most glorious King Charles." Would a person be able to govern your society if he or she could not write his or her name?

defeated. Other Germanic peoples tried to escape the Huns and migrated westward toward the borders of the Roman Empire. The Romans were too weak to keep the Germanic tribes from moving into their empire.

One tribe, the *Visigoths* (VIS-uh-goths), crossed the Danube River, raided Italy, and looted Rome. They moved on and settled Spain. Another tribe, the *Vandals* (VAN-d'ls), entered France, passed through Spain, and settled Roman North Africa. In the early 400's, *Angles* (ANG-gulz), *Saxons* (SAK-sunz), and Jutes (JOOTZ) invaded England. Everywhere in western Europe, Roman power collapsed because of the Germanic "barbarians."

In 451, the Huns attacked France, led by **Attila** (AT-'l-uh), their king. The following year, the Huns invaded Italy. In 453, Attila died and the Huns were leaderless and disunited. Their power was broken. Since Roman power also was destroyed, this left the Germanic peoples in control of almost all western Europe.

The last Roman emperor fled from Rome to a safer location in northern Italy. In 476 A.D., a barbarian general named Odoacer (ode-uh-WAY-sur) forced the emperor to give up the throne, and the Roman Empire in the west came to an end. For 300 years barbarian kingdoms rose and fell. Not until 800 A.D. was a ruler able to unite former Roman lands in the west and restore strong, stable government.

The Franks Most of the Germanic kingdoms disappeared but one Germanic tribe managed to form a powerful kingdom. This tribe was the *Franks,* who are the ancestors of the French. Under the leadership of several able rulers, the Franks established a large kingdom in what is today France.

In 481, a young warrior-prince named Clovis (KLOE-vus) set out to expand the small territory he held. France then was populated by several Germanic tribes. Clovis defeated the *Alemanni* (al-uh-MAN-ee) tribe and forced them back across the Rhine River into Germany. Clovis then attacked groups of Visigoths and drove them out of France, into Spain. In his next move, he overcame his rivals among the Franks. Clovis established himself as king of all the Franks and ruled until 511. Clovis was married to a Christian and decided to adopt his wife's religion. Following the king's example, all the Franks became Roman Catholics.

For 200 years after Clovis' death some member of the *Merovingian* (mer-uh-VIN-jee-un) family—Clovis' royal family—held the throne of the Franks.

Frankish rulers of the 500's and 600's were warrior kings. They brought under control the vast territory that includes modern-day France and parts of Germany and Spain. Because later Merovingian kings were weak, real power fell into the hands of royal officials. Eventually, one of these officials, Charles Martel (mahr-TELL), seized power for himself and passed it on to his descendants.

Charles Martel was the founder of a new royal line—the *Carolingians* (kar-uh-LIN-jee-unz). He was a successful military leader. He reunited the former Merovingian kingdom, but he never took the title of king. His son, Pepin (PEP-un), who ruled the Franks from 751 until 768, was first to assume the royal title. According to custom, Pepin left the throne to his two sons. One of them died within three years, and the surviving son became the most outstanding of all the Carolingian rulers.

He was Charles the Great, or **Charlemagne** (SHAHR-luh-mane), and ruled from 768 to 814.

Charlemagne   Charlemagne devoted more than thirty years to fighting sixty military campaigns. As a result, he doubled the size of the Frankish kingdom. At its height, his empire included all of modern-day France, Germany, lands to the east of Germany, parts of Spain, and much of Italy. (See the map below.) It included most of the land that was once ruled by the Roman Empire.

A New Roman Empire   Charlemagne helped to spread Christianity to all the territories under his control. He established a strong central government and ruled his vast empire from the city of Aachen (AHK-un) in Germany. In 800, when Charlemagne visited Rome, the pope (the head of the Catholic Church) declared that all the lands Charlemagne conquered and ruled were to be a new Roman Empire. Charlemagne was also declared emperor.

Charlemagne's empire did not last long after his death, however. Charlemagne's son, Louis the Pious (PIE-us), ruled from 814 until 840. He arranged for the empire to be divided among his three sons following his death. To one

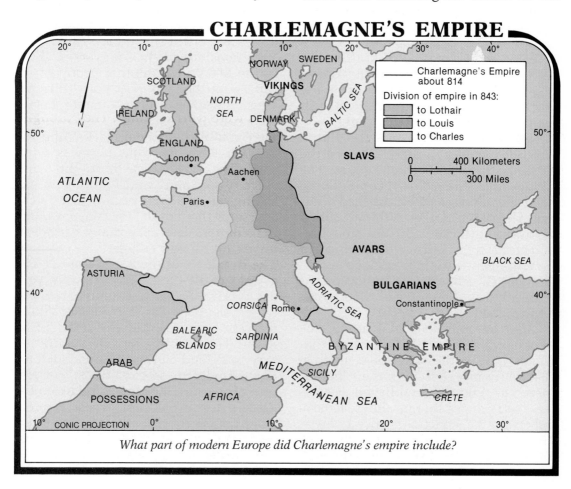

CHARLEMAGNE'S EMPIRE

What part of modern Europe did Charlemagne's empire include?

son, Louis, he gave the Germanic lands. To another, Charles, he gave France, and to the eldest son, Lothair (loe-THAIR), he gave an area between the two, together with much of Italy. (See the map on page 169.) Even though they were threatened by invasions from all sides, Louis, Charles, and Lothair refused to unite against their common enemies. As a result, the huge empire built up by their grandfather, Charlemagne, gradually collapsed.

The Invasions of the Vikings   The most serious threat to Europe came from Scandinavia and lands along the Baltic Sea. About 800, wave after wave of fierce, seagoing warriors from this region began raiding the coasts of Europe. These Scandinavian warriors were called *Vikings* (VIE-kings). The Vikings struck at western European towns and cities everywhere—from the North Sea to the Mediterranean—in fast boats called long ships.

Some Vikings crossed the Baltic Sea to Russia. There they followed the rivers southward in search of loot. The Vikings overthrew the people living along the rivers and established their own kingdoms. Other Vikings sailed westward, attacked Britain and Ireland, and then sailed to Iceland. In the tenth century, they founded settlements in Greenland. It is believed that as long ago as 1000 some of the Vikings even reached North America.

On the continent of Europe, the French probably suffered the most from Viking raids. In the early 900's, much of western France fell into their hands. There the Vikings established permanent settlements along the seacoasts and rivers. This part of France today is still called *Normandy* (NOR-mun-dee), which means "land of the Northmen." England, like France, suffered terribly from Viking raids. By the late 800's, much of eastern England had been conquered. The Vikings settled the lands and founded their own small kingdoms. They often warred with the native peoples of England.

The Invasions of the Muslims   The Vikings were not the only threat to Europe at this time. Beginning in 711, Muslim (MUZ-lum) invaders from North Africa crossed the Straight of Gibraltar (juh-BRAWL-tur). They quickly conquered most of the Iberian Peninsula. From their base in Spain, the Muslims threatened France. In the 800's, the Muslims moved from North Africa to Sicily and other Mediterranean islands. From there, they raided towns and cities of southern Italy.

The Invasions of the Magyars   Late in the 800's, still another group of invaders pushed into eastern Europe. These invaders were nomadic horsemen called the *Magyars* (MAG-yahrz). They established themselves along the Danube River in what today is Hungary. They raided northern Italy and parts of Germany and France that the Viking raids had not yet touched. In the course of their raids, the Magyars, like the Vikings, destroyed many European towns, cities, and villages.

The Break-Up of the Kingdoms   The attacks of all these invaders were very destructive. Paris, for example, was put under siege in 886 by 40,000 Viking warriors who sailed up the Seine (SEN) River. The Carolingian rulers found no way to defend Europe against such attacks. Under these conditions, the peoples of western Europe turned to local leaders for protection. These leaders were forced to take the law into their own hands. They constructed strong castles for defense against raids and tried to organize effective fighting forces. The castle became the focal point of rural European society. The horse became an important weapon of war because warriors on horseback were effective in fighting off Viking attacks.

Kings continued to rule, but they had little real authority. Western Europe slowly broke up into small, independent political divisions, each trying to defend itself. These divisions varied in size. Germany, for example, was divided into five sections, each the size of a small kingdom. Each section was ruled by a duke and was called a *duchy* (DUCH-ee). Other divisions were smaller. In Italy, for example, an independent political unit often was made up of no more than a walled city and the surrounding countryside.

SECTION REVIEW

1. Mapping: Using the map on page 165 and the information on page 164, name the geographical features of western Europe and explain how western Europe is distinguished from eastern Europe. Using the map on page 169, describe the extent of Charlemagne's empire and its division after his death.
2. In your own words, briefly define or identify: the Middle Ages, medieval, Visigoths, Franks, Merovingians, Charlemagne, Vikings, the Magyars, duchy.
3. Give two reasons why Charlemagne was an important figure in history.
4. What effect did the series of raids and invasions have on the people of western Europe during the 800's and 900's?
- What qualities do you think a ruler must have to be called "great"? Do you think a warlike ruler could be a great ruler? Why or why not?

THE FEUDAL SYSTEM

After the Germanic peoples conquered western Europe, Roman civilization almost disappeared. From about 500 until 1000, western Europe was plunged into a period that used to be called the **Dark Ages.** The name suggested that civilization and learning disappeared. It also was used to indicate that European life, in general, declined compared with what life had been under the Roman Empire.

The Dark Ages This period was a time of change for the Germanic peoples. They settled among the Romans, slowly gave up their nomadic way of life, and became farmers. However, this was also a time of almost constant warfare. Town life died out. Trade and travel decreased, and there was a breakdown in law and order. Under these conditions, learning also declined.

The Beginnings of Feudalism As you remember, there was a breakdown of centralized government because of invaders like the Vikings. The breakdown gave rise to a new political system. The Frankish rulers depended on the services of a great number of officials to fight their wars and govern their lands. These officials became known as nobles.

The Frankish kings often could not pay their officials in money. Taxes were collected in grain, animals, or service. Payment in land was a surer way to reward people for their services. So the kings furnished nobles with large estates of royal land from which to obtain a living. Each noble who received land was supposed to be the king's servant. He owed the king loyalty and service. For example, when called upon, he had to fight at the king's side and provide a band of armed knights. He was also ex-

Scenes of peasant life were a favorite subject of some early west European painters. This winter scene shows indoor and outdoor activities of peasant farmers. How does this painting compare with today's farm life?

Others, however, might be so small as to support only one knight (warrior) and his war horse.

Vassals Challenge Royal Power   Under the feudal system, vassals usually tried to accumulate wealth and increase their power. Only a strong king could keep his vassals under control. During the unsettled times that followed Charlemagne's death, royal vassals assumed all the political authority over their lands that formerly belonged to the king. Vassals eventually claimed the right to pass their lands on to their descendants. As a result, the king became a weak and unimportant figure to most people. The king's vassals were usually the most important people in a kingdom. The king's vassals, in turn, created vassals of their own, who served them just as they served the king.

The Peasants   During the Middle Ages, few people were nobles. Perhaps 90 percent of all the people in western Europe belonged to the peasant class. They farmed the lands held by feudal nobles. Some peasants rented the land they farmed. Most of the population, however, were serfs (SURFS). *Serfs* were usually not free to leave the land on which they had been born. They had to spend a lifetime working for the noble on whose lands they lived. In some cases, though, serfs were able to accumulate money and buy their freedom.

A Rural Society   After the fall of the Roman Empire, many towns and cities grew smaller. Some settlements were destroyed. Most of the early kings were never able to protect their own towns and cities or to keep roads and bridges in good repair. Bandits made travel unsafe. Few people were willing to venture far beyond the settlements in which they lived. In a lifetime, some people traveled no farther than the

pected to come to the king's court and give advice when requested, to help the king financially in special cases. This political system was called *feudalism*.

The nobles who received land from the ruler were called *vassals*. The land a vassal received was a fief (FEEF). A *fief* included the land and everything on it—even the peasants who farmed the land. Some fiefs were huge. Some of them were the size of a small kingdom.

boundary of the community in which they lived. As a result, trade declined and town life diminished. Small villages dotted the map of western Europe. Most people made their living from agriculture.

The Structure of a Manor Most peasant farmers and serfs lived in small villages on the estates of feudal nobles. These estates were called *manors*. A manor was self-sufficient because practically everything needed was either grown on the manor or made there. Most clothing, for example, was made from the wool of sheep raised on the manor. Weapons and tools were made in the blacksmith shop. And, of course, a manor raised its own food. The main crops were grains and vegetables. Grains such as wheat, barley, oats, and rye were common. Some of the chief vegetable crops were cabbage, peas, beans, turnips, and carrots. Potatoes were not known in feudal times. Fruits were available only when in season.

Part of every manor was set aside as pasture land. Cattle, sheep, and swine were raised. Pork was the most common meat consumed. Meats, as well as fish, were salted to preserve them. The plow was in widespread use, and oxen, not horses, were the beasts of burden. Like farmers in Asia, European peasants learned that the same crop could not be planted year after year without exhausting the soil. It was customary to let a field lie unplanted every third year to allow the soil to replenish itself.

A manor was governed by the feudal noble who owned the fief. He was lord of the manor. His home, the manor house, was often a castle. And it was usually built as a fortress to give maximum protection from raids. Usually it was surrounded by a water-filled ditch

known as a *moat*. Serfs and peasants who worked on the manor looked to the lord for protection. In case of danger, the castle was a place of refuge for these serfs and peasants.

Some of the land on each manor was set aside for the peasants' use from which they obtained a scanty living. The rest of the land belonged to the lord. The serfs were obligated to work on the land for a certain number of days each year. They were also required to perform other services the lord demanded. All peasants did not work in the fields. Some worked as millers, shoemakers, blacksmiths, or weavers.

There was no need for a school on a manor. Peasants passed their skills on

This painting shows the peasants working in the fields owned by the lord of the manor. Do you think the peasants had an easy time farming?

from generation to generation. The nobles were interested chiefly in the art of warfare, so there was little use for learning. All over Europe the number of people who could read and write had sharply declined since the fall of the Roman Empire. It was not unusual, therefore, to find high-ranking officials who were illiterate. Charlemagne himself was scarcely able to write.

The lord of a manor was expected to be skillful in the use of weapons. Most of his time was spent in fighting or preparing for war. In peacetime, the lord entered *jousting tournaments*, or contests between armored knights on horseback who fought with lances. These contests resembled mock battles and could be very dangerous.

The lady of a manor supervised the household routine and the kitchen. She watched over the servants. In her spare time, she might sew or play a musical instrument. When the lord, her husband, was away at war, the lady of the manor took his place. She had to manage the fief until his return.

Justice on a Manor   In general during feudal times, justice was often very harsh. Trials by battle or by ordeal were sometimes held. A duel was fought, and the outcome of the fight determined who was guilty and who was innocent. Guilt was also determined by the ordeal of holding a hot iron or plunging an arm into boiling water. If the wounds healed quickly, the person was judged innocent. If not, the person was found guilty. Justice on a manor was administered by the lord. He served as judge and settled disputes among his serfs and peasants.

The authority of a lord on the manor was unlimited. He had the right to tax. Many special taxes and "gifts" had to be presented to the lord of the manor at special times each year.

Peasants and serfs had to pay a variety of fees to their lord. For example, the lord provided a baking oven. No peasant family was permitted to have its own. As a result, the peasants had to have their baking done by the lord's baker. For this service, they had to pay a fee. Some lords collected fees from everyone using the manor's roads or bridges. Fees of this sort were deeply resented by those who paid them.

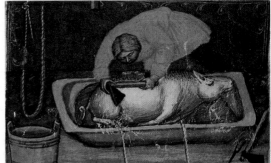

The serfs on a manor did a variety of chores such as threshing wheat, butchering a pig, and harvesting turnips. How have chores changed since the 1400's?

174

The Knights Sons of nobles spent many years in preparation to become knights. The training of a knight began at the age of seven. From seven to fourteen, the boy was a *page*— that is, a servant of the women of the house. Here he learned manners, basic reading and writing, and the behavior expected of a knight.

At the age of fourteen, he became a *squire* and was a servant of the men. In addition to the skills of war and hunting, he learned chess, poetry, and how to play the lute (a musical instrument used for courting). He cared for the knight's weapons, equipment, and horse. He accompanied his master wherever he went—even into battle. At the age of twenty-one, when his training as a squire was completed, a young man might become a *knight*, after demonstrating his skill at fighting with the weapons of that time, such as the lance and the sword. Admittance to knighthood was a solemn occasion. From that time on, the young knight was expected to abide by an unwritten code of conduct called *chivalry*. Chivalry stressed, among other things, politeness, courage, and respect for women and defeated enemies.

The Christian Church in Feudal Times
Not every young boy of noble birth became a knight. Sons of a feudal lord sometimes chose a career in the church. Even though a career in the church was open to anyone, *clergy*, or church leaders, from the noble class usually rose to higher positions in the church. Clergy often were very wealthy and powerful during the age of feudalism. The Roman Catholic Church was the only Christian church in western Europe, and it was a very important and influential institution within the community.

After the collapse of Charlemagne's empire, there was no political authority that tied together all the peoples of western Europe. Modern nations did not exist yet. The Roman Catholic Church was the only bond that held Europeans together. It was the common denominator of the Middle Ages. The loyalty people might have shown to a political leader often was given to the church instead.

The Organization of the Church The chief officials of the church were the *bishops*. Each bishop was responsible for all the Christians in a particular area. This area, known as a *diocese* (DIE-uh-sus), usually included a number of towns and villages. To care for each group of Christians within his area, a bishop appointed priests. Sometimes two or more areas were placed under the authority of a single bishop, known as an *archbishop* (ahrch-BISH-up).

The bishop of Rome was called the *pope*—a Greek word meaning father. The pope was considered the highest ranking of all bishops. He was, therefore, head of the church in western Europe. The pope gathered many advisers around him at Rome. Some of these were known as *cardinals*. When a pope died, it was the cardinals' responsibility to elect a successor. A vast and complex church organization grew up, with its center at Rome. In many ways, the organization of the church resembled the civil administrations of the Roman Empire and acted as a state with its own government. For example, the church collected a sort of tax. It established its own courts and had its own laws. And it dispatched ambassadors to all parts of Europe.

The church became powerful for several reasons. It accumulated great wealth, largely through gifts of land. In addition, the early Frankish kings cooperated with and helped spread the influence of the pope. Many Christians came to regard popes as more important than kings. Most people also depended upon the church because it continued to provide services that kings had been unable to do, such as caring for the poor and the sick.

Not all clergy were part of this vast and complex organization. Some followed a strictly disciplined life devoted to prayer, fasting, and hard work, and lived together in communities called *monasteries.*

The Role of Monasteries   A monastery, like a medieval manor, was self-sufficient. Members of the monastery were called *monks.* They followed a daily routine of prayer, study, and hard work. They raised food and made things they needed. The organization of a monastery included a leader called an *abbot.* The abbot governed the monastery and was equal in rank to a bishop. Members of a monastery were compelled to accept that abbot's decision as if he were lord of a medieval manor. As time went by, hundreds of monasteries were founded. Most observed their own special rules. Women also took up a monastic life. Members of their communities were called *nuns.* They lived in *convents,* governed by *abbesses.*

Accomplishments of the Church in Medieval Times   One of the church's greatest accomplishments was the preservation of learning inherited from Greek and Roman civilization. Libraries often were set up in monasteries or convents. There books were copied by hand. At that time, Europeans had not yet developed the printing press.

In the Middle Ages, the church performed many services that today would be performed by governments. For example, the poor looked to the church for assistance. The sick were cared for in hospitals operated by nuns. Since there were no hotels, travelers were given lodging in monasteries. The first schools were church schools. Some bishops and other clergy entered government, since there was no one else capable of ruling. Other bishops were military leaders or mayors of towns. They even served as diplomats, advisers to kings.

After about 1000, the power of kings slowly began to increase, and conflicts often broke out between the kings and the church. In these struggles the chief power of the pope was *excommunication* (eks-kuh-myoo-nun-KAY-shun), or the power to exclude a person from receiving communion. Excommunication was a dreaded punishment because in the Middle Ages Christians believed that salvation outside the church was impossible. The pope also had the power to declare an interdict (INT-ur-dikt). An *interdict* was a papal order closing the churches of a particular country. This too was a dreaded punishment.

SECTION REVIEW

1. Why did the kings of western Europe divide their land?
2. In your own words, define or identify: manor, fief, clergy, pope, monks, excommunication, interdict.
3. What purposes did the feudal system serve during the Middle Ages?
4. Describe how life was different for the lord and the serfs on a feudal manor.
5. Describe the training a young boy received before he became a knight.

⟩ You learned that in the Middle Ages, the church performed many services that government performs today. Do religious organizations provide any social services today?

THE CRUSADES

The former Roman province of Palestine (PAL-uh-stine), where Jesus had lived, was sacred to Christians during the Middle Ages. Christians called Palestine the *Holy Land.* Countless Christians, rich and poor, undertook the long and dangerous trip from western Europe to visit the places inhabited by Jesus during his lifetime. Such a journey was called a *pilgrimage* (PIL-gruh-mij) and the travelers were called *pilgrims.*

In the seventh century, the Holy Land fell into the hands of the Muslims. In general, Muslim rulers allowed Christian pilgrims to come and go as they wished. However, conditions changed after 1000, when the Holy Land was conquered by the *Seljuk* (SEL-jook) *Turks.* They settled in the region that is present-day Turkey and rapidly created a huge empire, which included the Holy Land. (You will learn more about the Seljuk Turks in the next unit.) Pilgrims returning to western Europe told stories of Christians who had been killed or tortured by the Turks. They also claimed that Christian churches were being destroyed or turned into Muslim places of worship. These stories spread widely in western Europe.

Meanwhile, the Seljuk Turks defeated the armies of the Roman empire in the East, which by this time was known as the **Byzantine** (BIZ-'n-teen) **Empire.** The Turks took much territory and threatened to take Constantinople, the capital city of the Byzantine Empire. In the face of this danger, the emperor appealed to the pope for help. In 1095, partly because of this appeal, Pope Urban (UR-bun) II called for a Holy War against the Muslims. The object of the war would be to capture the

Uniforms worn by the Crusader knights in battle included protection such as helmets, greaves (leg guards), and a protective suit made of chain mail. How does this uniform compare with uniforms worn by soldiers' today?

Holy Land and rescue the Byzantine Empire.

There was a quick response to the Pope's call for a huge Christian army. Thousands volunteered and they showed their dedication to the cause by sewing a cross on their garments. Thereafter, a volunteer was called a *Crusader* (kroo-SAY-dur). Military expeditions to the Holy Land were called **Crusades.** The terms crusade and crusader probably came from the word meaning cross. Beginning with the Crusade launched by Pope Urban II, a series of expeditions against the Muslims continued for 200 years. (See the map on page 179.)

Many volunteers joined the Crusades for deeply religious motives. Some believed, for example, that dying in battle for a holy cause would earn forgiveness of their sins. Other Crusaders, however, were seeking adventure. Some young knights longed to win glory on the battlefield. Serfs and peasants joined the Crusades to escape their hard work in the fields. They dreamed of gaining a fortune in faraway countries. High-ranking nobles and kings saw the Crusades as an opportunity to carve out new kingdoms for themselves from Muslim territories.

The First Crusade The First Crusade set out from Constantinople in 1097. The Crusaders marched overland into Muslim territories. The Muslims were unable to stop the Crusaders' advance. The city of Jerusalem (juh-ROO-suh-lum) fell to the Christians in 1099 after a terrible siege. A Crusader kingdom was set up in the Holy Land and named the Kingdom of Jerusalem. A French duke became its first king. The other chief nobles took lands for themselves, and bands of knights were organized to defend the new kingdom against the Muslims.

Meanwhile, Italian merchants transported Crusaders by ship between Europe and the Holy Land for profit. With this additional money, merchants purchased luxury goods in the Middle East and took them back to Europe. In this way, Europeans were introduced to many products from the Middle East.

The Second Crusade In the twelfth century, Muslim power was revived. Lands claimed by the Christian Kingdom of Jerusalem were captured by the Muslims. In Europe, there was fear that all the Holy Land might be lost to the Muslims again. As a result, a Second Crusade was launched in 1147. However, the Crusade was a failure because the Crusaders returned to Europe in 1149 without regaining the territories they lost to the Muslims.

The Third Crusade Later in the 1100's, a great Muslim general, Saladin (SAL-ud-'n), restored Muslim control over much of the Holy Land. In 1187, he captured the city of Jerusalem. In response to this, a Third Crusade was organized. German, French, and English Crusaders reached the Holy Land by 1191. However, when their leader died, the Germans gave up the Crusade and returned home. Then the French king, Philip II, quarreled with the English king, and the French went home. This left King Richard I (nicknamed "the Lion-Hearted") alone. His armies were able to capture the port city of Acre (AHK-ur) from the Muslims. But Jerusalem held out against the Crusaders, and King Richard and his troops returned home without accomplishing their goal of reclaiming the Holy Land.

The Fourth Crusade In 1202, a Fourth Crusade was launched. It was a failure, however. The Crusaders assembled in the Italian port of Venice (VEN-us), a major Italian trading city. Instead of sailing to the Holy Land, the Crusaders attacked a town on the coast of the Adriatic Sea. This Adriatic town had been part of Venice's empire, but it had revolted. News then arrived of a revolution in Constantinople. The Crusaders were asked to help put in power one of the rivals for the throne of the Byzantine Empire. The Crusaders reached Constantinople in 1203. They looted the city and seized it for themselves. In 1204, they established the Latin Kingdom of Constantinople which survived until 1261.

Crusades Continue The pope and other Christian leaders denounced the Fourth Crusade and called for another. In 1215, the king of Hungary organized a Crusade. The Crusaders invaded Egypt. However, the Crusader armies were defeated, and the Crusade ended in failure.

Later in the 1200's, another Crusade was undertaken. A German ruler,

Frederick II, was the leader of this army. Frederick did not lead his army against the Muslims. Instead, he negotiated a settlement with the Muslims, and as a result he was permitted to crown himself king of Jerusalem. In return for this, Frederick permitted the Muslims freedom of religion in his new kingdom. A Christian-Muslim truce was arranged, but it lasted less than twenty years. In 1244, the Muslims regained control of Jerusalem.

There were later Crusades against the Muslims in Egypt and Syria, areas surrounding the Holy Land. But they were not successful. The last Christian possession in the Holy Land was the city of Acre. It fell to the Muslims in 1291. After that, the Holy Land remained in Muslim hands until the twentieth century.

The Children's Crusade Probably the most famous crusade was the "Children's Crusade." In the early 1200's, a French peasant boy named Stephen called for a Children's Crusade. Many listeners came to share his opinion that perhaps children might be able to accomplish what adults had been unable to do. Scholars believe as many as 30,000

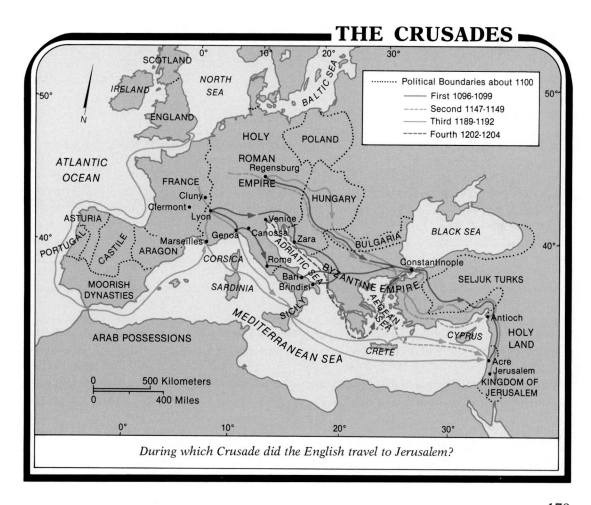

THE CRUSADES

During which Crusade did the English travel to Jerusalem?

French boys and girls joined Stephen's Crusade. A similar Crusade began among the Germans. About 20,000 children joined it. The French children marched to the port of Marseilles (mahr-SAY) in southern France. They hoped to find ships to carry them to the Holy Land. Unfortunately, most of them were carried away by ship captains, who sold them into slavery in Africa and elsewhere. The German Crusaders also met a terrible fate. Many died on the long march across the Alps from Germany into Italy. Other children boarded ships for the Holy Land and were never again heard from.

The Effect of the Crusades   The Crusades contributed to the growth of the pope's power. The age of the Crusades was probably the high point of the church's influence in western Europe. The Crusades also helped the kings of Europe in their struggle for power with the feudal nobles. Many nobles died or lost their fortunes in the Crusades. This weakened the power of the nobility and strengthened the power of the kings in the years following the Crusades.

The Crusades increased the availability in western Europe of luxury items from the East, such as spices and sugar. The great demand for these luxuries encouraged trade with the Muslim world. Due to the role that Italian merchants played in transporting Crusaders to the Holy Land, the cities of Italy particularly benefited because they became the chief ports for ships engaged in east-west trade. The Crusades also introduced new ideas from Muslim lands and other places visited by Crusaders. For example, during the Crusades, western Europeans learned about Arab philosophy, medicine, and mathematics and about Byzantine art and architecture.

1. Mapping: Using the map on page 179, describe the route of the four major Crusades.
2. In your own words, identify or define: Byzantine Empire, pilgrimage, Palestine, Children's Crusade.
3. What role did the Italian merchant ships play during the Crusades? Why were they important?
4. Why did the Crusaders fight the Muslims in the Holy Land? Did everyone who joined the Crusades do so for religious reasons?
▷ What meaning or meanings does the word *crusade* have today? Can you see any similarities between today's definitions of the word and the Crusades you read about in this section?

LIFE DURING THE MIDDLE AGES

Towns in the Middle Ages   Early in the Dark Ages, town life had almost died out. But by about 900, many old towns and cities had come back into existence. Meanwhile, many new towns were founded. Frequently they grew up around an easily defended site such as a castle, or a religious center such as a cathedral or church. Merchants were often the founders of new towns. They needed places to store the goods they sold, so they built warehouses. Sometimes villages sprang up around the warehouses and later grew into towns.

Despite wars and plagues that killed countless numbers of people, the population of western Europe steadily increased between 500 and 1000 A.D. This meant the work force was larger than was needed to work the land. Some peasants moved to towns where their skills in metalworking, stonecut-

This is a famous painting by Pieter Brueghel depicting city life in the Middle Ages. How does Brueghel's style differ from those of earlier artists?

ting, or weaving were in demand. Serfs often ran away from manors and found new kinds of jobs in the cities. In this way, towns steadily grew. The growth of towns increased trade because city dwellers had to manufacture goods to sell to the countryside in exchange for agricultural products. Towns traded their products with one another, and in time trade among different countries was revived.

Art During the Middle Ages The church usually was the most beautiful and impressive structure in every town. It also was the center of town life and a meeting place. The doors of the church were used as public bulletin boards where notices of all sorts were posted. Larger towns often boasted a cathedral.

Many of these medieval cathedrals are still standing today.

Until about 1100, most of the churches in western Europe were imitations of Roman structures, with massive walls and rounded arches. This style of architecture was called *Romanesque* (roe-muh-NESK). Around 1200–1300, a new style of architecture was introduced. It was called the *Gothic* (GAHTH-ik) style of architecture and was characterized by pointed arches and high steep roofs.

Church building and religious life encouraged the development of other art forms during the Middle Ages. Tapestry weaving for wall hangings, the production of stained glass for church windows, wood carving, sculpture, and painting

181

The church of La Madeleine at Vézelay, France, (left) is built in the Romanesque style. Romanesque architecture uses rounded arches and is built in the shape of a cross. The church of Sainte-Chapelle in Paris, France, (right) is in the Gothic style. The Gothic style tended to emphasize height by using pointed arches and tall slender columns. The Gothic style developed after the Romanesque style in northern Europe. How do these styles differ from today's styles in architecture? What information about your society can be found in the styles of architecture in your community?

for church decoration, and the composing of music to be sung during church services all flourished during this period. In addition, beautifully illustrated books were produced in the monasteries. Some of them survive and can be seen in museums today.

Learning During the Middle Ages As you read in Unit 3, the Greek philosophers were scholars who spent a lot of time searching for answers to questions such as "Why do we behave the way we do?" The philosophers in the Middle Ages asked some of the same questions, but they were influenced by Christianity. Often medieval philosophers were monks or priests who combined their knowledge of religion with their interest in philosophy. They had high regard for Greek and Roman learning. Their task was to make the wisdom of the earlier non-Christian thinkers acceptable to Christian believers of their own times. Thanks to medieval philosophers such as *Thomas Aquinas* (uh-KWIE-nus) and *Anselm* (AN-selm), much of the learning of the ancient world was preserved for modern times.

The feudal lords and serfs had little opportunity for much education in their daily lives. As a result, learning was left in the hands of the Roman Catholic Church. The Church recognized the need for educated clergy who could read and write and study the holy writings. Schools were established to prepare future clergy. The earliest schools were opened in monasteries. Then, from about 1000 to 1100, cathedral schools developed. Because they were usually located in towns or cities, they became the most important centers of learning. As years passed, the subjects taught in cathedral schools needed to be expanded. This led to the founding of the first universities in the 1200's.

During the Middle Ages, most people used two languages. One was a spoken, or everyday language, and the other was the written language of education, Latin. In ancient Rome, Latin was usually the language spoken. After the Germanic conquest of the empire, spoken Latin gradually disappeared. Written Latin, however, continued to be used everywhere throughout western Europe. Meanwhile, the language of the Germans blended with that of the Romans. Out of this mixture, new languages were born. Spoken languages continued to change, and it was not until 1200–1300 that ordinary, spoken languages developed as written languages. Even after that, Latin continued in widespread use, especially in fields such as science, medicine, and law. Latin is still widely used in the technical vocabulary of these professions today.

Medieval Law Important developments took place in law during the Middle Ages. Modern judicial (jooh-DISH-ul) systems of courts began. A form of modern jury was developed in the 1200's. King Henry II of England, who ruled from 1154 to 1189, made a major contribution to the jury system. It was his custom to send judges on regular travel routes throughout his kingdom. The judges went from place to place, called together a group of twelve people with good reputations, and had them speak out against persons suspected of crimes. This group later was called a *grand jury*.

If the grand jury's evidence convinced the king's judge that crimes had been committed, he held court and conducted a trial. Other reliable citizens were called to attend the proceedings. This group of citizens was called the *petit* (PET-ee) *jury*.

It discussed questions of innocence or guilt and assisted the judge in reaching a decision. The grand jury and the petit jury are important parts of the judicial systems today. In some parts of Europe, the Middle Ages also gave rise to political institutions that developed into lawmaking bodies called *legislatures*.

Medieval Government Following the example of the Frankish kings, rulers began to seek the advice of nobles. Out of this practice emerged the *king's council*, which was made up of a large group of nobles and clergy. The council met regularly and offered the king its opinion on matters of state. Therefore, the king's council shared in the governing of the kingdom.

Councils were formed in most of western Europe. As time went by, groups other than nobles and clergy demanded a voice on the council. So kings enlarged their councils. In England, for example, King Edward I, who ruled from 1272 to 1307, called together a large assembly that included representatives of the nobles, high-ranking clergy, townspeople, and rural landowners. This assembly was called **Parliament** (PAHR-luh-ment). Like the king's council, Parliament discussed affairs of state, approved new taxes, and generally assisted in the business of governing. But the nobles and high-ranking clergy preferred to meet apart from the townspeople and rural landowners, who were considered to be commoners. They formed a body known as the *House of Lords*. The commoners, the other members of Parliament, met together as the *House of Commons*. From that time on, the English Parliament has been divided into two houses or branches.

In France, the French king Philip IV ordered the clergy, nobles, and commoners to meet separately from the beginning. Each of the three groups or assemblies was called an *estate*. The First Estate represented the clergy. The Second Estate represented the nobles. All the rest of the people were represented in the Third Estate. Although they did not meet jointly, the three collectively were called the *Estates General*.

Representative assemblies such as England's Parliament or the Estates General in France sprang up in other countries during the Middle Ages. The earliest assembly in Scandinavia developed in Iceland. It first met in 930. Denmark's assembly was organized in 1282 and Sweden's in 1435. In Spain, the legislature was called the *Cortes* (KORE-tez). The Cortes' strength declined, however, and by the 1400's it possessed no real power at all. Although other parts of Europe saw the beginning of legislative institutions, the English and French models were the most successful.

SECTION REVIEW

1. Where were many of the new towns founded in the Middle Ages?
2. In your own words, identify or define: Gothic and Romanesque architecture, Thomas Aquinas, grand jury, petit jury, Parliament, Estates General.
3. How did the church contribute to learning in the Middle Ages?
4. Name and describe the type of legislatures that developed during the Middle Ages.
▷ Choose six nouns and look up their derivation in a dictionary. From what languages were they derived? What does this tell you about the English language?

chapter 9

Political Change in Western Europe

MONARCHY IN ENGLAND

From about 1095, the time of the Crusades, until about 1500, the kings in Europe gradually gained more and more power. The kings struggled with the nobles and clergy, who did not want to give up any of their wealth or privileges. By 1500, however, kings in England, France, and Spain had won the struggle. They created national states, each of which was under the control of a strong central authority. The strength of the nobles had been reduced, and the church lost much of its power and influence. England was one of the first kingdoms to develop a strong monarchy (MAHN-ur-kee). A **monarchy** is a country that is ruled by a *monarch* (MAHN-urk), or a king or queen.

Early English Rulers As you read in Chapter 8, England was invaded by Germanic tribes known as the Angles and the Saxons after the fall of the Roman Empire. These tribal people became Christians and set up their own kingdoms in England. The native peoples of England, the *Celts* (KELTS), were forced to move to Scotland, Ireland, and Wales.

England did not remain in Germanic hands for long, however. As you remember, during the 800's, Vikings also began to raid the Anglo-Saxon kingdoms. The most famous of the Anglo-Saxon kings, Alfred the Great, successfully protected his kingdom from the Vikings. In spite of Alfred's efforts, the Viking invaders settled much of eastern England. Finally, the Anglo-Saxons and the Vikings learned to live peacefully side by side.

In 1066, new invaders conquered all of England. This time the invaders were the Normans. The *Normans* were the descendants of the Vikings who had raided and settled the coastal regions of France. Their ruler, known as *William the Conqueror*, defeated the Anglo-Saxon king, Harold, at the Battle of Hastings. William then established his own ruling family. William the Conqueror laid the foundations of centralized government in England by making each feudal lord swear allegiance directly to him. In this way, all the noblemen became vassals of the king. William then distributed lands to Anglo-Saxon nobles as well as to his Norman supporters. Thus French-speaking Normans and Anglo-Saxon lords made up the ruling class of new nobles. As a result of this mixture, the modern English language became a blend of the Norman language and the language spoken by common people in England when the Normans arrived.

All the king's vassals were expected to assemble at court to offer the king advice. The *Great Council* of nobles was a very large group, however. William preferred to meet with a small group representing the nobles. This smaller body usually included the more powerful vassals, known as *barons*.

King William's son, *Henry I*, who ruled from 1100 to 1135, appointed a small group of advisers. They were personally loyal to him, and he depended upon them rather than upon the nobles to govern his kingdom. This group of advisers later came to be known as the *Privy Council*.

Throughout the Middle Ages, the nobles of England, led by the great barons, would seek to increase their own power and to reduce royal authority.

King *Henry II* reigned from 1154 until 1189. Henry II married Eleanor of Aquitaine (AK-wuh-tane) in 1152. Because of Eleanor's family holdings, she inherited vast lands in France and could call upon her French vassals there for an army. Henry II too inherited lands in France. This French military strength helped Henry II take the throne and reduce the power of the great nobles in England.

Henry II is remembered most for his reform of the judicial system in England. As you know, Henry II was responsible for our modern jury system. He was also among the first to establish a uniform code of laws for England. In trying to do this, however, he quarreled with church leaders.

At this time, the Archbishop of Canterbury (KANT-ur-ber-ee) was Thomas Becket. Becket had earlier served Henry II as an adviser. When Becket became archbishop, the king believed his friend would continue to support royal policies. However, Becket believed Henry's new law code took away the rights of the Roman Catholic Church, and he refused

to support Henry. The king spoke out in anger against the archbishop. A group of knights believed this meant the king wanted Becket killed. They therefore invaded a church where the archbishop was conducting services and murdered him. England was shocked. To retain his supporters, King Henry revised his law code. He also made public his regret for what his knights had done in his name.

From Henry II on, the kings and queens of medieval England looked upon the church and the barons as rivals for their royal power. Following Henry's death in 1189, his son, King *Richard the Lion-Hearted*, reigned. During most of his rule, Richard was not in England. He led an army in the Third Crusade. (See page 178.) While returning home, Richard was captured and held prisoner by the Germans until a huge ransom was paid. After that, he spent most of his time fighting wars on the continent. During his entire reign, Richard visited England only twice. However, the officials Henry had trained kept the government strong during the absences of Henry's son.

When Richard's brother, *King John*, came to the throne, he found the royal treasury almost empty. John could find no means to raise the armies he needed to protect his lands in France.

The Magna Carta John was an unpopular king who made many enemies. In 1215, a group of barons forced him to meet them at Runnymede (RUN-ee-meed). At this meeting, the king signed a document known as the **Magna Carta,** or Great Charter. The document was a list of things the king was forbidden to do. It was a statement of the rights claimed by the nobles and common people. For example, it stated that no unusual taxes might be collected without the consent of the Great Council.

This Norman castle shows from the top down, the dormitory, Great Hall, and guardroom.

It also declared that the king's subjects were entitled to the protection of the laws and a trial when accused of wrongdoing.

The Magna Carta has always been respected by the English people. It was important because it limited royal powers. King John promised to uphold the charter and agreed that if he failed to keep his promise, the nobles were justified in making war against him.

Following John's death, his son *Henry III* ruled from 1216 to 1272. The nobles believed King Henry was bound to keep the promises made by his father in the Magna Carta. Henry, however, challenged the barons. As a result, a baron named Simon de Montfort (MUNT-furt) organized an opposition to the king, and civil war broke out. Simon de Montfort summoned an assembly in order to discuss means for keeping the king under control. The assembly included representatives of the nobles, clergy, and common people.

Simon de Montfort's assembly may have influenced King *Edward I*, who ruled from 1272 to 1307. You have already learned that Edward summoned England's first Parliament. It was called the *Model Parliament.*

Since the reign of Edward I, Parliament has been a permanent institution in England. It was summoned on a regular basis. It continued to defend its right to share responsibility with the king or queen in governing the country.

War of the Roses   Later monarchs of the Middle Ages were weak rulers. *Edward II*, who reigned from 1307 to 1327, was overthrown by a revolt headed by his own queen. *Edward III*, who ruled from 1327 to 1377, was in constant need of money to fight a war in France.

Richard II, who reigned from 1377 to 1399, tried to rule without Parliament. The barons rose against him and placed *Henry IV* on the throne. King Henry IV, who ruled from 1399 to 1413, allowed Parliament to exercise all its powers. The House of Commons told the king how taxes were to be spent and even kept track of Henry's expenditures. His son, *Henry V*, reigned from 1413 to 1422 and faced opposition from a family named York, which claimed to have a better right to the throne than the Lancaster family of Henry V.

Henry V's son, *Henry VI*, reigned from 1422 to 1461 but was only an infant when he came to the throne. Powerful nobles began to take sides between the two families that claimed the throne, and a great civil war broke out. This war was called the *War of the Roses* because the emblem of the York family was a white rose and that of the Lancaster family a red rose. During the War of the Roses, 1455–1485, England had four kings.

The Tudor Monarchs   The War of the Roses ended at the battle of Bosworth Field in 1485 with a military victory for Henry Tudor. He was married to a member of the York family, but he based his claim to the English throne only on his military victory. It is said that at the battle of Bosworth Field Henry Tudor discovered the crown of the slain king on the ground. He placed it on his own head, and claimed the throne for himself. Henry ruled as *Henry VII* from 1485 to 1509. His family, the *Tudors*, gave England several of its strongest and most popular monarchs.

The Tudor family ruled England from 1485 until 1603. By governing wisely, Henry VII gathered together

IMPORTANT ENGLISH RULERS BEFORE 1600

Ruler	Dates of Rule	Important Aspects of Reign
William the Conqueror	1066–1087	Invaded England, defeated the Anglo-Saxons at the battle of Hastings, and established himself as king of all England.
Henry II	1154–1189	Established a court system using juries; struggled to reduce the authority of the church in England.
Richard the Lion-Hearted	1189–1199	Famous as a Crusader and a warrior knight.
John	1199–1216	Forced by feudal nobles to sign the Magna Carta in 1215.
Edward I	1272–1307	In 1295, summoned the first real law-making body, called Parliament.
Henry V	1413–1422	Won great victories in the war against France and established England as a first-rate power.
Henry VI	1422–1461	A civil war broke out during his reign between two families, each of which claimed the English throne. The war lasted from 1455 to 1485 and was known as the War of the Roses, because each family used a rose as a symbol.
Henry VII	1485–1509	Ended the War of the Roses by defeating his rivals in battle and established his own family, the Tudors, as a new dynasty. Also successfully established a strong central government.
Henry VIII	1507–1545	Broke England's ties with the pope and placed the church under royal authority with the king as head of the church.
Elizabeth I	1558–1603	During her reign, she encouraged exploration of the New World, destroyed the Spanish Armada, and promoted economic prosperity.

vast wealth, which he passed on to his son. During his reign, there were several plots against him by rivals who thought they had better claims to the throne. But King Henry VII suppressed them. He arranged marriages for his children with the royal families of Spain, Scotland, and France. By the time of Henry VII's death, the Tudor family was firmly established. And England was becoming one of Europe's leading nations.

This painting by Hans Holbein shows King Henry VIII as a powerful ruler. What are state portraits like today?

Henry VIII reigned from 1509 to 1547 and was one of the most powerful kings in England's history. He won a struggle with the Roman Catholic Church and broke England's ties with the pope. The church in England was then placed under royal authority, with the king as head of the church. King Henry VIII took much of the church's wealth, tore down many of its monasteries and convents, and divided lands owned by the church among his own political supporters. But in everything he did, Henry VIII always obtained the approval of Parliament.

The other Tudor monarchs were *Edward VI* and *Mary*. Edward's reign, from 1547 to 1553, was brief. He ascended the throne while a child and ruled with the assistance of certain nobles. Upon his death, his elder half-sister Mary, became queen. Her reign, from 1553 to 1558, was troubled.

The most able ruler among Henry VIII's children was his daughter **Elizabeth I.** Elizabeth I ruled from 1558 until 1603. Like her father, she governed with the cooperation of Parliament. Elizabeth permitted only the Anglican Church to exist in her kingdom and expected all her subjects to belong to that church.

The Elizabethan Age   The reign of Queen Elizabeth was a long and prosperous one. During the years she was on the throne, she encouraged voyages to the New World and the founding of colonies in what is now the eastern United States. The queen became a symbol of unity to her people. During her rule, the English took pride in their country, and the arts flourished. **William Shakespeare,** one of the greatest playwrights, lived and worked during this period, which is called the Elizabethan Age, after Queen Elizabeth.

Although England enjoyed peace during much of Elizabeth's rule, rivalry with Spain over the riches of the New World and English raids on Spanish ships finally brought England to war with Spain during the 1580's. A great invasion fleet, called the **Spanish Armada** (ahr-MAHD-uh), was sent to conquer England. However, the English fleet, with the help of a huge storm, destroyed the Armada. This great victory established England as a major sea power until modern times.

SECTION REVIEW

1. Mapping: Using the map on page 165, describe the location of England and the British islands in relation to the rest of western Europe.
2. In your own words, identify or define: monarchy, William the Conqueror, Henry II, War of the Roses, Elizabethan Age, Shakespeare, Spanish Armada.
3. Name the Tudor monarchs and describe their main contributions to England.
4. What was the significance of the Magna Carta?
 ◗ Wealth was important to the English kings if they were to have authority. Do you think wealth is important today in the United States in order to have political power? Explain.

MONARCHY IN FRANCE

Royal Authority in France   The kings in France faced greater difficulties in building royal power than did the English kings. In 987 the last Carolingian ruler died. France was split into numerous regions. Each region was ruled by a powerful feudal noble. These nobles chose a new royal family to replace the Carolingians. This new royal family was the *Capet* (KAY-put) family. It was headed by Hugh Capet, and it ruled from 987 until 1328.

The new kings of France were not among the great landowning nobles of the country. They were weak and seldom held more land or power than the nobles who were their vassals. William the Conqueror, for example, continued to be a vassal of the French king even after he had conquered England and made himself its king. One of William's descendants, Henry II of England, also was a vassal of the French king. In addition, Henry owned more than half of France as his fief. Under these circumstances, it was difficult for the French kings to have any authority over the great nobles. Before long, the early Capetian (kuh-PEA-shun) kings had lost their possessions to vassals with more power. All that was left to the kings was the area around the city of Paris. The early Capetians were figureheads, or kings in name only. The real power behind their thrones often were court officials, who grew so powerful that their positions became hereditary. The only allies the kings could find were clergy, because leaders of the Roman Catholic Church in France favored a strong, central government. They sided with the kings against the nobles, and offered what help they could.

From the 1100's onward, later Capetian kings regained control over their officials, reestablished law and order in their own territories, and tried to build royal authority in France. *Louis VI* (nicknamed the Fat) ruled from 1108 until 1137. He was the first Capetian fully to control his own lands. Louis tried to expand his power by bringing some of his vassals under control.

His son, *Louis VII*, ruled from 1137 to 1180. Louis VII joined the Second Crusade. This did nothing to build royal power. The Crusade was unsuccessful. Louis VII returned home defeated and humiliated. He married Eleanor of Aquitaine, who had inherited lands in France far greater than those held by the king. But in 1152 he divorced Eleanor. She then married Henry, the Duke of Normandy, who later became King Henry II of England. This divorce cost Louis VII control of the lands belonging to Eleanor. Louis' successors looked for ways to recover Eleanor's territories from the English.

Philip II reigned from 1180 to 1223. He was one of France's greatest medieval kings. Philip was a practical and hard-working ruler. He made an alliance with Henry II of England and went to war against vassals in France. In 1189, Henry II died. Not long after, Philip joined the new English king, Richard the Lion-Hearted, in the Third Crusade. When they reached the Holy Land, the two monarchs quarreled. Philip returned home to France. When Richard was taken prisoner on his return to England, Philip plotted against Richard. Richard never forgave Philip for this, and after his release, Richard tried to make war against Philip in France. However, he failed to defeat the French king.

The French Monarchy Gains Territory
When King John came to the English throne, Philip II took away the land in France that John had inherited. Few English nobles wanted to help John retake his lands in France. As a result, King Philip II was able to regain almost all the lands lost to the French when Eleanor of Aquitaine married the English king. Philip II attained lands in southern France by permitting his vassals in northern France to fight against

nobles in the south who defied him. Philip also fought enemy nobles in the north. In 1214, he acquired the territory of Flanders as a result of a great military victory. Thus Philip II became the first Capetian monarch to extend royal control over most of France.

By the reign of *Louis IX*, which lasted from 1226 to 1270, royal power had grown even more. Louis asserted his right to administer justice over all of France. Nobles who had acted as judges in the past were replaced with royal officials. The king took control of the towns and cities of France. He claimed the right to appoint local officials such as mayors.

French Government During the Middle Ages   Unlike English kings, the rulers of France did not have the authority to tax. However, *Philip IV*, who ruled from 1285 to 1314, set out to find new sources of income. He needed money to hire troops that could keep the French nobles under control. King Philip IV found various means to collect taxes from his subjects. He also succeeded in taxing the clergy of France. Under Philip IV, a sort of supreme court developed in the capital. It was known as the *Parlement of Paris*.

In 1302, Philip IV summoned an assembly that represented all the classes of his kingdom. The assembly was known as the *Estates General* (See Unit 8). The Estates General eventually developed into a legislature.

Following the death of Philip IV, the feudal lords tried to regain political power from Philip's three sons, who ruled from 1314 to 1328. The last to rule was *Charles IV*, who reigned from 1322 to 1328. Charles had no sons. Since it was French custom that a woman could not inherit the throne, Charles did not choose his sister but

In The Hundred Years' War, the French (on the left) are shown fighting with cross-bows while the English (on the right) use longbows. How do their fighting techniques compare with those used today?

chose a male cousin as his successor. This successor, Philip VI, founded a new royal family. This new royal family was the *Valois* (val-WAH) family.

The Hundred Years' War The English would not recognize *Philip VI* as the French king. Edward III, king of England, was a son of Isabella, sister of the dead French king, Charles IV. Edward III declared the French throne should have passed to his mother, and from her to him. He claimed the throne and in 1338 the English launched a war against France. This long conflict, called the *Hundred Years' War*, continued off and on from 1338 to 1453—for more than a century. Most of the fighting took place on French soil, and the French people suffered terribly.

Under the Valois king, *Charles V*, who reigned from 1364 to 1380, the English were almost driven out of France.

IMPORTANT FRENCH RULERS BEFORE 1500

Ruler	Dates of Rule	Major Events of Reign
Hugh Capet	987–996	Elected king by the great nobles. Since the city of Paris was the center of his lands, Paris became the New French capital.
Louis VII	1137–1180	When Louis divorced his queen, Eleanor, she married one of Louis's vassals who later became King Henry II of England. Henry II claimed the lands in France Eleanor had inherited. This began a rivalry between the English and French rulers.
Philip II	1180–1223	Went on Crusades with King Richard the Lion-Hearted of England. Took English lands in France away from England's King John. Increased his own power and territory as France's king.
Louis IX	1226–1270	Established a system of royal courts for France.
Philip IV	1285–1314	Was a member of the new royal Valois family. Established the custom of summoning a lawmaking body called the Estates General to assist the king.
Philip VI	1328–1350	Was a nephew of King Philip IV. The English king, Edward III, was a grandson of Philip IV. Both claimed they should be king of France. This quarrel led to the beginning of the Hundred Years' War in the year 1338.
Charles VII	1422–1461	Joan of Arc led his armies to victory against the English. The Hundred Years' War ended in 1453, with France retaking almost all the territories once held by the English.
Louis XI	1461–1483	Maintained a standing army and relied for support upon wealthy businessmen and townspeople. Was successful in his struggle with the nobles.
Charles VIII	1483–1498	Made France a great power in Europe. Invaded Italy.

However, *Charles VI*, who ruled from 1380 to 1422, became ill and was unable to govern. During his reign the war turned against the French.

The dukes of Burgundy (BUR-gun-dee)—powerful French nobles—deserted their king and joined the English. Burgundy made an alliance with King Henry V of England. He invaded France and won a great victory at the battle of Agincourt (AJ-un-kort). As a result, the French monarchy was forced to sign a treaty with King Henry. The provision of the treaty was that King Henry would become king of France when Charles VI died. But both Henry V and Charles VI died in 1422. So England and Burgundy declared the infant son of Henry V to be the new king of France. However, Valois supporters declared Charles VII, son of Charles VI, to be their new king.

Joan of Arc   At this point, a young peasant girl claimed it was her mission to lead France to victory over the English and the Burgundians. This girl was **Joan of Arc.** She helped lead the French soldiers to victories and escorted Charles VII to his coronation. She inspired the French people with a sense of patriotism. However, Joan was taken prisoner by the Burgundians. They turned her over to the English. She was tried as a witch and burned at the stake in 1431.

The French Drive the English Out of France   King *Charles VII* reigned from 1422 to 1461 and made use of the French people's desire to drive out the English. This desire strengthened his own position as monarch, and during Charles' lifetime, the English were indeed driven out of France. His successors, *Louis XI*, who reigned from 1461 to 1483, and *Charles VIII*, who reigned from 1483 to 1498, managed to reduce the power of the French feudal nobles.

SECTION REVIEW

1. Mapping: Using the map on page 165, describe the location of France in relation to England and the rest of western Europe.
2. In your own words identify or define: Capets, Philip II, Parlement of Paris, Estates General, Valois, Hundred Years' War, Burgundins, Joan of Arc.
3. What obstacles did the French kings have to overcome in order to build royal power in France?
4. Describe the relationship between France and England during the Middle Ages.
   D The early kings of France before Philip IV lacked the authority to tax their people. What purposes do taxes serve today? Do you think taxes are important? Explain your opinion.

SPAIN DURING THE MIDDLE AGES

Spain After the Fall of Rome Christianity entered Spain shortly after the collapse of the Roman Empire. At this time, Spain was overrun by a number of Germanic tribes. One of these, the Visigoths, controlled most of Spain during the 500's and 600's. The Visigoth kingdom did not last long. It fell to Muslim invaders from North Africa during the early 700's. The Muslims took control of all of Spain except the very mountainous areas in the northern part of the Iberian peninsula. There, several small Christian kingdoms were established. During the 700's, these kingdoms began a campaign to oust the Muslim conquerors from Spain.

The Muslim conquerors of Spain were known as the *Moors* (MOOHRZ). The Moors were able to maintain a strong central government in most of Spain for hundreds of years. Between

700 and 1000, they settled among their Christian subjects and intermarried with them. The Moors, however, always remained a minority in Spain.

The high point of the Muslim rule in Spain occurred in the 900's. After that, the strength of the Moorish government declined. In 1031 the central government collapsed. It was replaced by a number of small states. It was then easier for the Christian kingdoms of Spain to overcome their Moorish enemies. They turned the Moorish states against one another and conquered them one by one. The Christian struggle to reconquer Spain continued off and on for almost 500 years.

Toledo, in central Spain, was captured by Christian forces in 1085. Córdova, the former Muslim capital, was taken in 1236. Seville (suh-VIL) fell in 1248. This left only the kingdom of Granada (gruh-NAH-duh), in the southern tip of Spain, under the control of the Moors. However, Granada finally was conquered in 1492.

The long struggle to reconquer Spain produced many heroes. But none were more famous than an eleventh century knight known as *El Cid*—a Moorish word meaning lord or leader. "The Poem of El Cid" describes his heroic deeds.

Spain As a Nation-State   While the Spanish kings were fighting the Muslims, they were also trying to take power away from the Spanish feudal nobles. This proved to be difficult, because the kings usually had to depend on the help of the nobles in fighting the Muslims. To replace the military aid of the nobles, the kings often used townspeople as soldiers. In return, towns became allies of the kings rather than the nobles. The kings also tried to make an ally of the church. As a result, there was not the struggle between the king and church in Spain that existed in England and some other parts of Europe.

By the 1400's, the Muslims held only a small territory in southern Spain. Most of the Spanish kingdoms had united by this time under one of the two major Spanish kingdoms, Castile (ka-STEEL) or Aragon (AR-uh-gahn). In 1469, the future rulers of these two kingdoms were married. Later, as **Queen Isabella** and *King Ferdinand*, they united all of Spain under a strong central government and drove the last of the Muslims from the Iberian peninsula.

Queen Isabella is famous for financing the voyages of Christopher Columbus to the New World. The great wealth that later poured into Spain from the Americas in the form of gold and silver made the Spanish rulers the richest monarchs of their time.

Above are Queen Isabella and King Ferdinand entering Granada in 1496. How do today's leaders enter a city?

196

1. **Mapping:** Using the map on page 165, describe the location of Spain in relation to North Africa, France, and the rest of western Europe.
2. In your own words, identify or define: Moors, Castile and Aragon, Queen Isabella.
3. How did the final unification of all Spain as one nation came about?
   - Spain had a wide diversity of languages, religions, and cultures. How can such a diversity within a nation contribute to its heritage?

FAILURE TO UNIFY GERMANY

Although strong central governments were established about 1500 in England, France, and Spain, this did not occur in Germany. In Germany, the kings never succeeded in destroying rival dukes and other feudal nobles. Therefore, it was not until the 1800's that Germany became a nation under its own ruler.

A Strong Monarchy Fails to Unite Germany. Under Charlemagne, the empire of the Franks included not only France but also parts of modern Italy and Germany. Charlemagne's empire was later divided among his three grandsons. The Frankish lands in Germany were given to Charlemagne's grandson Louis. (See the map on page 169.) He and his successors were the kings of Germany until 911. By that time, Germany was divided into a number of large duchies. As you recall, a duchy was like a small kingdom. Each one was ruled by its own duke. The dukes were the strongest of the feudal nobles, whereas the king had become only a figurehead. During most of the Middle Ages, the German kings constantly tried to increase their power, wealth, and territory, while the dukes protected their own lands from the king and preserved their own authority.

The German nobles did not wish to invite a Carolingian from France or some other part of Europe to go to Germany and rule as king. Instead they chose German dukes to rule. *Henry,* Duke of Saxony, was elected in 919, and his reign lasted until 936. He and his successors are known as the Saxon emperors. They kept the German crown in their family until 1024.

The Monarchy Gains Strength Henry's son, *Otto I,* was one of the outstanding rulers of medieval Germany. During his long reign, from 936 to 973, he devoted most of his time to increasing royal power. He took some of the duchies into his own hands and placed others in the hands of his relatives. Otto also was a successful military leader. His armies ended the Magyar threat to Germany. (See page 170.) Otto realized that his position as king would never be safe. There was always a danger that the German nobles might band together against him. He needed allies, so he turned to the church.

Since they often distrusted the feudal nobles, the German kings made high-ranking clergy their vassals. German kings would grant land to the clergy because they knew that when a member of the clergy died, the land would go back to the crown. Clergy were not permitted to marry and thus did not have any heirs. On the other hand, if the king gave the land to a noble, it usually stayed in the noble's family after his death. In this way, a noble family could gain much power. Under the circumstances, the kings preferred the clergy for their allies. In addition, bishops and other clergy were skillful administrators. They provided the kings with educated officials. Some clergy were even able generals.

The Holy Roman Empire   In 962, the title of Roman Emperor was restored, and King Otto I was crowned Roman Emperor. Earlier, Charlemagne had assumed this title. Later, Otto's title was changed to Holy Roman Emperor to indicate that the German lands were Christian. But neither Otto I nor his successors could put together an empire as large as Charlemagne's. The opposition of the German feudal nobles was too great. They did not want another strong ruler like Charlemagne.

Otto used the title of emperor to imply that the king had the right to rule not only Germany, which at that time was only a collection of German-speaking states, but also parts of Italy, as Charlemagne had done. Otto's domain was then known as the **Holy Roman Empire.** (See the map on page 179.) Otto became involved in Italian affairs. Attempts to gain territory in Italy distracted Otto and succeeding German emperors from their duties. This weakened their control over the Holy Roman Empire.

Conflicts Between the Emperors and the Popes   A new line of emperors came to the throne in 1024. They were known as the Franconians (frang-KOE-nee-unz) or Salians (SAY-lee-uns). The emperors' reliance upon the clergy as allies in Germany eventually led to a conflict with the popes. The dispute between the popes and the emperors was over who should select the bishops in Germany. The popes claimed this was their right. The German emperors believed that if the popes placed their own supporters in these high church positions in Germany, the lands they received with these posts might fall under the control of the popes. The emperors also wanted the right to select bishops in order to make sure the bishops would support the crown against the nobility.

The conflict between emperors and popes came to a head during the reign of *Henry IV*, which lasted from 1056 to 1106. Henry realized that his only allies in Germany were the bishops and clergy, for they were willing to stand by him against the nobles. The emperor made appointments to church offices and paid no attention to attempts by the popes to control church affairs in Germany.

Gregory VII, a strong pope, was ready to challenge Henry IV. Although the pope knew the German clergy supported Henry and had little loyalty to the pope, Gregory VII decided that the German clergy were not likely to support Henry against the feudal nobles if the pope sided with the nobles. Therefore, Pope Gregory excommunicated Henry IV and announced that the German nobles were released from their feudal vows of allegiance to the emperor. As a result, Henry was taken prisoner and the German nobles set out to elect a new ruler.

Pope Gregory was on the verge of becoming a powerful religious leader in medieval Europe when Henry IV escaped. He made his way to northern Italy, where the pope was staying, and begged for forgiveness. As a religious leader, the pope had no choice but to remove Henry's excommunication. The emperor crossed the Alps and returned to Germany. To the German nobles it appeared that the pope had restored Henry to the office of emperor. Many nobles then joined Henry, and he was able to overcome his opponents. A few

Above, the excommunicated Emperor Henry IV is being absolved by Pope Gregory VII in 1077. How much influence did the Pope have over rulers then? Does the Pope still have this influence?

years later, Henry returned to Italy with an army and removed Gregory as pope. Not until the thirteenth century was a compromise reached by which popes and emperors shared in the selection of church officials.

Another line of emperors was founded in 1138. This was the *House of Hohenstaufen* (HOE-un-stow-fun). The Hohenstaufen emperors dedicated themselves to establishing a strong central government in Germany and reducing the power of the medieval popes.

The Papal States　But soon a new conflict arose. The German emperors wanted lands in Italy that belonged to the popes. In central Italy, the pope ruled a kingdom called the *Papal States*. In the middle of the eighth century, the pope asked the king of the Franks to help him against a Germanic tribe that was attacking Rome. The king conquered the tribe and gave its lands to the pope. These lands became the Papal States. They formed a belt across the center of Italy. (See the map on page 165.)

Emperor *Frederick I* invaded Italy six times and seized territory in the north. Later, Emperor *Henry VI* inherited parts of southern Italy from his wife's family. Eventually the emperors controlled territory north and south of the Papal States. Then the popes greatly feared the emperors. As a result, the popes decided to destroy the power of the emperors once and for all. They usually sided with the German feudal nobles against the German emperors or asked other countries in Europe to make war against them.

The Emperors Lose Power　Meanwhile, the emperors power in Germany was slowly slipping away. They were absent from Germany much of the time, carrying on wars or crusades. While they were away, the feudal nobles grew more powerful. The emperors had also lost the support of the church and exhausted themselves in trying to conquer Italy. For a time, the German nobles were able to prevent the election of an emperor, and this brought on a civil war in Germany. This period without a ruler was called the *Interregnum* (int-uh-REG-num). It lasted from 1254 to 1273.

The Interregnum ended when the nobles of Germany met in an assembly and elected a new emperor. After 1356, the election of new emperors was the duty of a group of seven high-ranking nobles and clergy. They were known as *Electors.*

The Electors were afraid to give too much power to one of their own members or to a strong member of the royal family. So for many years they elected only weak princes as emperors. For this reason the "Holy Roman Emperor" had little real authority. But because the office did have prestige, powerful princes often offered to give up some of their authority in order to be elected emperor. And in doing so, they further weakened their power.

Under these circumstances, there were few strong emperors. Political power remained in the hands of nobles and church leaders. The land they controlled eventually became independent states. The nobles and church leaders assumed their own titles and ruled their lands thereafter as monarchs. What we call Germany today was a loose collection of about 300 states of varying sizes, including some called kingdoms. Each one was governed by a different ruler. When one of these rulers was elected emperor, he actually ruled only the lands brought with him when he was elected. Therefore, though an emperor might claim to rule all Germany, he was actually ruling only a piece of the Holy Roman Empire.

A New Royal Family Takes Over In 1273, a member of the *Hapsburg* (HAPS-burg) family was elected emperor. The Hapsburg family was to provide most of the Holy Roman Emperors during the remaining 500 years that the empire survived. This royal family added to its territories through marriage, inheritance, and military conquest. By modern times it came to be one of Europe's most important ruling houses.

Probably the greatest of the Holy Roman Emperors was a Hapsburg, *Charles V*. Charles ruled from 1519 to 1556. By the end of his reign, he held the Hapsburg lands in Germany and what is today Austria, and had inherited the kingdom of Spain and all the Spanish lands in America discovered by Columbus and other explorers. Part of the old duchy of Burgundy, along with what is today Belgium and The Netherlands, was also part of Charles V's empire. In addition to all this, he inherited most of southern Italy and was crowned king of the lands in northern Italy that had formerly been claimed by medieval emperors. Thus Charles V's empire became far greater than the so-called Holy Roman Empire.

But Charles' empire was too large for any one ruler to manage. In 1556, Charles gave up his throne. His possessions in western Europe were given to his son, King Philip II of Spain. His position as Holy Roman Emperor, along with Hapsburg lands in Germany and Austria, was given to Charles' brother. Charles himself retired to a monastery.

SECTION REVIEW

1. Mapping: Using the map on page 165 and the Atlas of Europe, describe the extent of the Holy Roman Empire and compare it with the political boundaries of present-day Germany.

2. In your own words, identify or define: King Otto I, Pope Gregory VII, Papal States, Interregnum, Electors, Hapsburgs, Charles V.

3. What constituted the Holy Roman Empire? How were emperors selected?

4. Why did the German kings claim the right to rule Italy?

5. Why were there few strong emperors of the Holy Roman Empire? What specific situations limited the power of the emperors?

▶ Do you think a strong central government is good or bad for a community? Explain.

ITALY DURING THE MIDDLE AGES

Nation-State Fails in Italy   In the Middle Ages, Italy, like Germany, was not the unified nation we know today. The early Frankish kings and later the German emperors claimed the right to rule Italy. But they never were able to unite all the Italians. Like Germany, Italy did not become a nation under a single ruler until the 1800's.

When Charlemagne's empire collapsed, Italy fell into disorder. There was no central government, and for more than a century feudal lords ruled most of the land. In the 900's, the German emperor, Otto I, claimed Italy for himself when he took the title Roman Emperor. Succeeding German emperors had trouble upholding Otto's claim. They added parts of Italy to their possessions but never succeeded in taking over all of Italy and uniting it.

Northern Italy in the Middle Ages By 1100, northern Italy consisted for the most part of a number of small, independent republics, or city-states. Among them were Florence, Milan (muh-LAN), Venice, Pisa (PEA-zuh), and Siena (see-EN-uh). A city-state was made up of a city and the surrounding countryside under its control. Although most of the cities in the north of Italy recognized the claim of the German emperor to rule Italy, they found ways to escape German control. In their struggle to remain free, the cities were aided by the prosperity that swept the Italian peninsula during the Middle Ages. This prosperity was largely due to the role of Italian merchants during the Crusades.

The Italian city-states produced a new kind of ruler in the 1400's. These rulers were known as **despots** (DES-puts). They found ways to seize control of the city-states by their own effort. They hired *mercenaries*, or paid soldiers. Or they used murder, trickery, or other means to win power. The despots took full advantage of their position. They paid no attention to the rights of their subjects. The despots had won power and through force they kept their power. Their attitude could be summarized as "Might makes right."

Machiavellianism   *Niccolò Machiavelli* (NEE-koe-loe mak-ee-uh-VEL-ee), who lived from 1469 to 1527, believed in the despot's point of view. Machiavelli had served as an official for the republic of Florence. After leaving the city's service, he wrote a book, *The Prince*. It gave advice on how to win and hold on to power. Machiavelli saw no goodness in men and women. Instead, he focused on their weaknesses, greed, and shortcomings. He believed a

Machiavelli said leaders should protect their states by whatever means necessary. Should rulers follow Machiavelli's ideas? Explain.

prince could take advantage of human weaknesses to obtain and keep power. Machiavelli also believed a despot with unlimited powers provided better government for his or her subjects than did a republic or any other form of democracy. Many dictators after the Middle Ages followed Machiavelli's advice given in *The Prince*. The term **Machiavellianism** (mak-ee-uh-VEL-ee-un-izm) today refers to political behavior without morals or scruples.

Central and Southern Italy During the Middle Ages   The German emperors' desire to rule Italy was a constant threat to the popes. They feared that the German emperor might seize the Papal States. Southern Italy had been united since the eleventh century as a kingdom ruled by the Normans. Many Normans had gone to southern Italy during the Crusades. Norman knights seized southern Italy from the Byzantine Empire in the 1000's and drove the Muslim pirates from the island of Sicily. Sicily was then united with the southern mainland of Italy, forming the Kingdom of the Two Sicilies.

Attempts to Conquer Italy   As you have learned, the German emperors in the 1100's made plans to conquer all of Italy. Faced by this threat, the cities of northern Italy formed an alliance with the pope and with the Normans in the south. Together these powers were able to prevent a German take-over of Italy. Unable to win a military victory, Emperor Frederick I arranged a marriage between his son, Henry VI, and Constance of Sicily. Their son became Emperor Frederick II and in 1211, Frederick's wife inherited southern Italy. In this way, the German emperors added the Kingdom of the Two Sicilies to their possessions.

The German emperor *Frederick II*, who ruled from 1211 to 1250, used southern Italy as a base from which he tried to conquer all of the Italian peninsula. This danger reunited the cities of northern Italy with the Papal States against the Germans. Once again, the Germans failed to conquer Italy.

During the Interregnum, when there was no German emperor, the French seized the kingdom of the Two Sicilies. Later, the French were driven out by Aragon, one of the Spanish kingdoms. The Spanish made the island of Sicily a separate kingdom and renamed the territory on the mainland the kingdom of Naples (NAY-pulz). Naples was and still is an important port city. All of southern Italy remained in Spanish hands off and on until the 1800's.

By 1500, therefore, when England, France, and Spain already had become nations with strong central governments, the Italian people were still not united. Sicily and southern Italy were kingdoms. In central Italy, the pope ruled. And in the northern part of Italy, there existed numerous city-states. All of Italy was not united as a single nation until 1870.

SECTION REVIEW

1.   Mapping: Using the map on page 165 and information in your textbook, describe the three divisions of the Italian peninsula during the Middle Ages.
2.   In your own words, identify or define: Italian city-states, despots, mercenaries, Machiavellianism.
3.   Why was it difficult for the Italian people to unite as a single nation during the Middle Ages?
▷   What political and social factors do you think are necessary for people to be united as a nation?

chapter 10

Cultural and Religious Change in Western Europe

THE RENAISSANCE

As you know, town life in western Europe revived around 1000. The growth of towns and cities was stimulated by the Crusades, particularly in Italy. Italian cities took the lead in manufacturing and trade. The growth of cities created a wealthy new class of business leaders and merchants. This class between the nobility and the peasantry was called the *middle class,* or *bourgeoisie* (boohrzh-wah-ZEE).

The middle class was prosperous. It had both the leisure and the wealth to support the work of artists, writers, and scholars. Leisure and wealth created renewed interest in learning and culture. This renewal is called the **Renaissance** (ren-uh-SAHNTS), meaning re-birth. From the cities of northern Italy, the Renaissance spread to France, then to what is now Belgium and The Netherlands, and finally to the rest of Europe.

Interest in the Ancient World Grows During the Renaissance, interest in the cultures of ancient Greece and Rome was revived. This led to research into Greek and Latin writings. Scholars produced new translations of the Greek and Roman classics. Great collections of ancient writings also were assembled. In 1455, the papal library at Rome had only 352 Greek manuscripts. Only thirty years later, its collection had expanded to more than a thousand. Such collections and the research of scholars who made them enabled Europeans to understand more fully their ancient heritage.

Development of Humanism As Renaissance scholars learned more about ancient Greece and Rome, a freer, more critical way of thinking slowly developed. Scholars were less interested in religious matters. They focused on the importance of life here on earth. They believed every individual should develop his or her talents to the fullest extent, and they called for reforms to make the world a more perfect place. The attitude held by these individuals, or humanists, was called *humanism.*

The ideal of the humanists was the "universal man," an educated person skillful in many things. *Leonardo da Vinci* is a good example of the universal man. Da Vinci was an Italian scientist and inventor who lived during the fifteenth and early sixteenth centuries. He developed skills in mathematics, engineering, architecture, and other sciences. He also knew music and distinguished himself as an artist. One of his most famous paintings was the *Mona Lisa.* Da Vinci served as a model for others during the Renaissance.

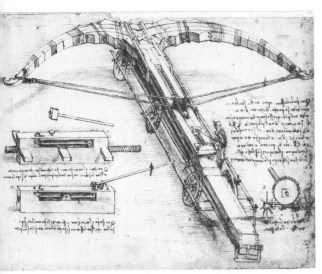

Leonardo da Vinci is known mainly for his painting. He was also highly skilled in architecture, mathematics, and engineering. Above is da Vinci's drawing of a great crossbow. What do you think its purpose was?

Modern Languages Come Into Their Own The Renaissance not only stimulated an interest in the classics but also encouraged the development of what are called the *vernacular languages.* "Vernacular" is a term used to distinguish the native language of a country or region. During the Middle Ages, Latin was the scholarly language of western Europe. All serious writing was done in Latin. However, people spoke the vernacular languages of Italian, French, or German every day, and they would use these languages in daily business. But whenever an official document was to be written, a poem created, or a scholarly work composed, people used Latin. Latin was considered superior to the vernacular languages.

Early in the 1200's, however, the vernacular languages began to be used in literature. The first important work written in the vernacular was *The Divine Comedy.* This long poem was written in Italian by the poet *Dante* (DAHN-tay). Later, another major Italian poet, *Petrarch* (PEH-trahrk), wrote works in Italian. His friend, *Giovanni Boccaccio* (joe-VAHN-nee boe-KAHCH-ee-oe), wrote a series of stories, called *The Decameron* (deh-KAM-ur-un), in Italian. *Geoffrey Chaucer* (CHAW-sur) wrote his *Canterbury Tales* in English.

The development of the printing press and the invention of movable type in the 1450's by *Johann Gutenburg* (YOE-hahn GOOT-un-burg), a German, also helped the spread of the vernacular. This made possible the publications of many works written in the vernacular languages. Between 1450 and 1500, 177 editions of the Bible were printed in Latin. However, fifteen editions were printed in German, thirteen in Italian, and eleven in French.

Renaissance Advances in the Arts Important developments in art also took place during this period. Painting and sculpture became more lifelike. Religious subjects were still favorites for many artists, but a number of artists became interested in nonreligious subjects. Paintings of scenes from Greek and Roman mythology, for example, were common. *Giotto* (JAH-toe), an Italian artist, introduced realism to painting. For many years, Italian artists such as *Botticelli* (baht-uh-CHEL-ee) and *Raphael* (RAHF-ee-ul) dominated Renaissance painting.

Sculpture reached new heights during the Renaissance. *Michelangelo* (mik-uh-LAN-juh-loe) was considered the leading sculptor of the period. But he excelled in several fields of art. His paintings of scenes from the Bible that decorated the ceiling of the Sistine (SIS-teen) Chapel, which belonged to the pope in Rome, are considered one of the most famous works produced during the Renaissance. Some of his works may still be seen today.

The Influence of the Renaissance
The Renaissance began in Italy in the 1200's and 1300's. It spread slowly to Germany, England, and other parts of northern Europe. Although the Renaissance had ended in Italy by 1500, it lasted longer in other parts of Europe. The effects of the Renaissance differed from country to country, but, in general, it can be said that it stimulated new ideas everywhere. And it produced new forms of literature and art.

The most influential humanist in northern Europe was a Dutch scholar, *Erasmus* (ir-RAZ-mus). He was a writer and reformer who corresponded with kings and popes and the leaders of Europe. Erasmus' most influential book was *In Praise of Folly.* It was a satire about life in the time of Erasmus. It attacked ignorance and hatred. Erasmus' friend, *Thomas More,* was the leading English humanist. His book *Utopia* attempted to describe an ideal society. The greatness of English literature was reached later, however, during the age of Elizabeth. Writers such as Christopher Marlowe, a dramatist, and Edmund Spenser, a poet, influenced literature during the Elizabethan Age. This also was the time of William Shakespeare, one of the greatest English writers. (See page 190.) One of the best-known humanists in France was *Rabelais* (RAB-uh-lay), who wrote collections of stories intended for common people. Another writer, *Montaigne* (mahn-TANE), was thought to be the greatest thinker and writer of the French Renaissance. Montaigne developed a new form of writing. He called it the essay. In Spain, *Miguel Cervantes* (mee-GEL sur-VAHN-tayz) wrote one of the greatest works of Spanish literature, *Don Quixote* (kee-HOE-tee). Cervantes was poking fun at knighthood, chivalry, and the Middle Ages—for the Middle Ages was dying out during Cervantes' own lifetime.

Science During the Renaissance
One of the most outstanding personalities in Renaissance science was *Nicolaus Copernicus* (koe-PUR-nih-kus), a Pole. He proposed a new theory of the solar system in the 1500's. Copernicus claimed the earth revolved around the sun. Until then, it was believed that all the planets and the sun too revolved around the earth. The earth was considered the center of the universe. Copernicus' theory might have remained only a theory had it not been for the work of *Galileo* (gal-uh-LAY-oe), an Italian mathematician. Galileo developed a telescope through which he

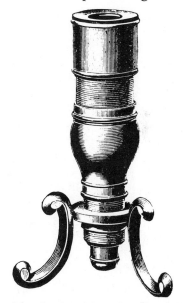

When Galileo developed his telescope and looked at the skies through it, he saw changes taking place in the heavens as well as on Earth. Can you list any scientific discoveries made in your lifetime that have changed the way people see the universe?

observed the solar system. His observations verified Copernicus' theory. They showed, beyond a doubt, that the earth was not the center of the universe.

The greatest advances made in science, mathematics, and medicine, however, were brought about after the close of the Renaissance. Individuals like *Sir Isaac Newton*, who developed our concept of gravity, lived and worked during the mid-seventeenth and early eighteenth centuries.

The Expansion of Trade Routes

Manufacturing and trade did more than create wealth to support artists like da Vinci. They also stimulated a demand for foreign imports, especially luxury goods from the Far East. This demand had been easily satisfied while Europeans controlled the Middle East. However, when Muslims regained control of that area after the Crusades, trade was more difficult and expensive. Goods passing through Muslim lands from the Far East were heavily taxed. The taxes increased the price of the goods when they were sold in western Europe. For this reason, Renaissance merchants looked for routes to the Far East that would bypass Muslim lands.

Two routes to the Far East seemed possible. One was by sea around Africa to India, China, and the rest of the Far East. The Portuguese were the first to discover this route around Africa. There was thought to be another route. Some Europeans thought they could reach the Far East by sailing directly westward from Europe. Christopher Columbus, sailing under the Spanish flag, followed the westward route and discovered the New World. The discovery of these routes made Portugal and Spain the new leaders in world trade. As a result, the Mediterranean ceased to be Europe's chief trade route, and the Italian cities lost the importance they had held in commerce since the Crusades.

Other Contributions of the Renaissance

The renewed interest in learning of the Renaissance continued during the 1600's and 1700's and resulted in great advances in scientific knowledge. The spirit of the Renaissance affected not only science but almost every field of learning during the 1600's and 1700's. Important contributions were made to philosophy, political science, economics, and history. In general, great curiosity, research, and progress characterized the 1600's and 1700's. Many people refer to it as a scientific revolution.

Some Things Remain Unchanged

Not everything changed during the Renaissance. Some things were no different from the way they had been during the Middle Ages. For example, people still were divided into social classes. As in medieval times, there were nobles, or **aristocrats,** who were the ruling class. They inherited special privileges along with their titles and positions in society. Their wealth was usually based on ownership of land they had inherited from their medieval ancestors. By early modern times, newcomers were added to the ranks of the aristocrats. These newcomers had acquired their wealth in business. They used it to buy land. Sometimes they married into aristocratic families. Regardless of their origins, all aristocrats could be identified by their education, dress, speech, homes, and wealth.

Most people in Europe were not aristocrats. They were called commoners because they inherited no special privileges and had no titles or high-ranking positions in society. The majority of commoners were peasants who

CONTRIBUTORS TO THE ADVANCE OF SCIENCE IN THE 1600's AND 1700's		
SCIENTIST	NATIONALITY	MAJOR CONTRIBUTIONS
Robert Boyle (1627–1691)	English	Founder of modern chemistry; developed a basic principle describing gases.
Benjamin Franklin (1706–1790)	American	Proved through experiments that lightning was a form of electricity.
William Harvey (1578–1657)	English	Discovered how blood circulated through the human body.
Robert Hooke (1635–1703)	English	Developed Hooke's Law of elasticity and identified cells in living matter.
Edward Jenner (1749–1823)	English	First to use the vaccination as a successful way to prevent disease.
Anton van Leeuwenhoek (1632–1723)	Dutch	Improved the light microscope, enabling him to prove the existence of bacteria.
Carolus Linnaeus (1707–1778)	Swedish	Invented a system of plant classification and identification.

made their living from agriculture as their ancestors had during the Middle Ages. Their life had changed little since medieval times. The peasants were the most important people in Europe. Without them to work the land and raise crops, the rest of Europe would have gone without food.

Not all commoners were peasant farmers. Many had been peasant farmers and had moved to the city to earn a better living. Some sold goods in shops of their own, became bankers, or opened businesses to manufacture goods. Some were able to obtain an education to enter professions like law, medicine, or teaching. In many instances, they became extremely wealthy and could afford to live in the luxurious style of the aristocrats. As in Italy, these wealthy commoners of a town or city made up a new class—the middle class.

SECTION REVIEW

1. Mapping: Using the map on page 165 and information on pages 203–206, describe the origin and the spread of the Renaissance in western Europe.
2. In your own words, define or identify: vernacular languages, Dante, *Canterbury Tales*, Cervantes, Leonardo da Vinci, bourgeoisie.
3. Why were the discoveries of Copernicus and Galileo important?
4. Support or dispute the following statement: "The invention of the printing press was the single most important development of early modern times."
5. How did the developments of the 1600's and 1700's illustrate the influence of the Renaissance on European life?
▶ What period in your own life has had the greatest influence on the way you live today? Why?

REFORMATION IN GERMANY

By the time Columbus discovered the **New World,** the church was facing a number of serious problems. Kings who had struggled to increase their own powers at the church's expense throughout the Middle Ages were hostile to the church. Land owned by the church was eyed jealously by kings and nobles. People also resented the worldly life many church leaders lived.

The headquarters of the church were located in Rome, and the popes were almost always Italian. As a result, Italians were frequently selected to fill important church positions. **Nationalism**—a sense of loyalty to one's own country—was growing and led some people to challenge the power that Rome and the Italians held in the church. Many people also resented the fact that a large part of the church contributions were shipped to Rome and set aside for the popes' use.

Often the ways in which contributions were collected caused scandal. In Germany, for example, a priest named Tetzel (TET-sul) traveled about during the early 1500's. Taking advantage of the peasants' lack of education, Tetzel offered them in return for money an *indulgence,* or a reduction in the amount of punishment due for one's sins.

Reports that Tetzel was selling indulgences outraged many people. Among the outraged was a priest named *Martin Luther* in the city of Wittenberg in northern Germany. In 1517, when Tetzel visited a nearby town selling indulgences, Luther denounced Tetzel's actions. No one could purchase the forgiveness of sins, Luther claimed. He challenged Tetzel to a public debate.

Johann Tetzel outraged many Christians, including Luther. How did Tetzel help bring about the Reformation?

Luther drew up a list of *Ninety-five Theses* (THEE-sees), or questions for debate, and posted them on a church door. One of the theses Luther wanted to debate was the sale of indulgences. Although Tetzel never accepted the challenge, Luther's theses were copied, printed, and widely circulated throughout Germany.

Luther's Points of View   Martin Luther was a deeply religious Christian. In the Ninety-five Theses, he criticized many things in the church that he considered wrong and in need of reform. His study of the Bible led him to conclude that Christian men and women could never earn salvation, or eternal life for their souls, by performing such good works as praying, fasting, and making pilgrimages, or by contributing money to the church. He concluded that only through faith could people gain salvation.

Luther's disagreement with the church created such a stir that the German emperor and the pope condemned him. He was excommunicated by the pope. In 1521, Luther was put on trial by the emperor for the things he had written and preached. At his trial Martin Luther refused to admit he had been in error. Instead, he took the position that a Christian had the right to read the Holy Scriptures and to follow his or her conscience, regardless of what the church taught. Many people were shocked by Luther's ideas. They were considered to be revolutionary. If a person were saved by faith alone, as Luther claimed, there appeared to be no need for a church, priests, or bishops.

The Reformation   Although Luther defied the church, he was permitted to return home after his trial. He was under the special protection of the Elector of Saxony, one of the most important German nobles. From then until his death in 1546, Luther continued to teach, preach, and write about his new interpretation of Christianity. The movement begun by Luther became known as the **Reformation,** because it set out to reform certain abuses within the Christian church. Those who supported Luther were called **Protestants,** or protesters. Later all western European Christians who were not Roman Catholics were called Protestants.

Luther Revolutionizes Christianity   Luther began a revolution. Because of the invention of the printing press, news of his stand against the church reached a wide audience. His doctrines were popular in Germany and Scandinavia. From Luther's ideas a new Christian church emerged. Preaching and teaching were considered among the most important functions of the church. Church organization and religious ceremonies were simplified. Protestant and Catholic forms of worship resembled one another, but in questions of belief, the two churches were far apart.

In 1526, the German Catholic emperor, Charles V, summoned the nobles of Germany to an assembly. There he issued a decree declaring that a local ruler could determine the religion of his subjects. Many German rulers had become Lutherans. (The Lutherans, as you know, were the first Protestants.)

These German rulers, great and small, took the lead in spreading Lutheranism. They claimed the right to decide which church their subjects would belong to. State-established churches appeared. At Luther's death in 1546, Scandinavia was Protestant and Germany was divided between Catholics and Protestants.

In 1546, a religious war between Catholics and Protestants erupted in Germany. It lasted until 1555. Both sides struggled to establish their own religious faith in all of Germany. This was the first in a series of religious wars between Catholics and Protestants that swept across Europe for almost 100 years. These religious wars were especially bitter and brutal, with participants deeply convinced that their beliefs were the only true ones.

Martin Luther disagreed with some of the beliefs of the Catholic Church. How did Luther's ideas reach a wide audience in Europe?

1. Using the map on page 217, describe the parts of Europe that became Lutheran Protestant areas by the 1600's.
2. In your own words, define or identify: indulgence, Ninety-five Theses, nationalism, Elector of Saxony, Reformation, Protestants.
3. Using evidence in the text, give some of the reasons a German man or woman in the early 1600's might have supported Luther's revolt against the church.
4. How did the new church founded by Luther differ from the Catholic Church?
◗ There are still religious conflicts in the world today. Do you think a religious conflict can be resolved? Why or why not?

THE RISE OF CALVINISM

A number of other reformers throughout Europe followed Luther's example. They completely broke away from the Catholic Church and founded their own churches. Soon there was a wide variety of Christian doctrines and churches in western Europe. The most influential Protestant reformer next to Luther was *John Calvin.* Calvin was born in France. Adopting some of Luther's doctrines, he fled to Switzerland and spent his life teaching, preaching, and writing as the head of the Protestant movement he founded. His version of Protestantism is known to this day as **Calvinism.** His teachings were collected in a book first published in 1536, *Institutes of the Christian Religion.*

Calvinism   Calvin agreed with Luther that no man or woman could earn salvation by performing good works.

Unlike Luther, Calvin said no one was saved by faith either. Calvin believed that God chose some men and women to enjoy eternal life. He called this group the *Elect.* No persons who had not been chosen already by God could belong to the Elect. No matter how many good works they might perform or how deeply they might believe in Christianity, they could not be saved unless they had been chosen by God as one of the Elect. This teaching is called *predestination* (pree-des-tu-NAY-shun).

A new Christian belief emerged based on the teachings of Calvin. All elaborate church ceremonies were eliminated. Preaching was the basis of Calvinist worship. Calvin insisted that services be simple. Crosses, stained glass windows, and other ornaments sometimes found in Catholic and Lutheran churches were removed.

Calvinists placed great importance upon proper behavior. They were convinced that God disapproved of music, dancing, and gambling. They also frowned upon wearing fine clothes or going to the theater. Great value was placed on hard work, and Calvinists set high moral standards for themselves. The Calvinist attitude toward life was called **Puritanism.** It greatly influenced Europe, especially the English-speaking peoples. Despite the sternness of its beliefs, Calvinism was popular and soon had spread through western Europe.

Switzerland was the center of Calvinism. From there it spread to France. French Calvinists were called *Huguenots* (HYOO-guh-nahts). In northern Germany and The Netherlands, Calvinism was the basis of the German and Dutch Reformed churches. In Scotland, the **Presbyterian** Church was established. This church was largely the accomplishment of *John Knox,* who had

Followers of Calvin had strict rules that governed their life. Their attitude toward life was called Puritanism. Many of Calvin's followers settled in the New World in the 1600's. How does this picture reflect their beliefs?

studied in Switzerland. Calvinism also spread to England, where its followers were known as *Puritans.*

Calvin differed with Luther on the relationship between church and state. Luther considered the state to be supreme. Luther had gone so far as to teach that a ruler had the right to determine the religion of his or her subjects. However, to Calvin and his followers, the church was supreme. Calvin taught that Christians should obey the law. However, Calvin approved of overthrowing a ruler who acted in defiance of God's laws. Calvinists believed every individual had to obey his or her conscience, even if it were in conflict with the government or the laws. Thus Calvinist beliefs contained the seeds of revolution.

In the 1530's, Calvin was invited by the Protestant city of Geneva in Switzerland to govern their city. Calvin accepted, and there he put into effect his teachings. The church was governed by a group of men called *presbyters* (PREZ-but-urs). The presbyters, together with Calvin, formed a council that made and enforced the laws.

Crime was punished in Geneva. But there also were penalties for other forms of misconduct. To miss church services or to laugh during a sermon was an offense. Individuals could be fined for dancing or playing cards or wearing clothes not considered to be modest. In Geneva, the leaders of the church were also the officials of the government. Such a government is known as a **theocracy** (thee-AHK-ruh-see).

SECTION REVIEW

1. Mapping: Using the map on page 217 and information in your textbook, describe the center of Calvinism by the 1600's and trace its spread across Europe.
2. In your own words, identify or define: Calvinism, *Institutes of the Christian Religion,* the Elect, predestination, Puritanism, Huguenots, presbyters, theocracy.
3. In what ways did Calvinism differ from Lutheranism?
   - What would be the advantages and disadvantages of being governed by a theocracy?

211

THE REFORMATION IN ENGLAND

The Reformation in England took a different form from the one it had taken in Germany or Switzerland. Religious changes in England were introduced by government officials rather than by church leaders. When the Reformation broke out in Germany, King Henry VIII of England supported the pope against Luther. Later however, Henry and the pope quarreled over Henry's demand for a divorce from his wife, Queen Catherine. Church authorities refused to permit the divorce, and Henry broke ties with Rome. He denied that the pope had authority over the church in England. And Parliament declared that King Henry was the head of the Catholic Church in England.

The Reformation under Henry VIII
Henry's reformation made drastic changes in church organization, but for the most part, there were few changes in Catholic ceremonies or beliefs. Major changes in church teachings were not introduced until after his death in 1547.

After breaking with the pope, Henry ordered the destruction of all monasteries and convents in England. He seized their wealth and distributed their lands among the nobles who supported him. This made Henry richer and won him many new allies. Most of the common people went along with the religious changes introduced by Henry. Many church leaders opposed what he was doing, but those who spoke out were quickly replaced by his supporters. Meanwhile, a new Parliament passed laws requiring subjects to swear to uphold the king's authority in religious matters. A number of English men and women, however, remained loyal to the pope. They could not bring themselves to support Henry and were executed. Sir Thomas More, a famous English humanist, was one of those executed. Most Englishmen, however, abided by the new laws and accepted the king as the head of the church in England.

After Henry's death, a group of church leaders who favored Lutheran and Calvinist ideas took control of the church. From 1547 to 1553, during the brief reign of Henry's son, Edward VI, radical changes were introduced in religious ceremonies and doctrines. These changes had been scarcely introduced when the sickly king died.

Upon Edward's death , his half-sister Mary became queen. Mary was a Catholic. She tried to reverse the changes that had been introduced under her father and half-brother. She restored the pope's authority in England. But she encountered fierce resistance to her actions. When many Protestants openly protested the return of Catholic ceremonies and beliefs, the queen launched severe religious persecutions. Several hundred Protestants were executed. As a result, Mary's Protestant opponents gave her the nickname "Bloody Mary." Mary's religious changes were cut short by her death in 1558. Mary was succeeded by her half-sister, Elizabeth.

The new queen tried to strike a compromise between English Catholics who remained loyal to the pope and English Protestants who wanted to introduce forms of Lutheranism and Calvinism. Elizabeth adopted religious ceremonies and beliefs from both sides in the hope of winning the support of all her subjects. She was determined that there would be only one Christian church in her kingdom. Catholics and Protestants, therefore, who refused to

212

follow the queen's leadership in religious matters were persecuted. However, most of the English accepted the idea of a "single church." They went along with the ceremonies and beliefs established for them by their queen.

SECTION REVIEW

1. Mapping: Using the map on page 217, describe what religions most of the people followed in England, Scotland, and Ireland by 1600.
2. In your own words, identify or define: Henry VIII, Sir Thomas More, "Bloody Mary."
3. How did the Reformation in England differ from the Reformation in Germany or Switzerland?
4. Why did Henry VIII destroy the monasteries in England?
5. After the Reformation, why was the church in England considered a "single church"?
▷ Many nations have constitutions that ensure the right of freedom of religion. What is the meaning and importance of religious freedom in today's world?

COUNTER-REFORMATION

Many Christians who wanted changes did not want to leave the Catholic Church. They decided to reform their church from within rather than create new churches as Luther and Calvin had done. They launched a movement called the **Catholic Reformation,** or the **Counter-Reformation.** Its chief aim was to correct the abuses that had been criticized by Luther and Calvin and win back the parts of Europe that had been converted to Protestantism.

The Society of Jesus   Ignatius Loyola (ig-NAY-shus loi-OE-luh), a Span-
iard who had been a professional soldier, founded a religious organization whose purpose was to bring Protestants back into the Catholic Church. The new organization was called the Society of Jesus, and its members were known as **Jesuits** (JEZH-uh-wutz) The Jesuits were organized, trained, and disciplined like soldiers. They worked ceaselessly to spread Catholic beliefs throughout Europe. In nations that were officially Protestant, the Jesuits had to work in secret. Many were forced to sneak into those countries in disguise and live in hiding while working there.

The Council of Trent   Catholic leaders also took steps to reform the financial and administrative abuses that had grown in the church. Many of these reforms were enacted at the *Council of Trent.* The Council was a general assembly of Roman Catholic church leaders from all parts of the world. It met in the city of Trent in northern Italy and lasted from 1545 to 1563. A sweeping restatement of Catholic beliefs was one of the Council's most important achievements. The restatement specified exactly what the teachings of the Catholic Church were. By doing this, the church hoped to avoid misinterpretations of its teachings as well as abuse by unscrupulous clergy such as Tetzel.

Other Accomplishments of the Catholic Reformation   The Catholic Reformation also created the *Index,* a list of books considered dangerous to the Catholic faith. A special organization was responsible for keeping this list up to date. Catholics were forbidden to read books listed in the Index. Nor could these books be sold in Catholic countries. Catholic rulers—especially the Spanish—prevented forbidden books from being smuggled into their countries.

The reforms ordered by the Council of Trent (above) helped to restore the position of Catholicism in Europe. But new religions continued to flourish. How have churches changed since the 1500's?

The Catholic Reformation also revived the *Inquisition,* which resembled a medieval court with a police force. It had been set up early in the Middle Ages by several monarchs. Its purpose was to seek out and punish persons guilty of heresy. In the 1500's, the Inquisition was brought back into use only in countries whose rulers approved of it.

The Restoration of the Catholic Church The reforms ordered by the Council of Trent and the missionary work of the Jesuits helped somewhat to restore the position of the Catholic Church in western Europe. In Spain and Italy, Protestantism was stamped out. The areas that are today southern Germany, Poland, Austria, and Belgium returned to Catholicism. But the Catholic Reformation could not turn back the clock and completely wipe out

the Protestant faiths. By the close of the 1500's Protestantism was firmly established in Europe. As a result, the religious divisions in Europe are essentially the same today. (See the map on page 217.)

(See the map on page 217.)

SECTION REVIEW

1. In your own words, identify or define: Loyola, Jesuits, Council of Trent, Index, Inquisition.
2. What was the purpose of the Catholic Reformation, or Counter-Reformation? What did it accomplish?
   ▷ What are possible reasons why the religious situation in Europe has changed little since the 1500's? Do any of these reasons pertain to the religious situation in your own community?

chapter 11

A Time of Conflict

THE RELIGIOUS WARS

Religious divisions created by the Reformation eventually gave rise to a number of wars in the 1500's and 1600's. Sometimes these wars were fought between nations. And sometimes they were civil wars fought within a nation.

The Huguenot Wars One of the worst religious wars broke out in France in 1562. It lasted until 1598—over thirty years. Many French nobles who resented the power of the king became Calvinists. They used the new religion to organize political opposition to the monarch. French Calvinists were called Huguenots. Huguenot opposition to the king was especially strong in southern France, and civil war broke out there. Catholic nobles and their supporters generally backed the royal power. They struggled with groups of Huguenot nobles and their supporters, who generally opposed the central government. During the war, religious intolerance was fierce and persecutions were bloody.

In 1572, a truce was arranged between Catholic and Huguenot nobles. The leading Huguenots gathered in Paris to attend the wedding of their chief, Henry of Bourbon, who later became King Henry IV. Henry was to marry the sister of King *Charles IX.* The king and his sister were Catholic, so Catholic leaders also attended the wedding. During the wedding celebrations, the king's mother, Catherine de Médicis (MED-uh-cheez) convinced King Charles that the Huguenots were plotting to kill him. Charles signed an order authorizing the massacre of all Huguenots. Shortly after midnight on August 24, armed mobs stormed through Paris breaking into Huguenot houses. They looted the homes and killed men, women, and children. Students murdered their teachers. Debtors sought out and killed the individuals to whom they owed money. At least 3,000 persons were killed in Paris—most of them Huguenots. Because August 24 was St. Bartholomew's Day, the attack upon the Huguenots became known as *St. Bartholomew's Day Massacre.*

The last Valois king died in 1589. The throne then passed to the nearest heir, *Henry IV,* who established the *Bourbon* family on the French throne. He was the leader of the Huguenot cause. King Henry IV ruled from 1589 until 1610. In the hope of ending the civil war and uniting his people, King Henry gave up his Protestant faith and became a Catholic. Since the French were overwhelmingly Catholic, he knew they never could accept a Huguenot king. But as the new ruler, he also issued the *Edict of Nantes* (NAHNTS) in 1598.

This edict was named for the city in western France in which it was issued. It granted religious freedom to the Huguenots. Through this edict, Henry restored peace in France.

War in The Netherlands Other countries also suffered from religious wars in the 1500's. The Spanish Netherlands was among them. In the 1500's, The Netherlands was a possession of Philip II, the king of Spain. Philip was a member of the Hapsburg family.

Calvinism spread through the northern part of The Netherlands. Philip II, a Catholic ruler, decided that it was his duty to stamp out the new religion. The religious persecutions he began sparked a war for independence from Spain. Religion and politics became inseparable. The people of the northern half of the Spanish Netherlands began their struggle against Spain in 1566. The king's army held the southern half of the country, which was mostly Catholic. The Protestant northern half of The Netherlands declared itself a new nation in 1581. With help from Protestant England, it was able to resist Spanish attempts to conquer it. The northern part of the Spanish Netherlands became the present-day country of The Netherlands, and its people are largely Protestant. The southern part of the Spanish Netherlands, on the other hand, is now known as Belgium, and its population is mainly Catholic.

The Spanish Armada Because Queen Elizabeth aided the Dutch, Philip II decided to make war on England. Philip planned to invade England with troops already stationed in the Spanish Netherlands. To accomplish this, a large fleet called an *armada* was dispatched from Spain in 1588. Before the armada reached its destination, it was attacked by the English fleet. In a great naval bat-

Philip II of Spain was a Catholic ruler and decided what religion the Spanish should follow. Should a ruler decide on his subjects' religion?

tle, most of the Spanish ships were sunk or crippled. Those that escaped the sea battle were destroyed later by storms. Philip II was forced to give up his plan to invade England. The Netherlands' struggle for independence lasted until 1609 with a victory over Spain.

The Thirty Years' War At this time, much of Europe was ruled by the Hapsburgs. They were a large and powerful German family with extensive territories in Germany and Austria. One of their territories included Bohemia. Most of Bohemia was Protestant by the early 1600's. *Ferdinand II*, a Hapsburg, became king of Bohemia in 1617 and ruled until 1637. In 1619, he was also elected emperor of the Holy Roman Empire. Upon his election, he set out to do what Philip II had tried to do in The Netherlands—restore the Catholic faith. The Bohemians resisted Ferdinand's plans. They took up arms in defense of their Protestant religion but

RELIGIONS IN EUROPE ABOUT 1648

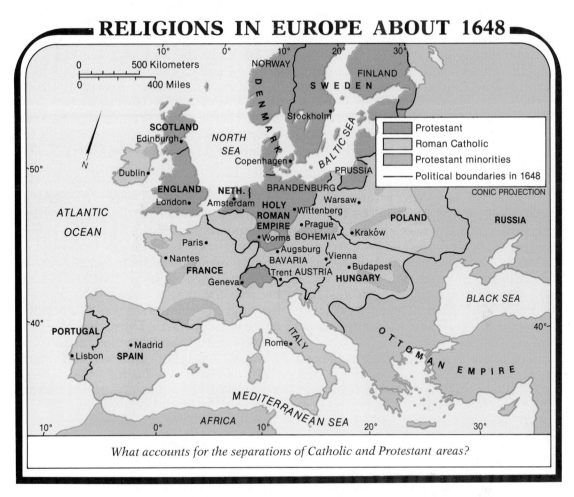

Protestant

Roman Catholic

Protestant minorities

Political boundaries in 1648

CONIC PROJECTION

500 Kilometers

400 Miles

NORWAY · FINLAND · SWEDEN · DENMARK · Stockholm · BALTIC SEA · PRUSSIA · NORTH SEA · SCOTLAND · Edinburgh · Dublin · Copenhagen · BRANDENBURG · Warsaw · ENGLAND · NETH. · London · Amsterdam · HOLY ROMAN EMPIRE · Wittenberg · POLAND · RUSSIA · Prague · ATLANTIC OCEAN · Worms · BOHEMIA · Kraków · Paris · Augsburg · Vienna · Nantes · BAVARIA · Budapest · FRANCE · Trent · AUSTRIA · HUNGARY · Geneva · BLACK SEA · PORTUGAL · Madrid · Rome · ITALY · OTTOMAN EMPIRE · Lisbon · SPAIN · MEDITERRANEAN SEA · AFRICA

What accounts for the separations of Catholic and Protestant areas?

What kinds of weapons and tactics were used during the Thirty Years' War?

217

were crushed in 1620 by the emperor and his Catholic allies.

The defeat of the Bohemians alarmed the Protestant rulers of the small kingdoms within the Holy Roman Empire. They feared Ferdinand II might attempt to remove them and restore Catholicism in the Holy Roman Empire. To prevent this, they banded together and sought foreign assistance against the Hapsburgs. Help was given by Denmark, Sweden, and France. The French king's chief minister was a high-ranking member of the Catholic clergy, **Cardinal Richelieu** (RISH-uh-loo). Aware that this struggle involved more than religion, Richelieu sent aid to the Protestant enemies of the Catholic Hapsburg rulers. He hoped to crush the Hapsburgs and increase the power of France.

The chain of events following Protestant Bohemia's revolt against the Catholic Hapsburgs led to the conflict called the **Thirty Years' War.** From 1618 to 1648, war waged more or less continuously throughout the Holy Roman Empire. At one time or another, almost all the major European countries were involved. The long struggle exhausted Catholic Spain and the Hapsburgs.

The Thirty Years' War caused many hardships in Germany. Lawless armies of many nations marched back and forth across Germany. They stole the crops and cattle of farmers for their armies' food. Civilians were treated brutally or killed. Entire villages were wiped out. Half the population of German towns died. It has been estimated that as many as seven and one half million people may have lost their lives in the German lands during the Thirty Years' War.

In 1648, the war ended with the *Treaty of Westphalia* (west-FAYL-yuh). The treaty actually consisted of many agreements. Most of these arranged territorial changes so that none of the participants in the long war would be left empty-handed. (See map on p. 217.)

After peace was restored in 1648, the Holy Roman Empire was little more than a name. The days of Spain's greatness were over.

Scandinavia's Role in the Thirty Years' War Scandinavia was also affected by the religious wars in Europe. In the 1500's, Sweden was under the rule of Denmark. The Reformation presented an opportunity for the Swedes to revolt against the Catholic king of Denmark. In 1523, they declared their independence. *Gustavus Vasa* (gus-TAY-vus VAH-suh) became the first Swedish king. During his reign, Lutheranism was established as the national faith. Throughout the rest of the century, Sweden was involved in wars with neighboring countries, especially Denmark. During the Thirty Years' War, Sweden played an important role on the Protestant side. By the late 1600's, Sweden had become one of Europe's leading military powers.

SECTION REVIEW

1. Using the information in this section, make a list of the major religious struggles and the countries in which they were fought.
2. In your own words, identify or define: Huguenots, St. Bartholomew's Day Massacre, Bourbon family, Henry IV, Edict of Nantes, Bohemia, Cardinal Richelieu, Treaty of Westphalia.
3. Why was the Spanish Armada organized? What was the result?
4. Why was the Thirty Years' War fought?
▷ During the 1500's and 1600's in Europe, religious differences resulted in many wars. What other causes can result in wars?

DYNASTIC STRUGGLES OF THE 1600's AND 1700's

Western Europe did not enjoy peace for long after the Thirty Years' War. Scarcely twenty years later, the major powers were at war once again. During the 100 years that followed, there was nearly always a major struggle underway somewhere in Europe. The dynastic wars of the 1600's and 1700's, however, were not fought for the same reasons as the religious wars. Some wars were waged by rulers who sought to add territory to their kingdoms. Other dynastic wars were fought to preserve the **balance of power** in western Europe. That is, nations often formed alliances that balanced or equalized each side's power to wage war. As a result of these alliances, no single nation or group of nations could easily dominate others. For example, if one nation grew too powerful, others might try to weaken it by war and thereby restore the balance of power. In the 1600's, France was almost in a position to dominate Europe. It was too powerful to be defeated by anything but a strong alliance of the other European powers. Therefore, other nations in Europe could not help regarding France as a threat to the balance of power. Several times European nations banded together in wars against France. (See chart on p. 227.)

Europeans Contend for Colonies Throughout the 1600's and 1700's, the European countries explored and colonized parts of the Americas, Africa, and the Far East. (The age of exploration and colonization will be discussed later in Unit 7.) During the period 1667-1783, European wars were often carried to colonial areas. The battles fought there were often as significant as those fought in Europe.

SECTION REVIEW

1. Using the chart on page 227, describe the alliances formed during each of the wars of the 1600's and 1700's. How did these alliances reflect the concept of balance of power?
2. According to the chart on page 227, which nations were most often at war in Europe during the 1600's and 1700's? Which nations appear to be leading rivals in most of the conflicts listed on the chart?
3. What were the chief differences between the religious wars of the 1500's and 1600's and the dynastic wars of the 1600's and 1700's?
▶ Do you think balance of power might have something to do with the relations between countries today? Explain your answer.

THE DECLINE OF MONARCHY IN ENGLAND

When Queen Elizabeth I died in 1603, *James I* (the son of Mary Stuart, Queen of Scotland) inherited the English throne. James ruled from 1603 to 1625 and authorized a lengthy translation now known as the King James Bible. King James firmly believed that kings and queens had a right to rule without any limits to their power. He felt that this right was given to all monarchs by God. Thus it was known as the divine right. Like other European kings of the 1600's, James I tried to strengthen royal powers. As a result, he became embroiled in a power struggle with Parliament. This lawmaking body was determined not to allow James to take away its share in the governing of England. King James, however, proceeded to govern as if there were no Parliament. He tried to collect taxes without Parliament's consent. He ignored judges who would not give verdicts in his favor. He went so far as to imprison his political

Here Queen Elizabeth is being carried on a litter by her soldiers. By what means do present-day leaders travel?

opponents. King James quarreled constantly with Parliament about nearly every aspect of government.

The Puritans versus the King   Just like Queen Elizabeth I who ruled before him, James I was determined that there would be only one Christian church in England. By the 1600's, all English subjects had to belong to the **Church of England.** James I was also constantly at odds with a Calvinist minority within the Church of England called the Puritans. Some Puritans wanted to remain part of the Church of England, but they demanded that the church be reformed and reorganized. Other Puritans wanted to leave the Church of England and organize their own separate churches. But King James insisted there be only one church in his kingdom and that all his subjects belong to it and accept its beliefs. He threatened to chase the Puritans out of England if they did not abide by his decisions in religious matters. As a result, many Puritans decided to leave the country to find religious freedom

elsewhere.

Among the Puritans who left England in search of religious freedom were the group who became known as the **Pilgrims.** They went first to The Netherlands and then to the unsettled English lands in North America to find a place where they could practice Calvinism freely. They sailed to North America aboard the "Mayflower" in 1620 and founded the English colony of Plymouth.

Civil War in England   James's son *Charles I* was a staunch believer in the theory of royal rule by divine right. He ignored the rights won by medieval parliaments to share in governing the kingdom. He would not acknowledge the House of Commons' demand for approval of taxes the king wished to collect. A showdown occurred in 1629 when Parliament issued the Petition of Right. This petition demanded, among other things, an end to imprisonment without cause, and to taxation without the consent of Parliament. Charles agreed to the petition then later broke his word. Charles was determined to rule without Parliament's interference. So he dismissed Parliament in 1629. For eleven years the king ruled England in this way, and as a result, many of his subjects turned against him.

Charles' religious policy also cost him support. He believed there must be only one church in his kingdom and that every subject must attend. As head of the church, King Charles introduced religious ceremonies that personally pleased him but offended Puritan members of the Church of England. Many began to believe the king was trying to reintroduce Catholicism. They became suspicious of the powers he gave the bishops of the Church of England.

Because of Charles' religious policy, he became involved in a war with Scotland. The Scots were strongly Calvinist and raised an army to fight against King Charles. An army crossed the border and invaded England. This brought Charles' singlehanded rule to an end. It was impossible to raise an army to fight the Scots without more taxes. And Charles had already used almost every possible way to raise money. Only a newly elected Parliament could persuade the people to accept additional taxes. So Charles was forced to summon a Parliament.

Taking advantage of the king's situation, Parliament tried to limit his powers before giving in to his demand. It arrested the king's chief minister, put him on trial, and executed him. It arrested the Archbishop of Canterbury and sent him to prison. Some members of Parliament proposed doing away with all the bishops in the Church of England. In response to this, the king invaded the House of Commons with 300 soldiers. He planned to arrest the leaders of Parliament who had spoken out against him, but they had escaped in time. Soon there seemed no way to settle the differences between the king and the elected representatives of the people. The conflict between the king and Parliament led to civil war in 1642.

During the war, the royal cause was supported by believers in the divine right of the rulers, by the Church of England, and by most of the upper classes and the rural population. Parliament was supported by opponents of strong monarchy, the Puritans, the middle class, and the city dwellers. Those who stood by the king were called *Cavaliers.* Those who sided with Parliament were called *Roundheads.*

Parliament's most able military leader was *Oliver Cromwell.* Under his leadership, troops of Parliament eventually defeated the king's army. Charles I was captured, put on trial, condemned to death, and executed in 1649.

The Interregnum For the following eleven years (1649-1660), there was no king. This period is called the *interregnum,* meaning "between reigns." During this time, Parliament shared power with Cromwell and his army, but actually Cromwell was the real ruler of England. He was respected abroad for his military power, but as a dictator at home he was never able to establish any form of permanent government.

During the interregnum, Cromwell went to Ireland at the head of an army. He put down an Irish rebellion against English rule that had been smoldering for many years. He treated the Irish cruelly. Cromwell's persecutions created a lasting bitterness toward the English that still exists today.

Scotland also suffered at Cromwell's hands. The Scots were an independent country and had no loyalty to

Cromwell ruled England with Parliament during the interregnum. Here he is shown dissolving Parliament in 1653. Do any world leaders today govern without an elected legislative body?

Cromwell. Charles II, the son of Charles I, was proclaimed king by the Scots.

Cromwell's army marched into Scotland. It defeated the Scots in every battle. Disguising himself, Charles II managed to hide from Cromwell's soldiers for forty days. Barely escaping capture, he sailed to France for safety.

To improve English trade, Cromwell had laws passed banning goods from entering the country except aboard English vessels. Many of the Dutch made their living transporting goods of other countries. This law hurt them economically, and they went to war against England. The two countries fought a naval war. The English won most of the victories and after two years of struggle, peace was restored.

Cromwell ruled as a dictator. He divided England into military districts, and army officers were appointed to govern each one. If Parliament disagreed with Cromwell, he dismissed it and called for new elections. Cromwell declined to be king, but he did take the title "Lord Protector of England" and decided that title was to be passed on to his descendants. But when Cromwell died, his son had no wish to fill his father's position.

The Restoration   After Cromwell's death in 1658, *Charles II*, the son of King Charles I, was called back to England. The return of the monarchy is called the Restoration. Charles II, who reigned from 1660 to 1685, knew that a monarch could not hope to govern without Parliament's support. Although he did not use force to get his way with Parliament, a group within Parliament did not trust his royal power. This group was called the *Whig Party*. There was another party in Parliament called the *Tory Party*. On most issues the Tories supported the king. The Whigs and Tories were the first real political parties in England.

Charles II did clash with Parliament on one issue—religious toleration toward Catholics. Charles tried unsuccessfully to end discrimination against Catholics. He also attempted to restore their civil rights. But Charles was unsuccessful. The Parliaments during his reign passed a number of measures against both Catholics and Puritans. Parliament wanted to restore the Church of England as it had been before the days of Cromwell.

In 1679, Parliament passed a measure of great importance to the later development of liberty for all English subjects. This act was a law known as the *Habeas Corpus Act*. It provided that judges, when requested to do so, must issue a document called a **writ of habeas corpus.** This document must be given to any person taken prisoner by government authorities. The writ directed the jailer to bring the prisoner forward before the judge and to offer reasons why he or she was being imprisoned. This law also provided for speedy trials and established the principle that no person set free by a court could be imprisoned a second time for the same offense. The Habeas Corpus Act later influenced American government and law.

The Glorious Revolution   Charles II was succeeded by his brother *James II* in 1685. The new king became a Catholic. James decided it was his duty to restore the Catholic religion in England. His decision was almost universally opposed. Even believers in a strong monarchy would not support the king on this issue.

Matters reached a crisis in 1688. James' queen—his second wife—gave birth to a son. Until then, the heirs to the throne were James' two Protestant daughters. But the birth of a son meant James' new heir would be a Catholic. This meant that Protestant England would have a monarchy that would be Catholic for many years to come.

A number of important politicians took matters into their own hands. They went abroad to ask James' eldest daughter Mary and her Protestant husband, William of Orange, to come to England as king and queen. William landed in England with an army in 1688. James' troops refused to fight William, so James fled to safety in France. This bloodless revolution in 1688 is known in England as the Glorious Revolution.

The revolution was a victory for Parliament. Parliament removed a king whose politics it disliked and replaced him with monarchs of its choice. William and Mary were not the hereditary heirs to the throne. They owed their position to Parliament. From that time forward, no English monarch could claim a divine right to reign. The Glorious Revolution proved monarchs ruled only by consent of the governed.

The Protestant Succession and Its Reforms   William and Mary ruled from 1688 to 1702. The English people looked forward eagerly to an end to the bitter religious and political controversies that plagued their nation. However, the English still had qualms about royal power. The new rulers, therefore, agreed to a document called the Bill of Rights, which was drawn up by Parliament.

The **Bill of Rights** was a statement denouncing practices that would be considered illegal thereafter. These were mainly things James II had done, such as suspending laws and keeping an army in peacetime without Parliament's consent. Other clauses concerned the right of English subjects to bear arms, speak freely in Parliament, and conduct free elections. No part of the Bill of Rights has ever been repealed. It is still a part of Britain's fundamental law and has greatly influenced American law.

William and Mary also agreed to a document called the *Act of Settlement*, which stated that the throne of England could be occupied only by a Protestant monarch. The purpose of this document was to ensure the place of Protestantism as the state religion and to prevent, as much as possible, future religious wars within England.

Since William and Mary had no children, Parliament provided that Mary's sister Anne should succeed William and Mary to the throne. During Anne's reign, from 1702 to 1714, the kingdoms of England and Scotland were united as one country. Together with Ireland and Wales, these territories became known as Great Britain. After Anne's death, the throne of Great Britain passed to German relatives of the royal family who

A Closer Look

THE BILL OF RIGHTS, 1689

Following the Glorious Revolution of 1688, the Parliament drew up a list of statements that denounced practices widely in use during the reign of James II. These statements, called the Bill of Rights, became laws that ensured the rights of English subjects and are still in effect today. The following are a selection of these laws:

That the pretended power of suspending laws by royal authority, without consent of Parliament, is illegal.

That levying taxes for the use of the crown without the permission of Parliament, or for a longer time or in other manner than shall be granted by Parliament, is illegal.

That the raising or keeping of a standing army within the kingdom in time of peace, unless it be with the consent of Parliament, is against law.

That the freedom of speech and debates in Parliament ought not to be questioned in any court or place out of Parliament.

That jurors must be used in trials and their verdicts listened to.

And that for the redress of all grievances and for the amending, strengthening, and preserving of the laws, Parliament ought to be held frequently.

Adapted from: Edward P. Cheyney. *Readings in English History*. New York: Ginn and Company, 1922 (as reproduced in *Like It Was—Like It Is*, Volume II. edited by Knox Mellon, Jr., and Miriam U. Chrisman. Glenview, Illinois: Scott Foresman and Company, 1972, pp. 305–306.)

1. What things was the king forbidden to do by the Bill of Rights?
2. What rights were preserved for each English citizen by the Bill of Rights?
3. What parts of the English Bill of Rights exist in the Constitution of the United States today?

ruled the German kingdom of Hanover.
The House of Hanover   When George of Hanover ascended the British throne as *George I*, he could not speak a word of English. So the governing of Britain gradually fell into the hands of his ministers. They made decisions for the king.

George did begin a new tradition, however. He made one of his ministers the chief, or prime minister. From the time of George I, the prime minister actually governed in the king's name.

Under George's son and grandson, *George II* and *George III*, the power of the English monarchy decreased. George II allowed the majority in Parliament to select the prime minister for him. George III was periodically insane during his reign and was, therefore, unable to take an active role in governing. After the reigns of the three Georges, the power of the British monarch slowly diminished. By the mid-1800's the monarch reigned as a symbol of the nation but had no real power to govern.

1. **Mapping:** Using the map on page 228, describe the relative location of Ireland, Scotland, and The Netherlands to England.
2. In your own words, identify or define: divine right, Pilgrims, interregnum, Restoration, Tory and Whig parties, writ of habeas corpus, Glorious Revolution.
3. What were some of the reasons why English Puritans opposed King James I and Charles I?
4. Describe the groups that sided with Parliament during the civil war in England. What groups supported the royal cause?
5. In your opinion, what were the most significant developments in English law and government during the reigns of William and Mary, Anne, and the three Georges?
   - Do present-day American ideas about law and government resemble the ideas of England during the 1600's and 1700's? Explain your answer.

SUPREMACY OF ROYAL POWER IN FRANCE

King Henry IV came to the French throne during the religious wars of the 1500's. He restored peace and prosperity to France. His successor, *Louis XIII,* was only nine years old when he ascended the throne. The nobles seized this opportunity to rebel against royal authority. Once again, bitter fighting broke out between Catholics and Huguenots, the French Protestants.

In 1624 Cardinal Richelieu became the chief minister of Louis XIII. Richelieu successfully suppressed the Catholic and Huguenot nobles. He established royal officials to supervise various parts of the country in the king's name. Richelieu put an end to the independence of the nobles and strengthened the monarchy. The cardinal was devoted to France, and he believed that a strong monarchy with unlimited powers was the best government for the nation. He entered the Thirty Years' War, hoping to gain territory for France and weaken its rivals, the Hapsburg emperors. By the end of the Thirty Years' War in 1648, France had become one of the strongest military powers in Europe. But Richelieu's policies had alienated many of the common people of France who were burdened with heavy taxation to support the government.

Louis XIV and Royal Absolutism   In 1643 Louis XIV, a five-year-old boy, succeeded to the throne. The government was in the hands of Cardinal Mazarin (maz-uh-RAN), Richelieu's hand-picked successor. During the first years of Louis' reign, the French nobles made their last attempt to reduce the power of the monarchy. From 1649 to 1652, there were a number of rebellions. But the king's enemies failed to unite the nation or offer France a better form of government. The royal army built up by Richelieu finally destroyed the king's opposition.

With the nobility crushed, Louis XIV realized that he was free to rule as he wished. As king, he now had absolute power. After Mazarin's death in 1661, Louis took personal charge of the government. Until his death in 1715, he ruled almost without opposition. Royal power became *absolute,* or unlimited. It was said that the king possessed a divine right to rule. His subjects, therefore, had no right to question what he did. There were no parliaments in France as there were in England, so there was no check on royal power and

225

Louis XIV

Louis always came to council meetings prepared. He had great patience listening to the advice of his ministers. But he never made a decision on the spur of the moment. His council was free to disagree with the king, although in the end he did what he pleased.

Once a decision was made, however, Louis would tolerate no limits on his power. In 1655, the Parlement of Paris met to discuss some of the king's decrees. Louis went at once to where the court was assembled. Entering the hall dressed in his riding clothes and top boots, whip in hand, Louis threated the judges. "The woes that courts like this bring on are well known to everyone. I order you to break up this assembly at once. You will not question my decrees. I forbid it." Later, Louis took away the functions of the court and gave them to a small committee he appointed.

Under Louis XIV, the place of nobles in government was radically changed. For his advisers and officials, Louis preferred the middle class. Nobles seldom were given posts.

Leading noble families were invited to leave their estates most of the year and attend Louis' court. He had built a huge palace at Versailles (ver-SIE), a short distance outside Paris. The court in 1664 consisted of about 600 persons. At certain times of the year, however, as many as 10,000 people might be found at Versailles attending some special occasion at the royal palace. The greatest of the nobles were royal guests and stayed at the palace. Lesser nobles built homes in Paris.

Each day after working on government business, Louis joined the court at 7:00 PM for amusements—music, dancing, cards, billiards. At any time, anyone might approach the king and speak to him but few took the liberty to do this.

Adapted from: Will and Ariel Durant. **The Age of Louis XIV.** New York: Simon & Schuster, 1963, pp. 15–18 and 31–32.

1. Basing your answer on the information above, do you think Louis XIV was an "absolute" monarch? Explain.
2. How were the French nobles treated by their king?
3. What advantage did Louis XIV attain by having his nobles under his watchful eye?

no representative body to make the people's wishes known. The king had cut himself off from his people.

Louis XIV wanted to expand the borders of France. His attempts to seize territories threatened the southern part of The Netherlands that was still in Spanish hands and the northern part of The Netherlands known as the Dutch Republic. Louis XIV fought three wars: the Dutch War (1672–1678), the War of the League of Augsburg (1668–1697), and the War of the Spanish Succession (1702–1713). (See the chart on page 227.) In each he faced the Dutch, who organized alliances to stop him.

EUROPEAN WARS OF THE 17TH AND 18TH CENTURIES

Dates	Conflicts and Major Contenders		Treaty Ending the Conflict
1667–1668	War of Devolution France	vs. England, Spain, Netherlands, Sweden	**Treaty of Aix-la-Chapelle** France kept about half the territory conquered by the French in the Spanish Netherlands. Other conquered territories were returned to Spanish control.
1672–1678	Dutch War France	vs. Netherlands, Spain, Austria, England	**Treaty of Nijmegen** France returned captured Dutch territory to the Dutch in return for future Dutch neutrality in case of war. From Spain, France took Franche-Comte and small parts of the Spanish Netherlands.
1689–1697	War of the League of Augsburg France	vs. England, Netherlands, Austria, Spain, Sweden	**Treaty of Ryswick** France gave up most of the territory gained since the Treaty of Nijmegen but was permitted to keep Alsace.
1702–1713	War of the Spanish Succession Britain Netherlands German states Austria Portugal	vs. France, Spain	**Treaty of Utrecht** Spain lost Gibraltar to Britain and gave the Spanish Netherlands and southern Italy to Austria. France gave some of its territory in North America to Britain.
1733–1735	War of Polish Succession Russia Austria	vs. Spain, France	**Treaty of Vienna** Southern Italy and Sicily were given to Spain. Parts of northern Italy were given to Austria.
1740–1748	War of Austrian Succession Britain Austria	vs. France, Prussia, Spain	**Treaty of Aix-la-Chapelle** Prussia kept territory in northern Austria conquered during the war. Britain and France exchanged territories seized from one another in India and North America.
1756–1763	Seven Years' War Britain Prussia	vs. France, Austria, Russia	**Treaty of Paris** France lost Canada to Britain and gave the Louisiana territory to Spain. Spain gave Florida to Britain. France lost almost all its colonial possessions in India.

EUROPE IN 1763

Hapsburg Possessions

CONIC PROJECTION

SCOTLAND

IRELAND
GREAT BRITAIN

NORTH
SEA

ENGLAND

NETH.

DENMARK

SWEDEN

BALTIC SEA

EAST
PRUSSIA

PRUSSIA

POLAND

RUSSIA

ATLANTIC
OCEAN

FRANCE

BAVARIA

AUSTRIA

HUNGARY

VENICE

BLACK SEA

PAPAL
STATES

PORTUGAL

SPAIN

SARDINIA

PAPAL
STATES

MONTENEGRO

OTTOMAN EMPIRE

NAPLES

MEDITERRANEAN SEA

500 Kilometers

400 Miles

Which parts of Europe were involved in wars of the seventeenth and eighteenth centuries?

The War of the Spanish Succession
The last war Louis fought was the *War of the Spanish Succession.* The king of Spain died in 1700, leaving no successors. Both Louis XIV and the Holy Roman Emperor, Leopold I, were related to the Spanish royal family. Each claimed the throne. Louis was willing to give up the throne himself, but he wished to make his grandson king of Spain. Other European powers were alarmed at the prospect of France and Spain being united under the Bourbons—the French royal family. As a result, other European powers went to war against France and Spain.

The war went on for twelve years.

The *Treaty of Utrecht* (YOO-trekt) restored peace in 1713. By that time, Louis XIV and his armies were almost exhausted. Under the terms of the treaty, Louis' grandson received the throne of Spain. However, the Spanish Netherlands were taken from Spain and given to the Hapsburgs. During the war, France had lost many of its colonial possessions to the English. The French had to agree that no one member of the Bourbon family ever would rule both France and Spain. Thus Louis XIV's reign did not end in victory or glory. The cost of his wars created a great financial debt from which later French kings were never able to recover.

Though Louis XIV may have been an enemy to other European kingdoms, French culture was imitated everywhere. French was spoken by the diplomats and by the upper classes of every country. Louis XIV was Europe's richest and most powerful monarch. His court and form of government were imitated by monarchs everywhere. French palaces, French styles in clothing, French literature and drama all became models for Europeans. France was acknowledged as the leader of Europe. In fact, the years from 1661 to 1715 have been called the Age of Louis XIV.

Problems Plague France   Royal absolutism continued in France after Louis XIV's death. But his two successors, *Louis XV* and *Louis XVI*, were not as interested or as skilled in matters of government as Louis XIV had been. Like Louis XIV, however, they lived a life of luxury, largely cut off from the problems of their subjects.

In 1788, King Louis XVI summoned the Estates General, which French kings had ruled without since 1614. Louis XVI expected the Estates General to help find solutions to the financial problems of France. His decision marked the beginning of the end of absolute monarchy in France.

The Enlightenment   In the 1700's a new movement, based on reform and reason, spread among the intellectuals in Europe. This movement was known as the **Enlightenment.** It was characterized by rationalism, skepticism, experimentation in social and political thought, and a questioning of authority. The center of the movement was France, and the writers and critics who spread demands for change were known as *philosophes* (fee-luh-ZAWFS) or philosophers. They believed that problems could be solved by reason and rational thinking. This is why the period is sometimes called the Age of Reason.

The scientific advances of the 1600's and 1700's influenced the philosophes. They believed that scientific methods could be applied to human ideas and customs. Some claimed that science had proved the universe was governed by natural laws. Some said God had created the world and made rules for all living creatures. But they claimed God took no further interest in human affairs.

Some philosophes criticized government. They called for freedom of speech and limits on the privileges of kings and nobles. A few of Europe's absolute monarchs were influenced by these new ideas, but little in the way of reform came about. However, the writers and critics of the Enlightenment were important because the ideas they spread became the basis for the American and French Revolutions later in the 1700's.

SECTION REVIEW

1. Mapping: Comparing the maps on pages 165 and 228, describe how western Europe had changed between 1550 and 1763.
2. In your own words, identify or define: absolute rule, Louis XIV, Treaty of Utrecht, Enlightenment.
3. What were the policies of Cardinal Richelieu designed to accomplish?
4. What brought about the War of the Spanish Succession?
5. Explain this statement: "Louis XIV's reign did not end in victory or glory."

⟩ During the 1700's, French culture was imitated throughout Europe. What country is most widely imitated in the world today? Why? What do you think leads people to imitate a foreign culture?

Reviewing the Unit

Unit Summary

After you have read the selection below, answer the questions that follow.

The fall of Rome and the invasions of Germanic tribes left western Europe in a state of political instability. Many individuals believed Europe had entered the "Dark Ages."

One Germanic tribe, the Franks, eventually restored political unity. Under Charlemagne, a large empire was created. Christianity spread rapidly, and the Catholic Church, headed by the pope in Rome, became an important institution. Town life, too, eventually revived. Trade increased. Following the Crusades a great revival of learning and culture began. This movement was known as the Renaissance, or re-birth. It made important contributions to a new European civilization.

After Charlemagne's death, his empire broke up and feudalism developed. Feudalism did not favor the growth of a strong central government headed by a single monarch. Feudal lords wanted weak kings in order to keep power in their own hands.

The 1500's were years of religious turmoil. In 1517, a German priest named Martin Luther began a revolt against abuses within the Catholic Church that resulted in the Reformation. Luther stimulated other reformers such as John Calvin, the founder of Calvinism. To halt the spread of Protestantism, the Catholic Church launched changes of its own and began a Counter-Reformation. Prostestantism was permanently established, however,

The Thirty Years' War was the last religious war. Following it, kings and emperors fought wars in order to gain territory. If one king grew too powerful, his enemies united against him to restore the balance of power.

By the 1700's, very different forms of government had developed in England and France. In the 1600's, the monarchs of both countries had claimed divine authority to rule without interference. But by 1688, Parliament held political power in England. In France, royal absolutism triumphed and reached its height under King Louis XIV. But royal absolutism was challenged in the 1700's by a movement known as the Enlightenment.

Developing Your Reading Skills

1. What in your opinion is the one main idea in the reading above?
2. In your own words, state the main idea in this reading about: **a.** feudalism, **b.** the Reformation, and **c.** government in England and France.

Developing a Sense of Time

Examine the time line below and answer the questions which follow it.

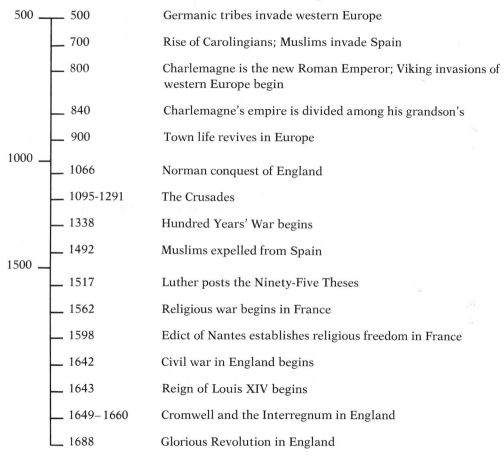

500	500	Germanic tribes invade western Europe
	700	Rise of Carolingians; Muslims invade Spain
	800	Charlemagne is the new Roman Emperor; Viking invasions of western Europe begin
	840	Charlemagne's empire is divided among his grandson's
	900	Town life revives in Europe
1000	1066	Norman conquest of England
	1095-1291	The Crusades
	1338	Hundred Years' War begins
	1492	Muslims expelled from Spain
1500	1517	Luther posts the Ninety-Five Theses
	1562	Religious war begins in France
	1598	Edict of Nantes establishes religious freedom in France
	1642	Civil war in England begins
	1643	Reign of Louis XIV begins
	1649–1660	Cromwell and the Interregnum in England
	1688	Glorious Revolution in England

1. Which monarchy was established first: Norman or Carolingian?
2. When did the Muslim invasion of Spain begin? When were they driven out of Spain?
3. What was happening in France at the time of the English Civil War?
4. When did the last Crusade end?
5. List three other key events from Unit 4 that could be added to this time line and give a reason for selecting each.

Recalling the Facts

1. Describe in detail the feudal system of medieval Europe.
2. What were the Crusades? How did they affect the development of medieval Europe?
3. What brought about a revival of town life during the Middle Ages?
4. Who were the five Tudor monarchs who ruled England?
5. Describe the realm of the Holy Roman Empire under Otto I.
6. Name four important Renaissance figures and offer examples of their contributions to western culture.
7. Give at least two examples of religious wars in Europe in the 1500's and 1600's. How did these end?
8. How did the governments of England and France change during the 1600's and 1700's? Why were these changes significant?
9. Give reasons why the Glorious Revolution has been called a victory for Parliament over the monarchy in England.

Using Your Vocabulary

1. Name the invaders of early medieval Europe. What effect did each have on western Europe?
2. What is meant by the "Dark Ages"?
3. Define the term "justice." What did the term "justice" mean to a serf or peasant on a medieval manor?
4. Distinguish between a pilgrimage and a crusade. Give reasons why a person might have joined either.
5. Define the term "parliament." Give examples of early parliaments in three countries of Europe.
6. What is meant by the term "despot"? What did the term mean in Italy during the Middle Ages? What did Machiavelli have to do with despots?
7. Explain the terms "Reformation" and "Counter-Reformation." In the 1500's, how might a Protestant and a Catholic have used these terms?
8. Define and give an example of the concept "balance of power."
9. Explain the terms *Enlightenment* and *philosophes*.

Using Your Geography Skills

1. How can western Europe be distinguished geographically from eastern Europe?
2. Using information in your textbook and the map on page 169, describe: **a.** the extent of the empire created by Charlemagne, and **b.** how it was later divided among his grandsons.
3. The Vikings were a sea-going people and good sailors. Using the information on pages 170–171 and the map on page 165, trace the various Viking raids.
4. Using the map on page 165, describe the relative location of the Papal States. How did these Papal States come into the possession of the popes?
5. Using the map on page 217, describe the religious divisions in western Europe by 1600.
6. Identify each country that participated in the Thirty Years' War. Locate each of these on the map on page 217. Where did most of the fighting take place during the war?

Developing Your Writing Skills

In this unit you have learned about the development of England and France from the early Middle Ages to the 1600's and 1700's. Using your knowledge of the very different forms of government that eventually developed in each country, consider the following:

FORMING AN OPINION

1. Suppose you had to make a choice between living under a form of government that had developed in England by the 1600's and 1700's, or the form of government that had developed in France. Which would you choose and why?
2. List as many characteristics as possible of the form of government you would choose.

SUPPORTING AN OPINION

In a short essay, explain why you selected this type of government. Using the list completed for question 2, begin your essay by completing the following topic sentence: I favor the form of government that developed in England (France) by the 1600's and 1700's because _____

Why Study the Past?

If it were possible to enter a time machine and go back in time to the Middle Ages in western Europe, is there any special person you would like to have met? What particular event of history would you have liked to alter? Would your alteration have changed today's world in any particular way?

Your History Bookshelf

Chamberlain, E. R. *Everyday Life in Renaissance Times.* New York: Putnam, 1969.

Byrne, Muriel St. C. *Elizabethan Life in Town and Country.* New York: Barnes & Noble, 1961.

David, Williams Stearns. *Life on a Medieval Barony.* New York: Harper & Row, 1951.

Easton, Stewart C. *The Western Heritage.* New York: Holt, Rinehart and Winston, 1966.

Hartman, Gertrude. *Medieval Days and Ways.* New York: Macmillan, 1965.

Packard, Laurence Bradford. *The Age of Louis XIV.* New York: Holt, Rinehart and Winston, 1966.

Trevor-Roper, Hugh. *The Rise of Christian Europe.* London: Harcourt Brace Jovanovich, 1965.

unit 5

The World of
East Europe and Islam

The following story was told by a German noble after his return from a visit to Russia during the 1850's. It is said to be a true account and was used by the noble to illustrate the character of the Russian people in the 1800's. "During the first days of spring it was the custom for everyone connected with the court of Tsar Alexander II to take a walk in the garden between the royal palace and the banks of the river. There one day the tsar noticed a sentry standing guard in the middle of a plot of grass. The soldier was asked why he was there when there was nothing for him to stand guard over. He could only answer, 'Those are my orders.'

"Therefore, the tsar sent one of his court officials to the guardhouse to ask for an explanation. Why was a sentry standing guard in the middle of a lawn every day? No one knew. The only explanation anyone could give was that a sentry had to stand there from winter to summer. But no one knew why. The original order to do this could no longer be found—if indeed it had ever existed at all.

"The matter was talked about at court. It reached the ears of the palace servants. One of these, an old man, came forward. He told the tsar that he thought he could solve the mystery. He said that long ago his father had once said to him as they passed the sentry in the garden, 'There he is, still standing guard over the flower.' It seems that on that spot the Empress Catherine II once noticed a wild flower in bloom. It had blossomed very early in the spring. She gave orders to the guards that it was not to be picked.

"This command had been carried out by placing a sentry on the spot to guard the flower, and ever since then a sentry had stood guard on that same spot."

This story of how a Russian soldier obeyed orders given to someone else long before he was born may seem foolish or even unbelievable to us today. But it does point out that the absolute rule of the Russian tsars was obeyed without question. Stories such as this can provide a personal view into the times, political situation, and histories of other people.

In this unit, you will read about the histories of the eastern Europeans, Muslims, and Russians during the Middle Ages and early modern times. The material in the unit traces the origins of each of these groups of people, showing their political, social, and economic relationships to each other and to western Europe. The influence of geography, foreign invasions, the rise and fall of empires and great leaders, wars, religious conflicts, and great contributions to western civilization are some of the themes that characterize the histories of each of these groups of people. As you read, watch for these themes. Using common themes historians are always interested in making comparisons, noting cultural influences, and citing differences in the development of different groups of people.

Unit Goals

1. To know the land and people of early eastern Europe and the present-day countries that comprise that region.
2. To be able to compare the government and religion of the Byzantine Empire with the government and religion of western Europe during the Middle Ages.
3. To understand the origin and character of Islam and the lives of Christians and Jews under Muslim rule.
4. To know which peoples invaded eastern Europe and their effect on the life of eastern European peoples during the Middle Ages.
5. To know the causes of the decline of Poland during the 1700's and the effect of its decline on the other powers of eastern Europe.
6. To understand the growth of Russia during medieval and early modern times.

Eastern Europe

10° 20° 30° 40° 50° 60°

60°

S W E D E N

FINLAND

Helsinki

Stockholm

Tallinn

★ St. Petersburg

ESTONIA

Novogrod

Riga

LIVONIA

Volga R.

LITHUANIA

Dvina R.

Moscow

RUSSIA

Vilnyus

EAST
PRUSSIA

BALTIC SEA

URAL MTS.

Oder R.

Vistula R.

★ Warsaw

POLAND

Ural R.

50°

gue

Kraków

Kiev

TRIA

Dniester R.

UKRAINE

Dnieper R.

COSSACKS

Vienna

CARPATHIAN MTS.

Don R.

★ Budapest

MOLDAVIA

HUNGARY

TARTARS

CASPIAN SEA

va R.

Belgrade

CRIMEA

CAUCASUS MTS.

BOSNIA

SERBIA

WALACHIA

Bucharest

Danube R.

BLACK SEA

BALKAN PENINSULA

Tirnovo

IC SEA

Sofia

BULGARIA

40°

ES

MONTENEGRO

Maritsa R.

Durazzo

Adrianople

RUMELIA

BOSPORUS

NIAN
SEA

SEA OF
MARMARA

★ Constantinople

AEGEAN
SEA

DARDANELLES

GREECE

O T T O M A N   E M P I R E

Athens

Navarino

CONIC PROJECTION

– – – – Political Boundaries in 1763

0   400 Kilometers

0   300 Miles

MEDITERRANEAN
SEA

20° 30° CYPRUS 40°

The Land and the Peoples of Eastern Europe

THE EASTERN EUROPEANS

In eastern Europe, the Roman Empire lasted for about 1,000 years after the western part of the empire had fallen to the "barbarians." However, the Roman Empire in the East became very different during the Middle Ages from what it had been in ancient times.

A number of new kingdoms were founded beyond the empire's frontiers in eastern Europe. As a result, the empire spent much of its energy and resources attempting to protect itself from these rival kingdoms. There were also threats of invasions by peoples from Asia, the Middle East, Russia, and western Europe. These strong enemies finally succeeded in undermining the power of the eastern empire, and it began to decline in strength and size.

By the 1500's, almost all the small kingdoms of eastern Europe disappeared along with the eastern Roman Empire. The eastern half of Europe was then divided among a few great new empires that had conquered the area and would continue to dominate it until modern times. (See the map on page 237.) While western Europeans were already beginning to develop modern nations, the formation of eastern European nations was delayed for hundreds of years as the people struggled to free themselves from their conquerors.

The Geography of Eastern Europe
If you were to draw an imaginary line on the Atlas of Europe extending from the Baltic (BAWL-tic) Sea southward along the Oder (ODE-ur) River to the city of Vienna (vee-EN-uh), and from there to the city of Trieste (tree-EST) on the Adriatic (ay-dree-AT-ik) coast, you would have a fairly accurate dividing line between eastern and western Europe. Looking again at the Atlas, you can also see that modern-day eastern Europe includes the following countries: Poland (POE-land), Czechoslovakia (check-uh-sloe-VAHK-ee-uh), Hungary (HUN-guh-ree), Yugoslavia (yoo-goe-SLAHV-ee-uh), Albania (al-BAY-nee-uh), Greece, Bulgaria (bul-GAR-ee-uh), and Romania (rooh-MAY-nee-uh).

Draw an imaginary line connecting the cities of Trieste and Belgrade (BEL-grade) in Yugoslavia, with Bucharest (BOO-kuh-rest) in Romania. The region south of this line is a mountainous area known as the Balkans (BAWL-kunz). The *Balkans* include parts of Yugoslavia and Romania, and all of Albania, Bulgaria, and Greece. The Balkan area is separated from Turkey and the rest of the Middle East by two waterways called the Dardanelles (dahrd-'n-ELZ) and the Bosporus (BAHS-puh-

238

rus). They connect the Aegean (ih-JEE-un) and the Black seas, and they form a dividing line between the Middle East and Europe. (See the map on page 237.)

To the east of Poland and Romania lies Russia. Even though it was cut off from contact with the rest of Europe until modern times, Russia had a great influence upon the history of eastern Europe. The heartland of Russia lies between its border with eastern Europe and the Ural (YOOR-ul) Mountains. This part is known as European Russia and has been the scene of the most important events in Russia's history. All of the territory of Russia that lies east of the Ural Mountains and stretches to the Pacific Ocean is called *Siberia* (sie-BIR-ee-uh).

The Peoples and Languages of Eastern Europe   Since ancient times, eastern Europe and Russia have been invaded again and again. This is because there are few natural barriers, such as high mountains or broad rivers, between Europe and Asia. (See the map on page 237.) Most of the invaders of the eastern Roman Empire pushed westward from central Asia into the richer, more fertile lands of eastern Europe. Some were nomadic people who raided settlements and then moved on. Others went to Europe as raiders but then settled down and became farmers or townspeople. Each group of invaders brought with them new customs and new languages.

As a result of these many invasions, the people of eastern Europe can today be divided into several groups, depending on their languages. There are many more languages spoken in eastern Europe than there are in western Europe.

Cultural Groups Were Scattered   In western Europe, people speaking the same language usually lived together in

This satellite photo shows the Dardanelles. What is the strategic value of this area?

the same area. For example, the people of France spoke French and those of Great Britain spoke English. But in eastern Europe, people speaking the same language did not always live in the same place. They were scattered from country to country. A number of different cultural groups, each speaking its own language, might be found in any one country. For example, in the early Middle Ages in the kingdom of Hungary lived Magyars (MAG-yahrz), who spoke Hungarian, Germans, who spoke German, and *Croats* (KROTES), who spoke Croatian.

In western Europe, where people speaking the same language lived in the same area, it was easier for them to unite and form a separate country with their own ruler. In eastern Europe this unity was more difficult to accomplish. Early eastern European kingdoms often included large groups of people speaking languages different from the national language. This mixture of languages often led to misunderstanding, unrest, and even to rebellion.

Religions in Eastern Europe Christianity was the major religion in eastern Europe but eastern Europe was never united by a single faith. Some eastern Europeans became Roman Catholics; some adopted the faith of the early Greek Christians, which differed from Roman Catholicism; others established their own national churches. Some people also became Muslims (MUZ-lums).

The Search for Independence In western Europe, the many nations that were established in the Middle Ages, whether large or small, survived to modern times. But the medieval kingdoms of eastern Europe were destroyed by the foreign empires that absorbed them. However, the eastern Europeans never gave up their longing for independence. They were proud of their early history, and they looked forward to the day when their territories might be re-established. History was important to them. It kept alive their pride, their sense of being different from their conquerors, and their hopes for freedom. Perhaps it is not surprising that some of the leaders in the struggle for independence in eastern Europe had first been historians who had studied the history of their own people.

240

SECTION REVIEW

1. Mapping: Using the map on page 237 and the information on page 238 of the text, describe the geographic boundaries that separate eastern Europe from western Europe and the Middle East. Using the Atlas of Europe, list the modern-day countries, major rivers, and mountain ranges of eastern Europe.

2. In your own words define or identify: Balkans, Dardanelles and Bosporus, European Russia, Siberia.

3. Describe three ways in which western European history has been different from eastern European history.

▶ Do you know of any groups of people living in the United States that speak languages other than English? List them. What kinds of problems do these groups face because they do not speak the national language? Why do many of these groups want their children to know both English and their own native language?

THE EASTERN LANDS OF THE ROMAN EMPIRE

As was discussed in Unit 3, the Romans once ruled a vast empire that included most of Europe, the Middle East, and North Africa. This empire was governed from the capital city, Rome. In 330 A.D. the Roman emperor Constantine (KAHN-stun-teen) founded a second capital in the eastern part of the empire named Constantinople (KAHN-stant-'n-OE-pul). It was located at the entrance to the Black Sea, on the ruins of an ancient city named Byzantium (buh-ZANT-ee-um). All ships entering or leaving the Black Sea sailed past Constantinople, and it became an important port.

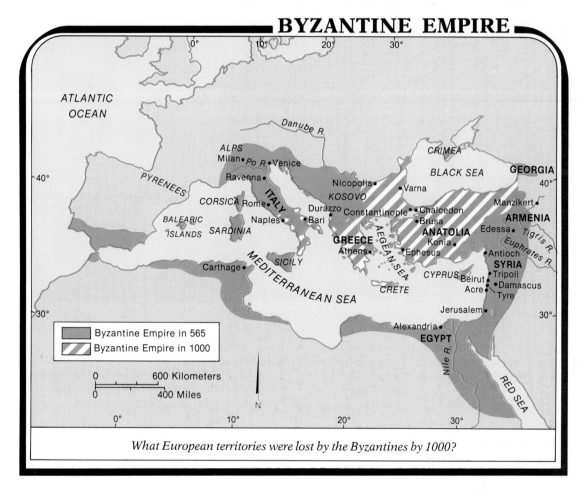

ATLANTIC OCEAN

Danube R.

ALPS
Milan • Po R. • Venice
Ravenna •
PYRENEES
CORSICA Rome •
ITALY
BALEARIC
ISLANDS SARDINIA
Naples •
• Bari

Nicopolis •
KOSOVO
Durazzo • Constantinople • • Chalcedon
• Brusa

CRIMEA

BLACK SEA
• Varna

GEORGIA

Manzikert •
ARMENIA
Edessa • Tigris R.
Euphrates R.

GREECE
Athens •
AEGEAN SEA
• Ephesus
ANATOLIA
Konia •

Antioch •
SYRIA
• Tripoli
• Damascus
Acre • Tyre

Carthage •
MEDITERRANEAN SEA
SICILY

CRETE
CYPRUS Beirut •

Jerusalem •

Alexandria •
EGYPT

Nile R.

RED SEA

Byzantine Empire in 565
Byzantine Empire in 1000

0   600 Kilometers
0   400 Miles

N

What European territories were lost by the Byzantines by 1000?

Emperor Constantine ruled the Roman Empire from 306 until 337. He came to realize the empire was too large to be governed efficiently by one person. After Constantine's death, one of his sons ruled the western half of the empire from Rome. The other son became the emperor at Constantinople and ruled the eastern half of the empire. Thus the eastern and western parts of the empire developed different ways of life. Although Constantinople was ruled by Roman emperors, the city's culture was mostly Greek. In time, Greek even replaced Latin as the official language of the eastern empire.

The Byzantine Empire   After the fall of Rome in 476 A.D., the eastern part of the Roman Empire became known as the *Byzantine* (BIZ-'n-teen) *Empire.* Some of the early Byzantine emperors tried to gain back the lands lost to the "barbarians" in western Europe. The emperor *Justinian* (juh-STIN-ee-un), who ruled from 527 to 565, restored much of the old empire's territory.

Justinian's Conquests   After the collapse of Rome, North Africa had fallen to the Vandals (VAN-d'lz), a Germanic people. In 533, Justinian dispatched an invasion fleet to North Africa. Landing at Carthage (KAHR-thij), the Byzantine

241

The emperor Justinian stands in the midst of his advisors. He thought of himself as a Roman emperor. How much of the old empire did he recover?

army defeated the Vandals and took the city. (See the map on page 241.) Carthage and parts of North Africa remained in Byzantine hands for about a century.

The Germanic "barbarians" who overran the Italian peninsula were known as the Ostrogoths (AHS-truh-goths), or East Goths. In 535, a Byzantine fleet sailed from North Africa and landed troops in Italy. This began a war against the Ostrogoths that dragged on for almost twenty years. The Byzantines successfully took control of Italy, but the long war nearly destroyed the Italian peninsula. There was great loss of life. Rome and other cities were left in ruins.

Justinian's generals also tried to reconquer Spain from the Visigoths (VIZ-uh-goths) in 554. But the imperial armies had little success. Only a small corner of southeastern Spain was taken. The emperor's goal of reconquering France, Britain, and parts of Germany had to be abandoned. As a result, the empire in the west that Justinian had won back was much smaller than the Roman Empire had been.

Justinian did not re-establish Rome as the capital of the western part of his empire. (See the map on page 241.) However, he did leave an official in Italy to govern in his name. Justinian died only a short time after the conquest of Italy.

The Code of Justinian Justinian's greatest accomplishment was the writing of a new code of laws. In 528, he appointed a small group of officials to sort through the laws from all corners of the empire. They were to simplify these laws, organize them, and produce a single law code for the whole empire. The result of their work is called the **Code of Justinian.** This new code was important because it preserved the legal advances made by the Romans.

Invasions of the Empire Justinian's attempt to reunite the eastern and western parts of the old Roman empire left the Byzantine treasury empty. His successors could not hold on to the lands Justinian had taken, and a few years after his death, another group of Germanic "barbarians" invaded Italy. These were the Lombards (LOM-bahrdz). Within seven years, the Lombards had overrun northern Italy, and by 605 all of Italy except for a few cities and the southern tip of the Italian peninsula had fallen to them. A short time later, the Visigoths retook the southeastern corner of Spain from the Byzantines. And by the early 700's, the Byzantines had lost all of North Africa to the Muslims. As a result, most of Justinian's conquests in the west were lost.

The Byzantine Empire was further threatened during this time from the north, across the Danube River, by peoples known as the *Slavs* (SLAHVZ) and the Avars (AH-vahrs), who were pushing into the Balkans. From the east, the Persians threatened the empire. However, early in the seventh century the Persians were replaced by a greater threat, the Muslims. Within 100 years, the Muslims had taken the eastern and southern parts of the Byzantine Empire. Muslim armies attacked Constantinople several times. Late in the 600's, another enemy of the Byzantines appeared in the Balkans—the *Bulgars* (BUL-gahrz). They settled the land known as Bulgaria. (See the Atlas of Europe.) Thus surrounded by enemies, the Byzantime Empire by 700 was in serious peril.

Leo III At this time of crisis, Leo III, who ruled from 717 to 741, came to the Byzantine throne. Leo, however, was an able general who beat back the Muslim attackers from Constantinople. He then reformed the government and the army. Leo's reforms paved the way for a revival of Byzantine strength in the 800's that lasted for almost 200 years. During this period of renewed Byzantine power, parts of southern Italy were retaken. The Bulgars were defeated, and the territories previously lost to the Muslims were reconquered.

Basil II The empire reached a high point under **Basil** (BAZ-ul) **II,** who ruled from 976 to 1025. Basil greatly expanded the boundaries of the empire. Contact with Russia also increased during this time. The Russians patterned their government after that in Constantinople and imitated Byzantine art and architecture. The Russians accepted Christianity from the empire's Orthodox missionaries.

Basil's reign was a prosperous time for the empire. Trade increased, businesses thrived, and Constantinople became the richest city in the Mediterranean (med-uh-tuh-RAY-nee-un) world.

The Decline and Fall of the Empire After the death of Basil II, the Byzantine Empire gradually declined and never recovered. The territories of the empire slowly shrank in size until nothing was left except Constantinople and the surrounding countryside. Then in 1453, Constantinople fell to the Ottoman Turks.

One reason for the empire's decline was its rivalry with the city of Venice (VEN-us). Venice had been able to preserve its independence when the German "barbarians" overran Italy. By the eleventh century, Venice was an important center of trade. It had built up its naval power and soon dominated the Adriatic Sea. Venice threatened to replace Constantinople as the commercial leader of the eastern end of the Mediterranean.

Also in the eleventh century, a new threat came from the *Seljuk* (SEL-jook)

Turks. They had moved into the Middle East from central Asia. They overran Persia, captured the Holy Land, and seized a large part of the eastern Byzantine empire. In desperation, the Byzantine emperor appealed to the pope in Rome for help. As a result, a series of Crusades were organized in western Europe to rescue the Byzantine Empire and restore Christian control over the Holy Land.

However, in 1204 the empire's rival, Venice, persuaded the Crusaders to attack Constantinople rather than march on the Holy Land. The Crusaders seized the city and set up a kingdom of their own, known as the *Latin Kingdom.*

The city of Constantinople and a small part of the Byzantine Empire made up the Latin Kingdom of the Crusaders. The rest of the Byzantine lands became small independent states, each with its own ruler. One of these rulers, *Michael Paleologus* (pay-lee-AH-luh-gus) conquered Constantinople in 1261. He took over the Crusaders' kingdom and restored the Byzantine Empire. He and his successors, known as the Paleologic (pay-lee-AH-loe-jik) emperors, ruled the empire until its final collapse in 1453.

The Paleologic emperors faced another menace. The empire of the Seljuk Turks fell to another Turkish tribe, the Ottomans (AHT-uh-MUNZ). The *Ottoman Turks* were attracted to the wealth of eastern Europe. In the middle of the fourteenth century, they moved from what today is Turkey into the Balkans. The Ottomans bypassed Constantinople. They slowly conquered Greece and Bulgaria and the other Balkan kingdoms. They were also able to turn back the armies sent against them from Hungary and other parts of Christian Europe. In the end, all of the Balkans fell to the Turks.

In 1453, the Ottoman Turks turned against Constantinople. The city was under attack for seven weeks. The Turkish army numbered from 140,000 to 160,000 men. The small Byzantine army defending the city was outnumbered twenty to one. The defenders could not hold out against the Turkish cannons, which used gunpowder. The cannons destroyed the city walls, and Constantinople fell. The last Byzantine emperor died during the Turkish seizure of the city. This brought the Byzantine Empire to an end.

SECTION REVIEW

1. Mapping: Using the map on page 237, locate by means of latitude and longitude coordinates the city of Constantinople. What territories did the Byzantines lose between 565 and 1000? (See page 241.)
2. In your own words, define or identify: Constantine, Justinian, Basil II, Latin Kingdom, Ottoman Turks, Michael Paleologus.
3. Which parts of the old Roman Empire was the Emperor Justinian able to recover? Which groups of people did he have to fight to do so?
   ◗ You have learned that Justinian and Basil II were considered great rulers of their times. Who do you think is a great political leader today? Why?

CONTRIBUTIONS OF THE BYZANTINE EMPIRE

The Byzantine Empire made a number of contributions to civilization. One of its most important contributions was its preservation of many of the advances of the Roman Empire.

Government in the Byzantine Empire

The Byzantine Empire inherited many of its principles of government from the ancient Romans. One of these principles was that the government should have control of almost every activity in the empire. The Byzantines accepted the idea that the emperor's authority was absolute, or unlimited. This style of government also influenced Russia and other parts of eastern Europe where rulers tried to imitate Byzantine government.

Christianity in the Byzantine Empire

The division of the Roman Empire led to a division in early Christianity. The Christians in the Byzantine Empire held basically the same religious beliefs as the Roman Catholics and worshiped in the same way. However, the Christians in western Europe were united into one church under the leadership of the pope. In eastern Christianity, each bishop or archbishop usually was an independent church leader. Some archbishops of the eastern church, however, were more important than others. These clergy were called **patriarchs** (PAY-tree-ahrks). After Rome fell to the "barbarians," some eastern Christians looked to Constantinople as the new center of Christianity. But the patriarch in Constantinople never possessed as much authority as the pope in Rome.

As in all other aspects of their subjects' lives, the Byzantine emperors' decisions in matters of religion were absolute. The emperors decided what should be believed by the members of the Christian church, and they chose the clergy. As a result, the clergy in the Byzantine Empire never became as powerful as that in western Europe.

The Iconoclastic Controversy During the reign of Emperor Leo III a serious controversy arose over the use of

Icons such as this one of the Madonna and child appeared in Orthodox churches. What is the purpose of religious art such as this?

statues and religious paintings, called *icons* (IE-kahnz), in Christian worship. In 726, the emperor banned their use. He believed the use of icons and statues was a form of *idolatry* (ie-DAHL-uh-tree), or idol worship. Leo ordered the removal of all statues from the churches. Church walls filled with icons were to be painted white, to cover the religious pictures. Leo's actions raised a storm of protest. Troops were used to enforce his orders in the east. Disputes over the use of statues and icons continued for more than 100 years and created greater hostility between eastern and western Christians. The dispute finally ended with the restoration of icons, but not statues, in eastern churches.

245

The Orthodox Church   Like the Roman Catholics in the west, eastern church officials were active in spreading Christianity in their part of the world. Because of their efforts, many people in eastern Europe accepted the Christian faith. As new kingdoms were created among these peoples, each kingdom formed its own church administration with its own bishops. These became independent national churches, such as the *Russian Orthodox* (AWR-thuh-doks) Church and the *Bulgarian Orthodox* Church.

The churches in eastern Europe used the word *orthodox* to distinguish themselves from the Roman Catholic Church. By the 1100's, the churches in eastern Europe had cut their ties with the Christian church in the west. In fact, they sometimes competed with the western churches in converting followers. From the Middle Ages onward, eastern and western Christianity developed separately.

Byzantine Art and Architecture
Byzantine art developed along different lines from art in western Europe. Byzantine art was almost exclusively religious. Its purpose was to stimulate religious emotions. An onlooker was expected to meditate on the subject matter, not to admire the work of art itself as a thing of beauty. Consequently, realism was not important to Byzantine artists. They devoted themselves chiefly to icon painting and the production of mosaics. *Mosaics* were pictures created by putting together bits of colored materials like wood, glass, or marble. Mosaics in Byzantine churches were a highly developed art form. Sculpture, however, did not advance among the Byzantines because of the iconoclastic controversy.

Byzantine architecture had an influence on other parts of Christian Europe. The most important Byzantine structures were churches. The model for many of these was the Hagia Sophia (HAH-juh soe-FEE-uh) Church, built in Constantinople by the emperor Justinian. The interior of this church was beautifully decorated, and its huge dome was considered an engineering marvel. Architects in Europe were influenced by the Byzantine style and many churches in Russia show Byzantine influences.

The Byzantine Empire as a Buffer Against the East   Western Europe owed a great debt to the Byzantine Empire because for centuries the empire protected western Europe from the Muslim advance. The Byzantine struggles with Muslim people to the east gave western Europe an opportunity to develop its own strength. Had Constantinople fallen before 1453, Muslim invaders might have pushed deep into western Europe before the kings had grown strong enough to halt the Muslims. Thus for more than 500 years, the Byzantine Empire was a buffer protecting Europe from the Middle East.

SECTION REVIEW

1. Mapping: Using the map on page 241, explain why Constantinople was ideally located as a trading center. Why was the Byzantine Empire a buffer zone?

2. In your own words, define or identify: Leo III, icons, mosaics.

3. Describe the absolute powers held by the Byzantine emperor in both government and religion.

▶ Would you have enjoyed living under the control of an absolute ruler? Why or why not? Is there a time when absolute government might be justified?

The Muslim Peoples

THE WORLD OF ISLAM

Most of the peoples living in North Africa and the Middle East today are Muslims. They live in more than a dozen modern countries, but they share a common religion. This religion is known as Islam (ISS-lahm) and was founded more than 1,300 years ago among the Arabs.

The Arabs   The *Arabs* were the inhabitants of the Arabian peninsula. Some of them lived in small towns, and some were nomads who roamed over the Arabian desert with their herds of sheep, goats, horses, and camels.

The Arabs were organized into tribes, each of which was governed by a leader called a *sheikh* (SHEEK). The Arabs were fiercely loyal to their tribes, but there was no larger political organization uniting them until after the year 610.

The Birth of Islam   About 610, a religious leader named Muhammad appeared. He had been born in 570 in Mecca (MEK-uh), one of the inland cities near the Arabian coast. (See the map on page 249.) The new faith he founded was called Islam.

Before Muhammad, the Arabs had been polytheists, or worshipers of many gods. The Arabs worshiped gods who they believed lived in water wells, trees, stones, the sun, the moon, the stars, and other aspects of nature. A special object of worship was often a large stone. There were several revered stones in Arabia, but the most important one was at Mecca. A cube-shaped temple was built around this stone, which was called the *Kaaba* (KAHB-uh). At the Kaaba, many of the Arab gods were worshiped, and Mecca, the site of the temple, came to be considered a holy city. Arabs from all over Arabia went to worship there by praying and offering animal sacrifices.

Once in a lifetime, a Muslim is supposed to make a pilgrimage to the Kaaba in Mecca. Do people of other religions make pilgrimages? Where do they go?

247

Muhammad   Historians believe that Muhammad belonged to a poor branch of Mecca's leading family, the Quraish (kur-AYSH). His parents died when he was a child, and Muhammad was reared first by his grandfather and then by an uncle. Almost nothing is known with certainty about Muhammad's boyhood. But historians do know that at age twenty-five Muhammad was married to a widow named *Khadija* (khah-DEE-jah).

Muhammad became a successful businessman. Like the other businessmen in Mecca, Muhammad was a trader; thus he had contact with many people from outside Mecca. It is likely that he learned about Judaism (JOOD-uh-iz-um) and Christianity (kris-chee-AN-ut-ee) through his trading activities. Muhammad's analysis of the differences between the ethical ideas of Judaism and Christianity and the polytheism of his own people may well have started him on his religious career.

It was Muhammad's custom to go once a year into a cave near Mecca to meditate. When he was forty years old, he returned from his meditation and announced that a revelation had been made to him. It was revealed to him that there was only one God, *Allah* (ahl-LAH), and that he, Muhammad, was Allah's prophet. In this way, Muhammad was called to preach and spread the new faith of Islam.

Muslim Relations with Jews and Christians   Like the Jews and Christians, Muhammad believed there was only one God. He taught that there had been other prophets before him. Among them were Moses and Jesus. But Muhammad claimed he was the last prophet sent by Allah. Believers who accept Muhammad as the Prophet of Allah are called *Muslims*.

There was no reason for the Muslims to hate the Jews and the Christians, according to Muhammad, because their religions also shared in Allah's truths. However, he said that the Jewish and Christian beliefs were incomplete and only the Muslims knew Allah's most recent truths. For this reason, Muslims were Allah's special people and were entitled to special privileges. Jews and Christians who wanted to practice their own religious beliefs might do so, but they had to expect to be treated as second-class citizens in any Muslim country. Efforts were to be made to convert people other than Jews and Christians to Islam. Muhammad also taught that a holy war might be declared to spread the faith or to defend Islam, if people of other religions attacked it.

The Koran   After Muhammad began to preach and teach, he had many additional revelations. He passed these on to his followers orally. After his death, these revelations were collected into the **Koran** (kuh-RAN), the scriptures of Islam.

Muslim Duties   In Islam, there has never been an organized clergy, as there is in the Christian or Jewish faiths. Instead, each Muslim community usually chooses one or more persons, called *muezzins* (moo-EZ-'ns), whose duty it is to call the faithful to prayers. There is also a person who leads the prayers in the **mosque** (MAHSK), or the traditional Muslim place of worship.

Regular prayers are required for Muslims, and on certain days they must fast. An entire month, called *Ramadan* (RAM-uh-dahn), is set aside each year during which a Muslim must not eat or drink between sunrise and sunset. Other moral duties are required

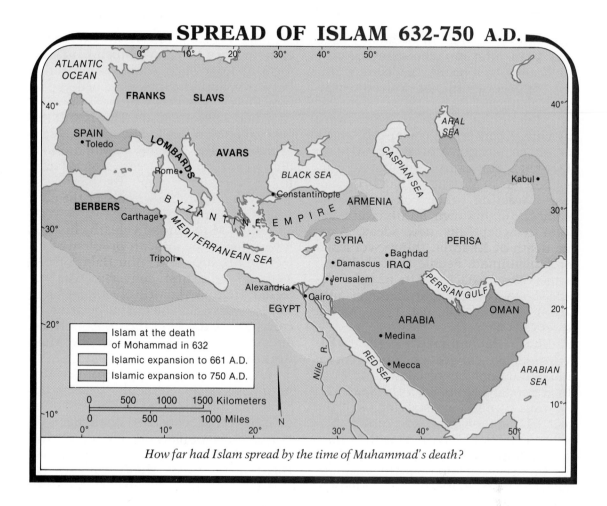

SPREAD OF ISLAM 632-750 A.D.

ATLANTIC OCEAN

FRANKS   SLAVS

SPAIN
•Toledo

LOMBARDS

Rome•

AVARS

BLACK SEA

•Constantinople

ARAL SEA

CASPIAN SEA

Kabul•

BERBERS

Carthage•

B Y Z A N T I N E   E M P I R E

ARMENIA

MEDITERRANEAN SEA

Tripoli•

SYRIA

PERISA

•Baghdad
•Damascus IRAQ

•Jerusalem

Alexandria•

•Cairo

EGYPT

ARABIA

•Medina

OMAN

•Mecca

ARABIAN SEA

Nile R.

RED SEA

PERSIAN GULF

Islam at the death of Mohammad in 632

Islamic expansion to 661 A.D.

Islamic expansion to 750 A.D.

0   500   1000   1500 Kilometers
0   500   1000 Miles

N

How far had Islam spread by the time of Muhammad's death?

during the year, such as giving money to the poor and offering hospitality to strangers. Alcoholic drinks and certain foods are forbidden to Muslims. The followers of the Prophet also believe that there is a life after death in which the wicked are punished and believers who obey the teachings of Muhammad will be rewarded.

In addition to the Koran, Muhammad's sayings and actions were recorded by his followers. These are also used as a guide for correct behavior. These traditions, called *Hadith* (hah-DEETH), are used to supplement the Koran and to help interpret it. Eventu-

ally a group of specially trained scholars, called *Ulema* (uh-leh-MAH), used the Koran and traditions to form the law for the Islamic countries. These Ulema still play an important role in Muslim countries because the dividing line between the functions of religion and government is not as clear as it is in the West.

The Spread of Islam   At first, Muhammad's teachings spread slowly. The Arabs worshiped many gods, and Muhammad's insistence that there was only one God offended believers in the old faith. Muhammad's teachings also threatened the city of Mecca, which

249

earned a large amount of money each year from pilgrims who came to visit the Kaaba. As a result, the leading citizens of Mecca did not welcome religious changes.

Muhammad's first converts were his wife, Khadija, his cousin Ali, and a merchant named **Abu Bakr** (AH-boo BAH-kur). However, Muhammad was not popular in Mecca and had little success attracting other converts. Most members of his own family were unable to accept his new ideas. After the death of Khadija, things worsened for Muhammad. People ridiculed him. Some threatened him. In 622, he decided to leave Mecca for Medina (muh-DEE-nuh), where he had been invited to settle.

Medina   Muhammad's *hegira* (HEJ-uh-ruh), or emigration to Medina, marks the birthday of Islam. The Muslim calendar begins with the year 622. Muslims count years starting with the year 622 as their first year rather than from the birth of Christ, as is the Christian custom.

In Mecca, his home town, Muhammad had been persecuted. In Medina, he was treated with great respect. He became the political and religious leader of the city. The citizens of Medina believed Muhammad possessed a divine authority to rule them. Many converted to Islam, including the nomadic desert tribes called *bedouin* (BED-uh-wun).

Muhammad's Return to Mecca Eventually, Muhammad was prepared to take over Mecca by force. In 630, he marched on Mecca at the head of a large army, and Mecca surrendered. Muhammad destroyed the idols in the Kaaba but left the temple itself. He decided to make the Kaaba the central place of worship for all Muslims. A pilgrimage to Mecca to visit the Kaaba became a duty for every Muslim to perform at least once. Mecca remained a holy city, and Muslims were ordered to face Mecca when they prayed, no matter where they might be. This is still the custom of Muslims today.

Muhammad's Death   Muhammad died in 632, only two years after returning to Mecca in triumph. By the time of his death, all Arabia was under the control of the Muslims.

After Muhammad's death, his followers faced the difficult problem of selecting his successor. Abu Bakr, one of Muhammad's first converts, was selected. He took the title of *caliph* (KAY-luf), or supreme ruler. The position of caliph carried with it the same political and religious authority over the Muslims that Muhammad had held.

After the death of the Prophet Muhammad, it was difficult to keep the Muslims united. Each of the first four caliphs faced constant challenges to his authority. The second caliph to come to power was Umar (OE-mur). He ruled until his assassination in 644. He was followed by Uthman (AHTH-mun), who was murdered in 656. His successor was Ali, Muhammad's cousin. Ali had married Fatima (FAT-uh-muh), Muhammad's daughter. Despite this, a civil war broke out against Ali, and in 661 he was assassinated.

Islamic Expansion During the reigns of the first four caliphs, Muslim armies rapidly spread Islamic political rule into the countries bordering Arabia. The Muslims conquered the Persian Empire and took away much of the Middle East from the Byzantine Empire. The Arabs respected the cultures of the peoples they conquered. Converts to Islam were given special privileges, including freedom from taxation. Jews

The tomb of Tamerlane the Great, the powerful Muslim ruler, stands in Samarkand in the Soviet Union. What does evidence such as this tell you about the expansion of Islam?

and Christians were permitted to practice their religions but were required to pay taxes.

Arabic eventually became the language of Muslims and non-Muslims in the conquered territories. Much of the knowledge of the ancient world was translated into Arabic. These translations helped to preserve the knowledge and spread it to other peoples.

The years from 632 until 750 were the period of Islam's greatest expansion. New believers helped to spread the faith after they themselves had been conquered and converted by the Muslims. In this way, the Muslim faith spread across Egypt, North Africa, and into Spain. It also spread across Persia to India and to southeast Asia and China. Many of the nomads of Asia, such as the Mongols and Turks, became Muslims (See the map on page 249).

The Umayyid Dynasty After the murder of Ali, the *Umayyid* (uh-MIE-yid) family seized the caliphate. They passed the position of caliph from father to son during the period of 661 to 750. They also moved the capital of the Muslim empire to the city of Damascus (duh-MAS-kus) in Syria. (See the map on page 249.)

During the period of Umayyid rule, the *Berbers* (BUR-burz), a native people of North Africa, converted to Islam. They in turn spread the new faith from Egypt in the east to the Strait of

251

Gibralter (juh-BRAWL-tur). Muslim armies invaded Spain and conquered the Visigoths. Then the Muslims pushed across the Pyrenees (PIR-uh-nees) into southern France. However, the Franks proved too strong for them, and the Muslims turned back to Spain.

Meanwhile, from Persia the Muslim faith was carried by conquering armies eastward. Islam expanded into central Asia and by the 700's reached India's borders. As you learned in Unit 2, most of India fell to Muslim invaders several hundred years later.

The Abbasid Dynasty In 750, the Umayyid dynasty was overthrown. It was replaced by the *Abbasid* (uh-BAS-ud) dynasty. This dynasty ruled until the thirteenth century from a new capital at Baghdad (BAG-dad), in modern Iraq. Under the Abbasid caliphs, the unity of the Muslim world was shattered.

In Spain, a caliphate was established that refused to acknowledge the Abbasids as rightful rulers of all of Islam. Later, other Arab and non-Arab peoples followed the example of Spain. In the 900's, a rival group of leaders established itself in Egypt and North Africa and challenged the power of the Muslim leaders in Baghdad. To maintain control over their lands, the caliphs had to hire troops from nomadic Asiatic tribes. One of these tribes was the Seljuk Turks who moved into the Middle East in large numbers about 1000 and were converted to Islam. By 1100, the Seljuks had become rulers of much of the Middle East. They organized their own state in what is now Turkey.

The Ottoman Empire The next 200 years in the Middle East were full of conflict. Then, at the beginning of the 1300's, the Ottoman Turks, another group of Muslim people, replaced the Seljuk Turks as the main power in the Middle East. Their rulers held the title of *sultan* (SULT-'n). The sultans looked upon the Byzantine Empire as their chief enemy. Although at first the sultans were unable to capture Constantinople, they did push back the frontiers of the Byzantine Empire. In 1345, they crossed the Dardanelles into eastern Europe. (See the map on page 253.) For more than 100 years after that, the Ottoman advance into Europe continued as the Turks conquered the Balkan kingdoms one by one. In 1453, after a long siege, Constantinople finally fell and the Byzantine Empire collapsed.

Sultan Muhammad II, who ruled from 1451 to 1481, moved his capital to Constantinople. Within a short time, the Turks had brought under their control all of the Middle East, the Balkans, Egypt, and much of Hungary. (See the map on page 253.) Under the strong leadership of the sultans at Constantinople, the quarreling rival states in the Muslim world were reunited.

The Government of the Ottomans Muslims believed that the laws of government should be based on the religious teachings of Islam. The Muslims felt that Christians and Jews who did not accept the beliefs of Islam could not be expected to obey all Muslim laws. Therefore, following Muhammad's pattern, the Ottoman sultans granted Christians and Jews limited authority to govern themselves under their own religious leaders.

The Ottoman Empire was divided into many provinces. Each province was usually under the direct control of the central government at Constantinople. The government at Constantinople appointed officials to act as provincial governors. In some places, how-

THE OTTOMAN EMPIRE FROM THE 15TH TO THE 17TH CENTURIES

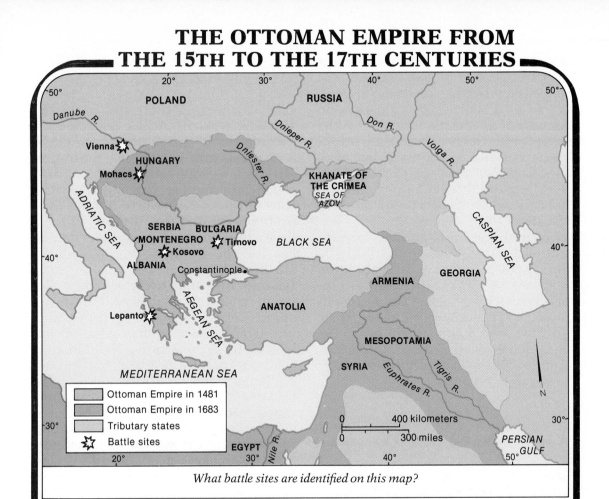

What battle sites are identified on this map?

ever, conquered rulers were allowed to continue governing their own people under Ottoman supervision.

The Ottoman Army   The control of such a vast empire required a large army. For their best troops, the sultans depended upon the conquered Christian population of eastern Europe. The sultans took a certain percentage of the male Christian children as a form of a tax. Every four years, from the late fourteenth to the early seventeenth century, youths from ten to twenty years of age were taken from Christian villages in the Balkans. The boys were taken as slaves to Constantinople and brought up in special schools to become Muslims. The most gifted of these children were educated for the sultan's government. Trained by the Turks, some of them rose to the highest ranks of the Ottoman government. Others became professional soldiers. These soldiers, known as *Janissaries* (JAN-uh-ser-eez), were among the finest troops in Europe during the 1400's.

Weakness in the Empire   There were many weaknesses in the structure of Ottoman rule that eventually created problems for the Ottomans. First of all, the crushing burden of taxation fell mainly on the peasants. Old-fashioned

253

agricultural methods practiced by the Turks produced small harvests. And the greedy tax collectors pressed the peasants so hard that whole villages were abandoned as people moved to the cities. Crafts were a large and profitable part of Turkish industry, but most of the artisans were the Christians or Jews because the dominant Muslim Turks thought such occupations were unworthy.

In addition, the Turkish government was mostly concerned with its military power and gave little attention to absorbing conquered peoples. Instead, minorities within the Ottoman Empire were allowed to make their own laws and follow their own customs. Some of the more important groups gained special privileges, which increased their power.

SECTION REVIEW

1. **Mapping:** Using the map on page 249, find the distance between each of the following cities: Mecca and Medina, Medina and Damascus, Mecca and Baghdad.
2. In your own words identify or define: Muhammad, Mecca, Kaaba, Koran, mosque, hegira, Ottoman Empire, caliph, sultans, Janissaries.
3. What were the main beliefs taught by Muhammad's new religion?
4. What was the Muslim conquerors' attitude toward: **a.** conquered peoples **b.** Christians and Jews?
5. How did the Byzantine Empire finally fall?
 A Muslim has many religious duties. Describe one of these duties and tell how it is similar to or different from religious practices in your own community.

CONTRIBUTIONS OF THE MUSLIM WORLD

One of the chief contributions of the Muslims was the Arabic language. It became the language of all Islam. The Koran was first written in Arabic, and Muslim law would not permit its translation into another language. As a result, Muslims everywhere had to learn Arabic because it was the duty of a believer to read the Koran. Thus Arabic became the common language of all Muslims.

Islamic Art and Architecture Religion strongly influenced the development of art everywhere in the Muslim world. Perhaps the greatest advances in art made by the Muslims were in architecture and decoration. The most important building designed by Muslim architects was the mosque. Domes and minarets (min-uh-RETS) were made part of the mosques and gave them a distinctive appearance. The *minaret* was a tall, slender tower from which a muezzin called believers to daily prayer.

Islam forbade the use of statues and paintings of humans or animals as decorations in the mosques. Instead, sculptors and painters excelled in decorating mosques with designs based on flowers, plants, leaves, geometric figures and words from Arabic.

Handiwork and crafts from many parts of the Muslim world were sought after eagerly in the Mediterranean countries. Carpets made in Persia were famous. Leather goods from North Africa and Spain were a special craft that the Muslims mastered. And Spanish swords made in Toledo (tuh-LEED-oe) were highly prized by medieval knights in Europe. Muslims were also noted for their trade in silks and other fabrics.

Islamic Science Muslim scholars contributed to the development of modern sciences such as chemistry, physics, and astronomy. Muslims were especially interested in astronomy. A knowledge of the stars was useful for navigation and for telling the times for prayers and festivals. Consequently, they built many observatories and invented the *astrolabe* (AS-truh-layb), the forerunner of the sextant, for measuring the movements of heavenly bodies.

The Muslims also contributed to the development of modern mathematics. The nine Arabic numerals were not invented by the Arabs. They were invented in early India. But the Arabs carried the Indian system to the Mediterranean world. The zero probably was invented by the Indians also. However, the Arabs combined use of the zero with other Arabic numerals to develop a modern system of numbers. This Arabic system replaced the old Roman numerical system.

The Arabic system of numbers was organized in the ninth century by a Muslim scholar named **Al-Khwarizmi** (ahl-kwah-RIZ-mee) and introduced to western Europeans in the 1200's. Al-Khwarizmi also helped lay a foundation for modern algebra. Muslim mathematicians were acquainted with geometry and trigonometry as well.

By 1000, the Muslims probably possessed the most advanced medical knowledge in the world. They had translated books on medicine from early Greece and built hospitals and large medical libraries where physicians could study. Their understanding of diseases was far greater than the knowledge in the Christian West. By 1000, the Arabs were acquainted with the treatment of such illnesses as mea-

The above is a detail from a Persian miniature showing a hunting scene. What does this tell us about life in the Middle East?

sles and smallpox. **Avicenna** (av-uh-SEN-uh), a famous Muslim philosopher from Persia, also studied medicine and compiled an encyclopedia of medical knowledge used in European medical schools until the eighteenth century.

255

Avicenna and Averröes (av-uh-ROE-eez), a Spanish philosopher and physician, were among the best-known Muslim philosophers. They studied the Greek writers, particularly Plato and Aristotle. Their goal seems to have been to find ways to reconcile the ideas of the early Greeks with the teachings of Islam.

Much of the scientific knowledge that the Muslims had gathered from the ancient world and from India was passed to the West through Spain and southern Italy around the time of the Crusades. At that time, most European scholars and scientists recognized the scientific and technological superiority of the Islamic world and eagerly sought translations of Muslim writings. Every intellectual discipline owes a debt to the scientific heritage of Islam.

Islamic Literature In the west, the best-known figure in Muslim literature was probably *Omar Khayyam* (OE-mahr KIE-yahm). Khayyam was a Persian mathematician. However, his poetry made him famous outside his home country. A collection of his poems entitled *Rubaiyat* (ROO-bee-aht) is his most famous work. Collections of folk tales and other stories were also popular in the Muslim world. *The Arabian Nights* was such a collection. These stories tell us much about life in early Baghdad and other Muslim cities.

SECTION REVIEW

1. Mapping: Using the map on page 253, describe the relative location of each of the following: Arabia, Persia, North Africa, Greece, Spain. How did people or products from each of these areas contribute to Islamic cultural development?

2. In your own words identify or define: mosque, minaret, Omar Khayyam, astrolabe.

3. Why was Arabic important in the Muslim world?

4. How did religion affect the art of Islam?

5. List the significant contributions made by Muslims.

In the Muslim world, religious beliefs had a great influence on art and artists. What affects art today? Why?

This example of calligraphy reads, "And I believe in Allah."

chapter 14

The Early Kingdoms of Eastern Europe

THE SOUTH SLAV LANDS

At the time of the Roman Empire, much of the land along the empire's frontier in eastern Europe was occupied by a people known as the Slavs. Little has been learned about the origin of the Slavs. They may have come from the plains and marshes of Russia or from somewhere in Poland.

Slav Migrations   About 500 A.D., the Slavs began to migrate to different parts of Europe. One group, the western Slavs, settled in Poland and Czechoslovakia. Other Slavs moved southward into parts of present-day Bulgaria and Yugoslavia. The east Slavs made their homes in Russia. (See the map on page 258.)

The Byzantine rulers tried to stop the Slavs from moving into the lands belonging to the empire. But the emperors were facing more dangerous enemies, such as the Persians, and were never able to stop the flow of Slavic peoples into Byzantine territories. By about 650, most of the Balkan peninsula, with the exception of Greece, was inhabited by Slavic tribes.

The Bulgars   Not long after the settlement of the Slavs, a group of people called the *Bulgars* pushed into the Balkans from Asia. The Bulgars were able to overcome the Slavs and occupy the land that today still bears their name—Bulgaria. In Bulgaria during the 800's and 900's, the Bulgars established an empire that was a rival in power to that of the Byzantines. (See the map on page 258.) The Bulgarian Empire reached its peak about 900. During its height, the Bulgarian Empire stretched from the Black Sea to the Adriatic Sea. Ambitious Bulgarian rulers warred against Byzantine emperors in the hopes of making themselves emperors.

One of the Byzantine emperors, Basil II, who ruled from 976 to 1025, inflicted a terrible defeat on the Bulgarian army. He captured 15,000 Bulgarian soldiers and blinded 99 out of each 100. The hundredth prisoner was allowed to keep the sight of one eye so that he could lead the other ninety-nine home. From that time on, Basil II was known as "the Bulgar slayer," and Bulgaria came under the control of the Byzantine Empire.

In the late 1100's, the Bulgarians freed themselves from Byzantine rule and once again established an empire. The second Bulgarian Empire, like the first, did not last long. By the 1300's, it was in decline and eventually split into several weak independent states, each with its own ruler. Meanwhile, the Bulgarian people had been adopting the language and customs of the Slavic

West Slavs
East Slavs
South Slavs

NORWAY

NORTH SEA

SWEDEN

DENMARK

BALTIC SEA

KURLAND

BALTIC PEOPLES

Novgorod

FINNS

KINGDOM OF KIEV (RUS)

Rhine R.

Elbe R.

Vistula R.

KINGDOM OF THE FRANKS

POLANIANS

Oder R.

GREAT MORAVIA

Prague

Velegrad

VISLANIANS

Kiev

Dnieper R.

KHAZARIA

Dniester R.

MAGYARS

SLOVENES

KINGDOM OF ITALY

CROATS

CORSICA (Arabs)

ADRIATIC SEA

SERBS

BULGARIAN EMPIRE

Danube R.

Tirnovo

Preslav

Ochrida

Constantinople

BLACK SEA

SARDINIA (Arabs)

MEDITERRANEAN SEA

SICILY (Arabs)

BYZANTINE EMPIRE

0   200 Kilometers
0   400 Miles

N

Which Slavic peoples had moved into eastern Europe by the ninth century?

tribes they had conquered. Christianity was introduced in the 800's, and by about the year 900, the language and customs of Bulgaria had become Slavic.

The Magyars   During the rise of Bulgaria, new invaders from Asia appeared in eastern Europe. They were the Magyars. The Magyars were skilled horsemen and fierce warriors. (See page 170.) Their raids spread terror for 100 years throughout eastern Europe, southern Germany, northern Italy, and parts of France.

The Magyars moved into Romania in 889. From there they raided Bulgaria but were turned back by the Bulgars. The Magyars left Romania, crossed the Carpathian Mountains, and overran the plains of Hungary, conquering the Slavs who lived there.

Magyar Settlement   After a serious defeat in 955 at the hands of the German emperor, Otto I, the Magyars gave up their nomadic life and settled down in Hungary. By 1000, they had adopted Christianity and were united under one Magyar leader. King *Stephen I*, who ruled from 997 to 1038, helped to found the modern Hungarian state. He spread Christianity and left behind a strong monarchy. Stephen's family, the *Ar-*

pads (AHR-pads), continued to rule Hungary until 1301.

After settling Hungary, the Magyars mixed with the Slavic peoples. Unlike the Bulgarians, the Magyars never gave up their native language and customs. Instead, the Magyar Kingdom of Hungary permanently divided the south Slavs from the west Slavs in Czechoslovakia and Poland.

The Croats   The Croats were a Slavic people that founded a kingdom, named Croatia (kroe-AY-shuh), in the northern part of present-day Yugoslavia in the early 900's. They were in contact with the Italians, Germans, and other western Europeans, as well as with the Byzantine Empire. The Croats became Roman Catholics and used the Latin alphabet to write their language. Scarcely a century after settling along the coasts of the Adriatic Sea, the Croats became skilled sailors. This was unusual, as most Slavs had never before been seagoing peoples. The early Croatian kings built fleets that were used at first for piracy and then later for trade.

Occupation by Hungary   The period of Croatian growth and prosperity came to an end by 1100. Croatia was located between two rising powers. On one side, at the tip of the Adriatic Sea, was Venice, an Italian trading center. On the other side of Croatia was Hungary, a strong kingdom ruled by the Arpads. Both Venice and Hungary were eager for a chance to acquire territory belonging to the Croats.

In 1089, the last Croatian king, Zvonimir (svon-OF-mir), died without leaving any heirs. A period of disorder followed his death, and the Hungarians saw their opportunity to take over Croatia. In 1091 the Hungarian army occupied Croatia, and in 1102 the Hungarian king made Croatia a part of Hungary. The Hungarian king appointed a governor to rule Croatia in his name and gave the Croatian nobles a great deal of liberty. In spite of this freedom, there were frequent rebellions against Hungarian rule. But it was not until the early 1900's that the Croats won complete independence from Hungary.

The Serbs   The *Serbs* (SERBZ) were closely related to the Croats and spoke the same language. A Serbian kingdom was founded in the southern part of present-day Yugoslavia in the late 1100's, long after Croatia had been conquered by the Hungarians. The founder of Serbia was *King Stephen,* who ruled from 1168 to 1196. The Serbs became Orthodox Christians, while their close relatives, the Croats, became Roman Catholics. Although Croats and Serbs spoke the same language, Serbo-Croatian, the Croats used the Latin alphabet and the Serbs used an alphabet similar to that of the Greeks. These religious and language differences have lasted until today.

In the 1300's, when the second Bulgarian empire declined, Serbia took over some Bulgarian territory. Also in the late 1300's, the Serbs took control of large parts of what are now present-day Greece and Albania. Serbia became a large and powerful kingdom. The greatest of Serbia's medieval kings was *Stephen IV*, who ruled from 1331 to 1355. Stephen IV grew so powerful that he planned to attack Constantinople and seize the Byzantine throne. Stephen IV died, however, in 1355 before carrying out his plans, and after his death Serbia's power rapidly declined.

The Slovenes   Another southern Slav people, the *Slovenes* (SLOE-veenz), moved into eastern Europe at about the same time as the Serbs and

Croats. Unlike the other south Slavs, the Slovenes did not establish a country of their own. They settled the northwest corner of what is today modern Yugoslavia. (See the map on page 258.)

The Slovenes fell under the influence of their German neighbors in the early 800's. Their nobles began to use the German language and imitate German culture. Only the peasants preserved the true Slovene customs. Eventually, the lands of the Slovenes were added to Austria.

SECTION REVIEW

1. Mapping: Comparing the map on page 258, with the Atlas of Europe, determine and list what modern countries were settled by the west Slavs, south Slavs, and the east Slavs.
2. In your own words, define or identify: Bulgars, Magyars, Croats, Serbs, Slovenes, Basil II, Stephen I of Hungary.
3. List the earliest kingdoms to appear in the southern parts of eastern Europe.
◗ Make a list of things that you think made the people of eastern Europe feel they were a nation. What things do you think make people in the world today feel they are a nation?

THE WEST SLAV LANDS

One of the earliest Slavic kingdoms was Moravia (muh-RAY-vee-uh). It was founded about 870 in what today is modern Czechoslovakia. The Moravian kingdom lasted less than 100 years, but one event of lasting importance took place there. In the late 800's, the Moravian ruler asked the Byzantine Empire for help against the Germans, who were constantly threatening Moravia. In addition, the Moravian ruler also asked for clergy who could teach his people about Christianity.

The Cyrillic Alphabet In response to the Moravian ruler's request, two monks familiar with Slavic languages were sent from Constantinople. These men invented an alphabet for the Slavs, who had none of their own. These two monks used Greek letters and some letters of their own design. The alphabet was named for one of its inventors, a monk named Cyril, and is still known as the **Cyrillic** (suh-RIL-ik) **alphabet.** Today it is used by all the Slavic peoples in the Soviet Union and by the Bulgarians and Serbs. However, the Slavs of present-day Czechoslovakia, for whom the alphabet was originally intended, now use the Latin alphabet.

At the end of the ninth century, Moravia began to enlarge its territory. (See the map on page 258.) However, an invasion of Moravia by the Magyars from Hungary destroyed the Moravian state, which finally fell to the Magyars in 906.

The Slav Kingdom of Poland. The early Slavic kingdom of Poland was founded perhaps as early as 960 by *Mieszko I* (MYESH-kaw). (See the map on page 237.) Mieszko founded the *Piast* (PEE-ahst) dynasty of kings and ruled Poland until 992. He united several Slavic tribes that lived between the Vistula (VIS-chuh-luh) and Oder rivers and also introduced them to the Roman Catholic religion. By 1000, the borders of Poland were roughly the same as those of Poland today.

Division of Poland Early Polish unity disappeared under the rule of the Piasts. For 200 years, Poland was split into a number of rival duchies (DUCHeez). Each duchy was a large territory under the control of a single noble known as a duke. During this period, the Polish people suffered greatly when raiders from central Asia terrorized southern Poland. After that, the Poles were too weak to resist German colonists, who poured into the southern region. German knights also settled Polish land along the Baltic Sea in what became known as East Prussia. The Germans in Prussia soon became a danger to their Polish neighbors because they wanted to link East Prussia and Germany by conquering the Polish land that was between the two. This would have cut the Poles off from the sea. (See the map on page 237).

Casimir the Great In the early 1300's, Poland was reunited under a strong king, *Casimir* (KAZ-uh-mir) *the Great.* Casimir ruled from 1333 until 1370. He gave Poland thirty years of peace, during which towns developed and prosperity returned. He made the city of Kraków (KRAHK-kow) his capital. There, in 1364, he founded the first university in Poland. It is the second oldest university in eastern Europe.

Unification of Poland and Lithuania In the late 1300's, the throne of Poland passed to a Polish queen whose husband was the ruler of Lithuania (lith-uh-WAY-nee-uh). The unification of Poland and Lithuania in 1386 created one of the largest and most powerful countries in medieval Europe. It stretched from the Baltic Sea to the Black Sea and from Poland's frontier along the Oder River eastward to the Dnieper (NEE-puhr) River. (See the map on page 237.) After the unification of Poland and Lithuania, Christianity spread to the people of Lithuania, and the Polish language and culture were adopted by the Lithuanian ruling class.

Modern newspapers in Russia are written in Cyrillic letters. What other peoples use an alphabet other than the Latin alphabet we use?

Another result of the unification was the crushing defeat of the Germans at the battle of Tannenberg in East Prussia in 1410 by the Poles and *Lithuanians.* Warfare continued off and on for fifty more years. Finally, in 1466, the Germans surrendered much of their land to the Poles. They kept East Prussia and were permitted to govern themselves, but their ruler became a vassal of the Polish king.

The Kingdom of Bohemia By about 1000, Bohemia (boe-HEE-mee-uh), another Slavic kingdom, had appeared in the western part of Czechoslovakia. Christianity was introduced there in the 800's. During much of Bohemia's early history, it was involved in a struggle to preserve its independence from its German neighbors to the west and

Otakar II was known as the "man of gold" but he was not elected Holy Roman Emperor. Why are money and politics often connected?

north. Civil wars broke out often in Bohemia because the Bohemian kings, who were elected, were constantly in conflict with the Bohemian nobles over control of the throne.

King Otakar One of Bohemia's greatest kings was *Otakar* (AHT-uh-kar) *II,* who ruled from 1253 to 1278. King Otakar reduced the power of the nobles and restored law and order. He then enlarged the size of Bohemia by adding German, Hungarian, and Italian lands to the south so that Bohemia stretched to the Adriatic Sea. Bohemia prospered, and the king became so wealthy he was called the "man of gold."

Because of his wealth and power, when the Holy Roman Emperor died, Otakar expected to be offered the va-

cant throne. But the small group of German rulers who elected the emperors feared having a powerful ruler like Otakar so in 1273 they picked Rudolf of Hapsburg (HAHPS-boorg) instead. The new emperor claimed some of the territories held by Otakar II, which caused a dispute that led to war. The Bohemians invaded Austria, and the rival armies met in battle near Vienna (vee-EN-uh). Otakar II was defeated and killed.

The outcome of this battle was significant because it made the reign of the Hapsburg family in Austria secure. Bohemia survived as a separate kingdom for almost 400 years after the battle. But from that time on, the kings of Bohemia no longer threatened Austria. Instead, the Hapsburg rulers of Austria were always trying to take the Bohemian throne for themselves.

The Decline of Bohemia The Bohemian ruling family died out in 1306. A royal family from western Europe took the throne and ruled Bohemia until 1437. During the rule of this royal family, known as the *Luxemburgs* (LOOK-sum-boorgz), Bohemia prospered. Science and other fields of learning were advanced. The first university in eastern Europe was founded at Prague (PRAHG) in 1348 by King Charles I, who ruled from 1347 to 1378. The king made his home in Prague and did much to make it one of Europe's most beautiful cities.

During the 1400's, conditions changed. Royal authority disappeared. Bitter civil wars and struggles for the throne broke out. In 1471, the Bohemian throne was taken over by members of the Polish ruling family. The Polish kings held the Bohemian throne until 1526. After that, the powerful Hapsburgs of Austria seized the Bohemian throne. Consequently, the territory held by the Bohemians remained an independent kingdom. But its kings were foreigners who also ruled the Austrian Empire.

The Thirty Years' War   You may recall that the Thirty Years' War was begun in Bohemia. (See page 216.) It started as a revolt against one of the foreign-born Hapsburg rulers. The incident that began the Thirty Years' War occurred in Prague. The Protestants of Bohemia refused to obey orders from their Catholic Hapsburg king, Ferdinand, who ruled from 1617 to 1637. Three Hapsburg officials were sent to warn the Bohemians. But the rebels threw all three out the window of a high castle. The three men fell 21 meters (70 feet) but landed safely because their fall had been broken by a huge pile of garbage beneath the castle. This act of rebellion was the signal for a revolt in Bohemia and the beginning of the long war that followed.

In 1620, the Bohemian rebels suffered a crushing defeat at the **Battle of White Mountain.** As a punishment for rebelling, Bohemia's separate status was revoked by the Hapsburgs. Thereafter, Bohemia was merely part of the Austrian Empire. The old nobility of Bohemia was stripped of their lands and position. They were replaced by a new, German-speaking ruling class from Austria.

The Problems of Hungary   In 1301, the last of Hungary's Arpad kings died. A period of disorder and civil war followed, as rivals struggled for the throne. However, these troubled times ended when a new royal family, the *Anjou* (AN-jooh) from western Europe, took power in 1308. Unfortunately for the Hungarians, the new Anjou kings dragged Hungary into the wars their large family had been fighting in western Europe.

These wars only created resentment on the part of the Hungarian people against the foreign monarchs, who spent much of their time away from Hungary.

The result of having a foreign monarchy in Hungary was a long period marked by struggles for power between nobles and kings, debates over the elections of new kings, mistreatment of peasants, and civil wars. The Anjous lost the throne and throughout the 1400's, it passed from one noble family to another. In 1516, Louis II came to Hungary's throne. Louis was only ten years old at the time, and royal power dissolved under his reign. Not long after Louis took the throne, the Protestant Reformation spread to Hungary. Consequently, Catholics and Protestants fought with one another, and this weakened Hungary even more.

Louis II of Hungary came to the throne at the age of ten. What are the dangers of having a young ruler?

263

1. Mapping: Using the Atlas of Europe, locate the following cities by latitude and longitude coordinates: Kraków, Prague, Warsaw, Vienna.
2. In your own words identify or define: Cyrillic alphabet, duchies, King Casimir the Great, Hapsburgs, Otakar II, Battle of White Mountain.
3. What are some of the problems Poland had to overcome in order to make itself a powerful nation?
4. Why do several Slavic countries today use an alphabet different from the alphabet used elsewhere in western and eastern Europe?

▷ How does an elective monarchy differ from a hereditary monarchy? Do you think it would be better for your country to have an elected leader or a hereditary leader? Give reasons to support your answer.

TURKISH CONQUESTS IN EASTERN EUROPE

For 1,000 years after the fall of Rome, the people of eastern Europe faced threats of invasion from several directions. In the west the Germans made war on the Slavs and settled on Slavic lands. From the east came tribes of Asiatic nomads who raided parts of Poland, Hungary, and Romania, leaving behind great destruction. The most terrible of these raiders were the Mongols (MAHN-guls). In 1241, they pushed across eastern Europe from Poland, through Hungary, and on to the Adriatic Sea before returning to Asia.

The most dangerous threat to eastern Europe came from the south, however. Eastern Europe was safe so long as the Byzantine Empire stood between the Balkans and the Muslim-held territories. But the gradual decline of the Byzantine Empire finally made it possible for the Ottoman Turks to invade the kingdoms of eastern Europe and conquer them one by one.

The Turks in the Balkans   The Ottoman Turks first arrived in Europe in 1345. They could not conquer Constantinople, so in 1366 they made Adrianople their capital. This city was located 224 kilometers (140 miles) west of Constantinople. From there the Turks invaded Bulgaria in 1369. By 1372, much of Bulgaria was in their hands and became part of the Ottoman Empire. Next the Turks began the invasion and conquest of Serbia. They defeated the Serbian army at the *Battle of Kossovo* (KAW-saw-vaw) in the year 1389. The Serbian king was killed, and the Serbs lost their independence to the Ottoman Turks. They did not become a free nation again until the 1800's.

Montenegro   One corner of Serbia was able to hold out against the Turks. This part of the kingdom was known as Montenegro (mahnt-uh-NEE-groe). (See map on page 237.) The territory of Montenegro was made up of rugged mountains, deep valleys, and dense forests. It proved to be a difficult area to conquer. Turkish armies tried to defeat Montenegro many times, but Montenegro remained free from Turkish control. The Serbs who lived in Montenegro organized it as their own small state and selected princes to rule it.

Isolated and always in danger from the Turks, the hardy people of Montenegro preserved their language, their Serbian Orthodox religion, and the use of the Cyrillic alphabet. Montenegro also supported the other Slavic peoples in their long struggle for independence.

The Defeat of Bulgaria   When most

of Serbia was defeated in 1389, the Ottoman Turks turned again toward Bulgaria. After a brave resistance, Tirnovo (TURN-uh-voe), the Bulgarian capital, fell. By 1396, the country was under Turkish control. In the 1400's, the Turks renewed their advance through the Balkans and in 1453 finally succeeded in capturing Constantinople.

Turkish Conquests The following seventy years were spent by the Turks in conquering the rest of southeastern Europe. In addition to Montenegro, only two countries, Albania and Romania, offered serious resistance to the Ottoman Turks. The Albanians were able to hold out for fifteen years after the fall of Constantinople. But the Albanian capital was captured in 1466, and by 1468 all of Albania had fallen to the Turks. Because of their conquest by the Turks, some Albanians and Yugoslavians still practice Islam.

The Turks also met stubborn resistance in Romania. The Romanians withstood repeated Turkish attacks throughout the 1400's. One of the famous heroes in the struggle to preserve Romania's freedom was Stephen the Great, who ruled from 1457 to 1504. Only after his death were the Turks able to conquer that country.

The Turks in Central Europe In the 1500's, it was Hungary's turn to face the Turkish threat. The Turkish sultan Suleiman (SOO-lay-mahn) invaded Hungary in 1526. A large Bohemian and Hungarian army fought the Turks at the *Battle of Mohács* (MOE-hahch) and were wiped out by the Turks. King Louis II of Hungary was killed on the battlefield, and Hungary was left defenseless. The Turks then overran most of the country. The Hapsburgs were able to hold on to only a narrow strip of western and northern Hungary. The

The Turkish sultan, Suleiman, overran Hungary in 1526. Why do you think he was called Suleiman the Magnificent?

Turks did not try to settle Hungary, but they tightly controlled the Magyars and forced them to pay heavy taxes. After the conquest of Hungary, Suleiman marched into Austria as far as the city of Vienna. There the Turks met a new enemy, the Germans of Austria.

The Turks and the Germans The Turks were stopped at last. They could neither take Vienna nor defeat the Germans. Ten years of warfare between the Germans of Austria and the Turks ended in a draw. An agreement was made to divide Hungary between the Hapsburgs and the Ottoman Empire. The German rulers of Austria also took the Bohemian throne.

The division of Hungary and the Hapsburg takeover of Bohemia left Poland as the last independent eastern

European state besides Montenegro. For the next 300 years, eastern Europe was dominated by the Ottoman Empire and several other powerful empires such as Austria, Russia, and Prussia.

Turkish Rule Often the common people in eastern Europe did not resent Turkish rule as much as they resented the mistreatment they had received at the hands of their own nobles. In Hungary and Serbia, for example, the big landowners had made life miserable for the peasant farmers. Whenever the Turks conquered an area, however, they usually destroyed or weakened the power of the ruling nobles. Then they replaced the nobles with Turkish governors. The governors often left the peasants to themselves. As long as taxes were not too heavy, the peasants seemed to have lived peacefully with the Turks.

Religious Toleration The Turks were tolerant of the religions of the peoples in their newly conquered territories. Jews and Christians had legal protection under Ottoman law. They could practice their religions in peace and carry on their business activities. Many Jews and Christians rose to high places within the Ottoman government. In general, most eastern Europeans remained true to their own religions.

One terrible thing that the Christians suffered was the tax they had to pay in children to the sultans every few years. As you learned, a certain number of Christian children were taken to Constantinople and brought up to become Muslim professional soldiers, or Janissaries. They became the sultans' elite troops. After 1600, however, discipline among the Janissaries broke down. They often meddled in politics and became mercenaries. The unruliness and corruption of the Janissaries seriously weakened the Ottomans.

Decline of Turkish Power After 1600, as the Ottoman Empire declined, the German rulers of Austria threatened to take advantage of the situation. The Turks were faced with the possible loss of their eastern European territories to Austria.

In 1683, the Ottomans invaded the Austrian part of Hungary, and again marched on Vienna. The fall of the Austrian capital was prevented by the timely arrival of a large army commanded by the Polish king, *Jan Sobieski* (soe-BYES-kee). He led a combined force of 60,000 Polish and German troops. Sobieski became a hero for his part in defeating the Turks.

The failure of the Ottoman Turks to capture Vienna marked the beginning of the Ottoman Empire's rapid decline as a military power in Europe. Within a few years, the Ottoman Turks signed a treaty turning the Turkish part of Hungary over to Austria. After that, the Turks were never again a danger to Europe.

SECTION REVIEW

1. Mapping: Using the map on page 253, list the areas that were acquired by the Ottoman Empire. In a separate list, name the other important powers that controlled territory in eastern Europe during the time of the Ottoman Empire.
2. In your own words define or identify: Ottoman Turks, Montenegro, Adrianople, Suleiman, Jan Sobieski.
3. Why were the Battles of Mohács and Kossovo important?
4. What caused the Ottoman Empire decline?
▷ What do you think it means to say that a nation has declined? What thing do you think could lead to a nation's decline today?

THE RISE AND DECLINE OF POLAND

The 1500's were a period of greatness for Poland. The country was prospering. Kraków, its capital, was a center of learning and culture, visited by artists and scholars from all parts of Europe. In addition, the country had become a great military power. It also was about this time that the Poles and Russians began a long struggle to determine who would control the territory along the Baltic Sea.

Poland Clashes with Russia Poland, at first, was successful in its struggle with Russia. The Poles defeated the Russian ruler, Ivan the Terrible, in a contest for Livonia (luh-VOE-nee-uh). Then under *Sigismund* (SIG-uh-smund) *III*, who ruled from 1587 until 1632, Polish armies invaded Russia and successfully occupied Moscow. Although Polish troops were eventually forced to withdraw from Russia, Poland kept large areas of western Russia under its control.

During the reign of King Sigismund, the southeastern corner of Poland was the source of almost constant trouble. This was an area where Poland, Russia, Turkey, and the lands of the Mongols met. This territory had been settled long before by the Cossacks (KAHS-aks). (See the map on page 258.)

The Cossacks The *Cossacks* were peoples from several parts of eastern Europe. Many were peasants who had fled to avoid serfdom. The term *cossack* came from a Turkish word meaning "fur person." The Cossacks made a living by farming, selling furs, and by fishing. There was never a single Cossack nation, but the Cossacks organized

A great Cossack hero of the seventeenth century was General Sahaydachny (sah-hah-DAHCH-nee). How does this drawing of the general on horseback reflect the things for which the Cossacks were famous?

themselves into large bands, elected their chiefs, and practiced a form of democracy. They became famous as soldiers and were willing to hire themselves out as soldiers or mercenaries.

The non-Cossack inhabitants of southeastern Poland usually sided with the Cossacks against the Poles. In 1654, a widespread peasant revolt broke out in Poland against the landowning class. The revolt was backed by the Cossacks. It developed into a bloody civil war in which the peasants and Cossacks were finally defeated by the Poles. The Cossacks appealed to the Russian ruler for his protection. This gave the Russians an excuse to make war on Poland. From this time the inhabitants of Cossack

267

lands tended to side with Russia during Polish-Russian disputes.

Threats from Sweden and Prussia Russia was not Poland's only enemy. Sweden had become a military power by 1600, and the *Swedes* were expanding southward along the coast of the Baltic Sea. The Swedes interfered in Polish politics and took control of territory that Poland was never able to recover. Poland lost Livonia to Sweden in 1660. (see the maps on pages 237 and 274.)

Another threat to Poland was presented by the Prussians. East Prussia came under the control of the Hohenzollern (HOE-un-zahl-urn) family that ruled Prussia early in the 1600's. Later in the 1600's, Prussia became a new military power in eastern Europe. Thereafter, Prussia was a threat to Poland, its neighbor.

The Decline of Poland A lack of patriotism among Poland's ruling class contributed to the nation's gradual decline. Landowning nobles often put self-interest ahead of what was good for the country as a whole. For example, they excluded towns from any role in the government and oppressed the peasant farmers with heavy taxes. The great nobles of Poland ruled their lands as if they themselves were kings. The nobles used their wealth to bribe members of the Polish parliament to make laws they wanted. Along with the parliament, they stripped the Polish king of most of his royal power. Once, the Polish nobles even refused to raise troops for the king in time of national danger.

The Polish Parliament The Polish parliament was made up of a group of aristocrats who had an unusual legislative power given to them by a Polish law. The law was called the *liberum veto* (LEE-bu-rum VEET-oh). It re-

quired that every proposal of the king must be approved by every member of parliament. Under this law, any single member of parliament had the power to veto any proposal made by the king merely by stating, "I do not wish it!" This veto was valid even if every other member of parliament sided with the king. Many parliament members used the *liberum veto* for their own selfish reasons. In addition to this problem with its legislative body, the Polish state was so loosely organized that it had no ambassadors, no regular army, and no organized group of officials to carry on the affairs of government.

The First Partition of Poland Under such conditions, Poland declined rapidly. In the late 1700's, Poland's more powerful neighbors, Russia, Prussia, and Austria, agreed to divide Polish territory among themselves. In 1772, the first partition of Poland took place. A *partition* is the dividing of a country into two or more areas.

The Poles were unable to stop the division of their country. Following the partition, however, the Poles who lived in the remaining portion of the Polish kingdom were stirred to strengthen their government. If their plans had been successful, Poland might have been restored as a major power. But Russia, Prussia, and Austria did not want that to happen, so in 1793 they seized more territory. Finally, in 1795, they had taken what remained of the Polish kingdom.

The fall of Poland was significant. It left eastern Europe at the end of the 1700's in the hands of Russia, Prussia, Austria, and the declining Ottoman Empire. It was not long until these strong powers began to quarrel among themselves over the control of all of eastern Europe.

SECTION REVIEW

1. Mapping: Using the map on page 237, list the countries that neighbored the kingdom of Poland. Which of these neighbors participated in the partition of Poland?
2. In your own words, define or identify: King Sigismund, Kraków, Cossacks, *liberum veto*, partition.
3. Describe how Poland, which was a strong nation, weakened and then declined.

   What reasons do you think there might be for one or more countries to want to take control of another country? Why is it difficult to end a country's existence even if its name is removed from the map?

EARLY RUSSIA

The early movements of the Slavs brought some of them into Russia. There they settled along the rivers. In time, the towns they founded became the trading centers for the exchange of goods with the *Scandinavians* and the Byzantines. Some historians believe that early Vikings from Scandinavia, who sailed the rivers, were invited to settle in Russia and rule over the Slavs. Other historians believe that a Viking chief named *Rurik* (ROOH-rik) took over the city of Novgorod (NAHV-guh-rahd) about 862 A.D. Other Vikings followed his example by taking over other Russian cities. However, none of them were able to unite all the Slavs of Russia. Instead, each Russian city-state had its own prince.

Kievan Russia   Kiev emerged as the leading city-state in Russia. Kiev was built on the banks of the Dnieper River, the major trade route connecting Russia with the Byzantine Empire. (See the map on page 274.) Commerce on the Dnieper River grew rapidly, and this contributed to Kiev's importance. The princes of Kiev were able to enlarge the territory they controlled, and eventually many of the other city-states acknowledged Kiev's dominance in a kind of lord-vassal relationship. As a result, Kiev established the first Russian state between the ninth and tenth centuries. This state was called *Kievan* (KEE-yef-un) *Russia.*

Kievan Russia was a loosely connected confederation of independent city-states. It reached from the Baltic Sea southward toward the Black Sea. (See the map on page 274.) All the people in this vast area recognized the prince of Kiev as their ruler and sent taxes each year to Kiev.

Vladimir the Great   *Vladimir* (VLAD-uh-mir) *the Great* ruled the city of Kiev from about 972 to 1015. Vladimir was a particularly important ruler because he introduced Christianity to the Russians about the end of the tenth century. Under his rule, Kiev also became the center of Russian culture.

Formal education came to Russia with the introduction of Christianity. Using the Cyrillic alphabet, clergy wrote the first literature in the Russian language. Sermons, saints' lives, and some histories were translated from Greek into Slavic. But most of Russia was cut off from the cultural influences of the ancient Greek and Roman classics that the Christian church in western Europe enjoyed.

Vladimir and his successors tried to imitate the Byzantine system of government. In its religion, alphabet, coinage, art, architecture, and government, early Russia reflected Byzantine influences. Vladimir proclaimed the divine right of Russian princes to rule without

St. Sophia stands in Kiev, Russia. How does its interior differ from those of churches in your community?

limits on their powers. He also kept the church under his tight control, and the church and state in Russia thereafter always remained closely linked.

Yaroslav the Wise   A son of Vladimir called *Yaroslav* (YUR-uh-slahv) *the Wise* ruled Kievan Russia from 1019 to 1054. He encouraged scholarship, beautified Kiev, and built churches. The most splendid church Yaroslav erected was the cathedral of St. Sophia in Kiev. He also collected the laws of Russia and ordered the writing of Russia's first law code. To help him in governing Kievan Russia, Yaroslav depended upon the warrior noble class, known as the *boyars* (boe-YAHRZ). The boyars served the ruling prince as officials in time of peace and provided him with military leadership in time of war.

The Mongol Conquest of Russia   The development of Russian culture was cut short during the thirteenth century by the Mongol conquest of most of the Russian city-states. The Mongols were an Asiatic people who inhabited territories north of China known as Mongolia (mahn-GOLE-yuh). As was discussed in Unit 2, the Mongols were united around 1200 by Genghis Khan (GENG-guh-SKAHN). (See page 87.) After their invasion of China, a large Mongol army was sent westward into Russia. It was led by *Batu* (BAH-too), a descendant of Genghis Khan.

Batu and the Mongol army entered Russia and in 1237 sent a message to the city of Ryazan (ree-uh-ZAN) demanding its surrender. The prince of Ryazan refused. The prince sent pleas for help to the other city-states of Russia. But no help came, and the city faced the onslaught of Mongols alone. Ryazan was captured, looted, and burned.

Batu's army of horsemen then rode against the city of Suzdal (SOOZ-dul) and destroyed its army. The Mongols also burned Moscow and besieged the city of Vladimir. Throughout this period, the Russians failed to unite against the invaders and never offered an effective defense. The Mongols were able to conquer Russia city by city. The citizens of the defeated towns were treated with terrible cruelty; the Mongols struck terror throughout Russia.

The Mongol army moved northward against the city of Novgorod in 1238. However, dense forest and numerous streams made them turn back. The Mongols then moved southward toward Kiev. On their march to Kiev, they destroyed several towns and cities. The Mongols stormed Kiev, captured it, and slaughtered thousands of people.

The Golden Horde　In their conquest of Russia, the Mongols realized it would be almost impossible for Mongol troops to occupy every city in order to keep them under control. With this in mind, the Mongols decided on a new plan for controlling Russia. They moved eastward to the Volga River, which was the eastern frontier of the Slav lands. There the Mongols established a capital city called Sarai (sah-RIE).

Sarai became the center of a new Mongol empire under the rule of the *Golden Horde.* The Slavic lands of Russia were left in the hands of native princes. However, the Russian princes had to send gold and silver as tribute to the Golden Horde each year. Any city that defied the Mongols' orders or did not send tribute was threatened with attack and destruction. Because the Mongols were so powerful, the defeated princes of Russia acknowledged Mongol domination.

Mongol Domination　Using this tribute system, the Mongols were able to dominate Russia for more than 200 years. During this long period, Russia was cut off from contact with western Europe.

In the eyes of Europeans, Russia was an Asiatic land. Many Russians married Mongols. Some adopted the Mongol language and customs and wore Mongol clothing. Russian princes imitated the Mongol system of government. The Russian Orthodox Church, however, was left undisturbed by the Mongols, and in return the church taught believers to be submissive to religious and political authority. This submissiveness took root permanently among the Russian peasants and made it simpler for later Russian rulers to exercise unlimited power over their people.

During the long period of Mongol domination, the princes of Moscow became the most powerful in all of Russia. They served the Mongols as tax collectors, but at the same time they built up their own strength so that they could eventually throw off Mongol rule.

Ivan the Great　Mongol power began to decline in the middle of the 1300's. When Russian princes dared to disobey Mongol orders, armies were sent from Sarai to punish the Russians. But by the 1400's, the Mongols were no longer certain of victory. Sometimes the Russian armies defeated the Mongols. Led by Moscow, the Russians struggled with the Mongols for more than 100 years until winning a final victory in 1480. **Ivan III,** who led the Russians to victory, was given the title Great.

The princes of Moscow replaced the Mongols as the conquerors of Russia. By destroying the independence of other city-states, Ivan the Great, who ruled from 1462 to 1505, laid the foundation for a new Russian state called *Muscovy* (muh-SKOE-vee). He united the Slavic cities of Russia under his rule and expanded the territories of Muscovy.

The Third Rome　Ivan the Great married the niece of the last Byzantine emperor and claimed to be the emperor's successor after the fall of Constantinople in 1453. Moscow was proclaimed the third Rome. This meant Moscow was the successor of Rome and Constantinople, which was considered to be the second Rome. Ivan tried to preserve the Byzantine system of government. He adopted the double-headed eagle, which had been the emblem of the Byzantines, and he took the title *tsar* (ZAHR). This term was Russian for caesar, a title used by emperors of the old Roman Empire.

Early Tsars of Muscovy   When the Russian tsars who ruled Muscovy imitated the Byzantine emperors they stirred up the opposition of powerful landowning nobles, or boyars. A rivalry between the boyars and the tsars went on until the power of the boyars was finally destroyed about the middle of the sixteenth century.

Ivan IV   Tsar **Ivan IV,** who ruled from 1533 to 1584, completed the destruction of the power of the boyars in Russia. Ivan was a grandson of Ivan the Great and was only three years old when the throne passed to him. The boyars saw this period of rule by a boy-king as an opportunity to win back some of the powers they had lost to earlier tsars. They began a bloody civil war in which boyars battled one another for land, wealth, and power. Ivan IV grew up in the midst of this violence. His mother's death was blamed on the boyars, two of his uncles were arrested by the boyars, and others close to the tsar's family were exiled or murdered. Ivan was often humiliated by the boyars and seemed to have grown up fearing them.

When he was old enough to take power into his own hands, however, Ivan IV set out to take revenge on the boyars. To accomplish this, he decided to create an entirely new upper class. These new boyars came from every part of Russian society. Some were commoners, some were of noble birth, and some were criminals. All of them were loyal only to Tsar Ivan and had to prove their loyalty by obeying any order the tsar might give them. They were rewarded for their loyalty and obedience with gifts of land and possessions taken by force from the old ruling class. The new nobles created by Ivan were known as *oprichniki* (oe-PRICH-nee-kee).

The Oprichniki   The oprichniki terrorized the former upper class. Whole families were murdered or were arrested and disappeared without a trace. Fear spread among the former boyars. No one knew where Tsar Ivan might strike next with his dread oprichniki.

In 1570, Ivan learned the people of Novgorod were plotting against him. Believing the plot was real, the tsar sent an army headed by the oprichniki to take over Novgorod. The people of Novgorod were massacred, and the city was burned. Novgorod never recovered its place as the leading city of northern Russia.

Even church leaders were not safe if they dared to oppose the tsar. In 1568, the *Metropolitan* (me-truh-PAHL-ut-'n) of Moscow, a high-ranking bishop, denounced Ivan face-to-face during religious services. A month later, the Metropolitan was seized in his cathedral by the tsar's men. He was dragged into prison and never heard of again.

During the reign of Ivan, legal serfdom was also instituted in Russia. Peasants were forbidden to leave their lands or to go to work for another landowner. This loss of freedom was a great hardship for Russia's peasant farmers.

Ivan the Terrible   The people came to dread Tsar Ivan. He was called "the Terrible." In spite of the things he did, Ivan IV was responsible for one of the greatest examples of Russian architecture. He built St. Basil's cathedral outside the *Kremlin* (KREM-lun) walls in Moscow. The cathedral stood at one end of a huge square, known today as *Red Square.* Its onion-shaped domes and style of architecture are uniquely Russian. (See the picture on page 235.) According to legend, Ivan the Terrible was so pleased with St. Basil's that he blinded its architect so that there could never be another masterpiece like St. Basil's.

Expansion of Muscovy Territory Ivan the Terrible expanded Muscovy's territory. Between 1552 and 1556, his armies attacked and conquered Mongol cities along the Volga River. He was unable to take the Crimean (krie-MEE-un) peninsula in southern Russia from the Mongols, but his victories gave Russia control of the Volga River. (See the map on page 274.)

In 1581, rich merchants sent a band of mercenary soldiers east across the Ural Mountains into Siberia. These soldiers had little difficulty defeating the nomadic tribes of the region. The explorations of these bands of soldiers established Russia's control over Siberia. This led eventually to Russia's expansion across Siberia to the Pacific coast and from there southward to the borders of China.

Ivan IV was not as successful in pushing Russian borders westward. In 1557, he invaded Livonia, which today is Estonia (eh-STOE-nee-uh), and Latvia (LAT-vee-uh). (See the map on page 274.) Poland, however, also wanted control of Livonia. Polish troops met Ivan's army at the *Battle of Polotsk* (poe-LOT-ski) in 1582 and won a victory over the Russians. As a result, Livonia had to be abandoned by Ivan. Not until 100 years later was Russia able to control this area.

The Succession Problem One day in 1580, Tsar Ivan struck his eldest son on the head with a staff during a fit of anger. His son, who was the heir to the throne, died. Ivan was grief-stricken. He fell ill and offered to give up the throne. He seemed never to recover from his son's death.

Ivan's two remaining sons were incapable of governing Muscovy, and the

Compare these pictures of Moscow in the 1600's (above) and in the 1700's (below). How did Moscow change in a century?

273

GROWTH OF RUSSIA FROM THE 14TH TO THE 16TH CENTURIES

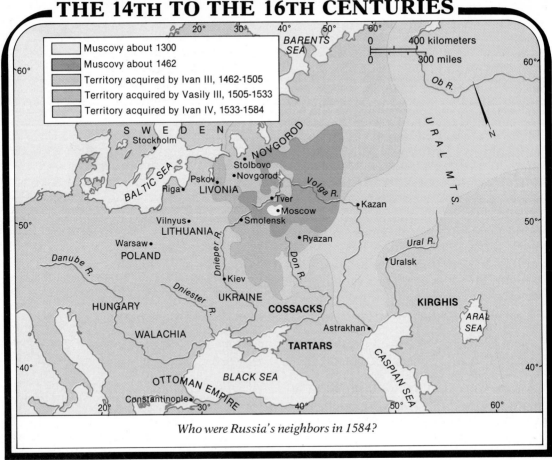

Legend:
- Muscovy about 1300
- Muscovy about 1462
- Territory acquired by Ivan III, 1462-1505
- Territory acquired by Vasily III, 1505-1533
- Territory acquired by Ivan IV, 1533-1584

Who were Russia's neighbors in 1584?

boyars preferred Ivan to his sons. After his son's death, the tsar lived only a few more years. He died in 1584 while playing chess with *Boris Godunov* (guh-doo-NAWF), his trusted adviser.

Ivan's son *Feodor* (fee-OE-dore) ruled from 1584 until 1598. He was weak, had no interest in governing, and turned his powers over to Boris Godunov. Besides having been an adviser to his father, Godunov was married to Tsar Feodor's sister.

In 1591, Feodor's younger brother *Dmitri* (duh-MEE-tree) died under mysterious circumstances. Dmitri was the last heir to the throne. Rumors circulated that Boris Godunov had murdered Dmitri in order to seize the throne for himself when Tsar Feodor died. Whether or not this is true, Godunov did, in fact, take over after the death of Feodor in 1598.

Boris Godunov   Tsar Boris ruled Muscovy for only seven years, from 1598 to 1605. Tsar Boris had many enemies among the boyars, and when famine struck Russia early in his reign, the peasants blamed the tsar for their suffering. Civil war broke out in 1604, and in the following year the tsar died.

Time of Troubles   After the death of Boris Godunov, Muscovy was thrown

274

into a period of disorder known as the *Time of Troubles.* Individuals pretending to be members of the old royal family claimed the throne. Weak tsars came and went, law and order broke down, and foreign armies marched across Russia with little opposition. During this period, Polish troops captured and held Moscow for two years.

The people who suffered the most during this civil warfare were the peasants. They had to pay high taxes and were forced to serve in the armies of the tsars and the nobles.

The Romanovs   The "Time of Troubles" finally ended in 1613 when Michael Romanov (ROE-muh-nahf) was made tsar. This youth of sixteen was the first of a great family of tsars who ruled Russia for more than 300 years. The *Romanov* line of rulers ended only with the Russian Revolution in 1917. Michael's reign united the Russians behind their new ruling family. Foreign invaders were driven out of Russia. Law and order returned. A period of new influence from western Europe was about to begin.

Peter the Great   In the seventeenth century, Russia was more of an Asiatic than a European nation. For generations, the country had been isolated culturally from the nations of Europe. The early Romanov tsars recognized Russia's isolation and set about trying to put Russia in touch with Europe. They invited foreigners to Muscovy with the hope that the scholars, merchants, and soldiers of other countries would teach the Russians to be as modern and prosperous as their neighbors in western Europe.

The most remarkable of these early Romanov tsars was **Peter the Great,** who ruled from 1682 to 1725. Peter the Great was a person of boundless energy. At various times during his life, he took up carpentry, shoemaking, cooking, clockmaking, ivory carving, etching, and even dentistry.

Peter was convinced that Russia needed quick and far-reaching changes if it was to catch up with the other European nations. Leaving the government in the hands of his officials, Peter traveled across western Europe to learn about things for himself. He studied shipbuilding, military science, and other practical matters. Wherever he went, he hired western European specialists and sent them back to Russia so that they could train his people in new skills.

In order to carry out the changes that were necessary, the Russian people were forced to give up many of their old ways. Since the word of the tsar was law, few dared to oppose the tsar's wishes. He made it a law that beards, which were not in style in western Europe, could no longer be worn by Russian nobles. He introduced a new calendar, so that dates used in Russia were more in line with those used in western Europe. He also reorganized the government, increased taxes, and made every noble serve the country for twenty years, either in military or government service. Even though many of these changes were bitterly resented, the tsars who followed Peter the Great continued to bring western ways to Russia for the next hundred years.

St. Petersburg   To complete his break with the past, Peter ordered the construction of a new capital in the northwestern part of Russia. He named this new capital city St. Petersburg and in 1703 moved the government there from Moscow.

The new capital put Russia in closer touch with western Europe. The

Peter the Great is shown here snipping off the beard of a noble, an action that symbolized Peter's efforts to modernize Russia. How does this picture compare with modern political cartoons?

acquire its Baltic ports. But Sweden stood in Peter's way.

In 1700, Livonia belonged to Sweden, whose king, Charles XII, was one of Europe's most able generals. When Peter's army marched westward into Livonia, the Swedes met the Russians at the *Battle of Narva*. Although outnumbered by the Russians five to one, the Swedes inflicted a crushing defeat on Peter's troops. Peter fled the battlefield before the fighting ended. The Battle of Narva taught him a lesson. He realized the backwardness of Russia's army in comparison with western Europe's troops. As a result, Peter set out to reform the army and to build a modern navy. By the end of his reign in 1725, Russia had become one of the strongest military powers in Europe.

Sweden's king, Charles XII, was killed in a battle in 1718. Sweden made peace with Russia and gave the Baltic lands of Livonia to Tsar Peter. From that time on, Russia replaced Sweden as the greatest military power in eastern Europe.

old capital, Moscow, was located deep inside Russia far from the centers of Europe. St. Petersburg, however, was located on the sea route that led through the Baltic Sea to the main ports of Europe. Ships could easily reach Russia's new capital. Peter considered St. Petersburg Russia's "window on the West."

War with Sweden   Peter's determination to have greater contacts with the West led to war with Sweden beginning in 1700 and lasting for twenty years. It was known as the *Great Northern War*. The cause for the war was an attempt by Tsar Peter to seize Livonia. Tsar Ivan the Terrible had tried to take Livonia but failed. (See page 273.) Peter hoped to conquer Livonia in order to

The Succession Question   Like Ivan the Terrible, Peter the Great killed his son, Alexis, who was the heir to the throne. Born in 1690, Alexis grew up unlike his father in many ways. They often quarreled, and as he grew older Alexis disagreed in public with his father's policies. As a result, Peter decided to disinherit him. Alexis, fearful about his safety, fled Russia and went to western Europe. Tsar Peter sent agents to find his son. In 1718, they located Alexis in Austria and persuaded him to return to Russia, promising him he would be safe. But upon his arrival at St. Petersburg, Alexis was thrown in prison and charged with treason. He died while being tortured upon his father's orders.

At that time, there was nothing in Russian law requiring that the throne be passed from a deceased ruler to his or her closest relative, and Tsar Peter did nothing to provide for his successor. Because there was no heir when Peter died in 1725, his second wife, Catherine I, seized the throne with the help of the army. Until the early 1800's, the death of each Russian tsar was usually followed by a struggle for power. The army overthrew several tsars and had the last say about who should take the Russian throne.

PEOPLE IN HISTORY

Catherine II

Catherine the Great plotted her takeover of the Russian throne for about six months. Her husband, Tsar Peter III, had shocked and offended everyone. He wanted to disband the three regiments of Russian soldiers that served as royal guards and hire more "trustworthy" foreign soldiers. Furious at this insult to their loyalty, the Russian guards preferred to see Catherine on the throne.

On June 28, the leader of the rebels supporting Catherine quietly left St. Petersburg for Peterhof to tell Catherine that she must leave right away to be proclaimed Russia's new ruler. Sneaking away from Peter and his spies, Catherine jumped into a carriage and rode with the rebel leader to the headquarters of the Izrnalylovsky (iz-MAHL-off-ski) Regiment, which protected the capital city of St. Petersburg. Catherine and the rebel leader were worried. But when a drum roll summoned the troops, the men at once shouted and cheered for Catherine. At about nine o'clock, barely three hours after beginning her dash to the capital, Catherine heard herself proclaimed ruler in a short church service.

It was not long until news of the revolution in St. Petersburg reached Tsar Peter. He was protected by 1,590 foreign troops at Peterhof, and he tried without success to find loyal units of the Russian army to reinforce them.

Once proclaimed ruler, Catherine set out immediately for Peterhof at the head of her guards. She put on the uniform of a guards' officer, carried a sword, and rode astride a white horse. Before she could reach Peterhof, two letters were brought to her from Peter III. In the first letter, Peter offered to share the throne with Catherine. In the second letter, he merely asked permission to leave the country safely. Catherine ignored both letters.

Knowing resistance was useless, Tsar Peter resigned. He was then taken away to prison where he was later murdered. Catherine returned to St. Petersburg and began her reign of twenty-four years.

Adapted from: Ronald Hingley. **The Tsars: 1533-1917.** New York: Macmillan and Co., 1968, pp. 190–192.

1. Upon whom did Catherine rely in order to take power in Russia?

2. What might Catherine's takeover have to do with "Might makes right"?

How does this picture of Peter the Great compare with one on page 276? Explain.

None of Peter's successors was able to match his accomplishments. After the death of Catherine I, who ruled from 1725 to 1727, a series of weak rulers followed who were only interested in their own pleasures. Between 1725 and 1800, the nobles were able to win back some of the power they had lost to Peter the Great. They continued to imitate western Europe. Anything French was especially admired. To speak French was considered to be a mark of education and dignity.

A Closer Look

SERFS FOR SALE

Below are some excerpts from advertisements for the sale of serfs that appeared in Russian newspapers in the 1790's.

For Sale-

Well-behaved craftsmen: two tailors, a shoemaker, a watchmaker, a cook, an engraver, a general handyman, and two coachmen. They may be seen and the price for them may be learned from their owner in the Third Part, Fourth Quarter [of the city] at house number 51. Also for sale: three young racing horses, one stallion, and a pack of about fifty hunting dogs, which will be one year old in January or February.

For Sale-

In the Fifteenth Part, Second Quarter, house 183 on Meshchanskai Street near the church, a worker about 25 years old. He is a trained woman's shoemaker and knows his profession exceptionally well. In addition, he performs all domestic, coachman's, and footman's duties, as well as waiting on the table during meals. He has a wife, 22 years old, who is expecting a baby. She sews, irons, starches, waits on the lady of house, and cooks.

For Sale-

In Part Twelve of the city, a 16-year-old girl, formerly belonging to a poor family, who knows how to knit, sew, iron, starch, and wait on the lady of the house. She has a pretty face.

Adapted from: Basil Dmytryshyn, ed. *Imperial Russia: A Source Book, 1700-1917*. New York: Holt, Rinehart and Winston, 1967.

1. What were some of the skills and qualities for which Russian serfs were valued?

2. Do you think a modern people could practice serfdom of this sort and still be civilized? Explain.

Catherine the Great From 1762 to 1796, Russia was ruled by another outstanding person, **Catherine II.** She, like Peter, earned the title Great because of her accomplishments. Catherine was a German princess who married the heir to the Russian throne. Her husband, Peter III, became tsar in 1762 but was overthrown six months later by Catherine. Even though she was not a Russian, Catherine was supported by the army and became tsarina.

In general, Catherine tried to imitate Peter the Great's system of rule. She ruled as an absolute monarch. Schools were built, laws were modernized, and Catherine improved local government by appointing nobles as local officials and closely supervising them. Catherine's reign was a golden age for the nobles of Russia. Under Peter the Great, they had owed the state twenty years' service, but under Catherine, the duty was abolished. In return, the nobles supported Catherine's claims to the throne.

While life for the nobles improved, the conditions of serfs worsened. Russia's serfs were reduced to slavery. Individuals or whole families of serfs were bought and sold like animals. The power of a noble over his or her serfs was unlimited.

Conditions of serfdom in Russia became so bad that a widespread peasant uprising broke out. This great revolt of 1773-1775 was led by an illiterate peasant named *Pugachev* (POO-kaw-chef). His revolt began along the Volga River and quickly spread across southern Russia. The peasants who followed Pugachev spread terror among the landowning class. Catherine's army, however, was too strong for Pugachev. He was captured and executed in 1775. This brought his revolt to an end. But Pugachev's revolt was not Russia's last peasant uprising. From that time on, the treatment of serfs brought about frequent revolts.

Expansion of Russia Catherine II strengthened Russia's army and navy and was able to expand Russian territory. She fought a series of wars with the Turks. As a result, Russia annexed the Crimean peninsula and the north coast of the Black Sea. (See the map on page 237.) This pushed Russia's western frontier to the Dniester River. Catherine also added vast territories in the west by destroying and partitioning the kingdom of Poland, with the help of Austria and Prussia. (See page 268.) Between 1772 and 1795, about one-third of Poland was added to Russia's territory and remained attached to Russia until after World War I.

SECTION REVIEW

1. Mapping: Using the map on page 274, make a list of early Russia's neighbors. Which tsars made large additions of territory to Russia from the 1300's to the 1500's?

2. In your own words, identify or define: Kiev, Muscovy, Ivan the Great, Ivan the Terrible, boyars, oprichniki, "Time of Troubles," Peter the Great, Catherine the Great, serfs.

3. What territory did Peter the Great add to Russia? What territory was added by Catherine the Great?

◗ Do you believe that Catherine and Peter are called great only because they added territory to Russia? Would you consider a present-day ruler great if he or she added territory to a country as a result of war?

Reviewing the Unit

Unit Summary

After you have read the selection below, answer the questions that follow.

After the fall of Rome, the eastern half of the Roman Empire came to be known as the Byzantine Empire and continued to exist for almost 1,000 years. Some of the early Byzantine emperors, such as Justinian, tried to recapture the former territories of the Roman Empire in the west but were unsuccessful.

Until the final fall of Constantinople in 1453, the Byzantine emperors faced hostile neighbors. Most of the Middle East fell to the Muslims by the end of the eighth century. The Muslims were followers of Muhammad, a leader who founded a new religion, Islam, in Arabia.

Among the peoples who converted to Islam were the Turks. They established the Ottoman Empire in the Middle East. When the Ottoman Turks were unable to capture Constantinople, they invaded the Balkans instead. There, the Turks conquered the Slavic peoples and defeated the Hungarians. In 1453, the Turks conquered Constantinople and made it their capital.

Long before their conquest by the Turks, the south Slavs had faced invasions by the Bulgars and Magyars. The east Slavs in Russia were overcome in the 1200's by the Mongols. The west Slaves were threatened by the Germans. Long struggles between Poles and Germans ended in the fifteenth century with a Polish victory. The Czechs of Bohemia lost to their German neighbors in The Thirty Years' War.

By 1500, the Russians had thrown off Mongol control and established an independent Muscovy. Ivan the Great united most of Russia, and his successor, Ivan the Terrible, destroyed the power of the Russian nobles. From that time on, the Russian tsars were absolute monarchs. Russia was cut off from the rest of Europe. Late in the 1600's, however, Tsar Peter the Great tried to modernize his country.

Under Tsar Peter and later under Catherine the Great, the territory of Russia was greatly expanded. By 1796, almost all of eastern Europe with the exception of tiny Montenegro had fallen to the Turks, the Russians, or the Germans.

Developing Your Reading Skills

1. What do you think is the main idea of this reading?
2. In your own words state the main idea from the reading about each of the following:

   a. Byzantine Empire
   b. Turks
   c. south Slavs
   d. west Slavs
   e. Russians

Developing a Sense of Time

Examine the time line below and answer the questions that follow it.

527	Emperor Justinian rules the Byzantine Empire
570	Birth of Muhammad
900	Magyars in Hungary; peak of Bulgarian Empire; Croats found a kingdom
1000	Russia becomes Christian
1100	Split of eastern and western Christian churches
1102	Croatia loses independence to Hungary
1237	Mongols invade Russia
1453	Fall of Byzantine Empire to the Turks
1462	Ivan III (the Great) rules Moscow
1584	Death of Ivan IV (the Terrible)
1605	Russian "Time of Troubles" begins
1620	Bohemia loses its independence to the Hapsburgs
1725	Death of Peter the Great
1762	Catherine II (the Great) rules Russia
1795	Last division of Poland among the great powers

1. Who ruled Russia first—Peter the Great or Catherine the Great?
2. When was the fall of the Byzantine Empire?
3. Which occured first: the Mongol invasion of Russia or the Turkish conquest of eastern Europe?
4. In which century was Muhammad born?
5. Choose three other key events or developments from Unit 5 that could be added to this time line and give a reason for selecting each.

Recalling the Facts

1. Why did it take most of the peoples of eastern Europe so long to establish their own independent states?
2. Describe the system of government in the Byzantine Empire.
3. How did Christianity in eastern Europe differ from Christianity in western Europe?
4. Explain the fundamental beliefs of Islam that distinguish it from other religions. How did Muslims treat Christians and Jews?
5. Name and identify each of the south Slav and west Slav peoples and the kingdoms they established.
6. Tell why each of the following battles was significant: Mohács, Kossovo, White Mountain.
7. What caused the decline of Poland?
8. What was the Russian "Time of Troubles"? How did it affect the peasants? How did it finally end?
9. How did Ivan III, Ivan IV, and Peter the Great change Russia?

Using Your Vocabulary

1. How were the terms *icon* and *idolatry* related, according to Emperor Leo III?
2. What does it mean when a ruler has absolute power? Give three examples of absolute rulers.
3. Briefly define or identify: Koran, Hadith, Kaaba, hegira, minaret, muezzin.
4. Describe the life of a Janissary.
5. What is the Cyrillic alphabet? Who uses it?
6. What do the terms *boyar* and *oprichniki* have in common?
7. How would a Russian tsar define the terms *freedom* and *ruler?* Would a Russian serf define them the same way? Explain any difference or similarity.
8. What might the terms *freedom* and *ruler* have meant to a sultan of the Ottoman Turks? How might the meaning change for people living under Ottoman rule?

Using Your Geography Skills

1. Using the Atlas, describe the political and physical geography of eastern Europe by naming the present-day countries, major rivers, mountain ranges, and bodies of water in the area. What countries make up the Balkans?
2. List all the territories included in the Byzantine Empire at its fullest extent.
3. Describe the spread of Islam. What territories became Muslim?
4. Trace the growth of the Ottoman Empire. As the empire expanded, which lands and peoples did the Turks conquer?
5. Describe the divisions of Poland in the late 1700's. To which European empires were Polish lands and people annexed?
6. How did the geographic location of St. Petersburg contribute to its being called Russia's "window on the West"?

Developing Your Writing Skills

Today we speak of Eastern Europe and Western Europe. European peoples still are classified geographically. It is also a common practice to classify the peoples of America geographically as North Americans, Central Americans, and South Americans. Why is this done? Can you think of any problems in trying to classify all peoples geographically? Is there a more accurate way to classify them?

FORMING AN OPINION

1. In your opinion, what were the major differences between east Europeans and west Europeans during the period you have studied?

2. What were the major similarities?

SUPPORTING AN OPINION

3. How many of the similarities and differences between east and west Europeans had to do with geography? Do you think there are any problems in classifying peoples by geographic regions? Answer this question in a paragraph or essay. Begin by completing the following topic sentence:
There is (is not) a problem in classifying peoples by geographic regions _____

Why Study the Past?

Constantinople was a well-run metropolis with free hospitals, lighted streets, and even a fire department. Its population reached nearly a million people, and unemployment and crime were major problems. In the center of Constantinople was the Hippodrome. It resembled a large football stadium and seated 60,000 spectators who went to see various sporting events. And when taxes rose too high, Constantinople's angry taxpayers used the Hippodrome to stage demonstrations. How could this description be used to prove the saying "The more things change, the more they remain the same"?

Your History Bookshelf

Andrae, Tor. *Mohammed: The Man and His Faith.* New York: Harper & Row, 1974.

Halecki, Oscar. *Borderlands of Western Civilization.* New York: Ronald Press, 1952.

Hussey, Joan M. *The Byzantine World.* New York: Harper & Row, 1973.

Isenberg, Irwin. *Eastern Europe.* New York: Scholastic Book Services, 1968.

Nazaroff, Alexander. *The Land and People of Russia.* Philadelphia: Lippincott, 1972.

Time Line

	3000		2000		1000		500		100 B.C.		100 A.D.		500		600		700		800	
		2500		1500		750		250				250		550		650		750		850

Unit 1

- Sumerian cities developed   • Hittite Empire falls   • Alexander conquers Egypt
- Old Kingdom in Egypt   • Solomon rules the Hebrew Kingdom
- Sumer's government declines   • Persian Empire established
- First pyramid begun in Egypt   • Egypt invaded by Assyrians
- Middle Kingdom in Egypt   • Height of Chaldean Empire
- Code of Hammurabi developed
- Hyksos invade Egypt
- New Kingdom in Egypt
- Hatshepsut's reign begins
- Hebrews invade Canaan

Unit 2

- Indus Valley civilization ends   • Ch'in Empire established in China
- Aryan tribes enter India   • Maurya Empire established in India
- Aryans begin to settle in India   • Fall of Han Empire in China
- Chou Dynasty replaces the Shang in China   • Gupta Empire established in India
- Buddhism founded in India
- Harsha rules in India
- T'ang Dynasty founded in China
- Printing invented in Chi

Unit 3

- The Trojan War   • Democratic government established in Athens
- Rome founded   • Rome defeats Carthage   • Christianity becomes a major religion of the Roman Empire
- The *Iliad* and the *Odyssey* are written down   • Fall of the Roman Empire
- Dark Age in Greece ends   • Augustus rules in Rome
- Jesus is born
- Roman Republic founded
- Peloponnesian Wars end
- Sparta defeats Athens
- Alexander the Great conquers Egypt
- Hellenistic Age in Greece begins

Unit 4

- Germanic tribes invade western Europe
- Carolingians come to po
- Muslims invade Spain
- Charler new Rom Emperor
- Viking of Europe
- D Cha emp

Unit 5

- Emperor Justinian rules the Byzantine Empire
- Muhammad is born

900	1000	1100	1200	1300	1400	1500	1600	1700	1800
950	1050	1150	1250	1350	1450	1550	1650	1750	

• Minamoto Shogunate established in Japan
• Kublai Khan rules China
• Kublai Khan's invasion of Japan fails

• Manchus conquer China
• Tokugawa shoguns continue to rule Japan

• First Crusade begins

• Fourth Crusade ends
• Holy Land remains in Muslim hands
• Hundred Years' War begins

• Civil War in England begins
• Reign of Louis XIV begins
• Cromwell and the Interregnum in England
• Glorious Revolution in England

• Muslims expelled from Spain
• Luther posts Ninety-five Theses
• Religious war begins in France
• Edict of Nantes establishes religious freedom in France

• Town life revives in Europe
• Norman conquest of England

• Magyars are in Hungary
• Peak of Bulgarian Empire
• Croats found a kingdom
• Russia becomes Christian

• Byzantine Empire falls to the Turks
• Ivan III (the Great) rules Moscow

• Last division of Poland among powers

• Eastern and Western Christian churches split
• Croatia loses independence to Hungary
• Mongols invade Russia

• Ivan IV (the Terrible) rules Moscow
• Russian Time of Troubles begins
• Bohemia loses its independence to the Hapsburgs
• Peter the Great dies
• Catherine II (the Great) rules Russia

unit 6

The World of
Early Africa

One of the most remarkable journeys ever recorded in history was the famous pilgrimage of Mansa Musa (MAHN-sah MOO-sah) from 1324 to 1325. This Muslim king, who ruled the empire of Mali (MAHL-ee) for twenty-five years, was anxious to visit the holy city of Mecca (MEK-uh). Great preparations were made for the pilgrimage. Food and supplies were gathered. And about ninety camel loads of gold dust, each weighing 135 kilograms (300 pounds), were collected for Mansa Musa to spend on his trip. When the caravan was finally ready to leave, several thousand of the king's subjects left with it. Some claim that 60,000 people accompanied Mansa Musa. Many were members of Mansa Musa's family.

During the journey, Mansa Musa, being a devout Muslim, was extremely generous with his wealth. He not only made huge donations to the cities of Mecca and Medina (muh-DEE-nuh) but also frequently gave gifts to people and officials he met along the way. Mansa Musa was so free with his gold that he ran out of money before the journey was over and had to borrow from the merchants of Cairo (KIE-roe). This generosity almost destroyed the Cairo gold market. The sudden increase in gold caused its price and value to fall drastically. According to one source, it took more than twelve years for the Cairo gold market to recover.

Mansa Musa and his pilgrimage caused such a sensation that they were remembered years after his death. A map drawn in 1375 for Charles V of France shows Mansa Musa. (See page 298.) The writing on the map reads: "This Negro lord is Musa Mali, lord of the Negroes of Guinea. So abundant is the gold that is found in his land that he is the richest and most noble king of all the land."

The 1375 map showing Mansa Musa and describing the immense gold resources of Mali had a great impact on European views of Africa. The majority of these views were based on exaggerations or distortions of facts about the African continent. For example, Europeans came to believe that Africa was overflowing with gold. Recent studies of African history have corrected many of the false impressions of Africa that have accumulated over the centuries.

In this unit, you will examine the early history of Africa as well as some of the false impressions that Europeans had about it. You will learn how the slave trade started, how it effected African life, and why it spread to other continents. This unit will also describe a typical early African village and some African customs. You will study about the various major empires of early Africa. These are shown on the map on the next page. You can use this map to locate these empires as you study them.

Unit Goals

1. To know the main geographical features of the continent of Africa.
2. To know the five major population groups to which most early Africans belonged and the location of the area inhabited by each group.
3. To understand the Bantu migrations and to know the importance of these migrations.
4. To identify the main early African empires and kingdoms, the modern African nations in which they were located, and the geographical features of the lands they occupied.
5. To list the outstanding characteristics of the early African empires of Ghana, Mali, Songhai, and Kanem-Bornu.
6. To know the difference between the life of slaves within early African society and the life of slaves owned by non-African masters.
7. To know how the triangular trade worked and to know what impact it had on early African societies.

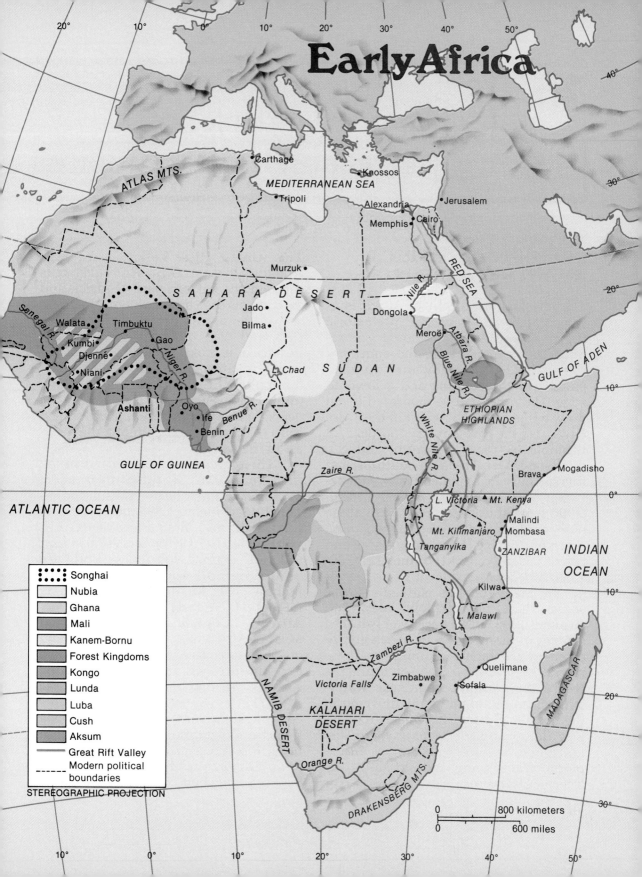

Early Africa

20° 10° 0° 10° 20° 30° 40° 50°

40°

ATLAS MTS.

MEDITERRANEAN SEA

•Carthage

•Knossos

•Tripoli

Alexandria •Jerusalem

Memphis •Cairo

30°

RED SEA

SAHARA DESERT

Murzuk•

20°

Jado•

Nile R.

Bilma•

Dongola•

Senegal R.

Walata•

Timbuktu•

Meroë•

Kumbi•

Gao•

Albara R.

Djenné•

Niger R.

L. Chad

SUDAN

Blue Nile R.

Niani•

10°

Ashanti

Oyo•

Benue R.

•Ife

ETHIOPIAN
HIGHLANDS

•Benin

GULF OF ADEN

GULF OF GUINEA

Zaire R.

Brava •Mogadisho

White Nile R.

ATLANTIC OCEAN

L. Victoria ▲Mt. Kenya

0°

Malindi

Mt. Kilimanjaro▲

Mombasa

L. Tanganyika

ZANZIBAR

INDIAN

OCEAN

Kilwa•

10°

L. Malawi

Zambezi R.

Quelimane•

Victoria Falls

Zimbabwe

MADAGASCAR

•Sofala

20°

NAMIB DESERT

KALAHARI
DESERT

Orange R.

DRAKENSBERG MTS.

30°

••••	Songhai
	Nubia
	Ghana
	Mali
	Kanem-Bornu
	Forest Kingdoms
	Kongo
	Lunda
	Luba
	Cush
	Aksum
———	Great Rift Valley
---	Modern political boundaries

STEREOGRAPHIC PROJECTION

0   800 kilometers

0   600 miles

10° 0° 10° 20° 30° 40° 50°

The Early Peoples of Africa and Their Empires

PREHISTORIC AFRICA AND ITS GEOGRAPHY

The physical geography of Africa is as varied today as it was in prehistoric times. According to the noted geographer, J. Desmon Clark, the continent can be divided generally into two main parts: a highland zone and a lowland zone. The zones can be separated if you draw a line from the mouth of the Zaire River to the present-day borders of Ethiopia (ee-thee-OE-pea-uh) and Sudan (soo-DAN). The area south of that line is mostly a plateau ranging between 900 and 1,500 meters (3,000-5,000 feet) above sea level, with some higher ridges and mountains. The area north of this line has mainly plains and basins usually 150-160 meters (500-2,000 feet) above sea level.

In many of the plateau's lower areas, there are shallow lakes and swamps filled with a variety of fish. The sources of many rivers in Africa are located in the higher mountains. These rivers eventually reach escarpments where they become rapids or waterfalls. From there, the rivers move on to the coastal plains. This makes navigation almost impossible for any long distance and has prevented many an explorer from going too far into the interior of Africa.

The Great Rift Valley A large trough called the *Great Rift Valley* cuts through the eastern part of Africa and extends across the continent of Africa, as well as across much of the Middle East and Asia. Located near this rift in Africa is Lake Victoria, the continent's greatest lake. Lake Tanganyika (tan-guhn-YEE-kuh) and Lake Malawi (muh-LAH-wee) were formed in the deeper parts of the Great Rift Valley. Both of these lakes are among the deepest in the world.

Three great mountains exist in the rift area. Two of these mountains, Mount Kilimanjaro (kil-uh-muhn-JAHR-oe), which is 5,895 meters (19,340 feet) high, and Mount Kenya (KEEN-yuh), which is 5,199 meters (17,058 feet) tall, are extinct volcanoes. Both are snowcapped all year round. The third highest peak, Mount Stanley, is 5,039 meters (16,795 feet) high.

Africa's Climate and Vegetation Most of Africa has a wooded grassland of deciduous trees (those which shed and produce new leaves each growing season). As one moves south of the equator, the winters or dry seasons become longer. Some last as long as six months. Vegetation can vary from dense forest to scattered bushes.

Just north of the equatorial forest is the Sudan belt. *Sudan* is the name

These chipped stones found in East Africa were used as hard axes by prehistoric humans. What do you think archaeologists can learn about prehistoric life by studying such fragmentary remains?

given to this grassland of West Africa by Arab geographers. (The term *Sudan* should not be confused with the present-day country of Sudan.) South of the Sudan is woodland-grassland vegetation where many kinds of animals such as antelopes, elephants, and species of buffaloes and horses live.

The areas north and south of those grasslands have a drier climate. They have fewer grasses and low bushes. Going farther in either direction, one encounters true deserts. The Sahara is to the north, and among others the Kalahari (kal-uh-HAHR-ee) to the south.

Prehistoric Remains Found in Africa Much of our evidence about the earliest humans comes from Africa. Archaeolo-gists believe they have found the remains of men and women who lived millions of years ago. (Refer to the section on Prehistoric People in the introduction.)

The Sahara Region Some scientists propose that from about 5500 B.C. to 2500 B.C. the Sahara was not desert. It had enough rainfall to sustain human, animal, and plant life. There was abundant vegetation that provided food, building materials such as wood, and other necessities. People of the early Sahara lived by hunting, farming, and herding. The rivers of the Sahara supplied fish.

After 2500 B.C., some scientists believe the Sahara gradually became drier. The climate may have changed drastically, or overgrazing may have destroyed the vegetation. As rivers and lakes dried up, most of the hunters and fishermen left the Sahara. They moved eastward toward Egypt, northward toward the Mediterranean, or southward into West Africa. (See the Atlas of Africa.) By the time the Sahara had developed into a desert, only the Berbers (BUR-berz), a nomadic people, remained there.

Ironworking Spreads to Early Africa
Around 2000 B.C., Egyptian and Asian metal workers discovered how to make bronze by mixing copper with tin. Bronze was the hardest metal then known to the ancient world. When the Hittites (HIH-tites) invaded Egypt, they brought iron, a harder metal, with them. The technique and knowledge of making iron gradually spread from Egypt throughout the rest of Africa. Black West Africans were working with iron by 200 B.C. The people of East Africa were making their own iron by 300 A.D. By 500 A.D., the knowledge of ironmaking had spread to the heart of south central Africa.

The effects of iron on African life were important and lasting. Africans who knew how to make iron tools and weapons dominated those who had none; a wooden spear was no match for an iron weapon.

Five Major Population Groups
While our evidence about the very earliest Africans is limited, we do know something about those that lived several thousand years ago. For instance, we know that by then the peoples of Africa were members of five major population groups. These groups shared similar physical characteristics, and they spoke related languages. These early groups were the *Black Africans*, the *San* (SAHN), also known as Bushmen, the *Pygmies* (PIG-meez), the *Mongoloids* (MAHNG-guh-loidz), and the *Caucasians* (kaw-KAY-zhuhnz). The Black Africans lived in the area called *sub-Saharan Africa*, or Africa south of the Sahara Desert. The San lived in east central and southern Africa. The Pygmies inhabited the humid forest regions of west central Africa. Mongoloid people settled mainly on the island of Madagascar (mad-uh-GAS-kur), which is located off the southeastern coast of Africa. They were probably related to the earliest inhabitants of the Mediterranean shores and the Middle East. The Caucasians settled in northern Africa and along the Nile River Delta. The Pygmies and the Mongoloid peoples each had very small populations. The Black Africans and Caucasians, however, numbered in the millions.

Little is known about the origins of these five population groups. Scholars guess that the Black Africans originated in the river valleys of present-day Nigeria (nie-JIR-ee-uh) and spread east, north, and south by means of the Bantu migrations. The Caucasians may have come from the Middle East. The Mongoloids may have sailed from southeast Asia to eastern Africa around 2,000 years ago. Even less is known about the beginnings of the San and the Pygmies. Some scholars wonder if the two groups had a common ancestor. More research must be done, before any definite opinions can be formed. Archaeologists such as Dr. Mary Leakey and her son, Richard Leakey, must find new evidence of the earliest Africans.

Farming and Cattle Raising of the Early Africans
Scholars do know some things about the activities of early Africans. Africans living in the Nile Valley changed their way of life

This painting was found on a rock wall in the Sahara Desert. Scholars believe it was created by people who inhabited the Sahara while it was still a green and fertile area. What evidence does the painting contain to support this theory?.

around 5000 B.C. They began to get food by farming and raising cattle rather than by hunting and gathering. Their knowledge of raising crops and cattle spread from the Nile Valley gradually west and south to the open plains of the grassland. People in western and central Africa had acquired this knowledge by 1000 B.C.

The Bantu Migrations　One of the most important events in early Africa was the great migration of the Bantu-speaking Black Africans. The *Bantu* (BAN-too) are one of the largest Black African groups today. They are also the largest group south of the Sahara whose languages have a common origin. *Ba* is an African prefix meaning "many" or "more than one;" *ntu* is a word for "human being." Thus *Bantu* means "many human beings" or "many people."

The Bantu probably originated in the river valleys of present-day eastern Nigeria or the area of Cameroon (kam-uh-ROON). (See the Atlas of Africa.) There they lived mainly by fishing.

They also hunted game, cultivated yams and palm trees, and grew some grains. They bred goats and some sheep and cattle. And they made pottery, cloth from bark, and fabrics of woven tree fibers.

The Bantu migrations were probably triggered by the movement of people from the Sahara into West Africa. Over the centuries as new peoples moved from the Sahara into the West African grassland, the Bantu moved southward into the tropical forests of present-day Zaire (zie-IR).

Loading their families, goods, and livestock aboard wooden canoes, they traveled along the rivers. Because these waterways made travel easy, a whole village could move a great distance in a short period of time. The forests were a good place to live because they furnished timber for housing and canoes. Game could also be found there for food. The marshes and rivers were teeming with fish. The mild climate was actually more pleasant than that of the harsh, dry grassland.

As far back as 2,000 years ago, the Bantu gradually populated the African continent south from ancient Benin (buh-NEEN) in the west to present-day South Africa in the south. (See the map on page 289.) As they moved mostly north to south, they displaced and absorbed most of the early San and Mongoloid cultures.

The Bantu migrations were so frequent that the Bantu also spread rapidly throughout the lower part of the African continent. Over a period of time, they settled in large numbers as far east as the Great Rift Valley, down the Zaire and Zambezi (zam-BEE-zee) rivers, and eventually migrated as far north as Somalia (soe-MAHL-ee-uh) and Lake Victoria.

When they acquired iron tools, the Bantu in eastern Africa began to cultivate new crops. They raised bananas and taro, a plant with broad leaves and a large, starchy root. Both plants had been introduced to Africa from southeast Asia. Bantus in southeastern Africa began to raise cattle on a large scale. The earliest Bantu people had been cattle raisers when they lived in the West African grassland. When they moved south into the forests, their herds were killed by the tsetse (TET-see) fly. The tsetse fly's bite caused a disease known as sleeping sickness, which resulted in death. As the Bantu moved out of the forests into other parts of Africa, they encountered the Khoi (KOY), who are also known as the Hottentots (HAHT-'n-tahts), and other cattle-raising people who taught them how to herd.

By the nineteenth century, the number of Bantu-speaking peoples had grown. From a relatively small group of forest dwellers, they had become a group large enough to speak over forty different but related Bantu languages.

SECTION REVIEW

1. Mapping: Using the map of Africa on page xxx and information on pages 290-292, briefly describe the physical geography of Africa.
2. In your own words, identify or define: Bantus, Sudan, Benin.
3. How did the Sahara region change after 2500 B.C.? How did that change affect the people who lived there?
4. Name the five major population groups of early Africa. Where did they settle?
5. Why are the origins of those five groups so obscure?
6. In your own words, briefly describe the Bantu migrations in Africa. Why were the migrations important?
◗ How can moving affect one's way of life and thinking? Explain your answer.

EARLY WESTERN AFRICAN EMPIRES

Early North Africa While the Egyptian civilization was developing, people in other parts of North Africa were also creating important civilizations. Among these North Africans were the inhabitants of Carthage (KAHR-thij). As you know, Carthage began as a Phoenician (fih-NISH-uhn) colony on the shores of northern Africa. When it was founded, the northern Sahara was still a lush grassland. Carthage was a very prosperous colony. It continued to grow and prosper after gaining its independence from Phoenicia. At the height of Carthaginian power, the population of the city was over 500,000.

The Punic Wars with Rome ended Carthaginian independence, making it a Roman colony. The Romans wanted to develop the plains outside Carthage into farmlands. There they hoped to grow grain to feed their expanding empire. Eventually, Rome dominated not only Carthage and its immediate surroundings but all of northern Africa.

The Berber Caravans By 400 A.D., Roman influence in North Africa had begun to decline. The Berbers, who had been pressured by the Romans to become farmers, resumed their nomadic way of life. The camel became very important to the Berbers because it was uniquely adapted to desert life. Its web-like hoofs kept it from sinking into sand, and it could store water internally for as long as three weeks.

Using camels to carry their goods, the Berbers set up an active trade with the Black Africans of the grassland south of the Sahara. By 1000 A.D., the Sahara was crisscrossed by caravan routes. The towns where routes crossed grew rapidly. Some cities such as Timbuktu (tim-buk-TOO), Walata (wuh-LAH-tuh), Djenné (jeh-NAY), and Niani (nee-AHN-ee) became important cities of West Africa. West African goods carried in Berber caravans found their way to markets as distant as Europe and the Middle East. Gold and salt were among the most important items for trading. (See the map on page 296.) Most trading took place in the Sudan region of West Africa and was stimulated by the civilizations that developed there.

This temple is evidence of the influence of Roman culture on North Africa. What foreign cultures have influenced your culture the most?

TRADE ROUTES IN WEST AFRICA 300-1400 A.D.

ATLANTIC OCEAN

NORTH AFRICA

MEDITERRANEAN SEA

Tripoli

Cairo

EGYPT

-30°

N

S A H A R A   D E S E R T

Nile R.

20°

NUBIA

-20°

Walata

Timbuktu

Djenné

Senegal R.

Niger R.

L. Chad

Kano

Niani

WEST AFRICA

10°

⬧	major gold fields
☐	major salt deposits
—	major trade routes
•	major trading cities

0   600 kilometers

0   400 miles

10°   0°   10°   20°   30°

Where were the major trading cities in West Africa?

The Empire of Ghana   One of the first civilizations to emerge in the Sudan was that of ancient Ghana (GAHN-uh). The empire of Ghana was located several hundred kilometers north of the modern state of Ghana. As early as 300 A.D., the inhabitants of ancient Ghana had mastered the art of iron-working. Like the Egyptians of the Nile Valley, the people of ancient Ghana used iron farm tools to cultivate crops of rice and millet, a wheat-like grain. Iron-tipped weapons made Ghana's soldiers superior to soldiers of neighboring states who had only weapons made of ebony.

The rulers of Ghana became powerful because they controlled the trade routes from West Africa to North Africa. Ghana controlled the area between the salt mines just below the Sahara and some of the gold deposits of the West African forests to the south. Until Ghana's decline around 1200 A.D., great caravans consisting of 500 to 10,000 camels journeyed throughout the empire. The rulers of Ghana taxed all the caravans, thus raising large sums of gold for their personal treasuries. With all this wealth, Ghanaian rulers were able to support thousands of soldiers. The soldiers were used to dominate the entire Sudan region.

The royal palace of Ghana was located in Kumbi (KOOM-bee), the largest city of ancient Ghana. Kumbi was actually two capital cities, 10 kilometers (6 miles) apart. The king lived in one city, inside a walled fortress. In the other city were mosques, markets of the Blacks and Arabs, and residential areas for merchants, teachers, craftspeople, and other workers. At its height, Kumbi's population was about 30,000.

Muslims in Ghana As you learned in Unit 5, Muslim (MUZ-luhm) Arabs had entered Egypt from the Middle East by 639 A.D. Soon after 700 A.D., they had conquered all of Africa north of the Sahara. The Muslims of North Africa greatly influenced Ghanaian religion and culture.

Although the majority of people in Ghana did not adopt the religion of Islam, a significant number did. The rulers of Ghana kept their traditional West African beliefs, but they allowed Muslim scholars to establish schools in the major cities of the empire. Muslims became close advisers to Ghana's rulers. Friendly relations with Muslim merchants of the north brought more money and more power to the empire of Ghana.

Ghanaian Royalty and Religious Beliefs According to legend, ancient Ghana had been ruled by at least forty-four kings by 300 A.D. Like most other empires that developed in the Sudan, the rulers of Ghana were believed to be the descendants of gods. Since the well-being of the king and that of the country were closely related, no ruler was allowed to die a natural death. When a ruler became seriously ill or grew old, the people feared that the country might suffer. The sick or aged king was either poisoned or suffocated in the course of elaborate rituals. At his burial, some of his wives, personal servants, and other members of the royal household committed suicide so that they might continue to serve the king in the next life.

Like most early Africans, the people of Ghana believed that the north and its inhabitants had been created by a supreme god. Lesser spirits were believed to respond to the prayers of the people. These deities had different names and functions in various regions. Many were associated with such natural objects or forces as the sun, the moon, thunder, animals, rivers, and trees. In this sense, the religious beliefs of the Ghanaians and other early Africans resembled those of the ancient Greeks and Romans. Dead rulers and important ancestors were believed to influence the affairs of the living. The variety and complexity of African religious beliefs are only beginning to be studied.

The Empire of Mali Soon after 1300 A.D., the empire of Mali became the most powerful in West Africa. It rose to this position by gaining control of some of the caravan routes and cities that Ghana had dominated. The Black African rulers of Mali created the second largest empire in the world at that time. It was surpassed in size only by the empire of the Mongols (MAHNG-guls) in Asia.

The Rule of Mansa Musa Mansa Musa ruled Mali at its height. Unlike the rulers of Ghana, he accepted the religion of Islam. Many court officials and some of the people also accepted Islam, but most villagers retained their traditional beliefs.

During his twenty-five year reign, from 1312 to 1337 A.D., Mansa Musa

Above, a section of a 1375 map of Africa shows Mansa Musa, emperor of Mali, seated on his throne and holding a gold nugget. Compare this map with current maps of Africa. What are the main differences?

brought many scholars to his capital at Niani. They came from places as distant as Egypt. Niani became a center of Muslim scholarship. Under Mali rule, Timbuktu in eastern Ghana became a renowned center of learning. Scholars flocked to its university. While Europe was in the Dark Ages, Timbuktu was flourishing as an educational center. Schools established by Muslims helped maintain order and stability.

Mansa Musa sent representatives from Mali to the area that is present-day Morocco (muh-RAHK-oe) and Egypt. It is possible that these ambassadors also traveled to more distant lands. As you have read, Mansa Musa

himself made a pilgrimage to Mecca in 1324. Mansa Musa's fame spread far and wide. In 1375, a European geographer made a map of Africa with a picture of Mansa Musa in the center. It was the first map of Africa known to have been made in Europe.

The Empire of Songhai   To the east of Mali was Songhai (SONG-hie). It eventually surpassed Mali and became the largest of all West African empires. By 1200 A.D., its rulers had created one of the best-trained armies in Africa. The Songhai defeated Mali in a series of wars. Around 1400, Songhai took control of the western Sudan and thus extended their empire beyond Mali to the Atlantic Ocean. (See the map on page 289.)

Sunni Ali (SOON-ee AH-lee) was the king of Songhai around 1464. He captured the important Mali cultural centers of Timbuktu and Djenné and made them part of his kingdom. He was considered a ruthless conqueror and was not liked by many of his Muslim subjects. When he died, his throne was seized by one of his officers, a Muslim named **Astia Muhammad** (AHS-tee-uh moo-HAHM-ud), who proved to be a capable leader. He divided the kingdom into a group of well-administered provinces and introduced several reforms. For example, he standardized weights and measures all over the kingdom and assigned a tax collector to each district. Under his leadership Timbuktu, Djenné, and Walata flourished as centers of learning, religion, and trade.

A Closer Look

YORUBAN WIT AND WISDOM

Yoruba storytellers were especially fond of beginning a storytelling session with proverbs and riddles. They did this to arouse the interest of their audiences. Some of those ancient proverbs or sayings follow.

Mouth not keeping to mouth, and lip not keeping to lip, bring trouble to the jaws. (Talk is silver, silence is gold.)

The thread follows the needle.

Peace is the father of friendship. Wrangling is the father of fighting.

The young cannot teach tradition to the old.

One who does not understand the yellow palm-bird says the yellow palm-bird is noisy. (Men are prone to despise things that they do not understand.)

We call the dead—they answer. We call the living—they do not answer. (Dry leaves sound when trodden on. Fresh ones don't.)

We are going to Ife—we face Ife. We are returning from Ife—we will face Ife. (Both climbing and descending a palm tree, one faces in the same direction.)

Two tiny birds jump over two hundred trees. (A man's eyes can carry him far.)

Adapted from: American Heritage Society. "Wit and Wisdom from West Africa," *The Horizon History of Africa*. New York: American Heritage Publishing Co., 1971, pp. 207-208.

1. What do these sayings seem to be teaching? Select three of them and tell what they could teach a person.
2. Do you think these sayings could be used as historical evidence about West African life? Explain.
3. Could sayings or proverbs used in your own society be used by historians 200 years from now as evidence about your culture? Explain.

Songhai was able to withstand attacks by Berbers and other neighboring peoples. But Songhai fell in 1596 to a group of people from Morocco equipped with a new kind of weapon—the musket. This superior enemy technology was as fatal to Songhai as it was to other empires.

The Empire of Kanem-Bornu   As Songhai declined, Kanem-Bornu (KAH-nem BORE-noo) developed to the east. (See the map on page 289.) With the copper mines around Lake Chad supplying wealth, Kanem-Bornu became the last great trading empire of the Sudan.

The empire of Kanem-Bornu was

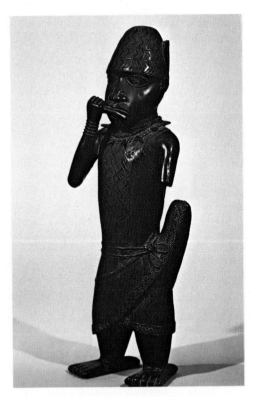

The West African empire of Benin was noted for its superbly crafted bronze sculpture. How does this piece compare to present-day sculpture?

famous for its mounted cavalry. By 1400 A.D., the cavalry were equipped with quilted armor, chain mail, and iron helmets. One ruler of Kanem-Bornu brought Turkish instructors from Tripoli (TRIP-uh-lee) in the north to train his soldiers to use muskets. Kanem-Bornu's highly trained armies were used to subdue all hostile or uncooperative neighbors in the east central Sudan. But as in the ancient empires of Ghana, Mali, and Songhai, wars with neighboring states and feuds within the empire gradually brought about the decline of Kanem-Bornu as a major power.

The Forest Kingdoms   While the various empires in the Sudan flourished and declined, forest peoples also organized states in the forested southern half of West Africa, especially along the Guinean (GIN-ee-un) coast. By 1200 A.D., these states were similar in some ways to the empires of the Sudan. The new states included the Ashanti (un-SHAN-tee) and the Yorubas (YORE-uh-buhs) at Oyo (OE-yoe), Ife (EE-fay), and Benin. (See the map on page 289.)

Each town within these kingdoms had markets where people from the surrounding countryside came to trade. The existence of dense forests and tsetse flies made camel and horse travel almost impossible, so most traders traveled by foot, carrying their goods on their heads.

The splendid sculpture of the Forest Kingdoms can be seen in museums today. Among the best-known examples of this art are the sculptures of *Nok* (NOK), which date back over 2,000 years. Sculptures from Ife and Benin, produced sometime after 1200 A.D., are also superb. The sculptors of Nok worked mostly in terra-cotta and those of Ife and Benin in bronze.

The wealth of the Forest Kingdoms came from vast deposits of gold and an abundance of elephant tusks and kola nuts. These commodities were among the most valuable articles in the trans-Saharan trade, and they regularly reached the port cities of the Middle East and Europe. Rulers of the Forest Kingdoms also traded cattle, cloth, and a few horses from the Sudan, and beads, copper, and cloth from central and northeastern Africa. Cowrie (KOW-ree) shells, which served as one form of money, came via Egypt from the Seychelles (SAY-shellz), islands in the Indian Ocean. Trade, which sometimes involved distances of over 12,800 kilometers (8,000 miles), was flourishing long before Marco Polo ventured into what Europeans regarded as the unknown lands of the Far East in the late 1200's.

SECTION REVIEW

1. Mapping: Comparing the map on page 289 and the Atlas of Africa, describe the location of the empires of Ghana, Mali, and Kanem-Bornu, and list which modern African states these empires seem to fall within.
2. In your own words, identify or define: Berbers, Mansa Musa, Timbuktu, Niani, Ife, Yorubas.
3. By 1000 A.D., what had happened within the Sahara?
4. Describe the religious beliefs of the ancient Ghanaians.
5. Summarize the trading activities of early West Africa.
◗ Could the conduct of a government leader affect the society he or she represents? Explain.

EAST AFRICAN EMPIRES

The Empire of Cush A Black empire emerged in northeastern Africa with the rise of *Cush* (KUSH). By 750 B.C., a Cushite leader and his son, Piankhi (PYANG-kih), had seized an area stretching from the headwaters of the Nile to Palestine (PAL-uh-stine). Once in control of Egypt, the *Cushites* also became pharaohs of Egypt. They ruled their vast empire until the invasion of Egypt by the Assyrians a century later. The Cushites learned ironworking from their Assyrian conquerors.

During the Assyrian invasion, the Cushites retreated southward. They established their capital city at Meroë (MER-uh-wee). By 200 B.C., Meroë had become one of the largest iron-producing areas of the ancient world. The Cushites of Meroë retained many Egyptian customs. They also developed their own alphabet based on Egyptian hieroglyphs, built beautiful palaces, and began a complex system of irrigation to expand their farmlands. The Cushites were active traders. They exported iron, slaves, ivory, ebony, wood, and ostrich feathers to the Middle East.

Meroë probably became the capital of the kingdom of Cush because of its strategic location. The city was built between the Nile and the Atbara (AT-buh-ruh) rivers. Thus Meroë benefited by the floods of both rivers, which left rich deposits of silt behind. The fertile soil made better agricultural production and greater grazing activity possible. In addition, Meroë was near a major crossroads for caravans loaded with goods to be traded in faraway regions. Although the people had a written language, we do not know what the words mean and, therefore, have only a limited knowledge of Cushite history.

The Empire of Aksum   The power of Cush was challenged by a rival empire called Aksum (AHK-sum), also called Axum, which was located in the northern corner of the Ethiopian highlands. (See the map on page 289.) The people of Aksum were a mixture of Caucasian and Black African peoples. By 1000 B.C., they had moved to Aksum from what is present-day Yemen (YEM-un). Their language resembled that of the Arabs and the Jews.

By 50 A.D., Aksum had become the center of the greatest ivory market in northeastern Africa. Aksum's extensive trade with the Middle Eastern and Mediterranean world brought it into constant contact with other peoples. The kings of Aksum learned Greek. They had excellent relations with the rulers of the Roman Empire. As Aksum's power grew through trade and wealth, Cush became more and more isolated from outside trade and contact with other peoples.

By 300 A.D., Aksum had become a Christian state that was controlled and protected by the Roman Empire. The link with Rome helped make Aksum stable. It also encouraged the expansion of Aksum's trade with Arabia, India, the Mediterranean world, the coast of eastern Africa, and even England. Around 350, Aksum defeated the Cushites and destroyed their capital city of Meroë. However, Aksum itself declined shortly thereafter. Its decline was related to the gradual collapse of Rome and its empire. What remained of Aksum was later to become what is present-day Ethiopia.

The Muslims in East Africa   After the fall of Aksum around 1000, much of the East African coast came under the influence of the Arab Muslims. Between 650 and 1000, the Arabs had expanded across North Africa as far west as the Atlantic Ocean. The also tried to extend their influence into the Sudan and along the East African coast. First the Arabs concentrated on controlling Nubia. But the *Nubians* (NOO-bee-unz) did not want this. To prevent war, the Nubians agreed on a peace treaty to send Nubian slaves to the Arabs and not to harm Arab traders. In return, the Arabs agreed to respect Nubia's independence and supply its people with such items as cloth and horses. Nevertheless, soon after this treaty, many Nubians moved westward into the Sudan and as far away as the Guinean coast.

During the attempted invasion of Nubia around 650 A.D., the Arabs also launched an attack against Aksum. The fighting continued off and on until 1415 when the Ethiopians finally managed to repulse the Arabs. With a new power base at the old Nubian capital of Dongola (DONG-goe-luh), the Christian Ethiopians managed to check the Arab invasion.

The Arabs were not able to subdue Ethiopia, but they did have successes farther down the East African coast. Between 1250 and 1492, Arabs gained control of cities that had existed long before their arrival. During this period, new Muslim Arab cities sprang up along the East African coast. These Muslim cities extended from Mogadisho (mahg-uh-DISH-oe) south to Sofala (soe-FAHL-uh). One of the most impressive cities was Kilwa (KIL-wuh) with its wide streets and beautiful palaces. Recent archaeological discoveries indicate that Kilwa had a royal palace with over 100 rooms and a bathing pool. Kilwa merchants controlled trade between the interior of Africa and ships from India and Arabia.

Above are the remains of the magnificent city of Kilwa. Africa's first mint was in Kilwa. Wealthy merchant leaders cast many coins of different denominations. Do you think the presence of a mint as well as Kilwa's control of trade affected its prosperity?

Islamic influence was especially evident in the areas that are present-day Somalia, Kenya, and Tanzania (tan-zuh-NEE-uh). (See the Atlas of Africa.) By 1500, the people of the East African coastal area were a mixture of Blacks and Arabs. They developed their own language, which is known as Swahili (swah-HEE-lee).

East African Trade   Trade was the main source of income for the East African coastal cities. From the interior came gold, copper, ivory, and slaves. These continued to be among the most valuable articles of trade until the 1800's. Cotton, camel-hair goods, and iron ore were also exported. Imports of East Africa were carried by Arabian ships and included cloth, carpets, jewelry, and porcelain made during the Sung and Ming dynasties in China.

For several hundred years, there was a vigorous trade between China and East Africa. During the period of prosperity under the Han Dynasty, China began to trade with cities as far away as the Red Sea. Chinese trade peaked during the early 1400's.

During the early 1400's, Cheng Ho (CHUNG HOE), a Chinese noble and admiral, began the first of his seven great voyages to East Africa. Between 1405 and 1453, he sailed his trading fleet to what is today India, Indonesia (in-duh-NEE-zhah), Thailand (TIE-land), the states of the Persian Gulf, and down most of the East African coast. In 1417, he sailed to Africa to bring the Black African ambassador from Peking home to what is now Kenya.

Trade links between East Africa and China did not last. Around 1450, the Ming Dynasty decided to close China's doors to foreigners. East Africans continued to trade across the Indian Ocean and Persian Gulf, however.

303

SECTION REVIEW

1. **Mapping:** Using the map on page 289, **a.** describe the relative locations of Nubia, Cush, and Aksum, and **b.** locate the cities of the East African coast by means of longitude and latitude coordinates.
2. In your own words, identify: Piankhi, Meroë, Dongola, Nubians, Cheng Ho.
3. What attempts did the Arabs make to control East Africa? How successful were they?
4. Give evidence from the text to show how and why the prosperity of the East African empires was tied to trade.
5. Describe the trade relations between China and East Africa.
    - Make a list of the major types of businesses found in your community. Based on this list, analyze to what extent the power and the prosperity of your society or your community are tied to trade.

CENTRAL AND SOUTHERN AFRICAN EMPIRES

While empires and trading cities were emerging in western and eastern Africa, the Bantu-speaking peoples of Africa were also building states. Among the most important of the Bantu trading states was the Luba (LOO-bah) Kingdom. Its people excelled in pottery making and metal work. It is possible that some of the *Lubas* were descendants of the migrating peoples who built the southern African city of *Zimbabwe* (zim-BOB-way) in the third century A.D. The ruins of Zimbabwe were not discovered by Europeans until 1868. The word *zimbabwe* is Bantu for "great stone house." Huge stone buildings were found there but archaeologists still do not know much about the people who built them.

The Luba Empire   As early as 800 A.D., the Luba lived in small, scattered states in south central Africa. Several hundred years later, *Kalala Ilunga* (ka-LAH-luh ih-LOONG-guh), a Bantu chief, united enough of these scattered kingdoms to create the Luba Empire. He introduced the idea of *bulopwe* (boo-LOP-way), a type of sacred kingship. All the descendants of his line were supposed to have a special kind of blood. It was so powerful that anyone with that blood had a right to rule. It was thought that only people with bulopwe could promote the fertility of crops and ensure the success of the hunt.

The Lunda Empire   The Lunda (LOON-dah) Empire, with its own trading cities, emerged to the southwest of the Luba. According to folklore, it began when a Luba man brought bulopwe to the *Lundas*, who were then governed by a young queen named *Rweej* (ruh-WEEJ). Rweej met *Kibinda Ilunga* (kih-BIN-duh ih-LOONG-guh), a handsome Luba hunter and prince, and married him. Because he had *bulopwe*, she let him rule. The Lunda state prospered and became an empire. The queen's twin brothers, however, were dissatisfied with the arrangement. They went to the region now called Angola (ANG-goe-luh) to carve out new territories for themselves.

The Kongo Kingdom   If the story is true, those brothers were the founders of the Kongo (KON-goe) Kingdom, located west of the Lunda and Luba Empires. (See the map on page 289.) By 1480 A.D., the Kongo Kingdom was a flourishing state. Pottery making, weaving, ironworking, and sculpture were fully established. A government-regulated monetary system with the

The great wall in this picture is among the remains of a culture that flourished in Zimbabwe in southern Africa many centuries ago. It is a mystery to scholars whether Zimbabwe was a city or a religious place. What mysteries do you think a historian writing about your society will encounter? Why?

cowrie shell as its basic unit of exchange was in use throughout the kingdom. The king of the Kongo had the power to depose any chief as well as all lower officials.

SECTION REVIEW

1. Mapping: Using the map on page 289 and the map of Africa in the Atlas, list the main geographical features of the Luba, Lunda, and Kongo kingdoms.
2. In your own words, identify: Kalala Ilunga, Rweej, Zimbabwe.
3. What is bulopwe? According to legend, how did it affect the history of the Lundas?
▶ How is the idea of bulopwe similar to the idea of hereditary monarchies of western Europe? Explain.

CITIES AND TOWNS IN THE EMPIRES

Each empire contained important cities and towns. Some were mainly religious centers and others were political or trade centers. Most emerged from one-time small villages and grew when more and more people could live there and support themselves.

We know how these towns grew, but there are things about them that we do not know. What did those early African cities and towns look like? What could their physical appearance tell us about the people who built and lived in such cities and towns? For hundreds of years, people living outside of Africa could not begin to answer such questions. In recent times, scholars of early Africa have been able to piece together

305

The houses shown here belong to members of the Kikuyu tribe, one of the largest tribal groups in East Africa. This type of housing has existed in parts of East Africa for centuries. Why is the housing well suited to the environment?

much of the puzzle of early African urban life, just as they have done with the history of early African empires.

One of these scholars, Richard W. Hull, made a special investigation of African urban society. His research reveals much about early Africans and their culture. Among his findings, three things about African cities and towns seem to stand out: their use of walls, of passageways, and of urban space.

The Use of Walls The use of enclosing settlements with outer walls can be found over much of the African continent. A classic example of the use of walls can be seen with the *Hausa* (HOW-suh) peoples, who lived in what is present-day northern Nigeria. Hausa walled towns could have begun when the inhabitants first used iron technology. As a town grew, its residents built a wall around it. The first outer walls probably served as a defense against attack or to protect the iron-smelting industries. When the towns continued to grow in size and population, more and higher walls were built.

Much of the food supply of the townspeople was grown by nearby farmers who sold or traded their crops in exchange for iron tools made by the townspeople. Since an enclosed area was necessary to store food during long sieges by enemies, a second outer wall was often built. One example of an outer wall can be seen at Kano (KAHN-oe) in Nigeria. By the 1800's, it was 6 meters (20 feet) wide at the base, 9 meters (30 feet) high, and 19 kilometers (12 miles) long. The total area was 47 square kilometers (16 square miles).

Outer walls around early African cities also had other purposes. They provided some protection against theft and allowed control of people entering and leaving a city. The larger the wall, the greater a leader's ability to control his or her subjects. Walls were even used to awe foreign visitors. Gates at the outer walls were sometimes the locations of toll booths. Taxes collected on goods coming into or leaving a city were used to provide funds to operate the city government or they were placed in a royal treasury.

One of the greatest outer walls to be found in Africa was at Zimbabwe. It had 10 meter (32 foot) high walls of cut stone laid in a variety of patterns and was built during the 1300's. The great outer wall had 5,460 cubic meters (182,000 cubic feet) of fine stonework and was over 240 meters (800 feet) in length. It is the largest single prehistoric structure south of the Sahara. Another great African wall was built at Benin around 1440. It extended 10 kilometers (6 miles) on one side of the town. The wall itself was about 3 meters (10 feet) in height. The Yorubas built walls surrounded by very deep trenches. Some cities had deep moats for protection instead of walls.

Inner walls often protected a royal compound where a king or queen and the royal family lived. Inner walls helped to keep intact the mysteries of divine kingship or queenship. The public could not see over such walls.

Located between the inner and the outer walls of many early African cities were many other walls. These helped to give the general public some sense of privacy. They even provided some areas where businesses could operate. **The Use of Passageways** Within this system of walls were passageways that took many forms. Some were narrow alleys that separated blocks of buildings. In large towns and cities, one could find avenues or wide streets. Alleys opened onto the avenues. Sometimes as one traveled down an avenue, you might encounter a large community plaza or a large marketplace. However, most avenues went to the center of the town or city. There one might find the royal palace, a main square, and the main marketplaces.

The Use of Space The use of urban space was as important to Africans as was their use of walls and passageways. Most Africans living south of the Sahara had a special feeling about the land. The believed that it belonged to their ancestors and that the roots of the living were in the earth. This belief made them especially careful to try to preserve something of a rural setting, even in their towns and cities. As a result, animals were allowed to wander about. Trees shaded streets and plazas. In some towns, people even raised crops along walkways or in open plots of land. Others even had parks in which no one was allowed to cut down trees and so homes and businesses had to be

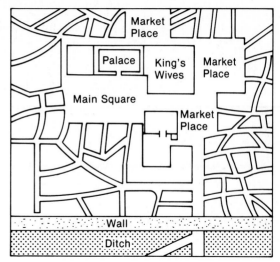

This is a drawing of a typical African city within walls. How does it compare with your city?

built around them.

These features of towns and cities gave them the appearance of overgrown African rural villages. How urban a town might appear usually depended on the size of the population, the market activity, and the number of people involved in highly specialized occupations, such as iron-working, pottery or cloth making, building, education, or the military.

SECTION REVIEW

1. How did outer walls in African cities develop? What purpose did they serve?
2. What were the purposes of inner walls in African cities?
3. Why did passageways develop in African cities? Describe them.
4. How did the early Africans regard and make use of urban space?
   ◗ Look at a map of your town or city. What does its basic plan look like? What do you think an outsider could learn about your town or city by studying its plan?

Village Life and Slave Trade

FROM EMPIRE-STATE TO VILLAGE LIFE

As you have seen, early African history involved great movements of peoples, such as the Bantu migration, and the emergence of important cities and powerful states. Equally important was the daily life of the people who lived outside the bustling cities and royal palaces. Most Black Africans lived in villages. These villages supplied the cities with food, goods, and raw materials that were necessary for their trade.

Village Society   In the typical early African village, as in much of Black Africa today, society is based on the family unit. We tend to think of the immediate family as father, mother, and children. This concept is called a *nuclear family.* According to this concept, relatives such as grandparents, uncles, aunts, and cousins are considered to be outside the nuclear family. In the traditional African society, however, the immediate family includes many of these relatives as well as the parents and children. Uncles and aunts have nearly as much authority over children as the children's parents. Cousins are treated as brothers and sisters, and grandparents are regarded as parents by the entire group. This concept of family is known as an *extended family.*

A member of an extended family is obliged to help care for the old people and the children and to build houses and plant crops.

If several extended families are descended from one set of ancestors, they are known as a *clan.* A group of clans with common ancestors makes up an *ethnic group.* Some ethnic groups, such as the Yoruba, have populations numbering in the millions.

Because of the importance attached to family life, Africans regard marriage as a union between two families, not two individuals. Therefore, before two people marry, certain rituals have to be followed—ancestors must be consulted by means of special rites, and bridewealth has to be paid. Bridewealth is paid by the groom or his family to the bride's family. This custom is supposed to ensure the success of the marriage. In some societies cattle are used as payment. Sometimes payment is merely symbolic. Often the bridewealth received by the bride's father is used as payment for a son's marriage.

In early Africa, the extended family usually lived together in a compound surrounded by its fields. Farming was the chief economic activity of the village. Main crops such as sorghum, millet, peas, yams, okra, pumpkins, watermelons, and cotton were grown in

Many skills such as the weaving of fish traps are passed down within a family. The older members of the family teach the crafts to the younger members. Have any skills been passed down in your family from generation to generation?

various parts of Africa. From Asia, the African villager acquired barley, wheat, beans, beets, onions, radishes, cabbage, lettuce, grapes, dates, figs, pomegranates, garlic, olives, rice, cucumbers, eggplant, bananas, mangos, ginger, and sugar cane. As Europeans began to explore and colonize the Americas, trade with Africa increased. Crops from the Americas were brought to Africa. Africans began to plant *maize* (MAZE), lima beans, peanuts, sweet potatoes, pineapples, squash, tomatoes, avocados, papaya, cacao, red pepper, and tobacco.

From Ethnic Group to Kingdom

Often when population groups grew large and powerful enough, the leaders became what we would call a king. Such kings ruled Ghana, Mali, Songhai, and Kanem-Bornu. The power of local leaders and kings was not absolute, however. It was usually limited in some way. Decisions about the governing of a kingdom were often made after consulting with advisers. Many African clans and ethnic groups had councils of elders. These councils had the power to remove a ruler who displeased the people.

309

SECTION REVIEW

1. Why do Africans attach so much importance to customs surrounding marriage? What marriage rituals are usually followed?
2. In your own words, define the following: nuclear family, extended family, clan, ethnic group.
3. How did many Africans limit the power of their kings or leaders?
4. What advantages would the extended family provide for people living in a small farming village? Answer using the information on pages 308 and 309.
▷ Which type of family group is most common in your community —nuclear or extended?

THE BEGINNING OF THE END: THE SLAVE TRADE

The growth of the slave trade probably disrupted the ancient African system of village life more severely than anything else. Even cities and empires felt its harmful effects.

African Slavery Slave trading had existed for a long time in Africa. The Egyptians, Greeks, and Romans had dealt in slaves from Africa. Slaves were also traded from one area of Africa to another by native African dealers. Black African slavery involved mostly war captives and criminals. Criminals were generally punished by being traded or sold out of their ethnic group. As time passed, the slave could become an adopted member of an extended family in his or her new ethnic group. The former slave would then be treated as family with the same social status as the other family members. Children of women slaves and free men were automatically members of their father's clan and, therefore, free. Slaves were expected to perform the hardest work. But their owners often worked alongside them in fields, and some slaves were more like domestic servants.

The Slave Trade Another system of slavery was the sale of Black Africans to non-African slave traders. Many African states engaged in this type of slave trade. Beginning in the 1400's, slaves exchanged for foreign goods were usually purchased from Black Africans by Arab traders. They were then sold to new owners in Arabia, Persia (PER-zhuh), and India. The trade in slaves with Asia, known as the *Indian Ocean Slave Trade,* was lucrative. The *trans-Saharan slave trade* provided African slaves to the Mediterranean world. North African Berbers collected Africans in West Africa and the Sahara to sell to traders from the Mediterranean.

This picture shows Black slaves being traded by Arab slave dealers at a market in Zanzibar. Can you tell by looking at this picture how the slaves were treated?

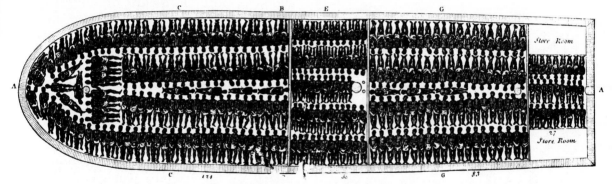

This diagram shows the interior of a ship that transported slaves to the Americas. What do you think these voyages were like for the slaves? Explain.

Europe Enters the Slave Trade
Until Europeans began to participate actively in the slave trade in the 1500's, the trade in African slaves was small in comparison to the trade in other items. As the market for slaves increased, so did the trade.

The Portuguese desire for more slaves to ship to Brazil gradually overshadowed their desire to Christianize the people of the Kongo and maintain friendly relations with them. The Portuguese began to train the Kongolese in modern warfare and urged them to wage wars to obtain captives for the slave trade. In 1540, one Kongo king, **Alfonso,** begged the Portuguese king not to encourage the Kongolese to take part in the slave traffic. His pleas, however, went unheeded. By 1575, the Portuguese were seeking slaves in all of the western portion of central Africa, especially in present-day Angola. Portugal used Angola as a base for supplying slaves to Brazil until the late 1800's.

The Portuguese also wanted to control the Indian Ocean trade of East Africa. The first city they attacked was Kilwa in about 1500 A.D. It was forced to pay large sums of money to the Portuguese as tribute and was later de-

stroyed. Other towns were seized, and trade centers which had once prospered declined because of mismanagement by the Portuguese invaders. When Portuguese power in Africa declined in the late seventeenth century, some of the trade was resumed, but it never regained its former status.

The Portuguese were not the only Europeans that helped increase the African slave trade with the Americas. By the 1650's, the Dutch, English, and French controlled slave-trading areas along the West African coastline from the Forest to the Kongo kingdoms.

The Role of Africans in the Slave Trade
European slave traders needed the cooperation of Africans because most were unable to reach the interior of Africa. Slave traffic throughout western and central Africa depended on coastal Africans. They captured other Africans who lived several hundred kilometers in the interior of the continent. Captives were then brought to coastal forts where the newly-enslaved were sold to European ship captains.

But non-Africans who eventually owned enslaved Africans generally cared less about the welfare of the slaves than a native African owner

311

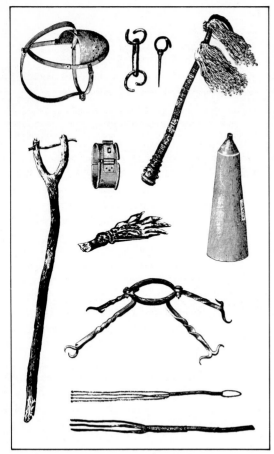

These instruments were used by slave traders to punish or control the slaves they were transporting. Why do you think such devices were necessary?

would have. Non-Africans closely packed slaves in their ships to save space and chained them together in order to prevent rebellion. Their food and water supply was scarce and sanitation was usually nonexistent. As a result, 20 percent of the slaves died during the voyage. Those who did survive were often separated from their families because they were sold to different owners.

In return for supplying Africans as slaves, the African captors, usually kings or merchants, received such items as cloth, hardware, and firearms. They used the firearms to secure more slaves. A pattern of wars was begun, which by the early 1800's had pitted one group of Africans against another until nearly the entire continent was involved.

Trade with Africa With European participation, the nature of the African slave trade changed. The African-Asian trade with Europe that was not monopolized by the Italians was in the firm control of the *Moors* (MOORZ), who were Muslims. They held northern Africa and much of present-day Spain and Portugal. (See pages 195-196.)

Portuguese Explorations for Trade A gradual loosening of the Moors' control over trade occurred just after 1400. The Portuguese and Spanish drove the Moors from the Iberian peninsula. Once this was accomplished, the Portuguese turned their attention to Africa. Even though North Africa was in Muslim hands, farther south, Guinea—known to Europeans as the Land of Gold—was not under Muslim control.

Portuguese seamen had learned a great deal about geography and navigation from Arab geographers. With this knowledge, *Prince Henry* of Portugal developed a new plan for trade with Africa and Asia. He wanted to outflank the Muslims by sailing around Africa to Asia. If he succeeded, the Portuguese could buy spices in greater quantities than ever before and at prices cheaper than those charged by the Venetians (vih-NEE-shunz) and Muslims. Henry also planned to send missionaries to Africa and Asia to convert the areas to Christianity. In 1445, his ships reached islands presently known as Cape Verde (VURD) and the mouth of the Senegal (sen-ih-GOL) River in western Africa. (See the Atlas of Africa.) The Portuguese soon colonized the Cape Verde Islands and made them a base for trade with the Empire of Mali.

In 1471, Portuguese seamen reached the Guinea coast, where they constructed forts. Eleven years later, they arrived at the mouth of the Zaire River and began to develop regular trade with the people of Benin.

During the years 1497-1499, **Vasco da Gama** (VAHS-coe duh GAH-muh) made a voyage from Portugal, around the Cape of Good Hope, up the coast of East Africa, to India, and back to Portugal. Portugal's maritime successes continued with the Portuguese defeat of a Venetian-led fleet in the Indian Ocean ten years after da Gama's voyage.

By the latter part of the fifteenth century, the Spanish had driven most of the Moors from Spain. Freed from the threat of the Moors, the Spanish king and queen could concentrate their finances and attention on voyages of exploration and trade to Asia.

Christopher Columbus   An Italian explorer in the service of Spain, **Christopher Columbus** was eager to find a westward route to Asia. However, he did not know that the continents of North and South America blocked a direct route to Asia. The existence of North America was unknown to most

EUROPEAN KNOWLEDGE OF AFRICA, 1682 AND 1816

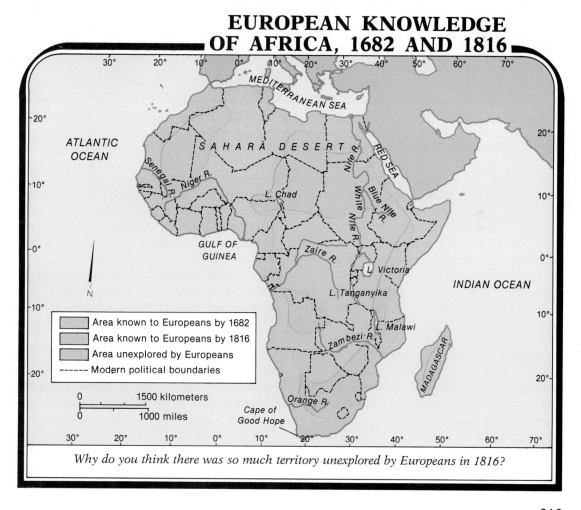

Why do you think there was so much territory unexplored by Europeans in 1816?

313

Many explorers traveled to parts of Africa. Here English explorer Mungo Park is guided down the Niger River. What do you think compelled people to explore foreign lands? Do we explore foreign lands today? Explain.

Europeans. When he sailed to the New World in 1492, Columbus thought he had actually reached Asia. He was convinced that present-day Cuba (KYOO-buh) was Japan. He based his conclusions on a map of the world most European scholars thought was accurate. This map was one drawn in 1474 by Toscanelli (tahs-kah-NEL-lee), an Italian mapmaker. The distance between Europe and Asia shown on the map was in reality the distance from Europe to present-day Mexico. Therefore, it was logical for Columbus to believe he had arrived at islands off the Asian mainland, rather than Cuba.

Columbus's voyages had an extraordinary impact not only on Europe but on Africa as well. Once Europeans realized that Columbus had discovered a new continent, the royal houses of Europe rushed to establish new colonies there. This hurried colonization was to affect millions of Africans. The establishment of colonies in the New World brought demands for slave labor.

The Trans-Atlantic Slave Trade   By the 1700's, Spain, Portugal, France, England, and the Netherlands all had colonies in the Americas. The Indians in the Americas rebelled at being forced into slavery, but the colonies needed slaves to work in mines and later in rice, sugar, and cotton fields. Spanish officials demanded even more slaves for the gold and silver mines of Mexico. During the late 1700's, the invention of the cotton gin and a new process for making granulated sugar increased the demand for slaves in the New World.

PEOPLE IN HISTORY

Abduhl Rahahman

In 1762, Abduhl Rahahman (ahb-DOOL RAH-hah-mahn) was born in Timbuktu. His father was Alman Ibrahim (ahl-MAHN ih-brah-HIM), King of Futa Jallon (FOO-ta ja-LON), a small kingdom near Timbuktu. Abduhl was educated in a manner befitting the heir to a throne. At the school he attended, Abduhl read, wrote, and studied geography, astronomy, calculation, Islam, and the laws of the country.

In 1781, Abduhl first saw a white man, John C. Cox, the English surgeon of a ship off the coast of present-day Sierra Leone (see-ER-uh lee-ONE). Separated from his companions, lame and ill, Cox was found and brought to Alman Ibrahim, who invited Cox to remain until he was able to travel.

While Cox was recovering, he and Abduhl became close friends. Six months later, Cox was well and wanted to go home to England. Ibrahim paid his passage and sent fifteen men to escort Cox.

Seven years later, wounded and captured in an ambush, Abduhl was taken prisoner and sold as a slave to Thomas Foster, in Natchez (NACH-uz) Mississippi. Abduhl, then called Prince, worked in the fields with other Africans. In time, he married. He learned to speak English and made the best of life as a slave.

Seventeen years later, Abduhl was sent to Washington, Mississippi, where he saw John Cox who embraced and took him to his home.

Cox offered to pay Foster $1000 for Abduhl's freedom. Foster refused because Prince was an excellent slave. Until his death in 1816, Cox tried to gain Abduhl's freedom. His son, William Cox, continued the attempt until his own death. But Foster refused to sell or free Abduhl. Finally, in 1829, with the help of the United States government, the African Colonization Society, and others, Abduhl and his wife were bought, freed, and sent to Liberia, West Africa, with 160 other emigrants. Liberia was founded as a new homeland for freed slaves sent from America.

Abduhl was sent to Liberia to help develop trade with the interior of Africa, to aid in Christian missionary work, and to secure the friendship of his relatives in Futa Jallon for the new colonists in Liberia.

Abduhl wrote to the Fulbe (Foohl-bee), his countrymen in Timbo, asking for money to help ransom his children and grandchildren, still slaves in America. The Fulbe remembered him and sent a band of men toward Liberia with $7000 in gold dust for Abduhl. However, before they reached Liberia, they met a trader who told them of Abduhl's death, caused by coast fever on July 6, 1829. When they heard this, the Fulbe men returned with their gold to Timbo.

Adapted from: Charles S. Snydor. "The Biography of a Slave," **The South Atlantic Quarterly**, XXXVI. January, 1937, pp. 59-73, copyright 1937 by Duke University.

1. Who was Abduhl Rahahman? What happened to cause him to become a slave?
2. How long did it take him to regain his freedom? What happened afterwards?
3. How can the term tragic be applied to this story? What might the story reveal about the enslavement of any people?

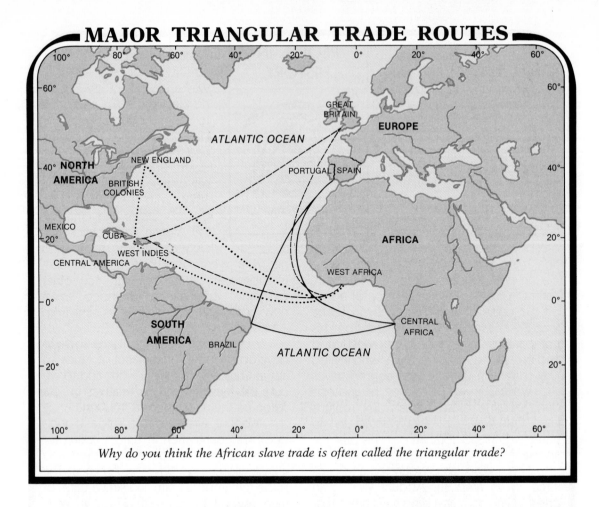

MAJOR TRIANGULAR TRADE ROUTES

Why do you think the African slave trade is often called the triangular trade?

The Portuguese were among the first to supply African slaves to the New World on a large scale. This was known as the *trans-Atlantic Slave Trade.* The Portuguese sent slaves to their colonies in Brazil and to the Spanish-held areas of the West Indies, Mexico, and Central America.

A study of the slave traffic to the New World presents historians with startling figures. Some historians estimate that in the 340 years from 1500 to 1840 between nine and eighteen million Africans were sold to slave traders along the coasts of Africa. Of that number, probably half were carried to the

Americas in English-owned ships. As a result of the interest in Africa generated by the slave trade, the European knowledge of Africa's geography expanded between 1682 and 1816. (See the map on page 313.)

Triangular Trade Routes　The magnitude of slave trade eventually gave rise to the *triangular trade routes.* They were typical of the major trade routes between Africa and Europe, and Africa and the Americas from 1600 to 1800, when the slave trade reached its greatest heights. (See the map above.)

One triangular trade route consisted of goods such as textiles and metal utensils that were shipped from England to West Africa. These goods were exchanged for slaves. The slaves were usually sent under the most inhumane conditions into the British-controlled West Indies. Merchants in the West Indies then exchanged the slaves for sugar or molasses, which was sent to England in exchange for metal goods and textiles. And so, the triangle was complete.

A second route involved the transportation of metal goods from Portugal to Africa in exchange for slaves. Those slaves were then sent to Portuguese-controlled Brazil, or they were traded in Mexico or Cuba for sugar, gold, or silver.

A third route shipped rum and manufactured products from New England to West Africa where the goods were traded for slaves. The slaves were then shipped to the West Indies where they were traded for sugar and molasses. The sugar and molasses were then sent to New England for the production of rum. And then the trade process was repeated. The rum was sold in West Africa for more slaves, and so on. Profits were made at each point of the triangular trade route.

By the early 1800's, many nations began to recognize the evils of trading human lives and took steps to stop it. In 1807, England approved a law forbidding any of its citizens to engage in the slave trade. Denmark and the United States outlawed the slave trade in 1808. By 1842, most other European and American countries had done the same. By that time, the British, and to some extent the French, had also tried to persuade African rulers not to export slaves to any other countries. Particularly noteworthy was England's use of its powerful fleet against nations still involved in shipping slaves. The actual practice of slavery was abolished in Mexico in 1829. It was not abolished in the United States until 1865, following the Civil War, and it was not outlawed in Cuba and Brazil until the 1880's.

As horrible as the slave traffic was, it did not, as many scholars previously believed, completely destroy the African societies involved in the trade. It is true that many West Africans and some East Africans were forced to leave their homelands. But the areas of West Africa that supplied the largest number of slaves had been the most densely populated regions of the continent and continued to be so after the trade stopped. The African spirit of independence and freedom survived even the slave trade.

SECTION REVIEW

1. Mapping: Using the map on page 313, and the information in the text, describe the way in which European knowledge of Africa expanded between 1682 and 1816.

2. In your own words, identify: King Alfonso, Cape Verde Islands, trans-Atlantic Slave Trade, Vasco da Gama, Christopher Columbus.

3. How were most slaves captured before being sent to Europe and Asia? Why were slaves needed?

4. How did slavery in Africa differ from African slavery in Europe and Asia?

5. What effect do you think the demand for more slaves in the Americas had on African village life?

▷ What would happen to your community if many of its men, women, and children were regularly kidnapped and sold into bondage with the help of people living in one of your neighboring communities?

Reviewing the Unit

Unit Summary

After you have read the selection below, answer the questions that follow it.

Africa is a continent of many contrasts. It has large areas of rain forests along the equator. North and south of the equator are grassland regions and even farther in each direction are deserts. The Great Rift Valley cuts a path across the African continent and has created some of its highest mountains and deepest lakes.

The peoples of Africa are as varied as its geography. Five main groups of people are located there: Black Africans, Caucasians, San, Mongoloids, and Pygmies. One of the most important events in the history of some of these peoples was the great migrations of the Bantu-speaking Black Africans. These migrations began as far back as 2,000 years ago and continued throughout the nineteenth century. The Bantu-speaking peoples gradually populated much of Africa south of the equator.

During the Bantu migrations, many empires developed and declined.

In North Africa were the Berbers. Among West African empires were those of ancient Ghana, Mali, Songhai, Kanem-Bornu, and the Forest Kingdoms. Each conducted trade across much of the continent. East African empires included ancient Cush, Aksum, Nubia, and other trade centers that developed under Muslim control during the years between 650 and 1000. Kingdoms in central and southern Africa encluded those of the Luba, Lunda, and Kongo empires.

The decline in the power of early African empires began with the introduction of the European slave trade in Africa. Africans sought captives to sell to Europeans as slaves. Those sold in such trades usually went to the Americas. The trade was not halted by Europeans and Americans until the early 1800's. By then, the slave trade had done great damage to many African cultures and societies, leaving them weakened to further European expansion on the continent.

Developing Your Reading Skills

1. Explain the main point about *each* of the following: **a.** the physical geography of Africa, **b.** the main groups of people in Africa, **c.** early African empires, **d.** the slave trade.

2. Give this reading a question as a title. Your question should represent as much of the reading as possible. What would your question be? Explain?

Developing a Sense of Time

Examine the time line below and answer the questions that follow it:

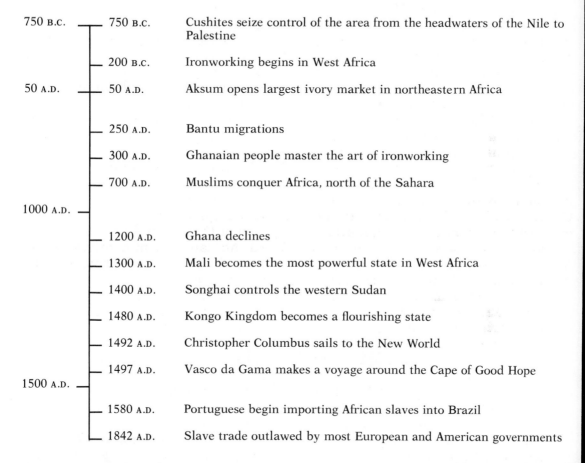

750 B.C.	750 B.C.	Cushites seize control of the area from the headwaters of the Nile to Palestine
	200 B.C.	Ironworking begins in West Africa
50 A.D.	50 A.D.	Aksum opens largest ivory market in northeastern Africa
	250 A.D.	Bantu migrations
	300 A.D.	Ghanaian people master the art of ironworking
	700 A.D.	Muslims conquer Africa, north of the Sahara
1000 A.D.		
	1200 A.D.	Ghana declines
	1300 A.D.	Mali becomes the most powerful state in West Africa
	1400 A.D.	Songhai controls the western Sudan
	1480 A.D.	Kongo Kingdom becomes a flourishing state
	1492 A.D.	Christopher Columbus sails to the New World
	1497 A.D.	Vasco da Gama makes a voyage around the Cape of Good Hope
1500 A.D.		
	1580 A.D.	Portuguese begin importing African slaves into Brazil
	1842 A.D.	Slave trade outlawed by most European and American governments

1. List two other key events from Unit 6 that could be added to this time line and give a reason for selecting each.
2. What are two conclusions you can form about African history from the information on your time line?
3. Do you think every student in your class would reach the same conclusions as yours? Explain.
4. Which happened first, Ghana's decline or Mali's emergence as a powerful state in West Africa? How are the two related?

319

Recalling the Facts

1. Describe the Bantu migrations. What is their importance?
2. In your own words, list what you think are the outstanding characteristics of each of these early African empires: Ghana, Mali, Songhai, Kanem-Bornu.
3. What was one special feature of each of the following early African empires: Cush, Aksum, Luba, Lunda?
4. List three special features of early African cities and towns. Describe the purpose of each.
5. Using the illustration on page 307, describe what a typical African village looked like.
6. What were the important differences between the fate of slaves within early African societies and the fate of slaves who were sold to non-African owners?
7. What effect did the triangular trade have on early African societies?

Using Your Vocabulary

1. Name the five main population groups to which most of the early Africans belonged.
2. Define the word *Bantu*.
3. What was bulopwe? Why was it important to the people of the Luba Empire?
4. What is a tsetse fly? How did it hinder early Africans?
5. What is the difference between a nuclear family and an extended family?
6. How do the words *clan*, *ethnic group*, and *kingdom* apply to early African societies?
7. How can *your* definition of religion, empire, civilization, and slavery be used to illustrate something about early African culture?
8. Define cowrie shells.
9. What is the purpose of bridewealth? Do we have a similar practice in our society?

Using Your Geography Skills

1. Using the map on page 289 and the Atlas of Africa and the information in your textbook, list *four* main features of the physical geography of Africa.
2. Using the map on page 289, locate the following early African cities by means of latitude and longitude coordinates: Kilwa, Mogadisho, Sofala, Timbuktu, Walata, Niani, Djenné.
3. Using the map on page 316 and information in the textbook, describe the triangular trade.
4. Using the map on page 289 and the Atlas, describe the geographical features of the area occupied by each of the early African kingdoms or empires. What can you surmise about how the physical geography of Africa affected the development of early African empires?

Developing Your Writing Skills

In this unit you have examined the cultures developed by early Africans living mostly south of the Sahara. You studied the rise and fall of empires created by Africans and about life within those empires. Now, consider the following:

FORMING AN OPINION

1. How would you define the word *unique?*
2. What would you consider to be five main features of African history (excluding Egypt) for the period 300 A.D.–1800 A.D.?

3. Based on what you have learned about the early histories of the peoples of the Middle East, Asia, Rome and Greece, and Europe, would you consider any part of early African history as examined in Unit 6 as unique?

SUPPORTING AN OPINION

Answer question three in a paragraph or essay, beginning with the completion of the following topic sentence: Early African history was (unique/ sometimes unique/never unique) because _____

Why Study the Past?

Is it possible that Africans reached the Americas before 1492? Consider the following and reach a conclusion: Columbus wrote that the Indians of Haiti told him of black traders who had spear points of a metal made in West Africa.

Mansa Musa claimed that his predecessor had disappeared during an expedition across the Atlantic Ocean. Scholars have found many pre-1492 sculptures in Mexico resembling early African sculptures.

Your History Bookshelf

Carlson, Lucille. *Africa's Lands and Nations.* New York: McGraw-Hill Book Co., 1967.

Clark, Leon, ed. *Through African Eyes: Cultures in Change.* (6 volumes) New York: Praeger, 1969– 1975.

Courlander, Harold. *A Treasury of African Folklore.* New York: Crown, 1975.

Dennis, R. Ethel. *The Black People of America.* New York: McGraw-Hill Book Co., 1970.

Hull, Richard W. *African Cities and Towns Before the European Conquest.* New York: W. W. Norton, 1976.

Kosova, Maria, and Stanovsky, Vladislav. *African Tales of Magic and Mystery.* New York: Tudor, 1971.

Oliver, Roland, and Fage, J. D. *A Short History of Africa.* New York: Penguin, 1962.

The New World

Many years ago, Big Eyes, a young woman from the Wichita tribe, was captured by an enemy tribe, the Tejas from eastern Texas. Big Eyes was frightened, but another captive from her tribe reassured her that some day they would return to their own land. But the Tejas kept moving farther and farther west. In their travels, they met the Pueblo people. The Tejas traded Big Eyes to the Pueblos as a slave.

The Pueblos were a peaceful people, but Big Eyes still longed to go back home. Finally, the opportunity to escape arrived when some Europeans on unusual animals called horses attacked the Pueblo village. They took Big Eyes and another Indian captive because they wanted them to serve as guides. These men were members of the Coronado expedition and were searching for gold in the area near Big Eyes' home. The Indians knew there was no gold, but this was their chance to return home.

One night, Big Eyes escaped and found her way back to her village. Months later, a group of Spaniards arrived in the Wichita village. They had traveled with De Soto, another explorer, and were looking for Coronado and his group. Big Eyes explained that she had left the other Spaniards about nine days' traveling distance from her village. She then sketched a map in the dust, showing the route she had followed. One of the Spaniards copied her sketch on a piece of paper.

The story of Big Eyes and her map spread throughout the Spanish colonies. From her map, the Spanish were able to make the first estimate of the amount of land on the North American continent, and Big Eyes became one of the most important early mapmakers in American history.

The relations and cultural conflict between the first people known to inhabit North and South America—the American Indians—and the Europeans who came to the Americas in the late 1500's, thousands of years after the Indians, will be one of the main themes of this unit. The origins of the Indians, what the cultures of the major Indian groups were like before the arrival of the Europeans, and how they were affected by European exploration and colonization of what the Europeans called the New World will also be discussed. In addition, you will see how the various European nations vied with each other for power and wealth in the Americas and how a third group, the Black Africans, played a vital role in the race for empire by supplying much of the labor on which the European nations—and later the independent nations of the Americas—built their wealth. As you study this unit, also keep in mind the part played by geography in the building of the New World.

Unit Goals

1. To identify the land masses, geographic features, and present-day countries that comprise the area that the Europeans called the New World.
2. To know what conclusions most scholars have reached about the origins of the American Indians and why they migrated to the Americas.
3. To identify the names of the major American Indian groups, their locations, and the chief characteristics of their cultures.
4. To compare and contrast the English, French, Spanish, and Portuguese styles of colonizing the Americas.
5. To describe the role black Africans played in the colonization of the Americas.
6. To describe the impact of European colonization on the Americas and the American Indians.

The New World

SIBERIA

BERING STRAIT

GREENLAND

ARCTIC

NORTHWEST
COAST

SUBARCTIC

NORTH AMERICA

PLATEAU
AND
GREAT
BASIN

NORTHERN
WOODLAND

CALIFORNIA

PLAINS

SOUTHWEST

SOUTHERN
WOODLAND

ATLANTIC OCEAN

GULF OF
MEXICO

TROPIC OF CANCER

20°

MIDDLE
AMERICAN

CARIBBEAN

PACIFIC OCEAN

0°

TROPICAL FOREST

SOUTH AMERICA

ANDEAN

20°

Routes of Indian Dispersal
Throughout the New World

TROPIC OF CAPRICORN

BIPOLAR CONIC PROJECTION

0   1500 Kilometers

0   1000 Miles

SOUTHERN

40°

120°   100°   80°   60°   40°   20°

The Earliest Americans

THE NEW WORLD

The *New World* is made up of two large continents, North America and South America, and a variety of nearby islands, including Cuba (KYOO-buh), Haiti (HATE-ee), Puerto Rico (pwert-uh REE-koe), Jamaica (juh-MAY-kuh), and others. The two continents are linked by a strip of land, which has become known as Central America. (See the Atlas of the Americas.)

Actually, the New World is not new at all. The New World continents are as old as the other continents on earth. People call North America and South America the New World because the continents were two of the last great land masses discovered by the Europeans. (Australia was the last.)

Geography of the Americas   The two land masses of North and South America are linked by a mountain "backbone," which runs from Alaska in the northern corner of North America to the southern tip of South America. (See the Atlas.) In North America, the highest parts of this mountain spine are called the Rocky Mountains. In South America, the highest peaks are found in the Andes (AN-deez). The narrowest land area joining the two continents is a strip in Panama (PAN-uh-mah) about 56 kilometers (35 miles) wide.

Bodies of Water   On all sides of the New World continents are great bodies of water. (See the Atlas.) To the far north is the Arctic Ocean. On the west is the Pacific Ocean, and to the east is the Atlantic Ocean. The Gulf of Mexico extends along the shores of the southern United States and Mexico.

Among the great rivers of the New World, two are of special importance. The Mississippi River system flows through the heart of North America. In South America, the Amazon (AM-uh-zahn) River begins in the Peruvian (puh-ROO-vee-un) Andes and flows first north and then east about 6,400 kilometers (4,000 miles) through northern Brazil (bruh-ZIL) to the Atlantic Ocean. These two great bodies of water serve as major arteries for transporting foods, goods, and people in North and South America.

Climate Regions   Climate and vegetation vary greatly on both continents. Generally, in the northern Canadian *tundra* (TUN-druh) area (a treeless region with permanently frozen subsoil) and in the forested areas of present-day Canada and Alaska, the climate is extremely cold in the winter and very cool in the summer. In the continental United States, the northern part of the country (including the lightly forested areas of the eastern coastline, the prairie of the Great Plains, and the heavily forested areas in the Far West) generally has cold or cool winters and warm summers. In the Southwest and in much of northern Mexico, the land is very dry. These regions have great stretches of desert. Tropical rain forests grow in southern Mexico, in much of Central America, and in Brazil—especially the area of Brazil that drains into the Amazon River. (See the Atlas.) Tropical grasslands stretch across the area south of the Amazon in Brazil. Northern Paraguay (PAR-uh-gway) and parts of Argentina (ahr-jun-TEE-nuh) and Bolivia (buh-LIV-ee-uh) consist of tropical bush country. Farther south, the climate changes again in the cooler and drier prairie grasslands of Argentina and Uruguay (YOOHR-uh-gway). At the southern extreme of South America, near Tierra del Fuego (TEE-er-uh del foo-AY-goe), is Cape Horn. It is a barren, cold, bleak coastal region with severe winds, which originate in Antarctica to the South.

THE ORIGINS OF THE EARLIEST AMERICANS

Scholars know very little about the first human inhabitants of the Americas. (See the Introduction to this book.) They have learned, however, that the migrations of early peoples to the New World occurred much later than other migrations in Europe, Asia, and Africa. **Migrations from Asia** There are several theories about the migration routes used by people moving into North America. However, much of the available evidence suggests that most of the early migrants crossed the Bering Strait from Siberia, in Asia, to Alaska, in North America. (See the At-

What does this petroglyph, or rock painting, suggest to you about early Indian life?

las.) Why these early people migrated is not known. There may have been pressure from other groups of people to move on. Famine may have made it necessary to find new food supplies. The herds that supplied meat and milk may have migrated east. Perhaps these migrating people sought milder climates, better living conditions, more abundant game, and a more plentiful food supply.

Whatever the reasons for the migrations, historians do know that the travelers migrated south from Alaska all the way to the southern-most part of South America. (See the map on page 325.) One great pathway taken by these early peoples lay along the western slopes of the coastal ranges of the Rocky Mountains into Mexico, down the Central American strip, and on into the southern continent. The migration through the Americas may have taken

327

as long as 40,000 years. The first human beings probably arrived in South America around 5,000 years ago. Because Christopher Columbus mistakenly believed he had reached the Indies in 1492, the decendants of these first Americans were called Indians by the first Europeans to encounter them.

Evidence of the Earliest Americans
Until 1926, few archaeologists (ar-kee-AHL-uh-jists) would have supported any theory that argued that human beings had been in America for more than a few thousand years. In 1926, however, an interesting discovery was made by George McJunkin, a Black cowboy in New Mexico. McJunkin found some fossil bones of an extinct bison and a flint spear point. This discovery helped archaeologists determine that people lived in America more than 12,000 years ago. Since then and with the introduction of more sophisticated methods of dating fossils, evidence has been examined that points to the possibility of people having inhabited North America for 40,000 years.

Carbon 14 Dating   One new method that has helped scientists determine the age of various archaeological finds is *carbon 14 dating*. This process measures the amount of radioactive carbon (radiocarbon) left in an object to find its age. All living things absorb radiocarbon from the air. Since radiocarbon is a radioactive substance, it gives off particles that can be detected with special equipment when it begins to decay. When a living thing dies, this radiocarbon loses radioactivity at a specific rate over a certain period of time. For example, the radiocarbon content in a substance such as a bone fossil is half gone in about 5,700 years. It continues to lose half of its remaining radioactivity every following 5,700 years. Thus

scientists using special instruments can measure the amount of radioactivity from radiocarbon left in a fossil's remains to find out how old it is.

Another method being used by scientists to determine the age of certain remains is *dendrochronology* (den-droe-kruh-NAHL-uh-jee), the name given to tree-ring dating. Using this method, archaeologists try to determine the age of wood remains by comparing an unknown wood remain with the growth rings in a tree trunk whose age is known. The most important factor in dendrochronology is to determine which ring patterns match in different wood remains.

Archaeological Finds   So far, archaeologists have not been able to locate any older traces of human life in the Americas than those from 40,000 years ago. However, there is ample evidence of the presence of early men and women in the Americas after that time. In the southwestern United States, archaeologists have found a number of ancient fire pits, or hearths. One of the hearths they discovered contained not only the charred bones of many ancient animals but also the earliest known spear points used by an American people. These are called *Clovis points*, from the name of the place in New Mexico where they were found.

Clovis Points   Clovis points were usually about fifteen centimeters (six inches) long. They were made by carefully chipping off flakes from a piece of flint. Although the prehistoric Indians lacked precision tools, the points were neat and sharp-edged. Clovis and other points found by archaeologists were parts of javelins used by prehistoric hunters to kill the big animals on which they depended for food. The most important of these animals were the

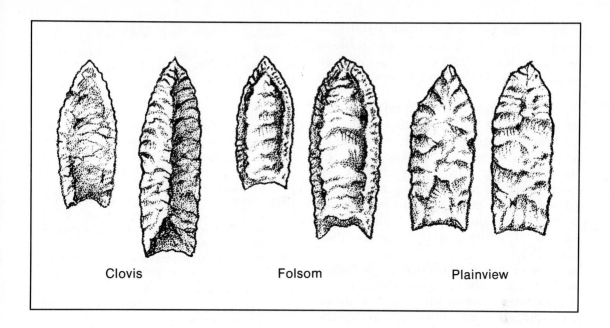

Clovis   Folsom   Plainview

mammoth (an ancestor of the elephant) and a very large bison. Both animals are now extinct. Most of the places where Clovis points have been found were once swamps or bogs. It is probable that prehistoric hunters chased any large animal they found into a swamp, where it would become trapped in the mud. When the animal was stuck there, the hunters would surround it and hurl their javelins into its sides. Scholars believe that this was the usual method of hunting huge animals.

When scientists tested the charred wood found near the Clovis points, they found that it was more than 37,000 years old. Other digging in the same region yielded more spear points. These are known as *Folsom points.* They were five centimeters (two inches) long, leaf-shaped spear points. (See the picture above.) After applying the carbon 14 dating process to charred bones found with the Folsom points, scientists have learned that hunters had probably camped there about 10,000 years ago.

The *Plainview point,* discovered in the Texas panhandle area, is another indication of the presence of people in the Americas many thousands of years ago. A single Plainview point was found when archaeologists uncovered the skeletons of about 100 bison. The skeletons were jammed together in an area about 30 centimeters (one foot) deep and 15,000 centimeters (500 feet) square. Among the tools found in this "bone bed" was a spear point about eight centimeters (three inches) long. Carbon 14 tests of the charred remains near this spear point revealed that the site was about 9,000 years old.

A Mysterious Discovery   One of the most mysterious discoveries relating to the ancestors of the American Indians was made in gravel pits near the Trinity River in east Texas. Between 1929 and 1939, two gravel contractors and a team of archaeologists discovered three carved stone heads. Since no tools or other signs of human life were found at the gravel pits, scholars have no idea who carved the stones or for what purpose. Using the dating tests available to them, archaeologists can only make an educated guess that the carvings are at least 20,000 years old.

Rock Paintings   Other evidence left by the earliest Americans are their cave and rock paintings. Like the rock paintings of ancient Africa, those of the Americas still show traces of the vivid colors used by painters long ago. These cave and rock paintings are perhaps as old as those found in the Sahara, and they deal with similar subjects. (See page 293.)

Another Type of Evidence   Scholars are curious about why the earliest Americans domesticated so few crops and animals before 1492. Except for the dog, and in cultures of the Andes Mountains the llama (LAHM-uh), the earliest Americans had no domestic animals. There were no horses, cattle, pigs, sheep, or goats. With the exception of *maize* (MAZE), or corn (see page 336), there were no domesticated cereal grains. It is known that during the Neolithic (nee-uh-LITH-ik) period, people on other continents did domesticate many of these useful animals and plants. This leads scholars to believe that the first Americans moved from ancient Asia before those crop and animal domestications occurred or at least before those who migrated to America had learned about them. This argument also seems to support the theory that the North American continent was joined with Asia at the Bering Strait by a "land bridge" and then separated from it about 20,000 years ago. The disappearance of the connecting strip of land could help to explain why many crops and animals did not reach the Americas until the arrival of European explorers after 1492.

SECTION REVIEW

1. Mapping: Using the text on page 326, briefly describe the different climate regions in North America and South America. Using the Atlas and the text on page 326, list the major mountain ranges and rivers on both continents.
2. In your own words, briefly define or identify: New World, carbon 14 dating, dendrochronology, Clovis points.
3. Where do most scholars believe the earliest Americans came from? What theories do they have for why people migrated?
4. What evidence have scholars discovered to support the theory that the ancestors of the American Indians came to the New World more than 40,000 years ago?
▷ Imagine that you are a scholar 5,000 years from now. Write a short summary of what life in the twentieth century must have been like based on the only evidence of that era so far discovered by archaeologists—a twentieth century American high school.

AN OVERVIEW OF EARLY INDIANS OF THE AMERICAS

Scholars cannot form a detailed picture of the earliest American way of life. But archaeologists and others who study Indian life have been able to piece together a somewhat detailed, yet in many ways incomplete, account of the cultures that dominated the Americas just before 1492.

Indian Languages   Scholars know that many different languages emerged among the various groups of American Indians. By 1492, there were about

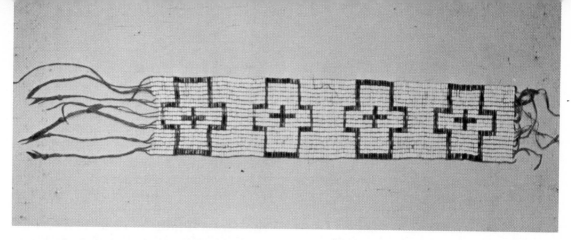

The formation of the Iroquois League in 1450 is commemorated by this wampum belt. How do we commemorate special events today?

200 languages spoken in North America north of the Rio Grande (ree-oe GRAND). In Mexico and Central America, 350 languages were used. In South America, there were about 1,450. These 2,000 native American languages represented about one third of all the languages of the world. Indian groups who spoke the same or similar languages usually banded together in nations, or leagues, such as those groups who made up the Shoshoni (shoe-SHOE-nee), the Apache (uh-PACH-ee), the *Sioux* (SOO), the *Iroquois* (IR-uh-kwoy), and the *Creeks*. Sometimes, however, tribes speaking the same language warred with each other. The Iroquois did this when they massacred their language kin of the Great Lakes region: the *Erie* (IR-ee), *Neutral, Susquehanna* (sus-kwuh-HAN-uh), and *Tobacco* tribes.

Indian Religious Beliefs   Religion played an important part in the lives of most Indians. Many Indians were monotheistic, believing in one *Great Spirit*. Some tribes had *shamans* (SHAHM-unz). These people were supposed to help interpret what the Great Spirit desired. Other Indians worshiped the sun. Several tribes also worshiped gods that represented aspects of nature.

Aspects of Indian Society   The Indians usually lived by the code that no one person should ever endanger the lives of all the people in the group. Life among most Indians centered upon the tribe, not upon the individual. Theft among members of the same tribe was very rare. However, stealing from an enemy was regarded as honorable. This was the task often given to a young warrior who wanted to achieve the status of manhood. Murder among the tribe members was punishable by permanent exile from the tribe. Other evils punished by banishment included allowing anyone in the tribe to go hungry, being disrespectful to the elderly, abandoning children of dead parents, or returning alone from war after one's commander had been killed.

Most tribes were divided into *clans* named after animals or birds. Clans usually chose their leaders from those who were descended from the oldest mother of the tribe. Like many other peoples of the traditional world, many Indian groups made slaves of war captives. Many slaves became adopted members of their captor's clan and intermarried with clan members.

Indians of the North   The northernmost group of Indians in the Americas inhabited the Arctic region at the far northern end of the North American continent. This is present-day Alaska. Throughout the centuries these Indian groups lived mainly by hunting and fishing. Their migrations over the cold northern regions of the continent took them as far east as Greenland. (See the map on page 325.) There, some of them may have made contact with the Viking explorers as early as 1000 A.D.

Stretching over much of Canada and Alaska is a region just south of the Arctic that geographers call the *subarctic*. (See the map on page 325.) There other Indians, such as the *Cree* (KREE), lived by hunting and fishing. Indians living in subarctic areas hunted big game, such as the caribou (KAR-uh-boo) and the moose. By 1500 A.D., the Indians of this area were still scattered thinly across Canada. They probably did not number more than 200,000.

Other early peoples lived on the northwest coast and in the plateau regions of North America. These regions include parts of the arctic areas of far-western Canada and Alaska and the present states of Oregon, Washington, northern Idaho, and western Montana. (See the map on page 325.) Indians in these areas, such as the Yakima (YAH-kee-mah), had few contacts with Europeans before the 1800's. They lived chiefly by fishing, and salmon was their main food. They were renowned for their superb basketwork and wood carving.

The Great Basin and California To the south and east, in the California and Great Basin areas, were bands of Indians who lived by trapping small game, such as rabbits and desert rodents, and by gathering wild foods such as acorns, berries, herbs, and roots. (See the map on page 325.) They sup-

plemented their diet with fish. These Indians, which included the *Yuma* (YOOH-muh) and the *Mohave* (muh-HAHV-ee), inhabited the present states of California, Nevada, southern Idaho, and western Wyoming and Colorado. The were also known for their skills in basket weaving. The baskets they made were often so tightly woven that water could be stored in them.

The Great Plains The Plains Indians lived in an area that extended from western Canada, east of the Rockies, to southern Texas. Most Plains Indian tribes were nomadic hunters. They included the Sioux and the Cheyenne (shie-AN). They roamed over a large area of the continent to the places where game was plentiful. Because they were always on the move, they had no permanent homes. Their lives were dependent on the buffalo. The buffalo furnished them with food, shelter—in the form of skins for tepees—and most of their clothing. Dried buffalo dung was burned as fuel. From buffalo bones and sinews (SIN-yoohs), the Plains Indians made most of their smaller weapons and tools. *Sinews*, made from buffalo muscles, provided the strings that were a basic part of the Plains Indian's standard weapon—the bow.

Because the various tribes of Indians on the Great Plains spoke different languages, the need arose for a common means of communication. This resulted in the use of sign language, which consisted of commonly understood gestures. Sign language has its limitations, however, since it could only be used to express uncomplicated ideas.

In order to survive their long journeys, the Plains Indians, as did many others, made one of the first forms of concentrated food. It was called *pem-*

332

Many early Indian peoples, who lived on the Great Plains of North America, depended on the buffalo for their food, fuel, clothing, and shelter. This buffalo shirt is one example of how the Indians used buffalo hides. What animals does your society depend on?

mican (PEM-ih-kun) and consisted of dried deer or buffalo meat pounded into a powder. When the Indians were ready to eat their pemmican, they mixed it with hot fat—a source of energy—and cut it into cakes. Sometimes they flavored the mixture by adding berries. Pemmican keeps for a long time and is very compact. Only a small amount is needed for survival.

The Northern Woodlands East of the Great Plains is the area that scholars call the northern woodland region. It includes southeastern Canada, the Great Lakes region, the northeastern United States, and part of the southern

United States. The people of this area were hunters. They farmed as well, but their harvests were too small to live on, and they had to rely on hunting, gathering, and fishing. Most of the Indians in the northern woodlands were seminomadic. They moved only when food supplies ran low or when they were threatened by more powerful neighbors.

The Iroquois were the largest group of northern woodland Indians. They consisted of five tribes—the *Mohawks* (MOE-hawks), *Oneidas* (oe-NIDE-us), *Onondagas* (on-un-DAW-gus), *Cayugas* (kee-YOO-gus), *Senecas* (SEN-i-kus).

A Closer Look

A French View of the Natchez Indians

As you read this description, try to decide whether it reflects the way of life of the Natchez Indians or whether it represents what the French expected they would find in America. Keep in mind that the French ruler, Louis XIV, who ruled from 1661–1715, was called the Sun King.

Maturin Le Petit, a missionary, reports after a visit in 1699:

To the Natchez, the sun is all important, and they cannot believe anything can possibly be above it. It is for this reason that the chief of the Natchez takes the name Brother of the Sun.

The Great Sun [Brother of the Sun] claims he came from the sun and has all power over his subjects. He can take their goods or their lives whenever he chooses. Yet in matters that concern the whole tribe, he does have to listen to the advice of the wise older men.

When the Great Sun dies, his wives, guards, and servants are expected to die also. The Natchez believe that when they die, they will go to live in another world. There, if they have been faithful to the Great Sun and his commands, they will have plenty to eat and live comfortably. If they have disobeyed the rules of the Natchez, they will have to live in a land entirely covered with water and mosquitoes; their enemies will make war upon them; and they will have nothing to eat but crocodiles and spoiled fish.

Adapted from: Allan O. Kownslar and William R. Fielder. "The Natchez," *Inquiring About American History*, Data Card. New York: Holt, Rinehart and Winston, 1972.

1. Do you think this report could be considered reliable evidence about the life of the Natchez? Why or why not?
2. Do you think a Natchez Indian would have described his or her society in the same ways? Why or why not?
3. Who might give the most accurate description of your society, you or a visitor from another country? Explain.

The tribes banded together to form a *confederacy*, or union, which, was known as the *Iroquois League*. The confederacy was so democratic that Benjamin Franklin used it as a model for what a representative government should be. By 1492, the Iroquois had also developed an elaborate trading system with other groups of Indians in North America.

The Southern Woodlands Indians of the southern woodland region were also among the most advanced peoples of North America. They included the *Natchez* (NACH-uz), the *Caddoes* (KAD-does), the *Five Civilized Nations of the Cherokees* (CHER-uh-keez), and the *Chickasaws* (CHIK-uh-sawz), *Creeks*, *Choctaws* (CHAHK-taws), and *Seminoles* (SEM-uh-noles). They lived in the area that now comprises the southern section of the United States and eastern Texas. The southern woodland Indians farmed and lived in towns. The Caddoes of Texas were among the most successful farmers in the New World. They maintained confederacies much like the one developed by the Iroquois. The Natchez of Mississippi and other tribes often had women rulers.

The Caribbean On the islands to the south and southeast of Florida's Seminole tribe lived the peoples of the Caribbean (kar-uh-BEE-un) area. With the exception of possible early encounters with the Vikings, the first Indian contacts with Europeans were probably between the Indians of the Caribbean islands and the explorers of the New World, beginning with Columbus. The Caribbean Indians, especially the peaceful *Arawaks* (AR-uh-wahks), farmed on a small scale. But chiefly they lived on fish and game or foods that grew wild.

Southwestern Area of North America In the area that is now the southwestern United States lived a group of Indian tribes known as the *Pueblo* (poo-EB-loe) peoples. They were called the Pueblo peoples because of their style of architecture. (See the picture below.) They represented a mixture of life-styles. Some, like the Mohave, remained nomadic hunters and traders. Others, such as the *Navaho* (NAV-uh-hoe) and *Hopi* (HOE-pee), established permanent settlements. Their economy was based on farming. They were skilled in the arts of weaving and pottery making. Large numbers of these people lived together in flat-roofed houses called pueblos, made of stone or sun-dried clay, or adobe (uh-DOE-bee) brick. At Pueblo Bonito (which means "beautiful town"), in Chaco (CHAHK-

The ruins of this great pueblo were found at Mesa Verde in Colorado. Some Pueblo peoples, such as the Navaho, still live in pueblos today. How are buildings such as these well suited to the environment?

oe) Canyon, New Mexico, stood the largest "apartment house" in prehistoric America. Built about 1000 A.D., it housed some 1,200 people. Its 800 rooms rose in horseshoe- shaped tiers from one to four stories high and were reached by ladders. In the middle was a courtyard in which stood several community halls. The stone walls of the pueblo were set in adobe cement. The interiors were marked off by poles and screens of woven willow and cedar. This pueblo was abandoned about 1300 A.D., probably because of a severe drought.

The Mayas   A number of advanced cultures flourished in the present-day regions of Mexico and Central America. (See the map on page 325). The Mayas (MIE-us) developed their civilization in the subtropical climate region of southern Mexico and Guatemala (gwaht-uh-MAHL-uh). By 100 B.C., the Mayas had made an important discovery—the domestication of maize. With the widespread cultivation of hearty and nutritious maize, the Mayas and other later Indian groups were able to make many cultural advancements. Large-scale farming of maize meant that the Mayas could settle in large communities and set up a division of labor among community members. Weaving and other crafts could be developed. Besides maize, the Mayas also cultivated beans, chili, various gourds, cacao (the main ingredient of chocolate), sweet potatoes, cotton, tobacco, and native fruits. They also learned how to produce cotton thread and fabric.

By 100 A.D., the Mayas had formed a triangular-shaped empire the end points of which were the cities of Palenque (puh-LENG-kay), Tikal (TEE-kahl), and Copán (coe-PAHN). This land was in the present-day territories of Honduras (hahn-DOOHR-us), northern Guatemala, and southeastern Mexico. About 500 A.D., Maya culture entered into what has been called the *Classic* period. It lasted until about 900 A.D. During this time, the Mayas developed a number system that included the idea of zero, a highly accurate calendar, an ideographic writing system in which symbols stood for ideas, and a method for predicting eclipses of the sun and the moon. Several cities and monuments were also built during this era.

In the 800's, however, the Mayan people began to abandon their cities and move north into the Yucatán (yoo-kuh-TAN) peninsula of Mexico. (See the Atlas.) No one is sure why they left. Some scholars have suggested that the Mayan population was growing too large for the available food supply. Others believe epidemics and wars may have killed much of the population.

In their new home in the Yucatán, the Mayas built city-states somewhat similar to those of ancient Greece. (See page 119.) One of those cities, Chichén Itzá (chee-CHEN eet-SAH), was built by the Mayas about 1,000 years ago. One of the most important structures left at the site of Chichén Itzá is a huge pyramid called *el Castillo* (el kah-STEE-yoe), or the Castle. It has four stairways, each with 365 steps, or one for each day of the year. Scholars believe that the Mayas probably built el Castillo and other tall pyramids because they wanted to climb as close as possible to their sun god.

Around 900 A.D., the Mayas entered into another cultural phase called the *Post-Classic* or *New Empire* period. It was characterized by new cultural influences, particularly the worship of a plumed serpent god borrowed from the Mayas' northern neighbors, the *Toltecs*

The great stone pyramids at Tikal were built by the Maya people of the Yucatan peninsula in Mexico. They had been abandoned for centuries by the time archaeologists found them. If you were an archaeologist, how might you go about investigating what they were used for?

(TOLL-tecks). At the end of the Post-Classic period, around 1200, the Mayas were conquered by the Toltecs, and their city-states went into a long period of decline. By the time the Spanish arrived in America in the early sixteenth century, most of the great Mayan cities were no longer occupied and had been covered over by rain forest.

The Toltecs During the Mayan Classic period in the tenth century, the Toltecs began to develop a culture that would later serve as the basis for the *Aztec* (AZ-teck) civilization. Toltec culture reached its height in the thirteenth century. The Toltecs set up their capital city at Teotihuacán (tay-oe-tee-wah-KAHN), near present-day Mexico City. Before conquering the Mayas, the Toltecs seem to have been greatly influenced by their culture. The Toltecs also

built large pyramids and cultivated corn and other crops.

The Toltecs probably introduced the practice of human sacrifice into Middle American culture. In their view, they were offering their gods the most precious of all gifts—life. This idea was not new. Human sacrifice as part of religious ceremonies was also being practiced at that time among peoples in Africa, Asia, and Europe. Invading Aztec peoples from the northwest soon adopted the custom of human sacrifice and also much of what the Toltecs had borrowed from the Mayas.

The Aztecs In the thirteenth century, the Aztecs became the dominant group in the valley of Mexico. The Aztecs referred to themselves as the *Mexica* people, and the lands they inhabited later became known as Mexico.

Calendar stones were designed by Aztecs.

Aztec power reached its height in the fifteenth and early sixteenth centuries.

From their capital city of Tenoch-titlán (tay-noch-teet-LAHN), the Aztecs created an empire that covered most of south-central and southern Mexico. According to Aztec legend, Tenochtitlán was located on the spot where the Aztecs had seen a heaven-sent eagle holding a snake in its beak, sitting on a cactus growing from a rock in a lake. This scene is pictured on the flag of modern-day Mexico, and Mexico City now stands on the site of Tenochtitlán.

Like the Toltecs and the Mayas, the Aztecs were great builders. Great temples and pyramids filled the city square of Tenochtitlán. Beautiful objects made of gold, silver, copper, lead, and bronze were produced by Aztec artisans and were sold in many of the capital city's colorful market places. The Aztecs were also fine weavers and skilled potters.

Education was highly valued in Aztec society. Sons of wealthy Aztec parents went to school at age fifteen to become priests or warriors. These were considered the two most important professions in Aztec society. Aztec history, written on long strips of paper called *codex*, was an important subject in school. In addition to schools for the wealthy, special schools enabled boys from poor Aztec families to prepare to be soldiers, landholders, or government officials. Some Aztec women were trained to become priests. Others took charge of booths in the marketplace or ran households.

Religion was an important part of Aztec life. The Aztecs had many gods and goddesses. *Huitzilopochtli* (WEET-zeel-oe-POTCH-tlee) was worshiped as the god of the sun and war. *Tlalóc* (TLAH-lok), the rain god, and *Quetzal-coatl* (ket-sahl-KOE-ah-tl), represented in the form of a plumed serpent, were also influential gods. The Aztecs believed that the world had been destroyed and created four times. The fifth and present recreation of the world was the result of Quetzalcoatl's sacrifice of his own blood. Because of this belief, the Aztecs felt that human sacrifices were necessary to keep the universe going.

In order to have enough humans to sacrifice, the Aztecs needed a large number of prisoners. As a result, they were constantly at war with other Indians. When the Spanish arrived in Mexico in 1519, many of the tribes conquered by the Aztecs were willing to join the Spanish to fight against their Aztec rulers. (See page 344.)

In summary, the Aztecs built a major empire which exhibited outstanding accomplishments in the development of architecture, agriculture, education, and the arts.

The Incas   Among the early peoples of the Andean area of South America were the *Incas* (ING-kus). (See the map

veloped a distinctive way of life in the highlands of Peru, with Cuzco (KOOZ-koe) as their capital city. The rise of the Inca Empire occurred about the same time the Toltec culture of Mexico was reaching its height in the thirteenth century.

By the sixteenth century, the Incas had conquered many of their neighbors. The Inca Empire covered about 988,000 square kilometers (380,000 square miles). Its territory extended from present-day Ecuador (EK-wuh-dawr) into central Chile (CHIL-ee) and eastward from the Pacific Ocean high into the mountains of Bolivia (buh-LIV-ee-uh). The empire also had a population of twelve million people who belonged to 100 different ethnic groups and had twenty different languages.

Unlike the Aztecs, the Incas absorbed the people they conquered into their own culture. Sons of the conquered rulers were brought to Cuzco to be educated in the Inca way. The Inca government also sent colonists into conquered lands to teach the new subjects the Inca way of life.

Political and religious power in the Inca Empire was in the hands of the supreme leader, who was called *The Inca*. The Inca's followers believed that he was a descendant of their sun god. The rest of Inca society was strictly divided into classes, or castes. The Inca and the royal family occupied the highest level of society. Nobles and warriors were on the next level, then artisans and farmers.

All Inca land was owned by the state as well as all means of production and distribution. Farm land was worked under a highly organized and centralized system that provided for the people who farmed the land as well as for The Inca and the upper classes. A complex irrigation system, land terrac-

ing, and efficient methods of food storage were features of Inca agriculture. Corn, white and sweet potatoes, and peanuts were the chief food crops.

Almost every aspect of an Incan individual's life was controlled by the state. Men were drafted into the army or had to spend time in the government's service. Women received specialized training in religion and household activities. Marriage was also regulated. If a man was not married by a certain age, he was urged to do so or a wife would be assigned to him.

The Incas were also highly skilled artisans known for their weaving, pottery, and jewelry making. They excelled in engineering, especially in architecture and road building. The Incas also had highly trained doctors who could set broken bones, perform amputations, and even do brain surgery. Coca (KOE-kuh), the plant from which cocaine is made, was probably used by their doctors as an anesthetic.

SECTION REVIEW

1. Mapping: Using the map on pages 325 and the Atlas, list the major Indian groups that inhabited the Americas in 1500 and the modern nations they were located in.
2. In your own words, briefly define or identify: clans, pemmican, Iroquois Leaque, el Castillo, codex, The Inca.
3. Give three examples of how the Indians of the Americas adapted to their environment.
4. How did the domestication of maize change Mayan life?

▷ Why do modern Americans often have a stereotyped view of the way of life of the earliest American? How can such views be a block to good communication and relations between Indians and other Americans?

chapter 18

Europe Explores and Colonizes the New World

EXPLORERS COME TO THE NEW WORLD

Spurred by the discoveries made in 1492 by Christopher Columbus, an Italian navigator sailing under the Spanish flag, many western European nations sent other expeditions to the New World. These explorers were interested in finding a "northwest passage" around or through North America to the Far East. They were also concerned with establishing claims and colonies in the new lands for their countries and securing gold, silver, and other valuable products. In addition, many of the explorers brought missionaries with them to try to convert to Christianity the people whom Columbus had called the "Indians."

Mercantilism Underlying the establishment of European colonies in the New World was a policy called **mercantilism.** It was a policy initiated in the fifteenth century that was accepted and practiced by all the major European governments. According to the mercantilist system, colonies were supposed to supplement a nation's economy. In this way, both the nation and its colonies could become self-sufficient. In order to maintain the system, the colonizing country would regulate the commerce and trade of the colonies. Ideally, the colonizing country would furnish manufactured goods, and the colonies would supply raw materials. Strict political control of the colonies by the colonizer was supposed to ensure that the system would work as smoothly as possible. In the end, the goal of mercantilism was the establishment of a growing and self-sufficient empire that existed for the benefit of the colonizing country and the colonies, but with the colonizing country the principal beneficiary of the system.

Major Powers During the 1600's and 1700's, the major mercantile powers of Europe were Spain, Portugal, England, France, and The Netherlands. Each of these countries tried to achieve wealth and power by promoting a favorable balance of trade among themselves, their colonies, and the rest of the world. Having a *favorable balance of trade* meant that each country had to sell or export more goods outside the empire than it bought or imported. If a country succeeded in exporting more than it imported, it could keep its profits high and retain its gold and silver. These high profits, in turn, could be used to keep a large army and navy for national defense. Without a strong army and navy, the colonizing country might be in danger of losing its colonies to more powerful nations.

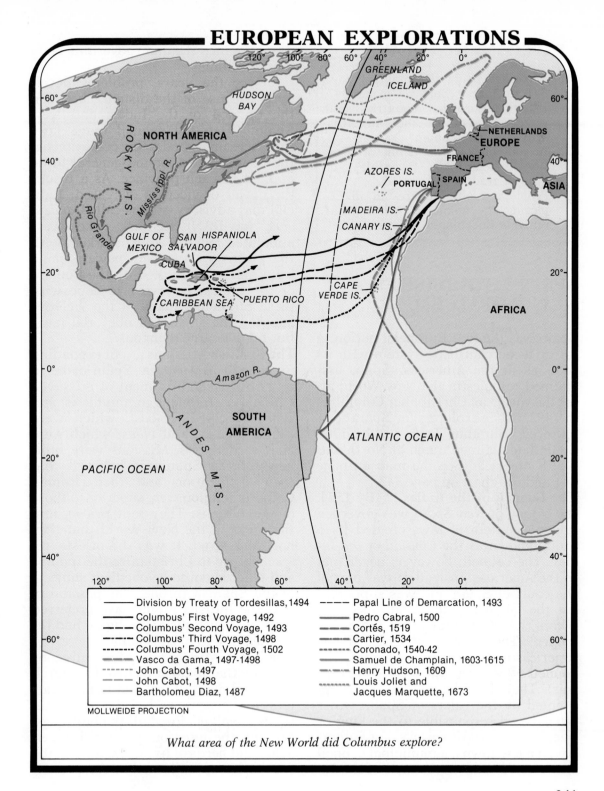

EUROPEAN EXPLORATIONS

GREENLAND
ICELAND
HUDSON BAY
NORTH AMERICA
ROCKY MTS.
Mississippi R.
Rio Grande
GULF OF MEXICO
SAN SALVADOR
HISPANIOLA
CUBA
PUERTO RICO
CARIBBEAN SEA
AZORES IS.
PORTUGAL
SPAIN
NETHERLANDS
EUROPE
FRANCE
ASIA
MADEIRA IS.
CANARY IS.
CAPE VERDE IS.
AFRICA
Amazon R.
SOUTH AMERICA
A N D E S   M T S.
ATLANTIC OCEAN
PACIFIC OCEAN

—— Division by Treaty of Tordesillas, 1494	– – – Papal Line of Demarcation, 1493
—— Columbus' First Voyage, 1492	—— Pedro Cabral, 1500
– – – Columbus' Second Voyage, 1493	– – – Cortés, 1519
–·–·– Columbus' Third Voyage, 1498	—— Cartier, 1534
······ Columbus' Fourth Voyage, 1502	······ Coronado, 1540-42
⟩⟩⟩⟩ Vasco da Gama, 1497-1498	—— Samuel de Champlain, 1603-1615
······ John Cabot, 1497	⟩—⟩— Henry Hudson, 1609
– – – John Cabot, 1498	······· Louis Joliet and
—— Bartholomeu Diaz, 1487	Jacques Marquette, 1673

MOLLWEIDE PROJECTION

What area of the New World did Columbus explore?

1. Mapping: Using the map on page 341 and the chart on page 347, list the European countries that sent explorers to the Americas. Why did they come?
2. In your own words, define or identify: mercantilism, favorable balance of trade.
   ◗ People are often interested in exploring the unknown. Why? What remains unexplored today?

SPAIN ESTABLISHES A NEW WORLD EMPIRE

Spain was the first European nation to set up a mercantilistic system with its colonies in the Americas. Spain first claimed colonies in the New World after the voyage of Christopher Columbus in 1492. Other explorers for Spain soon followed Columbus' lead, and by 1763 Spain had claimed much of North and South America. (See the map on page 341 and the chart on page 347.)

The Council of the Indies   By 1524, the colony of *New Spain* was governed under a system of laws created by a group known as the *Council of the Indies*. The council, however, never met in the Americas. Instead, it was part of the court of Spain and was supported by the Spanish king and queen to whom, it was assumed, the Indies belonged. The highest officials in the Americas responsible for executing the council's laws were the *viceroys* (VISE-rois). They, like the council, were appointed by the rulers of Spain. Other officials, all responsible to the king or queen, served at other levels of authority. In a few towns, a municipal council was elected, but the Council of the In-

dies remained the main governing body for the colonies.

Over the years, problems developed because of the distance between the Council of the Indies and New Spain. Often the council made laws that were unrelated to the conditions in the new territory or too general to be applied to each province. As a result, the power of viceroys increased. Judicial and advisory groups called *audencias* (ow-DANE-see-ahs), who were appointed by the king, worked with the viceroys, but their powers came from and were limited by the Council of the Indies. In trying to cope with these problems, many of the viceroys adopted the saying, "I obey the laws, but I don't carry them out."

The Spanish Missions   In expanding its control in America, Spain came to rely on the establishment of *missions*, which were religious communities, *presidios* (preh-SID-ee-oes), which were military posts, and *villas*, which were civil settlements. Missions were built because the Spaniards believed that their civilization and their Roman Catholic religion were superior to those of the Indians. They sent priests into the areas of the New World that they had conquered. It was the priests' responsibility to Christianize the Indians and teach them to be obedient subjects of the Spanish throne. The possibility that the Indians might have preferred their own customs and religion had little meaning to most Spaniards.

The First Missions   Most missions built by the Spanish included a church or chapel, workshops, and living quarters for priests and Indians. Sometimes a wall enclosed all the buildings. Around the mission were cultivated fields and herds of livestock. Among the first missions built within the present boundaries of the United States were those in or near San Antonio and El Paso, in Texas, and San Diego, Monterey, and San Francisco, in California.

The duty of the priests after Christianizing the Indians was to teach them a trade practiced by Europeans, such as cattle raising, carpentry, or the cultivation of new kinds of crops. The priests were also supposed to help guard the area against intruders, especially Portuguese, French, or English explorers who might try to claim the region.

Except in Texas and part of Paraguay, a mission was usually secularized within ten years after it had been founded. *Secularization* occurred when the use or control of the mission was transferred from the church or a religious organization to a civil authority. Often when the mission had performed its basic function in opening up a new area, it was dissolved, and a regular parish took its place. In some areas, when a mission was secularized, its lands were distributed to the resident Indians.

Spanish Missionaries The *Franciscans*, the *Dominicans*, and the *Jesuits*, three orders of Catholic priests and monks, were deeply involved in founding Spanish missions. In addition to being the most numerous in Spanish America, the Jesuits were also among the first explorer-priests for the French in North America. They moved up western Mexico and through the Baja California peninsula in present-day Mexico, founding missions along the way. The Franciscans traveled with the Spanish explorers. They moved northward from Mexico City, the new Spanish capital of the Americas, and entered New Mexico, Texas, the Great Plains area, and finally California. Using St.

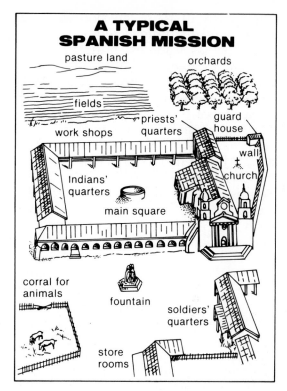

A TYPICAL SPANISH MISSION

pasture land

orchards

fields

work shops

priests' quarters

guard house

wall

church

Indians' quarters

main square

corral for animals

fountain

soldiers' quarters

store rooms

Augustine as a base, they also traveled from Florida into the Carolinas until the English drove them back into the Florida peninsula. South of Mexico City, the Dominicans worked with the Indians in Central America.

In South America, the Franciscans and Jesuits worked their way to the tropical forests of the upper Amazon River area. While the Franciscans attempted to Christianize Indians living in Argentina, the Jesuits ventured into Paraguay. All three groups of missionaries entered Chile.

Some missions established by these priests flourished for a time. The missions had herds of cattle and sheep that often numbered in the thousands. Sometimes a mission grew enough wheat to export to Europe. In many missions, the priests organized various manufacturing enterprises. The Indian

343

population in these mission factories wove blankets, tanned hides, and produced shoes, saddles, pottery, tallow for candles, wine, and olive oil.

Southwestern Missions Missions in the southwestern portion of the United States were usually built not far from the Indian villages and pueblos. Missionaries sought to make the Indian people living there subservient to them in civil and spiritual matters. The Spanish also tried to force nomadic Indians from nearby areas to settle down with the other Indians in the villages and pueblos and to join the Catholic church.

In the years that followed, however, the Spanish efforts to control these people failed. One reason for the failure was the way the Spanish abused those who tried to revive the native religion. Indian religious leaders were often whipped and put in prison, which greatly outraged followers. The Pueblo people also recognized a major weakness in the Spanish colonization program. Serious differences of opinion over how to treat the Indians existed between the Spanish civil leaders, who wanted to make the Indians slaves, and the church leaders, who wanted to save their souls. The Indians recognized this dispute and used it to their advantage.

The Pueblo Revolt In August 1680, nearly 30,000 *Rio Grande* and *Acoma* (ah-KOE-mah) Pueblo people rose against the Spanish colonial government. The **Pueblo Revolt,** as it has come to be called, was the first "American Revolution" against outside rule and oppression. During the revolt, *Popé* (poe-PAY), a Pueblo reformer, urged his people to abandon the customs of the Spanish and return to their old ways.

For about twelve years, the Pueblos succeeded in expelling the Spanish from their land. Eventually, however, the Spanish sent in fresh troops to reconquer them. After this time, the Pueblos were never again able to unite, and they remained in subjugation through centuries of Spanish, Mexican, and United States rule.

The Spanish and the Aztecs In 1519, a Spanish explorer named **Hernando Cortés** (kore-TEZ) set sail from the island of Cuba for Mexico with 508 soldiers, sixteen horses, several small cannons, and gunpowder. His arrival in Mexico marked the beginning of the end of the Aztec empire. (See page 337.) Because the Mexican Indians had never seen cannons or horses before, Cortés had a great advantage over them. The Aztecs also felt the arrival of Cortés was the fulfillment of an ancient prophecy. It had been predicted that Quetzalcoatl, the Aztec plumed-serpent god, would return to Mexico one day from the east, bringing ruin and destruction to the Aztecs. When the Aztec ruler **Montezuma** (mahn-tuh-ZOOM-uh), who was familiar with the prediction, heard about Cortés, he thought the Spaniard might be the plumed-serpent god coming for his revenge.

After landing in the present-day city of Vera Cruz, Cortés fought his way to the Aztec capital of Tenochtitlán. Some of the Indians who Cortés had fought and defeated along the way joined him in fighting the Aztecs. These were the people of the tribes that the Aztecs had conquered and forced to send tribute and humans for Aztec religious sacrifices. (See page 337.) With this group of Indians behind him, Cortés pushed toward Tenochtitlán. Although Montezuma had a large and powerful army, he decided to invite Cortés into the city instead of ambushing or attacking him.

Who do you think painted this scene of the Spanish and the Aztecs? Why?

Cortés, however, was in Mexico illegally. The governor of Cuba, Diego Velásquez (vah-LAHS-kez), had become convinced by Cortés' enemies that Cortés might not be loyal to the Spanish throne and might keep any riches he found for himself. Worried, Valásquez sent troops to Mexico to arrest Cortés. Hearing the news of the arrival of these troops, Cortés left Tenochtitlán to engage them. He managed to defeat them and enlist the survivors in his scheme to conquer the riches of Mexico.

Cortés and Montezuma While Cortés was away, his forces in Tenochtitlán had misinterpreted an Aztec ceremony as being hostile and had attacked their Aztec hosts. A battle followed, and in the process, Montezuma was overthrown by his people. Despite this, when Cortés returned, he still sought Montezuma's support. When Montezuma tried to persuade his people not to fight Cortés, however, they stoned him and pierced his body with arrows.

Shortly thereafter, Montezuma died. His successor died four months later of smallpox, a disease unknown in the Americas until the arrival of the Europeans. A new leader, *Cuauhtémoc* (kwa-TAY-mock), inherited the task of trying to expel the Spaniards.

The Final Defeat of the Aztecs Meanwhile, Cortés was regrouping his forces. With his soldiers who were equipped with cannons and muskets and an attack force of thousands of Indian allies, Cortés managed to capture Tenochtitlán after killing up to 120,000 of its Aztec inhabitants. Cuauhtémoc surrendered to Cortés and was hanged by the Spanish three days later. By 1521, two years after he had first landed in Mexico, Cortés had succeeded in defeating one of the strongest military societies of the Americas.

A sidelight to Cortés' conquests was the role played by *Malintzin* (mah-LIN-tsin), whom Cortés called *Doña Marina* (DOE-nyah mah-REEN-ah). She was

345

an Indian slave. Because she spoke both the Mayan and Aztec languages, she became an important interpreter for Cortés. Although she was loyal to the Spanish, Malintzin also sympathized with the Indians and made several efforts to help them survive the blows of conquest.

The Incas and the Spanish Other Indian groups in New Spain, as well as those throughout the Americas, suffered fates similar to those of the Aztecs. The powerful Inca empire was destroyed, primarily through the efforts of **Francisco Pizarro** (pee-ZAHR-oe), an illiterate Spaniard. Pizarro had traveled with other Spanish explorers in North America before he decided to try to conquer the Peruvian Incas. His first attempt failed because of a shortage of soldiers, munitions, and supplies. However, his second expedition, which began in 1530, succeeded beyond his wildest dreams. During the next five years, he and his men captured *Atahualpa* (ah-tuh-WAHL-puh), the Inca leader. They offered to ransom him to his people for 13,000 pounds of gold and 26,000 pounds of silver. The Incas paid the ransom. But Pizarro refused to release him. Instead, the Inca leader was charged with treason and condemned to die.

Through the wars that resulted from this action, Pizarro subjugated the peoples of present-day Peru, Ecuador, Bolivia, and Colombia. The Incas had no weapons to match the Spanish horses, muskets, and cannon. Cuzco, the Inca stronghold to the south, was sacked. There Pizarro built his City of the Kings, called Lima (LEE-muh).

Slavery in New Spain Over the violent objections of many priests, Spanish officials subjected many of the defeated Indian peoples to forced labor in gold and silver mines. This resulted in thousands of deaths. In order to replenish their labor supply, the Spaniards in the Americas began to import slaves from Africa. By 1570, Portugal, eager to profit from the African slave trade, had supplied Spanish officials in Mexico with at least 20,000 slaves. Over the years, more and more Africans followed in the inhumane slave traffic.

Slavery changed the composition of the populations of the Spanish-controlled West Indies and the northern rim of South America. A few Africans came to the New World with the earliest European explorers and remained there as free people. Many descendants of Africans, regardless of how or why they came, intermingled with the Spanish and Indian people of the Americas. The result of this mingling was the appearance of the mestizo, mulatto, and zambo populations prevalent in Latin America today. A *mestizo* (mes-TEE-zoe) is a person of mixed European and American Indian ancestry. A *mulatto* (muh-LAHT-oe) is part European and part Black African. A *zambo* (ZAHM-boe) is a mixture of Black African and American Indian.

A fourth major group to develop was the *Creoles* (KREE-olz). These were people of European descent born in the New World. As used here, the term *Creole* means persons of Spanish or Portuguese descent born in the New World.

Spanish Settlements To protect their New World frontiers, Spanish officials built presidios. The typical presidio was a military outpost occupied by professional soldiers. The primary role of the soldiers at a presidio was to protect nearby missions, friendly Indian people, and the Spanish subjects of a region. In addition to missions and presidios, the Spaniards established

EUROPEAN EXPLORERS

Explorer	Date of Voyage	Discoveries
Explorers for Spain		
Christopher Columbus	1492	Discovers America, returns and tells the story of his discovery
Amerigo Vespucci	1499–1501	Finds that the New World is not part of Asia
Vasco Núñez de Balboa	1513	Crosses the Isthmus of Panama and sees the Pacific Ocean
Hernando Cortés	1519–1521	Conquers the Aztecs in Mexico
Ferdinand Magellan	1519–1522	Sails around the world
Francisco Pizarro	1527–1536	Explores the west coast of South America, conquers Inca Empire
Hernando de Soto	1530–1542	Explores the southern part of North America, including Florida, Oklahoma, and Georgia
Francisco Vásques de Coronado	1540	Searches for gold and silver in southwestern North America
Explorers for Portugal		
Vasco da Gama	1497	Sails around Africa to India
Pedro Álvares Cabral	1500	Explores the coast of Brazil
Explorers for France		
Giovanni da Verrazano	1524	Explores the northeast coast of North America. First European to see New York harbor
Jacques Cartier	1534	Locates the St. Lawrence River
Samuel de Champlain	1608–1615	Travels on the St. Lawrence River to the Great Lakes
Jacques Marquette and Louis Joliet	1673	Explores the upper Mississippi River Valley
Explorers for England		
John Cabot	1497	Reaches Newfoundland
Francis Drake	1577–1580	Sails around the world
Martin Frobisher	1576–1579	Looks for a Northwest Passage through Labrador and Baffin Island
George Weymouth	1602–1606	Explores New England coast
Henry Hudson (also sailed for The Netherlands)	1610	Searches for a Northwest Passage

villas. These were small hamlets or towns. There were neither military nor religious establishments. The population of a villa was usually made up of laborers, farmers, ranchers, merchants, artisans, and government officials. All of these, in the eyes of the Spanish government, were the most desirable settlers for the American colonies. The villas and sometimes the nearby missions or presidios were often the foundation of such large cities as St. Augustine, Florida (1565); Sante Fe, New Mexico (1609); El Paso, Texas (1659); Albuquerque, New Mexico (1706); San Antonio, Texas (1718); San Diego (1769), Monterey (1770), and San Francisco (1776), California.

With the establishment of missions, presidios, and villas in Spanish America, a new culture emerged. It was a blend of three cultures: Indian, African, and Spanish. Spaniards were always a minority of the population. Together, these groups gradually formed the basis of a new population in Spanish-controlled America.

Spanish and Mexican Contributions Spanish and Mexican contributions to contemporary life in the United States have been important throughout our history. Language is one example. Spanish words have long influenced our vocabulary. Words such as *rodeo, frijóle, tamale, patio, enchilada, tortilla, fiesta, siesta, piñata, hombre, sombrero, hacienda, rancho,* and *serape* have become so familiar that we sometimes forget that they are of Spanish rather than English origin.

Many customs of the Southwest and Far West are also of Spanish or Mexican origin. Many cowboys, for example, learned their trade from Mexican *vaqueros* (vah-KAR-rose). Mexicans were pioneers in the use of irrigation in farming. Historians believe that cattle branding is Mexican in origin. Many of our laws guaranteeing rights of property to married women are of Spanish origin. In addition, many of our land laws originated during the Spanish and Mexican periods of western history.

SECTION REVIEW

1. Mapping: Using the map on page 350 and the Atlas, list the present-day countries that were once part of New Spain. What were the main reasons for Spanish exploration and colonization in the Americas?
2. In your own words, briefly define or identify: viceroys, audencias, missions, presidios, villas, secularization, mestizo, mulatto, zambo.
3. What problems did the Council of the Indies have in governing New Spain?
4. Why did the Spanish establish missions? Why did the Spanish efforts to control the Indians fail?
5. Why were Cortés and Pizarro able to conquer the powerful Aztecs and the Incas?
6. List five Spanish or Mexican contributions to life in the modern United States.
   The Spanish felt their culture was superior to any of the Indian cultures they encountered. How do you think the Indians felt about the Spanish?

PORTUGAL ENTERS THE RACE

Portugal became the second major European nation to enter the race to establish a New World empire. Portugal had been the first European country to make a serious attempt to send ships to sail around Africa in the hope of establishing a direct trade route with Asia. Early European visits to the Americas caused the Portuguese to increase their interest in the New World, and soon expeditions sailing under Portugal's flag were exploring the coastline of the Americas. Not long after the Spanish came to America, the Portuguese began to establish their own colonies in South America.

Spain and Portugal Divide the World Spain was not particularly interested in the eastern part of South America, but it did try to find some way to limit Portuguese territorial claims in the New World. At the urging of Spanish rulers, *Pope Alexander IV* (of Spanish birth) established what became known as the *Papal Line of Demarcation* (dee-mahr-KAY-shun) of 1493. This line encircled the globe, passing through the North and South Poles and lay about 424 kilometers (270 miles) west of the Cape Verde (VURD) Islands. (See the map on page 341.) All discoveries west of the line, made after 1493 and not already held by a Christian king, were to belong to Spain. The line acknowledged Spain's claim to practically all of the New World.

A year later, King John II of Portugal, who was understandably unhappy with this arrangement, convinced Spain to agree to a line about 1,600 kilometers (1,000 miles) west of the Cape Verde Islands. This line was set halfway between the Azores (AY-ZOREZ) and the West Indies. The agreement is known as the *Treaty of Tordesillas*(tore-day-SEE-yahs). Spain received exclusive rights to all New World lands west of the line. Portugal had similar claims in the area east of it. By this arrangement, Portugal obtained a claim to what is now Brazil. (See the map on page 350.) This area soon became the basis for the Portuguese empire in South America. Neither France nor England agreed to the establishment of this new line or the original line.

The Portuguese Captaincy System Portugal ruled Brazil somewhat differently from the way Spain managed its colonies. In Brazil, the Portuguese established the *captaincy system.* Under this system, Portugal granted interested citizens large tracts of land in South America. These tracts began along the Atlantic coast and extended inland for many kilometers. The person receiving the captaincy, or grant, was usually a wealthy man of some distinction. He had to be rich, since he had to develop his land with his own money. In the Americas, he served as captain and governor of the land. By the 1540's, some thirteen large captaincies had been granted, but only a few had actually been established. Landed estates on established captaincies became plantations. They resembled those that existed in the southern United States before the Civil War.

In established captaincies, many of Brazil's staple products were cultivated. The Portuguese began the sugar industry. Cotton production was begun, but only on a very small scale. Tobacco, a native American plant, was grown so successfully that it soon became one of Brazil's main exports.

Expulsion of the French and the Dutch Shortly after the establishment of these land grants, the Portuguese expelled two other groups of Europeans from Brazil. French Huguenots (HYOOH-guh-nahts) had made the area around Rio de Janeiro (REE-oe day zhuh-NER-oe) a center of trade. Their custom was to make occasional calls on Indian friends to trade for lumber and pepper. In return, the Indians received

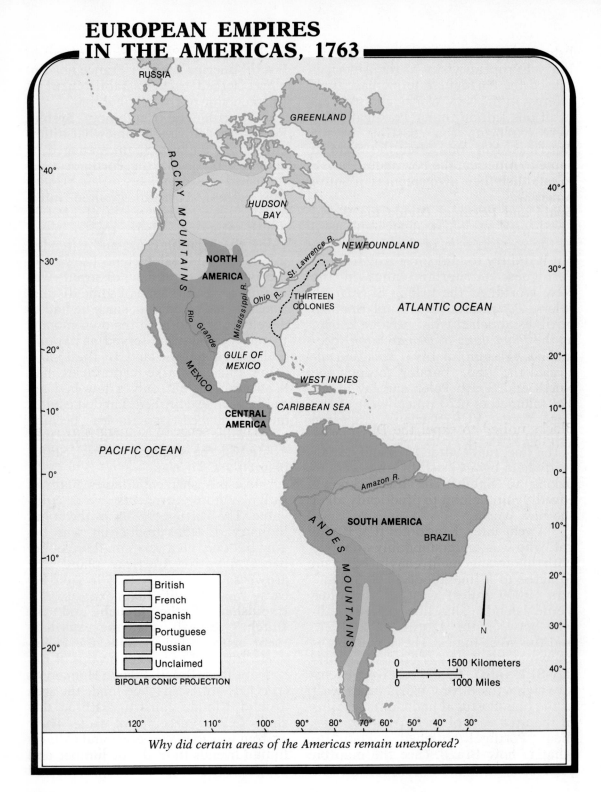

EUROPEAN EMPIRES IN THE AMERICAS, 1763

RUSSIA

GREENLAND

ROCKY MOUNTAINS

HUDSON
BAY

NEWFOUNDLAND

**NORTH
AMERICA**

St. Lawrence R.

Mississippi R.

Ohio R.

THIRTEEN
COLONIES

ATLANTIC OCEAN

Rio Grande

MEXICO

GULF OF
MEXICO

WEST INDIES

**CENTRAL
AMERICA**

CARIBBEAN SEA

PACIFIC OCEAN

Amazon R.

A N D E S   M O U N T A I N S

SOUTH AMERICA

BRAZIL

N

	British
	French
	Spanish
	Portuguese
	Russian
	Unclaimed

BIPOLAR CONIC PROJECTION

0   1500 Kilometers

0   1000 Miles

120° 110° 100° 90° 80° 70° 60° 50° 40° 30°

Why did certain areas of the Americas remain unexplored?

knives, axes, scissors, and the like. By the 1560's, the French had built a trading fort in the area. Faced with this French threat to their New World claims, the Portuguese used force to dislodge the French in 1567. Thereafter, Rio de Janiero was under Portuguese control.

Under the direction of a trading company, the Dutch decided in 1624 to establish themselves in Brazil. In a series of conflicts with the Portuguese, the Dutch managed to gain control of the sugar-producing areas of northeastern Brazil. But in 1651 the Dutch government in Europe had to make a choice. The English were threatening to destroy The Netherlands' large fleets of merchant vessels and warships that sailed the Atlantic. When the Dutch decided to use all their strength to fight the English, they had to abandon their efforts to hold Brazil. Soon the Portuguese settlers, native Indians, and Blacks united to expel the Dutch who had stayed in the area. This ended the last major threat to Portuguese control of Brazil until the early part of the nineteenth century.

Brazil's Colonial Population　A variety of people made up Brazil's colonial population by 1580. Portuguese settlers, Indians living in missions, and newly arrived Black African slaves numbered about 30,000 people. About half that number lived in or near four of the country's main cities: Pernambuco (per-num-BYOOH-koe) on the eastern bulge, Baía (bah-EE-uh) to the south, the port of Rio de Janeiro, and São Paulo (sown POW-loo) in the southeast. At that time, Baía was the capital city of Portuguese Brazil.

Labor Shortage　As the colonial population of Brazil began to expand, the colony faced a labor shortage. The economy of the colony had until then depended on the use of Indian labor. At first, the Indians had been treated as free people and encouraged to sell such items as logs to the Portuguese authorities. Then, when the sugar industry began to boom, the Portuguese needed a large labor force in order to carry it on. They attempted to enslave the Indians. But whether enslaved or free, not enough Indians were available to meet the labor shortage. Once the Indian labor supply had been depleted and the more wary Indians had retreated into the interior of Brazil, the Portuguese turned to another labor source—slaves from Africa.

Population Changes　The Portuguese became one of the major suppliers of African slaves to the New World. They brought about one million Africans to Brazil between the years 1530 and 1680. At least 25,000 Black Africans lived in Baía in the late 1700's.

The presence of so many slaves, as well as the arrival of other people lured by discoveries of minerals and diamonds, greatly changed the population of Brazil. As Portugal was less rigorous than Spain in enforcing immigration restrictions, many settlers besides Portuguese entered the colony. Native people of mixed Portuguese and Indian ancestry became a new group in Brazil. They were largely responsible for developing the region around São Paulo. The imported Africans, many of whom mixed with settlers, likewise changed Brazil's population. In time, the Blacks and mulattos were freed from slavery. Added to these groups were descendants of early French and Dutch settlers. There were also descendants of European Jews, who had been able to enter Brazil because of the more lenient attitude towards religious diversity.

Colonial Brazilians enjoyed a varied economy and worked out ways to adapt to New World realities.

SECTION REVIEW

1. Mapping: Using the map on page 341, locate the Papal Line of Demarcation and the line established by the Treaty of Tordesillas. What was the purpose of these lines?
2. How did the Portuguese captaincy system work?
3. Why did Brazil's colonial population change? Explain using examples.
▶ How do you think a varied population adds to the culture of a nation or state? Give examples of things that you do or use that come from cultures other than your own.

FRANCE BUILDS A NEW WORLD EMPIRE

By 1500, France had become the most powerful military power in western Europe. To become even more powerful and provide yet another economic outlet for its people, France joined England, Spain, and Portugal in a race for empire in the Americas. (See the map on page 350.) The French holdings in the New World were called *New France.* They were the results of explorations and colonizations by the French from 1524 to 1680. (See the chart on page 347.)

French Explorations The French explorers, like the Spanish, at first sought riches in America. Throughout the sixteenth, seventeenth, and eighteenth centuries, many Europeans continued to believe that gold, silver, and precious jewels were abundant in the New World. Missionaries also accom-

panied explorers and became explorers themselves in an attempt to Christianize the Indians.

In 1524, *Giovanni da Verrazano* (ver-uh-ZAHN-oe) sailed from France to the eastern coast of North America. He was followed in 1534 by *Jacques Cartier* (kahr-TYAY), who explored the St. Lawrence River valley. Later the French began their explorations in eastern Canada. By 1604, *Samuel de Champlain* (duh sham-PLAYN) had begun a journey that would eventually establish France's claim to the Great Lakes area. Gradually, the French also began to establish their strongholds along the Mississippi River. In the later 1600's, the French explorers *Jacques Marquette* (mahr-KET), a Jesuit priest, *Louis Joliet* (zhoe-LAY), *Louis Hennepin* (HEN-uh-pun), and *Robert de La Salle* (duh luh-SAL) traveled through much of the Mississippi River basin. The French Jesuits were active not only as explorers but also as missionaries. Many were killed by Indians who resented European trespassers on their lands and hunting grounds.

French Forts As France's land claims mounted in North America, the French began to build forts for the defense of their empire against the threat of the English. French forts were located at strategic places like Detroit and Ticonderoga (tie-KON-der-oe-gah). The main French settlements were established at Quebec (1608), Montreal (1642), and New Orleans (1718).

The Fur Trade The abundance of fur-bearing animals in the French colony made the fur trade an important source of wealth for France. The fur trappers and traders of New France referred to themselves as *coureurs de bois* (koo-RUR duh BWAH), or wood rangers. Many adopted the Indians' way of

PEOPLE IN HISTORY

Sacajawea

Sacajawea (sak-uh-juh-WEE-uh), a young Shoshone Indian, was one of the most famous members of the Lewis and Clark Expedition, which explored the North American continent between 1804 and 1806. The only woman of the group, Sacajawea acted as guide and interpreter for the expedition.

Sacajawea had been captured by the Minnetarri (min-uh-TAR-ee) Indians as a child and gambled away to a French guide named Toussaint Charbonneau (shar-buh-NOE) whom she later married. Both she and Charbonneau were engaged by Lewis and Clark as guides and spent the winter with them in the Dakota territory where Sacajawea's son, Baptiste, was born in February of 1805. In the spring, with her baby strapped to her back, Sacajawea led the party west into her own country.

Immediately recognized by her own people even after her long absence, Sacajawea persuaded them to help the expedition party. With guides from Sacajawea's tribe, the Lewis and Clark party finally reached the Pacific Ocean on November 7, 1805.

Historical accounts vary on the fate of Sacajawea. Some say she was the last survivor of the expedition, dying in her 90's in April of 1884. Clark wrote, however, in his **Cash Book for 1825–1828** that she had died at age 25 of a "putrid fever." Clark also took her son Baptiste to live with him. Later, Baptiste became a guide and interpreter in the West, helping among others Clark's own son.

Adapted from: Claire R. and Leonard W. Ingrahm. **An Album of Women in American History.** New York: Franklin Watts, 1972, p. 21.

1. How did Sacajawea help the Lewis and Clark expedition?
2. It is said that there are more statues of Sacajawea in the western part of the United States than of any other woman. Why do you think this is so?

---

life. They dressed like their Indian friends and married Indian women. In the process, they helped the French government maintain generally friendly relations with the Indians.

French Colonial Government The French colonial government set up an elaborate system of regulation and supervision of its colonists. For example, in return for grants of land, the colonists had to take their grain to the leading military officer's mill. Or they had to buy their flour from him, purchase the bread made in his bakery, or give him a portion of all fish they caught. The military officers thus became the New World counterparts of European feudal lords. This arrangement collapsed in the 1700's. At that time, most of the French colonists demanded and obtained the right to do with their land as they saw fit.

SECTION REVIEW

1. **Mapping:** Using the map on page 341 and the text on page 352, describe the areas that were explored by the French. Why were the French interested in America?

2. In your own words, define or identify: Samuel de Champlain, *coureurs de bois.*

3. What was French colonial government like?

▶ Many of the French fur trappers adopted the way of life of the Indians. To what extent do you think any foreigner or newcomer should adopt the ways of a new country or area? Give an example.

ENGLAND BUILDS A NEW WORLD EMPIRE

East and south of New France, the English were also busy building New World colonies. The English were late in entering the race for empire in the New World. Some explorers sailing under the English flag, including John Cabot (Giovanni Caboto) in 1497 and his son Sebastian Cabot in 1509, had explored some of the northern part of the New World. But the English did not make a serious attempt to colonize America until after the exploratory voyages of Sir Walter Raleigh to Virginia in 1584 and Henry Hudson to what is now Hudson Bay in Canada.

New England A string of English colonies, hugging the Atlantic coastline from present-day Maine to Georgia, finally emerged in the 1600's. (See the map on page 355.) The New England colonies of Massachusetts, Rhode Island, New Hampshire, and Connecticut made up the northernmost group of colonies. Their way of life focused on the town meetinghouse, where matters of government were discussed; the village green, which was common land; and the school, one of the most important institutions in the settlement. The people lived much as they and their ancestors had in England. They cultivated fields, lived in small villages, and used pasture and woodland in common with their neighbors. Some engaged in manufacturing on a small scale. Others fished and trapped fur-bearing animals. Still others engaged in boat building, shipping, or overseas trade.

The Middle Colonies South of New England were the middle colonies of New York, New Jersey, Pennsylvania, and Delaware. Colonists in that area, like their New England neighbors, raised corn, wheat, vegetables, and other crops. They shipped some of their products to England. Their main exports to England were tar, turpentine, hemp for rope, and ship masts. (See the map on page 355.) The colonists of this area also engaged in the triangular trade with England, Africa, and the West Indies. (See page 316.) Centers for this trade developed in Philadelphia and New York. Boston, in Massachusetts, and Newport, in Rhode Island, also became major slave markets.

The Southern Colonies The southern colonies included Maryland, Virginia, North Carolina, and Georgia. Most southern colonists did not come to the New World seeking religious freedom, as had many of the northern colonists. They usually came to obtain land in the New World. The plantation system was soon the South's dominant economic pattern. Plantations were huge tracts of farm land. They were usually cultivated by indentured servants from Europe and slaves from Africa. *Indentured servants* were persons who agreed, in return for their passage

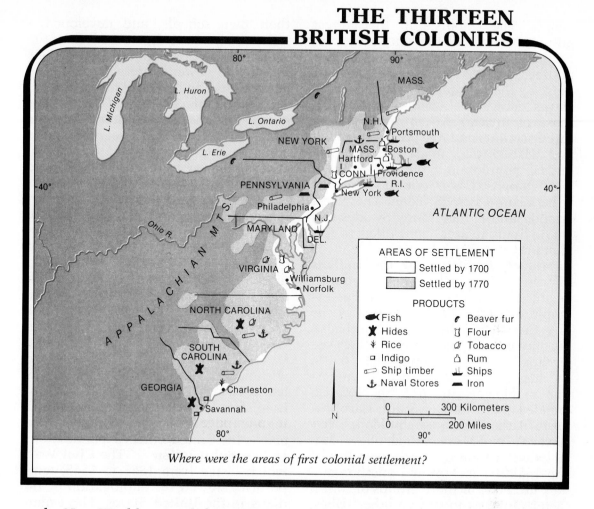

80°   90°

MASS.

L. Huron

L. Michigan

L. Ontario

N.H.

Portsmouth

L. Erie

NEW YORK

MASS. • Boston

Hartford

CONN. • Providence

R.I.

New York

PENNSYLVANIA

Philadelphia

ATLANTIC OCEAN

N.J.

Ohio R.

MARYLAND

DEL.

40°   40°

APPALACHIAN MTS.

VIRGINIA

Williamsburg
• Norfolk

NORTH CAROLINA

SOUTH
CAROLINA

GEORGIA

• Charleston

Savannah

AREAS OF SETTLEMENT

☐ Settled by 1700

▨ Settled by 1770

PRODUCTS

Fish	Beaver fur
Hides	Flour
Rice	Tobacco
Indigo	Rum
Ship timber	Ships
Naval Stores	Iron

0   300 Kilometers

0   200 Miles

N

80°   90°

Where were the areas of first colonial settlement?

to the New World, to work for someone for four to seven years, receiving only room and board. After that, they became free men and women. Indentured children had to work until they were twenty-one. Indentured servants were used in all the English colonies. Slaves from Africa and their children usually retained that status for life. As early as 1663, a group of slaves in Virginia attempted to rebel and free themselves. They were joined in their unsuccessful rebellion by some white indentured servants.

Some land grants to plantation owners were for no more than 180 hectares (450 acres). Southern plantations raised tobacco, rice, indigo, sugar cane, and some cotton. Tobacco remained the most profitable money crop throughout the colonial period. Under the prevailing mercantilist view, the British government naturally expected all products not needed for immediate use in their colonies to be sent to England. Beginning in the mid-1600's, a series of laws designed to promote that objective and protect royal or imperial interests was passed by Parliament. But the laws were not strictly enforced.

Colonial Population   By 1775, the population of the English colonies, like the colonial populations in Brazil and New Spain, was made up of a variety of

355

people. The colonists in the largest group—about half the total—were of English origin. The second largest number, about 20 percent, were Blacks, most of them brought from Africa as slaves. However, about 5 percent of those of African descent were indentured servants and free people. Scottish and Irish settlers made up the third largest population group. The fourth was composed of German colonists. Others came from Sweden, The Netherlands, and France, Many Swedes and Dutch living in areas controlled by England became British citizens.

Continued Problems for the Indians

All this new settlement, of course, meant trouble for the Indians. For example, the Cherokees were one of the Five Civilized Tribes of the Southeast. Europeans did not enter Cherokee territory as settlers until the 1690's. By then Spain had founded St. Augustine in Florida. In 1673, the English founded the colony of South Carolina. By 1679, the French were at Mobile Bay on the Gulf of Mexico. Each new colonial power encouraged the hostility of one Indian tribe toward another and they used one or more groups of southeastern Indians to war on other tribes. The Creeks, for example, aided the English in fighting Christianized Spanish-controlled Indians in Georgia and Florida. The Choctaw and Natchez were French allies until the French in 1732 decided to exterminate all the Natchez.

By the time the United States achieved its independence from Great Britain in 1783, surviving Indian tribes of the Southeast as well as groups east of the Mississippi were in danger of extinction unless they adopted European customs. Some groups—mainly the Five Civilized Tribes—tried to do this. The Cherokees wrote and approved a democratic constitution, established their own schools, and developed a written alphabet. It seemed that the Civilized Tribes would succeed in their efforts, but newer settlers decided they needed more Indian land for farms.

The Trail of Tears

The turning point for the southeastern Indians came in 1830. In that year, Congress passed a law that allowed the federal government to buy Indian lands and move the Indians farther west at government expense. Those of the Five Civilized Tribes who remained in the South were moved during the years 1832–1839 to what is now eastern Oklahoma. The journey became a nightmare when soldiers would not even allow the Indians to stop along the way to tend their sick or bury their dead. The Cherokees called the route from Georgia to Oklahoma *The Trail of Tears*.

Earlier, many other tribes living within the continental United States had met similar fates at the hands of English colonists. The process of forcing the Indians into submission continued as the United States expanded.

Indian Subjugation

The Civil War, which lasted from 1861 to 1865, temporarily slowed the subjugation of Indians in the United States. The Union victory, however, meant that the acquiring of Indian lands could begin anew. During the years following the Civil War, United States soldiers defeated what remained of the resisting Plains Indians. The last major battle with those Indians occurred at *Wounded Knee*, in South Dakota. There, in 1890, a detachment of the Seventh Cavalry killed more than 300 Sioux. Most of the victims were women and children who were heading for the Pine Ridge Indian reservation in search of food. Thereafter, most Indians in the United States were required to live on federal government reservations.

356

The Cherokees set out on their "trail of tears" after having been expelled from Georgia. By the time they reached Oklahoma, many had perished. How does this painting differ from other paintings of Indians you have seen?

Throughout all the years of conflict, both Indians and settlers inflicted horrible atrocities on one another. People on both sides—young and old, men and women— suffered and died. All Indians did not fight against the settlers, however. The Crows and Pawnees, for example, never engaged in wars against the newly arrived Europeans. Other Indians actually sought refuge with the Europeans against their hostile Indian neighbors. A group of Texas Indians, for example, lived in or near European settlements to obtain protection from the hostile Apaches.

The End of the Frontier   After the Wounded Knee killings, Indian-European violence subsided. Indians in both North American and South America tried to make new lives for themselves. In the United States, the Indian struggle to retain old tribal lands was a lost cause. Soon after the Wounded Knee battle, a historian named *Frederick Jackson Turner* stated that by 1893 the land frontier of the United States had ceased to exist. Americans from coast to coast had finally settled the continental United States to the extent that no large unclaimed land areas existed within its boundaries. The country would have to look elsewhere for new frontiers to conquer.

SECTION REVIEW

1. Mapping: Using the map on page 355, list the major trading centers and products of the English colonies.
2. In your own words, define or identify each of the following: indentured servants, Wounded Knee.
3. Describe three main characteristics of New England colonies, middle colonies, southern colonies.
4. List the different ethnic groups living in the English colonies by 1775.
5. Briefly summarize the problems between the Cherokees and the Europeans. What happened to the Indians after the Civil War?

> Has the population of your community ever changed? In general, were the newcomers welcomed or resented?

357

Reviewing the Unit

Unit Summary

After you have read the selection below, answer the questions that follow.

What the Europeans called the New World is made up of two large continents, North America and South America, and a number of nearby islands. Available evidence suggests that most of the first inhabitants of the Americas, the Indians, crossed from Asia through the Bering Strait to Alaska as early as 40,000 years ago. However, due to a lack of definite evidence, that date remains uncertain.

Scholars, however, do know many things about early Indian life. Tribes often varied greatly in life styles. Much of this had to do with the effects of the physical environment.

Trouble between the Indians and the European newcomers began soon after the arrival of Christopher Columbus in 1492. Beginning with the conquests of Cortés in the 1520's, the many groups of Indians that put up determined struggles against the Europeans continually lost.

Columbus' arrival in the Americas also resulted in a race for New World empires. Underlying the European colonization of the Americas was a policy called mercantilism. According to this policy, colonies were supposed to supplement a mother-nation's economy.

During the 1600's and 1700's, the major mercantile powers of Europe were Spain, Portugal, England, France, and The Netherlands. Spain's empire was located mainly in the present-day Southwest, Mexico, Central America, and the western part of South America. Its empire had its own government and used missions to help in establishing order. Portugal claimed present-day Brazil. It was dominated by a captaincy economic system. France's empire, until it was lost to the British in 1763, covered much of the Mississippi Valley and Canada. Before its collapse, the French had built up a profitable fur trade and improved relations with many Indian tribes. England, which soon squeezed out the New World interests of the Dutch, built a series of economic enterprises among thirteen colonies along the eastern coastline of the present-day United States.

Developing Your Reading Skills

1. What do you think is the main idea or point in this reading about *each* of the following?
   a. Indian origins
   b. Indian life
   c. The major mercantile powers and their colonial locations
2. Imagine that you had to give this reading a question as a title. What would your question be? Why?

Developing a Sense of Time

Examine the time line below and answer the questions that follow it.

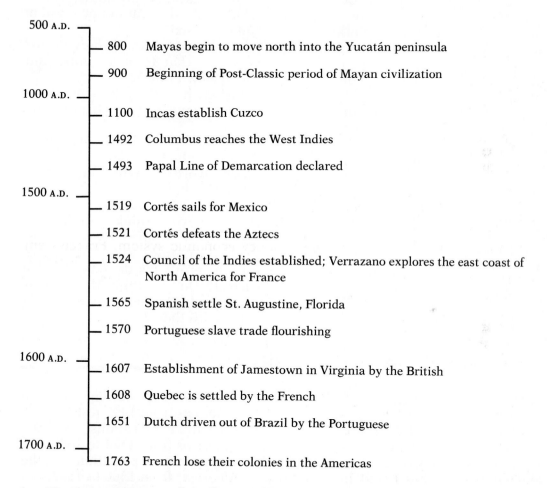

500 A.D.		
	800	Mayas begin to move north into the Yucatán peninsula
	900	Beginning of Post-Classic period of Mayan civilization
1000 A.D.		
	1100	Incas establish Cuzco
	1492	Columbus reaches the West Indies
	1493	Papal Line of Demarcation declared
1500 A.D.		
	1519	Cortés sails for Mexico
	1521	Cortés defeats the Aztecs
	1524	Council of the Indies established; Verrazano explores the east coast of North America for France
	1565	Spanish settle St. Augustine, Florida
	1570	Portuguese slave trade flourishing
1600 A.D.		
	1607	Establishment of Jamestown in Virginia by the British
	1608	Quebec is settled by the French
	1651	Dutch driven out of Brazil by the Portuguese
1700 A.D.		
	1763	French lose their colonies in the Americas

1. How many years after the voyage of Columbus did Spain establish the Council of the Indies?
2. Which event on this time line is directly related to Africa?
3. Pick two events off this time line and explain how they were related to events in Europe.
4. Pick three other events off this time line and explain what caused each one and how each event affected life in the Americas.

359

Recalling the Facts

1. List five of the major Indian groups of the early Americas, and describe their cultures in detail.
2. Summarize the conclusions scholars have reached about the origins and migrations of the Indians.
3. How did European exploration and colonization effect the American Indians? Summarize.
4. Summarize the Spanish colonial system.
5. What agreements did Spain and Portugal reach over settlement of the Americas?
6. Why did France wish to explore the Americas? What was its system of colonization?
7. Why were each of the three main areas of the English settlement founded in North America?
8. What role did Black Africans play in the colonization of the Americas? How did their way of life differ in the English, Spanish, and Portuguese colonies?

Using Your Vocabulary

1. How does mercantilism differ from colonization?
2. What were the distinctive features of each of the following in New Spain: missions, presidios, villas?
3. What was the captaincy system and who used it?
4. What does *coureurs de bois* mean? Why was that term an important one in New France?
5. Define each of the following terms in your own words: civilization, religion.
6. How do you think Hernando Cortés might have defined each of these words? What examples might he have used to prove his definitions were correct?
7. How do you think Montezuma might have defined these words? What examples might he have used to prove his definitions were correct? Do you think the Indians conquered by the Aztecs would agree with these?

Using Your Geography Skills

1. Using the map on page 325 and the descriptions on page 326, tell which land masses comprise the area Europeans called the New World.
2. How did the physical geography and climate of those land masses seem to affect the ways of life among the Indians by 1500 A.D.? Cite three examples.
3. Using the maps on pages 341 and 350 and the chart on page 347, what can you conclude about:

a. Spanish exploration of the Americas from 1492 to 1543.
b. French explorations of the Americas from 1524 to 1680.
c. Portuguese exploration of the Americas from 1500 to 1542.
d. English exploration of the Americas from 1497 to 1611.

4. Using the map on page 350, tell which countries dominated which areas of the Americas by 1763.

Developing Your Writing Skills

In this unit, you have examined the various Indian cultures of the Americas. You have also learned about the development of European-controlled empires in the Americas. Now consider the following.

FORMING AN OPINION

1. What generally happened to the Indians as they encountered the Europeans?
2. What do you think can cause a clash of cultures?

SUPPORTING AN OPINION

3. Do you think that the clash of cultures that took place in the Americas between the Indians and the Europeans was inevitable or could it have been avoided? Answer in a paragraph or essay, beginning with completion of the following topic sentence:

The clash of cultures in the Americas between the Indians and the Europeans was _____

Why Study the Past?

"In the name of the Indian people, I claim the right of discovery and take possession of this land." Lucky Eagle spoke these words in October 1973, as he stepped off a jet airliner in Italy. Lucky Eagle, whose "paleface" name is Adam Nordwall, is a teacher at a college in California. He was trying to show that Indians today have as little right to claim Europe as Christopher Columbus had when he claimed the Americas for Spain in 1492. Lucky Eagle argued, America had been there all along; thousands of Indians had discovered it many years before the arrival of Columbus. According to Lucky Eagle, how were the American Indians wronged by Columbus?

Your History Bookshelf

American Heritage Society. *The American Heritage Book of Indians.* New York: American Heritage Publishing Co., 1961.

Burland, Cottie. *North American Mythology.* New York: Hamlyn, 1965.

Bushnell, G. H. S. *The First Americans: The Pre-Columbian Civilizations.* New York: McGraw-Hill, 1968.

Farb, Peter and Alvin M. Josephy. *Red Power.* New York: American Heritage Publishing Co, 1971.

Hulpach, Vladimir. *American Indian Tales and Legends.* New York: Hamlyn, 1965.

National Geographic. *The World of the American Indian.* Washington, D.C: National Geographic Society, 1974.

The World of
Revolution

When we think of the French Revolution, an image that usually comes to mind is a square filled with working-class people who cheer as the blade of the guillotine does away with another French noble. Most of us do not realize that the guillotine was adopted in France because it was thought to be a symbol of equality.

This instrument for executing people had already appeared by the Middle Ages. It had been used in China, Italy, Germany, and Scotland. In France before the revolution, however, condemned nobles were beheaded by the sword, and common people were sentenced to be hanged. Dr. Guillotin, who introduced the guillotine in France, did not approve of these methods. He thought people sentenced to die should be treated equally. He believed all criminals, regardless of social class, should be executed in the same way. Dr. Guillotin recommended that they be beheaded by mechanical means.

The doctor claimed that the new beheading device was quick and painless. "The mechanism falls like thunder," he explained. "The head flies off; blood spurts; and the man [or woman] is no more."

Unfortunately, the machine that was designed to make public death quick, clean, and painless performed so well that death did not appear to be horrible at all. In fact, the instrument was so quick, so clean, and so painless that many Parisians were quite entertained by it. This new means of execution was used on thousands of people from all walks of life during the French Revolution. And the citizens of Paris rarely gave a second thought to the device that so efficiently did away with both noble and commoner alike.

The latter part of the 1700's and the 1800's were years of upheaval in Europe and the Americas. The American Revolution, which began in 1776, and the French Revolution of 1789 introduced ideas about liberty that encouraged people in other parts of the world to fight for their freedom. Following the examples of France and the United States, most of the countries of Latin America fought for and received their freedom during the first half of the 1800's. Beginning in 1848, there were also rebellions in Austria, Germany, Italy, and—once more—in France. Another great revolution was carried out by the Russian people, who fought for more political freedom and for improved economic conditions. While the political revolutions were taking place, another kind of revolution was in progress. This was the Industrial Revolution. It had far-reaching effects on the lives of almost all the people in Europe and the Americas.

In this unit, you will be reading about many different events in the history of the 1700's and 1800's, most of which are connected with economic or political revolution and social change.

Unit Goals

1. To know the conditions in America that brought about the American Revolution.
2. To know the conditions in France that brought about the French Revolution, and the major events that took place during the Revolution.
3. To know how the Latin American countries gained their freedom from Spain and Portugal.
4. To know what problems were brought about by the Industrial Revolution and how people tried to solve these many problems.
5. To understand the theories of Karl Marx.
6. To understand why Russia rebelled against the tsar and how a Communist government developed.

Revolution

CANADA (Brit.)

NORTH

AMERICA

UNITED
STATES
1775
1783

GREAT BRITAIN

SOVIET
UNION
1917

EUROPE

FRANCE
1789

PORTUGAL SPAIN

ATLANTIC OCEAN

MEXICO
1810
1821

HAITI **1794** 1804

CUBA (Sp.)

DOMINICAN
REPUBLIC
1808
1821

BELIZE
(Brit.)

HONDURAS
1839

GUATEMALA
1839

EL SALVADOR
1839

NICARAGUA
1839

COSTA RICA
1839

PANAMA
1903

COLOMBIA
1810
1819

VENEZUELA
1830

GUYANA
1966

ECUADOR
1830

PERU
1821

BRAZIL
1822

SOUTH AMERICA

BOLIVIA
1825

PARAGUAY
1811

AFRICA

PACIFIC

OCEAN

CHILE
1810
1818

URUGUAY
1828

ARGENTINA
1810
1816

1775	Date revolution began
1783	Date became independent
------	Modern political boundaries

MOLLWEIDE PROJECTION

60°

30°

0°

30°

60°

120°   90°   60°   30°   0°

chapter 19

The American Revolution

AN ERA OF REVOLUTION

People in the thirteen English colonies of North America began an era of revolution in the 1770's that soon freed most of the people in the Americas from European control. The idea of independence spread throughout the Americas and into Europe and influenced people of other countries to revolt against unjust rulers and to develop their own governments.

The French and Indian War   The causes of the **American Revolution** date back to the end of the **French and Indian War.** This war, called the *Seven Years' War* in Europe, began in 1756. (See the chart on page 227.) The war, which began in Europe, was fought from 1756 to 1763. At its conclusion, Great Britain acquired Canada from France. Soon after, the British Parliament passed the **Proclamation of 1763,** which stated that the colonists could not move west of the Appalachian Mountains. This proclamation angered many of the colonists, who felt the eastern seaboard was becoming crowded and who wanted to move west in search of new lands.

New Taxes   Because the British had spent so much money to finance the French and Indian War, they thought it was only fair that the colonists should help bear the cost of it. After all, they argued, the war had been fought for the benefit of the colonies. As a result of these feelings, England imposed many new laws and taxes on the colonists that they came to resent.

Parliament taxed the colonies on all goods shipped to or purchased from the non-English islands in the West Indies. This was designed to force the New England colonists to trade only for sugar that was produced in the British islands. In 1764, Parliament imposed the *Sugar Act.* This set new duties on molasses and sugar from non-British colonies. Angry colonial merchants saw their profits drop.

The Stamp Act   In 1765, Parliament passed a new law known as the **Stamp Act.** It imposed a tax on legal documents in the colonies. The Stamp Act also was the first direct tax (as opposed to indirect taxes such as customs duties) on the thirteen colonies, and it raised quite an uproar. The act required that a wide range of printed material be marked with a special stamp, for which a payment had to be made. For example, a school or college degree had to bear a stamp costing two pounds. A land deed had to have a stamp that cost from sixpence to five shillings. On each sheet of every copy of a newspaper a stamp had to appear

George Washington became an outstanding leader of the American Revolution and our first President. What qualities do you think our political leaders should have today?

Thomas Jefferson wrote the Declaration of Independence in 1776. What important principles did Jefferson proclaim in the Declaration of Independence?

that cost one halfpenny. To the colonists, these tax payments seemed unfair because the same taxes did not exist in England.

The Colonists Rebel While the colonists opposed these taxes, the British government sent more troops to the colonies and passed additional taxes. New taxes were imposed on glass, paper, paint, and tea purchased from abroad. Further changes in the laws on tea in 1773 led to the *Boston Tea Party,* in which a group of colonists, disguised as Indians, protested the tax by dumping tea from a ship into Boston Harbor. Parliament struck back by passing the **Coercive** (koe-UR-siv) **Acts.** These acts of 1774, which were aimed at punishing

the colonies for the Tea Party, were called the *Intolerable Acts* by the colonists. There were four acts. One act closed the port of Boston. Another canceled the charter of the Massachusetts colony. Another gave officials the authority to send a person to Great Britain for trial. This act angered the colonists because they would rather be tried by their peers, not by the British. The British were severe in their judgment against the colonists. And the last act required the colonists to quarter (house and feed) British soldiers.

The Quebec Act Still another act of Parliament that angered the colonists was the **Quebec Act** of 1774. It was intended not to punish the colonists but

367

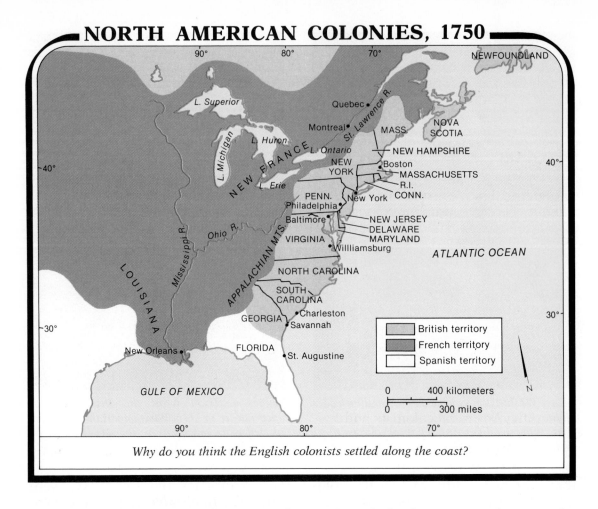

NORTH AMERICAN COLONIES, 1750

NEWFOUNDLAND

L. Superior

Quebec

Montreal

St. Lawrence R.

MASS.

NOVA SCOTIA

L. Michigan

L. Huron

NEW FRANCE

L. Ontario

NEW HAMPSHIRE

NEW YORK

Boston

MASSACHUSETTS

L. Erie

R.I.

CONN.

PENN.

New York

Philadelphia

NEW JERSEY

Ohio R.

Baltimore

DELAWARE

APPALACHIAN MTS.

VIRGINIA

MARYLAND

Mississippi R.

Williiamsburg

ATLANTIC OCEAN

LOUISIANA

NORTH CAROLINA

SOUTH CAROLINA

Charleston

GEORGIA

Savannah

New Orleans

FLORIDA

St. Augustine

	British territory
	French territory
	Spanish territory

GULF OF MEXICO

0   400 kilometers

0   300 miles

N

Why do you think the English colonists settled along the coast?

merely to update the Proclamation of 1763. The Quebec Act placed the country north of the Ohio River under control of the province of Quebec, in present-day Canada. It also put French civil law back into effect there in order to assure Roman Catholics their religious freedom. Despite the intentions of Parliament, the colonists saw the Quebec Act as another punishment. In addition, the colonists felt threatened because the province of Quebec was to be governed by an appointed council rather than an elected assembly.

First Continental Congress   These acts passed by Parliament served only

to disturb further many colonists who were already used to making their own laws. New Englanders had become accustomed to electing their own local officials at town meetings. In Virginia, the colonists had acquired the right to choose delegates to that colony's lawmaking body. The colonies showed their growing resistance to England by forming the *First Continental Congress* in 1774. Here the colonists expressed their grievances against British colonial policy.

Distance Is a Problem   In addition to the growing resistance to British rule, the geographic location of the

368

thirteen colonies continued to affect the situation. In the 1600's and 1700's, travel between Europe and North America took months. It was difficult for Great Britain to maintain strict control over people who lived thousands of miles away. Before 1763, few of Parliament's laws restricting colonial trade had been strongly enforced. However, after the French and Indian War, Parliament had become more interested in taxing the colonies. The colonists, on the other hand, were used to being left alone. They resented having their laws made by people who were so far away and who they felt did not represent them. One of the colonists' favorite sayings became "no taxation without representation."

Fighting Breaks Out   In 1775, British troops were sent to occupy Boston and enforce the British laws. The colonists rebelled against the presence of the troops. Open fighting broke out between the American colonists and British troops at Lexington and Concord in Massachusetts in April 1775. One month later, in May 1775, the *Second Continental Congress* assembled to prepare the colonies for war against England. The **Declaration of Independence** was drawn up by Thomas Jefferson and approved by the Continental Congress on July 4, 1776.

People Unite   People of many national backgrounds fought in the American Revolution and took part in making the new nation. Some, like George Washington, Thomas Jefferson, Betsy Ross, and Paul Revere, are now household names. The contributions of others have only recently been recognized. Crispus Attucks (AT-uks), a former slave, was killed in an early incident in the colonists' struggle against the British. This incident was called the Boston Massacre. Deborah Gannet, a black, fought as a soldier, like many other women. Haym Salomon (HIME SAHL-uh-mun), a Polish immigrant, gave most of his fortune to the patriot cause. Fredrich von Steuben (stoo-BEN), a German, and the Marquis de Lafayette (laff-ee-ET) of France served as officers on Washington's staff. On April 26, 1777, Sybil Ludington, a sixteen-year-old girl from New York, rode to spread the alarm about the advance of the English troops on Boston. Her ride was even longer than the famous ride of Paul Revere on April 18, 1775.

A New Nation Emerges   With the colonists' victory at Yorktown, Virginia, and French financial and military aid, America's victory over the British was decisive. By 1783, the new nation, called the United States of America, had extended its western boundaries to the Mississippi River. Thanks to the efforts of gifted leaders together with the hard work and adventurous spirit of their people, the former English colonies were united and beginning to emerge as an important world power.

SECTION REVIEW

1. Using the maps on pages 365 and 368, describe the colonial territories in the Americas belonging to England in 1750.
2. In your own words, briefly identify: the French and Indian War and the Declaration of Independence.
3. What seemed to be the main causes of the American Revolution?
▶ The American colonists rebelled against the king and declared themselves independent. Do you think a people are justified in rebelling against their rulers? Explain.

The French Revolution and Napoleon

THE FRENCH REVOLUTION

The successful struggle of the people of America against foreign control led to the establishment of an independent nation. In this new nation, the United States of America, a republic was established. Under this system, citizens governed themselves through elected officials. Power rested in the hands of the people. There were no nobles to enjoy special privileges, as there were in Europe. The American Declaration of Independence, the basis for the American Constitution, proclaimed that all citizens were equal and possessed certain rights that could not be taken away from them.

These ideas, which were exciting and revolutionary ones in the 1700's, had a profound influence on the people of Europe. In particular, the people of France felt these ideas could help them find ways to correct the injustices in their country.

The Old Regime in France　　**Old Regime** is a term used to describe French government, society, and life in the 1700's. The government of France was an absolute monarchy in which the king had absolute power. Under the Old Regime, the French people were divided into three groups. These groups were called **estates.** The *First Estate*, which made up less than one percent of the population, contained the churchmen. The *Second Estate*, which made up two percent of the population, was composed of the nobles. The *Third Estate* contained the rest of the population—the middle class or *bourgeoisie* (boohrzh-wah-ZEE), the peasants, merchants, professionals, and the workers.

The Estates　　The First and Second Estates enjoyed many privileges that originated in the Middle Ages. For example, nobles did not have to pay most taxes, which meant that nearly all the tax money had to come from the Third Estate. This was unfair to the people of the Third Estate who made the least amount of money and yet had to pay the bulk of the taxes. The clergy were also exempt from paying taxes, but they had the right to tax the members of the church. This meant that the Third Estate had yet another tax to pay.

This system was harsh and unjust. The lower classes did almost all the work but received few of the benefits. The upper classes enjoyed great wealth but paid little to support the government of France.

By the end of the eighteenth century, the Third Estate's resentment of the privileged French nobles had grown to the point of being unbearable.

The Philosophes Voltaire and other philosophes made new ideas about government popular during the Enlightenment. (See page 229.) The common people of France were now demanding reforms. They resented injustices such as heavy taxes and little personal freedom. Under the Old Regime, the people of the Third Estate had no rights. The king controlled everything.

The Bastille The king had the power to imprison anyone without a trial. A person might be sent to a royal prison without ever learning what crime he or she was charged with. For example, people could be secretly arrested and driven in closed carriages to the *Bastille* (ba-STEEL), an old royal prison in Paris. The prison wardens at the Bastille were forbidden to have any conversation with the prisoners.

Louis XVI During the late 1700's, France was ruled by Louis XVI, a weak ruler who was not prepared to deal with the complex affairs of state. When Louis XVI became king in 1774, he inherited a troubled country. The people were unhappy, and the treasury was empty. It is said that upon learning that he was the new king, Louis XVI exclaimed: "What a burden! At my age! And I have been taught nothing!"

King Louis XVI managed royal affairs so poorly that bankers were no longer willing to lend money to the king, who was already deeply in debt. Despite this, Louis, the queen, and the royal court continued to live in an extravagant, carefree style. The Austrian princess, Marie Antoinette (an-twah-NET), who had married Louis XVI, was so extravagant and ignorant of the misery of the people that she had a farmhouse built in the royal grounds at Versailles (vehr-SIE). There she and her ladies in waiting played as though they were peasants. They had no idea of what hardships French peasants actually faced.

IMPORTANT FRENCH PHILOSOPHES DURING THE ENLIGHTENMENT		
PHILOSOPHE	DATES	CONTRIBUTIONS
Voltaire	1694–1778	Wrote *Candide* and other works using satire to attack the injustices of his time; advocated religious tolerance and freedom of speech.
Montesquieu	1689–1755	French noble and author of *The Spirit of the Laws;* proposed that the power of government should be divided among legislative, executive, and judicial branches, which would check and balance one another.
Denis Diderot	1713–1784	Edited the *Encyclopedia,* a massive work that compiled the knowledge of the 1700's including new ideas about science and government.
Jean Jacques Rousseau	1712–1778	Wrote *The Social Contract;* stressed the goodness of human nature and suggested that good government should be based on the consent of the governed.

The Estates-General Louis XVI's ministers were unable to solve the country's money problems. Finally, King Louis decided to hold elections for an **Estates-General.** France's parliament had not met since 1614 because the French kings had become so powerful that they could rule without one. Now, however, the king hoped that the Estates-General, as elected representatives of the people, might be able to find more money for the monarchy. The Estates-General consisted of three assemblies. The churchmen of the First Estate elected 300 representatives to their own assembly, as did the nobles of the Second Estate. The representatives of the Third Estate were elected to represent all the other classes of France, who, of course, were the vast majority. King Louis decided to permit the Third Estate to elect as many representatives as the other two estates combined. However, according to tradition, the three estates had to meet and vote separately on matters brought before them.

The Estates-General met in May 1789, in Versailles, a town not far from Paris. The king expected the three estates to meet separately, as was the custom, but the Third Estate refused. Members of the Third Estate demanded that all three assemblies meet and vote as one. Otherwise, they said, the First and Second Estates could outvote the representatives of the vast majority on every issue by a vote of two against one. Some clergymen and nobles agreed with the Third Estate.

The National Assembly Is Formed King Louis tried to punish the Third Estate for its refusal to obey his order to meet as a separate assembly by locking its members out of their meeting place. This did not stop the Third Estate, however. Instead, the representatives gathered at a large indoor tennis court. There they took an oath, later called the *Tennis Court Oath*, not to disband until they had made political changes in France. Desperate for funds that could only be raised by the assemblies, the king finally decided to give in to the demands of the Third Estate. As a compromise, all three estates met together as one assembly, which promptly renamed itself the **National Assembly.**

The Storming of the Bastille A few months later, discontent in Paris broke out in violence. Shortages of grain in the country brought starving people into the city. The people believed that the nobles were the cause of the bread shortage. In July 1789, rumors began to circulate in Paris that the king was secretly planning to send troops against the city and disband the National Assembly. The people began to arm themselves, and on July 14, they attacked the old royal prison, the Bastille. The mob overcame its defenders, seized the prison, and released the six prisoners held there. Although none of the prisoners released had committed political crimes, the storming of the Bastille became a symbol of revolt against royal authority. Today the French people still observe July 14 as a national holiday.

The Great Fear The violence in Paris soon spread to the countryside. Homes of nobles were burned, and government officials, especially tax collectors, were killed. These uprisings frightened people more than the violence in Paris. The uprisings came to be known as the *Great Fear*. There was alarm among members of the National Assembly because the government seemed unable to put an end to peasant violence. It was up to the National Assembly to prevent violence from spreading. Its middle-class

This picture shows French revolutionaries storming the Bastille. What significance did this act have? Why is Bastille Day celebrated in France today?

members realized that to accomplish this, the assembly would first have to do away with the injustices the peasants had grown to resent.

The Citizens Receive Their Rights In August 1789, the National Assembly took action. It announced an end to the special privileges the nobles and other groups had held since the Middle Ages. **The Declaration of the Rights of Man** was issued, granting equality to all citizens. This document stated that all citizens had certain natural rights. It also declared that political power belonged to the people of France, not to the king. It promised freedom of speech, the press, and religion. This document was inspired by the American and British bills of rights and the philosophies of many French thinkers. Thomas Jefferson, who was then the American minister to France, was called upon for advice on the declaration.

A New Constitution When calm returned to France, the National Assembly set out to write a constitution. This was to make France a constitutional monarchy, in which a monarch rules but laws are made by representatives of the people. While the constitution was being drawn up, the assembly and Louis XVI shared in the governing of France.

The National Assembly also reorganized the government. The system of justice was improved. Restrictions on trade and on the conduct of business were done away with. Land owned by the church was confiscated and sold. The assembly also instituted the *Civil Constitution of the Clergy,* which put the church under state control. France was then divided into eighty-three administrative departments, each of equal size. Officials at all levels of local government were elected.

373

In 1791, many people in France believed the revolution was over. The country had undergone basic changes with relatively little violence. The king's power had been greatly limited, and many abuses of the Old Regime had ended. The middle classes were satisfied with the new government and wanted to prevent any more radical changes. But the peasants and city workers were still discontented. They wanted more wide-reaching reforms. Although the Declaration of the Rights of Man guaranteed equal rights, the peasants and workers still had no political power. This was because the new constitution stated that the right to vote was limited to citizens who paid a certain amount of taxes each year. The amount of taxes was set so high that most workers and peasants could not vote. Therefore the middle class had the most political power.

The National Assembly Is Upset Meanwhile, the nobles were looking for an opportunity to turn back the clock. Many of them left France with their families and went to neighboring countries. These nobles, known as *émigrés* (EM-uh-grayz), planned to return and restore the Old Regime. Others, who had remained in France, also hoped to restore the former powers of the king. Instead of accepting the moderate changes brought about between 1789 and 1791, Louis did his best to weaken the new government. He decided to flee France rather than accept his new role as limited monarch. In June 1791, the king and his family arranged an escape from Paris. Traveling in a carriage, they made their way across France toward the border, where foreign troops were waiting to escort them to safety in another country. Although Louis and Marie Antoinette had disguised themselves as a butler and a nursemaid, they made the mistake of traveling with a military escort. An alarm was sent ahead of the royal couple, and they were stopped by a detachment of troops and forced to return to Paris. After being returned to Paris, Louis XVI was treated as a prisoner of the National Assembly.

A New Assembly Is Formed The National Assembly finished the new French constitution by the end of 1791. The constitution permitted the king to remain at the head of the executive branch of the government, but it allowed him very little power. The lawmaking branch was elected by the taxpayers. It was named the **Legislative Assembly.** It met for the first time in October 1791.

Disagreement in the Assembly Within only a few months, the new government faced a serious crisis. There was wide disagreement in the new Legislative Assembly on the course of the revolution. The assembly was divided into three groups. One group, the *Girondists* (juh-RAHN-dusts), supported a constitutional monarchy. The radicals, dissatisfied with the constitution of 1791, pressed for a republic rather than a constitutional monarchy. Others had no program to propose at all. In the beginning, the radical members of the Legislative Assembly were able to assume leadership. They formed clubs in Paris that were centers of revolutionary propaganda. One of these clubs met in the house of the **Jacobin** (JAK-uh-buhn) Friars. Because of their meeting place, members of this radical club were called Jacobins.

The Jacobins The Jacobins' goal was to overthrow the monarchy and provide greater justice and opportunity for the common people. Soon Jacobin clubs sprang up all over France. The

Declaration of the Rights of Man, 1789

When the French National Assembly drew up a statement declaring the rights that all citizens possessed, it included ideas shared by the English and Americans. The French declaration is a positive statement of rights. The following are excerpts from the French declaration:

Citizens are born and remain free and equal in rights.

The aim of political institutions is the preservation of the natural and inalienable rights of citizens; these rights are liberty, property, security, and resistance to oppression.

Liberty consists in the freedom to do whatever causes no injury to others; thus the rights of a citizen have no limits except those that assure other citizens the enjoyment of the same rights; these limits must be determined by law.

Every citizen is presumed innocent until proved guilty.

The free communication of ideas and opinions is one of the most precious rights of citizens.

Adapted from: J. H. Stewart, trans. and ed. *A Documentary Survey of the French Revolution.* New York: Macmillan, 1951, pp. 113-115.

1. What rights did this document guarantee to all citizens?
2. How did this document establish equality for all French citizens?
3. What rights guaranteed to the French do you today possess?

three important leaders of the Jacobins were *Marat* (muh-RAH), *Danton* (dahn-TONE), and *Robespierre* (ROHBZ-pee-air). Marat founded a newspaper in which he carried on a campaign against social injustice. Robespierre was a lawyer and writer who wanted a new republic based on the ideals of virtue and justice. Danton was a gifted speaker in favor of the revolution. The Jacobins were able to draw large numbers of people all over France to their cause.

Opposition to Legislative Assembly Outside of France, there also was opposition to the Legislative Assembly, but for different reasons. Exiled nobles (*émigrés*) wished to see the downfall of the assembly and the restoration of the monarchy to full power. They had lost all their privileges under the laws passed by the new assembly and were hoping for a return to the Old Regime. Many of these exiled nobles spent their time plotting against the government of France and enlisting the support of foreign governments in attempts to overthrow the new regime.

France Becomes a Republic Weakened by internal disagreement and opposition from outside France, the moderate government under the Legislative Assembly was doomed to fail. The assembly feared Austria and Prussia would interfere and try to put the king back in power.

France Goes to War   In 1792, King Louis XVI was forced by the assembly to declare war on Austria. Shortly after, Prussia also entered the fighting. The rulers of these countries believed the weakening of the French monarchy was a threat to their own thrones. They intended to bring law and order back to France by restoring Louis XVI and the exiled nobility to their former position. They hoped an Austrian and Prussian victory would crush the revolutionary spirit that was spreading throughout Europe. But instead of restoring the power of the king and the nobility, the war did much to bring about their downfall. Moderate French people who favored a constitutional monarch objected to the return of absolute rule. They turned against the king and his supporters.

In the war, things at first went very badly for the French armies. France was in danger of foreign invasion. The French people reacted by staging an uprising in Paris in August 1792. Led by Jacobins and workers, they seized control of the city. The king was again taken prisoner, and the Legislative Assembly was ordered to pass a law abolishing the monarchy. Fearing the Parisian mobs that were controlled by the Jacobins, the assembly gave in. It took away all the king's powers and replaced him with a committee of six officials who would govern the country. Then the Legislative Assembly set the date for the election of a new assembly. Its task would be to decide the kind of government France should have and then to write a new constitution.

The National Convention   The new assembly was called the **National Convention.** It replaced the Legislative As-

sembly in September 1792. One of the first actions of the National Convention was to abolish the monarchy and establish the *First French Republic.* The Jacobin leader, Danton, became head of the government. Things also began to change on the battlefront. French armies were now winning victories over the Austrians and Prussians and declared they would assist other peoples who wished to overthrow their kings. To seal the fate of the French monarchy, the National Convention also put King Louis XVI on trial. Louis was declared guilty of treason and was beheaded by the guillotine on January 21, 1793.

Fear Spreads over Europe   Foreign rulers were frightened by the execution of the king. They feared that the French were planning to destroy monarchy everywhere and spread the French form of republicanism by force. For this reason, England, The Netherlands, Spain, and other countries joined with Austria and Prussia in the war against republican France. Of all these allies, England proved to be the strongest. From 1793 to 1815, England and France were at war almost continuously.

The Reign of Terror   While France was waging war against foreign enemies, the convention faced a number of revolts in and out of France against its authority. To meet these threats, the convention set up the *Committee of Public Safety.*

The Committee of Public Safety was headed by the Jacobin leader Robespierre. The first thing the committee did was to fortify the army. To do this, it started drafting all eligible men. The committee then launched a campaign to execute all the internal enemies of republicanism in France. Among the first victims to be guillotined during this pe-

During the Reign of Terror, many French men and women died under the blade of the guillotine. This picture shows Queen Marie Antoinette before she was executed. Why do you think so many people gathered to see this event?

riod was the queen of France, Marie Antoinette. This campaign was known as the *Reign of Terror*. It lasted from 1793 to 1794.

Soon, however, the committee began to use its power against anyone who tried to oppose the Jacobins. Thousands of French men and women, both monarchists and republicans, were arrested for political reasons and publicly executed without a fair trial. By the time the Reign of Terror was over, nearly 20,000 people had died under the blade of the guillotine.

The French People React While the country was in great danger, these harsh measures were accepted. But by the summer of 1794, internal revolts had been stopped, and the army was winning victories. This made the French people react and speak out against the Reign of Terror. However, many leaders of the revolution who dared oppose the policy of terror were executed. One of these was Danton. His ex-

ecution outraged many people. Public opinion turned against the executions and forced the National Convention to strip the Committee of Public Safety of its power. The Jacobins were suppressed, and their leader, Robespierre, and many of his followers were sent to the guillotine themselves. Another Jacobin leader, Marat, was murdered in his bathtub by Charlotte Corday, a young woman who wanted to deliver France from the radical Jacobins. After the execution of the Jacobins, the National Convention took a more moderate course. The people were anxious to see an end to terrorism and extremism.

The Directory Anxious to reestablish a moderate republic, the middle-class members of the National Convention drafted a new plan for a government called the **Directory.** Under the Directory, France was to remain a republic. Now it was to be governed by a lawmaking branch consisting of two houses. At the head of the government

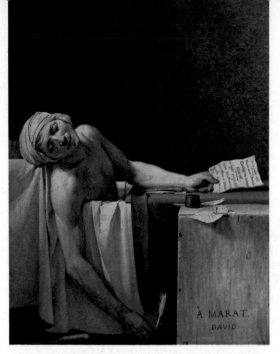

This painting by David shows the assassination of the Jacobin radical leader, Marat. Why are political leaders often the target for assassins?

was a committee of five directors, who were to carry out the laws. They were known as the *Directors.* The Directory governed France from 1795 to 1799. Unfortunately, the five directors in France's new government were unable to change the conditions that had brought about the revolution. The poor still lacked jobs and the necessities of life. Only the middle classes profited from the new laws made by the government. Corruption spread throughout the Directory, and the French people became discontented.

The End of the Republic   It was clear to the French people that the Directory had failed to solve France's problem. Debts, inefficiency, and corrupt political leaders continued to keep France in a weakened condition. Most people were tired of the war that had been going on since 1792. For solutions to these problems, the people of France turned to Napoleon.

The Rise of Napoleon   During the period 1795 to 1799, a young army officer named **Napoleon Bonaparte** (BOE-nuh-pahrt) came to be well known in France. Napoleon Bonaparte was born into a poor family in 1769 on Corsica, a French-controlled island about 112 kilometers (70 miles) from the coast of Italy. (See the Atlas.) At the age of nine, Napoleon began to study at military school, and as a young officer, he frequently distinguished himself in battle. In 1796, Napoleon married Josephine de Beauharnais (boe-ahr-NAY), a woman who had many important political connections.

In 1795, during the last days of the National Convention, Napoleon commanded troops that saved the convention from being attacked by a Paris mob. With the support of friends in the government, Napoleon was rapidly promoted. He was made a general at the age of 26. In 1796, he was placed in command of all the French troops fighting in Italy against the Austrians and other enemies.

Napoleon's Popularity Grows   By 1797, Napoleon had defeated France's enemies and forced them to make peace. He extended French control over all of northern Italy. Napoleon's growing popularity worried the Directors. So when Napoleon suggested that Britain could be weakened by cutting off its trade with the Near East, the Directors agreed. They felt that Napoleon's absence from France would reduce his popularity.

Napoleon was placed in command of an expedition that sailed to Egypt in 1798. The French had no trouble taking control of Egypt. But the expedition turned out to be a disaster. The French fleet supplying Napoleon's army was destroyed by the English Admiral

Nelson in the *Battle of the Nile*. Cut off from home, Napoleon realized he would be unable to win the victories he had hoped for. In 1799, he left his army in Egypt and managed to slip back secretly to France. There he joined a plot to overthrow the quickly deteriorating Directory.

The Consulate Is Formed On November 7, 1799, Napoleon and his supporters, backed by troops, overthrew the Directory in a *coup d' état* (kooday-TAH). A *coup d' état* is the removal of a government by force. Calling themselves *consuls*, Napoleon and two of his supporters took the place of the Directory. They established a military dictatorship known as the *Consulate*. Napoleon gave France another constitution. It preserved the republic and the elected lawmaking branch. The real political power, however, was in Napoleon's hands as First Consul. He was wise enough to realize he could not do away with many of the democratic changes that had come about in France since the revolution. He kept the reforms won by the French Revolution, but he found new ways to use them in establishing his personal dictatorship.

Code Napoleon Within France, Napoleon carried out many reforms the revolutionaries had worked on. He set up new and more efficient systems of government and tax collection. Public schools under government control were created, and a national banking system was established. A set of civil laws, the *Code Napoleon*, was the most important of Napoleon's reforms. It guaranteed that all citizens were equal before the law, and it reestablished their right to own property and worship as they wished. The Code Napoleon became the foundation for legal systems in other countries of western Europe.

Napoleon Bonaparte became First Consul of France in 1799. What impression of Napoleon do you get from this painting?

379

1. Mapping: Look at the size of France in the map on page 382. If you were to divide the French nation among the three estates discussed in this chapter, according to their power and wealth, how large a portion do you think each estate would receive? If you were to divide the French nation according to the percent of people belonging to each estate, how large a portion do you think each would receive?

2. In your own words, identify or define: Old Regime, First Estate, Second Estate, Third Estate, Louis XVI, Bastille, Jacobins, Estates-General, Reign of Terror, Napoleon.

3. Describe the economic and political position of the Third Estate in France before the revolution.

4. Why did the peasants in the country and the workers in the cities riot in 1789?

5. Who were the three outstanding leaders of the Jacobins? In what ways did the Jacobins discredit themselves with the French people?

6. In what ways did the Directory fail to govern France well?

7. What reforms did Napoleon introduce when he took power?

D Are there any advantages to having a government run by a dictator? Are there any disadvantages? Why would people want to live in a country where a dictator was in power? Explain.

THE AGE OF NAPOLEON

Napoleon was an ambitious leader. After firmly establishing his dictatorship as the First Consul, he proceeded to build France into an empire. Many French people believed that no one could take his place. They appreciated the strong government, order, and pros-

perity that Napoleon had restored in France. So in 1804, when Napoleon assumed the title of emperor, the French people approved of his action. During the coronation ceremonies in 1805, Napoleon, just as Charlemagne had done in the Middle Ages, took the crown from the pope and placed it upon his own head. In this way, he demonstrated that all political power was in his hands and that he owed his position to no one but himself. As emperor, Napoleon hoped to ensure that power would pass from one generation to the next generation in his own family.

Napoleon and the French Empire
Military conquests were an integral part of Napoleon's plan for building an empire. Just before Napoleon crowned himself emperor, war again broke out between England and France. Napoleon realized that while England's navy ruled the seas, he would never be able to dominate Europe completely. With this in mind, Napoleon planned to invade the British Isles. But the French navy was no match for the English warships. In 1805, the British fleet commanded by **Admiral Horatio Nelson** met the French and Spanish fleet at Cape Trafalgar (truh-FAL-gur), off the coast of Spain. During the **Battle of Trafalgar,** Nelson managed to destroy half of the French fleet without losing a single English ship. Nelson died in the course of the battle, but England's victory made that country the undisputed ruler of the seas.

Continental System After his failure to invade Britain, Napoleon decided to destroy England's power by cutting off its trade with Europe. Under his plan, which came to be known as the *Continental System,* Napoleon closed all ports under French control on the European continent to Britain. Al-

After crowning himself emperor, Napoleon then crowned his wife Josephine. What was the significance of this symbolic act?

lies of France were also obliged to cut off their trade with England.

France Expands Its Control Napoleon's other enemies were conquered one by one. Austria and Prussia were forced to sign peace treaties and give up lands to France. Napoleon made his brothers rulers of The Netherlands and Spain. By 1808, every major western European nation except England was either under French control or allied with France.

Reaction Against Napoleon On the surface it seemed that wherever it went, the French army brought the revolutionary ideas of liberty, equality, and fraternity, and Napoleon was cheered as a liberator. But the people conquered by the French quickly realized they had only exchanged one kind of absolute rule for another. Citizens were forced to house French soldiers in their homes, taxes were increased, and violators of French law were severely punished.

These conquered peoples were even drafted and sent off to fight Napoleon's wars. This treatment of the conquered peoples by the French encouraged the growth of national loyalty among the conquered people, loyalty to their homeland, not to Napoleon.

Napoleon Invades Spain In 1808, Napoleon's armies invaded Spain. He replaced the Spanish king with his brother, Joseph. This proved to be one of Napoleon's greatest errors. The Spanish people refused to accept a French ruler as king, and rebellion broke out. The British, wanting to put an end to Napoleon, sent help to the Spaniards. Resistance against the French continued for six years. This war was a strain on France's manpower. In 1812, with British help, the Spanish were able to drive the French out.

The Downfall of Napoleon When France went to war with England, the

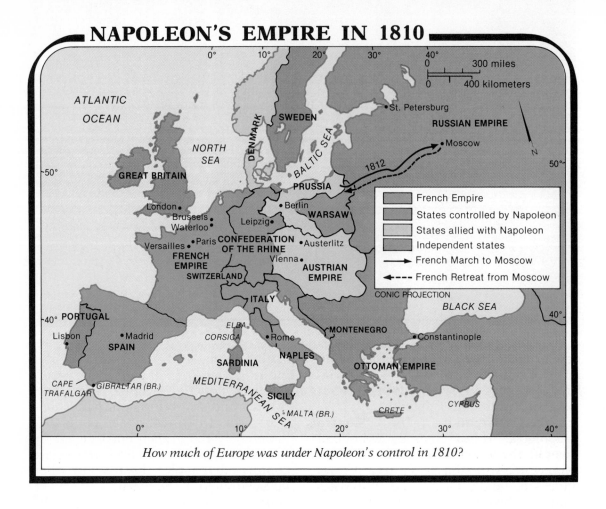

NAPOLEON'S EMPIRE IN 1810

ATLANTIC
OCEAN

NORTH
SEA

SWEDEN

DENMARK

BALTIC SEA

• St. Petersburg

RUSSIAN EMPIRE

• Moscow

GREAT BRITAIN

1812

50°

50°

London •

Brussels •
Waterloo •

• Berlin

PRUSSIA

WARSAW

Leipzig •

Versailles •
• Paris

CONFEDERATION
OF THE RHINE

FRENCH
EMPIRE

• Austerlitz

Vienna •

AUSTRIAN
EMPIRE

SWITZERLAND

	French Empire
	States controlled by Napoleon
	States allied with Napoleon
	Independent states
→	French March to Moscow
◄---	French Retreat from Moscow

CONIC PROJECTION

ITALY

BLACK SEA

40°

PORTUGAL

Lisbon •

• Madrid

SPAIN

ELBA

CORSICA

• Rome

MONTENEGRO

• Constantinople

40°

SARDINIA

NAPLES

OTTOMAN EMPIRE

CAPE
TRAFALGAR

• GIBRALTAR (BR.)

MEDITERRANEAN SEA

SICILY

• MALTA (BR.)

CRETE

CYPRUS

0°   10°   20°   30°   40°

How much of Europe was under Napoleon's control in 1810?

Russian tsar did not keep his promise to join Napoleon in the fight. Furthermore, in 1810, Russia started to trade with Britain. Napoleon, fearing that Russia's defiance might stir up resistance to French rule all over Europe, gathered an army of 600,000 soldiers and invaded Russia.

This invasion proved to be a disaster for Napoleon. The Russians retreated as Napoleon's army approached, burning their villages and fields as they went. The Russian army refused to meet Napoleon's soldiers in the field because they knew they were ill prepared to face the great French army. Instead, they con-

tinued to withdraw farther into the heartland of Russia. The two armies finally fought near Moscow at the *Battle of Borodino* (bor-uh-DEE-noe). The Russians were defeated, and Napoleon's path to Moscow was open. But when they arrived in Moscow, the French found the city almost deserted. Most of Moscow had been burned, leaving little shelter for the French army. **Napoleon in Moscow** Napoleon waited in Moscow, thinking Tsar Alexander would try to make peace now that the French had seized Russia's most famous city. Napoleon soon realized, however, that he was mistaken. The Russians were not going to make peace. They knew that time and the weather were on their side. After five weeks of waiting, Napoleon ordered a retreat. By this time, though, winter had set in. The lines supplying the French army with food and equipment were spread thin as the French marched through the ruined countryside. On the long march out of Russia, Napoleon's army suffered terrible hardships. The weather was severely cold and the Russian army frequently attacked the retreating French troops. Only 20,000 of Napoleon's soldiers lived to return from Russia.

Napoleon's Defeat   Napoleon hastened back to Paris before news of his failure in Russia reached France. Once in France, Napoleon began raising a new army to meet new alliances being formed against him. In 1813, Austria, England, Prussia, Russia, and Sweden made an agreement to make war on France once again. In October 1813, the armies of these allies attacked Napoleon near the German city of Leipzig (LIPE-sig) and inflicted a crushing defeat on him. In this battle, which has come to be known as the *Battle of the Nations,* Napoleon's allies deserted him. New revolts broke out in lands under French control, and the emperor was forced to retreat to France. In 1814, the allied armies captured Paris and Napoleon abdicated. The emperor was then sent into exile on *Elba*, a tiny island off the coast of Italy. He was sentenced to remain there for the rest of his life.

Battle of Waterloo   Nearly a year later, Napoleon escaped from the island of Elba and landed in France. He was greeted joyfully by the French people and soon raised another army. He again declared himself emperor, but his new reign lasted only 100 days. Alarmed by the reappearance of Napoleon, the allies formed an army, placing it under the leadership of the English general, the *Duke of Wellington*. Napoleon met this English army and the army of Prussia on a battlefield near the Belgian village of **Waterloo.** There the French army was defeated, and Napoleon surrendered to the allies. This time, Napoleon was taken to the island of *St. Helena*, off the west coast

After being defeated in Russia, Napoleon and his troops returned to France. What does this painting tell you about the hardships they suffered in Russia?

of Africa. He remained there under guard until his death in 1821.

Congress of Vienna   After Napoleon's defeat, peace returned to Europe. Leaders of the victorious powers met at the **Congress of Vienna** to try to agree on what was to be done with defeated France. The leading delegates at the Congress of Vienna were Tsar Alexander I of Russia, Lord Castlereagh (KAS-ul-ray) of Great Britain, Talleyrand (TAL-ee-rand) of France, and Prince von Metternich (MET-ur-nik) of Austria. **Metternich,** who acted as president of the Congress, arranged a series of lavish balls, hunts, festivals, and musicales for the entertainment of the delegates. The party-like atmosphere prompted one onlooker to exclaim: "The Congress dances but does not advance!"

Louis XVIII   In one of its first actions, the Congress replaced Napoleon with *King Louis XVIII*, a brother of the executed King Louis XVI. (Louis XVI's son was Louis XVII who died while still very young.) The lands conquered by Napoleon were taken away from France, along with some of its colonies, and the French boundaries were returned to about what they had been in the days of Louis XVI.

Europe Rearranged   At their meetings in Vienna, the leaders of the great powers rearranged the map of Europe. (See the map on page 386.) The British were allowed to keep many outposts they had seized during the long Napoleonic Wars. Austria gave up possessions in Belgium and southern Germany. In exchange, Austria took over territory in northern Italy and regained Polish lands once controlled by France. Russia took most of Poland, including much of what had belonged to Prussia. In exchange, the Prussians took land from the German kingdom of Saxony, which had been Napoleon's ally. All this shuffling of territory created mistrust and quarrels among the victors. Talleyrand, the French diplomat at Vienna, was able to secure favorable treatment for France through shrewd and skillful diplomacy. Before the Congress of Vienna, France had been a defeated country. Afterward, it was considered one of the important European powers.

The Balance of Power   Those who attended the Congress of Vienna were all guided by certain principles. They believed that the rights of the rulers of Europe before Napoleon should be respected and that their thrones should be returned to them. They also wanted to preserve peace in Europe and prevent further outbreaks of revolution. The way to do this, they believed, was to keep the balance of power from shifting in favor of any one nation. To prevent this they agreed to hold regular meetings to work out problems and thus avoid another war. They also pledged to take joint action against future revolutions wherever they might occur. All the upheavals, changes, and wars since the storming of the Bastille had created a fear of revolutions in the minds of many Europeans. They were terrified that others would follow the French example.

A New Period of Revolution   The ideas of the French Revolution, however, had not been forgotten. But the goals of the political reformers in Europe, who wanted more power for the common people, and the beliefs of the restored ruling classes were so far apart that compromise was almost impossible. For a while reformers continued to press their demands in a peaceful, nonviolent way. Rulers in western Europe rejected suggestions for reform.

Eventually, the reformers and their supporters revolted. The period from 1815 to 1848 was marked by almost constant revolution in Europe.

These revolutionary uprisings across Europe presented a serious problem to the great powers. Although they agreed that something should be done about the spread of revolution, they could not agree on how this should be done. The Russian tsar, for example, felt that the major powers should send troops into these countries to restore order. The British and others did not agree. They were not eager to establish a precedent that permitted large countries to interfere in the domestic affairs of others. This disagreement split the ranks of the great powers.

SECTION REVIEW

1. Mapping: Using the map of Europe on page 382, list the states controlled by and those allied with Napoleon in 1810.
2. In your own words, identify or define: Admiral Nelson, Leipzig, Elba, Duke of Wellington, Waterloo, Congress of Vienna, Talleyrand, Louis XVIII.
3. How did Napoleon's conquest of other countries encourage the nationalistic spirit of people in those countries?
4. How did the Russians defeat the great army of Napoleon in 1812?
5. How did the diplomats who attended the Congress of Vienna hope to preserve peace in Europe?
6. Why couldn't the great powers agree on a plan to suppress revolution in Europe?
> How do you think the leaders and people of a defeated country should be treated by the victors after a war?

EUROPE AFTER THE CONGRESS OF VIENNA

The restoration of European rulers to their rightful thrones was one of the major goals of the Congress of Vienna. However, this restoration did not ensure peace in the countries of western Europe. After the Congress of Vienna, European rulers found it almost impossible to turn the clock back to the days of the Old Regime. Some of the ideas that came out of the American and French revolutions had filtered down to the common people. However, the ruling classes opposed any kind of change. This brought them into conflict with many of the educated and liberal members of the middle class. Liberals were people who wanted constitutions, limiting the powers of government, and a parliament made up of elected representatives of the voters. They also believed in freedom of speech and freedom of assembly for all citizens.

Revolution Again Threatens France In France, the Bourbon family was restored to the throne after the defeat of Napoleon. But the powers of the Bourbon rulers were limited. This did not bother Louis XVIII, who ruled from 1814 to 1824. He was willing to let the people retain many of the reforms made between 1789 and 1815. In 1814, he granted his people a Constitution under which he agreed to share power with a *Chamber of Deputies* elected from the wealthier citizens and a *Chamber of Peers* made up of nobles.

Charles X When Louis XVIII died in 1824, his brother *Charles X* became king. Charles thought differently from his brother. He wanted to return to the ways of the Old Regime. Charles openly announced his intention of restoring the old privileges of the nobles

EUROPE AFTER THE CONGRESS OF VIENNA, 1815

ATLANTIC OCEAN

SWEDEN AND NORWAY

Stockholm

St. Petersburg

Moscow

RUSSIAN EMPIRE

NORTH SEA

GREAT BRITAIN

DENMARK

HELGOLAND (Br.)

50°

London

Amsterdam

NETH.

PRUSSIA

Berlin

Warsaw

RHINELAND (Pr.)

SAXONY

Paris

Carlsbad

FRANCE

Vienna

SWITZERLAND

AUSTRIAN EMPIRE

Budapest

Boundary of German Confederation

CONIC PROJECTION

BLACK SEA

PARMA

MODENA

TUSCANY

CORSICA

PAPAL STATES

MONTENEGRO

Adrianople

Constantinople

40°

PORTUGAL

Madrid

SARDINIA (Fr.)

Rome

Lisbon

SPAIN

BALEARIC ISLANDS (Sp.)

GIBRALTAR (Br.)

MEDITERRANEAN SEA

TWO SICILIES

OTTOMAN EMPIRE

Athens

CYPRUS

MALTA (Br.)

CRETE

0   300 miles
0   400 kilometers

N

50°

40°

Why did the other European nations divide France up at the Congress of Vienna?

and churchmen. He also wanted to repay them, using tax money, for the land that they had lost during the revolution.

In July 1830, Charles tried to abolish freedom of the press and take away the right to vote from his opponents. This was in violation of the Constitution, and the people of Paris revolted. Fighting broke out in the streets. Royal troops could not keep control of the capital, and King Charles was overthrown in what has been called the **Revolution of 1830.**

During this revolution, the city of Paris became a battleground. The peo-

ple set up overturned carts, boxes, tables, and whatever else they could find to barricade the streets. Armed revolutionaries crouched behind the barricades and fired upon the royal forces. From the roofs of the houses, families showered down brick, tiles, and rocks.

Louis Philippe Becomes King When Charles X was overthrown, many people in France favored setting up a republic once again. But the leadership of the new revolution was in the hands of liberals from the middle class. They favored a limited monarchy for France. *Louis Philippe*, a member of the Orleans family, was selected king. He ruled from 1830 to 1848. The liberals hoped that the supporters of monarchy would accept Louis Philippe because he was related to the Bourbon royal family. As a young man, Louis Philippe had volunteered to fight in the revolutionary army of 1792. This fact, it was hoped, would win support for him among the republicans.

Revolution Grows Again　As time went by, the government of Louis Philippe proved to be only a little more democratic than the government of Charles X. The right to vote was extended to the moderately wealthy middle class (substantial landowners), but the common people were not yet included. The working classes resented being overlooked by the government, and they resented the favor being shown their rich employers. As a result of government neglect, the workers began to turn to **socialism** as the solution to their problems. In a socialist society, the government, which represents the people, owns and operates the land and companies and handles the distribution of goods.

The Revolution of 1848　By 1848, Louis Philippe was facing growing opposition. In February 1848, the people of Paris again rose against the government. The king fled the capital. Mobs seized control of the government and proclaimed a republic. Middle-class moderates and working class radicals set up a temporary government and arranged for the election of a National Assembly, which would draw up a new constitution.

National Workshops　During this time, France was suffering an economic depression. To help the economy, the republicans and socialists promised that the government would provide jobs for all workers in projects called *National Workshops.* The promise of jobs brought about 100,000 workers to Paris. They remained idle, waiting for the government to fulfill its promises. But when it did, the jobs amounted to nothing. When the workshops failed to provide meaningful labor and were later abandoned, the people took to the streets again in bloody protest.

The Second Republic　The new wave of violence angered and alarmed people all over France. When order was restored, the National Assembly decided to draw up a plan for a democratic government and wrote a new constitution. The constitution gave back the rights the people had when Napoleon was in power. The people were to elect their own president to head the **Second Republic.**

In the first election in 1848, *Louis Napoleon,* a nephew of the former emperor, won the election as the new president of France by a large majority. Because of his overwhelming victory, Louis considered that he, rather than the new legislature, represented the will of the people. Louis Napoleon also wished to follow in the footsteps of his famous uncle, so he dissolved the government and declared himself emperor. Thus in 1852, the Second Republic gave way to the *Second Empire.* In less than fifty years, the French people had lived under three different forms of government: monarchy, empire, and republic.

1848—A Year of Revolution　When the French people rose in 1830 to overthrow King Charles X, the Belgians, Poles, Italians, and Germans also revolted in pursuit of greater liberty. In 1848, much the same thing happened. News of the successful revolution against the monarchy in France touched off a series of revolts in Austria, Italy, and Germany.

This painting shows Parisian citizens and the military fighting at the rue Culture Ste. Catherine during the Revolution of 1848. Do all revolutions lead to violence?

Hungary Revolts In the Austrian Empire, the Hungarians demanded independence. Louis Kossuth (KAH-sooth) led the Hungarians in their demands for independence from Austria. Kossuth was a great orator, and his speeches in the Hungarian lawmaking body inspired revolts throughout the empire. Taken by surprise at the degree of public support for the rebels, the Austrian emperor promised a constitution and the abolition of censorship. Revolution then spread to the non-German areas of the Austrian empire. The Slavic people of Bohemia demanded the right to govern their own affairs, which Emperor Ferdinand granted. In northern Italy, Austrian troops were under attack by Italians.

Before the end of 1849, the new Austrian emperor, Franz Josef, who ruled from 1848 to 1916, took the offensive and suppressed the rebels. The Russian tsar, fearing the revolt would spread to Russian Poland, helped Austria. The Russian tsar also sent his troops to put down the revolution in Hungary. Many Hungarians who surrendered were executed by the Russians. Austrian troops then restored order in other parts of the empire.

Italy Revolts In northern Italy, the rebels tried to drive out Austrian forces. Under the leadership of Giuseppe Mazzini (MAHT-see-nee), an attempt was made to unite the Italian peninsula as a republic. Violence broke out in many parts of Italy. Republics were es-

388

tablished in Rome and Florence. Many people in Europe were angered when the rebels seized the pope and took over Rome. When Louis Napoleon sent troops to rescue Rome from the rebels, many Italians had already turned against the revolution and were ready to side with the foreign invader. As in Austria, revolution in Italy failed partly because of foreign intervention.

Germany Revolts   Germans wanted to end Prussia's control over them. Liberals began to plan for a national assembly to draft a constitution. Rioting took place in Berlin between the army and revolutionaries. Following this, the Prussian king promised government reforms. Among the reforms promised were a parliament, a constitution, and support for a united Germany. Representatives from all over Germany met in the city of Frankfurt to plan a government that would unite all the German-speaking kingdoms.

Despite the revolutionary talk at the Frankfurt Assembly, very few real gains resulted. The assembly's idea of what the government should be differed from what most people wanted. Because of this the people's support lessened. This weakened the assembly, and supporters of King Frederick Wilhelm IV had a chance to rally their forces and undo the reformers' work. The army, which remained loyal to the king, was soon in control of Berlin. The Frankfurt Assembly was disbanded in June 1849. At that time, the king issued his own constitution, which kept nearly all of the power in the hands of the king and the ruling classes.

SECTION REVIEW

1. Mapping: Using the map on page 386 and the information in the text, name those countries that had rebellions in 1848. What proportion of the lands in western Europe were involved in these rebellions?
2. In your own words, identify or define: the Bourbon rulers, Louis Philippe, the liberals, Louis Napoleon, Mazzini, Franz Josef.
3. Why did the rulers of Europe find it almost impossible to return to the ways of the Old Regime after the Congress of Vienna?
4. Why were Italy and Germany unsuccessful in their attempts at unification?
    Sometimes one country interferes with the internal happenings of another country. Do you think a country has the right to do this? Explain.

chapter 21

Other American Revolutions and Growth of the Americas

INDEPENDENCE SPREADS

Soon after the American and French revolutions, colonists in South America began to act to free themselves from Spanish rule. After reading the two documents that were the products of both the American and French revolutions—the Declaration of Independence and the Declaration of the Rights of Man—the Spanish colonists felt that they too were entitled to determine how they would be governed. Spain, afraid of rebellion, tried to suppress all information about the revolutions. Because of this, copies of the American and French declarations had to be smuggled into South America.

Injustices in Latin America There were many social injustices in the South American colonies. For example, like French society during the Old Regime, Latin American society was strictly divided into classes. The upper class consisted of the officials who were born in Europe and held high government jobs in the colonies and of the higher clergy. The next group was made up of the *creoles* (KREE-oles), people of Spanish descent who had been born in the colonies. The *mestizos* (me-STEE-zoes), those with mixed White and Indian blood, were next on the social scale, followed by the

Indians. Class lines were rigid. It was not possible to cross from one class to another. This meant that only those born in Europe could have a say in the government. Because of Spain's mercantilist policies, the colonies were forced to trade only with Spain. These things, together with the news of the American and French revolutions, caused wide unrest throughout Latin America.

Haiti's Success Before 1800, there was only one successful revolt in South America. This revolt occurred on the western part of the island of Hispaniola (his-pun-YOE-luh), which was controlled by France. In 1791, under the leadership of *Pierre Dominique Toussaint L'Ouverture* (TOO-sa^n LOO-vur-tyoor), the slave colonists tried to take over the island. But the French were able to capture Toussaint L'Ouverture, who eventually died in prison. Soon the colonists rose up again, this time under another former slave, *Jean-Jacques Dessalines* (day-suh-LEEN). Weakened by malaria and yellow fever, the French soldiers were defeated by Dessalines. He and his army of former slaves, aided by the British, drove out the French. By 1804, the island became an independent nation known as *Haiti* (HAY-tee).

South Americans Free Themselves The revolutionaries in South America,

Pierre Dominique Toussaint L'Ouverture led the people of Haiti in a rebellion against French rule. What characteristics do you think are necessary to be a rebel leader?

Spaniards then rebelled against their French ruler. While Spain was in this weakened position, revolutionaries in some South American colonies seized upon this turn of events to proclaim themselves free of Spanish rule. This started many revolutions throughout South America.

Mexico Becomes Independent When the Mexicans learned that Joseph Bonaparte had become king of Spain, they felt the time was right to seize their independence. Their fight for independence began with a priest named *Miguel Hidalgo* (ih-DAHL-goe). For years, Hidalgo had been interested in the ideas put forth by the French revolutionaries. Hidalgo, together with his Indian parishioners, planned an uprising against Spanish rule that began in 1810. Several victories brought Hidalgo and his army to Mexico City, the capital. But Hidalgo's forces were defeated by Spain's loyal army. In 1811, Hidalgo and some of the revolutionaries were captured and executed.

The fight for independence was continued under another priest, *José Morelos* (moe-RAY-lose). Morelos called for a congress of rebels to meet in a small town in southern Mexico. On November 6, 1813, they declared themselves free and independent of Spanish or any other European rule. However, the mostly Indian forces of Morelos were finally defeated, and Morelos was captured and executed in 1815.

Creole Involvement In 1820, a revolt occurred in Spain that was basically an uprising of the army. General Rafael del Riego (dell ree-AY-goe) headed the revolt against King Ferdinand VII's regime. To end the rebellion, the king was forced to abide by the liberal Constitution of 1812. This limited the power of the Spanish king

and the thousands who joined them, finally received their opportunity to revolt when Napoleon (nuh-POLE-yun) rose to power. As you know, by 1808 Spain was conquered by Napoleon, and his brother Joseph was placed on the Spanish throne. Many

Spurred by the independence movements in France and the United States, Simón Bolívar (left) of Venezuela and José Francisco de San Martín (right) of Argentina rose to lead their people in their struggle for independence. How have political movements in other countries affected your society?

and the Roman Catholic Church. This turn of events in Spain influenced the creoles in Mexico to act.

The creoles were a conservative group. They liked the position they held in Mexico's society. They supported the church and the king, and they wanted things to remain the same. Realizing that the weakening of the king's and church's authority threatened their own position, the creoles decided to separate from Spain. They needed to declare Mexico's independence so things would continue to be in their favor. *Agustín de Iturbide* (ee-toor-BEE-thay), the son of a Spanish immigrant and a creole mother, became the creoles' leader. During the revolts led by Hidalgo and Morelos, Iturbide had fought for Spain; now his loyalties to Mexico and the Roman Catholic Church made him a rebel against the *Cortés* (the lawmaking body) in Spain. He succeeded in uniting much of Mexico against Spanish policy. By 1821,

Mexico had become an independent country.

Bolívar and San Martín In 1811, revolutionists in Paraguay declared their independence from Spain. Argentina and Uruguay followed, declaring their freedom. **Simón Bolívar** (buh-LEE-vahr) began the fight for independence in Venezuela (ven-uz-WAY-luh). Bolívar tried to attack the Spanish army by sea, but the attempt was a failure. He then decided he might stand a better chance of victory if he attacked by land. Bolívar attacked the Spanish armies' weakest point, which was at New Granada. To do this, Bolívar and his army made a dangerous crossing of the Andes Mountains. Joining forces with revolutionaries at New Granada, Bolívar defeated the Spanish army. This victory cleared the way for Venezuela's independence. Bolívar came to be known as the Liberator. By the early 1820's, he had helped to lead Colombia, Peru, Venezuela, and Bolivia to independence. (See map on p. 394.)

Other South American colonists achieved independence when *José Francisco de San Martín* and his forces crossed the Andes Mountains and helped to free Chile and Peru. Chile became independent in 1818 and Peru in 1821. Bolívar and his forces came to the aid of San Martín. When the two leaders joined, they could not agree on how to drive the Spanish from the rest of Peru. In 1822, rather than endanger the independence movement in a clash with Bolívar over leadership, San Martín quietly retired from the scene.

Spain's Control Crumbles Through the efforts of revolutionaries, the Spanish empire in South America had crumbled by 1825. In only a few years, the countries of present-day Latin America had emerged.

Many of the leaders of Latin American independence movements hoped to see a union of Spanish-speaking states in Latin America, much like the United States of America. However, this dream of unity never came to pass. Rivalries and geographical barriers, among other things, managed to split regions into smaller nations. When Simón Bolívar died in 1820, conflicts had broken out in Latin American nations. "I have plowed the sea," Bolívar said on his deathbed, meaning his work for a united Latin America failed.

Brazil Becomes Independent Portugal suffered the same fate as Spain in South America. As he had unintentionally done in the Spanish colonies, Napoleon also helped the independence movement in Brazil. Brazilian independence began with *Dom João* (ZHWOW), who had managed the Portuguese throne for his mother, the queen. In 1808, Dom João and many members of the Portuguese royal court were forced to flee Napoleon's troops and sailed to Brazil. Dom João remained in Brazil for about thirteen years. His presence there changed the status of Brazil from a colony to a kingdom. Brazil was now equal with its former ruling country, Portugal.

When Napoleon's forces had finally been defeated in Europe, the people of Portugal demanded that their ruler come home. Dom João had become ruler of Portugal as well as Brazil upon the death of his mother in 1816.

However, before he returned to Portugal in 1821, João arranged for his son to remain in Brazil. João had sensed the growing spirit of independence in Brazil and favored it. But he suspected that the Cortes (the Portuguese lawmaking body) would not allow Brazil to remain a kingdom. If Brazil became independent, João wanted his son to head the new government there.

Brazil Declares Its Independence João's suspicions were correct. After his arrival, the Cortes attempted to make Brazil a colony again. The Cortes also demanded that the king's son, *Dom Pedro*, return to Portugal. Instead, Dom Pedro, with the backing of many Brazilians, proclaimed Brazil independent of Portugal in 1822. Portugal was in no position to fight a war and recognized the independence of Brazil. This was the only colony to declare its independence without war.

The Americas Continue to Grow The success of revolutions in North and South America inspired many people in Central America to demand independence. Led by *José Mateas Delgado* (mah-TAY-ahs dell-GAH-doe), a convention was called at Guatemala City in 1821. The representatives proclaimed themselves independent of

NEW NATIONS OF LATIN AMERICA, 1840

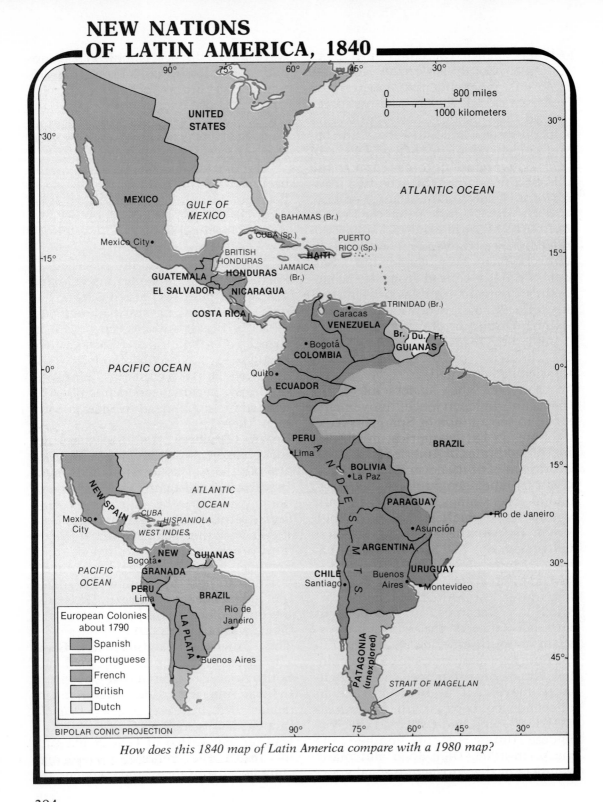

0 ——— 800 miles
0 ——— 1000 kilometers

UNITED STATES

ATLANTIC OCEAN

MEXICO

GULF OF MEXICO

Mexico City •

BAHAMAS (Br.)

CUBA (Sp.)

PUERTO RICO (Sp.)

BRITISH HONDURAS

JAMAICA (Br.)

HAITI

GUATEMALA   HONDURAS

EL SALVADOR   NICARAGUA

COSTA RICA

TRINIDAD (Br.)

Caracas •

VENEZUELA

Br. Du. Fr.
GUIANAS

• Bogotá
COLOMBIA

PACIFIC OCEAN

Quito •

ECUADOR

PERU
• Lima

BRAZIL

A N D E S   M T S.

BOLIVIA
• La Paz

PARAGUAY

• Rio de Janeiro

• Asunción

ARGENTINA

URUGUAY

CHILE
Santiago •

Buenos Aires •

• Montevideo

PATAGONIA (unexplored)

STRAIT OF MAGELLAN

Inset map

ATLANTIC OCEAN

NEW SPAIN

Mexico City •

CUBA   HISPANIOLA

WEST INDIES

GUIANAS

NEW GRANADA

Bogotá •

PACIFIC OCEAN

PERU
Lima •

BRAZIL

Rio de Janeiro •

LA PLATA

Buenos Aires •

European Colonies about 1790

- Spanish
- Portuguese
- French
- British
- Dutch

BIPOLAR CONIC PROJECTION

How does this 1840 map of Latin America compare with a 1980 map?

Spain. Their reasons for seeking freedom were the same as those that had led the Mexicans to revolt, and for a short time the Central Americans accepted the rule of Mexico's new leader, Iturbide. In the late 1830's, however, political divisions were established in Central America. Representatives from the countries of Guatemala, El Salvador, Honduras, Nicaragua, and Costa Rica met and formed the *United Provinces of Central America.*

Panama Becomes Independent
Panama was the last independent Central American country to be created. Panamanian independence came about for different reasons. In 1903, the United States acquired the right to build a canal across the narrowest part of Panama that would connect the Atlantic and Pacific oceans. Ships going from one coast of North America to the other could pass through the canal and would not have to sail around the dangerous southern tip of South America. This would save sailing a distance of some 12,800 kilometers (8,000 miles). Because of the number of jobs that such an undertaking would offer, the people of Panama wanted the canal built. However, Panama was a province of Colombia, and when it was reported that Colombia had rejected the proposed treaty with the United States, the people of Panama revolted against their rulers. Colombia attempted to send troops into Panama to put down the uprising, but Theodore Roosevelt, who was President of the United States at the time, ordered the United States fleet to block the path of the Colombian troops. Roosevelt argued that he was carrying out the terms of a treaty Colombia had agreed to in 1846. At that time, Colombia had granted the United States the right to ship goods across

Panama and to protect their transport.

The Revolution Is Successful
Because of Roosevelt's intervention, the Panamanian revolt was successful, and in 1903 President Roosevelt signed a treaty recognizing Panama as a new country. In return, Panama gave the United States possession of a strip of land called the *Canal Zone.* This zone extended for 8 kilometers (5 miles) on either side of the canal and remained a United States possession until 1979, when it was given back to Panama.

Self-Rule for Canada Far to the north, Canada remained a colony of England at the end of the French and Indian War. In the early 1800's, some groups of Canadians demanded that the British Parliament allow more local representation. Two rebellions by Canadians wanting more independence occurred, but they were not successful. Britain asked Canada's governor general, Lord Durham, to survey conditions in Canada and to make a report. As a result of *Durham's report,* Canadian provinces were granted self-rule. Canadian demands continued until 1867 when Parliament united the provinces into the *Dominion of Canada,* which remained a self-governing part of the British Empire. In 1921, it became an independent member of the *British Commonwealth of Nations.* Canada remained a sovereign state under the English monarch until 1982.

The End of Colonial Rule With few exceptions, most of the colonial empires had disappeared in both North and South America by the mid 1800's. However, Canada, the Bermudas, Jamaica, and several other islands in the West Indies were still under British rule. The Dutch, French, and British each had managed to retain a strip of the Guianas in South America. For the

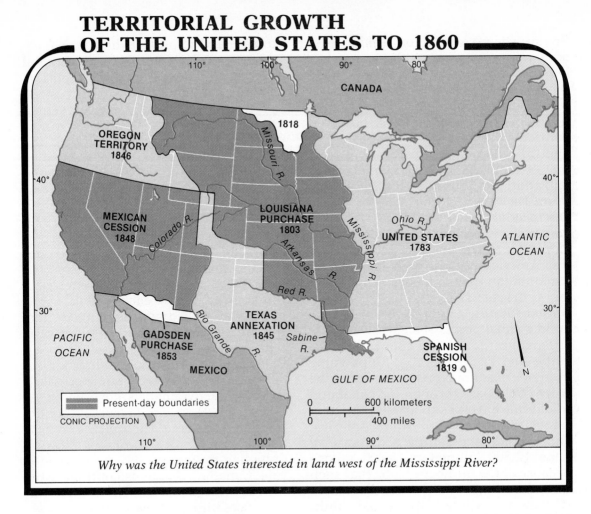

TERRITORIAL GROWTH OF THE UNITED STATES TO 1860

CANADA

1818

OREGON TERRITORY 1846

MEXICAN CESSION 1848

Colorado R.

LOUISIANA PURCHASE 1803

Missouri R.

Arkansas R.

Ohio R.

Mississippi R.

UNITED STATES 1783

ATLANTIC OCEAN

Red R.

PACIFIC OCEAN

GADSDEN PURCHASE 1853

Rio Grande R.

TEXAS ANNEXATION 1845

Sabine R.

SPANISH CESSION 1819

N

MEXICO

GULF OF MEXICO

Present-day boundaries

CONIC PROJECTION

0   600 kilometers

0   400 miles

Why was the United States interested in land west of the Mississippi River?

rest of the nations of the Americas, their position was clearly stated in 1823 when United States President James Monroe issued a warning to European nations against attempts at colonization or interference in the Western Hemisphere. This pronouncement came to be known as the **Monroe Doctrine** and has been a basis for American foreign policy for more than 150 years.

Expansion of the United States Besides his indirect role in Latin American independence movements, Napoleon also had a part in the expansion of the United States. Napoleon was anx-

ious to sell the American lands he had acquired from Spain in the Napoleonic Wars. He needed money to finance his wars on the European continent, and in 1803 he found a buyer—the United States. President Thomas Jefferson purchased the *Louisiana Territory* from France.

After the War of 1812, Great Britain and the United States reached an agreement on part of the American-Canadian border. Today this border is the longest undefended political boundary in the world. In 1819, the United States acquired East and West Florida from Spain.

ALIGNMENT OF STATES AND TERRITORIES IN 1861

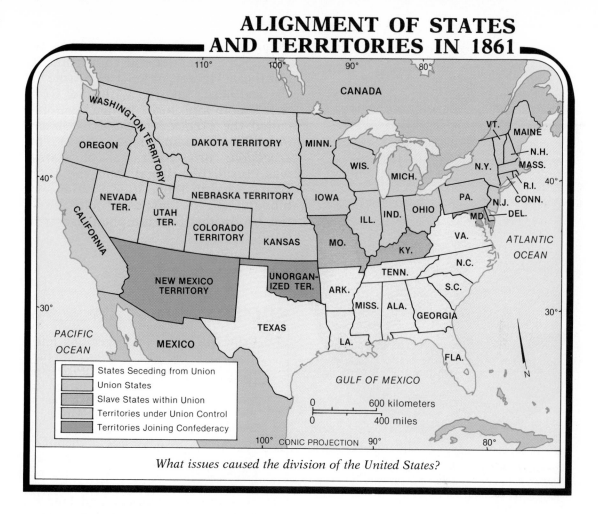

What issues caused the division of the United States?

Texas Declares Its Independence Texas declared its independence from Mexico in 1836. Under the leadership of Sam Houston, Stephen F. Austin, and Lorenzo de Zavala (zuh-VAHL-uh), Texas won its independence. It remained a republic for nine years and then became a part of the United States in 1845. A year later, the United States waged a successful two-year war with Mexico over the proper boundaries between the two countries. As a result of the war, the United States acquired the territory that is now the states of New Mexico, Arizona, Nevada, California, southern Colorado, and Utah. The *Oregon Settlement* with Great Britain in 1846 granted the United States full claim to the present states of Washington, Oregon, and Idaho, and parts of Montana and Wyoming. In 1853, the United States acquired from Mexico a section of land in present-day Arizona and New Mexico. This acquisition, known as the *Gadsden Purchase*, set the present continental boundaries of the United States.

The Civil War The development of newly acquired lands by the United States led to a need for a large labor supply. In turn, this led to increased slavery in the United States. Slavery

397

On April 14, 1865, five days after General Lee's surrender, Abraham Lincoln was assassinated. What do you think Lincoln's assassination meant to the nation?

major needs of the South would be ignored by the federal government. Southern leaders urged the people in the southern states to withdraw from the Union and form a new country called the *Confederate States of America.* (See the map on page 397.) The *secession,* or withdrawal of states, was considered illegal, and the Civil War started in 1861. After a bitter and bloody struggle that lasted four years, the Union finally triumphed over the Confederacy.

eventually came to be one of the issues that caused the outbreak of the **Civil War.**

Northerners who opposed the institution of slavery pointed out the evils of such a system. There were few slaves in the North, mainly because slavery was not profitable there. In 1860, Abraham Lincoln was elected President by voters who were opposed to the expansion of slavery into the new territories.

To many southerners, Lincoln's election meant that slavery would never be allowed to exist in any states created from the newly acquired western lands. Many also were sure that the

SECTION REVIEW

1. Using the maps on pages 365 and 394, and the information in the text, describe colonial territories in the New World belonging to Spain and Portugal. Between which years did the countries of Latin America receive their freedom?

2. In your own words, briefly identify: Simón Bolívar, Joseph Bonaparte, Canal Zone, Confederate States of America.

3. How did the American and French revolutions affect the independence movements in Latin America?

4. What effect did the expansion of Napoleon's power in Europe have on the countries of Latin America? on the United States?

5. How did the expansion of the United States become one of the causes of the Civil War?

◗ The people of the Americas all achieved independence from the European countries that controlled them, but they revolted for many different reasons. Do most people rebel because of a single reason or for many reasons? Explain your answer.

chapter 22

The Industrial Revolution in the West

WHAT WAS THE INDUSTRIAL REVOLUTION?

The **Industrial Revolution** is the name given to a series of changes in manufacturing and trade during the eighteenth and nineteenth centuries. Over a period of about 100 years, new inventions and ways of producing goods developed more rapidly than ever before. Key changes first took place in England during the 1700's. In the 1800's, similar changes came about in other countries of western Europe, North America, and Latin America.

Population Shifts The Industrial Revolution was not simply a wave of new inventions. It was much more than that. The whole pattern of economic life in England, western Europe, and America was changed. Simple, hand-operated tools were replaced by machines. No longer were goods made at home by individual workers. Large-scale production was carried on in factories that employed great numbers of workers.

The Industrial Revolution also brought about a shift in the population. People gradually moved from rural areas to the cities where factories were being built and jobs being offered. Old cities became crowded. New cities were founded and grew rapidly. Merchants searched for new markets for machine-made goods and new sources of raw materials. Better methods of trade, transportation, and business organization had to be developed to keep up with the large-scale system of production now operating.

Changes in Agriculture As feudalism and serfdom slowly died in Europe, the ownership of land changed. By the 1700's, the farm lands of Europe no longer were in the hands only of the noble families. Part of the farm lands now belonged to independent peasant farmers and wealthy merchants. Farming methods, however, had not changed. There had been few improvements in farming since the Middle Ages. The medieval *three field system* was still in use. Under this system, one third of a farmer's land was cultivated each year, another third was used for pasture, and one third was left unplanted to let the soil restore itself. *Strip farming* also was commonly practiced. Medieval villages had divided the land among the peasants so that each household received one strip of good soil, one strip of poor soil, and so on. The strips, however, were not necessarily near one another, which resulted in a great waste of time.

Medieval tools like the hoe were still being used in the 1700's by farmers to prepare the soil for planting. When a crop was planted, the farmer simply walked across the fields throwing seeds by hand to all sides. Many farmers were content with this method, which had been handed down to them over the generations.

New Farming Methods   In the early 1700's, however, a number of people began seeking ways to improve farming. Among them was an Englishman named *Jethro Tull*. After experimenting on his own, Tull concluded that most crops grow best in soil that is broken up thoroughly before seeds are planted. To prepare the soil, he suggested the use of machines called cultivators.

Tull also invented a machine for planting seeds. This machine dug holes in the ground, placed seeds in the holes, and covered them up with dirt. This new method of planting proved to be very efficient. But it was difficult to persuade farmers to change old methods.

Another English pioneer in agriculture was *Charles Townshend*, a nobleman. Townshend proved that a field need not lie unplanted every third year to prevent soil exhaustion. Instead, such crops as clover or turnips could be planted once every three years to enrich the soil. The clover and turnips then could be harvested and fed to livestock in winter. Most farmers slaughtered their livestock in winter from lack of feed for the animals. Townshend's proposals meant that livestock would not have to be slaughtered.

Improvements were also made in the breeding of cattle and sheep as sources of food. *Robert Bakewell*, another English farmer, developed methods for breeding that produced larger, heavier animals that could be raised for meat. Until then, livestock was mainly for dairy products, hides, and wool.

Large Landowners   The large landowners were the leaders in introducing agricultural changes. The new discoveries and improved methods of farming promised them great income from their lands. For this reason, large landowners were willing to set aside fields or pastures for experiments. They also were able to invest money in trying out new machines. When the changes in agriculture proved to be successful, large landowners were eager to buy more land to place under cultivation. They bought the farms of small landowners and purchased uncultivated lands. The government in England, for example, helped them by allowing the purchase of common or public lands. This takeover of common lands by landowners was known as the **enclosure movement.** It took its name from the practice of enclosing or fencing the land. The enclosure movement reached its peak in England between 1750 and 1810, when laws were passed by Parliament making it possible for individuals to purchase common lands. By 1850, all the open fields of England were gone.

Resistance to Change   The small farmers of England resisted the changes being made in agriculture and they could not afford to set aside fields or grazing lands for agricultural experiments. Nor did they have the money to invest in machines. Many were hurt by the enclosure of common lands that they had used as pastures freely until the land was sold to large landowners. Many small farmers in England had to give up farming. Some sold their land and moved to the cities. There, many found jobs in the new factories. Others became workers on the farms belonging to the large landowners.

At the same time many small farmers were giving up farming, the use of

DEVELOPMENTS IN AGRICULTURE AND INDUSTRY
18TH AND 19TH CENTURIES

Inventor	Invention/Year	Importance
Charles Townshend	Four-year rotation of crops and fields — 1700's	Helped nourish soil by introducing new crops. Led to increased production.
Jethro Tull	Developed an efficient seed drill — 1700's	Planted seed deep and in straight rows, thereby wasting less seed and insuring that seeds grow into plants. Led to increased efficiency in agriculture.
Thomas Newcomen	Developed a practical steam engine — 1705	Developed the first practical steam engine. It was also used to pump water from coal mines.
Abraham Darby	Developed the process of coking to remove chemical impurities from coal — 1713	Coke was used in smelters to make iron. Use of iron was one of the important advances in industry.
John Kay	Flying shuttle — 1733	The time required to weave cloth from yarn was cut in half.
James Hargreaves	Spinning jenny — 1770	Made it possible to spin many threads at the same time.
James Watt	Improved the steam engine for industrial use — 1769	Produced power to drive all kinds of machines.
John Wilkinson	Boring machine — 1775	Made it possible to drill a precise hole in machinery to increase efficiency.
Edmund Cartwright	Steam-powered loom — 1785	Replaced hand-operated loom to produce woven cloth faster than before.
Eli Whitney	Cotton gin — 1793	Eliminated the need to pick seeds out of cotton by hand. This increased the amount of cotton available for textile plants.
Richard Trevithick	Built the first steam locomotive — early 1800's	Made it possible to haul freight and passengers faster than horse-drawn methods. Amount of time needed to transport goods and people was cut down.
Robert Fulton	Steamboat — 1807	Made it possible to sail ships by using steam.
George Stephenson	Improved the steam locomotive — 1829	Made it possible to haul heavier loads at faster speeds.
Cyrus McCormick	Reaper — 1834	Eliminated the need to cut wheat by hand.

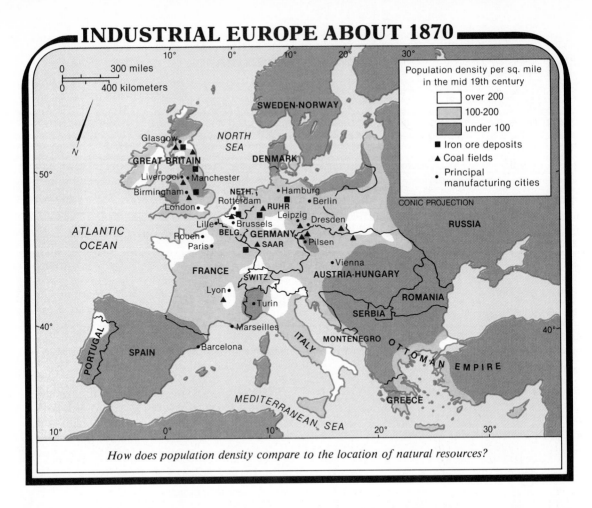

Population density per sq. mile in the mid 19th century

- over 200
- 100-200
- under 100
- ■ Iron ore deposits
- ▲ Coal fields
- • Principal manufacturing cities

CONIC PROJECTION

How does population density compare to the location of natural resources?

efficient, modern methods of farming spread rapidly. This brought about an increase in the amount of food produced in England. Thus even though each year fewer and fewer people may have been engaged in farming, the amount of food produced was greater than ever before.

The Industrial Revolution Starts in England The improvements in English agriculture were important in making possible the beginning of an Industrial Revolution in England. These new methods enabled a smaller group of farmers to produce all the food England required. Many of the people

who gave up farming moved to the cities in search of work. A large supply of labor was on hand to fill the jobs created by the new factories. England's adequate supply of food and large number of workers, among other factors, made possible the beginning of the Industrial Revolution.

Raw Materials Available England was also fortunate in possessing large supplies of raw materials such as coal, tin, iron ore, and wool. It would not have been possible to establish new industries without such supplies. Other raw materials were available from England's many colonies. Before factories could be built, however, another essential ingredient had to be made available—**capital.**

A Supply of Capital   Capital is the money business people spend on the purchases of land, the building of factories, the invention of machines, and all the other things necessary in starting a new industry. Business people who invest in this way are called *capitalists*. England had many wealthy merchants and landowners who were willing to invest money in new kinds of businesses. Of course, they expected to make a profit from their investment. This explains why business people were so eager to pay for new, efficient machines to use in manufacturing goods. Machine-made goods could be produced in greater quantities and at lower costs than handmade goods. And having more goods available to sell meant that more profits could be made.

Some Early Inventions   In the eighteenth century, the production of textiles was one of England's largest and most prosperous industries. To meet the needs of growing cities, wealthy owners of textile factories increased their production of textiles. Since they had money to invest in new machinery, some of the first new inventions appeared in the textile industry.

In the textile industry, improvements in one part of the manufacturing process led to improvements in other parts. A hand-operated loom called the *flying shuttle* was invented by *John Kay* in 1733. This device cut in half the time required for a weaver to weave cloth from yarn. As a result, there was a demand for more yarn to keep the new flying shuttles busy. This led an English inventor named *James Hargreaves* to develop a machine in 1770 that he named the *spinning jenny*. It was a device by which a number of rolls of thread could be spun into yarn at the same time. The amount of yarn a single worker could produce was increased since he or she could spin from several reels of thread rather than only one.

Richard Arkwright, another English inventor, improved the spinning process. About 1769, he produced a machine for spinning yarn that was water-powered. This machine was known as the *water frame*. The water frame could be used to spin yarn from pure cotton thread, something the spinning jenny could not do. Later in 1779, *Samuel Crompton* combined features of the spinning jenny and the water frame to produce a water-powered machine known as the *spinning mule*. This machine was able to produce the yarn needed for the finest textiles such as muslin and other sheer materials.

At this point, the spinning process was ahead of the weaving process. Since hand looms could no longer keep pace with the amount of yarn being produced for weavers to use, factory owners saw the need for power-driven weaving looms. *Edmund Cartwright* produced such a loom in 1785.

Advances in the textile industry increased England's demand for cotton. To increase the production of cotton, cotton growers searched for a means to separate cotton seeds from the cotton fiber. In 1793, a young American inventor, *Eli Whitney*, produced the *cotton gin*. This was a device that separated cotton seeds from the cotton fiber far more quickly than a worker could by hand. Using the cotton gin, a single worker was able to turn out 100 pounds of cotton per day, resulting in a great increase of cotton available for the textile plants. The southern states of the United States, where cotton was grown

The invention of the cotton gin by Eli Whitney in 1793 made it possible for one person to do the work of fifty. What other inventions can you think of that have cut the amount of time and people needed to do one job?

and the cotton gin was introduced, became the main supplier of England's cotton.

New Sources of Power   Up until the eighteenth century, England depended upon animals for farm work and water mills for power and upon wood as a source of fuel. This was sufficient until the early 1700's when England faced a fuel shortage. The forests were nearly exhausted and a new source of fuel had to be found. Coal, which England had rich deposits of, filled the new need. Water in the underground shafts made mining difficult, but in 1705, a pump

for removing the water was developed by *Thomas Newcomen.*

Newcomen's engine used a new source of power—steam. His engine used coal to heat water, then used steam to operate the pump. This was useful in the coal mines because the large amount of coal needed to operate the pump was right there. But it needed improvements for practical use outside the mines.

The Steam Engine   A Scottish inventor, *James Watt*, made improvements on Newcomen's pump and developed the modern *steam engine* in 1769. The steam engine was a major invention in the Industrial Revolution. At first it was used in coal mines, then in textile factories, and eventually it provided a major source of power for a wide variety of industries and forms of transportation.

Improvements   in   Transportation   Because of the changes in production and distribution during the Industrial Revolution, there was a need for an efficient, low-cost method of transporting raw materials to the factories and delivering manufactured products to the markets. Overland transportation by horse-drawn wagon was slow and expensive. For example, in 1750 it took four days or more to go between Manchester and London—a distance of about 320 kilometers (200 miles). England needed a faster, cheaper means of transportation.

Canals   Improve   Transportation   Between 1761 and 1830, a series of canals were built to speed up the transport of heavy raw materials like coal, timber, stone, and clay. The first canal covered a distance of only 19 kilometers (12 miles), connecting a coal mine with the city of Manchester. This canal was a financial success and soon other canals were begun. By 1790 over 4,800 kilometers (3,000 miles) of canals connected the major industrial centers of England like London, Manchester, and Birmingham. The cost of transporting goods by canal was about one third the cost of overland transportation.

Railroads Develop   The canals improved England's transportation system. But the real need for cheap, rapid transportation was met by the development of railroads. About 1801, *Richard Trevithick* (TREH-vih-thick), an Englishman, tried to adapt Watt's steam engine so it would move the wheels of a wagon along iron rails. Trevithick's invention—the locomotive—worked, but it lacked the power needed to pull heavy loads. Later, in 1825, *George Stephenson* built a steam locomotive able to pull heavy loads along a 64 kilometer (40 mile) track. Stephenson's locomotive, the Rocket, made its first trip in 1829 from Liverpool to Manchester at the great speed of 46 kilometers (29 miles) an hour! This was the beginning of the railroad industry.

The Spread of the Industrial Revolution   The Industrial Revolution spread slowly to continental Europe because the necessary raw materials and large markets were often lacking and capitalists were hesitant to invest. After a late start, France did develop some industries, especially those connected with textiles, iron, and mining. Germany was even slower in developing because the German states were not politically united.

Developments made by Britain in manufacturing and transportation spread rapidly to the United States, however. The United States had all the elements necessary for rapid industrialization: political unity, a vast supply of natural resources, a large population, skilled labor, and a spirit of enterprise, which made people willing to try new things and to plan for the future.

America's Contributions   Americans made important contributions to industry. Eli Whitney's invention, the cotton gin, efficiently separated the fibers of raw cotton from the seeds. An-

In the early nineteenth century, trains frightened many people. How have trains changed over the years? Why?

405

Fulton's steamboat made it possible to sail the inland waterways of the United States and revolutionized transportation. What other inventions made the world smaller?

other, perhaps lesser known, contribution of Whitney was his experiments with standardizing machine parts. Standardized, or interchangeable, machine parts are one of the essentials of mass production.

In the field of transportation, *Fulton's steamboat, the Clermont*, which was tested in 1807, made it possible for paddle-wheelers to sail the inland waterways of the United States. People and goods could be transported farther and faster than ever before.

The invention of a practical sewing machine in 1846 had a revolutionary effect on both home and industry. Women no longer were required to spend endless hours hand-sewing gar-ments. The widespread use of this machine also led to other developments. For example, dealers in sewing machines were among the first to promote installment buying and to guarantee service on their machines.

Other inventions in the field of agriculture occurred in the United States. Among these was the *reaper*, developed by *Cyrus McCormick* in 1834. The reaper harvested grain so it was no longer necessary to cut wheat by hand. Next came the mechanical thresher which separated the grains of wheat from their stalks. Later came improved methods of food processing, such as canning and refrigeration, and in the twentieth century, frozen food.

1. **Mapping:** Using the map on page 402, list the location of the major deposits of iron ore and coal in western Europe. Describe the relationship between these deposits and the major manufacturing centers that developed during the 1800's.

2. In your own words, define or identify: Industrial Revolution, Jethro Tull, capital, spinning jenny, spinning mule, James Watt, Eli Whitney, George Stephenson, Cyrus McCormick, *Clermont*.

3. Explain why the Industrial Revolution began in England. Include in your answer three things necessary for the development of industry.

4. Name three American inventions made during the Industrial Revolution and explain their importance.

▶ The English in the 1700's faced a fuel shortage when supplies of wood began to run low. As a result of this crisis, the English turned to coal as a new source of fuel. Faced by an energy crisis today, how do you think the United States should go about solving its fuel shortage?

EFFECTS OF THE INDUSTRIAL REVOLUTION

The Industrial Revolution had both good and bad results. Many of the inventions that were created in the nineteenth century saved both time and money but they also, often indirectly, created many problems. One example of this was the cotton gin. Because the cotton could be cleaned and made ready for factory use faster, more slaves were necessary to pick the cotton. This increased the demand for slaves, and the illegal slave trade flourished.

The Growth of Capitalism In the 1700's and 1800's, capitalism developed along with the changes of the Industrial Revolution. (See page 403.) Capitalists expected the expenses of operating their businesses to be less than the income. The difference between expenses and income was profit. Part of this could be reinvested. Profits might be used to purchase more raw materials, build new factories, or restablish new businesses. Profits used in this way would expand the business and lead to greater profits. The profit motive proved to be the greatest encouragement for the rapid development of manufacturing, transportation, trade, and businesses of many kinds.

Capitalism was not a new form of business enterprise. It had existed in Europe since the end of the Middle Ages. But until the 1700's, it was held back by government regulation and control of economic activity. This made it difficult for capitalists to make profits. Governmental regulation and control of industry were part of an economic system called *mercantilism* (MUR-kun-teel-iz-um). (See page 340.) In the 1700's, mercantilism began to give way to a new economic system known as **free enterprise.**

The Free Enterprise System Supporters of the free enterprise system were convinced that businesses would produce the greatest amount of goods and services when capitalists were allowed to operate with a minimum of interference from government. They believed in economic freedom as well as free trade between nations. This system is also known as *laissez-faire* (leh-say-FAR) capitalism, which is French for "let them [businesses] do as they please." Among the supporters of free enterprise was *Adam Smith*, whose

Industrial cities in the nineteenth century were crowded and dirty. Do large cities today face similar problems? Why?

book *An Inquiry into the Nature and Cause of the Wealth of Nations* greatly influenced the thinking of people in the late 1700's and 1800's.

In Smith's view, there were economic rules that governed all economic activity. These included supply and demand, and also competition. In business, prices (therefore, profits) are determined by the relationship of supply and demand. If there is a great demand for a particular good, and that good is scarce, buyers will pay a high price for it. As a result, profits from the sale of this good will increase. When this happens, individuals with capital are likely to invest in the manufacturing of the scarce good in order to earn profits. Soon many manufacturers may be producing this good and its supply becomes plentiful.

To make sales when the supply is plentiful, manufacturers compete with one another. They offer customers lower prices or a higher quality product, or both, while trying to keep operating expenses low. If too many manufacturers produce the same good, prices may became so low that some manufacturers will not earn a profit or even meet their expenses. This forces some people out of business. However, after these manufacturers leave the business, the supply of the good they were selling will decrease. This decrease in supply will make prices rise. Then the better organized and more efficient manufacturers will make profits.

Thus, Adam Smith argued, everyone gains from free enterprise. Manufacturers produce the goods demanded by buyers, workers have jobs, investors and business owners earn profits, and buyers receive better quality goods at lower prices.

Entrepreneurs   The free enterprise system allowed anyone, regardless of his or her social or economic background, to go into business. Individuals who founded or developed successful businesses of their own are referred to as *entrepreneurs*. In capitalist countries, there were many people of poor economic origin who were able to rise to the top of the business world in the 1800's. Andrew Carnegie was such an individual.

Andrew Carnegie was probably one of the best known entrepreneurs of the nineteenth century. He was born in Scotland to a poor family and immigrated to the United States when he was a boy. Carnegie, by the age of thirty, had acquired a fortune through the steel industry. By 1900, Carnegie's company produced most of the steel products in the United States.

There were entrepreneurs like Carnegie in all the capitalist countries. Other famous American entrepreneurs included John D. Rockefeller, a pioneer in the oil industry; Cornelius Vanderbilt, a developer of railroads; and Henry Ford, a founder of the automobile industry.

For entrepreneurs great or small, starting a business or factory in the 1800's was difficult and risky. It required a great deal of capital. Sometimes an individual could raise enough money to become the owner of a new firm. Often, two or more individuals joined together in a partnership in order to do business on a large scale.

Stockholders Sometimes in order for a business to expand, the owners sold stock to investors. The investors, known as *stockholders*, did not take a day-to-day role in managing the business. For the use of their capital these stockholders were paid periodically a sum of money called a *dividend*. A business in which shares of stock were sold to increase the amount of operating capital was called a *joint-stock company*. Today it is called a *corporation*.

Standard of Living As Smith predicted, the free enterprise system helped bring about the greatest industrial growth in the world. It produced prosperity and a high *standard of living* for the capitalist nations of western Europe and America.

The term *standard of living* is used to describe how economically well off the people of a particular nation are. Standard of living often is measured by dividing the total production of a nation's goods and services by its population. For example, if a country's productivity is great and its population is small, there are many goods and services available to everyone. In such a case, the country is said to have a high standard of living. In the late 1700's and 1800's, the capitalist countries of western Europe and America had

During the Industrial Revolution, children worked in factories and mines, such as this coal mine. Do you think the employment of children should be regulated by law today?

higher standards of living than other countries because they were able to produce more. This increased production was due in part to the technological advances made during the Industrial Revolution.

In addition to the availability of modern technology, productivity is likely to be high in countries with rich natural resources, an abundance of skilled labor, and an economic environment favorable to individual initiative and effort.

The prospect of earning profits, for example, is a strong motivating factor that encourages people to go into business, take risks, and work hard in the hope of gaining wealth. This leads to the production of more goods and services.

Some countries, such as the Soviet Union, have the resources and labor to support high productivity and achieve a high standard of living. Yet their economic system does not reward hard work with personal profit. This is one reason why productivity is less and the standard of living lower than in capitalist countries of western Europe and the United States.

Industrial Growth Capitalism and the free enterprise system helped to industrialize western Europe and America. Certain things are necessary in order for industrialization to occur. A country needs natural resources, a large labor pool, capital, and a market. Britain had all these things in the late 1700's. Britain also had a government that encouraged private enterprise and laws to protect private property. This combination of factors explains why the Industrial Revolution began in Britain. Until the twentieth century, many considered Britain the industrial leader of the world.

France lagged behind Britain. However, under laissez-faire governments in the early 1800's, the French began to develop industries, especially in textiles, iron, and mining. After Germany was united in the late 1800's, German industrial production grew dramatically. But by 1900, the United States had replaced Britain as the industrial leader of the world.

Economic growth of the United States The economic growth of the United States in the 1800's was due to a combination of factors. The United States was a vast country with a rich supply of natural resources and sources of energy. It had a large supply of willing labor, and its population was growing. Most Americans believed in freedom and laissez-faire capitalism. They possessed great technological skill and inventiveness. There were many entrepreneurs and able business organizers, as well as people with capital willing to take risks. In addition, the United States had traditions and laws that respected the individual's right to private property. And its government encouraged private enterprise. This combination of factors helped the American economic system to accomplish a remarkable growth. There was a tremendous increase in the production of goods and services. Efficient American farmers produced enough grain and other foodstuffs for export to worldwide markets. In addition, manufacturers in the United States were producing low-priced goods for foreign customers. Basic industries were quickly established and the United States became the world leader in the quantity and value of goods produced. This created great prosperity and made possible a continually rising standard of living.

The United States today remains an industrial leader of the world. Its economic system still is based on the principles of capitalism and free enterprise. Willingness to invest in new industries in hopes of making profits has contributed to recent advances in fields such as computer science and medical technology.

Capitalism Changes In the late 1800's, European farmers were demanding that their governments protect them from foreign competition. They were unable to compete with the farmers of the United States whose products poured into agricultural markets at lower prices than European products.

One way in which European governments tried to reduce American competition was by placing a tax on agricultural imports. This tax, called a *tariff*, made foodstuffs from other countries more expensive and thus protected the European farmers from foreign competition.

European industries demanded

the same form of government protection. Germany's government placed a high tariff on industrial imports in 1879. The French in 1892 imposed a high tariff to protect both manufacturing and agriculture. Eventually, all the industrial countries resorted to tariffs as a form of economic protection. This was helpful to new industries that could not compete with foreign competition. This also meant the decline of free trade.

The decline of free trade forced nations that manufactured goods for exports such as Britain, Japan, and the United States to begin a worldwide search for new markets. This competition for new markets contributed to the rise of imperialism. (See page 449.)

Big Business Grows Bigger The decline of free trade was not the only way capitalism began to change in the late 1800's. Businesses grew larger in order to meet the challenges of growing competition. As businesses grew bigger, they often cooperated with other large firms in their own fields of activity. Instead of competing with one another, they looked for ways to share markets and to charge fixed prices for the same goods.

This kind of cooperation among businesses led to new forms of organization in which the competing firms were combined. A large business might buy out its competitors. This new, larger firm was called a *trust*. If all the firms in a particular industry were combined in a trust, it was called a *monopoly*. Some trusts combined business enterprises in several countries. These international trusts were called *cartels* (kahr-TELZ).

Trusts, monopolies, and cartels played an important role in expanding the economies of Western nations in the 1880's and 1890's. They introduced new business techniques and greater production efficiency. These business combinations, however, were unpopular with the general public because they did away with competition, and fixed prices. This hurt the consumers.

Government Intervention in Economic and Social Life Farmers and industry were not alone in demanding government protection in the late 1800's. The rise of organized labor and the formation of workers' political parties led to demands that government intervene in economic and social matters.

New laws were passed to regulate competition and protect the public from price-fixing or other economic abuses that arose as competition disappeared in some parts of the business world. The United States government tried to break up monopolies and trusts. The number of laws and government regulations affecting business activity increased significantly in western Europe and the United States after 1890.

By 1900, many people demanded that the government assume an even greater responsibility for the welfare of society. British government provided housing for some of the needy and established tax-supported public schools. In Germany, by 1889 government welfare programs provided workers with health care and insurance against accidents and unemployment. Eventually, most European governments offered their citizens a wide variety of welfare programs. In the United States, presidents such as Theodore Roosevelt and Woodrow Wilson accepted an enlarged role for government in the economic and social life of the country. Many people, especially the poor, benefitted from this. However, increased taxation to support these programs decreased company profits.

The Quality of Life Changes   The Industrial Revolution brought about tremendous changes in the lives of the working people. No longer did most workers labor outdoors as farmers and live in small isolated farming communities. The majority worked in factories or mines, and they generally lived in large, crowded cities. Workers did not simply move from farms to cities overnight. This was a gradual process.

Conditions at Home   This movement of people into the cities caused many problems. The working class districts of early nineteenth century English cities were dirty, ugly, crowded slums. Most workers lived in small, one-family houses. In some cities, entire blocks of houses were built side to side and back to back so that the only windows were in the front of the house. This crowding created a high risk of fire. The housing was unsanitary, and airless. All these things contributed to the rapid spread of diseases.

However, to many workers, life in the city was an improvement over the villages from which they had come. The rural housing of farm workers was usually unsanitary, and ill-equipped. While urban housing may have been no better, life in the city held greater opportunity for some than did rural life.

Conditions at Work   At work, hours were long, wages were low, and working conditions were poor. Factories were noisy, dirty places. Little was done to ensure the safety of workers. If a worker was injured and unable to work, he or she did not receive wages.

The normal workday lasted fourteen to sixteen hours. An average week's wages for an adult male worker was from $5.00 to $9.00. Women and children made even less. Wages were so low that workers were able to save little money to fall back on when they were out of work.

Though factory workers were paid little, they nevertheless earned higher wages than before the Industrial Revolution. It was for higher income that many workers moved to cities and took factory jobs. Jobs were more plentiful in the cities. Sometimes entire families worked, including children. As a result, the total earnings in the city were usually higher than they had been in the country.

Perhaps the worst feature of the early Industrial Revolution was child labor. In some countries, young children worked long hours in coal mines and cotton mills under unhealthy and unsafe conditions. This occurred because many families could not afford to feed and house themselves unless their children worked too.

Conditions Gradually Improve   The living and working conditions for most European workers gradually improved. The factory owners themselves were responsible for some improvements. For example, owners often provided housing located near factories and mines for their workers. Such company-owned housing usually was better than what workers could obtain elsewhere.

The government also played a role in improving working conditions. Britain's Parliament passed the *Factory Act of 1819*. This act prohibited children under the age of nine from working in cotton factories. It also kept employers from working older children for more than twelve hours a day. In the late 1800's, Britain also regulated the number of hours employees could work each week.

In the long run, however, it was the increased production of goods brought about by the Industrial Revolution that most improved the lives of workers. Between 1800 and 1900, the standard of living steadily improved in the capitalist nations of Europe and America. While this gradual change was taking place, however, many workers turned to union movements or to socialism as ways of improving their lives.

The Union Movement   The union movement developed slowly. Not until the 1890's did unions in Europe and the United States experience a rapid growth in their memberships. Unions were organized to represent workers in a particular industry or workers having the same skills. Unions tried to get higher wages and better working conditions for their members.

The unions' main weapon for obtaining reforms was the strike. The strike is a form of protest in which workers stay away from their jobs until their demands are met. Another important weapon of the workers was the vote. In countries with representative governments, such as France and Britain, union leaders realized that the right to vote was the key to improving workers' conditions. As a result, late in the 1800's workers' political parties were formed. These parties usually were influenced by the workers' unions. Many of them also were influenced by **socialism.**

The Socialists   Early in the 1800's, some reformers believed the only way to improve the conditions of the working people was to abolish capitalism. These reformers proposed an economic system called socialism. Most *socialists* believed it was unjust for factory owners to have such great economic control. Thus, socialists opposed private enterprise. Some proposed doing away with private property. They favored government ownership of factories, mines, and railroads. All socialists rejected the economic principles of Adam Smith.

Utopian Socialists   Some of the early socialists were called *utopian socialists* because they wanted to do away with competition and to create utopias or perfect communities. **Robert Owen** was a leading utopian socialist.

Robert Owen was a Welsh businessman who believed in the natural goodness of all people. However, he said, people had been corrupted by their surroundings. If people could live in a society based on cooperation, in which there was no selfishness or competition, the true nature of men and women would be able to emerge. Owen tried to put his theories into practice. He bought a cotton mill in Scotland and turned the factory town nearby into a clean, safe community with good schools and a high standard of living. However, later attempts to set up ideal communities, one in England and one in the United States at New Harmony, Indiana, failed.

Other famous utopian socialists were Francois Charles Fourier (FOOR-ee-ay) and the Comte de Saint-Simon, both from France.

Karl Marx and Communism   Socialists like Robert Owen had little influence at first. However, in the second half of the 1800's, socialism became an important force in Europe. This was due mainly to a German named **Karl Marx** (MAHRKS). Karl Marx was the most important of all the nineteenth-

413

Karl Marx

The father of modern communism, Karl Marx, was born into a middle-class family in Prussia in 1818. Because Marx's father was a lawyer, his family hoped Marx would study law. In 1835, Marx entered the University of Bonn, but after a year he transferred to the University of Berlin where he became interested in philosophy and politics. As a result, Marx joined a student-professor group that criticized the Prussian government and called for revolutionary changes.

Marx received his doctorate in philosophy in 1841. Unable to find work as a teacher, he became a journalist. The revolutionary newspapers and magazines he helped to write, however, were suppressed by the government. After his marriage in 1843, Marx and his wife left the country. From 1843 to 1848, they lived in France and Belgium. During this time, Marx met Friedrich Engels, who was also a German revolutionary. Engels was forced to leave Prussia in 1844 and went to work in one of his father's factories in England. But he became friends with Marx, and together they worked on several articles and books.

Marx returned to Germany in 1848 and began working on a radical journal. He became known throughout Germany as a revolutionary. When the revolution of 1848 failed, Marx fled to England where he spent the rest of his life.

Marx considered himself a professional revolutionary. Because of this, he did not take a job or work for a living. Occasionally, Marx did write articles for newspapers, but he, his wife, and their six children depended on the money Engels sent regularly.

Marx was a well-educated person, dedicated to his beliefs. He was intolerant of criticism and contradiction and was often considered opinionated and conceited. Because of this, he had few friends except for Engels. He broke contact with his family in Germany but was devoted to his wife and children. Marx died in March of 1883 and was buried in London.

Marx's major work was **Das Kapital.** He spent thirty years writing this four-volume work. The first volume was published in 1867. The second and third volumes were published with Engels' help after Marx's death. The last volume consisted only of scattered notes Marx had completed. Based on these works, communist countries today consider Marx one of the greatest thinkers of all times.

Adapted from: R. L. Heilbroner. **The Worldly Philosophers: The Lives, Times, and Ideas of the Great Economic Thinkers.** New York: Simon and Schuster, 1955.

1. What in Marx's background prepared him to become a "professional revolutionary"? How does he compare with other revolutionaries?

2. What was the relationship between Marx and Engels?

3. Who do you consider the greatest thinker of all times? Why?

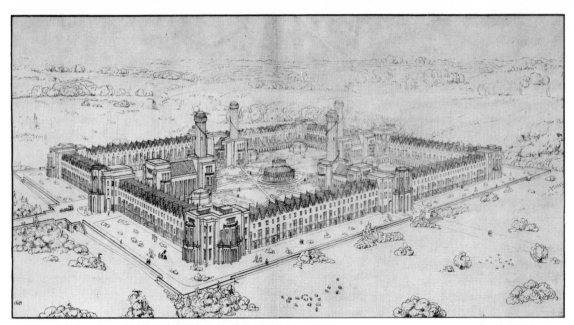

This shows Robert Owen's proposal for New Harmony, Indiana. It was a place where people were supposed to have worked together and share the goods they produced. What are the advantages and disadvantages of such a system?

century socialists. His theories became the basis for communism today. Marx, with the help of Friedrich Engels, wrote a famous book called *Das Kapital*. In it, he attacked capitalism. This book and Marx's other writings, such as the *Communist Manifesto*, are the basis for the political and economic systems of most modern communist nations.

Marxist Views Differ from Early Socialists The socialism of Marx differed from that of the early socialists in two important ways. First, while the early socialists believed that there should be a gradual and peaceful development toward ideal conditions for the workers, Marx forecast a sudden and violent uprising in which the workers would capture the government and use it to secure their own welfare. The early socialists intended to work within the capitalistic system to achieve their aims. But Marx predicted the destruction of the capitalistic system and its replacement by a communistic system in which all people shared equally in the goods produced. Marx believed that throughout the past there have always been two groups, or classes, of people involved in producing goods. One group has controlled the wealth and political power while the other group has done all the work. Marx said this could be seen during the Middle Ages when serfs were exploited by the landowning nobility. The struggle of serfs against nobles lasted for hundreds of years. Capitalism developed out of this struggle. Under capitalism, Marx said, workers have replaced serfs, and factory owners have taken the place of the landowning nobility. But the struggle between these two classes continues. In this class struggle, according to

415

Marx, the workers would eventually overthrow the factory owners.

Class Struggle After capitalism has been destroyed by the workers, a form of socialism would be established. All men and women would be equally provided with everything they needed. No one person would be permitted to take economic advantage of another. Competition would be replaced by cooperation. Since all capitalists would have been eliminated, only one class would remain—the workers. Therefore, class struggle would come to an end. Everyone would work at whatever he or she was able to do. In exchange for their work, all people would have their needs taken care of. Eventually, there would be no need for a government, and it would disappear.

Since Marx's death, there have been several socialists who have interpreted Marx's theories in different ways and added new ideas of their own. Today several different forms of communism exist. Not all communist leaders agree with one another, so communism differs greatly from one country to another. However, almost all communists hold the belief that capitalism is doomed and will be overthrown by a communist-led revolution of some kind.

Marxism in Russia The first country to put Marxism into practice was Russia. In 1917, a communist-led revolution in Russia sezied control of the government. Russia's new socialist leaders declared an end to capitalism and set out to promote communist-led revolutions in all the capitalist nations. Since 1917, this has remained a goal of the Soviet Union.

The worldwide influence of the Soviet Union has steadily increased. More than a dozen communist govern-ments have been established. Today about one third of the world's population live under Marxist political and economic systems. In the early 1980's, the U.S.S.R.'s influence was especially strong in the Middle East and parts of Europe. China, a communist state since 1949, was Russia's major rival for influence in Asia. Since the early 1960's, communist Cuba has played a major role in promoting revolutions in Central and South America. Some communist countries have also given assistance to revolutionaries in Africa.

The Soviet Economic System In the late 1700's and 1800's, Russia was among the last European countries to be affected by the Industrial Revolution. As a result, Russia in 1917 still was an agricultural nation with little industry. After the communist revolution, Russia's new rulers decided to rapidly industrialize the country in order to catch up with capitalist Europe and the United States. To accomplish this goal, the communists set out to abolish capitalism and do away with the right to private property in Russia. They also tried to take land away from millions of Russia's farmers.

At first, the communists failed. It was very difficult to change Russia into a socialist nation. Not until after Joseph Stalin came to power was socialism firmly established. Stalin did not hesitate to have millions of his own people killed in order to impose a new economic system. (See pages 482–483.)

In other countries, many people were horrified by what took place in the Soviet Union. Others, however, overlooked the human suffering. They were impressed by the fact that Marxism had transformed Russia from a backward agricultural country into a major industrial power.

416

The Command Economy   Today, the capitalist free enterprise system of the United States is known as a *market economy*. This name is taken from the markets in which buyers and sellers freely exchange goods. In contrast, the Soviet Union is known as a *command economy*.

In a command economy, there is little freedom. Only a few individuals participate in economic decision-making. The government determines how much shall be produced and what shall be produced.

In a command economy, the great majority of citizens simply obey government directives. They follow economic plans drawn up for the country by the government. The production and distribution of goods are planned in advance. All business is government-owned. Thus, there is no competition and the laws of supply and demand do not operate. Nor is there a profit motive. Almost all goods and services are in the government's hands. Little is privately owned other than automobiles and clothing.

Soviet Economic Problems   The development of the Soviet Union's basic industries, oil, steel, coal, and transportation, has been remarkable. However, the resources of the country have been used primarily to meet the goals of Russia's leaders rather than to meet the needs and wants of the Soviet citizens. This has created a shortage of consumer goods, resulting in a lower standard of living in the U.S.S.R. than in the United States and countries of western Europe.

The Soviet Union's command economy has not been able to solve the problem of agricultural productivity. Incentive is lacking. The average output of a Soviet farmer continues to be dramatically small in comparison with farm production in western Europe and the United States. Communist U.S.S.R. is still searching for ways to surpass the capitalist countries.

SECTION REVIEW

1. Mapping: Using the map on page 402, how can you account for the differences in population density in western Europe? Do you think this map would have shown the same population pockets in 1660? Why or why not?
2. In your own words, define or identify: capitalism, free enterprise system, tariff, cartels, monopolies, socialists, Karl Marx, communism.
3. In what ways did the workers try to improve their conditions during the Industrial Revolution?
4. Briefly describe Marx's theory about the destruction of capitalism and the development of a form of socialism. Has Marx's theory come true?
    ▷ Do economic differences still affect the ways people think and behave? Explain your answer.

chapter 23

The Beginnings of Revolution in Russia

RUSSIA IN THE NINETEENTH CENTURY

After the death of Catherine the Great in 1796, Catherine's son, Paul, came to the throne. Paul's reign was brief. In 1801, he was overthrown and murdered by a group of his political enemies, who then placed Paul's son, Alexander, on the throne in his father's place.

Alexander I Rules   Alexander ruled Russia until 1825. Russia's victory over France in 1815 and the defeat of Napoleon brought glory and fame to *Alexander I*. (See page 382.) He became popular in many parts of western Europe. In Russia, however, Alexander did very little to improve conditions for the people. As a result, discontent spread.

The Need for Reform   Russian officers who fought in western Europe, especially those who occupied France, returned to Russia convinced that reforms should be made so that Russians could enjoy the freedom and rights enjoyed by western Europeans. These officers formed secret organizations devoted to reforming Russia.

The Decembrist Revolt   When Alexander I died in 1825, the throne passed to his brother, *Nicholas I*. Nicholas I was opposed to any change that would help the people, which made him very unpopular. Due to this change in leadership, the leaders of the secret organizations inside Russia saw an opportunity to strike a blow for revolution. However, they had little support from the people except a few of the troops in the capital, St. Petersburg. The rebels had acted hastily, without a plan, and the rebellion was soon put down by troops loyal to Nicholas. The leaders of this revolt were executed or exiled to Siberia. Because this attempt at revolution had taken place in the month of December, the unsuccessful rebels were called *Decembrists*.

Results of the Decembrist Revolt   Instead of reforms, the Decembrist Revolt brought about a ruthless suppression of individual freedoms in Russia. To make sure there would be no future revolts, Tsar Nicholas established a secret police. Its job was to locate the tsar's enemies and send them to Siberia, where they would not be a threat. Controls over the press and speech were tightened, and a huge network of spies reported any activity considered dangerous to the government. Anyone who spoke out against the tsar might be executed, imprisoned, or exiled. Under these conditions, there was little hope for reform in Russia.

Many people who did favor reform decided to leave Russia rather than stay behind and risk punishment for their beliefs. The Decembrist Revolt was not forgotten by reform-minded Russians; it inspired other revolts.

The Crimean War   Nicholas I was also interested in expanding the territories of Russia. He wanted to increase his influence over the peoples of eastern Europe and to take territory from the Turks in the declining Ottoman Empire. When Tsar Nicholas threatened to declare war on the Turks in 1854, Britain and France decided to side with the Turks. This resulted in the *Crimean War* (krie-MEE-uhn), with the French, British, and Turks fighting against the Russians. Most of the war was fought in the Crimean peninsula, which is in the southern part of Russia on the Black Sea. (See the map on page 421.) The war lasted from 1854 to 1856. The tsar had expected Austria to become Russia's ally, but that country decided to remain neutral. The war went badly for Russia without allies, and Tsar Nicholas I died in the midst of the conflict.

Florence Nightingale   During the war, reports of terrible hospital conditions in the Crimean peninsula reached England. A group of nurses led by *Florence Nightingale* was sent to the war zone. There she set up clean hospitals and for the first time England's wounded received good care away from home. Until this time, there were few properly trained people to care for the wounded, nor were proper sanitary conditions being provided for them. Nurse Nightingale is considered one of the founders of modern nursing.

Freeing the Serfs   Nicholas I's son, Tsar *Alexander II*, who ruled from 1855 to 1881, quickly made peace and ended the Crimean War. He believed the war had seriously weakened Russia, and he

During the Crimean War, Florence Nightingale risked her life to care for the wounded. Why do you think people risk their lives for others?

also realized that the government must somehow be reformed. Alexander made many reforms, however, they were not all successful.

Alexander II began his reforms in 1861 with the emancipation of the serfs. This granted freedom to all serfs and it allowed them to purchase farmlands. Because of this reform Alexander is known as the *tsar liberator*. The reform, however, did not work. The former serfs were seldom able to purchase enough land to make a comfortable living. Those who did buy land often were unable to make the payments on it. Besides this, the former serfs were still under the control of their villages. The villages had the legal right to determine how farmlands might be used, to collect taxes, and even to prevent peasants from moving away.

Other Reforms Freeing the serfs was not Alexander II's only reform. During his rule, trial by jury was introduced to Russia and education became more available. Alexander also modernized the army and gave local governments new responsibilities. Elected governing bodies were created for towns, cities, and counties. Freedom, however, was still limited because the tsar would not permit any sort of national parliament.

Demands for Change in Russia About the time of Alexander II's reforms, a number of different organizations appeared in Russia, each demanding changes. Their goals, ideas, and ways of achieving their aims differed. One group insisted that reform must come from the tsar without any changes in the economic and political systems of the country. This group was made up chiefly of the upper class. Another group, called *liberals*, consisted mainly of the middle class. They believed that citizens like themselves should be given a greater share in governing the country.

Some people believed the only way to reform Russia was by *nihilism* (NIE-ul-iz-um). It emphasized the need to destroy Russia's political and economic systems. Any means, no matter how violent, could be used. Only by starting completely over could Russia be reformed. Many young, educated Russians were attracted to nihilism. They joined the *"To The People" movement* and went to live and spread their political beliefs among the peasants. But the peasants, to whom so much was promised, turned their backs on the young revolutionaries. In many cases, they handed the young revolutionaries over to the secret police.

Government Control Tightens Some revolutionaries began a series of assassinations of government leaders. The tsar himself was a target, and after many attempts, Alexander II was murdered by a band of young revolutionaries in 1881. The new tsar had the murderers executed and destroyed their organization.

Alexander III The murder of Alexander II convinced the new tsar, *Alexander III*, who ruled from 1881 to 1894, that permitting reforms or any sort of change had been a mistake. He and some of his advisers believed that western ideas such as democracy, constitutions, elections, freedom of speech, and freedom of the press were dangerous. The government made every effort to stamp out the revolutionaries and to silence anyone who proposed reform or political change.

The clock was turned back in Russia, and during the 1880's and 1890's conditions were not very different from what they had been in the days of Tsar Nicholas I. Many of the reforms of Alexander II were abolished. In their place, Alexander III instituted new harsh measures. Political parties and labor unions were forbidden. This regime also allowed religious persecution of Jews. Books and newspapers were not permitted to criticize the government or to suggest political reform. The secret police spied on people and reported to the tsar everything that was said or done. The Russian people had no share in governing themselves.

Russian Expansion While conditions at home worsened, Russia continued to expand its already vast territory. The Caucasus (KAW-kuh-sus) and the desert area in central Asia beyond the

GROWTH OF RUSSIA FROM THE 17TH TO THE 19TH CENTURIES

BERING SEA

BARENTS SEA

KARA SEA

LAPTEV SEA

BALTIC SEA

50°

St. Petersburg

Vilnyus•   •Petrozavodsk   •Archangel

•Minsk

Moscow•

Kiev•   •Nizhni
        Novgorod

Lena R.

Verkhny-Kamchatsk•   50°

SEA OF OKHOTSK

Yakutsk•

Yenisey R.

SIBERIA

•Kazan   Ob R.   •Tobolsk

Volga R.

BLACK SEA   •Samara   •Tsaritsyn

•Yeniseisk

Orenburg

Astrakhan•   •Orsk   •Troitsk   •Omsk

URAL MTS.

L. Baikal

Amur R.   •Khabarovsk

•Petropavlovsk

Akmolinsk•   Irkutsk•   •Nerchinsk

40°

40°

CASPIAN SEA

ARAL SEA   Semipalatinsk•

ALTAI MTS.

•Vladivostok

SEA OF JAPAN

L. Balkhash

•Petrovsk

Samarkand•   •Tashkent

	Russia at the end of 16th century
	Acquired during 17th century
	Acquired during 18th century
	Acquired during 19th century

0   600 kilometers

0   500 miles

N

LAMBERT'S PROJECTION

60°   80°   100°   120°

How does a map of Russia today compare with one from the sixteenth century?

Caspian Sea were both added to Russia's empire in the mid-1800's. Russia had claimed Alaska as a territory in the 1700's. However, because Alaska was so far from Russia that control was difficult, it was sold to the United States in 1867 for just over seven million dollars. From the mid-1800's, the Russians also were interested in exploring and settling Siberia, along the coast of the Pacific Ocean. (See the map above.)

Russia in China   In the 1850's, the Russians took some of China's territories. Since China had been defeated in wars with Britain and France, Russia had little difficulty in forcing the weakened Chinese to give up lands north of the Amur (ah-MOOR) River and along the Pacific coast. The Russians made these lands their own. At the southern end of the territory, they founded the port city of *Vladivostok* (vlad-uh-vuh-STAHK). By the end of the nineteenth century, Vladivostok had become very important, largely because in 1891 the Russians began to build a railroad across Siberia connecting Vladivostok with the European part of Russia.

Russia Struggles to Catch Up   By that time, there was a great interest in developing Russia's trade and manufacturing. Russia always had been an agricultural country. But after the middle of the nineteenth century, some thoughtful Russians realized the need to build factories and to develop the country's natural resources such as coal, iron, timber, oil, and cotton. There were countless problems to solve before Russia could develop industry. But by the 1800's, a start had been made. Many Russians hoped their country one day might catch up with such industrial nations as Great Britain and Germany.

This picture shows Russian peasants working in a coal-pit in the late 1800's. Do you think life was easy for them? Explain.

1. **Mapping:** Using the map on page 421, list the territories added to Russia in the 1700's and in the second half of the 1800's. How were these territories added to Russia?

2. In your own words, identify or define the following: Alexander I, Decembrist, Nicholas I, Crimean War, Alexander II, Alexander III, Florence Nightingale, nihilism, Vladivostok.

3. Describe the beliefs of revolutionaries in Russia during the late 1800's.

4. In what ways did Russia in the 1880's and 1890's resemble Russia during the days of Nicholas I?

5. Why did Russia sell Alaska to the United States?

◗ In what ways did Russia's expansion on the Pacific coast resemble the western expansion of the United States? Are there any ways in which the expansion of these two countries was different?

THE REVOLUTIONARY MOVEMENT IN RUSSIA

After the death of Alexander III in 1894, his son, *Nicholas II,* became tsar and ruled until 1917. Nicholas continued a one-man government; all power was in his hands. But Russia had become a vast empire that scarcely could have been governed by one man. Nicholas II was a weak ruler who was easily influenced by others and had a difficult time in reaching decisions. His refusal to make any sort of political reform or change eventually led to the outbreak of a revolution in the early 1900's.

Political Parties Rise   In spite of the tsar's restrictions, the liberals again be-

Tsar Nicholas II is shown here with his wife Alexandra, and their children Olga, Marie, Anastasia, Alexis, and Tatiana. How does this picture compare with present-day pictures of royalty?

came politically active. They proposed that, in imitation of the western European countries, Russia should establish a parliament called the *Duma* (DOO-mah). Revolutionaries also became active again early in Nicholas II's reign. They turned toward socialism and set up political parties, one of which, founded in 1898, was called the *Russian Social Democratic party*. The members of this party were known as Social Democrats and operated secretly for years. In 1903, a conference of the Social Democratic party was held. At that meeting, the party split into two opposing groups. One of these was headed by a man who used the name **Lenin** (LEN-un).

The Bolsheviks and Mensheviks
Lenin proposed that the revolutionary movement be led by a small, special group of professional revolutionaries.

All party members would have to obey orders from above without questioning them. Lenin called his supporters **Bolsheviks** (BOLE-shuh-viks), which means members of the majority. Lenin's opponents wanted a party with membership open to anyone, not just revolutionaries. They also disliked Lenin's suggestion that members give up the right to think for themselves. Lenin's opponents called themselves **Mensheviks** (MEN-shuh-viks), or members of the minority. Both Bolsheviks and Mensheviks accepted the teachings of Karl Marx.

Socialist Revolutionary Party
During the 1890's, another group of socialists created a political party called the *Socialist Revolutionary party*. The members of this party shared some ideas with the Bolsheviks and Mensheviks. The Socialist Revolutionaries

423

Lenin is shown here addressing a crowd of Bolsheviks. Why do you think so many people followed Lenin?

also accepted the principles of Marxism, but they changed Marx's teachings to fit conditions in Russia.

The two parties differed over the importance of the peasants in creating a revolution in Russia. The Socialist Revolutionary party believed the peasants would bring about the Russian revolution. They wanted immediate change and established a terrorist organization that planned and directed political murders. The Bolsheviks and Mensheviks, on the other hand, considered the workers to be the only true revolutionaries, as did Marx. They believed that the middle class would take power when the tsar was overthrown by the workers. Then the workers would have to seize power later. They also believed that assassinations and violence distracted revolutionaries from more important tasks.

Discontent Grows Russian industry experienced a decline in the years 1899 to 1903. Business failures and factory shutdowns left many people out of work and caused great suffering among the working class. Before Russia could recover economically, the government went to war with Japan. *The Russo-Japanese War* began in 1904, and peasants from rural areas that produced Russia's food had to be drafted. This resulted in severe food shortages. (See page 460.) The news that reached Russia from the fighting fronts in the Far East was also bad. The war was going against Russia. Dissatisfaction spread everywhere.

The Revolution of 1905 Discontent came to a head in January 1905, when the Social Democrats convinced the factory workers to strike. A strike involving thousands of workers broke out in St. Petersburg, the capital. On January 9, many of the striking workers joined a protest march to tell the tsar their grievances. Although the crowd was peaceful, troops were called out. They blocked the march and then opened fire on the crowd, killing and wounding hundreds of people. This day is known as *Bloody Sunday*. Immediately, new strikes occurred in the city, and then spread to Moscow and to other towns. A new wave of terror broke out. The tsar's uncle was murdered, and in February, revolts broke out in farming areas. These outbreaks became known as the *Revolution of 1905*. On top of all this, the army and navy were shaken by defeats in the war against the Japanese. Morale was low in the armed forces and a great many Russian soldiers and sailors were influenced by revolutionary propaganda.

The October Manifesto With his world falling to pieces around him, Tsar Nicholas II did not seem to know what to do. In October 1905, a soviet, or assembly, of delegates representing workers from the factories of St. Petersburg was formed. It demanded self-government for the city. Nicholas was forced to issue the *October Manifesto*. This document promised the people fundamental liberties, including freedom of the press, freedom of speech, and election of a national Duma (parliament).

The Tsar Regains Control With the war against Japan over and the return of troops, order was soon restored in Russia. The tsar was now feeling stronger and took steps to reduce the powers that the October Manifesto had given the people. The tsar dismissed the first two Dumas when they tried to make some reforms. Then the tsar changed the qualifications for the next election. As a result, the third and fourth Dumas represented only the wealthy landowners. They did manage to pass some reforms. These reforms, however, benefited the rich, not the poor. Soon it was clear that nothing had been won by the 1905 Revolution.

Parties Rise Again After the Revolution of 1905, political parties began to rise again. The liberals divided into two new political parties. One was the *Constitutional Democratic party*, which demanded power for the Duma and hoped the Duma would bring about reform. Members of this party were called *Kadets*. Some of them favored a constitutional monarchy for Russia. Many, however, decided a republic would be best for the country. The other political party was made up of middle-class and noble members who were content with the results of the 1905 Revolution. These individuals were known as *Octobrists*. For the most part, Octobrists were constitutional monarchists.

Supporters of the Tsar Opposed to both liberals and revolutionaries was a group made up largely of nobles, great landowners, high-ranking government officials, churchmen, and army officers. These formed several political parties, elected their members to the Duma, and encouraged the tsar to maintain a policy of absolute rule. Nicholas II welcomed this advice. Within three years of the 1905 Revolution, he had broken most of the promises made in the October Manifesto.

The End of Monarchy in Russia It is impossible to say how long the absolute rule of the tsars would have lasted had it not been for World War I. Due to Russia's part in the war, the Russian people were exposed to great hardships and sufferings. There were food shortages in the cities and on the battlefields. Russian troops suffered unbelievable defeats and the number of dead and wounded was estimated at more than two million.

Rasputin Meanwhile, the tsar's wife, Empress Alexandra, who greatly influenced the tsar, seemed to ignore the hardships her people were suffering. The Russians did not trust the tsar's wife because she was a German and easily influenced by an adventurer from Siberia named *Rasputin*. Rasputin, who claimed to be a Russian Orthodox monk, held the empress's trust because she believed he could heal her son, who suffered from hemophilia. Many believed that Rasputin could get official appointments for anyone, even those not qualified, if paid enough. Because of this use of his influence, Rasputin helped to destroy respect for the royal family and confidence in the tsar's leadership. By the end of 1916, corruption and inefficiency had exhausted the patience of almost

Rasputin had a great deal of influence over the tsar and tsarina. Does Rasputin appear to be a leader in this picture?

everyone, even those who had supported the tsar. Russians now openly criticized the throne. Nobles, hoping to save the tsar from further criticism, assassinated Rasputin in 1916.

Petrograd Soviet At the beginning of March 1917, a series of strikes broke out in Petrograd, the capital (the new name of St. Petersburg). Troops had to be called to break up the mobs roaming the streets. Some of the troops did obey orders, but many of the soldiers were in sympathy with the rioters. On March 12, some of the army units in the capital arrested their officers and joined the revolution. Representatives of the workers organized an assembly, as they had during the 1905 Revolution. It was known as the *Petrograd Soviet*. With the cooperation of the rebel troops, the Petrograd Soviet was able to take control of the city.

Nicholas II Resigns Before this takeover occurred, the Duma had been dismissed by the tsar. But the members of the Duma ignored the order to disband and established a temporary committee to set up a new national government. On March 1, 1917, this *Provisional Government* sent messengers to Tsar Nicholas II, who was away on the battlefront, urging him to give up the throne. The tsar tried to return to the capital, but striking railroad workers refused to permit his train into the capital. Nicholas discovered no one was willing to support him, not even members of the nobility and the armed forces. On March 15, Nicholas II resigned in favor of his brother. But the tsar's brother turned down the honor. With no one to claim the throne, Russia ceased to be a monarchy. A provisional government was set up until a permanent system of government could be established. Nicholas II and his family were imprisoned, and in 1918, after the Bolsheviks took control, they were shot.

The Petrograd Soviet The tsar's resignation left Russia in a confused situation. Political authority was divided between the Provisional Government, headed by *Alexander Kerensky* (kuh-REN-skee) and the Petrograd Soviet. The Provisional Government supposedly represented the middle class, while the Petrograd Soviet claimed to speak for the workers and the soldiers. The leaders of the Petrograd Soviet were Marxists.

The Bolshevik Revolution For a while the Socialist Revolutionaries, Mensheviks, and Bolsheviks agreed to tolerate the non-Socialist Provisional Government. The end of cooperation came in April 1917, when Lenin returned to Russia from exile in western Europe. As a leader of the Bolsheviks,

Lenin used his influence to persuade them to end their support of the Provisional Government and prepare to take control of the soviets throughout Russia. He wanted them to do everything in their power to prepare for the coming socialist revolution, which he believed would be the next step in the revolution.

Lenin's views were accepted by the Bolsheviks. They began a propaganda campaign to discredit the Provisional Government and weaken its authority. The Bolsheviks promised an end to Russia's part in World War I, an adequate food supply for the city populations, and more land for the peasants. Their slogan was "Peace, Land, and Bread." The popularity of the Bolsheviks continued to grow. Meanwhile, the Provisional Government lost support among the Russian people because it continued to insist that Russia fight on in the war until a final victory was won.

On the night of November 6, 1917, the Bolsheviks, supported by some troops of the regular army, seized key points in Petrograd in the name of the soviet. They surrounded the Winter Palace of the tsars, which had become the seat of the Provisional Government. The next morning, the city awoke to find the Bolsheviks in control and a new national government with Lenin as its head. A Communist form of government was established, which remains in force in Russia to this day.

The storming of the Winter Palace in Petrograd, led by the Bolsheviks, occurred in 1917. After this, a communist form of government was established in Russia. On what other occasions was Russia's government overthrown by revolutionaries?

Reviewing the Unit

Unit Summary

After you have read the selection below, answer the questions that follow.

Late in the eighteenth century, the English colonies of North America revolted, won independence, and established a republic based on a written constitution. The American Revolution probably had a great impact on many French who resented the injustices and abuses of their own Old Regime. In 1789, this resentment broke out in revolution. The Old Regime was destroyed, the powers of the king were limited, and a constitutional monarchy was established. King Louis XVI refused to accept limits on his power. Therefore, he was executed in 1793, and a republic was established. In 1799, the republic was overthrown by Napoleon Bonaparte.

With Napoleon's brother on the Spanish throne in the 1800's, the colonists in South America declared their independence. Spain's colonies revolted and set themselves up as independent nations, as did Brazil, a Portuguese colony in South America.

Many army officers who fought in western Europe during the Napoleonic Wars returned home to Russia convinced that Russia must be reformed. In 1825, secret revolutionary organizations believed the time for revolution had come. Although their attempt failed, the idea of revolution did not die. By the late 1800's, secret revolutionary organizations were seeking to overthrow the government. Revolution erupted in 1905, and Tsar Nicholas II had to make concessions in order to keep his throne. In 1917, revolution again erupted. Lacking support even from his troops, Nicholas resigned and a Provisional Government was set up. However, in November 1917, Lenin and the Bolsheviks seized control of Russia's government and set out to establish a Marxist dictatorship.

Meanwhile, in Europe and the Americas, the Industrial Revolution, which began in England, was rapidly changing the methods for manufacturing goods. A new way of living developed for the workers who flocked to the cities to work in the new factories that appeared.

Developing Your Reading Skills

1. What in your opinion is the one main idea in the reading above?
2. In your own words, state the main idea in this reading about each of the following:

   a. The revolutions in North, Central, and South America.
   b. The French Revolution.
   c. The revolutions in Russia.
   d. The Industrial Revolution.

Developing a Sense of Time

Examine the time line below and answer the questions that follow it.

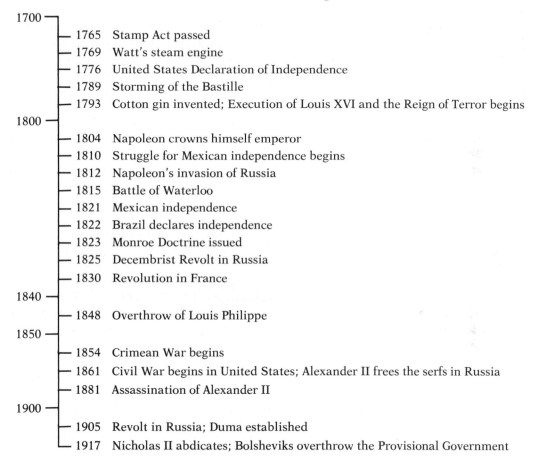

1700

— 1765   Stamp Act passed

— 1769   Watt's steam engine

— 1776   United States Declaration of Independence

— 1789   Storming of the Bastille

— 1793   Cotton gin invented; Execution of Louis XVI and the Reign of Terror begins

1800

— 1804   Napoleon crowns himself emperor

— 1810   Struggle for Mexican independence begins

— 1812   Napoleon's invasion of Russia

— 1815   Battle of Waterloo

— 1821   Mexican independence

— 1822   Brazil declares independence

— 1823   Monroe Doctrine issued

— 1825   Decembrist Revolt in Russia

— 1830   Revolution in France

1840

— 1848   Overthrow of Louis Philippe

1850

— 1854   Crimean War begins

— 1861   Civil War begins in United States; Alexander II frees the serfs in Russia

— 1881   Assassination of Alexander II

1900

— 1905   Revolt in Russia; Duma established

— 1917   Nicholas II abdicates; Bolsheviks overthrow the Provisional Government

1. Where did revolution occur first—in the American colonies or in France?
2. What was taking place in the United States at the time Alexander II freed the Russian serfs?
3. Which occurred first—the American Civil War or the Crimean War?
4. What other key events or developments from Unit 8 could be added to this time line? Name three such events or developments and give a reason for selecting each.

429

Recalling the Facts

1. How did the American Revolution differ from the fight for independence in Latin America? In what ways was it similar?
2. Describe the conditions in France under the Old Regime.
3. Describe Napoleon's rise to power in France. What brought about his downfall?
4. Name three major leaders in the Latin American revolutions.
5. How were manufacturing and agriculture changed during the Industrial Revolution?
6. List two social problems brought about by the Industrial Revolution. How were they solved?
7. List four important inventions during the Industrial Revolution and tell their significance.
8. Explain how the beliefs of Marx and Owen differed.
9. What brought about the Decembrist Revolt of 1825 in Russia? the Revolution of 1905? the Bolshevik Revolution of 1917?
10. How did monarchy in Russia come to an end? Why?

Using Your Vocabulary

1. What is meant by the term *Old Regime?*
2. What is meant by the term *Reign of Terror?* How did it apply in France?
3. How might a factory worker during the Industrial Revolution have defined the meaning of revolution? Do you think a person living in Mexico under Spanish colonial rule would have the same definition?
4. What is nationalism? How did Napoleon contribute to the development of nationalism?
5. Explain the terms *trust, monopoly,* and *cartel.*
6. Explain the following inventions: the flying shuttle, the cotton gin, and the water frame.
7. How are the terms *capitalism* and *free enterprise* similar? How do they differ?
8. How does the Industrial Revolution differ from other revolutions you have studied? What similarities were there?
9. How are the terms *socialism* and *communism* similar? How do they differ?

Using Your Geography Skills

1. Using the information in your text and the map on page 382, list the areas added to Napoleon's empire.
2. Using the map on page 382 and the information in your text, describe the march of Napoleon's army into Russia in 1812. How far is it from the Russian border to Moscow?
3. Using the map on page 365, identify the countries of Central and South America and the years they won independence from Spain and Portugal in the 1800's.
4. What parts of the United States were added during American expansion in the 1800's? How was each of these areas added?
5. Describe the location of the Panama Canal. Why is its geographic location significant?

Developing Your Writing Skills

In this unit you have learned about the great variety of revolutions that took place in Europe and the New World in the 1700's, 1800's, and early 1900's. Many of these revolutions resulted in violence and warfare, but they produced significant political changes in Europe and the New World. Using your knowledge of these revolutions, consider the following:

FORMING AN OPINION

1. Suppose you had to make a choice between living under a form of government you considered unjust or joining a revolutionary movement to bring about political changes. What would you do? Why?
2. What means other than revolution might bring about political change?
3. In your opinion, is revolution ever justified?

SUPPORTING AN OPINION

In a short essay, explain your answer to question 3. Begin your essay by completing the following topic sentence: Revolution is (is not) a justified means for bringing about change because ____
____

Why Study the Past?

It has been said that people who do not learn from the mistakes of the past are doomed to repeat those same mistakes.

Which of the events in this unit are examples of mistakes you would not want to see repeated?

Your History Bookshelf

Berlin, Isaiah. *Karl Marx: His Life and Environment.* New York: Galaxy, 1959.

Cash, Anthony. *Russian Revolution.* New York: Doubleday, 1969.

Crump, Kenneth G. *Napoleon Bonaparte: What Are the Consequences of Power?* New York: Scholastic Book Service, 1974.

Lawson, Don. *American Revolution: America's First War for Independence.* New York: Abelard-Schuman, 1974.

Liverside, Douglas. *The Day the Bastille Fell:* New York: Watts, 1972.

Prago, Albert. *The Revolution in Spanish America: The Independence Movements of 1808–1825.* New York: Macmillan, 1970.

Reeder, Red. *Bold Leaders of the Revolutionary War.* Boston: Little, Brown, 1973.

Rooke, Patrick. *The Industrial Revolution.* New York: John Day, 1972.

unit 9

The World of
Nationalism

Flying was quite different in the days of World War I from the way it is today. Airplanes were fragile, single-engine machines with open cockpits. Before the days of jet engines and heavy bombers, flying was in many ways more adventurous. In a letter written to his parents, the pilot of an American plane during World War I recounted the following adventure he had while flying as an observer over enemy lines. Observers used to take photographs of enemy movements.

"I had the thrill of my life yesterday. The plane I was flying had two guns on it, one for the pilot and one for the observer (called Fiske). Fiske was standing up on the seat in back of me, shooting away at an enemy scouting plane that was flying around us. At the same time, I put the plane into a dive so I could also get a shot at the enemy with my gun. As soon as I did this, I heard a sort of crash behind me. After I had straightened the plane out, I looked around to see what it was. Lo and behold, a man in a leather coat was hanging onto the tail of my plane.

"Fiske had fallen out of his cockpit when his gun broke loose from its fastenings and I had nosed over. I wondered if he had the strength to hold on until I was able to land the plane. I put the plane into a gentle glide and started for home, as I could not land where I was. Fiske at this time was able to hook his legs over the tail and, sliding his body up toward his seat, finally reached it. He dove into the cockpit head first.

"Today Fiske is resting in bed, having been excused from all flying. He will never come any nearer to death at the front."

Nationalism, the feeling of pride in one's country, was one of the most important political, social, and economic forces in the world during the 1800's and early 1900's. Nationalism took on many different forms and symbols during those years and spread to all parts of the world. It was also related to the period of intense colonization in Africa and parts of Asia and the Pacific. This race for colonies—a source of raw materials and markets for manufactured goods—by the industrialized nations of the world is called imperialism.

In this unit, the relationship between imperialism and nationalism will be explored. How these two forces combined and led to wars between nations will also be discussed. Further, this unit will deal with what impact these forces had on the unification of Italy and Germany, the causes and results of World War I, the Chinese Revolution, the change in the balance of power in Europe and Asia after World War I, the rise of dictators in Germany and Italy, and the outbreak, battle plans, and outcome of World War II.

Unit Goals

1. To define the terms *imperialism* and *nationalism* and to know how these two forces are related to each other.
2. To understand how imperialism and nationalism often led to conflict.
3. To trace the causes of World War I and to understand how the peace treaty following that war was partly responsible for conditions leading to World War II.
4. To describe the rise of Hitler and Mussolini in the period between World War I and World War II.
5. To understand the events most directly responsible for the outbreak of World War II in Europe and Asia.
6. To identify major events during World War II and describe the peace treaties and the formation of the United Nations.

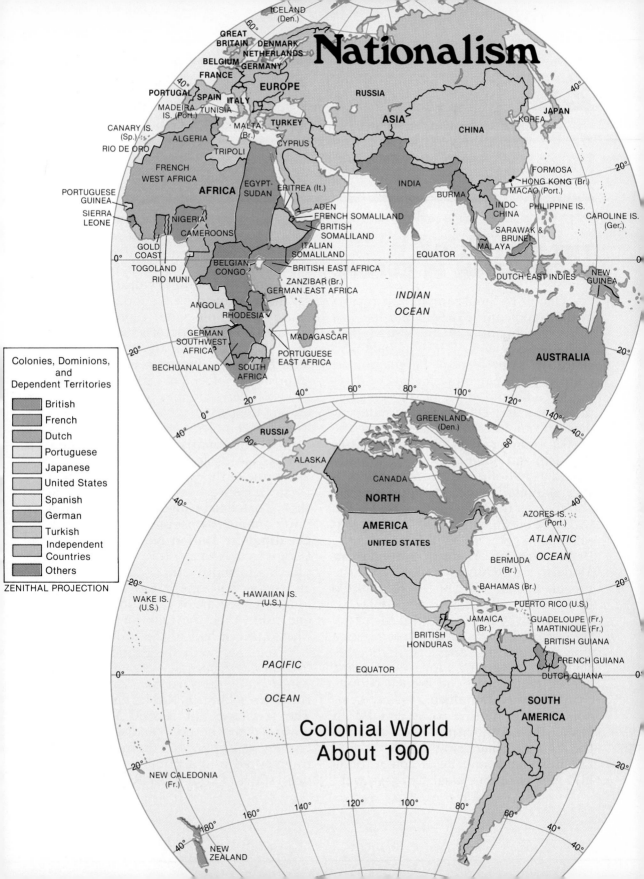

Nationalism

Colonies, Dominions, and Dependent Territories

- British
- French
- Dutch
- Portuguese
- Japanese
- United States
- Spanish
- German
- Turkish
- Independent Countries
- Others

ZENITHAL PROJECTION

Colonial World About 1900

EUROPE
ICELAND (Den.)
GREAT BRITAIN
DENMARK
NETHERLANDS
BELGIUM
GERMANY
FRANCE
PORTUGAL
SPAIN
ITALY
MADEIRA IS. (Port.)
TUNISIA
MALTA (Br.)
CANARY IS. (Sp.)
ALGERIA
RIO DE ORO
TRIPOLI
TURKEY
CYPRUS
RUSSIA
ASIA
CHINA
KOREA
JAPAN
FORMOSA
HONG KONG (Br.)
MACAO (Port.)
PHILIPPINE IS.
CAROLINE IS. (Ger.)

FRENCH WEST AFRICA
AFRICA
EGYPT-SUDAN
ERITREA (It.)
ADEN
FRENCH SOMALILAND
BRITISH SOMALILAND
ITALIAN SOMALILAND
INDIA
BURMA
INDO-CHINA
SARAWAK & BRUNEI
MALAYA

PORTUGUESE GUINEA
SIERRA LEONE
NIGERIA
CAMEROONS
GOLD COAST
TOGOLAND
RIO MUNI
BELGIAN CONGO
BRITISH EAST AFRICA
ZANZIBAR (Br.)
GERMAN EAST AFRICA
EQUATOR
DUTCH EAST INDIES
NEW GUINEA

ANGOLA
RHODESIA
GERMAN SOUTHWEST AFRICA
BECHUANALAND
SOUTH AFRICA
MADAGASCAR
PORTUGUESE EAST AFRICA
INDIAN OCEAN
AUSTRALIA

GREENLAND (Den.)
RUSSIA
ALASKA
CANADA
NORTH AMERICA
UNITED STATES
AZORES IS. (Port.)
ATLANTIC OCEAN
BERMUDA (Br.)
BAHAMAS (Br.)
WAKE IS. (U.S.)
HAWAIIAN IS. (U.S.)
PUERTO RICO (U.S.)
JAMAICA (Br.)
GUADELOUPE (Fr.)
MARTINIQUE (Fr.)
BRITISH HONDURAS
BRITISH GUIANA
FRENCH GUIANA
DUTCH GUIANA
PACIFIC OCEAN
EQUATOR
SOUTH AMERICA
NEW CALEDONIA (Fr.)
NEW ZEALAND

Modern Nationalism

THE REVIVAL OF NATIONALISM IN EUROPE

One of the most important results of the Napoleonic Wars in Europe was the revival of nationalism. **Nationalism** is the sense of unity felt by people who share the same history, language, and culture. Nationalism was also the driving force behind many of the struggles in Europe and elsewhere for independence from foreign rulers during the 1800's. Among the French, English, Spanish, and others who were already united as nations in the nineteenth century, nationalism became more intense and took on the form of increased pride in each nation-state and its accomplishments.

Beginnings of Modern Nationalism Modern nationalism began with the French Revolution. During the French Revolution, all classes of people became involved in the political life of the country. The goals of the revolution—liberty, equality, and brotherhood—inspired a strong loyalty toward France that united the French people.

Symbols of Nationalism New symbols of nationalism were created in France during this time. The display of the national flag, singing of the national anthem, and large celebrations in honor of the national holidays were signs of increased national pride. The French were also the first in modern times to have a military draft. Military service became a citizen's duty and because all people were represented in the army, French victories were looked upon as victories for the entire nation.

New States The presence of French troops on foreign soil, however, aroused new feelings of nationalism among the people whose land had been invaded. Napoleon also unintentionally inspired nationalism by creating new unified states for the Italians, Poles, and some of the Germans. Even though these states were under French control, their existence brought forth a spirit of unity among the people living there.

Creating the Italian Nation At the Congress of Vienna, Italy had been divided into many states and provinces and since that time, many Italians had longed to see all of Italy united under one ruler. (See the map on page 437.) The southern half of the Italian peninsula together with the island of Sicily (SIS-uh-lee) became known as the *Kingdom of the Two Sicilies* and was ruled by a king in Naples (NAY-pulz). The territories of central Italy were governed by the pope and were called the *Papal States*. Northern Italy was fragmented into a number of independent states. *Parma* (PAHR-muh), *Mod-*

ena (MAWD-un-uh), *Lucca* (LOO-kuh), and *Tuscany* (TUS-kuh-nee) were duchies, each with its own ruler, while the *Kingdom of Sardinia* included the island of Sardinia and the regions of *Savoy* (suh-VOY), *Piedmont* (PEED-mahnt), and *Nice* (NEES) on the mainland. The remaining states in northern Italy were *Lombardy* (LOM-bahrd-ee) and *Venetia* (vi-NEE-shee-uh), which had been given to Austria by the Congress of Vienna. In addition, Austria also protected some of the absolute rulers who governed the duchies in northern Italy. As a result, in the eyes of Italian nationalists, Austria was the chief obstacle to their goal of the unification of the Italian peninsula.

Mazzini   One of the early leaders of the *risorgimento* (rih-zor-jih-MEN-toe), or unification movement, in Italy was *Giuseppe Mazzini* (juh-SEP-ee maht-SEE-nee). Mazzini was a revolutionary writer and thinker who favored uniting the Italian peninsula as a republic. He founded a patriotic organization called *Young Italy*, and as revolutions swept across Europe in 1848, Mazzini's followers staged uprisings in Italy. When they seized Rome, Pope Pius IX fled, and Mazzini proclaimed an Italian republic in early 1849.

UNIFICATION OF ITALY, 1859-1870

Legend:
- Kingdom of Sardinia 1859
- Ceded to France in 1860
- Kingdom of Italy 1860
- Added to Italy in 1866
- Added to Italy in 1870

Which Italian kingdom led the struggle for unification?

Mazzini was one of the leaders of the Italian unification movement. What kind of government did he want to establish in Italy?

Mazzini Is Defeated Many Italians, however, refused to support Mazzini. Some believed that monarchy was the best form of government for Italy and feared republicanism. Meanwhile, in northern Italy, Austrian troops suppressed Mazzini's revolutionaries. The final blow came in April 1849, when an army of more than 8,000 troops was sent to Italy by Louis Napoleon, the president of France. Mazzini's army, led by *Giuseppe Garibaldi* (gar-uh-BAWL-dee), tried to defend Rome, but after two months Garibaldi gave up and fled into exile. The French took control of Rome, maintaining troops there for twenty years. They restored the power of the pope over the Papal States in central Italy.

Cavour and the Unification of Italy
After the failure of the 1848 Revolution in Italy, leadership of the *risorgimento* passed to **Count Camillo di Cavour** (Kuh-MEE-loe dee kuh-VOOR), the prime minister of the Kingdom of Sardinia. Sardinia had been the only Italian state to strongly resist the Austrians during the Revolution of 1848. After the revolution was over, the king of Sardinia became popular with many Italians because he granted his people a liberal constitution and Sardinia became a prosperous modern state under Cavour's leadership.

Unification by Annexation Cavour was a shrewd politician who realized that foreign help against Austria would be needed in order to create an Italian nation. When Britain and France went to war against Russia in the Crimea (krie-MEE-uh) in 1854, Austria refused to join them. Cavour saw this as an opportunity to win the friendship of the French and entered the *Crimean War* on the side of the French.

After the Crimean War, Cavour maneuvered Austria into declaring war on Sardinia in 1859. To win France as an ally against Austria, Cavour offered to give the territories of Nice and Savoy to Louis Napoleon, who by that time called himself Emperor Napoleon III. Consequently, French and Italian troops invaded the Austrian-held parts of Italy. After bloody battles in Lombardy, Napoleon III decided to negotiate for an end to the war. Under the peace terms he arranged, France took Nice and Savoy, but Austria had to give up Lombardy. Venetia, however, remained under Austria's control. With French approval, Sardinia annexed Lombardy, as well as Tuscany, Parma, Modena, Lucca, and a large part of the Papal States. (See map on page 437.)

Garibaldi   While this was taking place, Garibaldi, the former leader of revolutionaries in Rome, organized an army of 1,000 Italian nationalists. With these soldiers, Garibaldi invaded the island of Sicily. King Francis II of Sicily had a large army with which to stop Garibaldi, but he was unpopular with many of the people of southern Italy and with his own troops. As a result, within six months Garibaldi captured Sicily. When Garibaldi's army crossed to the mainland, the king of the Two Sicilies fled from Naples. At this point, Cavour sent Sardinian troops south to seize a large area of the Papal States and to prevent Garibaldi from attacking Rome. Cavour then persuaded Garibaldi to permit the unification of the Two Sicilies with Sardinia.

Final Unification   After the fighting ended, almost all the Italian peninsula was united. *King Victor Emmanuel* (eh-mah-noo-EL) II, the ruler of Sardinia, was proclaimed king of Italy in 1861. The final additions of Venetia in 1866 and Rome in 1870 completed the formation of the modern Italian state. When the capital of Italy was moved to Rome in 1870, a section of the city was set aside for the pope's use. Today, the pope continues to govern the *Vatican City*, a small nation-state located in Rome.

Creation of the German Nation   After Napoleon's final defeat, there were still about thirty separate German states, each with its own ruler. During the Revolution of 1848, the goal of the German revolutionaries had been to unite Germany under one ruler. Although the revolutionaries failed, they did not give up their goal. Some nationalists wanted Prussia to head a united Germany. Others believed Austria should unite the German states.

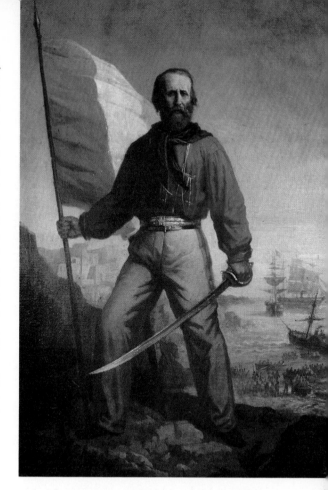

Why are revolutionary leaders, such as Garibaldi (shown here in his famous red shirt), often thought of as romantic heroes?

Prussia Unites Germany   Germany was finally united by the kingdom of Prussia. At the beginning of the 1700's, Prussia was a small kingdom. During this century, Prussia's rulers added territory, and under Frederick II, Prussia emerged as one of Europe's major military powers. In the Napoleonic Wars, Prussia suffered at the hands of the French. After the wars, Prussia enlarged its territory at the expense of some of Napoleon's former German allies. Prussia's sudden rise to power made it Austria's chief rival among the

439

The policies of Otto von Bismarck were important factors in the unification of Germany and had great influence on the course of German history in the twentieth century. Can you think of any policies formulated in the nineteenth century in the United States that have influenced us today?

German-speaking states by the middle of the nineteenth century.

Bismarck   Leadership in uniting all the German states passed to **Otto von Bismarck** (BIZ-mahrk), who became prime minister of Prussia in 1862. Bismarck realized that Prussia would never be the leading German state until it proved itself more powerful than the Austrian Empire. Bismarck devoted himself to building the Prussian army because he believed he needed a war to achieve unification.

In 1864, Bismarck persuaded Austria to join with Prussia in a war against Denmark. The purpose of this war was to take from Denmark the provinces of Schleswig (SHLES-wig)

and Holstein (HOLE-stine), which were inhabited by Germans. The small Danish army was easily defeated, but disagreements between Prussia and Austria soon arose. Prussia complained about Austria's administration of some of the conquered territory, and in 1866 provoked Austria into a war.

The Seven Weeks' War   Prussian troops invaded Austrian territory and met the Austrian army in Bohemia, where they won an important victory at the *Battle of Sadowa* (zah-DOE-vuh). Austria never recovered from this defeat and had to surrender. The war lasted only seven weeks.

As a result of the *Seven Weeks' War,* Prussia was able to take over some of the small states in northern Germany. The rest of northern Germany was united in an alliance called the *North German Confederation* under Prussian control. Only four southern German states remained outside the confederation, but they were tied to Prussia by military alliances.

The French   Prussia's sudden rise alarmed France. The French realized that if Bismarck could unite all of Germany, the new German nation would be one of the largest and strongest countries in Europe. Bismarck expected France to do everything possible to prevent the unification of Germany. He realized France was the next obstacle to be overcome.

The Franco-Prussian War   Prussia and France went to war in 1870. Bismarck was chiefly to blame for the outbreak of the fighting. He deliberately altered a telegram he had received that described a meeting between the king of Prussia and the French ambassador at the German city of Ems. Bismarck released the telegram to the press after altering it in such a way as to make the French believe their country had been insulted by the Germans, and to make the Germans believe they were being threatened by France. Within a short time after the telegram appeared in French and German newspapers, war was declared.

As in the war against Austria, the Prussian army was ready for immediate action. Prussian troops quickly invaded France. The French were badly defeated at the *Battle of Sedan* (sih-DAN) in northern France and Emperor Napoleon III was taken prisoner. When Paris finally surrendered after holding out against the Germans for more than three months, the war ended.

In the *Treaty of Frankfurt,* Bismarck imposed harsh peace terms on France. The French had to give up two important coal- and iron-rich territories—Alsace (al-SAS) and Lorraine (luh-RAYN). France also had to pay an *indemnity,* or a large sum of money, before German troops would withdraw from French soil.

A New German Nation   After the war, all the independent states of southern Germany joined those already annexed to Prussia to form a new nation. On January 17, 1871, a new Germany was proclaimed at ceremonies held in the great palace at Versailles built by the French king, Louis

UNIFICATION OF GERMANY, 1865-1871

150 kilometers
100 miles

SWEDEN

DENMARK •Copenhagen

BALTIC SEA

NORTH SEA

Kiel•

Königsberg

Danzig•

•Hamburg

NETHERLANDS

Amsterdam•

•Hanover

•Berlin

•Warsaw

RUSSIAN EMPIRE

Brussels•

BELGIUM

•Cologne

Dresden•

Breslau•

Frankfurt•

AUSTRIAN EMPIRE

LUXEMBOURG

•Paris

FRANCE

•Strasbourg

Munich•

SWITZERLAND

	Prussia 1865
	Annexed to Prussia in 1866
	Joined Prussia in North German Confederation 1867
	Joined Prussia and NGC States in German Empire 1871
	Alsace-Lorraine, annexed 1871
—	Boundary of German Empire 1871

What German state pushed for German unification?

XIV. Having such a German ceremony held in the palace that was a symbol of former French power and wealth was a great humiliation for the French people, and the French and Germans remained bitter enemies.

The Rise of Germany   During the period from unification until the outbreak of World War I in 1914, Germany became one of Europe's most powerful countries. Some of the changes brought about by Bismarck as prime minister were a common monetary system, a central bank, coordination of the railroad and postal system, and improved efficiency of the legal and judicial systems. Germany's industries grew rapidly and its population increased. Its army became the finest in Europe, and its navy was enlarged. To prevent the spread of socialism and avoid the danger of revolution, the German government enforced good working conditions in factories, mills, and mines. It also insured workers against illness or accidents. Meanwhile, Germany entered the race for trade and territory. It was able to establish colonies in Africa, Asia, and the Pacific area.

The Rise of the Second French Republic   The reign of Napoleon I in France was recalled by the French people as an age of glory, when France had been almost undefeated and had conquered most of Europe. A republic had been established after the 1848 Revolution in France, and Napoleon's nephew was elected its president. A few years later, he dissolved the republic and crowned himself **Emperor Napoleon III.** The *First Empire* in France had been the creation of Napoleon I. Napoleon III called his government the *Second Empire.* He worked hard to restore the glory France had known earlier. Under him, France was again the strongest nation on the European continent.

France Declines   But France's power slowly declined. Napoleon III attempted further foreign conquests. He wanted to unite his people behind him and hoped these adventures would appeal to French nationalism. Victory over Russia in the Crimean War did bring France military glory, but not all of Napoleon's plans worked out so well.

Emperor Maximilian   One of the worst mistakes Napoleon III made was in Mexico. In 1861, Napoleon sent troops to Mexico to seize the government and set up a new one under his control. He placed a member of the Austrian royal family on the new Mexican throne as *Emperor Maximilian* (mak-suh-MIL-yun). Almost immediately Mexican nationalists, led by *Benito Juárez* (WAHR-ays), struggled to drive the French out of Mexico. At the *Battle of Puebla* (poo-EB-luh) in 1862, the Mexicans inflicted a defeat on the French army. But Juárez's forces were not powerful enough to retake control.

Napoleon III was the nephew of Napoleon I. Using this photograph as a guide, do you think he thought of himself as a military leader or a civil leader?

The puppet of Napoleon III of France, the Emperor Maximilian, was finally executed by his unhappy Mexican subjects. Empress Carlotta was in Europe at the time. Do you think one country should impose a ruler on another? Why or why not?

The United States Steps In While the French were invading Mexico, the United States was engaged in the Civil War. But when that war ended in 1865, the United States, fearful of European armies in the Western Hemisphere, decided to force the French from Mexico. Napoleon III withdrew his troops rather than risk war with the United States. But the French left behind the unfortunate Maximilian. He was shot by Mexican forces in 1867.

The Fall of the Second Empire Only a few years later, the Second Empire was destroyed by the Prussian victory against France in the Franco-Prussian War. After the war was over, it was not certain what sort of government France would have. France probably would have remained a monarchy had it not been for disagreements over who should be at its head. Some people wanted to place a member of the Bourbon family on the French throne. Some supported the son of Louis Philippe, of the Orleans family. Others favored the son of Napoleon III. Because the three groups could not agree on who should be king, the *Third Republic* was proclaimed in 1871.

French Nationalism In the late 1800's and early 1900's, strong feelings of nationalism again united the French people. Almost all of them wished to take revenge on Germany for the humiliating defeat France had suffered in the war against Prussia. They also demanded that Germany return the French territories of Alsace and Lorraine, which Germany had taken over after that war. Nationalist feelings in France remained intense until the beginning of World War I in 1914. They drew France into the scramble for colonies along with the other powers, and France succeeded in creating an overseas colonial empire in Africa, Asia, and the Pacific that was second only to that of the British.

SECTION REVIEW

1. Using the maps on page 437 and 441, list the areas of Italy and Germany that later became part of each nation. What were the key factors in uniting both areas?

2. In your own words, identify or define: nationalism, Cavour, Victor Emmanuel II, Bismarck, Napoleon III.

3. How did Napoleon I stimulate nationalistic feelings in Europe during the early 1800's?

4. How did each of the leaders of the *risorgimento* contribute to Italian unification?

5. How did Bismarck use war as a tool in unifying Germany?

6. How did the overseas adventures of Napoleon III in Mexico affect the Second Empire?

◗ List the national characteristics that unite the people in your country today. What are some of your country's national symbols?

NATIONALISM IN THE NON-WESTERN WORLD

The beginnings of nationalism in Africa and Asia can be traced back to the 1800's, but nationalism developed fully in those parts of the world only in the twentieth century. The economic and political domination of western nations was partly responsible for the growth of nationalism in the non-western world. Nationalism sprang from the pride of a people in their civilization, and from their humiliation at being conquered and ruled by foreigners.

The Western Powers in China At the beginning of the 1800's, the Chinese were a proud people. China was called the Middle Kingdom as if it were the center of the civilized world. The Chinese regarded themselves as people who shared a superior civilization. Thus people who were not Chinese were thought of as barbarians. Foreign peoples had invaded China many times. Some, like the Mongols or the Manchus, had conquered China and set up their own ruling dynasties. Until the coming of Europeans to China in the 1800's, however, foreign invaders had respected China's long history and way of life. It was, therefore, a shock to the Chinese when they met "white barbarians" from the West who knew little about China and had no regard for its culture.

Manchus Come to Power The Manchus overthrew the Ming Dynasty in 1644. They made Peking their capital and placed their own rulers on the Chinese throne. Through most of the seventeenth and eighteenth centuries, the Manchus provided strong, capable leaders who governed China. However, a series of weak emperors came to the throne in the 1800's. They were more concerned with the pursuit of pleasure than with governing their empire.

Tz'u Hsi In 1861, the imperial throne passed to a five-year-old boy whose mother quickly seized control of the government and, thereafter, ruled China as the power behind the throne. This woman, *Tz'u Hsi* (TSOOH-SHEE), remained in actual control of the Chinese government off and on for more than fifty years. Tz'u Hsi's chief concern was keeping her own family in power. It was more important for her to see her sons and nephews on the throne as emperors than to look after the welfare of China. Thus throughout most of the nineteenth century, strong leadership in China was absent. This made it easier for foreign powers to take advantage of the Chinese.

The Opium Wars China fought two wars with western nations in the 1800's. The first of these was the *Opium War* against the British. The Opium War began in 1839 when the Chinese tried to control the importation of opium into China by British merchants. The opium was grown in India, which was then under British control. The British government dispatched a war fleet to China to protect British subjects there and British-Chinese hostilities resulted in a short war. The Chinese were no match for the powerful British army and navy. The Chinese government surrendered in 1842 and signed the *Treaty of Nanking.*

Peace did not last long. In 1856, the Chinese went to war with the British and the French. The western powers charged the Chinese with mistreatment of Europeans. This short war ended with China's surrender in 1860 and the signing of the *Treaties of Tientsin* (tee-EN-SIN) in order to restore peace.

The Unequal Treaties In both wars, Chinese troops had been no match for the Europeans and were badly beaten. The series of treaties that were signed after the end of these two wars gave almost all the European nations economic and political privileges in China. China was forced to open its ports to trade with the West. But it could not raise taxes on goods imported from the West without the consent of the Europeans. Europeans were also granted the privilege of *extraterritoriality.* This

The flags flying over this Chinese harbor reflect the trading interests in China in the early nineteenth century. These trading rights, however, were imposed on the Chinese. Do nations ever have the right to force other nations to trade with them?

485

meant that Europeans accused of crimes in China could not be put on trial in a Chinese court. Instead, they were to be returned to their home countries for judgment. The Chinese also had to permit western merchants and missionaries to travel wherever they liked in China. The Chinese came to call these treaties the *Unequal Treaties*.

Revolution in China While China was suffering at the hands of foreigners, a civil war swept across half the land. From 1848 to 1864, rebels, called the *Taipings* (TIE-PINGS), controlled much of southern China and gradually extended their control northward until about half of China was in their hands. The Taipings were determined to oust the Manchus, whom they considered foreigners, and to modernize China. The Taipings won supporters from all classes in Chinese society. Leaders of the rebellion enjoyed early military victories. However, when it appeared possible that the Manchu Dynasty might collapse, the European powers decided to give aid to the Chinese government. The Taipings were unable to resist the combined European and Chinese force thrown against them.

The Manchus Weaken Although the Manchus finally won, the civil war weakened the imperial government. The Chinese were slow in realizing the necessity of modernizing China. Unlike the Japanese, who quickly learned new ways from the western powers that were ready to overwhelm Japan, the Chinese continued to cling to their old way of life. They relied on their old traditions to provide solutions to their new problems. This attitude lasted in China for almost all the 1800's. The Chinese never lost their feeling that they were more civilized than the westerners.

War Between China and Japan Aware of China's weakness, Japan made war on China in 1894. China and Japan were rivals for influence over the Korean government. This rivalry led to war, and China was badly beaten. Japan's army and navy had been modernized and used western equipment and weapons. This defeat at the hands of another Asian country alarmed the Chinese government. Many educated Chinese now realized that the only way to save themselves was to follow the Japanese example. They agreed that China would have to modernize, using western learning and methods. In the 1890's, many Chinese revolutionaries called for the overthrow of the Manchus. They pointed out that the Manchus were foreigners, and they blamed them for China's misfortunes. These revolutionaries were developing a form of Chinese nationalism that continued to grow throughout the early 1900's. The father of Chinese nationalism was a revolutionary leader educated in the West named **Sun Yat-sen** (SOON YAHT-SEN).

The Boxer Rebellion Chinese resentment against foreigners became violent in 1900 in the *Boxer Rebellion*. The Boxers were members of a secret organization whose aim was to kill foreigners or drive them from China. The name *Boxer* came from the series of postures and exercises that members performed to harmonize mind and body in preparation for combat. Although the Manchu government at Peking decided to support the Boxers, their combined forces failed to overcome the western troops from many nations that joined together to put down the revolt.

The Chinese Revolution The western powers blamed the Manchus for the

446

Boxer Rebellion. Under the peace terms that followed the rebellion, large indemnities were imposed on China. At last, the Manchu government seemed convinced of the necessity to reform and modernize. But now it was too late.

The Chinese Revolution began in October of 1911. Almost all of China joined the revolution, and the Manchu emperor was forced to give up the throne. A Chinese republic was formed. However, at that point the unity of the revolutionaries disappeared. A general named *Yüan Shih-k'ai* (yoo-AHN SHIR-KIE) was made head of the new government. He was about to set himself up as emperor when he died in 1916. No one could be found to take his place. China was plunged into disorder and the central government simply ceased to exist. Local governors or military commanders, called *warlords,* seized control of provinces and ruled with the support of their private armies.

The Rise of Chinese Nationalism Most educated Chinese disliked what was happening to their country. Some, like Sun Yat-sen, who had been one of the leaders of the 1911 Revolution, knew that nationalism had to develop and a strong central government had to be established before China could become powerful. The goals of the western powers fighting Germany in World War I excited the Chinese nationalists. The western democracies declared that the war was being fought for the freedom of peoples like the Chinese. But when the war ended, they learned that the victorious democracies had no intention of giving up their colonies. Nor did they intend to withdraw from their influential position in China.

The Nationalist Party When the promises of the western democracies did not materialize, the Chinese reacted

Educated in the United States, Sun Yat-sen was later one of the leaders of the Chinese revolution. How do you think his experiences in the U.S. might have influenced his ideas?

strongly. A wave of nationalism swept the country. The *Nationalist party* was founded by Sun Yat-sen, who was considered the father of the modern *Republic of China.* Among the party's goals was the reunification of China. Sun Yat-sen realized his political party could not accomplish this reunification without foreign help. Knowing the western nations were not friends of China, he turned to his neighbor, Soviet Russia, for aid.

Communist Russia sent money, military equipment, and advisers to assist Sun Yat-sen's government. In exchange, Sun permitted members of the new, small Chinese Communist party to take key roles inside his own Nationalist party and the government he hoped to establish for all China.

Chiang Kai-shek Sun Yat-sen did not live to see the army of his Nationalist party reunite China. He died in 1925, and leadership of the party

447

passed to **Chiang Kai-shek** (jee-AHNG KIE-SHEK). Chiang had been placed in command of the Nationalist army before Sun's death, and in 1926 he launched a military campaign that was intended to destroy the power of the warlords and extend Nationalist control over all China.

It was not long before Chiang Kai-shek and the Chinese Communists grew to mistrust one another. The Communists were alarmed by Chiang's growing power as head of the army. When Russia withdrew its support of Chiang, the Chinese Communists plotted to overthrow him. After learning of the Communists' intention to take over the government of the new Chinese republic, Chiang Kai-shek decided to use force to destroy communism in China. In April of 1927, he began a long and bloody civil war between the Nationalists and the Communists. He forced the Soviet advisers in China to leave the country but was never able to crush communism completely in China.

This is a picture of the Nationalist leader, Chiang Kai-shek and the Communist leader, Mao Tse-tung. How did the split between these two men and their parties lead to the creation of "two" Chinas?

Chiang made war for ten years, from 1927 to 1937, against the Communist-held areas of China. The Communists, under a new leader named **Mao Tse-tung** (MOW-DZU-DOONG), in the twelve-month Long March of 1934 retreated to a far north-western corner of China.

Japan Invades China   The Nationalist-Communist struggle was halted in 1937 when Japan invaded China. The Nationalists and Communists temporarily put aside their hostilities to unite against the foreign invader. But the Chinese were unable to drive out the Japanese, who held a large part of China from 1937 throughout World War II.

SECTION REVIEW

1. Using the map on page 452, list the countries that held territory or had spheres of influence in China. Why were they able to gain this power?

2. In your own words, identify: Manchus, Opium War, Taipings, Boxer Rebellion, Sun Yat-sen, Nationalist party, Chiang Kai-shek, Mao Tse-tung.

3. How did the Unequal Treaties increase the power of foreign nations in China and limit the power of the Chinese government?

4. Why did the Chinese turn away from the western democracies after World War I? What was the result?

▷ Do you think the treatment of China by the western nations during the 1800's was justified? Do you believe a nation ever has the right to conquer another to improve its own economic condition? Explain your answer.

The Rise of Imperialism

WHAT IS IMPERIALISM?

Imperialism is another word for empire building, and this was a policy that the governments of many European countries, the United States, and Japan followed during much of the nineteenth and early twentieth centuries. Imperialism involved the expansion of a country's borders, the spread of its culture, and the economic or political domination of people in other areas.

Imperialism Declines Few European countries were interested in new overseas territory until late in the 1800's. Many of them already had established colonies abroad, but the colonies were not expected to make a profit for the ruling country. After the long Napoleonic Wars of the early 1800's, most European nations were more interested in solving their internal problems, building their industries, and trying to get along peacefully with their neighbors. The newly-formed United States had no thoughts of overseas expansion either. Its people were busy establishing themselves as a nation and settling the western frontier.

A New Interest in Imperialism Colonization became a major concern again of the European powers and the United States late in the 1800's. By then the Industrial Revolution had spread throughout Europe and had reached America. New inventions and production methods had brought about a tremendous increase in the amount of industrial goods. To continue producing more goods, manufacturers needed fresh sources of cheap raw materials. They also had to find new markets in which to sell their products. Business interests sought new places where they could invest capital profitably. The underdeveloped continents of Africa and Asia seemed to provide an answer to all of these needs.

Political Reasons There were also political reasons for the rise of imperialism. As national pride increased, countries became rivals in the race for power and prestige. It was generally believed that to be a great power, a nation had to create a vast empire. European nations considered it vital to compete with one another in empire building. One French statesman even said that the acquiring of colonies was a "matter of life and death" for his country!

Imperialism was popular among the common people also. News of their country's victories in faraway, unfamiliar places was exciting to those in the crowded factory cities of Europe. People were proud of their nation's success in conquest and colonization.

This poster for an opera reflects the interest of the British people in their army's exploits abroad. How does the media today reflect the current political situation?

Sometimes territory was seized for which there was no immediate use. For example, colonial powers took over African lands that stretched for thousands of kilometers into unexplored wilderness. Political leaders, explorers, and other imperialists of the 1800's believed such territory should be held as future investment. Henry Morton Stanley, the African explorer, expressed the attitude of English business toward overseas markets when he made the following statement: "There are forty million people beyond the gateway of the Congo, and the cotton spinners of Manchester are waiting to clothe them. . . ."

The Benefits of Civilization Supporters of imperialism considered Africa and Asia backward compared to Europe. They believed it was the duty of the wealthy industrialized nations to bring the benefits of their civilization to the less developed parts of the world. Many Europeans and Americans also believed they had a moral obligation to spread Christianity among the non-Christian peoples of Africa and Asia. Thousands of Catholic and Protestant missionaries sailed to distant lands, hoping to convert the natives to their own faith.

SECTION REVIEW

1. Mapping: Using the map on page 435, list the European nations that had colonies about 1900. What continents were these colonies in?
2. In your own words, define the term *imperialism*.
3. Why was there little interest in imperialism in the early 1800's?
4. What were the economic, political, and social reasons for imperialism?
5. Give two examples of imperialism that you have read about in other units of this text.
▷ Some people today still speak of imperialism. Do you know of any nations that still have an interest in imperialism? Explain briefly.

IMPERIALISM IN INDIA

In the 1500's a Muslim people, the Moguls from central Asia, invaded India and established the *Mogul Empire*. The most famous of the Mogul rulers was *Akbar* (AK-bar). Akbar was remembered not only for his great conquests but also for his religious tolerance and the wisdom with which he governed his empire from 1556 to 1605.

The Empire Declines   Unfortunately, Akbar's descendants did not rule the empire as carefully. Eventually, the growing religious intolerance of the Muslim rulers toward their Hindu subjects created resentment and turned most of the Indian people against them. Rebellions were frequent, especially in southern India. Hindus fought Muslims and by the 1600's the Mogul dynasty was seriously weakened. Parts of the empire broke away to set up their own independent states with their own local rulers. By the end of the 1700's, the Mogul emperors had lost most of their former territory.

The Coming of the Europeans   In 1498, the Portuguese explorer Vasco da Gama (dah GAM-uh) discovered a direct sea route for trading with India. At first, the Portuguese held several ports along India's coasts and controlled the seas around India. But as Portuguese power gradually declined, the interest of the British and the French in India began to increase.

In the 1600's and 1700's, all British trade with India was carried on by the *British East India Company*. As the Mogul Empire declined, the company built forts in several Indian cities. Local governors turned those cities over to the British without a struggle, even permitting them to collect taxes and to administer nearby territories.

Meanwhile, the French were also establishing trading centers in India. The *French East India Company* became the chief rival of the British. Both companies wanted to extend their trade and their power in India. While England and France were at war in Europe during the 1700's, the armies of the French and British East India companies fought one another in India. In 1757, forces of the British East India Company under the command of *Robert Clive* defeated the French and their Indian allies in the *Battle of Plassey* (PLAS-ee). This was a decisive victory for the British, and by 1763, the British had completely overcome the French in India.

After the British victory over the French, fighting broke out between the British and the Indians, but the British, armed with superior weapons, defeated the Indian armies.

The British East India Company   Through the 1770's, the power of the British East India Company continued to grow. Many of the company's officials took advantage of their positions and made themselves rich from taxes, fees, and bribes. To correct these abuses, the British government tightened its control over the company's activities in India.

British Expansion   By the time of the French Revolution in 1789, the British East India Company had authority over only a few Indian cities and southern territories taken from the French. But when Napoleon I came into power, the British feared that the French might try to recapture their former territories in India. This gave the East India Company an excuse to expand. Rulers of the Indian states were forced to accept treaties that gave control of their foreign affairs to the British

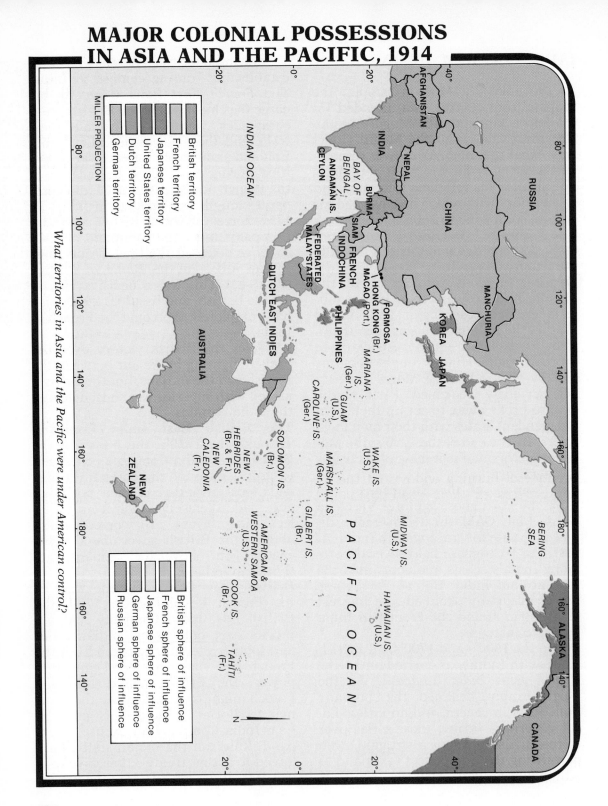

MAJOR COLONIAL POSSESSIONS IN ASIA AND THE PACIFIC, 1914

MILLER PROJECTION

British territory
French territory
Japanese territory
United States territory
Dutch territory
German territory

British sphere of influence
French sphere of influence
Japanese sphere of influence
German sphere of influence
Russian sphere of influence

What territories in Asia and the Pacific were under American control?

AFGHANISTAN

INDIA

NEPAL

RUSSIA

CHINA

MANCHURIA

KOREA

JAPAN

INDIAN OCEAN

BAY OF BENGAL

CEYLON

ANDAMAN IS.

BURMA

SIAM

FRENCH INDOCHINA

FEDERATED MALAY STATES

DUTCH EAST INDIES

MACAO (Port.)

HONG KONG (Br.)

FORMOSA

PHILIPPINES

MARIANA IS. (Ger.)

GUAM (U.S.)

CAROLINE IS. (Ger.)

WAKE IS. (U.S.)

MARSHALL IS. (Ger.)

AUSTRALIA

SOLOMON IS. (Br.)

NEW HEBRIDES (Br. & Fr.)

NEW CALEDONIA (Fr.)

GILBERT IS. (Br.)

AMERICAN & WESTERN SAMOA (U.S.)

COOK IS. (Br.)

TAHITI (Fr.)

MIDWAY IS. (U.S.)

HAWAIIAN IS. (U.S.)

PACIFIC OCEAN

NEW ZEALAND

BERING SEA

ALASKA

CANADA

N

452

East India Company, and much of southern India came directly under the company's control. However, after Napoleon's final defeat at Waterloo, some of the Indian states tried to throw off the company's rule. They failed, and by 1850 the company had imposed its political control over all of India.

Resentment Grows   From the 1820's until the 1850's, the East India Company improved its system of government in India. Telegraph lines and a postal system were introduced. Roads were built and canals dug for transportation and irrigation. Perhaps most important of all, a network of railroads was built. These benefits of British imperialism, however, were not welcomed by all Indians.

Along with its expanding political control, the East India Company attempted to impose British traditions and customs on the Indians. Consequently, the British tried to introduce several reforms. Among these was outlawing *suttee* (suh-TEE), the Hindu practice of burning widows on the funeral pyres of their dead husbands. Slavery was also forbidden. Unfortunately, these and other changes were often introduced without much knowledge or understanding of Indian customs and traditions. Many of the Indian people resented this interference in their way of life and felt that the British were treating them as inferiors.

The Sepoy Mutiny   In 1857, there was a mutiny of the Indian troops called *sepoys* (SEE-poiz) serving in the East India Company's army near Delhi. The sepoy rebels seized Delhi and proclaimed the re-establishment of Mogul authority over India. By the end of 1858, however, the rebels were defeated and the British once again were in full political control.

British woman fights off rebels during the Sepoy Mutiny. Do you think this etching above was done by an English or Indian artist? How can you tell?

Despite its failure, the *Sepoy Mutiny* had important results. The British Parliament abolished the East India Company and placed British territories in India directly under royal authority. From then on, governors and other high officials were given orders from London. In those areas outside British control, Indian rulers were promised that the government would respect the treaties the East India Company had made.

British Versus Indian Nationalism After the Sepoy Mutiny, the economic development of India continued under British direction. However, because Britain thought of India as a market for its manufactured goods, India's traditional industries greatly suffered. Many skilled Indians found themselves out of work and blamed the British. Many other Indians felt that there were great inequalities between the standards of living and opportunities for the British in India and those for their Indian subjects. For example, only the British could hold high positions in government, schools stressed European history and culture rather than Indian, and many important businesses in India were controlled by the British.

The Indian National Congress Because of the growing resentment and unrest, a group of Indians began the *Indian National Congress* in 1885. The Congress was originally established to give Indians more voice in their government and to provide an opportunity for better jobs. However, as time progressed and dissatisfaction with British imperialism increased, some of the members began to insist on complete self-government for India.

When World War I broke out in 1914, Indian troops fought on the side of the British. The Indians hoped that after the war the British would relax their restrictions and control in appreciation for their Indian allies services. But when the war ended, Britain continued to limit the freedom of the Indian people.

Mahatma Gandhi Into this uneasy situation came the Indian leader **Mahatma Gandhi** (muh-HAHT-muh GAHN-dee). Gandhi's plan for winning independence involved nonviolent resistance to British rule through such means as peaceful protest marches and the refusal to pay taxes. Gandhi was a devout Hindu and also sought reforms within his own religion. He encouraged equal rights for all men and women. Eventually, Gandhi became the leader of the Indian National Congress, and for the rest of his life he worked to bring an end to British imperialism in India. In 1947, two years after the end of World War II, India finally became an independent republic, ending British imperialism in·that country.

SECTION REVIEW

1. Mapping: Using the map on page 452, list the British possessions in the Pacific and Asia. How did the British establish themselves in India?
2. In your own words, identify: Mogul Empire, British East India Company, Battle of Plassey, Sepoy Mutiny, Indian National Congress.
3. What benefits did British imperialism bring to India?
4. Why did some Indians resent British rule?
5. What was Gandhi's plan for winning India's independence?
▷ Imperialism often brought benefits and problems to both the ruling country and its colonies. Do you think imperialism is ever justified? Explain.

IMPERIALISM IN AFRICA

Until about 1800, Europeans had little contact with people in Africa except for the Muslim peoples, who lived along the Mediterranean Sea. Early in the 1800's, however, the French established a colony in Algeria (al-JIR-ee-uh) in northern Africa. The rest of North Africa was part of the Ottoman Empire at that time.

Exploration of Africa The western coast of Africa had been explored by Europeans seeking a new route to India as early as the 1400's, but almost nothing was known about the vast interior. A few explorers had pushed into uncharted inland areas; the rest of Africa remained largely unexplored by the Europeans.

New Interest in Africa Beginning in the 1870's this situation changed. With the emergence of imperialism came a

454

EUROPEAN COLONIAL POSSESSIONS
IN AFRICA, 1914

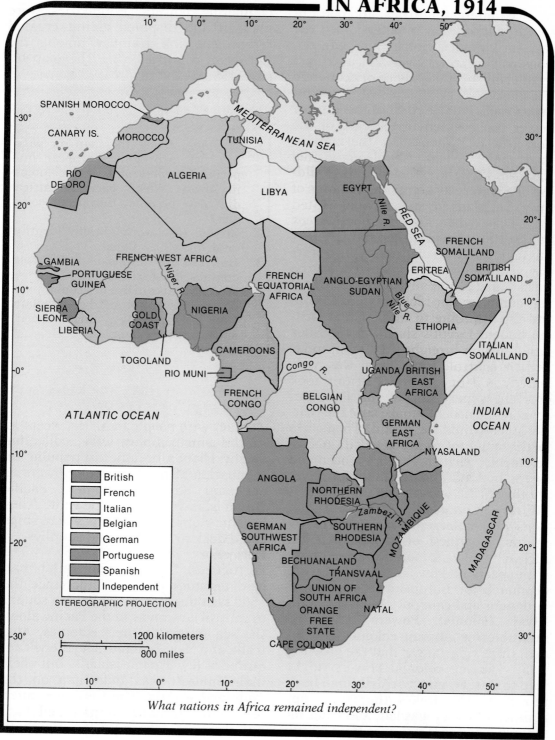

SPANISH MOROCCO

CANARY IS.

MOROCCO

RIO DE ORO

ALGERIA

TUNISIA

MEDITERRANEAN SEA

LIBYA

EGYPT

Nile R.

RED SEA

FRENCH SOMALILAND

GAMBIA

PORTUGUESE GUINEA

FRENCH WEST AFRICA

Niger R.

FRENCH EQUATORIAL AFRICA

ANGLO-EGYPTIAN SUDAN

ERITREA

BRITISH SOMALILAND

SIERRA LEONE

LIBERIA

GOLD COAST

NIGERIA

Blue Nile R.

ETHIOPIA

TOGOLAND

CAMEROONS

RIO MUNI

Congo R.

UGANDA

BRITISH EAST AFRICA

ITALIAN SOMALILAND

FRENCH CONGO

BELGIAN CONGO

ATLANTIC OCEAN

GERMAN EAST AFRICA

NYASALAND

INDIAN OCEAN

ANGOLA

NORTHERN RHODESIA

Zambezi R.

MOZAMBIQUE

MADAGASCAR

GERMAN SOUTHWEST AFRICA

SOUTHERN RHODESIA

BECHUANALAND

TRANSVAAL

UNION OF SOUTH AFRICA

ORANGE FREE STATE

NATAL

CAPE COLONY

	British
	French
	Italian
	Belgian
	German
	Portuguese
	Spanish
	Independent

STEREOGRAPHIC PROJECTION

N

0   1200 kilometers
0   800 miles

What nations in Africa remained independent?

renewed interest in Africa, and one European nation after another joined the race for colonies. Some European nations gained power over African rulers by offering military advice or economic assistance.

Suez Canal   The effect of this kind of power can be seen in the case of the *Suez* (soo-EZ) *Canal*. (See the map on page 544.) When Napoleon visited Egypt in 1799, he envisioned the building of a waterway across the Isthmus of Suez. Yet plans for such a canal waited until 1854, when *Ferdinand de Lesseps* (leh-SEPS), a French diplomat, got permission from the ruler of Egypt to start the venture. It was organized as the Suez Canal Company, and the Canal was completed in 1869. Anxious to control the sea route to India, Great Britain bought Egypt's shares in the Suez Canal, which brought the Canal under British control. But Egypt was very heavily in debt to Britain. Britain took over the supervision of the Egyptian economy in order to make sure the British loans would be repaid. Then, in a further attempt to protect Britain's investment, British troops occupied Egypt in 1882 and Egypt became yet another British possession.

Military Conquest   European nations also enlarged their empires by military conquest of African peoples. African armies, sometimes armed only with spears or bows and arrows, were no match for European troops armed with guns and cannon.

Rival Colonial Powers   As the scramble for African colonies continued, there was danger that the growing rivalry among colonial powers might lead to war. So much of Africa had been seized by the 1890's that little unclaimed territory was left, and what remained was eagerly sought after by the competing powers. Boundaries were unclear, and disputed claims created resentment and jealousy among the European countries. (See the map on page 455.)

SECTION REVIEW

1. Mapping: Using the map on page 455, list each of the European imperialist powers and their colonies in Africa. Which parts of Africa did not become European colonies?
2. In your own words, briefly identify or define: Suez Canal.
3. How did the Europeans build their empires in Africa?
◗ Would you like to live in a country under the control of another? Explain your answer using political, social, and economic examples.

IMPERIALISM IN THE PACIFIC AND ASIA

In the nineteenth century, collecting Pacific islands became as popular an occupation of the European powers as annexing African colonies. Pacific Ocean islands had strategic value. They became stopping-off points where ships could dock to take fuel and supplies.

Europeans in the Pacific   The Portuguese, Spanish, and Dutch had held territory in the Pacific since the 1500's. In the 1800's, the British sought to control new areas in the Pacific along the sea routes to their colonies, Australia and New Zealand. The French acquired a few Pacific islands, but their main interest was Indochina on the mainland of Asia. The Germans failed to establish colonies on mainland Asia, but they did take over the Marshall,

Mariana (mar-ee-AN-uh), and Caroline islands in the Pacific. (See the map on page 452.)

American Imperialism The United States entered the race for colonies in 1893, when it supported rebels in Hawaii who overthrew *Queen Liliuokalani* (luh-lee-uh-woe-kuh-LAHN-ee). American Marines landed in Hawaii to preserve order and to protect the many Americans living there. In 1894, a republic was proclaimed in Hawaii, and four years later the United States Congress annexed it. Soon after that, Puerto Rico, Guam, and the Philippines passed from Spanish to American control as a result of the *Spanish-American War*. Cuba was designated an American protectorate.

European Imperialism in Asia India became the most important colony in the British Empire. Britain's policy in Asia was, above all, to protect India from other imperialist powers. By the late 1800's the rapid Russian push through Muslim lands east of the Caspian Sea brought Russian armies within striking distance of India. This alarmed the British. As a countermeasure, Britain tried to take control of Afghanistan (af-GAN-uh-stan) and make it a buffer zone between India and the Russians. A *buffer zone* is an area that separates the territory of rival powers. The Afghans resisted British domination. This led to a series of wars, during which Russia sided with the Afghans against the British. For a time, war between Russia and Great Britain seemed ready to erupt. Fortunately, both countries were willing to settle their differences by negotiation, and peace was preserved. This did not end the rivalry between Britain and Russia in that area, however, and they continued to mistrust one another.

Queen Liliuokalani was the last monarch to officially rule in Hawaii. What other parts of the United States were once separate nations?

The French in Vietnam Under Napoleon III, the French tried to extend their control over southeast Asia. With the excuse that they had to protect the Christians of Indochina from persecution, the French landed troops in Vietnam (vee-et-NAHM) and seized Saigon (sie-GAHN) in 1860. The emperor of Vietnam signed a treaty with the French in 1862, which placed control of southern Vietnam in French hands. After that, the French gradually extended their control into the rest of Indochina. They took the city of Hanoi (ha-NOI), and by 1885 all Vietnam was under their control. Not long thereafter, Cambodia (kam-BODE-ee-uh) and Laos (LAH-ose) also were added to the

457

French colonial empire. Laos, Cambodia, and Vietnam together were known thereafter as *French Indochina*.

A Buffer Zone Between 1824 and 1855, the British fought a series of wars with Burma (BUR-muh), which lay east of India, and made it a colony. Between Burma and French Indochina lay the kingdom of Siam (sie-AM), which is known today as Thailand (TIE-land). Unlike its neighbors, Siam did not become a European colony. Instead, it was left as a buffer zone between the British in Burma and the French territories in Indochina. The British also established themselves in the port of Singapore (SING-uh-pore), off the southern end of the Malay (muh-LAY) peninsula. The Malay States thereafter came under British control. (See the map on page 452.)

Spheres of Influence Most of the European powers had carved out spheres of influence in China by the late 1800's. A *sphere of influence* is an area dominated by one of the powers and treated like a colony without being annexed officially. Technically, China continued to be independent, but its rulers had no control over those regions that had become European spheres of influence. Moreover, the Chinese government realized it lacked the technological and military power to defy the western nations.

Japanese Imperialism in Asia Japan had been plagued by civil wars that lasted from 1330 until 1573. This long period of disorders came to an end when the position of shogun was taken by *Tokugawa Ieyasu* (TOE-KUH-GAH-WAH EE-YEH-YAH-SUH) and a strong central government was restored. The emperor continued to hold the throne of Japan and no attempt was made to remove the royal family. But Tokugawa Ieyasu and his successors, as shoguns (SHOE-guns), were the real rulers of Japan for more than 200 years.

The policy of the Tokugawa family was to shut out foreign influences from Japan. For many years they were successful. From the early 1600's, Europeans were permitted to visit only the city of Nagasaki (nahg-uh-SAHK-ee), and the shoguns succeeded in stamping out Christianity as a rival to the older religions of Japan.

Japan Opens Its Doors By the nineteenth century, the power of the old samurai (SAM-uh-rie) class was declining and the Japanese farmers were no longer able to grow enough food to support the growing population. As a result, many Japanese were searching for new ways to change their country. During this period, a U.S. fleet commanded by *Matthew Perry* visited Japan in 1854. Perry asked for permission to open up trade. The Japanese government of the shogun feared that if it refused, the western nations might overpower Japan as they had China. Therefore, for the first time in about 250 years, Japan opened its doors to contact with other nations.

The Meiji Restoration This renewed contact with the West led to a civil war that ended in the overthrow of the shogun's military government in 1867. The revolutionaries called for an end of the shogunate and a return of political power to the emperor and his court. This political revolution in Japan is known as the *Meiji* (MAY-jee) *Restoration*, because the Emperor Meiji held the throne at that time.

The Meiji Restoration placed control of Japan in the hands of a group of new political leaders, who governed the country in the name of the emperor. Realizing Japan's weakness against the

United States Admiral Matthew Perry "opened the doors" of Japan to world trade. How have Perry and his men been portrayed in this portrait and banquet scene? What was the artist's point of view?

western powers, the new leaders of Japan launched a series of changes that transformed the old ways of life in Japan. Western developments in transportation, education, journalism, health care, and technology were adopted. The Japanese army and navy were reorganized. By 1900, Japan had become the most modern and westernized nation in Asia.

Japanese Imperialism Japan was a small country with a very large population. Gaining new territory was not only desirable but necessary in the eyes of Japan's new leaders. Japan joined the ranks of the imperialist nations with its decision to expand its influence into Korea.

Korea In the late 1800's Korea was under Chinese domination. China and Japan competed in assisting the weak Korean government. In 1894, rivalry led to war between China and Japan. The Japanese invaded China, destroyed the Chinese fleet, and threatened to capture the capital. In the face of this, China surrendered and the war ended in 1895. Japan won control of the island of Formosa (fore-MOE-suh) from China and part of the Chinese mainland. Korea gained its independence from Chinese domination.

459

The Russians and the Japanese
Before Japan could proceed with its conquest of Korea, Russia stepped in. Posing as China's friend and backed by France and Germany, Russia demanded that Japan return China's mainland territory and respect Korea's independence. The Japanese yielded, for their army and navy were no match for those of the western powers. Shortly after this, the Russians took control of the region. Japan had been forced to return Korea to China, and the Russians began to extend their influence over Korea. This created resentment in Japan. For the next ten years, relations between Japan and Russia grew worse.

The Russo-Japanese War   In 1904, Japan broke off diplomatic relations with Russia, and in a surprise attack on the naval base at Port Arthur on February 8, the Japanese were able to destroy most of Russia's Pacific fleet. Japanese troops landed and a series of bloody battles began between Japanese and Russian troops on Chinese soil. In 1905, Russia's Baltic Sea fleet reached Japanese waters after sailing for months from Europe around the southern tip of Africa. Much to the world's surprise, this Russian fleet was almost totally destroyed in the *Battle of Tsushima* (tus-shu-SHE-mah). Despite these naval victories, however, Japan could not win the war on the mainland of China.

President Theodore Roosevelt of the United States contacted both of the warring sides and brought about the beginning of peace talks. When the fighting ended, diplomatic representatives of Russia and Japan met in New Hampshire and drafted the *Treaty of Portsmouth* in September 1905. Japan regained the Russian-controlled territory on the Chinese mainland, along with the valuable Russian railway and mining rights in southern Manchuria. Korea was annexed by Japan in 1910.

SECTION REVIEW

1. Mapping: Using the map on page 452, describe the extent of European domination of the Pacific islands and Asia by listing the countries represented in the Pacific region and in Asia. Which areas in Asia and the Pacific became colonial possessions of a non-European nation? Which part of Asia did not become a colony?

2. In your own words, identify: buffer zone, sphere of influence.

3. What caused the rivalry in Asia between Great Britain and Russia? Between Russia and Japan?

   Would a nation today be justified in establishing a sphere of influence for the purpose of trade? Why or why not?

The Rise of Nation-States

INDEPENDENCE MOVEMENTS IN EASTERN EUROPE

The 1800's were a period of struggle for freedom by many of the different peoples in eastern Europe who lived under the rule of the Ottoman and Austrian empires. In spite of a growing sense of national identity, however, it was not until the end of the 1800's, and in some cases until after World War I, that these peoples managed to free themselves from foreign domination. Usually this was because peoples of the same culture did not live in the same region but were scattered throughout several countries. They had great difficulty in unifying, and in most cases independence came only after the intervention of the great powers.

Struggles for Independence Within the Ottoman Empire   In 1804, a revolt started in Serbia (SUR-bee-uh) that succeeded in driving out the Turks. Although fighting between the Turks and the Serbs continued for more than twenty years, the Turks never again gained complete control over the Serbs. In 1829, Russia decided to interfere in the conflicts between the Serbs and the Turks. In the treaty settlements that resulted, it was agreed that Serbia should remain part of the Ottoman Empire.

However, the Russians demanded that the Serbs be given the right to govern themselves. This compromise meant that Ottoman control over Serbia was essentially at an end. The Turks were forced to recognize *Miloš Obrenovich* (MEE-LOSH uh-BREN-uh-vich), a revolutionary leader of the Serbs, as the hereditary prince of Serbia.

Greek Independence   In 1821, the Greeks began their war of independence. Many Europeans had great respect for the history and culture of ancient Greece, and they had little goodwill toward the Turkish ruler. For this reason, Russia and other Europeans entered the struggle on the side of Greece. Although the Turks almost won the war, they were finally defeated at sea in the *Battle at Navarino* (nav-uh-REE-noh) off the Greek coast in 1827, and on land by the Russian army. At last, in 1829, the Turks surrendered and formally recognized an independent Greek kingdom in 1830.

The British Support the Turks   During the war between Greece and Turkey, Russian troops had marched almost to Constantinople. The British were alarmed by this. They were afraid that if the Russians defeated the Turks, Russia would seize Constantinople and occupy Turkey. This move into Turkey had long been a goal of the Russian

NATIONALITIES IN CENTRAL AND EASTERN EUROPE ABOUT 1914

Political boundaries 1914

FINNS

SWEDES

ESTONIANS

LETTS

LITHUANIANS

GREAT RUSSIANS

GERMANS

WHITE RUSSIANS

POLES

CZECHS

SLOVAKS

RUTHENIANS

LITTLE RUSSIANS

HUNGARIANS

SLOVENES

CROATS

SERBS

ROMANIANS

BULGARS

ALBANIANS

ARMENIANS

GREEKS

TURKS

50°

40°

20°

30°

N

0   200 kilometers

0   200 miles

CONIC PROJECTION

Did political boundaries in Eastern Europe correspond to nationalities?

462

tsars because while the Turks held Constantinople, Russia could never become a great naval power. Russian ships could not sail from Russian ports along the coast of the Black Sea to the Mediterranean (med-uh-tuh-RAY-nee-un) Sea except by passing through the Bosporus (BAHS-puh-rus) and the Dardanelles (dahrd-'n-ELZ). In times of war, the Turks could close these vital waterways to Russian ships. (See the map on page 462.) Control of these waterways could also put Russia in a position to threaten Britain's trade routes to India.

Because it feared and distrusted Russian power, the British government decided to support the Turks. The Russians feared the spread of British power. They thought that if the British chose to eliminate Russian competition for trade, the British would force the Turks to close the Bosporus and the Dardanelles. If this happened, the Russians might lose the right to sail on the Mediterranean Sea.

Pan-Slavism Because the British backed the Ottoman Empire, the peoples in eastern Europe of Slavic origin believed that Britain opposed their independence. Since the Russians opposed the Turks and also were Slavs (SLAHVZ), the Slavic people of eastern Europe looked to Russia for help. The feeling that all Slavic peoples should assist one another is called **Pan-Slavism.**

Romania Wins Its Independence Ever since the 1700's, the Ottoman Turks had sent Greeks to govern Romania (rooh-MAY-nee-uh). These Greek governors were known as *phanariots* (fuh-NAR-ee-ahts). The phanariots did not know how long they might hold their positions, so they tried to make themselves rich as quickly as possible while they were still in office. They collected all kinds of unjust taxes and kept their Romanian subjects in poverty. Finally, the Romanian people could stand their condition no longer, and in 1821 they revolted. For over thirty years after that, Romania remained in disorder. In 1858, a meeting of diplomats from the great powers recognized the right of the Romanians to self-government. Two new states called *Moldavia* (mahl-DAY-vee-uh) and *Walachia* (WAH-LAY-kee-ah) were created. Each of these was to be independent and ruled by its own prince. However, the next year the peoples of both states chose the same prince, *Alexander Cuza* (COO-zah), as their ruler. This put an end to the separation of Moldavia and Walachia. In 1862, Napoleon III of France urged the great powers to recognize the union of Moldavia and Walachia as one nation and the Turks had no choice but to go along with the decision. Later, in 1881, Romania declared itself to be a kingdom.

The Bulgarians Revolt By the middle of the nineteenth century, Turkish power had declined so greatly that the Russian tsar referred to Turkey as the "sick man of Europe." Taking advantage of the Turks' weakness, the Bulgarians revolted against them in 1876. But the revolt was put down brutally and whole villages were slaughtered. In 1877, Russia went to war against Turkey in support of Christians who had rebelled in Bulgaria (bul-GAR-ee-uh). The Russian army marched almost to Constantinople before the Turks made peace. The *Treaty of San Stefano* (STEF-uh-noe), signed in 1878, ended the fighting and created an independent Bulgaria.

The Congress of Berlin Bulgarian nationalists were disappointed, however. The great powers refused to permit the creation of a new, large Bulgarian state. The British, in particular, feared that the new country would become an ally of Russia. For this reason, Britain demanded a new treaty. The diplomats of the great powers met in Berlin later in 1878. In place of one large Bulgarian state, the *Congress of Berlin* created two new smaller states. Each of these was to manage its own affairs but remain under the rule of the Turks. Faced by a union of the British, French, Austrians, and Germans, there was little that Russia could do except agree to the arrangements made by the Congress of Berlin. However, these limits on Bulgarian independence did not last long. In 1885, in spite of Turkish opposition, the two states were combined into the new nation of Bulgaria. The Bulgarians chose a German noble to rule as their first king, and he used the title "tsar" in imitation of Russian rulers. Sofia (SOE-fee-uh) became the capital of the new Bulgarian nation.

Hungarians Revolt Against Austria   In 1848, several nationalities were living within the Austrian Empire. Germans made up 23 percent of the population; then came the Magyars (MAG-yahrz) with 14 percent; the Czechs and Slovaks made up 19 percent; and the remaining groups were Poles, Romanians, Italians, Slovenes (SLOE-veenz), Croats (KROTES), Serbs, and Ukrainians (yoo-KRAY-nee-unz).

Nationalism was becoming an important idea among some of these people and they longed for independence. The most serious revolt against Austrian rule took place in Hungary in 1848. One of the chief rebel leaders, *Louis Kossuth* (KOS-suth), proposed that the Hungarian kingdom of the Middle Ages be restored and ruled by the ethnic majority, the Magyars.

The Croats and Romanians living in Hungary did not support this idea. They did not believe they would be better off if they traded German rulers for Magyar rulers, so they joined the Austrians against the Hungarian rebels. When Russian Tsar Nicholas I sent an army into Hungary to assist the Austrians, the rebels were beaten. The Hungarian rebel army surrendered, its leaders were taken prisoner and brutally executed by the Russians.

The Ausgleich   When Austria went to war in 1866 with Prussia and suffered a crushing defeat, the Hungarians saw this was an appropriate time to again demand their freedom. The emperor, *Franz Josef I*, realized that the demands of the Hungarians would have to be met if he were to keep this throne. In 1867, a compromise was reached. The Hungarians were given their independence, but the Austrian emperor was to be their king. This decision divided the Austrian Empire in order to create a new Hungarian state. The event was known as the *Ausgleich* (ows-GLIESH), or separation.

The Magyars Govern Hungary   After Hungary became independent in 1867, the government of the new kingdom was controlled by the Magyar upper class. The Magyars ignored the poverty and other problems of the non-Magyar peoples living in Hungary. The Hungarian government also insisted that there should be one national language. Only Magyar was to be used in the schools. Since most non-Magyars could not speak that language, a child belonging to another cultural group could not get an education. Because all government offices also used Magyar, people who did not speak that language could not defend their rights. This pol-

Louis Kossuth is shown here receiving a hero's welcome in New York City in 1851. Why were leaders of revolutions often sympathetically received in the United States in the nineteenth century?

icy created resentment and helped strengthen independence movements among the non-Magyar population of Hungary.

The Creation of Yugoslavia In addition to the non-Magyar peoples of Hungary, other peoples living in eastern Europe, including the Slovenes, Croats, and Serbs, searched for independence in the late nineteenth century. The territory of Bosnia (BAHZ-nee-uh), which was under Turkish rule, was inhabited by the Serbs. In 1878, the Austrian emperor obtained permission from the Turkish ruler to govern Bosnia. In 1908, Bosnia was made part of the Austrian Empire. Serbs everywhere resented this. A Pan-Slavic movement, calling for a union of Bosnia and Serbia, sprang up. The Russian government, which was angered by the Austrian annexation of Slavic

peoples, sided with the Serbs but could do nothing to win independence for Bosnia without going to war against Austria. This problem was not solved until after World War I. In 1918, the Slovenes, the Croats, the Serbs, and the Montenegrans (mahnt-un-NEE-grunz) were united in a country called Yugoslavia (yoo-goe-SLAHV-ee-uh) or "land of the south Slavs."

Czech Bids for Independence There were many problems involved in the Czech (CHEK) attempt to gain independence. Many Germans lived in the same lands as the Czechs, and since the Thirty Years' War, the Germans had been the ruling class. They did not want the Austrian emperor to give any privileges to the Czechs. Thus, no matter what the Austrian government decided, neither the Czechs nor the Germans would be satisfied.

465

In her autobiography, Marie Curie, the famous Polish scientist, talks about her hatred of the Russians who occupied her homeland. How did the Russians treat the Poles who were under their control?

Polish Independence Because Poland had been divided among Russia, Prussia, and Austria in the late 1700's, the Polish people found it difficult to unite in a common independence movement. In 1830 and again in 1863, the Poles living under Russian rule revolted against the tsar. The revolts were brutally punished, and the Poles lost even more of their freedom as a result.

In both the Russian and Prussian parts of Poland, the Poles were forbidden to use their own language. As in Hungary, only the national language was used in all schools, law courts, and offices of the government. In the Russian section, many Polish rebels were sent into exile in Siberia. Many Poles fled to other countries when the Russian government tried to do away with the Polish upper class and neglected the needs of the peasants. The result of the oppression by tsarist Russia and militaristic Prussia was the widespread growth of Polish nationalism and ethnic pride.

In the Austrian part of Poland, conditions were better. Poles under Austrian rule had won some self-government by the late 1800's. In some parts of the empire, the Polish and German languages were used equally. There were Polish schools, and the Polish population had privileges not enjoyed by their fellow Poles under the rule of other nations.

In the 1880's and 1890's, a number of Polish political parties with different goals were organized in Prussia, Russia, and Austria. However, they met with little success in gaining freedom for the Poles. An independent Polish republic was finally proclaimed after the fall of the monarchies in Austria, Germany, and Russia after World War I.

The Czechs believed that these lands, which had once been part of the kingdom of Bohemia, rightly belonged to them. They also believed that they should be allowed to speak the Czech language and not forced to speak German. They regarded the Germans living in Bohemia, including the rulers in Vienna, as intruders. Some Czech leaders looked toward Russia for help in gaining their freedom from Austria. But it was not until 1918, when Austria-Hungary was defeated in World War I, that the nation of Czechoslovakia was formed. It united the lands inhabited by the Czechs with those inhabited by the Slovaks, another west Slav people.

1. **Mapping:** Using the map on page 462, list the various culture groups of people living in eastern Europe in 1914. Under the rule of which empire did each of these groups live?
2. In your own words, briefly define or identify: Congress of Berlin, *Ausgleich*.
3. After the Hungarians won their independence from Austria, how did they treat the non-Hungarian people in their own kingdom?
4. Why did the Czechs, Slovenes, Croats, and Poles have trouble in winning their independence?

▷ The Pan-Slavic movement united the Slavic peoples of eastern Europe in a common cause. Do you know of any movements working toward a common cause? What are they? How do such movements start?

THE JEWS IN EASTERN EUROPE

Like the Slavs, Germans, and Magyars, many Jews moved into eastern Europe during the Middle Ages. They also were searching for new homes. Although they never established a kingdom of their own in eastern Europe, the situation of the Jews resembled that of the peoples they lived among. They too often formed a distinct group, with a culture that was different from that of the people whose country they settled in.

Jewish Life in the Middle Ages In ancient times, the Romans conquered the homeland of the Jewish people and named it Palestine (PAL-uh-stine). Be-cause of their harsh treatment and the fact that they were forbidden by the Romans to practice their religion, large numbers of Jews left Palestine and traveled to new lands.

Most of the Jews outside Palestine lived under Muslim rule in the Middle East or North Africa after the Roman Empire collapsed. Many of the others outside Palestine moved to eastern Europe. The Jewish people in medieval eastern Europe often settled in their own all-Jewish villages. They prayed in their own houses of worship and lived according to their own beliefs and customs. Jews everywhere tended to marry only persons of their own faith. They also founded their own schools and used their own languages.

Anti-Semitism This separation of the Jews from the other peoples in the countries where they lived often caused trouble. People suspected and mistrusted what they did not understand. Often these misunderstandings, in the case of the Jews, led to anger and hatred. Prejudice against Jews is called *anti-Semitism* (an-tie SEM-uh-tiz-um).

Jewish settlements in some countries, especially in western Europe, entirely disappeared as a result of persecution. Jews were forced to leave England about 1300, and they had to leave Spain and Portugal at the end of the 1400's. Jews were also exiled from France, southern Italy, and hundreds of German cities during the period from 1300 to 1500. Most of these Jews moved eastward. They settled in large numbers in the countries of eastern Europe, especially in Poland and Lithuania (lith-uh-WAY-nee-uh).

The Jews in Russia When Russia added parts of Poland to its territory in the late 1700's, it became the nation with the largest Jewish population in

This interior of a synagogue in eastern Europe was painted in the nineteenth century. Why did many Jews settle in the eastern European countries?

Europe. The Jews were treated harshly by the Russians. They were allowed to live only in certain territories. Often they were forced to leave their villages and towns to be resettled elsewhere by the tsar's government. Jews were taxed twice as much as other subjects of the tsars. The Russian government also tried to prevent Jews from practicing their religion. In the early 1800's, Jewish children sometimes were taken from their families to special schools and reared as Christians.

To escape this harsh treatment, many Jews left Russia. About three million Jews came to the United States during the 1800's. Most of them came from Russia and other parts of eastern Europe where governments were hostile toward them.

SECTION REVIEW

1. Mapping: Using the appropriate maps in the Atlas, describe the location of the original homeland of the Jews. Then describe the region in eastern Europe where most of the western Jews settled.

2. In your own words, briefly define anti-Semitism.

3. How were the Jews treated in Russia?

▶ Anti-Semitism is a form of prejudice. What is prejudice? Can you give any examples of how prejudice has affected your life or community?

World War I

THE COMING OF THE WAR

By the beginning of the twentieth century, there were few lands left in the world for the major powers to seize or dominate economically. The imperialist nations of Europe had been able to carve up Africa without serious conflict among themselves. They, along with the United States and Japan, had also annexed territory and established colonies and spheres of influence in Asia. The scramble for colonies among the imperialist powers, however, sometimes led to dangerous rivalries that threatened to end in war.

Alliances Between the World Powers In order to preserve the balance of power among the nations of Europe and prevent war, the powers entered into a *system of alliances*. These alliances were designed to protect members in case of attack by a country outside the alliance. If one member nation was threatened, all the other members of the alliance agreed to join together to fight the attacking country. It was believed that an aggressive nation would hesitate to declare war if it meant fighting against several countries, rather than just one. By 1914, the major countries were divided into two rival alliances: the **Triple Alliance,** made up of Germany, Austria, and Italy; and the **Triple Entente** (ahn-TAHNT), made up of Great Britain, France, and Russia. In spite of the alliance system, threats of war in Europe continued to grow.

Tension Grows Between Germany and Britain In 1888, *Wilhelm II* became ruler of Germany. He decided to make Germany a great sea power by increasing the size of the German fleet. This alarmed the British, who had no intention of losing their position as the world's greatest naval power. To compete with the Germans, the British enlarged their navy. On land, the same

As emperor, Wilhelm II dressed in military uniform on public occasions. Why do you think German emperors wished to identify themselves so closely with the German army?

kind of military buildup was going on. When one country built up its military strength, other nations felt obliged to do the same.

Nationalism Leads to War While this military buildup was going on, the spirit of nationalism was also drawing countries closer to war. The spirit of nationalism had led the peoples of eastern Europe to fight for independence from the Ottoman and Austrian empires during the 1800's. The new nations of Greece, Romania, and Serbia were created from former Ottoman territory. However, winning independence was not always enough. When the Serbs of the Ottoman Empire had become an independent nation, they demanded freedom for Serbs living under Austrian rule. The Serbs believed that all Serbs should be united.

The Balkans Austria had lost its leadership of the movement for German unification. When the new German nation was created, Austria was not included and so it looked toward eastern Europe in its search for new territories. The decline of the Ottoman Empire provided the opportunity for Austria to take land from the Turks. Following Turkey's defeat in a war with Russia, Austria took the territory of Bosnia. However, Bosnia was inhabited by Serbs and other Slavic peoples. The Serbs believed Bosnia should have been made part of Serbia.

Russia was brought into this conflict because the Russian government had appointed itself protector of the Slavic peoples in the Balkans. The Russians hoped to dominate eastern Europe. Russia, therefore, wanted the Ottoman Empire weakened but did not want Austria to expand into the Balkans. If this happened, Austria might threaten Russia's influence

there. Austria's annexation of Bosnia in 1908 increased Russian hostility toward Austria. With good reason, Europeans began to call the Balkans the "powder keg of Europe."

SECTION REVIEW

1. Mapping: Using the map on page 472, list the nations that were members of the Triple Alliance and the Triple Entente. Which European nations remained neutral?
2. In your own words, briefly identify: Wilhelm II, Bosnia.
3. How was the European alliance system expected to preserve peace?
4. Why did rivalry increase between Germany and Britain? between Russia and Austria?
   Before World War I, the Balkans were called the "powder keg of Europe." Is there an area of the world that could be considered a "powder keg" today? Explain your answer.

THE BEGINNING OF WORLD WAR I

In the summer of 1914, the heir to the Austrian throne, *Archduke Franz Ferdinand*, decided to pay a goodwill visit to Bosnia. This territory had been annexed to the Austrian Empire in 1908. The people of Bosnia were Serbs, and feelings of Serbian nationalism were strong there.

The archduke and his wife visited the city of Sarajevo (sahr-uh-YEH-voe) on June 28. They rode through town in an open-topped automobile so they could wave to the crowds that lined the streets. As the archduke's auto passed

Archduke Franz Ferdinand and his wife, Countess Sophie, are shown here entering the touring car in which they were later assassinated in Sarajevo. How are leaders today protected from attempts on their lives?

through the streets, a bomb was thrown at Franz Ferdinand and his wife, exploding a few meters behind their car. Neither of the royal couple was injured, but they were urged to leave the city for their own safety. Before leaving, though, the archduke insisted on visiting the hospital to see an assistant who had been injured by the bomb earlier that morning. On the way to the hospital, the driver of the car in which Franz Ferdinand and his wife were riding unexpectedly made a wrong turn. The driver slowed the car and pulled toward the curb in order to swing the vehicle around in the right direction. At that moment, a young Serbian nationalist named *Gavrilo Princip* (gahv-REE-loe PREEN-tseep) moved forward and shot the archduke and his wife, killing them both. The assassination sparked a chain reaction that led Europe into World War I.

War Between Austria and Serbia

The Austrian government had reason to believe that the assassination was a plot by a nationalist organization inside Serbia. There was some evidence that the Serbian government knew of the plot but had not stopped it. Austria was willing to risk fighting with Serbia, but it wanted a small-scale war involving only itself and Serbia. For assurance, the Austrian government contacted Germany, its ally. Because the Germans believed that any war Austria started would be kept in the Balkans, they offered unlimited support to Austria. With this strong backing, the Austrian government sent a list of demands to the Serbian government, warning that all anti-Austrian activities in Serbia must be stopped. These demands were to be met within forty-eight hours, or Austria would declare war on Serbia. A list of demands such as these with a time limit is called an *ultimatum* (ul-tuh-MATE-um).

The Serbian government did not fear war with Austria. Serbia was certain Russia would take its side should a war begin. Serbia, therefore, agreed to almost all of the Austrian demands. This clever move placed war-ready Austria in a difficult position. It had to back down and accept Serbia's compromise or declare war.

The War Spreads to Other Nations
On July 28, 1914, Austria declared war on Serbia. With French support, Tsar Nicholas II of Russia and his generals began their mobilization of the Russian army on July 30. In 1914, *mobilization*,

or making preparations for war, was almost the same thing as declaring war.

When the Germans heard about the Russian mobilization and of France's support, they began to review their plan for fighting a two-front war with France on their western border and Russia in the east. Germany at once demanded that the Russians stop their preparations for war and that France promise to remain neutral. These nations refused, however, and Germany declared war on Russia on August 1 and on France on August 3.

The position of Great Britain now came into question. The British did not want a European war but realized they

EUROPE IN 1914

How did the alliance system contribute to the outbreak of war in 1914?

472

could not stay out of one if Austria, Germany, Russia, and France were determined to fight. What the British leaders needed was a cause to stir up the British people against Germany. The attack on Belgium by Germany provided that cause.

Belgium Many years earlier, the major European powers, including Germany, had signed an agreement to respect Belgium's neutrality. However, Belgium's location was of great importance to Germany's plans for winning a two-front war. The flat coastal plain on which Belgium is located borders both France and Germany and provides the easiest terrain in that part of Europe to be crossed by an invading army.

As soon as Germany had declared war on France, German troops moved across Belgium to invade France. The British protested, insisting that Belgium's neutrality be preserved, but the Germans ignored their pleas. Britain declared war on Germany on August 4, 1914.

Other Nations Japan had an alliance with Britain and entered the war against Germany. Italy, however, could not decide whether it should join the **Central Powers** (Germany, Austria, Turkey, and Bulgaria) or the **Allied Powers** (Britain, France, Serbia, and Russia). In 1915, Italy entered the war on the side of the Allied Powers after being promised territory in Austria when the war was over.

Later, other nations entered the war. In 1917, the United States entered on the side of the Allied Powers, as did a dozen other countries. What had started out as a local war had thus turned into a world war and the European alliance system, which had been formed to ensure peace, had helped instead to bring on a war.

SECTION REVIEW

1. Using the map on page 472, describe the relative location of Germany, France, Great Britain, Russia, and Belgium. Which countries would Germany fight in a "two-front" war? Why was it necessary for the Germans to invade Belgium before attacking France?

2. In your own words, briefly identify: Archduke Franz Ferdinand, ultimatum, Central Powers, Allied Powers.

3. Austria wished to fight a small-scale war with Serbia only. How did this small conflict finally become a world war?

▶ The European alliance system was supposed to prevent war. Do you think protective alliances between countries are a good way to maintain peace today? Explain your answer.

FOUR YEARS OF WAR, 1914–1918

German success in winning the war depended on a swift invasion of France through Belgium. But the Belgians delayed the German invasion by putting up a heroic resistance, which gave the French extra time to prepare for battle. The French were also aided by a hasty Russian offensive in the east.

At first, the French slowly retreated before the German advance into France. When the French had withdrawn to about 40 kilometers (25 miles) from Paris, they made a stand in the *Battle of the Marne* (MAHRN). They stopped the Germans, and Paris was saved.

The Western Front Stalled in France, the German army turned westward toward the English Channel. Once again, their advance was halted. This time they were stopped by British and Belgian troops in the *Battle of Flanders* (FLAN-durz). At that point, fighting came to a standstill. Both sides dug trenches and took up defensive positions along a 960-kilometer (600-mile) line that stretched from Switzerland to the North Sea. This area of fighting was known as the *Western Front.* In the first four months of trench warfare along

This photograph shows what life was like in the trenches on the front for the average soldier during World War I. Study the photo for a few minutes and then write a few sentences describing your thoughts as if you were the soldier in the photograph.

the Western Front, more than 1.5 million men were killed and wounded.

The Eastern Front   On Germany's eastern frontier, the Russian army launched an invasion. The Russian advance, however, left them open to attack from the north or the south. *General Paul von Hindenberg* (HIN-dun-burg) ordered German attacks on the Russians, causing them terrible losses. At the *Battle of Tannenberg* (TAN-un-burg), about 100,000 Russian soldiers were killed or captured, and an enormous quantity of guns and equipment was lost. In the first year of the war, the Russian army suffered nearly 4 million casualties. Russian soldiers were so ill-equipped that they sometimes went into battle armed with nothing more than a bayonet tied to a stick.

The Russians were more successful in fighting against the Austrians. They won the *Battle of Lemberg* (LEM-burg) in September 1914, and by the end of the year occupied a great deal of Austrian territory. However, their advance toward Berlin failed. Along the *Eastern Front*, both sides took up defensive positions and began the same kind of trench warfare that was being fought in the west.

The War at Sea   Not long after the war began, most of Germany's ships were captured or were bottled up in German ports. Britain and its Allies controlled the seas and blockaded the German coast. Since Germany was unable to protect its colonies, they were seized by the Allied Powers. At the *Battle of Jutland* (JUT-lund), which took place in the Baltic Sea in 1916, the German fleet was forced by superior British naval strength to return to the protection of its ports. It remained there for the rest of the war.

Britain's naval power was an important factor in the final victory of the Allied Powers. British control of the seas forced the Germans to resort to submarine warfare. One of the victims of a German torpedo was the British liner *Lusitania* (loo-suh-TANE-ee-uh), which sunk off the Irish coast in 1915. In this incident, over 1,000 people lost their lives, including more than 100 Americans. This act of war helped unite public opinion in the United States against Germany.

In the beginning of Germany's submarine warfare, its subs were a serious threat to the British fleet, but the British soon developed methods of pro-

This was the headline in The New York Times *the day after the sinking of the Lusitania. How do you think people seeing this headline would have felt about the Germans? How can the media affect public opinion?*

The New York Times.

THE WEATHER
Fair today and Sunday; fresh to strong southwest to west winds.

VOL. LXIV... NO. 20,923.   NEW YORK, SATURDAY, MAY 8, 1915.—TWENTY-FOUR PAGES.   ONE CENT In Greater New York, Jersey City and Newark.

LUSITANIA SUNK BY A SUBMARINE, PROBABLY 1,000 DEAD; TWICE TORPEDOED OFF IRISH COAST; SINKS IN 15 MINUTES; AMERICANS ABOARD INCLUDED VANDERBILT AND FROHMAN; WASHINGTON BELIEVES THAT A GRAVE CRISIS IS AT HAND

SHOCKS THE PRESIDENT

Washington Deeply Stirred by Disaster and Fears a Crisis.

BULLETINS AT WHITE HOUSE

Wilson Reads Them Closely, but Is Silent on the Nation's Course.

RUMOR OF CONGRESS CALL

Loss of Lusitania Recalls Firm Tone of Our First Warning to Germany.

CAPITAL FULL OF RUMORS

Roosevelt Calls It An Act of Piracy.

Special to The New York Times.
SYRACUSE, N. Y., May 7.—Colonel Roosevelt tonight characterized the sinking of the Lusitania as "an act of piracy."

"I do not know enough of the facts," said the Colonel, "to make any further comment or to say what would be proper for this Government to do in the circumstances.

"I can only repeat what I said the other day when the Gulflight was attacked. I then called attention to the fact that months before the German war zone was established, and deeds such as the sinking of the Lusitania were threatened, that if such deeds were perpetrated that

Admiralty Puts Embargo On News Dispatches

LONDON, May 8.—It is stated that the British Admiralty is not withholding any verified facts regarding the Lusitania, but declines to pass dispatches based merely on rumor.

It is expected that the Admiralty will issue a statement as soon as authenticated facts are available.

DEATH OF FROHMAN IS FEARED IN LONDON

"What Is America Going to Do About It?" Asks British Colleague of Manager.

SOME DEAD TAKEN ASHORE

Several Hundred Survivors at Queenstown and Kinsale.

STEWARD TELLS OF DISASTER

One Torpedo Crashes Into Doomed Liner's Bow, Another Into the Engine Room.

BOATS PROMPTLY LOWERED

But Ship Goes Down So Quickly Many Must Have Gone with Her —No Officers Reported Saved

tecting their ships. The Germans finally decided to carry on unrestricted submarine warfare, which meant that they would attack the ships of neutral nations as well as those of the belligerents. This turned many neutral nations against Germany and helped convince the United States to enter the war on the side of the Allied Powers.

A Long, Hard Struggle   In 1915, the Allied Powers were hopeful of victory. They had halted the German advance and begun one of their own. The Allies tried to drive the Germans back across northern France and Belgium. Their offensive failed, however, because it cost too many lives. In order to push the Germans back only 5 kilometers (3 miles), the French lost 300,000 men!

The Allied Powers also failed in an attempt to land troops along the Turkish coast in 1915. The Allies planned to knock Turkey out of the war and to force the Germans to withdraw troops from the Western Front, sending them into the Balkans. But the Allied plans were poorly carried out. The Turks put up a strong resistance and the Allies withdrew in January of 1916.

Verdun   In 1916, the Germans again launched an offensive. They attacked the French at *Verdun* (vur-DUN) with all of their available troops. Meanwhile, their Austrian allies were to drive into Italian-held territory. At the beginning both attacks went well, but the French finally were able to halt the Germans. The Italians retreated at first. Then they made a stand, and the Central Powers gave up their offensive. During the Battle of Verdun, the Germans had captured 338 square kilometers (130 square miles), but they had lost 330,000 men. By the end of 1916, the war on the Eastern Front once again was at a standstill.

Zeppelins were used for the first time during World War I. What other new weapons came into use during "the war to end all wars"?

New Weapons   During World War I, many new weapons were tested in battle. Airplanes were used for observation and an occasional bombing run. The Germans raided London many times using *zeppelins* (long cigar-shaped airships), but they did very little damage. On the battlefield, the machine gun made it impossible for soldiers to advance very far out of their trenches. Poison gases, introduced as a weapon by the Germans in the spring of 1915, were also used for the first time, but they proved to be unpredictable, depending on which way the wind was blowing.

Another new weapon introduced late in the war was the tank. The name *tank* originated when the vehicles were shipped from Britain to France in crates labeled "water tank" to fool German spies. However, when either side in the fighting introduced a new weapon, such as the tank or poison gas, the other side quickly developed the

476

same weapon or something to counteract it, such as the gas mask. Since both sides had the same weapons, the stalemate on the Western Front continued.

Russia Withdraws On the Eastern Front, the Central Powers had been pushing back the Russians since 1915. During the course of the war, more than 9 million Russian troops had been killed, wounded, or taken prisoner. The Russian government had not been able to replace their great losses in guns and equipment. At home, the Russian people were war-weary and were suffering severely from shortages of food and other essentials. This situation led to the abdication of Tsar Nicholas II in March of 1917. The revolutionary government that replaced the tsar attempted to continue the fighting on the Eastern Front, but it had little success. In November 1917, it was overthrown by the Bolshevik (BOLE-shuh-vik) Revolution.

The Bolsheviks withdrew Russia from the war. They made a separate peace with Germany and Austria and had to give up vast territories. Russia's new leaders signed the *Treaty of Brest-Litovsk* (brest-luh-TAWFSK) in March 1918, in which Russia agreed to cede to Germany and Austria territories in Poland, the Baltic lands, the entire Ukraine, Finland, and some land in the region of the Caucasus Mountains.

Not long after Russia's withdrawal from the war, Romania also surrendered to the Central Powers. By early 1918, German and Austrian troops, no longer needed along the Eastern Front, were being moved to the west for a showdown with the Allied Powers.

The United States Enters the War In April 1917, the United States entered the war on the side of the Allies. The Central Powers realized this meant that additional troops and supplies soon would reach the British and French. For this reason, German and Austrian leaders decided to launch a great offensive in the spring of 1918. In the *Second Battle of the Marne*, the Germans were unable to break the Allies' defensive positions. As the Germans retreated into Belgium, they suffered a series of defeats along the way.

By early November 1918, the German army was exhausted. Fresh American troops had reinforced the Allies. Recognizing the hopelessness of their situation, the general in charge of the German troops asked his government to arrange an end to the fighting. On November 11, 1918, an armistice was signed, ending the hostilities.

SECTION REVIEW

1. Mapping: Using the map on page 472, describe the location of the Western and Eastern Front lines. Who did Germany fight in the West? in the East?
2. In your own words, briefly identify: Western Front, Eastern Front, Battle of the Marne, Battle of Jutland, Treaty of Brest-Litovsk, Second Battle of the Marne.
3. How did German submarine warfare influence the United States to enter World War I?
4. Why did Russia withdraw from World War I?
▶ The number of casualties in World War I was far greater than those of any other war before World War II; 22 million people were dead, wounded, or missing before the war was over. Why do you think the losses of life and property in World War I were so much greater than in previous European wars?

PLANNING THE PEACE

It was decided that the victorious nations would meet in Paris to draw up peace treaties and then present them to the defeated nations. By the end of the war, more than thirty nations had joined the Allied Powers. Only six of these, however, had carried the major burden of the war. They were Great Britain, France, Italy, Russia, Japan, and the United States.

The Paris Peace Conference   At the time of the peace conference, Russia was in the midst of a civil war and its former allies were supporting the anti-Communist side. As a result, Russia was not represented at the *Paris Peace Conference*. Japan attended, but the Japanese were interested only in Asia and the Pacific area. This left most decisions at the peace conference up to the *"Big Four"*—Britain, France, Italy, and the United States. Each of these nations was represented by the head of its government. During the peace conference, **Georges Clemenceau** (klem-un-SOE), the seventy-seven-year-old French prime minister, was shot in the chest by an assailant. He recovered, and for a time dominated the peace conference from his bed.

From the beginning of the Paris Peace Conference, it was clear that each country had different ideas about what should be done. The Italian prime minister, **Vittorio Orlando** (or-LAN-doe), was interested chiefly in obtaining new colonies and territory for Italy. These had been promised to Italy by Britain, France, and Russia when Italy entered the war in 1915. Clemenceau, the French leader, was interested mainly in keeping Germany weak. He wanted Germany to pay a large indemnity to France for its losses during the war.

The British prime minister, **David Lloyd George,** was interested in preventing France from becoming the most powerful nation in Europe now that Germany was defeated. He also hoped to find ways to settle future international disputes without going to war. President **Woodrow Wilson** of the United States had stated his goals in a document called the **Fourteen Points,** which he issued in January 1918, as the basis for keeping peace in the future.

The Fourteen Points   Among the things Wilson proposed in his Fourteen Points was that a "general association of nations" should be formed to settle future international disputes. Wilson wanted this association, or league, to have the power to prevent countries from going to war. Wilson called also for disarmament, freedom of the seas, an end to secret agreements, and the removal of international trade barriers.

Wilson made "self-determination" one of the key terms at the peace conference. *Self-determination* is the right of a people with a common background to form their own nation and select their own government. But the Paris peacemakers discovered it was very difficult to redraw the boundaries of Europe so that each country contained a single nationality group. This was especially true in eastern Europe, where nationalities were too scattered to make it possible. As a result, self-determination was not applied in every case.

The Treaty of Versailles   The peace treaty with Germany was signed at Versailles, in the palace of Louis XIV, where German unification had been proclaimed in 1871 after the German victory in the Franco-Prussian War. The Germans called the treaty a dictated peace because they had had no voice in its composition. The Germans

Beginning fifth from the left, seated, Wilson, Clemenceau, and Lloyd George are in the Hall of Mirrors of Versailles. What were the results of the treaty they negotiated?

were especially angered by the *war guilt clause*, which stated that the Germans accepted full responsibility for having caused the war.

Other provisions of the treaty forced Germany to give up territories. (See the map on page 482.) Alsace and Lorraine, taken by Germany in the Franco-Prussian War, were returned to France. Germany lost its colonies.

Germany was compelled to reduce the size of its army and navy, destroy its fortifications, and give up its submarines and aircraft. Since Germany was considered responsible for the war, it was forced to pay an indemnity for each country's damages and losses. This was a huge financial burden.

Similar treaties were signed with the other members of the Central

Powers. The treaty with Turkey was not concluded until 1923, because the Turkish sultan had been overthrown. There also had been political changes in Germany. A revolution there shortly before the end of the war in 1918 overthrew Kaiser Wilhelm II, who fled the country. The representative of the new *Weimar Republic*, which had been set up after the revolution, signed the Versailles Treaty for Germany. The emperor of Austria, too, lost his throne. After the war, Austria became a republic.

The League of Nations The association of nations President Wilson had proposed was set up after the war. It was located in Geneva, Switzerland, and was called the **League of Nations.** Much to Wilson's disappointment, Congress voted against U. S. membership in the League because many members of Congress were afraid of becoming involved in European politics. Most of the other major powers joined however. The League was formed to find solutions, short of war, for international disputes. But it was up to member nations whether or not they would abide by the League's decision.

In the 1920's, the League successfully settled several disputes that could have led to war. However, the major test it faced came in the 1930's when the League was unable to prevent the outbreak of World War II.

New Nations Created The Paris Peace Conference created several new nations in eastern Europe from territories that formerly belonged to Germany, Russia, and Austria-Hungary. (To locate these countries, compare the maps on pages 472 and 482.) The Ottoman Empire also lost vast territories from which new states—Syria, Lebanon, Jordan, and Palestine —were carved. The League of Nations placed these under the supervision of Britain and France until they achieved full independence after World War II. Turkish territory farther east became Iraq. Both Iraq and Egypt remained under British control until the 1930's.

SECTION REVIEW

1. Mapping: Using the map on page 482 and the text on page 479, describe the location of those territories that Germany was forced to give up after World War I. How had Germany acquired these lands?

2. In your own words, briefly identify: Paris Peace Conference, Fourteen Points, self-determination, Treaty of Versailles, Weimar Republic, League of Nations.

3. Name the "Big Four" powers at the Paris Peace Conference. What did each of the powers intend to accomplish at the conference?

4. Why did Germany resent the Treaty of Versailles?

5. Why was it difficult to apply President Wilson's policy of self-determination to the peoples of eastern Europe?

▷ If you had been one of the Big Four powers, how would you have treated Germany after World War I? Why? How should any defeated nation be treated by the victors of a war?

Creating World War II

THE BALANCE OF POWER IN EUROPE

World War I destroyed the Austrian Empire and changed the balance of power that existed between Great Britain, France, Germany, and Russia. Because of the war guilt clause, the victorious powers expected Germany to pay for much of the cost of the war. In 1921, Germany owed the Allies $32 billion in war damages. Most Germans, however, did not accept responsibility for World War I. The war guilt clause was regarded as an insult to German honor, as was the payment of reparations (a form of indemnity), forced on Germany by the Versailles Peace Treaty.

Germany after World War I The Weimar Republic, which replaced the rule of Wilhelm II shortly before the war ended, tried to introduce democracy in Germany during the 1920's, but it had to struggle against serious economic and political problems. Other European countries did everything possible to prevent a renewal of German strength. Within Germany, the republic faced threats from political groups opposed to democracy.

The Nazis Like other industrial countries, Germany was struck by the worldwide financial depression of the late 1920's and early 1930's. Overcome by such problems as unemployment, loss of trade, and a drop in wages, many Germans were willing to surrender their political freedom in exchange for leadership that promised to put Germany back on its feet. This partly explains why antidemocratic groups, such as the Communists and the **Nazis** (members of the *National Socialist German Workers party*) became popular. The Nazi party came to power in 1933. Under Nazi leadership from 1933 to 1939, Germany became a dictatorship. Its military strength was rebuilt, and economic conditions gradually improved.

Soviet Russia after World War I After the Communist government was established in Russia in 1917, the country was called the *Soviet Union*. The former allies of the Soviet Union could not forgive it for making peace with the Central Powers and withdrawing from the war. Nor were they inclined to trust Russia's Communist leaders, whose goal was to create revolutions in other countries in order to spread communism.

The Communist leaders of the Soviet Union devoted their efforts to increasing the nation's strength. Lenin was the first Communist dictator of Russia until his death in 1924. Under

EUROPE AFTER WORLD WAR I

| 0 | 500 kilometers |
| 0 | 400 miles |

Areas lost by:
- Russia
- Austria-Hungary
- Germany
- Bulgaria
- Turkey

ATLANTIC OCEAN

NORWAY
Oslo • Stockholm •
SWEDEN

FINLAND
Helsinki •
• Tallinn
ESTONIA
Riga • LATVIA
LITHUANIA
Danzig • Kovno •
EAST PRUSSIA (Ger.)

• Moscow

NORTH SEA

GREAT BRITAIN
IRELAND
Dublin •

DENMARK
Copenhagen •

Amsterdam •
London •
NETH.
Brussels •
BELG.
Berlin •
GERMANY
• Warsaw
POLAND
SOVIET UNION

Paris •
LUX. Prague •
FRANCE
CZECHOSLOVAKIA
Bern •
Geneva • SWITZ. AUSTRIA
Vienna •
• Budapest
HUNGARY
ROMANIA
Bucharest •

Belgrade •
YUGOSLAVIA
BULGARIA
• Sofia

BLACK SEA

PORTUGAL
Lisbon •
• Madrid
SPAIN
CORSICA (Fr.)
Rome •
ITALY
SARDINIA (It.)
Tirana •
ALBANIA

• Ankara
TURKEY

GIBRALTAR (Br.)
MEDITERRANEAN SEA
SICILY (It.)
GREECE
• Athens
DODECANESE IS. (It.)
CRETE (Gr.)
CYPRUS (Br.)

Which country lost the most territory after World War I? Why?

Lenin, civil war ended and foreign armies withdrew from Russian soil. Lenin tried to introduce the Communist form of socialism to the Russian economy. However, the peasants refused to give up their land, and industrial production declined under government control. Because of this, Lenin temporarily abandoned his plan for making Soviet Russia into a Socialist country.

Stalin Lenin was followed by **Josef Stalin** (STAHL-un), who ruled Soviet Russia like an absolute monarch until his death in 1953. Stalin launched an ambitious plan to modernize Russian agriculture rapidly and increase the output of Soviet industry. At the same time, Stalin was determined to complete Lenin's goal of establishing socialism in Russia. Under Stalin's first *"Five Year Plan,"* which began in 1928, the Soviet government took control of the farms of the Russian peasants. Labor unions were abolished and all workers were placed under government supervision and control. Every aspect of Russia's economic life became part of a plan drawn up by the Communist party leaders.

Lenin had not been strong enough to bring about these changes in Soviet

482

life. Stalin, however, turned the army and his secret police against his own people. During Stalin's rise to power and the introduction of socialism, 5 to 10 million people may have been killed. He silenced all opposition within the Communist party by executing former comrades, including revolutionary leaders who had helped bring the Bolsheviks to power in 1917. By the late 1930's, Stalin had emerged as the most powerful ruler Russia had ever known.

The Soviet Union had been changed from an agricultural nation into an industrialized one by the 1930's. The people, however, paid a high price for this change. Their standard of living was kept low. The government controlled the economy, and citizens were expected to sacrifice personal comforts to pay for the development of new industries.

France and Great Britain after World War I   Of all the nations in Europe, France perhaps suffered the most during World War I, because most of the fighting in western Europe took place on French soil. To preserve peace after the war, the French insisted that Germany be prevented from ever again becoming a military power. The French also wanted Germany to pay the costs of rebuilding France and restoring it to its former position.

The British had a different point of view. They believed the best way to preserve peace in Europe was to allow Germany to regain its place as a world power. They agreed with France that Germany should not again be permitted to build up military strength, but they did not want to suppress the German economy. The British wanted trade with Germany, and they were willing to sign various agreements with the German government.

Since the British did not share France's fear of Germany, the French sought ways of protecting themselves in the future. French leaders tried to create alliances that would shift the balance of power in Europe in favor of France. Alliances tied the French to Germany's other neighbors, Poland and Czechoslovakia. The French hoped these alliances would make the Germans hesitate before taking aggressive action against France or any of its allies. Although the British and French followed different policies, the French also remained convinced that the two nations must stand together in the future against common enemies.

SECTION REVIEW

1. Mapping: Using the map on page 482, describe the relative locations of France, Germany, Poland, and Czechoslovakia. Why did the French make an alliance with the Poles and the Czechs after World War I?
2. In your own words, briefly identify or define: balance of power, Nazis, Stalin, Five Year Plan.
3. Why did many Germans support the Nazi party in 1933?
4. What means did Stalin use to make the Soviet Union into a Socialist country?
5. How did Britain's attitude toward Germany differ from that of France?
   - Some people believe that to preserve world peace today, a balance of power has to be maintained between the Soviet Union and the United States. Do you agree? Are there other nations or factors to be considered? Explain.

GERMANY UNDER ADOLF HITLER

After World War I, the Germans were a discouraged and defeated people. The Weimar Republic was under constant attack for its failure to solve Germany's problems. Some people claimed that the republic was failing because Germans were not used to democracy. Others, including the National Socialist German Workers party, blamed the government for accepting the huge World War I debt. This debt, they claimed, was ruining Germany. Inflation was Germany's most serious economic problem, and in January of 1923, one United States dollar was worth 8,695 German marks. Almost a year later, it took six trillion marks to equal one dollar!

Hitler's Plan for Germany   **Adolf Hitler** was an Austrian-born former army corporal who fought in World War I. After the war, he entered politics and became a writer and fiery speaker. Hitler was one of the leaders of the small, growing National Socialist German Workers party. He proposed that the German parliament, the *Reichstag* (RIKE-schtahg), be abolished because it was weak. Hitler said that the Reichstag contained too many Communists and others who were not interested in restoring the power of the German nation.

If Germany were to be strong, Hitler asserted, it would have to be ruled firmly by a single master. In place of the Reichstag, Hitler proposed a form of government that would aid the working classes by controlling all business and by breaking up large estates. All opposition to the government would be suppressed. The economy would be strictly controlled. Society would be re-organized. Hitler and his followers claimed that the German people were a *master race*, and under a dictatorship would someday rule the world. The political ideas of Hitler—which glorify one race and nation and propose government by a dictatorship—are called **fascism** (FASH-iz-um).

The Rise of Hitler   Hitler organized large meetings where he expressed his ideas. At these meetings he gained many followers who were called Nazis. One group of his followers, known as the *Storm Troopers* or *Brown Shirts*, carried weapons and wore brown shirts. They served as Hitler's private army and often used violence against rival political parties. In the German city of Munich in 1923, Hitler and his followers failed in an attempt to overthrow the government. Hitler was convicted of treason and jailed for eight months. In prison, he wrote a book about his life and ideas called *Mein Kampf* (*My Struggle*).

Widespread economic depression sent the world's economy into a tailspin between 1929 and 1933. In the midst of this confusion, Germans lost confidence in their republican government. To gain popularity with the middle class, Hitler changed some of his ideas about government and turned against the workers and the unions, because they were supporters of the German Communist party. Hitler's Nazi party grew more and more popular. Tired of inflation and afraid of a Communist revolution, the middle class and the wealthy turned to Hitler with financial and political support. The Nazi party made large gains in the 1932 elections for the German Reichstag. In 1933, Hitler was appointed *chancellor* or prime minister, succeeding World War I hero, Hindenberg.

Hitler Becomes a Dictator Hitler formed a new government, but he needed to have a new election to gain a majority of Nazi members in the Reichstag. Shortly before the election, the Reichstag building was set on fire. Hitler announced that the Communists had set the fire and thousands were arrested to stop what the Nazis claimed was a great "Communist conspiracy."

When the new elections were held for the Reichstag, the Nazis received enough votes for Hitler to control the government. Hitler was made dictator. He dissolved the labor unions and abolished all political parties except the Nazi party. He also established censorship of the press, radio, and motion pictures. He thrilled the nationalistic Germans with parades, rallies, and speeches. He spoke of the glory of war and the "racial superiority" of the fair-skinned people of northern Europe. Hitler repeatedly referred to the Germans as the "master race." He warned them not to mix with races he regarded as mentally and physically inferior, such as the Jews and the Slavs. A secret police force called the *Gestapo* (guh-STAHP-oe) searched out all who opposed the new government. Many church leaders who objected to Hitler's ideas were persecuted.

The Persecution of the Jews One of the results of the belief in German racial superiority was the persecution of the Jews in Germany by the new Nazi government. The German people were told that the Jews were a "subhuman" race. Jews were blamed for Germany's defeat in World War I and for most of the country's other problems. Germans were warned against doing business with Jewish shops and stores; and Jewish lawyers and doctors were barred from practicing their profes-

Large rallies were part of Hitler's show of strength prior to World War II. Here Hitler is shown with some of his important deputies. Why do you think Nazism grew in Germany?

sion. Signs declaring "No Jews Allowed" were posted outside villages and towns and in stores and restaurants everywhere. Frightened by this persecution, large numbers of Jews left Germany. By the end of Hitler's second year in power, nearly 60,000 Jews had emigrated to other countries.

In 1935, the Nazi regime passed the *Nuremberg* (NOOR-um-burg) *Laws.* These laws were designed to frighten even larger numbers of Jews into leaving Germany. Through them, Jews were stripped of citizenship. They could no longer call themselves Germans, nor were they permitted to use the German national flag. Marriage between Jews and non-Jews was prohibited. Jews could no longer employ non-Jews. Jewish musicians even were forbidden to play musical compositions by non-Jewish composers.

Kristallnacht When Hitler came to power in 1933, there were about 500,000 Jews in Germany. They represented only one percent of the total population, and they thought of themselves as Germans. Over four fifths of them had been born in Germany. Between 1933 and 1938, Hitler's persecu-

tion drove about 150,000 of Germany's Jews to leave their homeland. However, this did not satisfy Hitler. On the night of November 9, 1938, all over Germany violence against the Jews broke out. Jewish homes and places of worship were burned. Jewish shops and stores were looted and destroyed. Jews were attacked, beaten, and killed. This night of violence later was called the *Kristallnacht* (kris-TAHL-nahkt), which means "Night of Broken Glass."

Concentration Camps After the Kristallnacht, Hitler's regime made no secret about its intention to drive all Jews from Germany. Within a twelve-month period, another 150,000 Jews left the country. Those who remained behind were forced to identify themselves in public by wearing the Star of David, the six-pointed star that is a symbol of Judaism. Jews were forced to leave their homes and had to live together in neighborhoods or *ghettos*, separated from the non-Jewish population in each community. After World War II began, the Nazis began shipping Jews from Germany to the areas of Poland conquered by the German army. There Jews were confined in large *concentration camps*. By mid-1943, the Nazis proudly announced that Berlin and most of Germany was free of all Jews.

After the start of World War II, the Nazi leaders in Germany decided to destroy all the Jews in every European country that had fallen under Germany's control. This terrible policy was referred to as the *Final Solution*. All over Europe, Jews were rounded up along with other peoples the Nazis considered inferior, and mass executions began. Many Jews and Slavs were sent to death camps that had been established especially to exterminate "infe-

Over six million European Jews and other "inferior peoples" were herded into concentration camps by the Nazis and then killed. Do you think Nazism could rise in the world today?

THE HOLOCAUST

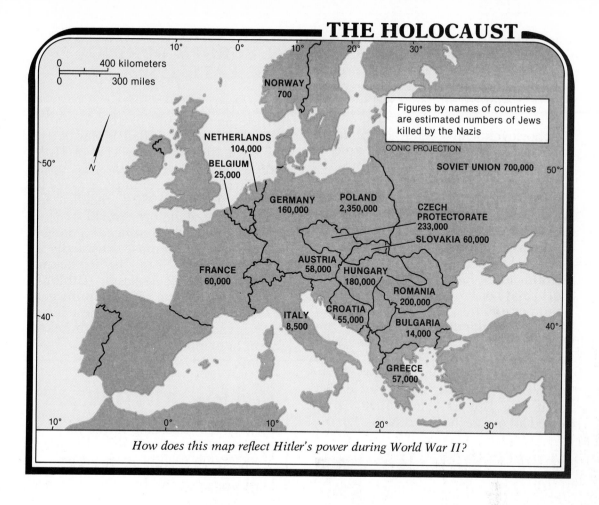

Figures by names of countries are estimated numbers of Jews killed by the Nazis

CONIC PROJECTION

- NORWAY 700
- NETHERLANDS 104,000
- BELGIUM 25,000
- SOVIET UNION 700,000
- GERMANY 160,000
- POLAND 2,350,000
- CZECH PROTECTORATE 233,000
- SLOVAKIA 60,000
- FRANCE 60,000
- AUSTRIA 58,000
- HUNGARY 180,000
- ROMANIA 200,000
- ITALY 8,500
- CROATIA 55,000
- BULGARIA 14,000
- GREECE 57,000

0 400 kilometers
0 300 miles

How does this map reflect Hitler's power during World War II?

rior" peoples. By 1944, Nazi officials boasted that about 6 million Jews had been killed. They claimed that 4 million of these had died in the concentration camp at *Auschwitz* (OWSH-vits), in southern Poland. In addition to Jewish victims, it is believed the Nazis murdered at least 6 million non-Jews. Most of these were Slavs, who died in the death camps alongside Jewish victims.

The dreadful attempt by Hitler's Nazi regime in Germany to wipe out all the Jewish people of Europe has been given the name *Holocaust* by the Jews themselves. The term *holocaust* means a great destruction of life. It is an ap-propriate word to describe the destruction of millions of innocent people by the Nazis.

German Aggression   One of Hitler's first acts after coming to power in 1933 was to withdraw Germany from the League of Nations. In March 1935, Hitler denounced the restrictions in the Versailles Treaty on the size of the German armed forces. He then rapidly built up the German army and navy. He also violated the Treaty of Versailles by moving German troops into the Rhineland, a German area on the border with France. In 1936, he sent aid to General Franco, the rebel leader who

487

was trying to overthrow the government of Spain. In March 1938, after promising to recognize Austria's independence, Hitler ordered his troops into that country and annexed it.

Hitler next demanded that Czechoslovakia give him the *Sudetenland* (soo-DATE-un-land), the area of Czechoslovakia inhabited mainly by Germans. The Czechs refused. To prevent war, the British and French met with Hitler and **Mussolini** (moo-suh-LEE-nee), his Italian ally, in Munich, Germany. Prime Minister *Neville Chamberlain* (CHAME-bur-lun) of Great Britain and *Edward Daladier* (duh-LAH-ee-ay) of France agreed to Hitler's demands and told the Czechs to give up the Sudetenland. The British and French treatment of Hitler was called *appeasement*. The British and French appeased Hitler because they believed he would reunite only former German territories. But in March 1939, Hitler seized all of Czechoslovakia.

SECTION REVIEW

1. Mapping: Using the map on page 487, list which areas of Europe suffered the greatest loss of their Jewish population.
2. In your own words, briefly define or identify: fascism, appeasement.
3. What things in Hitler's proposals show that Germany under Hitler was a Fascist government?
4. Trace the persecution of the Jews in Nazi Germany. Why were they persecuted?
  ◗ During the Holocaust, nearly 6 million Jews were killed by the Nazis. Have there ever been any other "Holocausts" in history? Do you think it is possible there will ever be another "Holocaust"? Explain.

TERRITORIAL CHANGES IN EUROPE DURING THE LATE 1930's

Many territorial changes were made in Europe as a result of the Versailles Peace Treaty that ended World War I. But with the ambitious rise of Hitler and Mussolini, the new European boundaries did not remain the same for long. In the late 1930's, the last few years of peace before World War II, there were some significant changes. Some of the areas most drastically affected were the Saar, the Rhineland, Austria, the Sudetenland, Ethiopia, and Czechoslovakia. The map on page 489 shows when each of these areas were invaded before the outbreak of war in September, 1939.

SECTION REVIEW

1. Mapping: According to the map on page 489, when did Germany move into each of these areas?
  a. Saar
  b. Rhineland
  c. Austria
  d. Czechoslovakia
  e. Sudetenland
2. Look at the map on page 462, showing some of the nationality groups of central Europe. What do you think the information on that map could have to do with nationalism and the territorial changes of the 1930's?
  ◗ If you had been head of the government of a major world power during the 1930's, would you have permitted these territorial changes or would you have tried to prevent them? Give reasons for your decision.

TERRITORIAL CHANGES IN EUROPE DURING THE 1930'S

NORWAY

SWEDEN

ESTONIA

NORTH SEA

DENMARK
Copenhagen

BALTIC SEA

Riga • LATVIA

Moscow •

LITHUANIA

Kovno •

GREAT BRITAIN

Amsterdam

London •

NETHERLANDS

Danzig EAST PRUSSIA

SOVIET UNION

GERMANY

Berlin •

BELGIUM

Brussels •

Saar Jan. 1935

Sudetenland Sept. 1938

Czechoslovakia March 1939

• Warsaw

POLAND

LUX.

SAAR

Rhineland March 1935

Prague • CZECHOSLOVAKIA

Paris •

FRANCE

Austria March 1938

to Hungary March 1939

Bern • SWITZ.

Geneva •

AUSTRIA

• Vienna

• Budapest

HUNGARY

ROMANIA

• Belgrade

• Bucharest

BLACK SEA

ITALY

CORSICA (Fr.)

YUGOSLAVIA

BULGARIA

• Sofia

• Rome

Albania April 1939

• Tirana

ALBANIA

SARDINIA (It.)

Ankara •

GREECE

TURKEY

SICILY (It.)

Athens •

Invasion of Ethiopia Oct. 1935

DODECANESE IS. (It.)

CYPRUS (Br.)

MEDITERRANEAN SEA

Axis Powers

Axis Controlled Area September 1, 1939

0   250 kilometers

0   200 miles

LIBYA (It.)

What was Hitler's excuse for taking over Czechoslovakian territory?

489

Mussolini is shown here reviewing troops by the Arch of Constantine in Rome. How did Mussolini rise to power?

ITALY UNDER MUSSOLINI

Italy experienced many difficulties after World War I. Political parties were unable to reach a compromise on national issues and there was a rapid succession of leaders. Moreover, Italy believed it had not received its fair share of territory after the war. Economic problems such as inflation and unemployment also plagued the Italian nation.

Mussolini and the Italian Fascists Following World War I, Benito Mussolini formed the *Fascist* party in Italy. Mussolini derived the word *fascist* from the symbol of authority in ancient Rome, the *fasces*, a bundle of rods surrounding an ax. The Fascists demanded the end of democracy and communism in Italy. They favored nationalism and dictatorship.

By fighting against the Socialists and Communists, the Fascists won the widespread support of the middle class. From the factory and landowners, Mussolini secured funds for his party, arms for his private army, and jobs for his followers. As the problems of Italy increased, the Fascists in 1922 decided to march on Rome and seize the government. To restore order, the Italian king, Victor Emmanuel III, invited Mussolini to form a government, and the parliament granted Mussolini emergency powers for one year to deal with Italy's pressing problems. However, Mussolini as *Il Duce* (DOO-chay), or the leader, remained a dictator for twenty-one years.

Italy under Fascism The Fascists transformed Italy into a total dictatorship with Mussolini as the leader. They disbanded all opposition parties and dropped all non-Fascist members from the cabinet. Under the Fascists, personal liberties disappeared and Mussolini told the people that they must "believe, fight, obey."

Mussolini Invades Ethiopia To win prestige for Italy, Mussolini began a war of conquest against Ethiopia (ee-thee-OE-pee-uh) in eastern Africa. The League of Nations failed to prevent his takeover of that nation, and in 1936, Mussolini announced that the king of Italy was also emperor of Ethiopia.

Soon after that, the League of Nations acted. It had already condemned Hitler when he began to rearm

Germany in defiance of the Treaty of Versailles. The League had also condemned an act of aggression by Japan in 1931 when it invaded Manchuria. Neither condemnation had had much effect, though, and Germany and Japan had replied by withdrawing from the League. This time, however, the League went further. It punished Italy by forbidding League members to trade with the Italians. Unfortunately, the other members of the League did not abide by the League's restrictions. In 1937, Italy followed the example of Japan and Germany and withdrew from the League of Nations. The failure of the League to punish Italy only demonstrated its inability to stop aggression.

The Spanish Civil War After his success in Ethiopia, Mussolini sent his troops to aid General Francisco Franco in the Spanish Civil War, which had broken out in 1936. At that time, Spain was a republic. When Socialists and Communists won control of the Spanish parliament, General Franco and other army leaders began a revolt. During the long civil war that followed, Italian and German troops fought in Spain on the side of the rebels, while Soviet Russia's Communist government sent troops to aid the Spanish parliament. The civil war ended in 1939 with General Franco's victory over the government. He set himself up as dictator of Spain and remained so until his death in 1975.

Albania Mussolini did not withdraw his troops from Spain until May of 1939. Meanwhile, Mussolini had decided to seize Albania. The Italians had considered Albania their sphere of influence since 1931. In April 1939, the Italian navy bombarded the coastal towns of Albania and troops were landed. The Italians quickly took over control of the whole country. Albania's king fled to Turkey, and Albania was annexed to Italy.

SECTION REVIEW

1. Mapping: Using the map on page 489, describe the location of Ethiopia and Albania in relation to Italy. Do you think this had any effect on Italy's decision to invade these two countries?
2. In your own words, identify: fascism, Mussolini, Spanish Civil War, Franco.
3. How did Mussolini come to power in Italy?
4. How did Fascists change Italy?
   If you had been a member of the League of Nations in 1936, how would you have punished Italy for its invasion of Ethiopia? Why is forbidding trade between countries sometimes hard to enforce?

BRINK OF WAR: 1939

By 1939, Europe was on the brink of another war. Czechoslovakia's seizure by Hitler had alarmed the British and French. Some of their leaders had been able to understand Hitler's demands for territory like Austria and the Sudetenland; the people there had been German. But in taking over the rest of Czechoslovakia, Hitler had annexed non-German peoples. Britain and France feared Hitler would annex Poland because many Germans lived there. So the British and French governments promised to stand by the Poles.

The British-French-Polish alliance presented Germany with the threat of another two-front war such as the Germans had faced in 1914. However, this would happen only if the Soviet Union stayed neutral or decided to join the British, French, and Poles. If the Soviet Union were to side with Germany, Poland would be caught in a German-Russian trap.

Stalin's Problem   Early in 1939, German diplomats rushed to Moscow to try to win the Russians to their side. At about the same time, a group of British and French diplomats set out for the Soviet Union in the hope of doing the same thing. The Russians kept their meetings with the Germans secret from the British and French, just as talks with the British and French were kept secret from the Germans.

By this time Stalin, the Communist dictator of Soviet Russia, knew from the writings and speeches of Hitler that Germany was no friend of the Soviet Union. It was clear that Hitler hated communism as much as he despised the Jews. Stalin probably realized that someday Hitler would make war on the Soviet Union.

On the other hand, Stalin mistrusted the British and French. They had done nothing to stop Hitler when his troops entered the Rhineland in 1936. They had stood by as Hitler annexed Austria in 1938. In 1938, the heads of the French and British governments had met with Hitler in Munich and permitted him to annex the Sudetenland. The rest of Czechoslovakia was annexed in early 1939.

At this point, Stalin must have considered what might happen to the Soviet Union if Britain refused to send its troops across the English Channel to fight the Germans. He must have also thought about the problems Russia would face if France decided to protect itself behind its great network of forts and trenches along the border between Germany and France. If neither Britain nor France launched an invasion of Germany, Hitler would not have to fight on two fronts. He could then hurl Germany's armies against the Poles and Russians. Poland would certainly fall, and the Soviet Union would face a German invasion.

Stalin then considered remaining neutral or declaring himself a friend of Germany. If he stood by and let the Germans conquer Poland, Hitler's armies would be a step closer to the Russian border. If Britain and France went to war against the Germans alone and were defeated, it would be Russia's turn to face the Germans. Hitler could defeat the small nations of Europe one by one, saving the Soviet Union until last. The Soviet Union was in a very dangerous position in 1939 so Stalin decided to join Hitler in order to gain time and strengthen the Russian army.

The German-Russian Non-aggression Treaty   Late in August 1939, much of the world was surprised to learn that Nazi Germany and the Soviet Union had just signed a treaty of friendship. They secretly planned to partition Poland between them. The diplomatic talks between the Germans and Russians had been kept secret, so people continued to believe that Nazis and Communists were bitter enemies. It seemed unbelievable that they could become allies. In some countries, Communist party members quit the party in protest. They refused to support Stalin's treaty with Hitler.

Hitler Invades Poland   On September 1, 1939, a week after the signing of the German-Russian treaty, war began when Hitler ordered German troops to invade Poland. German tanks and war planes swept across Poland in what was known as the *Blitzkrieg* (BLIT-skreeg) or "lightning war." About two weeks later, Hitler's Russian

THE TREATY BETWEEN NAZI GERMANY AND THE SOVIET UNION

Below is an excerpt from the treaty signed by Nazi Germany and the Soviet Union in Moscow on August 23, 1939. Note that part of the treaty was kept secret and not made public until after the end of World War II.

1. Both nations promise to avoid any act of violence, any aggressive action, and any attack on each other . . .
2. Should either Germany or the Soviet Union be attacked by a third nation, the other shall in no matter lend support to the third nation.
3. The Governments of Germany and the Soviet Union shall in the future maintain . . . contact with one another . . . to exchange information on problems affecting their common interests.
4. Neither Germany nor the Soviet Union shall become a member of any group of powers that is directly or indirectly aimed against the other . . .
5. The present treaty is concluded for a period of ten years. . . .

SECRET ADDITION TO THE TREATY

1. Should territorial changes be made in the Baltic states (Finland, Estonia, Latvia, Lithuania), the northern borders of Lithuania shall be the new boundary between the German and Soviet spheres of influence and domination.

2. Should territorial changes be made for Poland, Poland shall be divided between the German and Soviet spheres of influence and domination.

3. The question of whether Germany and the Soviet Union desire the continuation of an independent Polish state can only be determined in the course of further political developments, and both Governments shall resolve this question by means of a friendly agreement.

4. This Treaty shall be signed by both countries as strictly secret.

1. Summarize the public version of the treaty.
2. Summarize the secret section of the treaty.
3. Why wasn't the whole treaty revealed to the rest of the world?

ally also invaded Poland. Caught between German troops in the west and Russian troops in the east, Poland quickly collapsed. Although no military help for Poland came from Britain or France, they kept their promise to support Poland by declaring war on Germany. World War II had begun. But there was no invasion of Germany. Hitler was not facing a two-front war.

SECTION REVIEW

1. Mapping: Using the map on page 489, describe the locations of Poland and Czechoslovakia. Which nations bordered them?
2. In your own words, identify Josef Stalin.
3. Why was the Soviet Union in a dangerous position in 1939?
4. What was the immediate cause of World War II?

▷ If you had been a French or British leader in 1939, would you have called for a declaration of war against Russia as well as Germany? Explain your answer keeping the map of Europe in mind.

WORLD WAR II BEGINS IN ASIA

While Hitler and Mussolini were waging war in Europe, Japan was also preparing for conquests in Asia. The Japanese government had decided that the path to political power and prosperity lay in expanding onto the Asian mainland. Militarists in the government pushed a plan of aggression against China in the 1930's. The first step came in 1931 when the Japanese seized Manchuria, a part of northern China. In 1937, the Japanese struck again at China. Their troops seized most of the Chinese coast. The Chinese government retreated for safety to central China, making a new capital at Chungking (CHOON-KING). From there, Chiang Kai-shek's government tried to carry on the war against Japan.

Japanese Militarism The United States imposed limitations on trade with Japan because it had attacked China. In particular, the shipment of any U.S. oil to Japan was forbidden. At that time, Japan depended heavily on American oil.

The militarists in Japan, led by *General Tojo* (TOE-JOE), rose in anger and called for greater war preparations. The Japanese premier attempted to reach an agreement with the United States, but under pressure from the military leaders, he resigned in October 1941. General Tojo then became premier. The anti-American campaign in Japan intensified. There were warnings of a possible Japanese attack on the United States. Nevertheless, Japanese representatives were sent to Washington for talks to help maintain the peace.

The Axis Powers Demands were made by Japan that the United States remove its limitations on trade, stop aiding China, and recognize Japan's dominant position in Asia. The United States answered by demanding that

The militarists in Japan were led by General Tojo. What are the disadvantages of having the military in control of the government?

494

Japan withdraw from China, recognize the independence of China, sign a pact of non-aggression with all the powers in the Pacific area, and withdraw from its alliance with Hitler and Mussolini. Germany, Italy, and Japan were called the **Axis Powers.** They had signed a friendship pact on September 27, 1940.

Japan Attacks Pearl Harbor   The tensions between the United States and Japan began to mount toward the end of November 1941. At the same time, Japanese naval and air forces were secretly moving toward the Hawaiian Islands and other small islands in the South Pacific.

On December 7, 1941, while Japanese representatives were preparing for more peace talks in Washington, the Japanese air force launched a surprise attack on the chief U.S. naval base at Pearl Harbor, Oahu, Hawaii. The United States suffered tremendous losses in life and military equipment —

2,343 people died as a result of the attack, 1,272 were wounded, and nearly 1,000 were reported missing. After the attack, the United States declared war on Japan. With that, World War II spread to Asia.

SECTION REVIEW

1. Mapping: Using the scale of kilometers on the map on page 503, give the approximate distance between Hawaii and Japan. Why was Pearl Harbor important?
2. In your own words, identify: Manchuria, General Tojo, Axis Powers, Pearl Harbor.
3. In what ways were the reasons why Germany went to war similar to the reasons why Japan went to war? How did their reasons differ?
◗ Would aggression like the Japanese attack on Pearl Harbor ever be justified? Explain.

How does this picture reflect the war in the Pacific arena?

chapter 29

World War II

THE PROGRESS OF THE WAR, 1939–1941

In September 1939, the Poles called upon their allies for help against the Russians and the Germans, but the British and French did nothing. The Polish army fought bravely, but by the end of September Polish resistance had collapsed. The Germans took control of western Poland, while the Russian army occupied the eastern half of the country that had been promised to them in the secret German-Soviet treaty of August 1939.

War in Finland After the fall of Poland, British and French forces in France prepared for a German attack. But the German army made no aggressive moves. However, in November 1939, Hitler's Russian ally invaded Finland. To the surprise of most nations, the Finns inflicted a series of defeats on the Russian invaders and fought them to a standstill. The British and French governments decided to send troops to help the Finns against the Soviets. But before this force could be sent, the fighting there ended. In March of 1940, Finland and the U.S.S.R. signed peace terms.

Dunkirk Because the Germans still had made no aggressive moves, many people in the west began to believe there would be no fighting. Some started to call the war a "Phony War." Then, in April 1940, German troops attacked neutral Denmark and Norway. Denmark was easily conquered. The Norwegians valiantly resisted but were overwhelmed.

The fall of Denmark and Norway alarmed the British. Prime Minister Chamberlain resigned in May 1940, and his place as Britain's wartime leader was taken by **Winston Churchill.** On the same day Churchill took office, the German army began an offensive in western Europe. German troops crashed into The Netherlands and Belgium. Within four days, Dutch resistance ended and the Dutch queen fled to England. Belgian resistance lasted longer because of the support of British and French troops. The *Blitzkrieg* tactics that had defeated the Poles helped the Germans break through British-French defenses. German forces poured into France. A large number of Belgian, British, and French troops were cut off and trapped by the Germans. The Belgians surrendered on May 27, 1940, and the British and French retreated to Dunkirk (DUN-kurk). From there they were rescued by a remarkable assembly of both warships and private vessels that carried them across the English channel to safety.

In a show of power, the Germans marched under the Arc de Triomphe in Paris in 1940. How do you think the French people felt on that day?

The Fall of France The remainder of the Allied forces in France fought bravely, but they were no match for the German army. The Germans advanced rapidly into France, capturing Paris in June, and the French government fled south to Vichy (VISH-ee). *Henri Pétain* (pay-TA^n), a military hero of World War I, took over the French government. Believing it was hopeless to resist any longer, Pétain's government surrendered to the Germans.

Under the peace terms, only southeastern France remained under French control, with a new capital at Vichy. The rest of France, including Paris, was occupied by the German army. Many French were humiliated by their country's defeat and by the fact that their government at Vichy was a puppet of the Germans. French troops who had escaped to England were reorganized into a new fighting force. Led by **General Charles de Gaulle** (duh GOLE), they called themselves the *Free French* and promised to liberate France from the Germans.

The Battle of Britain After the fall of France in June 1940, Great Britain stood alone as the only country at war with the Axis Powers. Because the British navy still controlled the seas, a German naval invasion of Britain appeared to be impossible. Instead, Hitler decided to use his air force to defeat the British. Hitler was sure that bombs from German planes could persuade the British to surrender. In the summer

497

of 1940, the *Battle of Britain* began. Although German air attacks destroyed cities and killed thousands of people, the Germans could not destroy the British will to resist. By late 1940, the British were producing new planes faster than the Germans. Their air force was also taking its toll of German planes.

While the Battle of Britain was underway, Hitler struck at the British in Egypt, hoping to seize the Suez Canal. German and Italian forces attacked Egypt from Libya. Although Axis forces drove deep into Egypt, they were never able to reach the Canal. Throughout 1940 and 1941, the desert fighting in North Africa was a seesaw contest.

Hitler Moves Against the Soviets
After the failure of the Battle of Britain, Hitler's next move was against his ally, Soviet Russia. Hitler hated communism and considered the Russians an inferior race. Plans were prepared for an invasion of Russia in the spring of 1941. However, the invasion was delayed in order to send German paratroopers into the Balkans to rescue Hitler's ally, Mussolini.

Mussolini had decided to win glory by conquering Greece. In October 1940, Italian forces invaded Greece from Albania. But instead of winning a victory, Mussolini's army was pushed out of Greece, and by early 1941 the Greeks had seized part of Albania.

Meanwhile, in April 1940, German troops had poured into the Balkans. Hungary, Romania, and Bulgaria were forced into alliances with Germany. Yugoslavia was overrun in 1941 and the German forces took control of Greece within a few weeks.

In June of 1941, the Germans invaded Soviet Russia. At first, the Germans won victory after victory.

Great numbers of Russian prisoners were taken. German forces pushed deep into Russia, and by October, the Germans had reached Moscow and Leningrad. At that point, their rapid advance came to a halt. Russian resistance stiffened and the Germans suffered terribly from the effects of the Russian winter. As the weather worsened, the Soviet army began a series of attacks against the invaders. These attacks prevented the Germans from capturing either Moscow or Leningrad.

One of the chief German goals was the capture of the city of Stalingrad on the Volga River. The *Battle of Stalingrad*, during which the Russians endured a siege from August 1942 till the German surrender on February 1, 1943, was a turning point in the war. It marked the end of the German advance into Russia. After Stalingrad, the Germans began a slow retreat.

SECTION REVIEW

1. Mapping: Using the map on page 489 and the text on pages 492–498, describe the course of German aggression in World War II from the invasion of Poland until the Battle of Stalingrad. By 1941, which nations had been conquered by Hitler? Which nations were his allies? Which nations were fighting against him?

2. In your own words, identify: Winston Churchill, Vichy, Pétain, Dunkirk, Free French, Battle of Britain, Stalingrad.

3. How did Mussolini affect German plans to conquer Europe?

▶ Despite all of Britain's suffering during the Battle of Britain, the British did not surrender. What keeps people going under such conditions?

THE PROGRESS OF THE WAR, 1941–1945

On December 8, 1941, the day after the attack on Pearl Harbor, U.S. President **Franklin D. Roosevelt** appeared before Congress to request a declaration of war against Japan. Germany and Italy, Japan's allies, then declared war on the United States. On December 11, Roosevelt asked for and received from Congress a declaration of war against Germany and Italy. With that action, World War II began for the American people.

World Involvement   World War II did not involve every nation in the world, but it did include all the major powers of that time. Those fighting in the war were divided into two large opposing groups. They were called the *Allied* and the *Axis Powers*. (See the chart below.) The Soviet Union was originally allied with Germany. However, in June 1941, when Hitler launched an attack on Russia, Britain and the United States immediately aided Russia and the Soviet Union moved to the Allied side. The maps and charts on pages 500–503 document the

This poster was displayed shortly after the attack on Pearl Harbor. What does it tell you about how the United States reacted?

THE ALLIES		THE AXIS
The United States	Denmark	Germany
Britain	Greece	Italy
France	The Netherlands	Japan
The Soviet Union	New Zealand	
Australia	Norway	*Later joined by:*
Belgium	Poland	
Brazil	South Africa	Hungary
Canada	Yugoslavia	Romania
China (now		Bulgaria
Nationalist China)		

WORLD WAR II—ALLIED VICTORY IN EUROPE AND NORTH AFRICA, 1942-1945

1. Nov. 8, 1942–May 13, 1943. North African Campaign. An invasion force under General Dwight D. Eisenhower lands near Casablanca, Oran, and Algiers. Eisenhower's army advances east to Tunisia, while British troops under Field Marshal Bernard Montgomery defeat the Germans at El Alemain and push them westward to Tunisia. On April 7, the Allied armies meet near Gasfa, encircling the Axis forces. The Axis forces surrender on May 13.

2. Feb. 2, 1943–May 1944. Russian Counteroffensive. After retaking Stalingrad, the Russians begin to push the Germans out of Russia. Kiev is taken in November 1943; the Russians then drive into Poland, Romania, Yugoslavia, and Bulgaria.

3. July 10–Aug. 17, 1943. Invasion of Sicily. Anglo-American forces under Montgomery and U.S. General George S. Patton overrun the island in five weeks.

4. Sept. 3, 1943–June 4, 1944. Invasion of Italy. Anglo-American forces invade Italy. After months of heavy fighting, the Allies gain control of central Italy and liberate Rome on June 4.

5. Jan.–May 1944. Air offensive. The Allies launch a strategic air offensive from Britain, crippling German air power. Berlin is bombed.

6. June 6, 1944. Invasion of Normandy. Allied forces under Eisenhower storm the Normandy coast (Operation Overlord) and sweep across France. On August 25, Paris is liberated, and the Allies drive on to Belgium and Luxembourg.

7. Aug. 15, 1944. Invasion of Southern France. Allied forces land in southern France and move up the Rhone Valley to join the Normandy invaders at Paris. They then proceed to Austria and Germany.

8. Dec. 16–26, 1944. Battle of the Bulge. The Germans counterattack against U.S. troops in Belgium. After pushing 50 miles into Belgium, the Germans are checked at Bastogne.

9. March 7–May 8, 1945. Fall of Germany. From the west, Eisenhower's army pushes into Germany and overruns its industrial heartland. From the east, the Russian army takes Warsaw and crosses into Germany. On April 25, American and Russian troops meet at Torgau on the Elbe. Berlin falls on May 2, and on May 8 Germany surrenders (V-E Day).

WORLD WAR II ALLIED VICTORY IN EUROPE AND NORTH AFRICA, 1942–1945

ATLANTIC OCEAN

ICELAND (Den.)

SWEDEN

NORWAY

FINLAND

Oslo

Stockholm

Helsinki

Leningrad

ESTONIA

LATVIA

Moscow

NORTH SEA

GREAT BRITAIN

Dublin

IRELAND

DENMARK

BALTIC SEA

LITHUANIA

EAST PRUSSIA

Danzig

Russians

SOVIET UNION

London

Amsterdam

Berlin

Warsaw

Kiev

Stalingrad

(2)

NETH.

GERMANY

(9)

POLAND

Allies

(5)

Brussels

BELG.

Bastogne

Torgau

Russians

Normandy

(6)

(8)

LUX.

Paris

Rhine R.

Prague

CZECHOSLOVAKIA

Vienna

Budapest

FRANCE

Vichy

SWITZ.

AUSTRIA

HUNGARY

ROMANIA

CRIMEA

(7)

Danube R.

Belgrade

Bucharest

BLACK SEA

CORSICA (Fr.)

ITALY

YUGOSLAVIA

Sofia

BULGARIA

Rome

(4)

ALBANIA

Ankara

SARDINIA (It.)

Allies

SICILY (It.)

GREECE

TURKEY

Lisbon

PORTUGAL

Madrid

SPAIN

(3)

Athens

Allies

CRETE (Gr.)

CYPRUS (Br.)

SYRIA

IRAQ

Allies

Casablanca

Oran

Algiers

Tunis

TUNISIA

Gasta

MEDITERRANEAN SEA

DODECANESE ISLANDS (It.)

British

PALESTINE

TRANS-JORDAN

MOROCCO

ALGERIA

(1)

Tripoli

LIBYA

British

El Alamein

Alexandria

Cairo

EGYPT

SAUDI ARABIA

RED SEA

Legend

→ Allied offensives

--→ Allied air offensives

① Battle sites or campaigns

Neutral

Axis territory in 1939

Maximum extent of Axis control

Controlled by Allies

0   500 kilometers

0   400 miles

CONIC PROJECTION

N

Where did the main Allied offensives engage the Germans?

WORLD WAR II—ALLIED VICTORY IN THE PACIFIC, 1942-1945

1. **May 7-8, 1942. Battle of the Coral Sea.** U.S. pilots thwart a Japanese attempt to seize Port Moresby in southern New Guinea.

2. **June 3-6, 1942. Battle of Midway.** U.S. Admiral Chester Nimitz repels an enemy attempt to take Midway.

3. **Aug. 7, 1942-Feb. 9, 1943. Guadalcanal.** Marines land on Guadalcanal and seize the airport. Months of fighting follow. In the battle of Guadalcanal (November 25), American forces prevent the Japanese from landing reinforcements, making possible the American conquest of the island.

4. **March 24-Aug. 15, 1943. The Aleutians.** American troops force the Japanese from the Aleutians.

5. **July-Nov. 1943. Solomons Campaign.** American forces move up the Solomons from Guadalcanal and bombard Rabaul, the Japanese stronghold, cutting off all its supply lines.

6. **Nov. 1943-Feb. 1944. Central Pacific Campaign.** Nimitz successfully assaults the Gilbert and Marshall islands.

7. **Jan.-Sept. 1944. New Guinea Campaign.** General Douglas MacArthur moves up the New Guinea coast from Port Moresby to take Hollandia. After months of fighting in Hollandia, Japanese resistance ends.

8. **June 15-July 21, 1944. Saipan and Guam.** Nimitz continues his Pacific advance, taking Saipan (July 9) and Guam (July 21), in the Marianas.

9. **Oct. 20, 1944-Feb. 23, 1945. Philippines.** Beginning his drive, MacArthur invades Leyte. In the battle of Leyte Gulf, the Navy virtually wipes out the Japanese fleet. American forces retake Manila on February 23.

10. **Feb. 19-March 17, 1945. Iwo Jima.** Americans take the island, just 750 miles from Tokyo.

11. **April 1-June 21, 1945. Okinawa.** Americans seize Okinawa, main island of the Ryukyus.

12. **May-July 1945. U.S. Air Offensive.** The Air Force bombs the Japanese home islands.

13. **Aug. 6 and 9, 1945. Hiroshima and Nagasaki.** Americans drop an atomic bomb on Hiroshima. Three days later, another bomb is dropped on Nagasaki.

WORLD WAR II ALLIED VICTORY IN THE PACIFIC, 1942-1945

Japanese controlled
Allies
Line of maximum Japanese control Dec. 1942
Japanese advances
Allied advances
Allied air offensive
① Battle sites or campaigns

MILLER PROJECTION

ALASKA (U.S.)

SOVIET UNION

BERING SEA

SEA OF OKHOTSK

SAKHALIN

ALEUTIAN IS.
④
1943
1942

KURIL IS.

MONGOLIA

Peking

CHINA

Chungking

KOREA
JAPAN
Tokyo
Hiroshima
Nagasaki
⑬

PACIFIC OCEAN

1942

Attack on Pearl Harbor Dec. 7, 1941

OKINAWA
⑪
FORMOSA

INDIA
BURMA
Hong Kong
FRENCH
THAILAND INDO-
CHINA
SOUTH CHINA SEA

⑫
⑩ IWO JIMA

1941

② MIDWAY

HAWAIIAN IS.

1945 1942

1945

MARIANA IS.
SAIPAN
GUAM
⑧
TRUK
CAROLINE IS.
1942

WAKE

Nimitz 1944
MARSHALL IS.
⑥
1941-42
⑥

Nimitz

Manila
LEYTE
⑨
MacArthur
1944-45
PHILIPPINE IS.

MALAYA
Singapore
SUMATRA
BORNEO
CELEBES
DUTCH EAST INDIES
JAVA

BISMARCK SEA

GILBERT IS.
1943

Hollandia
⑦
NEW GUINEA
Port Moresby
Darwin

⑤ SOLOMON IS.
1942
③ GUADALCANAL
① 1942

CORAL SEA

NEW CALEDONIA

INDIAN OCEAN

MacArthur
1942

AUSTRALIA

Sydney

0   2500 kilometers

0   1500 miles

NEW ZEALAND

How did geography affect the kind of war fought in the Pacific?

503

progress of World War II after the entrance of the United States into the European and Pacific theaters of conflict.

Japanese-Americans   Shortly after the Japanese attack on Pearl Harbor, thousands of Japanese-Americans were arrested and placed in government prison camps. In spite of the fact that a majority of the people arrested were native-born Americans, this was done because some people believed that since these Americans were of Japanese ancestry, they would sympathize with or aid the Japanese cause in the war. Many Japanese-Americans, however, fought very bravely for the United States in Europe during World War II.

The End of the War   The Allies finally defeated the Axis after a prolonged and costly war. Italy surrendered on September 8, 1943. On April 28, 1945, Italians who supported the Allies killed Mussolini. Hitler committed suicide in Berlin on April 30, 1945. Seven days later Germany surrendered, and May 8th has become known as V-E Day, for Victory in Europe. After the United States dropped atomic bombs on the Japanese cities of *Hiroshima* (hir-uh-SHEE-muh) and *Nagasaki* (nahg-uh-SAHK-ee), Japan surrendered on August 14, 1945. Japanese representatives signed the surrender aboard the U.S. battleship *Missouri* on September 2, 1945. That day is known as *V-J Day*, for Victory over Japan.

The Costs of the War   World War II was the most destructive war in history. It has been estimated that about 40 million civilians and soldiers died as a result of the war. Several million refugees, uprooted by the war, also needed help in rebuilding their lives. Further, it has been estimated that the war cost about $4,000,000,000,000 or 4 trillion dollars. Of course, these figures do not reflect the amount of suffering experienced by the peoples of almost sixty nations that were involved in the war.

SECTION REVIEW

1. Mapping: Using the maps and charts on pages 500–503, briefly describe the progress of World War II as it was fought in North Africa and Europe, and Asia and the Pacific area, between 1942 and 1945.
2. In your own words, identify: Allies, Axis, Nagasaki, Hiroshima, V-E Day, V-J Day.
3. What happened to Japanese-Americans during the war?
    World War II lasted six years. Make a list of ways in which you think it changed people's lives.

BATTLE DEATHS OF SOLDIERS

The Major Allied Powers

The United States	295,904
The British Commonwealth	452,570
The Soviet Union	7,500,000
France	200,000
China	2,200,000
	10,648,474

The Major Axis Powers

Germany	2,850,000
Italy	300,000
Japan	1,506,000
	4,656,000

ALLIED EFFORTS TOWARD WORLD PEACE

Even before the Japanese attack on Pearl Harbor, the United States had been aligning itself on the side of the Allies who were under attack by Germany. On August 14, 1941, President Franklin D. Roosevelt and British Prime Minister Winston Churchill issued what has become known as the **Atlantic Charter.** In it, both leaders declared their goals to be: self-determination for all peoples, freedom of the seas and trade, freedom from fear and want, and the abandonment of armed force in international disputes. In that same year, the United States also began to loan Britain ships and supplies to be used in its battle against Germany.

Planning for Postwar Peace   Once the United States had entered the war, many plans were formed for winning the war and for keeping peace afterward. These plans were discussed and agreed upon at a series of meetings attended by the three major Allied leaders—Winston Churchill, Josef Stalin, and Franklin D. Roosevelt. At the *Casablanca Conference,* held in North Africa on February 12, 1943, Churchill and Roosevelt agreed that unconditional surrender was to be demanded of all Axis Powers. No harm was intended to the common people of those nations, but their "guilty and barbaric" leaders would be punished. The Allied leaders expressed their desire to restore to all conquered peoples their sacred rights.

At the *Moscow Conference* of October 1943, the major Allied Powers agreed to continue working together and cooperating on plans for maintaining the peace and security of the world at the end of the war. They decided to establish an international organization

In 1945, two of Japan's largest cities, Hiroshima and Nagasaki, were destroyed by atomic bombs. How has the invention of the atomic bomb changed the world?

for maintaining world peace. They stated that democratic government must be restored to Italy, and they agreed upon a program to bring this about. They warned the Nazis who had been responsible for or agreed to participate in massacres and executions of Jews and others that they would be tried in court for their crimes.

During the *Cairo Conference* of November 1943, Roosevelt, Churchill, and Chiang Kai-shek of China reached further agreement on the war against Japan. When defeated, Japan was to be stripped of all island and mainland territory it had seized since 1914. Korea was to become an independent nation.

At the *Tehran Conference* of December 1943, Stalin, Roosevelt, and Churchill agreed on plans to complete a drive by the United States and England against Germany by landing troops in western Europe. Iran would

Churchill, Roosevelt, and Stalin met at Yalta, Russia, in 1945 to discuss post-war plans. Why didn't they wait for the war to be over first?

receive economic aid for allowing goods to flow through its country to Russia. The three leaders also wanted to get Turkey to declare war on the Axis Powers. Turkey managed to remain neutral throughout most of the war. It maintained trade and commercial relations with both Allied and Axis powers. However, when the Allies decided that only nations that had actually taken part in the war would be asked to join in planning the United Nations, Turkey chose to declare war formally on Germany in 1945. This was at a time when Germany was all but defeated and the war was almost over in Europe.

During the **Yalta Conference** held in Russia in February 1945, Roosevelt, Churchill, and Stalin agreed that after the war Great Britain, the United States, and Russia would help the European nations to do three things: re-establish democratic governments, rebuild their economies, and achieve the goals of the Atlantic Charter. Germany would be disarmed and divided into sectors. The United States, Great Britain, the Soviet Union, and France would each administer one sector of Germany and the capital city, Berlin.

506

Germany would be expected to pay war costs and damages.

Franklin D. Roosevelt died on April 12, 1945, and Harry S Truman became President on that day. Truman represented the United States at the last of the major World War II conferences. It was held from July 17 to August 2, 1945, at *Potsdam* in Germany. At the meetings, Truman, Clement Attlee—the new British prime minister who replaced Churchill—and Stalin established a council of foreign ministers to prepare the peace treaties. Italy had surrendered on September 8, 1943, and Germany on May 7, 1945.

Creation of the United Nations The last major development as a result of World War II was the creation of the **United Nations.** (See the chart below.) It replaced the League of Nations. The United Nations received overwhelming support in the United States. The U.S. Senate ratified the UN Charter that had been drawn up by member nations meeting in San Francisco in December 1945, after only six days of debate. Following is an excerpt of the Charter: "We

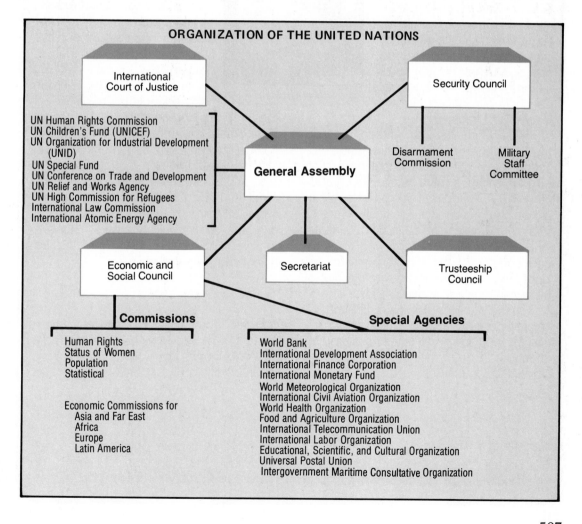

ORGANIZATION OF THE UNITED NATIONS

International Court of Justice

Security Council

UN Human Rights Commission
UN Children's Fund (UNICEF)
UN Organization for Industrial Development (UNID)
UN Special Fund
UN Conference on Trade and Development
UN Relief and Works Agency
UN High Commission for Refugees
International Law Commission
International Atomic Energy Agency

General Assembly

Disarmament Commission

Military Staff Committee

Economic and Social Council

Secretariat

Trusteeship Council

Commissions

Human Rights
Status of Women
Population
Statistical

Economic Commissions for
  Asia and Far East
  Africa
  Europe
  Latin America

Special Agencies

World Bank
International Development Association
International Finance Corporation
International Monetary Fund
World Meteorological Organization
International Civil Aviation Organization
World Health Organization
Food and Agriculture Organization
International Telecommunication Union
International Labor Organization
Educational, Scientific, and Cultural Organization
Universal Postal Union
Intergovernment Maritime Consultative Organization

507

the people of the United Nations are determined to save future generations from the scourge of war, which twice in our lifetime has brought untold sorrow to mankind. We are determined to reaffirm our faith in fundamental human rights, in the dignity and worth of the human person, and in the equal rights of men and women and of nations large and small. We are determined to estab-

PEOPLE IN HISTORY

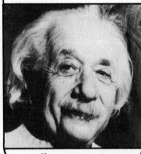

Albert Einstein

Albert Einstein was born on March 14, 1879, in Ulm, Germany. His family soon moved to Munich, where Einstein's father and uncle ran a small electrochemical factory. Einstein was no child prodigy. In fact, he was unable to speak fluently at age nine and developed a deep dislike for school. Much of his real education began at home where his uncle introduced him to algebra and geometry.

When he was sixteen, Einstein tried to enter the Federal Institute of Technology in Switzerland but he had to take the entrance exam twice. After graduating in 1900, Einstein had great trouble in obtaining employment. He finally went to work in the patent office in Bern, Switzerland. In Bern, Einstein continued to study and completed the requirements for his doctorate. There he also wrote the first of his revolutionary scientific papers.

In the years that followed, Einstein accepted positions at universities in Germany and his work began to attract widespread attention. In 1921, he was awarded the Nobel Prize in physics.

During the 1920's and early 1930's, Einstein accepted many invitations to lecture abroad. Fortunately, he was in California in 1933 when Hitler came to power. As a famous Jew, Einstein was a prime target for Nazi hostility. He then accepted a position at Princeton University in New Jersey.

In July 1939, Einstein signed a letter to President Roosevelt drawing attention to the danger of the Nazis' developing a uranium bomb. However, when Einstein's famous equation $E = mc^2$ was finally demonstrated with the dropping of the atomic bomb on Hiroshima in 1945, Einstein, the humanitarian, was deeply shocked and distressed. For a long time, all he could utter was "Horrible, horrible." On April 18, 1955, Einstein died in Princeton, New Jersey.

Adapted from: Roger H. Stueiver. "Albert Einstein," **The McGraw-Hill Encyclopedia of World Biography,** Volume 3. New York: McGraw-Hill, 1973, pp. 540–542.

1. How did Einstein feel about school?
2. What is one reason why Einstein is so famous?
3. Einstein was a genius. What rules should any genius follow when making known his or her theories or discoveries? Do you think this question could serve as a main point for discussion about the biographical sketch on Einstein? Tell why or why not.

lish conditions under which justice and respect for the duties arising from treaties and other parts of international law can be maintained. We are determined to promote social progress and better standards of life in greater freedom. To achieve these goals, we will practice tolerance and will live together in peace with one another as good neighbors. We are also determined to unite our strength to maintain international peace and security, and to insure that armed force shall not be used except in the interests of all. And, finally, we are determined to use international means to promote the economic and social advancement of all peoples. To accomplish these aims we have resolved to combine our efforts. And so our Governments, through representatives assembled in the city of San Francisco, have agreed to the present Charter of the United Nations. And they do hereby establish an international organization to be known as the United Nations.''

Today some Americans have mixed feelings about the UN. Some people note that the United States pays for about one fourth of the total UN budget, more than any other member. Yet those same people say that many members use the UN as a place to denounce the policies of the United States. Many UN countries openly violate the charter of the UN.

Other Americans claim that the UN provides a forum for member countries to discuss their differences in a peaceful manner. These people also argue that many of the UN agencies provide, among other things, valuable help to needy children, development of international trade, health care, and a means for gathering needed statistics on many topics.

SECTION REVIEW

1. Mapping: Using the Atlas, list the countries in which each of these cities is located: Moscow, Cairo, Casablanca, Yalta, Tehran, Potsdam, San Francisco.
2. In your own words, state the significance of the following: Atlantic Charter of 1941, Casablanca Conference of 1943, Moscow Conference of 1943, Cairo Conference of 1943, Tehran Conference of 1943, Yalta Conference of 1945, and Potsdam Conference of 1945.
3. According to its Charter, what are five goals of the United Nations?
4. Using the chart on page 507 as a guide, what are the six major bodies in the structure of the United Nations? To which body are all the others tied? Using the chart as evidence, what are the concerns of the United Nations?
   Do you think people and different countries and cultures should be able to work together peacefully?

Reviewing the Unit

Unit Summary

After you have read the selection below, answer the questions that follow.

Nationalism has been defined as the sense of unity among people with the same history, language, and culture. During the nineteenth century, nationalism inspired many people to fight for independence from foreign rulers. The Greeks, Serbs, and Bulgarians were among the East European peoples who won independence from the Ottoman Empire. The Magyars and the Czechs also demanded their independence from the Austrian Empire. Inspired by nationalism, the Italians and Germans, who never had been united as a single nation prior to the nineteenth century, established their own national states late in the 1800's.

Many people in the 1800's came to believe that great nations should possess colonies. As a result, imperialism revived among the European nations. Nationalism had much to do with this revival.

Conquest by imperialist countries helped to stimulate a sense of nationalism in Africa and Asia. China's mistreatment by imperialist powers produced a strong sense of nationalism by the early twentieth century.

Nationalism and imperialism threatened to bring countries into serious conflicts. The scramble for colonies in Africa brought the danger of war. Early in the 1900's, national rivalry between Austria and Russia threatened to cause a war as both powers tried to extend their influence in eastern Europe. The Balkans became the powder keg of Europe. There, in 1914, World War I quickly erupted.

One of the underlying causes of World War I was nationalism. Peacemakers after the war hoped to prevent another conflict. However, the new national boundaries established after the war helped to revive hostilities between some countries. Hitler came to power promising to reunite all Germans once again in a new Reich, or empire. Hitler's form of nationalism was one of the underlying causes for World War II.

After World War II, peacemakers once again sought ways to prevent another similar conflict. As a result, an international organization, the United Nations, was formed.

Developing Your Reading Skills

1. What do you think is the main idea of this reading?
2. In your own words, state the main idea about each of the following:

   a. definition of nationalism
   b. positive results of nationalism
   c. negative results of nationalism
   d. formation of United Nations

Developing a Sense of Time

Examine the time line below and answer the questions that follow it.

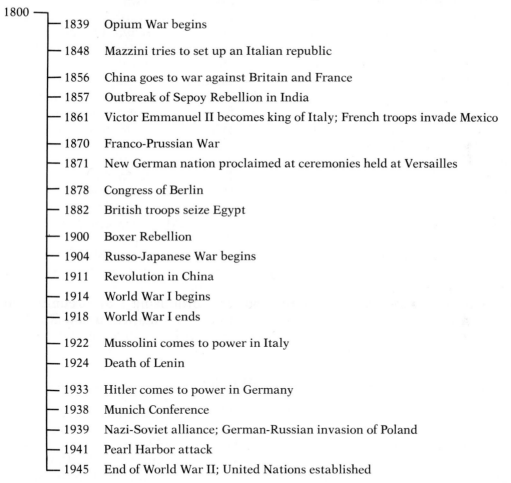

1800

—	1839	Opium War begins
—	1848	Mazzini tries to set up an Italian republic
—	1856	China goes to war against Britain and France
—	1857	Outbreak of Sepoy Rebellion in India
—	1861	Victor Emmanuel II becomes king of Italy; French troops invade Mexico
—	1870	Franco-Prussian War
—	1871	New German nation proclaimed at ceremonies held at Versailles
—	1878	Congress of Berlin
—	1882	British troops seize Egypt
—	1900	Boxer Rebellion
—	1904	Russo-Japanese War begins
—	1911	Revolution in China
—	1914	World War I begins
—	1918	World War I ends
—	1922	Mussolini comes to power in Italy
—	1924	Death of Lenin
—	1933	Hitler comes to power in Germany
—	1938	Munich Conference
—	1939	Nazi-Soviet alliance; German-Russian invasion of Poland
—	1941	Pearl Harbor attack
—	1945	End of World War II; United Nations established

1. Who came to power first—Hitler or Mussolini?
2. How many times did China go to war with foreign nations between 1839 and 1945?
3. How many years separated the end of World War I and the beginning of World War II?
4. What other key events or developments from Unit 9 could be added to this time line? Cite three and give a reason for selecting each.

Recalling the Facts

1. How did nationalism contribute to the unification of Germany and Italy?
2. How did the alliances made by the major powers prior to World War I bring about that war?
3. How did the Treaty of Versailles help bring about World War II?
4. What did each of the "Big Four" at the Paris Peace Conference after World War I represent?
5. Describe the relationship between Germany and the Soviet Union before the outbreak of World War II.
6. Why were the Jews persecuted by the Nazis? What was the Holocaust?
7. What event was most directly responsible for the beginning of World War II in Europe? in Asia?
8. Who were the "Big Three" leaders of the Allies during World War II? Why did they meet?
9. Describe the purpose of the United Nations.

Using Your Vocabulary

1. What is imperialism? Give three examples of imperialism.
2. What is nationalism? Explain the relationship between nationalism and imperialism.
3. How do you think Kaiser Wilhelm II of Germany would have defined imperialism and nationalism? How might Sun Yat-sen have defined these terms?
4. How do "spheres of influence" differ from "buffer zones"?
5. What was the Meiji Restoration? In your opinion, was this event a revolution?
6. Define the term "Pan-Slavism." Why did Pan-Slavism threaten the British in the 1800's?
7. Why did Europeans call the Balkans the "powder keg" of Europe before World War I?
8. What is meant by "self-determination"?
9. Define fascism. How was German fascism similar to Italian fascism?

Using Your Geography Skills

1. Identify the countries in East Europe that managed to break away from the Ottoman Empire in the 1800's.
2. Identify the peoples within the Austrian Empire who wanted independence in the 1800's.
3. Identify the political divisions of the Italian peninsula and who controlled them at the beginning of unification in the 1800's.
4. Which European powers had colonial possessions in Africa before World War I?
5. Which imperialist nations extended their control into the Pacific region? into Asia?
6. Identify the Central Powers in World War I. What countries were on Germany's two fronts?
7. How large was Hitler's Reich before the end of World War II?

Developing Your Writing Skills

In this unit, you have learned about imperialism in modern times. Each nation practiced imperialism in its own way, yet as a movement imperialism had a great impact on the peoples of Asia, Africa, and the Pacific. Keeping in mind the areas into which imperialist nations spread their influence, consider the following:

FORMING AN OPINION

1. In your opinion, what were some of the negative effects of imperialist rule in Asia and Africa? Give examples.
2. What were some of the positive effects? Give examples.

SUPPORTING AN OPINION

3. Do you think imperialism is ever justified? Answer this question in a short essay. Begin by completing the following topic sentence: Imperialism is (is not) justified because _____

Why Study the Past?

1. List three ways in which your study of imperialism and nationalism can be of value to you today. How might your study of this period of history help you predict what will happen in the next five or ten years?
2. How can historians learn about present-day diplomacy between nations by studying the relations between countries before World Wars I and II?

Your History Bookshelf

Brown, Harry. *Hitler and the Rise of Nazism.* New York: Roy, 1969.

Davenport, Marcia. *Garibaldi: Father of Modern Italy.* New York: Random House, 1957.

Dawidowicz, Lucy. *The War Against the Jews 1933–1945.* New York: Holt, Rinehart and Winston, 1975.

Esterer, Arnulf and Louise. *Sun Yat-sen: China's Greatest Champion.* New York: Messner, 1970.

Hersey, John R. *Hiroshima.* New York: Knopf, 1946.

Kamm, Josephine. *Explorers into Africa.* New York: Macmillan, 1970.

Rickenbacher, Eddie. *Fighting the Flying Circus.* New York: Avon, 1969.

Reeder, Red. *Bold Leaders of World War I.* Boston: Atlantic-Little, Brown, 1974.

Ryan, Cornelius. *A Bridge Too Far.* New York: Simon and Schuster, 1974.

——. *The Longest Day.* New York: Simon and Schuster, 1975.

Solzhenitsyn, Alexander. *August 1914.* New York: Bantam, 1974.

——. *One Day in the Life of Ivan Denisovich.* New York: Praeger, 1963.

Your World

Because of her very special qualities, Arabella had been selected to participate in Skylab, a unique space age experiment. She was light, delicate, agile, and skilled in making elaborate constructions out of virtually nothing. Furthermore, while most space travelers have had trouble with the change in gravity in a spacecraft, Arabella appeared to take weightlessness in stride. Life in the spacecraft scarcely seemed to affect her. Everyone in the Skylab project agreed that Arabella the astrospider gave a spectacular performance. The Skylab project was part of the U. S. space exploration program designed to gather information about outer space.

Through Skylab, scientists learned more about how people adapt to another environment, how many days they can remain in space without ill effects, and how space travel affects the human body. They discovered, for example, that the change in gravity caused astronauts' spines to lengthen about 2.5 centimeters (1 in.). The change was only temporary, however. Skylab also yielded a wealth of knowledge about Earth. Photographs taken from space revealed untapped mineral deposits and new fishing grounds. And in the Skylab photos of Mount Ararat in Turkey, scientists found clues that may help solve a centuries-old mystery—the location of Noah's Ark.

All experiments with Skylab came to an abrupt end on July 11, 1979, when Skylab, weakened earlier by unusual solar storms, made its final plunge toward the earth. As Skylab fell apart in the earth's atmosphere, pieces of it landed on central Australia and in the Indian Ocean. Fortunately, no one was injured by the pieces of Skylab, which failed to burn up before hitting the earth.

Exploration has been one of the absorbing pursuits of the twentieth century. Skylab was only one of many exploratory voyages. Other explorations have taken people far below the surface of the world's oceans to look at life on the floor of the sea. Still other explorers have done their work close to home. These include the scientists who explore the mysteries of life using microscopes and other instruments . . . the political, social, and economic thinkers who explore new forms of human social life . . . the historians who explore the past for clues to the present and future . . . and the artists, philosophers, and religious thinkers who explore new answers to the questions people have been asking themselves for centuries.

In this unit, you will continue your exploration of human history. You will be exploring the world of the twentieth century—your world.

Unit Goals

1. To list five important developments within the United States during the twentieth century and to explain why you think that one of these developments is the most significant of the five.
2. To describe, in as much detail as possible, the relations between the nations of North and South America, Asia, Africa, and Europe during the twentieth century.
3. To list five important developments in eastern and western Europe after World War II and to explain why you think that one of these developments is the most significant of the five.
4. To make a general statement that tells what you think the most important development has been in Asia since the end of World War II.
5. To make a general statement that tells what you think the most important development has been in Africa during the twentieth century.
6. To list five ways in which important developments in the world have influenced your life in the past or will influence it in the future.

Your World

WORLD POPULATION

☐ This amount of space on land represents a population of 1 million people.

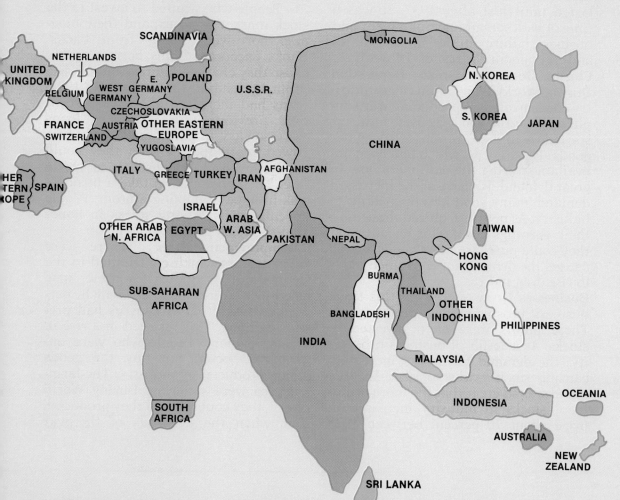

CANADA

U.S.A.

MEXICO

CUBA

OTHER CARIBBEAN

CENTRAL AMERICA

VENEZUELA

COLOMBIA

OTHER S. AMERICA

BRAZIL

CHILE

ARGENTINA

SCANDINAVIA

NETHERLANDS

UNITED KINGDOM

BELGIUM

WEST GERMANY

E. POLAND GERMANY

U.S.S.R.

MONGOLIA

N. KOREA

CZECHOSLOVAKIA

FRANCE

AUSTRIA OTHER EASTERN EUROPE

SWITZERLAND

YUGOSLAVIA

CHINA

S. KOREA

JAPAN

HER TERN OPE

SPAIN

ITALY

GREECE TURKEY

IRAN

AFGHANISTAN

ISRAEL

OTHER ARAB N. AFRICA

EGYPT

ARAB W. ASIA

PAKISTAN

NEPAL

TAIWAN

HONG KONG

SUB-SAHARAN AFRICA

BURMA

THAILAND

OTHER INDOCHINA

BANGLADESH

PHILIPPINES

INDIA

MALAYSIA

SOUTH AFRICA

INDONESIA

OCEANIA

AUSTRALIA

NEW ZEALAND

SRI LANKA

The United States in the Twentieth Century

THE GREAT DEPRESSION AND RECOVERY

Much of what occurred during the mid-twentieth century in the United States was related to the severe financial depression that began in 1929 and lasted until just after 1937. It was a time of widespread unemployment and business failure in the United States and throughout the rest of the world.

Causes for the Great Depression During World War I, American industry concentrated on producing war supplies. When the war was over, industry started again to produce consumer goods. These goods, which had been unavailable during the war, were now in great demand. Because of the increased demand, many good jobs opened up in industry. As people acquired these jobs, their earnings rose. This meant that they could purchase more goods, which caused the demand for consumer goods to rise even more.

Businesses Grow During this time, business prospered and profits grew. These profits were often invested in stocks. As a result of business prosperity, the demand for stocks increased, causing stock prices to rise. The demand was so great that the more prominent stocks in industry increased in price about 70 percent between 1923 and 1925. For example, stock worth $100 a share in 1923 sold for $170 in 1926.

As more goods and stocks were sold, industry expanded by building additional plants to produce more goods. Ultimately, more goods were produced than could be sold.

People who wanted to invest in the stock market or to expand their business borrowed money from banks. Banks encouraged this borrowing because they charged interest and made a profit by lending the money. By 1927, loans had increased about 66 percent over previous times. Because loans were so easy to get, many people borrowed more money than they could easily pay back and used it to speculate. To *speculate* is to take a business risk in hope of making a profit. People speculated by buying stocks in hopes that the stock prices would go up.

Unemployment Rises There were other factors which contributed to the depression. As industries grew, new machines were installed which performed tasks that employees had previously done. This resulted in a rise in unemployment. People who were unemployed could not buy the goods being produced by industry. The farmers also were suffering. During World War I, they could sell all they produced. But when the demands of the war ended, the price of farm produce fell sharply. With little or no profits, the farmers were unable to buy as much as they had in the past.

Stocks Begin to Drop In the autumn of 1929, industrial production fell. Some corporations were investigated and it was discovered that their stock prices were too high as a result of speculation. These events shook the confidence of a group of important investors, and several large operators on the New York Stock Exchange began to sell their stock early in October 1929, causing stock prices to drop.

Frightened by the decline in stock prices, many smaller stockholders panicked and began to sell their stocks on October 24, 1929. This caused the stock prices to drop even further. On October 29, the bottom fell out of the market.

Banks Lose Money Banks had loaned much of their money for stock purchases. They were afraid that if the values of stocks dropped, people who had borrowed money to buy stocks would not be able to pay back their loans. Many banks decided to call for immediate payment of loans, before it was too late. But stock values dropped too fast and stocks became worthless.

Most stockholders lost all that they had and could not pay back their loans.

Businesses Go Bankrupt Many businesses had invested a large part of their money in stocks. When the stock market fell, they lost a great deal of this money. Corporations had also invested so that they could expand. When banks called for immediate repayment of loans, most businesses did not have the money. Furthermore, once the depression began, people were buying fewer products. Thus businessmen could not sell the goods they manufactured. Many businesses declared bankruptcy.

When businesses closed, employees lost their jobs. They had trouble buying food and clothing, and paying rent. They could not afford to buy expensive items such as cars or iceboxes. When people stopped buying, businesses had to lay off more people. This caused unemployment to rise higher than ever.

Farmers Hit First The farmers, who did not earn profits in the 1920's, felt the effects of the depression more quickly than other people. Many did not own their farms, they were *mortgaged;* that is, the farmer had agreed to pay for the farm in installments, or parts, over a period of time. The bank

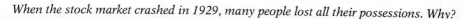

When the stock market crashed in 1929, many people lost all their possessions. Why?

Unemployment was probably the major problem the United States faced during the Depression. Through agencies like the Works Progress Administration (WPA), thousands of jobs were created. Should the federal government ever create such jobs?

owned the farm until the mortgage was paid. When the depression struck, many farmers could not meet their mortgage payments. If this happened, the bank had the right to *foreclose* on a mortgage: to demand full payment of the remaining cost of the farm. If the farmer could not raise the money, the bank took over the farm and sold it for whatever price it could. Many farmers lost their farms in this way, leaving them with no place to go and little or no money.

Banks Fail   As the depression developed, many people began to pull their savings out of banks. The banks had loaned some of this money to individu-

als and corporations. These people could not meet their obligations to the banks. Consequently, the banks could not pay people their money, and many banks were forced to close. People who had deposited money in these banks lost all their savings. By the winter of 1929–30, the Great Depression began.

Priming the Pump   In 1932, Franklin D. Roosevelt, a Democrat, was elected President, and by 1933 his program called the *New Deal* was in full swing. Through a series of legislative programs, Roosevelt began to pour federal money into the American economy. This process was called *pump priming*. It involved the hiring of the unemployed to work on federal conservation and public works projects; federal aid to farmers, banks, and businesses; federal loans to homeowners; slum clearance; fairer labor standards; the creation of a Social Security agency; and the establishment of new agencies to regulate the buying and selling of stocks and bank loans. In spite of this, by the time the United States entered World War II, most of the nation was still suffering from the Great Depression.

SECTION REVIEW

1. In your own words, briefly identify or define: to speculate, mortgaged, foreclose, pump priming.
2. Name three main causes of the depression in the United States which lasted from 1929 to 1937.
3. How did Roosevelt deal with the Great Depression? Explain.
   D When the American stock market crashed in 1929, its impact was felt worldwide. How could such an event in the United States have such global impact?

CONTINUED DOMESTIC GROWTH AND TURMOIL

After 1945 and well into the 1950's, the United States continued to experience astonishing change and rapid growth. This was also a difficult period of adjustment for the nation. The United States had just won a war. As a result of the victory, it emerged as a leading world power. But with the victory and leadership in world affairs came new responsibilities and problems, as the United States increased its political and military involvements around the world. Furthermore, Americans at home faced a number of important, difficult, and controversial questions about the nature and future of their society. They were forced to re-examine the values and institutions they had taken for granted for so long. Yet while the problems and questions were numerous, the answers and solutions were few.

Growth Brings Problems and Responsibilities   Strong leadership was needed to deal with the change and growth at home, and the problems and responsibilities abroad. President Roosevelt had died in April 1945, making Vice-President Harry Truman President. Truman served from 1945 to 1953.

Eisenhower   Truman was followed by Dwight D. Eisenhower. Eisenhower, a Republican who was in office from 1953 to 1961, came to the presidency as a national hero. During World War II, he had served as Supreme Commander of the Allied forces in Europe. Eisenhower was considered largely responsible for the defeat of Hitler and the Axis.

When Eisenhower took office, American troops were fighting once again on foreign soil—this time in Korea. (See pages 535–537.) In other parts of the world, Eisenhower committed the United States to the principles supported by the United Nations. Through the actions and policies of John Foster Dulles, Eisenhower's Secretary of State, the United States became more and more deeply involved in the affairs of other nations.

A Breakthrough in Civil Rights   It was during Eisenhower's first administration that the United States had its first major breakthrough in the area of civil rights in nearly 100 years. In 1954, the Supreme Court, in the case of *Brown* vs. *the Board of Education of Topeka, Kansas,* ruled that "separate but equal" education for Blacks was unconstitutional. As a result, all school districts were ordered to desegregate. President Truman had already desegregated the United States armed forces and called for the creation of a federal government office to enforce civil rights. He had urged the passage of laws guaranteeing voting rights in federal and state elections and laws against discrimination in employment, public and private education, housing, public and private health facilities, and all other public services. His recommendations were later adopted between 1964 and 1968, when Congress made them into law.

Civil Rights Leaders   A year after the Brown decision, *Dr. Martin Luther King, Jr.,* a Black minister from Montgomery, Alabama, began a bus boycott protesting the local practice that required Blacks to ride only in the back of public city buses. King's boycott was a success, and the buses were desegregated. Dr. King became one of the foremost leaders in the civil rights movement. Some other leaders included

Martin Luther King, Jr., shown here in one of the long marches he led in the south, was a noted civil rights leader. Why do you think people followed him?

César Chávez (SAY-sahr SHAH-ves), the head of the United Farm Workers Union; Russell Means, leader of the American Indian Movement; and Betty Friedan and Gloria Steinem, spokespersons for the movement favoring more guarantees of rights for women.

Recent Supreme Court Rulings During the late 1970's, the U.S. Supreme Court made several new rulings on the subject of civil liberties. One was in the *Alan Bakke* (BAHK-ee) case of 1978. Bakke, a White engineer, argued that the University of California at Davis Medical College had denied him admission while less qualified minority students had been accepted. The Court, in a five to four decision, agreed with Bakke in his claim of reverse discrimination. It also upheld the legality of flexible, not firm, race-based affirmative action plans. The admission plan at Davis Medical College was considered extreme in that it had a firm quota of 16 out of 100 places for minority students.

Another case, *United Steelworkers of America* vs. *Weber*, in 1979 allowed the Supreme Court to deal further with the issue of reverse discrimination. Brian Weber, a White chemical laboratory analyst, sued his employer and his union. Weber claimed that he had been illegally excluded from a company training program for higher-skilled jobs. The corporation and the union had set aside half the places in that program for minorities. Weber argued that such a practice was reverse discrimination. The Supreme Court, in a five to two decision, ruled against Weber. The court majority felt that employers had the right to give minorities special preference for jobs that had previously been for Whites only. In other words, a private company could use an affirmative action program to solve racial imbalance in employment.

A Time of Tragedy The 1960's were a time of tragedy for the United States. *John F. Kennedy*, a Democrat, was elected President in 1960. When he was assassinated on November 22, 1963, Vice-President Lyndon Johnson was sworn in as President. Congress, at Johnson's urging, passed most of the civil rights legislation recommended earlier by Truman and sought by Kennedy.

522

Other Americans were also assassinated during the 1960's. *Medgar Evers*, field secretary of the National Association for the Advancement of Colored People (NAACP) in Mississippi, was murdered on June 12, 1963. *Malcolm X*, a Black leader, was shot during a rally in New York City in 1965. In April 1968, the Reverend Martin Luther King, Jr., was killed in Memphis, Tennessee. In June of the same year, *Senator Robert F. Kennedy*, a brother of John F. Kennedy, was shot and killed while campaigning for the presidency in California. Attacks on public figures continued into the 1970's. In the summer of 1972, *Governor George C. Wallace* of Alabama was shot while campaigning in Maryland for the Democratic nomination to the presidency. Wallace lived but was paralyzed below the waist.

New States and New Amendments Americans witnessed many other changes as well in the 1960's and 1970's. Two new states, Alaska and Hawaii, were admitted to the Union in 1959. Several new amendments to the Constitution were ratified. In 1964, the *Twenty-fourth Amendment* abolished the poll tax as a requirement for voting in national elections. The *Twenty-fifth Amendment* provided for the removal of the President from office if he were deemed incapable of performing his duties. In 1971, the *Twenty-sixth Amendment* granted citizens between the ages of eighteen and twenty the right to vote in national elections. One proposed amendment continued to make news in the 1970's. The *Equal Rights Amendment* was sent from Congress to the states in 1972. The purpose of this amendment, according to its

The 1977 National Women's Conference was held in Houston, Texas. Many well-known American women such as (left to right) Betty Friedan, Liz Carpenter, Rosalynn Carter, Betty Ford, Elly Peterson, Jill Ruckelshaus, and Bella Abzug showed up to support the Equal Rights Amendment. What were the advantages and the disadvantages of ERA?

SOME DISCOVERIES AND INVENTIONS IN THE TWENTIETH CENTURY

	Who	What	Importance
1901	Guglielmo Marconi	Invented equipment that sent first transatlantic wireless telegraphy message	Led to regular transatlantic telegraphic service in 1903.
1903	Orville and Wilbur Wright	Developed the first workable motor-powered aircraft	Led to the use of aircraft for transporting people and mail in shorter time.
1904	Marie and Pierre Curie, A. H. Becquerel	Investigated radioactivity	Isolated a radioactive element for the first time; paved the way for development of X-rays.
1926	John L. Baird	Demonstrated the first successful television picture	Led to modern television, a major source of information and entertainment.
1928	Alexander Fleming	Discovered penicillin	Led to the widespread use of drugs in the fight to control disease.
1930's	Lise Meitner and Otto Hahn	Split the uranium atom	Led to experimentation with atomic chain reactions.
1930	Clarence Birdseye	First to package frozen foods	Led to the development of the frozen food industry.
1942	Enrico Fermi	Produced first controlled atomic chain reaction	Proved that nuclear energy could be harnessed.
1946	J. P. Eckert and J. W. Mauchly	Demonstrated the first electronic computer	Began era of widespread use of computers.
1948	Physicists at the Bell Telephone Laboratories	Developed the transistor	Made possible the transistor radio, portable television, pocket calculator and other portable electronic devices.
1954	Jonas E. Salk	Developed the Salk vaccine	Prevented polio.
1957	Russian scientists	Launched Sputnik	Marked the beginning of space exploration.
1960	Theodore Maiman	Perfected the laser	Made possible delicate cutting and welding procedures in industry and medicine.
1961	Yuri Gagarin	First person to orbit Earth	Made possible future space exploration.
1967	Christiaan Barnard	Performed first human heart transplant	Enabled people with damaged hearts to live longer.
1969	Neil Armstrong	First person to walk on Moon	Enabled scientists to study the chemical make-up of the moon.
1970	British researchers	Concorde supersonic jet	Enabled people to travel twice the speed of sound.
1970's		Microsurgery	Made possible delicate surgery for the reattachment of limbs.
1970's	Allan MacLeod Cormack, Godfrey Newbold Hounsfield	Computerized axial tomography (CAT Scan)	Combined a computer with X-rays to give a picture of sections of the body.
late 1970's		Solar energy	Research and development increased so we could decrease our dependence on fossil fuels.
Future		Artificial organ and limb replacement	Development of artificial organs and limbs to replace non-functioning parts.

In 1981, many women's groups were pleased to see Sandra Day O'Connor become the first female member of the U.S. Supreme Court. What women today hold high political office?

supporters, was to protect the rights of women. Opponents of the proposed amendment, led by Phyllis Schlafly (SHLA-flee) who formed STOP ERA, claimed it would do just the opposite or that such rights already existed. The proposed *ERA* (Equal Rights Amendment) provided equality of rights for all sexes under federal and state jurisdiction. Section 2 of the proposed amendment allowed for federal enforcement of its provisions. The proposed amendment was not ratified by its extended 1982 deadline. However, it was reintroduced in Congress that same year.

Exploring Space   The United States and Russia have long competed with one another. This is especially true when dealing with space exploration. The American space program took a great step forward on May 5, 1961, when *Alan B. Shepard, Jr.*, became the first American to enter space. He was followed by *Colonel John Glenn,* who on February 20, 1962, became the first American to orbit the earth. From then on, the U.S. space program grew by

leaps and bounds. During a mission in 1965, astronaut *Edward White* walked in space. On July 19, 1969, astronauts *Neil Armstrong, Edwin Aldrin,* and *Michael Collins* reached the moon after a nine-day journey. On July 20, Armstrong and Aldrin became the first humans to walk on the moon. Six more space projects and five more moon landings followed the first walk on the moon. In 1975, *Apollo-Soyuz,* a joint United States-Soviet space flight, took place. This flight showed how two powerful countries could work together to benefit all.

By 1982, the space shuttle program had completed its testing phase with the flights of *Columbia.* This spacecraft can be reused to advance space science and technology. The U.S. plans to include astronauts from other countries in future flights.

The United States has also sent unmanned spacecraft to photograph and gather data on Mars, Jupiter, and other planets of our solar system. Several of those space missions proved to be very important. *Viking I,* for example,

Pictured below is Columbia, *the reusable space shuttle. Why might such a space vehicle be important?*

landed on Mars in July of 1976 and sent back many photographs of that planet's surface. *Voyager II* in 1979 passed Jupiter and its moons, giving scientists close-up photographs of things never before known, such as the volcanic activity on one of Jupiter's moons.

SECTION REVIEW

1. In your own words, briefly identify: Harry S Truman, Dwight D. Eisenhower, Martin Luther King, Jr., Gloria Steinem, Betty Friedan, the Twenty-sixth Amendment, ERA, Phyllis Schlafly.
2. What was the significance of *Brown* vs. *the Board of Education of Topeka, Kansas?* of the Alan Bakke case? the Weber case?
3. What were some notable space achievements by the United States between the years 1962 and 1983?
 During the struggle for civil rights in the 1960's, many riots occurred. Do you think acts of violence help or hinder a cause? Explain.

UNITED STATES POLITICS IN MID-TWENTIETH CENTURY

Richard M. Nixon, a Republican, was elected President in 1968 and reelected in 1972. In the middle of 1974, through the research of Carl Bernstein and Bob Woodward, two reporters from *The Washington Post,* the public learned that members of the 1972 Nixon Re-election Committee had been involved in an attempted burglary of the Democratic party's election headquarters. The attempted burglary, which took place in the Watergate office building in Washington, D.C., became known as the **Watergate Affair.**

The President's Involvement The attempted burglary led to an investigation of the election committee. The committee was found to have received numerous illegal campaign contributions, mostly from large corporations. Some Democrats were also found to have accepted such donations, but these sums were small compared to those received by the Nixon committee. As the investigation continued, more corruption was exposed. It was learned that the President himself and some of his staff had attempted to destroy or cover up evidence of their own criminal activities during the election. This shocked and outraged the public.

Agnew Resigns As government prosecutors dug deeper into the investigation, more accusations of corruption in Nixon's administration began to pile up. Government prosecutors charged that Vice-President *Spiro Agnew* had failed to pay federal income taxes on alleged illegal payments made to him by some Maryland contractors. To these criminal charges, Agnew pleaded "no contest." He then became the first Vice-President in U.S. history to resign while under duress. He was sentenced to three years' probation and fined $10,000. Upon Nixon's recommendation, Agnew was replaced by *Gerald R. Ford,* a Republican congressman from Michigan.

A President Resigns After a long investigation, a majority of the House Judiciary Committee charged Nixon with obstruction of justice and abuse of his power as President. He was also forced, by the United States Supreme Court, to turn over all tape recordings and documents needed in the investigation. Faced with possible impeachment by the House of Representatives and a decline in his credibility and popular support, Nixon became the first President in American history to resign while in office. Gerald Ford succeeded Nixon and granted him a full pardon for any criminal acts he may have committed in regard to the Watergate Affair. In December of 1974, upon Ford's recommendation, *Nelson A. Rockefeller*, the Republican governor of New York, was confirmed by Congress and sworn in as the new Vice-President. For the first time, the United States had a President and a Vice-President neither of whom had been elected by the people.

Campaign of 1976 Because of the Watergate Affair, the presidential campaign of 1976 was closely watched. The Democrats selected Georgian Jimmy Carter, Jr., for their presidential choice. Carter narrowly defeated Ford, with 50.08 percent of the popular vote. After his election, Carter faced many problems. They included rising rates of inflation, energy shortages, a growing governmental bureaucracy, foreign involvement in the Middle East, and worries about arms control.

Campaign of 1980 Carter served only one term in office. In the 1980 presidential election, he and Vice-President Walter Mondale, were defeated by Republican Ronald Reagan and running mate, George Bush. Some people thought Reagan's victory was mainly due to voter dissatisfaction with Carter's policies. Others regarded it as a renewal of conservatism in America. As President, Reagan had to deal with the problems of inflation, federal government growth, unemployment, arms control, and continued turmoil in the Middle East.

In March 1981 President Reagan

Ronald Reagan was elected President in 1980. Why were some voters dissatisfied with Carter?

was the target of an assassination attempt in Washington, D.C. Besides the President, his press secretary, a policeman, and a secret service agent were wounded. All four survived.

SECTION REVIEW

1. What was the Watergate Affair and what resulted from the government investigation?
2. Who was elected President of the United States in 1976? In 1980? What problems did each President inherit?
◗ What problems does the United States face today? What do you think is the cause of these problems?

INFLATION AND OTHER DOMESTIC AFFAIRS

Inflation is said to take place when the cost of living rises faster than workers' salaries or their ability to buy needed or desired goods. This means that many people do not make enough money for proper food, clothing, and shelter.

Some Causes of Inflation   One major cause of inflation in the United States was the additional money that the federal government printed in the postwar period. This money was used to pay for such things as increased foreign aid, new social welfare and ecology programs, farm subsidies, an expanded space program, military equipment, low-income housing, Social Security benefits, and higher salaries for federal workers. The money was printed and circulated without any resources to back it.

The U.S. government also spent heavily during the Vietnam War of the late 1960's and early 1970's. The defense budget increased from about 72 billion dollars in 1967 to over 92 billion dollars in 1976. The Vietnam War was a conflict that enlarged the American armed forces by about 900,000 people. To pay the costs of the war, the federal government issued new currency without resources to back it. This money was used for the manufacture of airplanes, bombs, guns, ships, and tanks, as well as for the salaries and care of everyone fighting the war.

High Demand, Low Supply   All that additional money—which amounted to billions of dollars—was soon in circulation. Since ready cash was available, people purchased more goods. However, because the demand was greater than the supply, the price of goods skyrocketed. For example, the low supply of oil and natural gas during part of the 1970's made the costs of these fuels soar. Whenever there is a shortage of any desired commodity, its price goes up. Price increases help to cause high inflation rates.

Spiraling Inflation   Related to the desire for certain goods in short supply was the desire for affluence. *Affluence* is the higher standard of living people usually enjoy as their earnings in-

THE UNITED STATES FEDERAL BUDGET

Billions of Dollars (Approximate)

Year	Budget
1960	95
1965	120
1970	190
1975	310
1980	600
1985 (Estimated)	800

crease. The depression of the 1930's caused many governments, including that of the United States, to seek solutions. They provided programs and followed policies that would keep unemployment as low as possible. These programs and policies were generally successful in restoring the prosperity of many Americans. As prosperity returned, so did people's material goals —better food and housing, travel, higher education, and improved medical care. To meet those goals, workers went deeply into debt and counted on rapid wage increases to cover their payments. Management often did not resist such wage-increase demands but simply passed on the costs in the form of higher prices to the consumer. But workers are also consumers. To pay the higher prices, they needed new wage increases. And so inflation spiraled higher and higher.

The 1979 Energy Crunch   Perhaps one of the greatest causes of inflation and the rise in the prices of many goods has been our consumption of energy sources—especially that of oil. To help supply our need for oil, the United States had the *Trans-Alaska pipeline* built. In June 1977, oil began to flow from Prudhoe (PROO-doe) Bay to Valdez (vahl-DEZ); from there it was shipped to refineries in other states.

Oil Imports   Statistics on oil production, importation, and consumption help to illustrate part of the energy problem within the United States. In 1950, for example, the United States produced 52 percent of the oil in the world. In 1970, the United States produced only 21 percent of that oil. By 1980, the United States was importing over half of the oil it needed—a dramatic rise of about 1,000 percent since thirty years earlier.

OPEC   Compounding the problem has been the price policy adopted by the *Organization of Petroleum Exporting Countries.* Created in 1960 and called *OPEC*, its members include Saudi Arabia, Algeria, Iran, Iraq, Ecuador, Kuwait (kuh-WATE), Libya, Gabon (gah-BO^n), Nigeria, Qatar (KAT-ur), United Arab Emirates (im-MIR-uts), Indonesia, and Venezuela. OPEC is an oil cartel, a combination of independent commercial enterprises designed to limit competition. It has raised its price of oil from $1.50 a barrel in the early part of the 1970's to over $30.00 a barrel by 1980. This rise in prices, combined with the reduction in oil production by OPEC in 1973 and 1979 and America's strong dependence on oil consumption, caused long gasoline lines in the United States and a rapid rise in the price of gasoline and oil products.

Alternatives   In July of 1979, President Carter reacted to the U.S. energy crisis by calling for the adoption of many proposals. In essence, he asked for expenditures of over $140 billion to free the nation's dependence on foreign oil by 1990. That large sum was to come from windfall profits taxes placed on oil companies, whose prices were to be totally decontrolled by the early 1980's. Carter proposed the creation of an Energy Security Corporation and a Solar Bank. He also proposed that the nation's utility companies reduce their use of oil by one-half during the 1980's; the government would spend more to develop public mass transportation and automobile fuel efficiency; a standby gasoline rationing plan would be set up; and oil imports would be limited so that none were greater than the amount imported in 1977. President Carter's proposals also included grants to continue developing nuclear and solar energy. President Reagan placed more emphasis on continued oil and natural gas exploration than on development of other energy sources. He was helped in the early 1980's by the reduced consumption of oil products by Americans and more energy-efficient automobiles.

SECTION REVIEW

1. Mapping: Using the maps in the Atlas, list and locate the countries belonging to OPEC.
2. In your own words, explain: inflation, affluence, OPEC.
3. What were some of the major causes of inflation in the United States during the 1960's, 1970's, and early 1980's?
▷ What would you suggest as a way to control rapid inflation? Would anyone suffer from your suggestion or suggestions? Would anyone benefit? Explain.

THE UNITED STATES AND OTHER WORLD PROBLEMS

Population Growth Demographers, or population experts, estimate the number of human beings who have ever existed upon the planet Earth at between 69 billion and 96 billion. In the 1980's, Earth had about 4 billion people living on it. With the world's population swelling at the rate of 100 persons a minute, that total is expected to reach 6.5 billion by the year 2000. Population is growing but food production is not, thus causing a food shortage in some nations.

Feeding the World's People In response to the current worldwide food problem, richer nations—especially the United States—have considered what they can or should do to deal with food shortages. Some people argue that our extra food should be sent only to those nations that will become self-sufficient as a result of U.S. aid. Others insist that the issue is not who we share food with but whether we should share our food at all. This group maintains that if we share our food with the rest of the world, we will probably end up with a food crisis of our own. Yet another viewpoint in the debate suggests that it is our duty to share all our food with the rest of the world during the 1980's. The food problem is a complex one that cannot be solved easily.

The United Nations has recently estimated that as many as 1 billion people throughout the world may be suffering from malnutrition or starvation by 1984. The United Nations also reported that many thousands of children die every year of starvation.

Government officials in the United States continue to be concerned about population growth when it is not running parallel to economic growth. Overpopulation and food shortages create a low standard of living.

SECTION REVIEW

1. In your own words, describe the dilemma facing the nations of the world with respect to food production.
2. How many people does the United Nations believe are now suffering from malnutrition or starvation?
▷ How might you begin to resolve the problems noted about food supply and distribution?

31

United States Foreign Relations in the Twentieth Century

THE COLD WAR

During the post-World War II period, the United States continued to be active in foreign affairs. Part of that involvement included participation in two additional wars—in Korea and Vietnam. Other foreign commitments were made in the form of military and monetary aid and advice to nations around the world.

Rebuilding Europe   In 1943, the *United Nations Relief and Rehabilitation Agency* (UNRRA) was formed. The main goal of this organization, made up of forty-four nations, was to prevent famine and disease in war-shattered Europe. Through various forms of aid, the United States gave over $11 billion to *UNRRA* from 1945 through 1947. However, critics objected to the large amount of relief sent to eastern Europe, now dominated by communist Russia.

The Marshall Plan   In June 1947, Secretary of State George C. Marshall suggested a broader plan of economic assistance to all of Europe. This became known as the *European Recovery Program* or *Marshall Plan*. Congress allotted $21 billion for this program over a three-and-one-half-year period. In defense of his plan, Marshall explained: "Our policy is not directed against any country or doctrine but against hunger, poverty, desperation, and chaos." The aim of the Marshall Plan was to revive Europe's economies, "so as to permit the emergence of political and social conditions in which free institutions can exist."

The Truman Doctrine   A serious situation developed in Greece at the end of World War II. When the Germans retreated from Greece in 1944, the Greek government, supported by British forces, returned from exile. Noncommunists won the election in 1946. Shortly afterwards communist rebels, supplied by the communist governments of Albania (al-BAY-nee-uh), Yugoslavia (yoo-goe-SLAHV-ee-uh) and Bulgaria (bul-GAR-ee-uh), began a fierce guerrilla war in northern Greece. Britain could not afford to continue fighting this war and had to withdraw. President Truman decided the United States should take over for the British. He believed that if the communists took over Greece, Turkey would be at the mercy of the Soviet Union. This would cause the balance of power to be drastically changed. (See the Atlas of Europe.) With American aid, the Greek government was able to put down the communist revolt.

On March 12, 1947, Truman appeared before Congress to announce what has become known as the *Truman Doctrine*, the most far-reaching statement of American foreign policy since the beginning of the twentieth century. First, Truman proposed a program of major economic and military aid to Greece and Turkey. This, he felt, would prevent them from becoming dominated by the Soviet Union. Then, he stated that "it must be the policy of the United States to support free peoples who are resisting attempted subjugation by armed minorities or by outside pressures." This presidential statement committed the United States to intervene in revolutions anywhere in the world. Some historians believe Truman's policy was not wise because it drew the United States into situations over which American leaders had little or no control. Some also believe that Truman made no distinction between real military threats to American interests and revolutions that arose from local conditions.

The Zhdanov Doctrine   At this time, a similar statement was made in the Soviet Union by *Andrei Zhdanov* (zh-DAN-awf), a member of the Politburo (puh-LIT-byoor-oe), the Soviet Union's highest governing body. Zhdanov proclaimed that the world was divided into two camps, one socialistic and one capitalistic, and that the camps could never be brought together.

The Roots of the Cold War   Some historians believe it was the Truman and Zhdanov statements that caused the "Cold War" between the United States and the Soviet Union. But the Cold War—actually a war of politics and economics—had its beginnings before World War II. It originated when communism became a dominant political system in many eastern European countries.

During World War II, the United States and the Soviet Union were allied against the major Axis Powers—Germany, Italy, and Japan. At the end of the war, each of the major Allies received control of a part of Germany. In addition, the Soviet Union was able to gain influence over all of the eastern European states that had been occupied by Germany during the war, with the exceptions of Finland and Greece.

The Iron Curtain   Gradually, the Soviet Union and the other Allies abandoned their wartime policy of mutual support and friendly relations. Before long, an invisible boundary existed between eastern and western Europe. Winston Churchill called this invisible boundary the **Iron Curtain.** It divided Europe into two hostile groups. The western group of European countries favored and supported the policies of the United States. The eastern group favored the policies of the Soviet Union.

NATO and the Warsaw Pact   In Europe, the Cold War division between East and West was marked by the formation of two new alliance systems. One was the **Warsaw Pact** of 1955. It was composed of the communist nations dominated by the Soviet Union: Albania, Bulgaria, Czechoslovakia, East Germany, Hungary, Poland, and Romania. The West had the **North Atlantic Treaty Organization** (NATO), formed earlier in 1949. Its members were the United States, Canada, Iceland, Norway, Britain, The Netherlands, Denmark, Luxembourg (LOOHK-sum-boohrg), Italy, Portugal, Belgium, and France. In 1952, Greece and Turkey joined; in 1955, West Germany joined, and later, in 1982, Spain gained membership. Members of both alliances agreed to assist one another if attacked by any member of the other alliance.

Germany Divided   After World War II, Germany had been divided into two

EUROPE AFTER WORLD WAR II

0 500 kilometers
0 400 miles

N

FINLAND

NORWAY
SWEDEN
ESTONIA
SOVIET UNION
LATVIA
BALTIC SEA
LITHUANIA

NORTH SEA
DENMARK

IRELAND
GREAT BRITAIN

NETH.
Berlin
Stettin
POLAND
EAST GERMANY
Oder R.
Neisse R.

ATLANTIC OCEAN

BELG.
LUX.
WEST GERMANY
CZECHOSLOVAKIA

FRANCE
SWITZ.
AUSTRIA
HUNGARY
ROMANIA

SPAIN
Trieste
ITALY
YUGOSLAVIA
BULGARIA

BLACK SEA

ALBANIA
TURKEY
GREECE

MEDITERRANEAN SEA

BERLIN
(Fr.) (Soviet
(Br.) Union)
WEST EAST
(U.S.)

Occupied by Western Allies
Occupied by the Soviet Union
Territory transferred from Germany to Poland
Territory annexed by the Soviet Union

Why was Germany divided after World War II?

parts, pro-western West Germany, and pro-Soviet East Germany. Berlin, located 176 kilometers (110 miles) inside East Germany, was also divided into sectors after World War II. The United States, England, and France controlled West Berlin, and the Soviet Union controlled East Berlin. Soon after this division, trouble began. The West wanted all of Germany to become a democracy, but Russia wanted it to remain under Soviet domination. In June of 1948, the Soviet government threw up a blockade around Berlin, cutting the city off from all land traffic from the West. The United States and Great Britain air-

lifted food and coal to the blockaded area. A year later, the Soviet Union ended the blockade. Historians consider the *Berlin Blockade* another event that led to the Cold War.

In a further attempt to squeeze the western forces out of West Berlin and make it a communist-dominated city, the East German government, with the backing of the Soviet Union, built a wall separating West Berlin from East Berlin in 1961. The purpose of the **Berlin Wall** was to keep East Germans from escaping to freedom in West Berlin. President Kennedy responded to this by increasing the number of

The Berlin Wall was built in 1961. It divides the city of Berlin into two parts, east and west. What do you think it's like to be separated from friends and family who live on the other side of the wall?

American troops in Berlin. He believed this show of force would serve as a warning to East Germany. In speaking of the wall, Kennedy declared that West Berlin "is more than . . . an island of freedom in a communist sea. It is even more than a link with the free world, a beacon of hope behind the Iron Curtain, an escape hatch for refugees. . . . It has now become . . . the greatest testing place of Western courage and will. . . ." And indeed, even though the Berlin Wall remains to this day, so does the determination of the West Berliners to remain non-communist.

SECTION REVIEW

1. Mapping: Using the map on page 533, describe the division of Europe among the major powers after World War II; then describe the division of Berlin.
2. In your own words, identify: UNRRA, Marshall Plan, Truman Doctrine, NATO, Warsaw Pact, Iron Curtain, Berlin Blockade.
3. What was the Cold War, and what seemed to cause it? What conflicts occurred between East and West as a result of the Cold War?
    What do you think might cause a "cold" war to become a "hot" war?

THE UNITED STATES AND ASIA

In Asia in the 1950's and 1960's, the Cold War became hot, involving the clash of opposing armed forces.

Revolution in China   In Unit 9, you read about the growing mistrust between the Chinese Nationalists and Communists. This mistrust erupted in revolution in 1934 when the Chinese Communists, under the leadership of Mao Tse-tung (MOW-DZU-DOONG), broke away from the Nationalist government of Chiang Kai-shek (JEE-AHNG-KIE-SHEK).

The People's Republic of China   Mao's movement was disciplined, efficient, and alert to the needs of the majority of the Chinese people. The regime of Chiang Kai-shek, on the other hand, had become increasingly corrupt, inefficient, and authoritarian. The United States advised Chiang to begin reforms, but he resisted. President Truman sent General George C. Marshall to China to try to bring the Nationalists and Communists together, but Marshall's mission failed. War erupted in which the Nationalists suffered a series of military defeats. The Communists won the support of millions of Chinese with their promises of reform, and in October 1949, the *People's Republic of China* was proclaimed at Peking (PEA-KING). Chiang and the remainder of his Nationalist government fled to the island of *Formosa* (for-MOE-suh), today known as *Taiwan* (tie-WAHN). When Mao Tse-tung took control of mainland China, America's influence there came to an end. Until the establishment of diplomatic relations with the People's Republic of China in 1979, the United States continued to recognize the government of Taiwan as the official government of all China.

Other Problems in Asia   Following World War II, both the Soviet Union and the United States had stationed troops in Korea. The Soviet Union had moved troops into the north and the United States into the south. By 1949 the United States and the Soviet Union had withdrawn their troops. They left behind two Koreas, separated by the 38th parallel of latitude, under two different governments. (See the map on page 536.) All efforts by the United Nations to reunite the two Koreas failed, and the differences between them continued to grow. Korea's industry and mining were located in the north. Its best agricultural lands were in the south. The *Democratic People's Republic of Korea*, in the north, was headed by *Kim Il-sung*. It boasted a large Soviet-trained and equipped army. The *Republic of Korea*, to the south, adopted a constitution in 1948. Its government was headed by *Syngman Rhee* (SING-mun REE).

Korean Conflict   The desire for reunification was strong in both parts of Korea. Each side had repeatedly threatened to use force to achieve this. In June 1950, the North Koreans acted. They sent their army across the 38th parallel and attacked the unprepared South Korean forces. The American response was prompt. Truman put U.S. forces into the field to aid the South Koreans. The United Nations Security Council condemned North Korea as an aggressor and authorized "a police action to restore peace . . . and to restore the border." The United Nations also sent an international armed force to Korea to join the American and South Korean armies. The combined forces were commanded by General Douglas

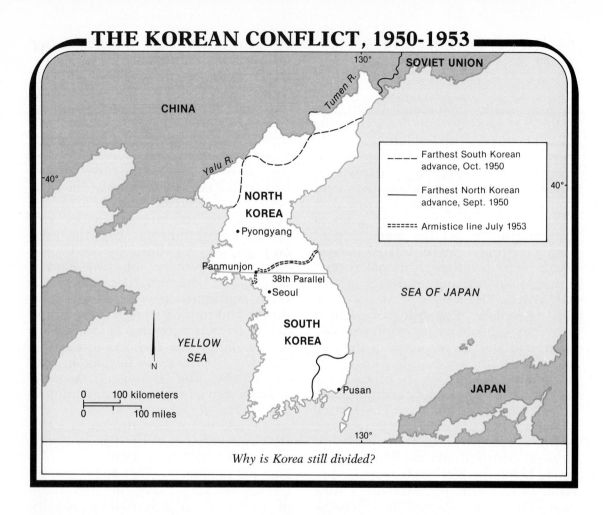

THE KOREAN CONFLICT, 1950-1953

130°
SOVIET UNION
CHINA
Tumen R.
40°
Yalu R.
NORTH
KOREA
• Pyongyang
40°

Farthest South Korean
advance, Oct. 1950

Farthest North Korean
advance, Sept. 1950

Armistice line July 1953

Panmunjon
38th Parallel
• Seoul

SEA OF JAPAN

N

YELLOW
SEA

SOUTH
KOREA

0   100 kilometers

0   100 miles

• Pusan

JAPAN

130°

Why is Korea still divided?

MacArthur. Communist China's army then entered the war on the side of North Korea with military equipment from Russia.

Fighting Ends After thirty-seven months of fighting, the two sides signed an armistice on July 27, 1953. The fighting had been bloody and destructive. More than 54,000 Americans died in the war and the cost to American taxpayers was over $22 billion. Moreover, the war ended without reunifying Korea. The boundary between North and South Korea stayed at the 38th parallel. Today, Korea remains divided into two hostile camps.

SEATO After the Korean Conflict, the *Southeast Asia Treaty Organization* (SEATO) was formed to oppose takeovers in that area by Communist nations or groups. Members in 1954 were the United States, Australia, France, Great Britain, New Zealand, Pakistan, the Philippines, and Thailand.

The Pueblo Incident One tragic incident between the United States and North Korea began in January 1968. Four North Korean patrol boats seized the American ship *Pueblo*. The *Pueblo*, carrying radar and other electronic equipment, had been cruising near the shores of North Korea in the

536

Sea of Japan. North Korea insisted that the ship had violated the 19-kilometer (12-mile) limit of territorial waters. The United States denied the charge. The United States urged the Soviet Union to persuade North Korea to release the *Pueblo* and its crew. Meanwhile, North Korea issued supposed confessions by the *Pueblo's* commanding officer, *Lloyd Bucher* (BOO-kur), and his crew. A year after the seizure of the ship, Bucher and the crew were released. Investigations cleared them of any charges of treason. Other incidents between the United States and North Korea continued through the 1970's.

Korea Today   In the 1980's, almost 40,000 U.S. soldiers were stationed in South Korea. They were there to help enforce the 1953 armistice with North Korea. People who supported U.S. assistance to South Korea argued that without continued American aid, South Korea would fall under the control of its communist neighbor to the north. Critics of such aid pointed out that the United States had lost too many lives and spent too much money in fighting wars in Asia. Whatever the case, no U.S. troop withdrawals from South Korea were planned under President Reagan.

The situation in Korea became more unstable when President *Park Chung Hee* was assassinated in November of 1979. A trial was held that concluded Park was assassinated by a member of the South Korean Central Intelligence Agency, Director Kim Jae Kyu (KIM JAY KYOO). Fearful of another North Korean invasion, Choi Kyu Hah (CHOY KYOO HAH) became acting president until a presidential election could be held. Chun Doo Hwan took office after the December 1979 election.

South Korea's president, Chun Doo Hwan, is shown here arriving for a visit with President Reagan in 1981. What issues do you think they discussed?

SECTION REVIEW

1. Mapping: Using the map on page 536, locate the 38th parallel and describe its significance.
2. In your own words, identify the following: Mao Tse-tung, Chiang Kai-shek, Formosa, People's Republic of China, Kim Il-sung, Syngman Rhee, SEATO, Lloyd Bucher, Park Chung Hee.
3. Explain the major U.S. involvements with North Korea and South Korea since 1950.

▷ Do you think the United Nations should send armed forces to a country that is fighting a civil war? Explain.

UNITED STATES INVOLVEMENT IN ASIA

In the years following the Korean War, the United States became more deeply involved in Southeast Asia. President Eisenhower sent $400 million in aid to Laos with the hope that Laos would support the West in world affairs. However, Eisenhower's plan did not work. The *Pathet Lao,* a communist movement supported by the Chinese Communists, gained political power and moved to take over the country. Fearful that a civil war would lead to increased Chinese influence in Laos, President Kennedy, with the support of the Soviet Union, sent 5,000 American troops to Thailand, a country bordering Laos. This move led the Laotian civil war leaders to agree to set up a coalition government with both sides represented. However, internal strife continued. In the latter part of 1975, the Pathet Lao movement seized power and set up the *Lao People's Democratic Republic,* a communist government.

Trouble in Vietnam Involvement with Vietnam in Southeast Asia presented the United States with many new problems. The country of Vietnam is more than 1,000 years old. In its long history, it has been invaded repeatedly by foreigners and for centuries it was under the domination of China. In the nineteenth century, it came under French rule. (See page 457.)

The Vietminh League At the end of World War II, most Cambodians, Laotians, and Vietnamese wished to be free of French rule. The *Vietminh League,* led by *Ho Chi Minh* (HOE CHEE MIN), a Vietnamese communist, emerged as the most important of many groups that hoped to secure independence for Vietnam. In 1945, Ho Chi Minh proclaimed the establishment of the Democratic Republic of Vietnam, with Hanoi as its capital.

The French, however, did not want to give up their colony. They set up an independent, non-communist government in South Vietnam as a rival to Ho Chi Minh's communist regime in the north. In 1946 war broke out. The fighting continued until 1954, when the French army suffered a great defeat by the Vietminh at Dien Bien Phu (dyen byen FOO). At this time the French agreed to negotiate, and in 1954 the *Geneva Accords* were settled upon. The United States and South Vietnam refused to sign the Accords; however, they did agree to abide by them.

The Geneva Accords Under the Geneva Accords, Vietnam was to be temporarily divided into two zones. (See the map on page 540.) The northern zone was to be governed by the communist Vietminh. The southern zone was placed under the control of the French-backed state of Vietnam. The Geneva Accords also provided that

For more than a quarter of a century, Vietnam was torn apart by war. Civilians, as well as soldiers, were drawn into the destruction and bloodshed. How does this photograph show the impact of the Vietnam conflict on civilians and soldiers?

elections to decide the future government of all Vietnam were to take place in 1956. But these elections were never held. All efforts to reunite the two Vietnams failed.

Civil War Starts In 1955 *Ngo Dinh Diem* (noe den ZEE-em), the French-educated, American-backed leader of the southern zone, proclaimed it a republic. He became its first president. Diem failed to make needed reforms in government and the economy.

National Liberation Front Diem's regime quickly lost popular support. Many nationalists, who opposed Diem, joined with communists to form the *National Liberation Front* (NLF). The NLF received encouragement from Ho Chi Minh. The goal of the NLF was to overthrow Diem's government and re-unite north and south Vietnam. The military wing of the NLF was the *Vietcong*. In 1957, the Vietcong began a campaign of terrorism in the south, and a long and bloody civil war began.

The United States had been training the South Vietnamese Army since 1956. Now it supplied aid to Diem's forces against those of Ho Chi Minh.

Diem Overthrown Diem's efforts to cope with the civil war failed. In November 1963, the government of Ngo Dinh Diem was overthrown by a group of South Vietnamese generals. Diem was murdered and his family was forced to flee South Vietnam. The murder of Diem and the change in government, however, did not bring an end to the war, and Ho Chi Minh increased North Vietnamese aid to the NLF.

THE VIETNAM CONFLICT

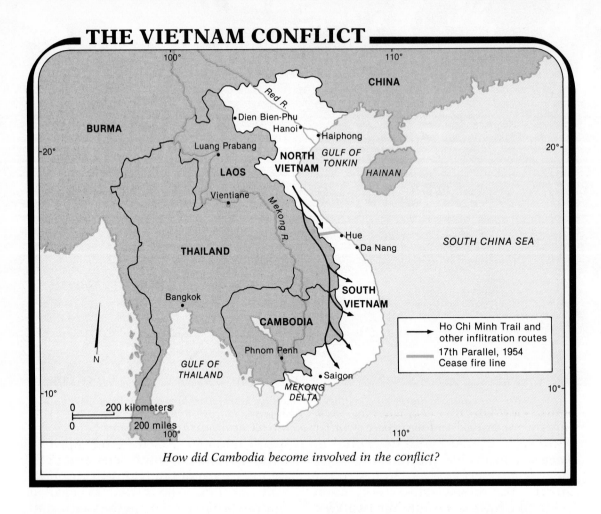

How did Cambodia become involved in the conflict?

Vietnam Conflict American troops became active in the war in 1961 when President Kennedy put 18,000 troops in South Vietnam as "advisors." As the United States continued to commit troops to what had started as a civil war, North Vietnam became increasingly involved on the side of the NLF.

North Vietnamese Troops Invade The South North Vietnamese involvement caused the U.S. forces to begin heavy bombardment of North Vietnam in 1965. (See map above.) By 1970 the United States had extended its bombing and search for North Vietnamese hideouts into neutral Cambodia.

Americans Protest U.S. Involvement in Vietnam By the latter part of the 1960's, more Americans were unhappy with the conflict, which had not officially been declared a war. Many felt it was a no-win conflict of containment. Others protested against any U.S. military involvement in Southeast Asia. As many as 117,000 young male Americans became draft evaders and deserters from what they regarded as an immoral war. The protest became so intense that President Lyndon Johnson, who since 1963 had been increasing the number of U.S. troops in Vietnam, decided not to run for reelection.

540

Cease-Fire   In 1969, Richard Nixon became President on a platform that promised a speedy end to the Vietnam conflict. Yet the costly war went on, as did the peace negotiations. For years, representatives of the United States, South Vietnam, North Vietnam, and the Vietcong met in Paris to discuss possible avenues to peace. A cease-fire was finally agreed to in 1973. Under the terms of the cease-fire, all U.S. troops were to be withdrawn from Vietnam, and U.S. prisoners of war were to be returned. The United States continued to send money and military supplies to help the South Vietnamese in their continuing struggle against the North Vietnamese and Vietcong. By 1975, the total of additional Vietnamese casualties had risen to well over 300,000.

On April 30, 1975, fighting ended when North Vietnam forced the complete surrender of the government of South Vietnam. In 1976, the two Vietnams were united to form the *Socialist Republic of Vietnam* with its capital in Hanoi.

Cost of the Conflict   By the time the United States had withdrawn from South Vietnam, over 56,000 Americans had been killed, more than 300,000 had been wounded, and $150 billion had been spent on the Vietnam conflict. This conflict proved to be one of the costliest in U.S. history.

Amnesty Granted   A partial amnesty for Americans who evaded the military draft or deserted the armed forces was offered by President Ford in 1974. Under his terms, any draft dodgers or deserters could receive amnesty by working for two years in public service jobs at home. However, many evaders were opposed to Ford's offer. They claimed that only total, unconditional amnesty would be acceptable.

They still believed they had been right in refusing to fight a war they considered immoral. Most chose to remain in hiding or to live in exile in such places as Canada and Sweden. In 1977, President Carter pardoned most draft evaders from the Vietnam conflict.

U.S. Involvement in Cambodia   Cambodia gained independence from France in 1953. Its ruler, *Prince Norodom Sihanouk* (NOR-uh-dum SEE-hah-nook), permitted the North Vietnamese and Vietcong to keep troops and supplies in Cambodia during the civil war in South Vietnam. In 1970, pro-U.S. prime minister *Lon Nol* seized power and demanded the removal of North Vietnamese troops. Sihanouk fled to Peking and became an ally of the North Vietnamese and Vietcong forces. In Peking he set up a government in exile.

To be sure of the North Vietnamese withdrawal and to destroy their supply depots, President Nixon sent U.S. troops into Cambodia on a "search and destroy" mission. It lasted from April to June 1970. After that, Nixon promised that he would not send any more troops into Cambodia. However, the United States continued bombing North Vietnamese and Vietcong forces hiding in Cambodia. U.S. military and financial aid to Lon Nol's government also went

This Vietnam Veterans' memorial was dedicated in 1982 in Washington, D.C. Why do we have war monuments?

on. Meanwhile, Cambodian communist forces known as the *Khmer Rouge* (k'mare ROOZH) began a civil war against Lon Nol's government.

After the U.S. withdrawal of troops from South Vietnam, the Khmer Rouge forces continued to seize large portions of Cambodia. By April 1975, with the capture of the Cambodian capital, Phnom Penh, they had succeeded in controlling the country. Lon Nol fled and Cambodia became a communist nation headed by *Pol Pot*.

The new government forced people to leave cities and towns, sending almost the entire population to clear jungles and forests. It is believed that almost one million persons were executed by the communists or died of hardships between 1975 and 1978. Many thousands of Cambodians fled to Thailand or Vietnam.

The Mayaguez Incident   The U.S. again became involved with Cambodia in May 1975 when the *Mayaguez*, an American-owned cargo ship, and its crew were seized by Cambodian gunboats in the Gulf of Siam. The Cambodians claimed that the *Mayaguez* was violating Cambodia's territorial waters. President Ford, hoping to avoid another *Pueblo* incident, sent troops to retake the *Mayaguez* and search for its captured crew members. After bitter combat, the Cambodians released the *Mayaguez* crew. President Ford explained the U.S. action by stating that freedom of the sea—a right possessed by all nations—was at issue.

Fighting Continues   War in Southeast Asia continued long after 1975. Many incidents occurred between Vietnam and Cambodia. The fighting went on into 1978 and 1979, with the Soviet Union backing Vietnam and Communist China backing Cambodia.

Soon, Vietnam had occupied much of the land area of Cambodia.

By 1978, Vietnam also had to contend with China. In July of that year, China ended all its economic aid to Vietnam. A month later, Chinese and Vietnamese forces began full-scale war along their border in the Friendship Pass area. Both sides claimed that intrusion by the other caused the conflict. The real causes stemmed from Vietnam's invasion of China-backed Cambodia and the mistreatment of Chinese living in Vietnam. The conflict faded after China had taken and then withdrawn from much of the northeastern part of Vietnam in the early part of 1979. Pol Pot, who had aligned himself with China, was overthrown by Cambodian insurgents and Vietnamese troops in 1979, and the communist *People's Republic of Kampuchea* (kampoo-CHEE-uh) was established. To ensure the survival of this new government, Vietnamese troops stayed in Kampuchea.

The Boat People and Other Refugees
The continued fighting in Southeast Asia produced more than 800,000 refugees between the years 1975 and 1980. The first group of about 135,000 left Vietnam when the United States withdrew. Soon after, over 200,000 ethnic Chinese were forced to leave Vietnam for China. Over 300,000 people have sought escape from the continued wars in Laos and Cambodia. At least another 300,000 Vietnamese, most unhappy with communist rule, fled their country in very crowded, unsanitary, and leaky boats. Known as the *boat people*, many of these refugees died on the open seas.

What to do with these refugees caused international problems. By 1980, the United States had taken in nearly 300,000, France over 50,000,

At the end of the Vietnam conflict, many people unhappy with communist rule fled their country in small, unsafe boats. What do you think life was like on one of these boats?

SECTION REVIEW

1. Mapping: Using the maps on pages 536 and 540, list the areas of U.S. involvement in Asia. Why do you think the North Vietnamese used Cambodia to keep troops and supplies?
2. In your own words, identify the following: Pathet Lao, Vietminh League, Ho Chi Minh, Geneva Accords, Ngo Dinh Diem, NLF, Vietcong, Lon Nol, Prince Norodom Sihanouk, *Mayaguez*, boat people.
3. How did the United States get involved in the affairs of South Vietnam during the 1960's? How did this involvement end?
4. What has been U.S. involvement with Cambodia during the 1970's?
5. Who were the boat people? What problems did they present?
   ◗ Under what circumstances do you think the United States should commit itself to an undeclared war?

Australia about 25,000, Canada about 15,000, Thailand more than 200,000, Malaysia about 80,000, Hong Kong over 60,000; smaller numbers moved to other countries. The United States in particular urged other countries to admit more of the refugees. President Carter doubled the United States' 1980 quota from 7,000 to 14,000 per month. Many other countries, however, failed to do the same.

THE UNITED STATES AND THE MIDDLE EAST

Major events in foreign policy during the mid-twentieth century involved the United States in the Middle East. Many of these policies have had a great impact on the United States, especially because of the U.S. dependency on oil, which America imports mainly from the Middle East, and because of its support of the state of Israel.

The Creation of Israel Many of the hostile relations in the Middle East date back to 1948. In 1948, the British-controlled territory of *Palestine* became the new Jewish state of *Israel*. Jews from all over the world, the new *Israelis*, poured into the new state, stirring up great hostility among the Arab

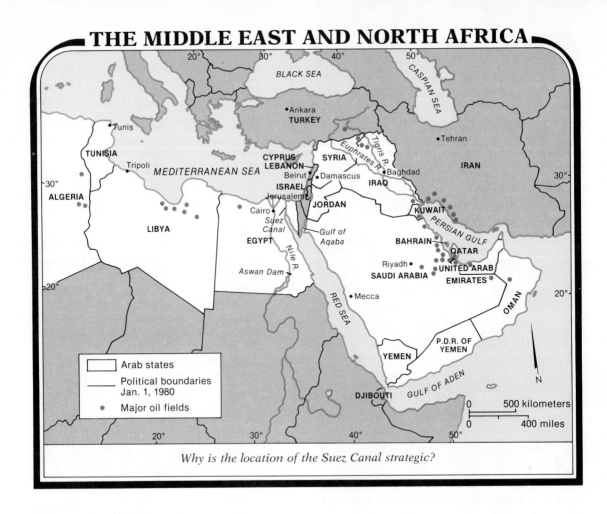

20° 30° 40° 50°

BLACK SEA

•Ankara
TURKEY

CASPIAN SEA

•Tunis

•Tehran

TUNISIA

CYPRUS SYRIA
LEBANON

IRAN

Tripoli MEDITERRANEAN SEA
Beirut •Damascus •Baghdad

Euphrates R. Tigris R.

30° ISRAEL IRAQ 30°
Jerusalem

ALGERIA Cairo•
Suez
Canal JORDAN KUWAIT PERSIAN GULF

LIBYA Gulf of
Aqaba BAHRAIN
EGYPT QATAR

Riyadh• UNITED ARAB
Aswan Dam SAUDI ARABIA EMIRATES

20° Nile R. 20°

•Mecca OMAN

RED SEA

P.D.R. OF
YEMEN

Arab states

Political boundaries YEMEN
Jan. 1, 1980 GULF OF ADEN N

• Major oil fields

DJIBOUTI 0 500 kilometers

0 400 miles

20° 30° 40° 50°

Why is the location of the Suez Canal strategic?

Palestinians who had occupied the land for centuries. Many Palestinians were Muslim. Many left or were expelled from Israel when it became a state.

In 1948, the five Arab countries of Egypt, Jordan, Syria, Lebanon, and Iraq invaded Israel. Israel successfully repelled this invasion, but it was only the first of many invasions and raids launched by Israel's Arab neighbors.

Aswan Dam　In 1955, *Gamal Abdel Nasser,* head of the Egyptian government, asked Russia and the West for aid in building the *Aswan Dam* on the Nile River. At first, the United States agreed to help finance the project.

However, in July 1956, when it was learned that Egypt had purchased Soviet military equipment, the United States withdrew the offer. This action humiliated Nasser. In response, he seized the Suez Canal in Egypt from its foreign owners. Britain, France, and Israel then invaded Egypt to seize control of the Canal but failed, leaving the Canal in Nasser's hands. In the end, the Aswan Dam was built with financial aid from the Soviet Union.

Israel vs. the Arab States　Trouble in the Middle East flared up again in 1967. At Nasser's request, the United Nations withdrew its peacekeeping forces from the Egyptian-Israeli borders and the Sinai (SIE-NIE) peninsula—forces that had been placed there after the fighting between Egypt and Israel in 1956. Egyptian soldiers took over the UN positions, including a post overlooking the Strait of Tiran (tir-AHN) at the southern end of the Red Sea. By holding that position, the Egyptians could prevent ships from carrying goods to and from Israel through the Strait. Israel called the blockade an act of war.

The Six Day War Soon afterward, Arab forces began to assemble along Israel's borders. Israeli forces, armed by the United States, in a lightning attack defeated the armies of Jordan, Egypt, and Syria in the *Six Day War*. As a result of the war, which lasted from June 5 to June 10, 1967, the Israelis occupied the Gaza (GAHZ-uh) Strip and the Sinai peninsula up to the Suez Canal, and closed the Canal. They also captured Old Jerusalem, Syria's Golan (GOE-lahn) Heights, and the West Bank of the Jordan River. A cease-fire urged by the United States and provided by the UN temporarily halted the fighting.

The October War Joining forces, Egypt and Syria launched simultaneous attacks on Israel on October 6, 1973. Shortly thereafter, the U.S. stepped in and helped establish a cease-fire agreement between the three countries.

Civil War in Lebanon During the end of 1975 and the early part of 1976, Lebanon became a trouble spot. Back in 1958, the United States had sent 14,000 Marines to Beirut, the capital of Lebanon, because pro-Nasser Arab nationalists had threatened Lebanon. Due to economic, social, political, and religious differences, Muslim and Christian groups in Lebanon again became involved in a bitter, bloody civil war. The United States, however, did not intervene directly in this war and Lebanon's regular army was unable to suppress the conflict. Order was restored only after President *Hafez al-Assad* of Syria intervened, assuming the role of peacemaker.

The fighting, however, continued for the next year and a half. The Syrian peacekeeping forces fought with Lebanese Army regulars and Christian militia. In February of 1978, intense fighting occurred between Christian militia and Palestinians living in southern Lebanon. During those battles, the Christian militia received aid from the Israelis.

The PLO Additional trouble came from the *Palestine Liberation Organization (PLO)*, led by *Yassir Arafat* (YAH-sir AH-rah-faht). The PLO is an Arab group committed to using any means, even terrorism, to regain the territory held by Israel for the Palestinian Arabs. The PLO claims to represent the Palestinian refugees. Most Palestinian refugees live either in Lebanon or Jordan, both of which border Israel.

The PLO gained world attention with terrorism both in Israel and in other countries. Its members often hijacked airlines or killed Israelis visiting abroad. One of the worst attacks was the assassination of eleven Israeli athletes at the Olympic Games in Munich in September 1972. Such terrorist tactics caused the Israelis to respond by bombing suspected PLO positions, mostly in southern Lebanon.

Israel Aids Lebanese Christian Forces In March of 1978, Israel sent ground forces into southern Lebanon with air and naval support. The aim of Israel was to eliminate what the Israelis regarded as terrorist bases used by

Yassir Arafat is leader of the Palestine Liberation Organization (PLO). The PLO uses terrorist tactics to gain attention. Why do you think they resort to violence?

Palestinian guerrillas for attacks within Israel. During the invasion, Lebanese Christian forces welcomed the Israeli troops.

The United Nations Steps In   During the latter part of March 1978, the UN Security Council voted unanimously to adopt a United States-sponsored resolution asking for the withdrawal of Israeli forces from Lebanon. Israel complied with the United Nations' wishes in April. The resolution also established a 4,000-member UN force to police a cease-fire in the area of southern Lebanon. Yet even with the UN peacekeeping forces present, occasional fighting continued, especially between Lebanese Christian militia and members of the more radical elements of the PLO. Throughout the conflict, the United States continued to urge all factions to arrive at peaceful settlements for their disputes.

Negotiations Start   Problems with the Arabs brought about a call for a change of government in Israel. In 1974, Premier Golda Meir, Defense Minister Moshe Dayan (MOE-shuh die-AHN), and Foreign Minister Abba Eban (AHB-uh EE-bun) were forced to resign. A new government was formed under the leadership of a former Israeli general named *Yitzhak Rabin* (YIT-zahk rah-BEEN). When Rabin became involved in a scandal, he resigned, and *Menachem Begin* (Meh-NAHK-um BAY-gun) became Israel's sixth prime minister in June of 1977. Soon afterward, Begin and President *Anwar Sadat* (AHN-wahr suh-DAHT) of Egypt began a series of negotiations designed to bring peace between the two countries.

In late 1977 Sadat became the first Egyptian leader to visit Israel. In exchange for recognition of Israel, he urged the Israelis to withdraw from occupied Arab lands and to recognize the rights of the Palestinians. Begin praised Sadat for his courage and replied that Israel desired to protect its existence as a nation. Meanwhile, most of the Arab states condemned Sadat's peace moves toward Israel. In particular, the leaders of Algeria, Iraq, Libya, Syria, South Yemen, as well as the PLO called Sadat's actions high treason to the Arab cause. Egypt then ended diplomatic relations with those countries but kept up its dealings with the PLO.

The Peace Treaty   More formal efforts to shape an Egyptian-Israeli peace treaty began in Cairo in December of 1977. Representatives from Egypt, Israel, the United States, and the United Nations were present.

After a series of meetings between Begin, Sadat, U.S. Secretary of State *Cyrus Vance*, and President Carter, a peace framework for the Middle East was signed in September of 1978 by Begin and Sadat, with Carter serving as a witness to the agreement. Most of the details for that framework were formed at a special summit meeting held among the three leaders at the presidential retreat at Camp David, in Maryland.

Conditions of Peace The framework for peace negotiated at Camp David was complicated and had many parts. Egypt and Israel agreed to sign a peace treaty; Israel would remove its troops from the Sinai, and normal diplomatic relations would begin between the two countries. Once all Israeli troops left the Sinai peninsula, the area would be demilitarized. The Camp David framework also provided that Israel, Egypt, Jordan, and the PLO would begin to negotiate how territories, taken by Israel in its wars, were to be controlled.

Yassir Arafat, the PLO leader, and many other Arab leaders denounced the Camp David accord. All felt it did not go far enough in providing a homeland for the Palestinians. For their efforts, however, Begin and Sadat both received the *Nobel Peace Prize* in 1978. With the backing of the United States, Israel and Egypt continued to work out some of the differences between their two countries. In October of 1981, however, President Sadat was assassinated by members of the Egyptian army who opposed his peace policy.

Israel Invades Lebanon Peace in the Middle East did not last long. In 1982, the Israeli army again invaded Lebanon. The aim of Israel was to wipe

Pictured above are Anwar Sadat of Egypt, Jimmy Carter, and Menachem Begin of Israel meeting at Camp David, Maryland, to form a peace framework for the Middle East. Why do you think an outside power stepped in to settle Egypt's and Israel's dispute?

547

out PLO bases used for attacks on Israel. The Israelis were supported by their Christian allies in Lebanon. Fierce fighting broke out. The city of Beirut was left in ruins, and thousands of civilians were killed. On September 16, 1982, Lebanese Christian forces entered Palestinian refugee camps and killed several hundred civilians.

U.S. President Ronald Reagan took a leading role in trying to stop the warfare. United Nations troops, including U.S., French, and Italian forces, were sent to Lebanon to enforce a cease-fire. PLO fighting forces were evacuated and sent to other Muslim nations. Talks continued between the PLO and the Arab countries on establishing a homeland for the Palestinians. Despite this, peace in the Middle East looked shaky.

Events in Iran   While involved with the peace moves between Israel and Egypt, the United States became concerned with other major problems in the Middle East including the changing political scene in Iran. Iran is the world's fourth largest oil producer and has one of the largest oil-exporting industries among all petroleum-producing countries. Until recently, Iran had been ruled under a constitutional monarchy. Its ruler was *Shah Mohammad Reza Pahlavi* (RAY-zuh puh-LAHV-ee), commonly called the Shah by the world's press. During the 1970's, the Shah of Iran attempted to modernize the country and to make it more democratic. At the same time, the Shah jailed many Iranians who disagreed with his policies. Some of those jailed without due process of law were tortured and killed.

The Shah Is Opposed   As opposition to the Shah's policies began to mount, he declared martial law and used force to put down mass demonstrations

The Shah of Iran is shown here with his wife and family in their ceremonial dress. Why, over the centuries, have some leaders felt it was important to dress so elaborately?

against his rule. Much of the opposition to the Shah came from Islamic religious leaders who felt the Shah would soon destroy many beliefs, customs, and laws of Islam.

Khomeini Returns   Finally, after much bloodshed, the Shah was forced to flee from Iran in 1979, leaving Prime Minister *Shahpur Bakhtiar* (shah-POOR BAK-tee-ahr) in charge. By then, a majority of the Iranian work force had shut down most of Iran's industries, including the state-owned oil company. Popular demand allowed the *Ayatollah Ruhollah Khomeini* (ie-uh-TOLE-uh roo-HOLE-uh kuh-MANE-ee), a seventy-eight-year-old Muslim religious leader, to return from exile in France to Iran. (*Ayatollah* is a title for a person recognized as having reached the highest degree of holiness.)

Bakhtiar tried to meet with Khomeini to arrange a transitional government, but Khomeini refused. Bakhtiar also faced great opposition from Khomeini's followers. On January 28, 1979, Bakhtiar supported the army when it fired on unarmed demonstrators. The struggle between Bakhtiar and Khomeini continued for weeks. When Bakhtiar finally lost control of the situation, he fled to France.

Khomeini quickly appointed a new government as well as special Islamic revolutionary councils to supervise the affairs of the country. As a result, hundreds of former supporters of the Shah's government were imprisoned and many executed on orders by Khomeini's religious trial councils. When some moderate Iranians protested Khomeini's attempt to impose strict Islamic rules on all people living there, he refused to listen to them.

Problems for the United States
Iran's revolution against the Shah's rule presented special problems for the United States. One dealt with the location in Iran of several key American radar installations used to monitor military activity and developments within the Soviet Union, which borders Iran. With the Shah's ouster from power, those special radar-monitoring stations were closed. This meant the United States would have to seek other locations for these very important radar-monitoring stations.

Another problem for the United States occurred when Iran's oil industry all but closed down during the revolution against the Shah's rule. Prior to that, Iran had supplied the United States with about 5 percent of its needed oil imports. The sudden cut in that 5 percent oil supply helped to create an energy shortage in the United States during the summer of 1979.

Iran under Khomeini   When Khomeini took control of the government, he demanded that the Shah return to Iran to be tried and executed for the injustices he had committed while in power. When the Shah came to the United States for medical treatment in October of 1979, many Iranians became outraged. They felt that the United States should not have allowed the Shah into the country. The United States refused to force the Shah to leave and on November 4, 1979, Iranian militants who were followers of Khomeini took over the U.S. Embassy

In 1979, after the Shah fled the country, the Ayatollah Ruhollah Khomeini returned from exile to Iran. What prompted his return?

549

in Tehran, capturing those in the embassy. The militants refused to release the hostages until the United States returned the Shah. Finally in December 1979, the Shah left the United States for Panama. This, however, did not satisfy those controlling the U.S. Embassy. The Shah died in July 1980, while living in Egypt.

At the same time, Khomeini's government was troubled by serious internal disunity. Khomeini's new constitution established him as absolute ruler over Iran for life. Disputes over the new constitution arose in many regions of Iran. For example, in the Azerbaijan (ah-zar-bie-JAHN) region the Turkish-speaking minority, following Ayatollah Mohammad Kazem Shariat-Madari (SHAH-ree-ut-muh-DAH-ree), another Muslim leader, protested vigorously for self-rule.

While trying to contain the growing unrest in the country, Iran was attacked by Iraq in September 1980. Though Iran was able to repel the attack, the country was growing economically and politically weak. In January 1981, the U.S. hostages were finally freed.

Events in Afghanistan Troubles in Afghanistan (af-GAN-is-tan) were equally alarming to the United States and many other countries by 1980. The Soviet Union, using its armed forces, helped to carry out a take-over in Afghanistan during which the president and his family were executed. Babrak Karmal (BAB-rak Kahr-MAHL) became the new leader. One reason for the take-over was to keep Muslim nationalist groups from regaining control of the government they had lost two years earlier. Many Muslims vowed to fight unceasingly to rid Afghanistan of the Russians.

SECTION REVIEW

1. Mapping: Using the map of the Middle East in the Atlas, describe the physical and political geography of the area. Then choose three key locations in the Middle East and tell what happened in each between the 1950's and the present.

2. Briefly identify the following and state their significance: Gamal Abdel Nasser, the PLO, Yassir Arafat, Anwar Sadat, Menachem Begin, Ayatollah Khomeini, Babrak Karmal.

3. How has the United States been involved in the Arab-Israeli conflicts since 1948?

4. How was the United States involved with Israel and Egypt during 1978 and 1979?

5. How did events in Iran during the late 1970's affect the United States?

◗ To what extent do you think the United States should have been involved in Middle Eastern affairs during the period from 1955 through the 1970's? Why?

THE UNITED STATES AND DETENTE

The United States began to improve relations with the Soviet Union and Communist China in the early 1970's. To accomplish this, each side had to make compromises.

The Cold War Eases As a step toward improved relations with the Soviet Union, President Eisenhower in 1959 invited **Nikita Khrushchev** (KROOSH-choff), the leader of the Soviet Union, to visit the United States. Khrushchev arrived in September 1959. His cordial talks with President Eisenhower at Camp David, Maryland, eased some Cold War tensions.

The U-2 Incident   In May 1960, less than two weeks before a series of United States-Soviet talks were to begin in Paris, the Soviet Union announced that an American U-2 spy plane had been shot down over Russia. Washington claimed the plane had been gathering information on the weather. The Sovet Union, however, demonstrated that it had not been a weather plane, and the pilot confessed he had been on a spying mission for the U.S. *Central Intelligence Agency (CIA).* In the end, President Eisenhower assumed full responsibility for the *U-2 incident.* He said the United States conducted such missions to protect the "free world" from attack by the Soviet Union. As a result of the U-2 incident, the Paris talks failed. During the next ten years, detente did not progress very much.

Detente in the 1970's   By the early 1970's, **Leonid I. Brezhnev** (BREZH-nef) had replaced Khrushchev as *First Secretary of the Communist party* in Russia, and *Aleksei N. Kosygin* (koe-SEE-gin) had become the premier. Efforts to improve relations with Russia came to be known as a policy of **detente** (day-TAHNT). In striving for detente, both sides made compromises. By so doing they hoped to lessen tensions that might otherwise lead to conflict.

With President Nixon's approval, Brezhnev and Kosygin arranged to purchase a huge shipment of U.S. wheat. This was to help offset the results of a poor wheat harvest in Russia. The Soviet Union also negotiated with America's privately owned Ford Motor and Pepsi-Cola companies for the opening of branches of these firms in the Soviet Union. In 1972 and again in early 1974, President Nixon visited Moscow. There he concluded successful talks on a variety of matters with the leaders of the Soviet government.

Brezhnev then made a trip to the United States in 1973. In late 1974, President Gerald Ford met with Brezhnev in Siberia in an effort to slow down the arms race. A joint American-Soviet space mission took place in 1975.

Setback in Detente   In 1975, detente between the United States and the Soviet Union underwent a serious setback. It occurred when the United States was preparing to grant the Soviet Union what is called *most-favored-trade status.* This means that high tariffs on many goods coming into the United States from Russia were to be lowered, especially on such Soviet goods as caviar, furs, sponges, wood pulp, and some manufactured items. The United States would have sent technicians to the Soviet Union to as-

When Gerald Ford was President, he met with Leonid I. Brezhnev to discuss the arms race. What is the status of the arms race today?

sist in building new Russian peacetime industries. The United States would also have loaned the Soviet Union money at low interest rates.

A majority approval of the U.S. Congress is needed before any trade agreement is approved. Congress wanted the trade agreement to have at least one basic condition—a guarantee by the Russian government that all citizens of the Soviet Union be allowed to emigrate from Russia without harassment, persecution, or imprisonment for their desire to leave. The Soviet government in 1975 decided it could not agree to such a condition and withdrew from the trade pact.

The SALT Treaties Since 1949, when the Soviets exploded their first atomic bomb, the Soviet Union and the United States have been in an arms race. During the 1970's, the United States and Russia managed to conclude several *strategic arms limitation treaties* known as *SALT*. The United States and Russia concluded *SALT I* in 1974. It served as only a beginning step in seeking to control the development and production of weapons. Some of these weapons are the multiple independent re-entry vehicle (MIRV) or a missile with numerous warheads that can be independently targeted, and nuclear warheads on intercontinental ballistic missiles (ICBMs).

SALT II Jimmy Carter and Leonid Brezhnev concluded SALT II in 1979 in Vienna. SALT II called for additional weapons arrangements between the two countries. The treaty, slated to last until the end of 1985, required that each side be limited in the amount of missiles and bombers they have and in new developments that may take place. It was hoped that this SALT treaty would lessen the possibility of nuclear destruction and help to ensure world peace.

Other parts of the treaty were equally complex. The United States, for example, agreed not to deploy, test, or launch any ground or sea cruise missiles until 1982. The Soviet Union by 1982 was to destroy about 270 of its old missiles and the United States would destroy about 35 mothballed B-52 bombers. SALT II also allowed both sides to position new air-launched cruise missiles and develop new submarine-based missiles.

On a more informal level, Brezhnev told President Carter that Russia would limit production of its medium-range Back-fire bomber to thirty a year. Most important was that both countries agreed on a statement of principles to guide the negotiations for *SALT III*, which could be formulated by 1985.

Senate Concerns Before SALT II could be finalized, the U.S. Senate had to ratify it. The Senate had many concerns about the treaty. Some senators felt the treaty would, by 1985, allow the Soviets to actually have a greater arsenal than the United States. Some were concerned about effective ways to verify the provisions of the treaty. Many worried that the Back-fire bomber issue was not included in the treaty. Others felt it did not go far enough in limiting arms on either side and that it still gave each country an overkill of about 10,000 nuclear warheads. Because of the Russian seizure of Afghanistan, American-Soviet relations became more strained and SALT II was not ratified. U.S. detente with Russia was seriously threatened.

The United States and China After twenty-three years of hostile relations and often bitter confrontations, the United States and the People's Republic of China also took steps toward detente. (See page 535.) In October 1971, the United Nations accepted the People's Republic of China as a member and expelled Nationalist China. On February 21, 1972, President Nixon arrived in Peking for an eight-day visit to China that he called "a journey for peace." The visit ended with a joint announcement by the United States and China that both would work to improve relations. They also agreed to an exchange of visits by scientists, artists, journalists, and athletes, and to an increase in trade between the two nations. President Ford later made his own trip to China in another effort to strengthen U.S.-Chinese relations.

By the time Jimmy Carter had become President of the United States in 1977, relations with China had improved considerably. After Mao's death in 1976, **Teng Hsiao-p'ing** (DAHNG-SHOW-PING) became the new vice-premier of China, and his government agreed to normalize relations with the United States by January 1, 1979. By then, both countries had exchanged ambassadors. Communist China in the meantime had replaced Nationalist China on the UN Security Council.

The United States, in return for full diplomatic recognition by Communist China, agreed to break diplomatic ties with Taiwan. The United States also agreed to end its mutual defense treaty with Taiwan, a move which angered many conservatives in America. As part of the overall agreement, Communist China stated that it would not interfere with U.S. investments in Taiwan, and seemingly promised not to use force in attempting to gain control of the Nationalist government on that island. These promises and those dealing with new trade agreements received further

Richard and Pat Nixon are shown here during the 1972 presidential visit to Peking. The purpose of this visit was to improve U.S. relations with China. How have relations improved since then?

support when Vice-Premier Teng made a visit to the United States in 1979.

The Nuclear Arms Race　　Despite efforts at detente, the nuclear arms race has continued to expand. In 1963, to slow the pace of the arms race, the United States, the Soviet Union, and many other nations signed a treaty banning nuclear tests in the atmosphere, outer space, or under water. In 1970, they agreed to the *Nuclear Nonproliferation Treaty*. This agreement was designed to halt the spread of atomic weapons. France, India, and China, however, did not sign these treaties because they did not have as many nuclear weapons as the other major world powers.

By the 1970's, other nuclear agreements had been reached, especially between the United States and Russia. For example, in May of 1976, the two countries signed a treaty that limited the size of underground nuclear explosives for peaceful purposes. The treaty, although probably unenforceable, also provided for on-site U.S. inspections of Soviet nuclear testing. By January of 1978, fifteen nations, including the United States and the Soviet Union, had agreed to new nuclear export safeguards. These were rules for exporting nuclear technology so as to halt the spread of such weapons. The rules, however, proved to have problems. By 1980, Pakistan managed to produce its own nuclear weapons as a safeguard against its enemy, India. And by the early 1980's, it was becoming apparent to many that yet other countries might soon build or had already secretly produced such weapons. Those countries included Israel, South Africa, and Brazil. Thus the nuclear bomb-building race continued.

In the 1980's, the nuclear arms race had also become the topic of a lively debate in the United States. Some Americans called for a freeze on the manufacturing of all nuclear weapons by all countries that now have them. They argued that this could serve as the first step in nuclear disarmament. Other Americans, also horrified at the thought of nuclear war, felt that the United States could not begin a nuclear arms freeze unless all the other countries involved did so. Moreover, they claimed the Soviet Union had shown no intention of actually placing a freeze on its manufacturing of nuclear arms.

SECTION REVIEW

1. Mapping: Which major powers have not signed the Nuclear Nonproliferation Treaty? Using the maps in the Atlas, do you think the location of any of these nations might have been responsible for this decision? Which nations? Why?
2. In your own words, define detente.
3. What was the "U-2 incident"? How did it serve to delay detente between the United States and the Soviet Union?
4. What are the SALT treaties?
5. Give two examples of the way the United States and China engaged in a policy of detente during the 1970's.
▷ What dangers do you think exist from the spread of nuclear weapons? How might their spread be stopped?

chapter 32

Latin America and Canada in the Twentieth Century

INDEPENDENCE IN LATIN AMERICA

During the 1800's, most European colonies in Latin America proclaimed their independence and became new nations. Simón Bolívar (buh-LEE-vahr), a revolutionary leader, had dreamed of an organization of South American republics. Each was to cooperate with the others to increase prosperity and give aid to the underprivileged. However, Bolívar's dream was not to come true.

Foreigners Control Latin American Resources By the early 1900's, twenty new republics had emerged in South and Central America. They had developed nationalistic attitudes and wanted no part of a federation of Latin America. Each of the new countries had become increasingly dependent on investments from Europe and the United States. By 1914, through such investments, foreigners controlled most Latin American plantations, public utilities, sources of oil, gas, and electric power, transportation, cattle ranches, meat-packing plants, and mines. (See the map on page 557.)

Growth in South America By the early part of the twentieth century, however, most of the major natural resources and agricultural products of Latin America had not been greatly developed. One reason was that, during the late 1800's and the early 1900's, most of South America had not been enlarged by any sizable immigrant population. The two major exceptions were Argentina (ahr-jun-TEE-nuh) and Brazil (bruh-ZIL). As the demand for more wheat and beef cattle grew, a flood of immigrants poured into Argentina. By 1910, nearly three-fourths of the adult population of Buenos Aires (bway-nuh-SAR-eez), the capital of Argentina, had been born in Europe. By the mid-1970's, Argentina's population was 97 percent European in origin.

Urban Areas Grow All of the people who moved to Latin American cities during the twentieth century, however, were not immigrants from abroad; many people from the rural poverty areas of the interior also flooded the urban areas. By 1950, about a third of the populations of Argentina, Uruguay (YOOR-uh-gway) and Chile lived in the capital cities of those countries. More than a fifth of the Mexican population lived in Mexico City—a metropolitan area that had grown from about 150,000 people in 1910 to over 12 million by 1980. Continued increases in the urban populations of Latin American cities only served to increase the problems of unemployment, poverty, and

Shacks like this can be found on the outskirts of large South American cities. Why do such extremes of poverty and wealth still exist today?

inadequate living standards.

The Indigenista Movement After World War I, a new spirit of cultural independence emerged in Latin America. It was caused in part by the success of the Mexican Revolution of 1910.

The Mexican Revolution helped to advance the *indigenista* (in-dee-hen-EE-stuh) *movement*. This was an attempt to make the large indigenous (in-DIH-jin-us), or native, Indian and mestizo populations of all Latin America proud of their ancient American heritage. Just after World War I, *José Vasconcelos* (vahs-kone-SAY-loss) of Mexico helped to make the indigenista idea popular there. He argued that Latin America could also make a unique contribution to world culture by boasting of its mixed heritage of Old and New World peoples. He was joined by many others, some of whom preferred to promote only the indigenista pride in Indian culture as the basis for Latin American nationality.

Economic Dependence and Independence in Latin America Although Latin America did experience a cultural revolution after World War I, most countries there were not able to free themselves immediately of economic dependence on Europe and the United States. Investors from those two areas continued to control many of the natural resources of Latin America until the Great Depression in 1929. Once the depression began in earnest, European countries and the United States were forced to abandon their sources for raw materials, especially in South America. As a result, exports from South American countries were cut to a third. This in turn caused massive unemployment in South American cities.

Self-sufficiency Begins In one way, the Great Depression proved to be a mixed blessing for Latin American nations. With the loss of most of their foreign markets, many began to be more economically self-sufficient. In the larger countries of Mexico, Brazil, Argentina, Colombia, and Chile, the governments began a policy of industrialization. Mexico helped to lead the way.

Mexican Business Grows From the years 1934 to 1940. President *Lázaro Cárdenas* (LAH-zah-roe CAR-dayn-as) encouraged Mexicans to begin their own businesses. To encourage more free enterprise at the local level, he gave more land to the peasants than all his predecessors combined had done. He also nationalized his country's oil industry in 1938, eliminating all foreign oil interests in Mexico.

Portillo Heads Mexico Many of the policies set forth by Cardenas were carried on by later presidents of Mexico, especially *José Lopez Portillo* (LOE-pes

ECONOMIC ACTIVITY IN LATIN AMERICA AND THE CARIBBEAN

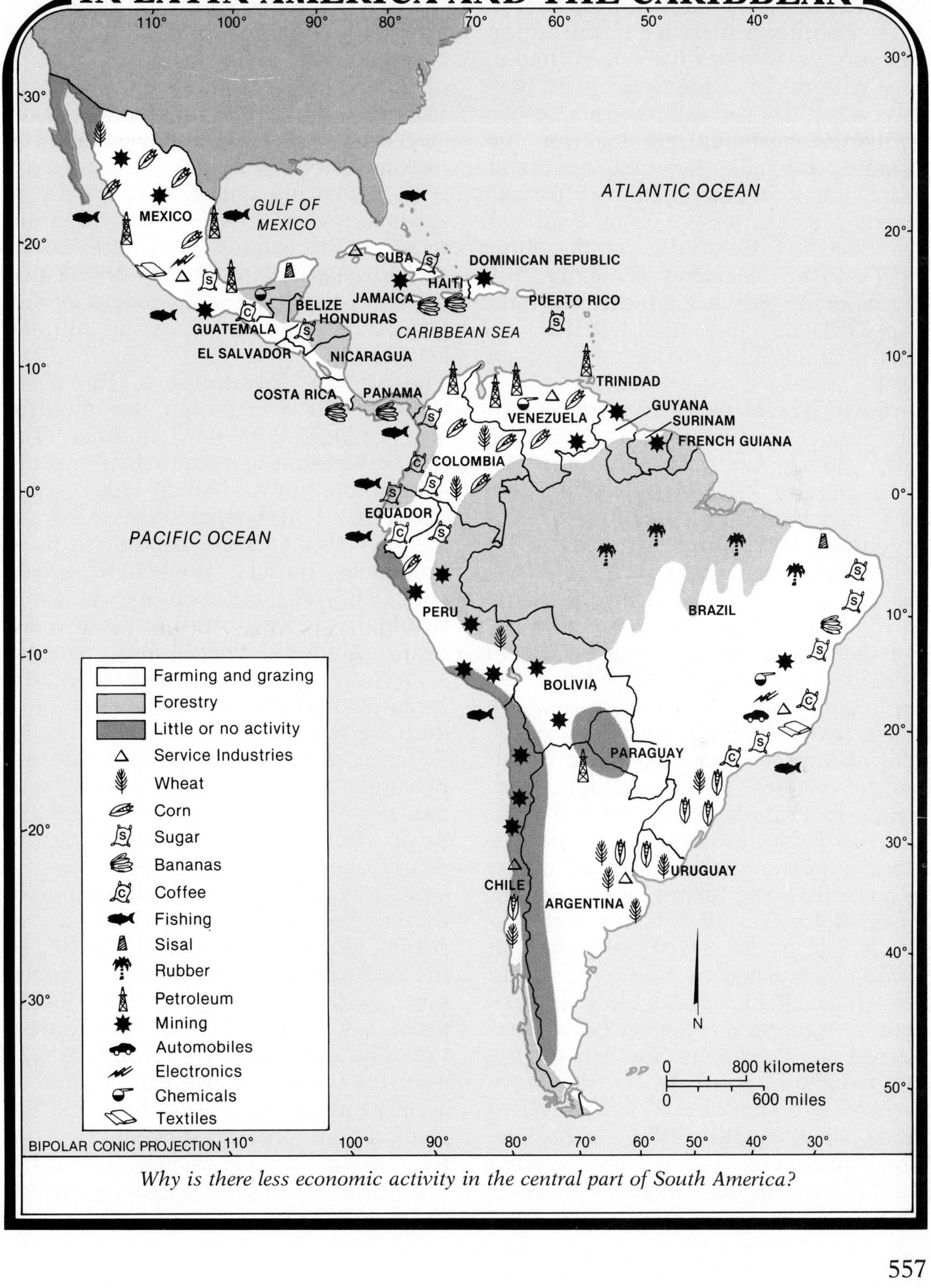

ATLANTIC OCEAN

GULF OF MEXICO

MEXICO

CUBA

DOMINICAN REPUBLIC

HAITI

JAMAICA

PUERTO RICO

BELIZE
HONDURAS

CARIBBEAN SEA

GUATEMALA

EL SALVADOR
NICARAGUA

COSTA RICA PANAMA

TRINIDAD

VENEZUELA

GUYANA
SURINAM
FRENCH GUIANA

COLOMBIA

EQUADOR

PACIFIC OCEAN

PERU

BRAZIL

BOLIVIA

PARAGUAY

CHILE

ARGENTINA

URUGUAY

N

Legend:

	Farming and grazing
	Forestry
	Little or no activity
△	Service Industries
	Wheat
	Corn
Ⓢ	Sugar
	Bananas
Ⓒ	Coffee
	Fishing
	Sisal
	Rubber
	Petroleum
	Mining
	Automobiles
	Electronics
	Chemicals
	Textiles

0   800 kilometers
0   600 miles

BIPOLAR CONIC PROJECTION

Why is there less economic activity in the central part of South America?

557

por-TEE-yoe), who became president in 1976. Portillo, a member of the ruling *Institutional Revolutionary party*, had to cope with massive unemployment, poverty, a rapidly rising birth rate, and a population growing too fast for the economy to handle. He and his political party unsuccessfully planned to use revenues from massive oil and natural gas deposits discovered in the mid-1970's to aid Mexico's economy. His successor, Miguel de la Madrid Hurtado (mee-GEL day lah mah-DREED ur-TAH-thoe), faced the same problems in 1982.

Perón in Argentina   In their search for greater economic independence, some South American countries became dictatorships. Many of the dictators had military backgrounds. In Argentina, for example, an army colonel named *Juan Perón* (HWAHN pay-RONE) became dictator in 1946. He used the financial crisis created by the depression to gain power. Perón formed a coalition that included the rural poor, the labor unions, and the army. By so doing, he antagonized Argentina's large landowners and urban middle classes. When he fell from power in 1955, however, he had done little to help the rural poor, and the labor unions and the army had begun to quarrel among themselves for power.

Perón Returns   Perón went into exile in Europe for seventeen years. In 1972, he returned to Buenos Aires. In September 1973, he was elected president of Argentina. His wife, *Isabel*, was elected vice-president. She became the first woman in South American history to hold a high political office. When Perón died in July 1974, Isabel became president — the first woman chief-of-state in the Americas. In 1976,

she was deposed by a military coup.

The Falklands   By 1982, *General Leopoldo Galtieri* had become President of Argentina. In that year, he sent troops to seize the Falkland Islands, east of the coastline of Argentina. The Falklands had long been claimed by both Argentina and Great Britain. A ten-week war resulted with Britain retaking the islands. Soon after, *General Reynaldo Bignone* (ray-NAHL-doe big-NON-ay) became President of Argentina. He was backed by the military leadership.

The Cuban Revolution   By 1959, Cubans had overthrown one dictator and replaced him with another. The Cuban Revolution began when a young communist lawyer named Fidel Castro (fee-DEL KAHS-troe) succeeded in ousting the corrupt dictatorship of Fulgencio Batista (fool-HANE-see-oe bah-TEES-tah) on January 1, 1959. Gradually, Castro transformed Cuba into a Marxist society. This involved some sweeping changes. Castro began a program requiring all school-age children, as well as many illiterate adults, to learn to read and write. However, privately-owned farmlands and businesses were seized by the new government. Freedom of the press disappeared and political opponents of Castro were imprisoned. Thousands of Cubans fled the island to escape persecution. Many of these Cubans settled in the U.S. Meanwhile, Castro's experiment with Marxism has had severe problems. Crop and industrial production has consistently declined. Moreover, the Cuban government has had to accept huge loans or gifts from the Soviet Union in order to survive.

Revolution Spreads in South America The intial success of Castro's revolution in Cuba and the continuing general dissatisfaction with economic conditions encouraged small Marxist-oriented groups in rural South America to seek power. They operated mainly as rural guerrilla bands. These guerrillas generally failed in their efforts. By 1967, most of their work seemed to have collapsed. In that year, the Bolivian Army killed *Che Guevara* (CHAY gwuh-VAH-rah), a South American Marxist hero and rural guerrilla leader.

But the failure of Che Guevara did not discourage revolutionary movements by other Castro sympathizers in the cities of South America. Many of those groups resorted to urban terrorism. They often assassinated or kidnapped prominent government officials and foreign businessmen. Largely as a result of such acts of violence, Brazil, Bolivia, Peru, and other nations came to be ruled by military regimes opposed to supporters of Castro.

Venezuela Another Latin American revolution of major importance occurred in Venezuela. It took place at the same time as Castro's revolution in Cuba. In 1958, Venezuela overthrew the dictatorship of *Colonel Marcos Perez Jimenez* (hee-MANE-es). *Rafael Caldera* (kahl-DER-uh) was elected its new president. During the first years Caldera was in office, small bands of communist-inspired guerrillas staged numerous raids within Venezuela. In 1969, Caldera offered the terrorists amnesty and free tickets to the foreign country of their choice. He also legalized the Communist party and established diplomatic relations with the Soviet Union. A year later, organized guerrilla activity in Venezuela was practically at a halt; but during the mid-1970's, urban guerrilla groups

again surfaced. In 1976, Venezuela, a chief supplier of oil to the United States, nationalized its oil industry, that is, the government took over control. That policy continued under the presidencies of *Carlos Andres Perez* (puh-REZ), and by 1980, *Luis Herrera Campins* (ay-RAY-rah KAHM-peens).

Chile Chile was among the last of the South American countries to come under military rule during the mid-twentieth century. It did so in September 1973, when the socialist-oriented civilian government of President *Salvador Allende* (ahl-YEN-day) was violently overthrown. He was reported by the new military regime to have committed suicide during the takeover. A year later, William E. Colby, then director of the U.S. Central Intelligence Agency, revealed that the Nixon administration had spent more than $11 million for CIA undercover operations in Chile to undermine Allende's Marxist government.

The new military government in Chile soon began a policy of imprisoning many of its political opponents. Under the leadership of *President Augusto Pinochet Ugarte* (ow-GOOS-toe peen-oe-CHATE oo-GAHR-tay), many people were denied all due process of law, arrested without benefit of trial, and tortured. This action was formally condemned by the UN Commission on Human Rights in 1975.

Uruguay Political turmoil occurred in Uruguay during the 1970's. In June of 1976, Uruguay's military leaders ousted *President Juan M. Bordaberry Arocena* (bore-dah-BAY-ree ah-roe-SEE-nah) from power and named *Aparicio Mendez Manfredin* (ah-pah-REE-see-oe MANE-dase mahn-FRAY-deen) as president. Mendez suspended the political

Pictured above is Canadian Prime Minister Pierre Elliott Trudeau. What problems did he face in the early 1980's?

rights of the leaders of all political parties in Uruguay.

Other South American Countries   In 1952, the Bolivian middle classes and miners overthrew a military regime. The new government was soon forced by Indian peasant uprisings to begin reforms. These reforms gave the rural farmers more land and better schools. By 1964, however, Bolivians were again living under military rule until 1982, when Hernan Siles Zuazo (air-NAHN SEE-less soo-AH-soe) became President of a new leftist civilian government. Paraguay, Bolivia's neighbor, has had a military dictatorship since it defeated Bolivia in a border dispute that ended in 1935. Both Peru, in 1980, and Ecuador, in 1979, had replaced military governments for civilian ones. However, government forces in Peru had to fight a Marxist guerrilla movement in 1982.

Puerto Rico   In 1952, Puerto Rico became a self-governing U.S. commonwealth. This allowed Puerto Ricans to come to the United States without immigration restrictions. Many Puerto Ricans want Puerto Rico to become our 51st state. However, not all Puerto Ricans agree.

Developments in Canada   The Dominion of Canada came into existence on July 1, 1867, by a proclamation of the British North American Act. It set up a federal system of government for Canada, modeled after the British system of a parliament and a cabinet under the crown. This alliance with Britain remained until 1931, when Canada became a self-governing Dominion within the British Empire. After that, Canada became an independent country.

Problems in Canada   In recent years, Canada has experienced some unique problems. Most of Canada is English-speaking, but 30 percent of the population is French-speaking. The majority of the French-speaking Canadians live in the province of Quebec, which was originally a French colony. Many have joined a group called the *French-Canadian Separatist Movement.* This group demands the right to determine whether Quebec should remain a part of Canada. Its members want French to be the official language of Quebec. The English-speaking Canadians, who are in the majority, counter, as did former Canadian Liberal Prime Minister *Pierre Elliott Trudeau* (troo-DOE) in 1978, that any attempt by Quebec to secede from Canada would be met by federal force. They also insist that English should be the official language of the country, pointing out that more than one official language creates communication problems. This remained one of the biggest political problems facing Progressive Conservative *Joe Clark*, who became prime minister of Canada in 1979. Clark, however, lost the confidence vote later that year, and Trudeau was reelected in 1980.

SECTION REVIEW

1. Mapping: Using the map on page 557, list the natural resources of Latin America. How were they developed in the 1970's?
2. In your own words, briefly identify or describe: indigenista movement, José Vasconcelos, Lazaro Cardenas.
3. What have been two significant developments in Mexico since 1934?
4. What roles did Juan and Isabel Perón play in Argentina's political life?
5. What was involved in the Falklands dispute?
6. What is the current status of Puerto Rico?
7. Who is Fidel Castro? Why is he important in Cuban history?
8. Why are each of the following important in Canadian history: Separatist Movement, Pierre Trudeau?
> Throughout history, military dictators have been in power in certain countries. Why do you think they gain political power?

LATIN AMERICA AND THE UNITED STATES OF AMERICA

After the Spanish-American War, the United States occupied Cuba. In 1901, the *Platt Amendment* was approved. This amendment called for the withdrawal of U.S. forces, it made Cuba independent, and it allowed the United States to intervene if order was threatened in Cuba.

U.S. Intervention in Latin America Since 1901, the United States has expanded the purpose behind the Platt Amendment for sending troops or agents to Latin American countries at different times. Those sent were usually given the task of protecting property owned by U.S. citizens or to suppress domestic disturbances. The United States intervened in the affairs of Haiti between 1915 and 1934, in Mexico just after 1915, in Honduras between 1916 and 1924, in Nicaragua between 1912 and 1933, and in Guatemala in 1954.

Nicaraguan Problems Nicaragua has had special political problems. During the time the United States stationed troops in Nicaragua, *Anastasio Somoza* (ah-nah-STAH-see-oe soe-MOE-sah) served as president. He was supported by a U.S.-trained national guard. In 1967, his son also named *Anastasio Somoza* became president.

President Somoza's problems began about 1970 when a group of left-wing *Sandinistas* (sahn-dee-NEES-tahs) started to challenge his strong-man rule. The Sandinista guerrillas got their name from a rebel Nicaraguan Army officer who fought against the U.S. Marines there during the early 1930's. When Somoza had some of his political opponents jailed, Nicaraguans started to protest. Then in 1978, the editor of the only opposition newspaper in Nicaragua was shot and killed, and anti-government rioting broke out.

Anastasio Somoza was forced to flee his country in 1979 by the Sandinista National Liberation Front. How do you think a group like that could become so powerful?

During other anti-government protests, many participants were killed or injured by government troops called the national guard.

The Sandinistas Grow The Sandinistas managed to capitalize on such internal turmoil and continued to enlarge the scope of their attacks, possibly with some communist backing. Their efforts brought success. After much bloodshed on both sides in which about 20,000 people died, President Somoza formally resigned his office on July 17, 1979, and went into exile in Miami, Florida. With his departure, the *Sandinista National Liberation Front,* as it called itself, organized a new government.

Elsewhere in Central America, leftist and rightist groups continued to involve themselves in guerrilla-type warfare in Guatemala, Honduras, and El Salvador. Fighting between the various groups in the country of El Salvador had cost about 40,000 military and civilian lives by the early 1980's.

Bay of Pigs The United States was involved in Cuba during 1961 and again in 1962. Many of Castro's changes angered Americans, especially when he seized property owned by U.S. citizens without paying them. By 1960, relations between Cuba and the United States had completely deteriorated. They grew rapidly worse after the *Bay of Pigs* incident. On April 17, 1961, an army of Cuban exiles who opposed Castro's regime landed at the Bay of Pigs in Cuba. The exiles, trained by the Central Intelligence Agency, were confident that the Cuban people would rally to their side and help them overthrow Castro. But the whole operation was a disaster. No popular uprising took place. Castro's army defeated and captured the invaders. They were not released until the United States paid Castro a large ransom for their return from Cuba.

War Avoided The next U.S. involvement with Cuba took place in October 1962 when the United States discovered that the Soviet Union was building missile bases in Cuba. With these bases, nuclear attacks could be launched against the eastern part of the United States and against neighboring Caribbean nations. President Kennedy set up a naval blockade around Cuba to prevent any additional Soviet supplies from entering. He told Premier Khrushchev of the Soviet Union that if a single missile was fired from Cuba, the United States would retaliate with a missile attack on Russia. Kennedy demanded that the missiles be removed and that shipments of weapons to Cuba cease immediately. The Soviet Union backed down. Soviet ships bringing missiles to Cuba turned around and returned to Russia. Kennedy then lifted the military blockade around Cuba.

More Trouble in Cuba New troubles with Cuba occurred in 1979, when the United States learned that a Soviet combat unit of about 3,000 soldiers had been stationed on the island. Many U.S. senators demanded that President Carter have Russia remove its troops from Cuba. The President, however, said the Soviet Union assured him the troops were manning a training center and offered no direct threat to the United States. In response, Carter increased U.S. military presence in the Cuban area to keep better watch on activities there.

Trouble in the Caribbean The United States became involved in other Caribbean affairs during President

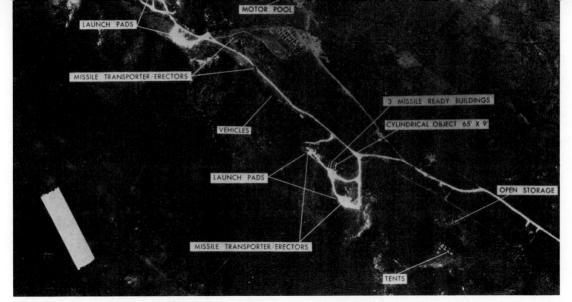

LAUNCH PADS

MOTOR POOL

MISSILE TRANSPORTER/ERECTORS

VEHICLES

3 MISSILE READY BUILDINGS

CYLINDRICAL OBJECT 65' X 9'

LAUNCH PADS

OPEN STORAGE

MISSILE TRANSPORTER/ERECTORS

TENTS

This is an aerial shot taken in 1962 of the missile base in Cuba. The missiles at this base had a range of 1,760 kilometers (1,100 miles). Why did the United States react so strongly to its location?

Johnson's administration. In 1963, *Rafael Trujillo* (troo-HEE-yoe), long-time dictator of the Dominican Republic, was assassinated. For the first time in years, the country had free elections and *Juan Bosch* (BAHSH) was elected president. Seven months later, he was removed from office by the army. The generals behind the army takeover accused Bosch of "being soft on communism."

In 1965, the generals who had deposed Bosch staged another revolt. This time it was against the Dominican government of *Donald Reid Cabral* (kuh-BRAHL). A younger group of officers organized a popular movement to restore Bosch. The supporters of Bosch were close to victory when 22,000 U.S. troops arrived and halted their efforts at a takeover of the government. President Johnson announced that the troops had been sent to protect American citizens there. However, it soon became clear that the United States had intervened to prevent Bosch and his supporters from regaining control. To explain this action, the State Department released a list of fifty-eight communists who it claimed had seized control of the Bosch movement.

The United States and Panama With help from the United States, the people of Panama gained their independence from Colombia in 1903. In return, the United States signed a treaty with Panama. Under the terms of that treaty, the United States acquired rights over a 16-kilometer (10-mile) wide zone of territory in Panama. The United States agreed to pay Panama $10 million plus annual fees that increased to $2 million a year.

The Panama Canal   After a tremendous and costly feat of engineering, the United States in 1914 opened the Panama Canal to the shipping of the world. Since then, the Panama Canal has operated without an increase in the tolls charged to ships using it. About 70 percent of the goods that have passed through the Canal went to or from the

563

Late in 1979, U.S. and Panamanian officials signed the treaty turning over the Canal Zone to Panama. By the year 2000, Panama will gain complete control of the Canal. Why do you think many Americans were reluctant to give up control of the Canal?

United States. The Canal has also made quick passage possible for U.S. warships between the Atlantic and Pacific oceans. Panamanians, too, have benefitted from the Canal. About one-third of all income in Panama comes from it.

Takeover in Panama   In 1968, *General Omar Torrijos* (OE-mahr toe-REE-yos) seized power in a military coup in Panama. Shortly after assuming power, General Torrijos began to complain about the U.S. presence in the Canal Zone. Torrijos wanted the United States to either amend or end the 1903 treaty and to sell or give the Panama Canal to Panama.

United States Turns Over Canal to Panama   The Ford and later the Carter administrations negotiated for new Panama Canal treaties. In September of 1977, President Carter and Torrijos signed the new treaties in Washington, D.C. The U.S. Senate ratified the treaties in 1978. By the terms of the treaties, the U.S. Canal Zone became Panamanian territory in 1982. Panama is not to gain complete control of the Canal until the year 2000. However, the treaties state that U.S. troops can enter the Panama Canal Zone after 2000 if Panama or any other country or group closes it. After Panama gained the Canal, Torrijos died in a plane crash. Shortly thereafter, Ricardo de la Espriella (es-pree-AY-yuh) became president.

Improving Relations Between the United States and Latin America
There have been attempts by some Presidents of the United States to promote peaceful relations with Latin America. President Franklin Roosevelt, for example, inaugurated what he called the **Good Neighbor Policy,** by which he hoped to preserve order in Latin America without using military force. He sought to use trade as a means of bringing stability to this area. The Good Neighbor Policy resulted in a series of conferences between 1933 and 1947. They were attended by most of the countries of the Americas. At these meetings, the participants agreed that no one state had the right to intervene in the domestic or foreign affairs of another American state. They also agreed that the American republics would consult one another in case of a threat to the security of one. Finally, they provided for mutual consultation and defense in the event that one or more of the American countries was attacked by a nation outside the Americas.

OAS   A major attempt at American unity came with the creation of the **Organization of American States (OAS)** in 1948. All the American nations except Canada and Cuba are members. In the OAS charter, the member nations agreed that settlement of disputes among the American countries should be attempted by the organization before the problems were taken to the United Nations. The OAS nations also agreed to consult each other before one member took action against another. On occasion, member nations have violated both of these agreements. However, the OAS has remained an active influence in the Western Hemisphere. Most recently, it helped pave the way in 1977 for the United States to ease a complete embargo on all goods to Cuba. In 1979, it strongly recommended with U.S. backing, that President Somoza of Nicaragua resign from office in order to avoid more fighting there.

Alliance for Progress　In 1961, at President John F. Kennedy's suggestion, the United States put into effect two new development programs in Latin America. The first was the *Alliance for Progress,* by which Congress appropriated $20 billion to aid Latin American nations for a ten-year period. The money was intended to strengthen the economies of those countries and to improve their housing, medical, and educational facilities. Kennedy hoped the Alliance for Progress would prevent other Latin American countries from following the example of Cuba. The program did help somewhat. But it has not been able to make the rate of economic growth match the high rate of population growth in Latin America.

Peace Corps　A second major program of foreign aid created during Kennedy's presidency was the *Peace Corps.* Initiated in 1961, it is still in operation today. Through the Peace Corps, the United States, at its own expense, sends volunteer workers to other countries. The volunteers— mostly young people—teach school, educate people in practical skills such as agriculture and medicine, and help

A Peace Corps volunteer is shown here teaching two Latin Americans how to weigh a pig. What other skills do these volunteers teach?

to build new community facilities of all kinds. The volunteers go only to countries that ask for their help. Among the first areas to which Peace Corps volunteers were sent were South America and Africa.

SECTION REVIEW

1. Mapping: Using the map on page 557, and the maps in the Atlas, identify the areas of Latin America in which the United States became involved in the twentieth century. Why is the United States worried about communist involvement in South America?

2. In your own words, identify and tell the significance of each of the following: Anastasio Somoza, Sandinistas, Fidel Castro, Bay of Pigs invasion, Juan Bosch, Omar Torrijos, Good Neighbor Policy, Organization of American States, Alliance for Progress.

What are some policies any "Good Neighbor" should follow?

Europe and the Modern World

THE SOVIET UNION AND EASTERN EUROPE

Europe was changed drastically by World War II. Much of the European continent had been severely damaged by the fighting. Furthermore, the war had shaken up European politics, producing new centers of power.

Soviet Union after World War II The people of the Soviet Union suffered greatly during and after World War II. It is estimated that during the four years of war, 20 million people of the Soviet Union, both civilian and military, were killed. More than 1,700 cities and towns were left in ruins, and 70,000 farm villages were totally destroyed. About half of the factories the Russians had struggled so hard to build during the 1930's were destroyed in the war. By 1945, when peace was restored, about 25 million people in the Soviet Union were left homeless.

The Policies of Stalin Many of Russia's people thought victory would bring a new way of life. But they were soon disappointed. From the end of the war until his death in 1953, Stalin, Russia's Premier, returned to his policies of the 1930's. Millions of people filled the slave-labor camps. The secret police were everywhere and heavy emphasis was placed on rebuilding indus-

try. Improvements in the standard of living were sacrificed for industrialization. To justify those sacrifices, the Russian people were told that America had replaced Nazi Germany as a threat to the Soviet Union. As the Cold War got under way, the eastern European countries that had been invaded by the Soviet Army during its fighting with the Germans were made part of Stalin's "empire." To rebuild Russia's economy, these countries were looted of everything of value.

Tito Led Yugoslavia Yugoslavia, under *Marshal Tito*, a communist wartime hero, objected to Stalin's domination. Tito maintained that he was still a communist but he wanted Yugoslavia to be independent of the Soviet Union. Stalin, fearing that the United States might aid Tito, hesitated to send troops to invade Yugoslavia. Yugoslavia was expelled from the *Cominform* (Communist Information Bureau) in 1948, and was allowed to remain a communist state that was independent of Soviet control.

De-Stalinization In March 1953, Stalin died. His death was followed by a struggle within the Communist party over who would take power. It was not until about 1956 that *Nikita Khrushchev* emerged as the new leader of the Soviet Union. Early in 1956, realizing how un-

Yugoslav leader Marshal Tito was a wartime hero. What other war heroes have become leaders of countries?

hind the Iron Curtain, where there was great resentment over Russian domination. The reforms made by the communist governments of eastern Europe were not enough to satisfy the people, however, and relaxation of government control led to open revolt.

Eastern Europeans Rebel Against Soviet Domination In 1953, riots by workers in East Berlin led to a widespread anti-communist rebellion, which Soviet troops quickly put down. This rebellion in East Germany had alarmed the Soviet leadership. They feared that the example set by independent Yugloslavia had inspired the Germans to revolt.

In 1956, anti-soviet rebellions also spread through Poland. Khrushchev, eager to prevent Poland from breaking away, flew to Warsaw to visit *Wladyslaw Gomulka* (VLAH-dee-slaw guh-MOOL-kuh), the new Polish Communist leader. Khrushchev returned to Moscow after Gomulka promised to remain loyal to the Soviet Union, and order was restored.

After the Polish rebellions were put down, Khrushchev faced another revolt. A new leader was at the head of the Hungarian government, *Imre Nagy* (EEM-ray NAHZH). Nagy had promised his people reforms, and he wanted to be free of Soviet domination. Nagy organized a new government and called on the United Nations for help. But the United Nations did nothing. This time, however, Khrushchev did not try to reach a compromise with the Hungarians. Instead, he sent Russian tanks and troops to crush the Hungarian rebels. Nagy was arrested, taken to Russia, and later executed. A new communist leader was installed, and Hungary again came under Soviet domination. About 200,000 Hungarians fled

popular a continuation of Stalin's policies would be, Khrushchev denounced Stalin, exposing many of the terrible things he had authorized during his long rule. Khrushchev then began a program of *"de-Stalinization."* This program promised the Soviet people an improvement in their standard of living, the release of prisoners from slave-labor camps, a greater availability of consumer goods, and for a while, greater freedom of speech and freedom of the press. Some people called this brief period of freedom *the Thaw.*

De-Stalinization was also carried into the eastern European countries be-

In 1982, Yuri Andropov became Secretary of the Communist party in Russia. What problems did the U.S.S.R. face in the 1980's?

their country to seek safety from the Soviet's revenge.

Many years went by before another eastern European country dared to imitate Yugoslavia by proclaiming its independence from Soviet Russia. However, this changed in 1968. A new Communist government took over in Czechoslovakia under the leadership of *Alexander Dubcek* (DOOB-check). He promised greater freedom to the people of Czechoslovakia. Dubcek also promised to remain friendly toward the Soviet Union, and he tried to establish better relations with non-communist nations.

Brezhnev Doctrine   Khrushchev was deposed in 1964 and Leonid I. Brezhnev became the new Soviet leader. Brezhnev treated Czechoslovakia as Khrushchev had treated Hungary. He launched a sudden, massive Soviet invasion of Czechoslovakia in 1968. The Czechs had no opportunity to resist.

Dubcek was removed from office by the Soviets and a new Communist leader was installed. A purge of Dubcek's supporters was begun. To justify what the Soviets had done to Czechoslovakia, the new Soviet leader announced the *Brezhnev Doctrine*. He claimed the Soviet Union had the right to interfere in any eastern European "satellite" nation if the U.S.S.R. considered itself in any way threatened by that satellite.

Trouble broke out again in Poland in 1980. Labor unions banded together in a series of strikes to protest food shortages and other government policies. By 1981, the Soviets were becoming concerned about the situation. The Polish army stepped in and seized control of the government. Martial law was declared, and the protest movement was suppressed. President Reagan and other world leaders promptly denounced this violation of the Polish people's freedoms.

Peaceful Coexistence   Before Nikita Khrushchev fell from power in 1964, he had come to realize that atomic war between the Soviet Union and the United States would only destroy both nations. He gave up Stalin's belief that war between these two giant powers had to take place. Khrushchev instead called for **"peaceful coexistence."** There must be no war, he said. However, America and Russia would continue to be rivals. In the long run, Khrushchev believed, the Soviet Union would defeat the United States by overtaking America in economic production and scientific knowledge, and by providing the world's people with a better way of life.

Brezhnev continued Khrushchev's policy of peaceful coexistence until his death in 1982. Brezhnev tried to improve relations with America through detente. One important reason why the

U.S.S.R. is eager for detente with the U.S. is because it is fearful of the People's Republic of China.

Chinese-Soviet Rivalry The People's Republic of China was established before Khrushchev came to power. Mao Tse-tung and other Chinese Communist leaders were Stalinists. They remained so even after Khrushchev launched his de-Stalinization program. Mao did not agree with Khrushchev's policies. "Peaceful coexistence" alarmed Mao, as he believed the communist world should pool its resources for a struggle with the West. Mao also resented Khrushchev's refusal to give China the financial help it needed to industrialize and become a modern military power.

The government in Moscow was determined to keep its dominant position. The Soviet Union soon discovered, however, that it could not force its policies on China as it had on Poland, Hungary, and Czechoslovakia. Since Soviet tanks and troops did not frighten Mao, the Soviet leaders had to find other ways to dominate China. They did this by recalling Soviet specialists and scientists from China, refusing to give China knowledge about nuclear power, cutting back trade, and refusing loans.

The Russians moved large numbers of troops into position along the Russian-Chinese border. When a border dispute broke out between them, both countries were willing to use force to back up their own claims. The Chinese-Soviet dispute started while Khrushchev was in power, but it became even more serious after Brezhnev took control. Border disputes led to fighting between Chinese and Soviet troops in 1969. Although war was avoided, military clashes have continued to the present day.

SECTION REVIEW

1. Mapping: Using the map on page 533, identify the countries of eastern Europe that the Soviet Union occupied after World War II. Which countries are dominated by the Soviet Union today?

2. In your own words, identify and state the significance of each of the following: Nikita Khrushchev, de-Stalinization, the Thaw, Wladyslaw Gomulka, Imre Nagy, Alexander Dubcek, Leonid I. Brezhnev, Mao Tse-tung.

3. Describe in as much detail as possible the impact of World War II on Soviet Russia.

4. What was the result of rebellions against Soviet rule in eastern Europe?

5. What is the policy of "peaceful coexistence"? Why has the Soviet Union pursued this policy with the United States?

▷ Does any nation have the right to interfere in the affairs of a neighboring country? Explain.

EUROPE OUTSIDE SOVIET INFLUENCE

The main task facing western Europe after World War II was the rebuilding of its shattered way of life. Due to tremendous amounts of aid from the United States through the Marshall Plan, the war-torn states of Europe were able to make a rapid recovery. By 1952, western Europe was producing about twice what it had produced before World War II.

The Common Market This rapid recovery was also due partly to a willingness among European nations to cooperate for their mutual economic

François Mitterand became President of France in 1981. To which political group did he owe his victory?

benefit. For example, in 1957, six countries joined together in the *European Economic Community*, also known as the **Common Market.** They were France, West Germany, Italy, Belgium, Luxembourg, and The Netherlands. These countries agreed to do away gradually with taxes on the imports of one another's products and to work toward the free movement of goods and workers between countries. With the addition of Great Britain, Denmark, and Ireland in 1973, and Greece in 1981, the Common Market has become an economic power second only to the U.S.

In 1979, the nine Common Market nations held elections to select members for the European Parliament. Membership in this international body was determined by the population of each country represented. The European Parliament has powers over the budget of the Common Market and over its bureaucracy. But the Parliament cannot make laws and can only offer advice to member nations. Despite its limited powers, supporters of Parliament predict it will lead to future political unity of Common Market nations.

De Gaulle and French Supremacy
As Europe gradually recovered from World War II, the Soviet threat to Europe appeared to diminish. By the 1960's, peaceful coexistence and the Chinese-Soviet split had convinced President **Charles de Gaulle** of France that there was no longer any danger of Russia expanding by seizing European territory. He therefore pulled France out of the North Atlantic Treaty Organization (NATO) and began to improve France's relations with the Soviet Union and the People's Republic of China. De Gaulle opposed a continuation of American and British influence in European affairs. He believed western Europe should unite under French leadership to become a world power equal to the United States, Soviet Russia, or China. To carry out his policies, de Gaulle broke several treaties with the United States and forced Americans out of U.S. military bases in France. De Gaulle also developed nuclear power for France.

In 1968, de Gaulle was unable to deal with severe domestic problems. Riots and strikes occurred throughout France. Workers wanted higher wages and better working conditions. De Gaulle promised reforms and increases in wages, thereby ending the strikes. He resigned in 1969 and *Georges Pompidou* (PAHM-pee-doo) succeeded de Gaulle as president. Pompidou died in 1974 and was succeeded by **Valéry Giscard d'Estaing** (val-eh-REE JEES-kahr deh-STAHⁿ).

The policies of Giscard d'Estaing were similar to those of de Gaulle and

Pompidou, but he faced powerful opponents. The popularity of socialists and communists in France was growing. In 1972, the socialists and communists formed an alliance. After working for one another's elections, they won a majority of city and local offices in 1976. In 1981, their alliance won the presidential election. Socialist leader François Mitterand (frahn-SWAH mee-teh-RAHn) defeated Valery Giscard D'Estaing. Mitterand repaid his communist supporters by appointing communists to his first cabinet.

Great Britain's Postwar Problems While de Gaulle was trying to revive France, some of the other great European powers went into decline. The economic recovery of western Europe did not spread to Great Britain. World War II marked the end of the vast empire Britain had once ruled. Self-government was gradually introduced to most of Britain's colonies, starting with Australia, Canada, New Zealand, Newfoundland, South Africa, and the Republic of Ireland, all in 1931. It was Britain's hope that after independence had been granted to these colonies, close ties, especially for trade, could be kept. Most of these ex-colonies joined a voluntary association called the *British Commonwealth of Nations*.

Welfare State At home Britain's problems after the war were chiefly economic. More and more demands were placed on the government for higher wages and better health, housing, and social welfare programs. In the 1945 election, the British people elected the Labor party to office by a large majority. Under its leadership, the government took over operations of many basic industries and created a **"welfare state"** whereby the government intervened in the social and economic affairs of its citizens in order to maintain a predetermined standard of living. This provided the British people with a wide variety of services, including free medical care. However, it was difficult for the government to find tax resources to pay for such services. Exports of British goods were falling behind the amount of imported goods, creating an unfavorable balance of trade.

The Conservative party came back to power from 1951 to 1964, and again from 1970 to 1974. Although the Conservatives returned the steel industry to private hands, socialism in Britain changed little. In 1979, the Conservative party leader **Margaret Thatcher** became Britain's first woman prime minister. Thatcher's platform pledged an end to socialism in Britain, but her government still faced many difficult problems.

Margaret Thatcher made many speeches before she was elected prime minister. What other methods do politicians use in trying to get themselves elected to office?

571

Britain in Ireland To add to Britain's worries, tensions between the Protestant majority and the Catholic minority in Northern Ireland has resulted in violence since 1968. Large numbers of British troops, at great cost to the British government, have been stationed in Northern Ireland to try to prevent rioting. In recent years, *Irish Republican Army (IRA)* terrorists seeking to unite Northern Ireland with the Republic of Ireland have carried out a continuing campaign of terrorism. Over 1,300 people have been killed as a result of terrorist activity, and no peaceful solution has yet been found.

In addition to the problem in Ireland, Britain faced a war with Argentina in 1982 over control of the Falkland Islands. (See page 558.)

The Recovery of Germany While the British were searching for ways to solve their serious economic problems, West Germany underwent a remarkable recovery from World War II. From the destruction of Hitler's government until 1949, Germany was occupied by Allied armies. In 1949, West Germany established a democratic republic called the *Federal Republic of Germany*. However, this new government remained under the influence of France, the United States, and Great Britain until 1955. Its government at Bonn was headed by Chancellor *Konrad Adenauer* (AH-den-ow-er) until 1963. East Germany, still under Russia's influence, also established a government in 1949, the *German Democratic Republic*.

West Germany Under Adenauer, West Germany grew to be one of Europe's major industrial powers and a strong ally of the United States. Reunification of Germany seemed impossible, since neither side would agree on any compromise.

When *Willy Brandt* (BRANT) became chancellor in 1969, he promised to improve West Germany's relations with East Germany and other communist states, especially the Soviet Union. Reunification would come about only if an East-West agreement were achieved. Brandt, therefore, worked to bring about better understanding between communist and non-communist Europe. To begin with, Brandt signed a treaty with Poland accepting the borders that had been drawn up for Germany after World War II. He did this even though it meant agreeing to a great loss of former German territory. This led to the establishment of formal relations between East and West Germany. Brandt resigned as chancellor in 1974, and **Helmut Schmidt** (HEL-mut SHMIT) replaced him.

West Germany continued to enjoy great economic prosperity under Schmidt. Since the 1950's, its industrial production has continued to grow. West Germany became the leading member of the Common Market. In 1982, however, Schmidt's government lost the support of the German parliament and Schmidt was replaced by Helmut Kohl (HEL-mut KOLE).

Italy Is Faced with Severe Problems Italy was a defeated nation after World War II and was unable to make a fast economic recovery. In 1946, by a small majority, Italian voters approved a republic for Italy ending the monarchy under which all of Italy had been united. For several years, *Alcide de Gasperi* (ahl-CHEE-day day GAHS-per-ee) headed the Italian government. Under de Gasperi, industry grew and reforms occurred in education and in the tax structure. After de Gasperi left politics in 1953, there seemed to be no strong leader to take his place, and the Com-

Members of an Italian terrorist group, the Red Brigades, are shown here being arrested. Why do such organizations exist?

munist party in Italy greatly increased in strength.

In the 1950's and 1960's, due to U.S. aid and membership in the Common Market, Italy was able to make economic progress. However, this did not last. Since 1966, the country has been plagued with economic troubles —strikes and disorders have often crippled progress. No political party has been able to offer the Italian people strong leadership. Elections became frequent in the 1970's, and no government has been able to remain in office for long.

Italy's Communist Party Grows
The Italian Communist party benefitted from this political instability. It became the largest and best-organized

communist party in western Europe. In the 1976 national elections, the Communists won over 35 percent of the seats in the Italian parliament. To win greater popularity for the Communist party, its leader, *Enrico Berlinguer* (berling-GER), promised to respect the constitution if the communists take over Italy's government in the future. There is a constant battle for control among the Christian Democrat, Socialist, and Communist parties.

A revolutionary organization known as the *Red Brigades* was formed in the 1970's. The Brigades' actions were mild when the group was first formed, but gradually they became more violent. In 1978, they kidnapped and murdered *Aldo Moro*, a former

573

prime minister of Italy. This and other acts of violence continued through the 1970's.

Portugal After almost forty years, the Portuguese dictatorship of Prime Minister *Antonio Salazar* (SAHL-uh-zahr) ended when he suffered a stroke in 1968. *Marcello Caetano,* who replaced Salazar, faced many problems. Portugal's African colonies were in revolt, demanding independence. The cost of putting down these rebellions was high for Portugal. *General Antonio de Spinola* (speen-OE-luh) led army officers in the overthrow of the Portuguese government in 1974. As president, Spinola promised democracy to the Portuguese people and independence to Angola. General Spinola resigned later that year due to pressure from the Communist party in Portugal. His resignation caused political confusion and instability. Government leaders changed many times after this. In 1979, *Maria Pintassilgo* (peen-tah-SEEL-goe), who did not belong to a political party, became prime minister. Pintassilgo had represented Portugal in the United Nations. She became the second woman in western Europe—after Margaret Thatcher—to be appointed prime minister.

Government Changes in Spain Portugal's neighbor Spain also had been a long-time dictatorship under *Francisco Franco.* In 1969, Prince **Juan Carlos,** a member of the royal family that had once ruled Spain, was chosen by Franco to follow as head of the government. When Franco died in 1975, Juan Carlos became king, and the transition to the new government was easily accomplished. The new king made it clear that he wanted Spain to become a more democratic state. A constitution was written, political parties were established, and free elections were held.

The popularity of the socialists steadily increased. In the October 1982 election, they won a sweeping victory and took over the government of Spain.

To add to Spain's political troubles, some *Basques* (BAHSKS) of northern Spain demanded independence. The Basques were a minority group near the Spanish-French border. Riots, demonstrations, and strikes caused by the Basques swept northern Spain. In 1980 the Basques won self-government, but their territories remained part of Spain. This did not end the violence, however. A campaign of assassinations and bombings continued, killing many people.

SECTION REVIEW

1. Mapping: Using the map of Europe in the Atlas, identify the European nations that form the Common Market. Which of these nations made the best economic recovery after World War II? Explain.

2. In your own words, identify each of the following: Common Market, Valéry Giscard d'Estaing, British Commonwealth of Nations, welfare state, Margaret Thatcher, IRA, Bonn, Konrad Adenauer, Willie Brandt, Red Brigade, François Mitterand, Helmut Kohl, General Antonio de Spinola, Francisco Franco.

3. Describe the policies of Charles de Gaulle from 1958 to 1969.

4. Do you think it is likely that the German people will accept a permanent division of their country into East and West Germany? What historical reasons can you give to support your conclusion?

▷ What are the advantages of being a welfare state? What are the disadvantages? Explain.

chapter 34

Asia and the Modern World

ASIAN INDEPENDENCE IS ACHIEVED

World War II marked the beginning of the end of Western imperialism in Asia and the Pacific. Nationalism had begun to grow among most Asian peoples by the early 1900's, particularly in Malaya, Indonesia, Burma, India, and Indochina. Many Asians expected an end to Western imperialism after the war since Western nations had fought Japan for trying to build an empire through conquest. After the war, when colonial powers tried to regain control, many Asian nations fought for their independence.

The Dutch in Indonesia   After World War II, the Dutch tried to reestablish control over their colonial possessions in Indonesia. By then, however, their former colony had declared its independence. It had set up a republican government, headed by President *Achmed Sukarno* (AHK-med soo-KAHR-noe). Fighting and negotiations went on between the Indonesians and the Dutch until 1949, when the Dutch finally granted independence to all of Indonesia except Dutch New Guinea, also called West Irian (ir-EE-ahn). (See the Atlas.) New Guinea joined Indonesia in 1963.

An Independent Indonesia   Sukarno was Indonesia's president from the time it gained its independence until 1968. During this time, Indonesia faced many problems. The country's population rose higher than its food supply, and Sukarno's policies resulted in economic setbacks that created unrest. Various revolts in 1958 caused Indonesian-American relations to worsen. Sukarno believed America was supplying aid to the rebels, so he started to favor communist nations and follow anti-American policies. Sukarno then started to accept aid from Russia. He also involved his country in a dispute over territory claimed by both the new nation of Malaysia (muh-LAY-zhuh) and Indonesia. In 1965, when Malaysia was elected to the United Nations Security Council, Sukarno withdrew Indonesia from the United Nations.

Indonesia's communist party became the third largest in the world. When it was learned in 1965 that the communist party planned to seize control of Indonesia's government, the army, led by *General Suharto* (soo-HAHR-toe), crushed the attempt. A widespread purge of communists followed, during which nearly 500,000 persons were killed. The army suspected that Sukarno was behind the communist attempt to seize the government, so they stripped him of all his power, leaving him with only the title of president. General Suharto was named head of the army and given total power. Suharto was elected president in 1968, reelected in 1973, and again in 1978. Under Suharto, Indonesia ended the Sukarno policy of hostility toward Malaysia, reopened relations with the West, and slowly improved economic conditions.

Malaysia and Singapore Malaysia gained its independence from Great Britain in 1957. In 1963, Malaysia united with Singapore and northern Borneo (BOR-nee-oe) to form the *Federation of Malaysia*. The Federation, however, faced ethnic difficulties. The majority of the population were Malays, who controlled the government. The rest of the population consisted of Chinese, who controlled most of the business and wealth, and a small percentage of Indians. Fearful that the Chinese, who dominated Singapore, would try to control the government, the Malays forced Singapore to secede from the Federation in 1965.

India Achieves Independence Nationalism had developed among the people of India before World War I. But two factors held back the growth of nationalism: lack of unity among the various regions of India, and hostility between Hindus and Muslims. India supported Britain during World War I, expecting to receive self-government in return. Britain, however, only gave India partial powers. This caused great unrest among the Indians, and a movement toward independence began.

Independence Leaders The greatest leader of the Indian independence movement was **Mahatma Gandhi** (muh-HAHT-muh GAHN-dee) also called Mohandas. Gandhi tried to bring Hindus and Muslims together. He preached civil disobedience, fasting, and nonviolent protest as the means of resisting British rule in India. Another Hindu leader in the struggle for independence was **Jawaharlal Nehru** (jah-wuh-HAHR-lal NAY-roo), who would become India's first prime minister. The Muslim leader for independence was *Muhammad Ali Jinnah* (JIN-uh). He became spokesman for the Muslim minority in India and maintained they were actually a separate nation.

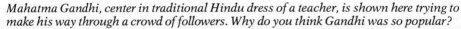

Mahatma Gandhi, center in traditional Hindu dress of a teacher, is shown here trying to make his way through a crowd of followers. Why do you think Gandhi was so popular?

India Is Divided   The struggle of Hindus and Muslims for independence from Britain had reached a critical point by the beginning of World War II. The British promised independence for India after the war if the Indians joined them in their fight against Japan. The British kept their promise. In 1946, the British government proposed that India become a federal union made up of states. But Jinnah and the Muslims rejected this and demanded separate Hindu and Muslim nations. Ill-will between Muslims and Hindus erupted in riots and disorders, causing the British to leave India and turn political power over to two governments, one Muslim, one Hindu. Thus, in 1947, British India was partitioned into the independent nations of India, containing mostly Hindus, and Pakistan, containing mostly Muslims. (See the map on page 579.)

Following this division, more than 10 million people fled their homes for fear of religious persecution, making their way to either Muslim or Hindu territory. Unfortunately, riots broke out between the Hindus and Muslims because of religious intolerance, and thousands were killed. At this point, Gandhi spoke out for religious toleration. In 1948, he was shot to death by a Hindu who disagreed with his views.

Nehru Governs an Independent India
Nehru was prime minister of the new Indian republic from 1950 until his death in 1964. Nehru successfully annexed colonial territories in India still held by Portugal. However, he met humiliating defeat when he tried to retake territory claimed by both India and China, creating deep-seated hostility between the Indians and the Chinese. Nehru also failed to settle India's dispute with Pakistan. In 1965, a short war broke out over disputed territory,

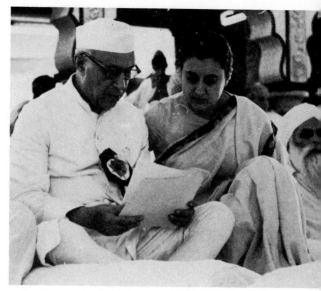

India's president Jawaharlal Nehru is giving a speech on non-violence at a luncheon in Bombay. He is sitting at a dais with his daughter, Indira, and some officials. How long was Nehru Prime Minister of India?

which caused Indian-Pakistani relations to worsen.

India Becomes a Major Power
When Nehru died in 1964, India's Congress chose a successor, *Lal Bahadur Shastri* (LAL BAH-huh-dur SHAH-stree). When Shastri died in 1966, Nehru's daughter, **Indira Gandhi** (in-DIR-uh GAHN-dee), became India's prime minister. Under her leadership, India became a major power. However, she could find no quick solution for India's overpopulation and poverty. In the 1970's, India suffered from political disunity, strikes, and disorder. Hundreds of political murders and serious food shortages occurred in 1972. In some places provincial governments collapsed, and the national government had to take over. These conditions led Prime Minister Gandhi to declare a state of emergency in 1975, which gave

577

Indira Gandhi

Indira Gandhi, the only child of Kamala (kuh-MAY-luh) and Jawaharlal Nehru, was born in the northern Indian city of Allahabad (AL-uh-huh-bad) in 1917. She spent a great deal of her childhood at her family home of Anand Bhavan, which means "abode of joy." Her early years were greatly influenced by her grandfather Motilal (MOTE-ul-ahl) and by Mahatma Gandhi, a frequent visitor. Both Indira's father and grandfather were committed to India's nationalist movement and, because of this, Indira was constantly surrounded by political activity while she was growing up. One experience during those years that left its mark on her was sitting, at age four, on the lap of her grandfather during his trial by the British for treason.

Indira left India to attend Oxford University in England. She returned after her graduation and in 1942 she married Feroze (FER-ose) Gandhi (no relation to Mahatma Gandhi). Shortly thereafter, they were both imprisoned for their active involvement in the campaign to free India from Britain's rule. Most of Indira's family had at one time or another been imprisoned for the same reason. After India gained its independence, Feroze Gandhi became a lawyer and newspaper executive and a member of independent India's Parliament. Indira and Feroze had two sons, Rajiv (RAH-jeev) and Sanjay (SAN-jaye).

After Indira's father became India's first prime minister in 1947, she served as his hostess. When her husband died in 1960, Indira spent all of her time and energy helping her father. After her father's death in 1964, Indira became the Minister of Information and Broadcasting.

In January of 1966, Indira became the third prime minister of independent India. She assumed office at a critical time in India's history. The nation was in the midst of a two-year drought. This resulted in severe food shortages and a deepening economic crisis. She persevered and was again elected in 1972. During both terms, Indira faced major problems in the areas of food production, population control, land reform, regulation of prices, unemployment, and industrial production.

Indira Gandhi's problems, however, only became greater by 1975. An Indian court found her guilty of using illegal practices during her 1971 election campaign. She appealed the decision. Fearing chaos in the country, she imposed almost-dictatorial rule. She had the Indian Supreme Court suspend the right of **habeas corpus.**

As a result of her actions, she was defeated in the parliamentary elections of March, 1977. In 1978, she was again elected to Parliament but was imprisoned for allegedly blocking a probe of her son Sanjay's 1975 business dealings. She was soon released, and in 1980 she again became India's Prime Minister.

1. What goals did Indira Gandhi try to achieve for India? What problems did she face as Prime Minister?
2. How were her actions undemocratic?
3. Should the suspension of civil liberties, such as freedom of speech or the right of **habeas corpus,** ever be imposed?

her the power to arrest her political opponents, restrict freedom of the press, and to control prices and industrial production.

Prime Minister Gandhi was severely criticized in 1976 for her actions during the time of emergency rule. Her supporters claimed her actions were the only means available to prevent the complete breakdown of Indian society. However, opposition to Prime Minister Gandhi increased until, in 1978, *Morarji R. Desai* (MORE-uh-jee duh-SIE) replaced her as prime minister. After Prime Minister Gandhi's fall from power, a government investigation began to look into the question of her improper use of power during her emergency rule. Desai restored political freedom, and some of Prime Minister Gandhi's unpopular measures were abolished. In 1979, however, with problems of food distribution, floods, droughts, and religious conflict, the government of Desai resigned. The new government lasted only three weeks. Then in January 1980, Indira Gandhi became prime minister for the second time.

Pakistan Is Divided Pakistan became an independent nation in 1947, when it was separated from India. Pakistan, however, was divided into

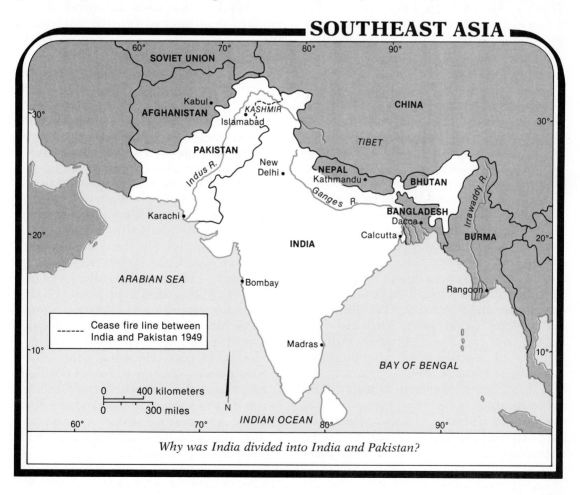

SOUTHEAST ASIA

Cease fire line between India and Pakistan 1949

Why was India divided into India and Pakistan?

two regions that were 1,600 kilometers (1,000 miles) apart. (See the map on page 579.) This division caused problems in governing. The eastern part of the country wanted a greater share in the government. In 1971, civil war broke out. The rebels wanted to become independent from West Pakistan. Because of the continued dispute with the Pakistani government, India decided to back the rebels of East Pakistan. By 1971, there was full-scale war between Pakistan and India. Pakistan lost control of its eastern lands, made peace with India, and East Pakistan became *Bangladesh* (bang-gluh-DESH).

China's "Great Leap Forward" By the mid-twentieth century, China was one of the three great powers of Asia, along with India and Japan. In the 1950's, China was faced with the Soviet Union's refusal to help it industrialize. Chairman Mao Tse-tung then decided to follow Stalin's example of the 1920's and industrialize without foreign help. To improve China's output of agricultural products, land was taken from the peasants and huge government-owned farms called *communes* were created. This agricultural increase would provide the capital that was needed to establish heavy industry in China. The Chinese people, however, were asked to work longer hours at lower wages and to make other sacrifices in order to industrialize their country. This plan was called the **"Great Leap Forward."** It turned out to be a terrible failure. China's production did not increase and the Chinese were forced to buy food from Western countries to avoid famine.

Conflict in China In the aftermath of the Great Leap Forward, some leaders within the Chinese Communist party began to question Mao's leadership. The party slowly divided into Maoists and anti-Maoists. One of the questions that divided them was whether it was more important to be a dedicated communist or to be an expert. Maoists insisted that the most important qualification for a job any man or woman could have was a knowledge of the communist doctrine. Anti-Maoists disagreed. It didn't matter to them how dedicated to communism someone was so long as he or she had skills that could be used to help modernize China. There were many other issues on which Maoists and anti-Maoists differed. By the early 1960's, anti-Maoists had gained control of important positions within the party and the government. Mao was now criticized and ridiculed openly.

China's Great Proletarian Cultural Revolution To recapture control in China, Mao and his supporters launched the *Great Proletarian Cultural Revolution*. Because the army refused to take sides, Mao organized high school and college youths into the *Red Guards*. They held huge rallies, demonstrations, and marches. Schools were shut down, and the teachings of Mao Tse-tung were used as a guide to all situations.

Mao's opponents tried to organize their own Red Guards, but they had little success. They found no effective way to fight Mao. Mao's appeal to the masses for support was apparently successful. Many of his opponents gave up the positions they held and were replaced by Maoists. Because of the growing number of clashes between the Red Guards and the peasants, the Chinese Army had to step in to disband the Red Guards and restore order. China's industry then began to pick up and schools were reopened.

The Chinese government sent out dance groups, such as the one above, to teach about Mao and communism. How is media used today to spread political beliefs?

Shortly thereafter, China's policy toward the United States took a dramatic turn. After Chinese-Soviet border struggles, the Soviet Union became the great enemy of the Chinese, and China sought detente with the United States. (See page 553.) President Nixon visited China in 1972 in the spirit of detente.

After Mao's death in 1976, a power struggle developed. The struggle was won by a group of leaders who hoped to modernize China rapidly. They also favored better relations with non-communist countries. In 1979, the United States established diplomatic relations with the People's Republic of China, opening the door to increased trade between these two nations. By 1982, *Hu Yaobang* (HOO YOW-BAHNG) was leader of the Chinese Communist Party and *Zhao Ziyang* (JOW ZIH-YAHNG) head of China's government.

SECTION REVIEW

1. Mapping: Using the map of the Far East in the Atlas, describe the geographic features of the following: Malaysia, Vietnam, the land through which the India-China border runs, Bangladesh. How are geography and a nation's power related?

2. In your own words, identify: Sukarno, Suharto, Mohandas Gandhi, Nehru, Indira Gandhi, communes, the Red Guards, the "Great Leap Forward."

3. What are the reasons for hostility between India and Pakistan?

4. Why was the Great Proletarian Cultural Revolution launched in China? Was it successful? Explain.

When making a judgement about another person, what do you consider more important: what he or she believes or the abilities he or she possesses? Explain.

chapter 35

Africa and the Modern World

EUROPEANS IN AFRICA

The modern history of Africa is closely intertwined with the history of the European exploration of that continent during the 1800's. Indeed, exploration, and not conquest, stimulated European interest in the continent. By 1875, much of Africa had been explored by the Europeans. Adventurers such as Mungo (MUN-goe) Park, Henry M. Stanley, Sir Richard Burton, Heinrich Barth (BAHRT), John Hanning Speke (SPEEK), and René Caillié (ruh-NAY kay-YAY) brought information back to Europe about Africa. For example, Europeans discovered Mounts Kilimanjaro and Kenya during the late 1840's and the source of the Nile in the early 1860's. Malaria, an infectious disease generally transmitted by the bite of an infected mosquito, kept many explorers and prospective colonists away. But in 1854, when it was learned that quinine from South America was an effective drug for combating the deadly effects of the disease, the pace of exploration and colonization quickened.

Perhaps one of the best examples of the hazards that the European explorers faced can best be illustrated by the example of an English adventurer, Henry Stanley. It was reported that when he explored the Congo River dur-ing the 1870's—now called the Zaire River—he lost 69 men through disease, 14 by drowning, and 58 through battle and murder. There were 8 who starved to death, one who was caught by a crocodile, and 13 listed only as "missing."

The British in East and West Africa
Before 1875, most European countries lacked interest in colonizing vast areas of Africa because it was considered too costly. Most of the Europeans who went to Africa during the mid-nineteenth century were scientists and explorers, or missionaries and physicians. The only major efforts by European countries to gain control over any sizable areas of African land prior to 1880 were made by Great Britain and France. As the British began to commit themselves to maintaining trade links with West Africa, they also began to exert their influence, especially in Nigeria (nie-JIR-ee-uh). During the 1850's, the British forced local Nigerian rulers to send raw materials to the seacoast where they could be bought and sold by British traders. The French did much the same in Senegal (sen-ih-GAWL) during that period.

Sayyid Said   British efforts to control trade in East Africa were especially evident in the area stretching from Mombasa (mahm-BAHS-uh) in Kenya to the Mozambique (moe-zam-BEEK) border. (See the Atlas.) During the early 1800's, the region had been under the control of an Arab sultan named *Sayyid Said* (SIE-yid SED). He had built a vast empire from the sale of East African slaves, cloves, and ivory. The ivory and cloves were usually shipped to Great Britain and India. The slaves were sold to Arab plantation owners in Zanzibar (ZAN-zuh-bahr), French sugar producers on the islands off Madagascar (mad-uh-GAS-ker), or to sheikhs in Arabia.

Many nations, including Great Britain, took steps in the early 1800's to abolish slave trading. In 1822, the British forced Sultan Said to restrict much of his slave trade. In return, the British agreed to use their navy to protect him from foreign invasions. When the sultan died in 1856, the British split his empire into two parts, Muscat (MUS-kat) and Zanzibar, placing a sultan over each. Thereafter, British officials in Zanzibar justified their control of Said's empire by stating that they were controlling the slave trade.

The British in Egypt   The British also expressed an interest in the northeastern part of Africa—Egypt. The location of the Suez Canal along its eastern border provided a vital trade link from the Red Sea to the Mediterranean. The British feared that another nation might seize Egypt and along with it, take over the Canal. So the British intervened and gained control of Egyptian affairs in 1882. (Refer to page 456.)

Europeans Colonize Africa   Large-scale European imperialism in Africa began in 1884 when *Otto von Bismarck* (BIS-mahrk), the German chancellor, called a conference at Berlin. The *Berlin Conference*, which lasted from November 15, 1884, to February 25, 1885, was attended by fourteen Euro-

Explorer Henry M. Stanley is shown here preparing for an expedition into Africa's interior. What supplies were necessary for this kind of trip?

pean nations. (See page 464.) Plans were made at the conference for the completion of European colonial conquest of Africa. Each country claimed rights to part of Africa and rules were made for future occupation of the coasts. (See the map on page 455.) During the thirty years following the Berlin Conference, European nations tightened their grip on the African continent. Most of Africa remained within that grip until the middle of the twentieth century.

Europeans Reap Africa's Riches   At the Berlin Conference, it became clear that European countries could take great riches from the African continent even in the face of African resistance. After dividing Africa among themselves, the European colonial powers began harvesting the wealth of gold, salt, copper, rubber, diamonds, ivory, palm oil, cocoa, and spices in Africa.

Under the Berlin arrangements, the Congo was recognized as an independent state, open to all nations for trade. The Congo, however, was put under the control of *King Leopold II* of Belgium. The Congo, an area about eighty times the size of Belgium, was prized by Leopold as a potentially rich source of rubber and copper. Leopold and Belgium were soon reaping vast profits from the exploitation of the Congo's natural resources. This was all done at the expense of native Africans living there.

The British in South Africa   In the area farther south were the *Afrikaners,* whom the British called the *Boers.* They were descendants of the first Dutch and Flemish (people from northern Belgium) settlers to come to South Africa in 1652. The Boers were mainly farmers and cattle raisers. The southern tip of Africa, the Cape Colony, had been under the protection of the Dutch until 1814, when Great Britain gained control after the Napoleonic Wars. In 1834, Britain abolished slavery in this area, thereby freeing all the slaves owned by the Boers.

During the following two years, the Boers, who were angered by this and other British measures, moved across the Orange River onto the high grassy plains called the *veld* (VELT). Their *Great Trek* resulted in the establishment of several independent republics. Already living in those republics were the Bantu people. The Bantu were no match for the well-armed Boers and were soon defeated. Those who moved northeast of the Cape Colony had to contend with the more warlike Zulu people. After winning a series of battles, the Boers established the Republic of Natal (nuh-TAL). This area, however, soon became a British colony. Other Boers established the republics of Transvaal (trans-VAHL) in 1852 and the Orange Free State in 1854.

The Boer War   For a short time, there was peace between Britain and the new republics. *Cecil Rhodes*, the British diamond-mine millionaire and industrialist, established a trade empire in South Africa. In 1890, he became Prime Minister of the Cape Colony. Rhodes wanted to expand the Cape Colony northward. However, the Boer republics stood in his way. When he encountered opposition from the Boers in 1895, he sent his own private troops against the Boers. Because of his actions, British Parliament forced Rhodes to resign. Three years later, the British annexed territory claimed by the Boers. The annexation resulted in the Boer War of 1899–1902. The Boers surrendered in May 1902 when they signed the Treaty of Vereeniging (vooh-RAY-nih-ging). The republics then became British colonies.

As a goodwill gesture, the British allowed the Afrikaners to decide if the right to vote should be extended to Black Africans in the two Boer states that were now controlled by the British. The Afrikaners, however, believed in White supremacy: they thought that Whites were superior to Blacks. This is sometimes known by the Afrikaners term, **apartheid** (uh-PAHR-tide). Under apartheid, Blacks are not allowed to vote in elections or hold any important or high governmental or business positions. These privileges are reserved for the White minority. Blacks are also forced to live in areas separate from those inhabited by Whites, and their movements are severely restricted. The Afrikaners, therefore, denied the right to vote to the Black Africans. When Britain created the Union of South

The Boer farmers on the right are shown surrendering to the British, thus ending the Boer War in 1902. Why do you think the British displayed such military might?

Africa in 1910, it allowed the Boers partial self-rule under British supervision. Despite the limitations of this system, the Boers joined with other Whites in denying all South African Blacks the right to vote or to serve in any high government office.

Britain's Colonies Grow   The English had other imperialistic plans during this period. They began to extend their African colonial empire southward from Egypt. In 1898, an English-Egyptian army under *Lord Horatio Kitchener* advanced into the Sudan and defeated all African opposition. During the fighting, about 20,000 Sudanese lost their lives. Soon afterward, England also gained control of Uganda, East Africa, and Rhodesia. To the west, the British acquired the Gold Coast, Sierra Leone, and Nigeria.

Other European Nations Move into Africa   While Belgium and England consolidated their colonial gains in Africa, other European countries completed the process of European colonization of Africa on the eve of World War I.

Portugal had tight control on Angola (ang-GOE-luh), Guinea, and Mozambique, while France had taken the greater part of the African continent above the equator, especially in the Sahara, and West Africa. The French Foreign Legion, an army composed largely of European volunteers, controlled areas of the Sahara, including Algeria. Germany controlled German West Africa, and Italy had gained control of Eritrea (ar-ih-TRAY-uh) along the Red Sea, Somaliland (soe-MAHL-ee-land) on the eastern coast of Africa, and Libya on the shores of the Mediterranean Sea. Spain retained its earlier claims to Rio de Oro (REE-oe day OE-roe) on the Atlantic side. By 1914, European colonization of Africa had been completed. (See the map on page 455.)

Germany's defeat in World War I only slightly rearranged the pattern of European colonialism in Africa. Parts of Germany's Togoland and Cameroons (kam-uh-ROONZ), for example, were divided between Britain and France, and Germany's East African possessions were split between Britain which received Tanganyika (tan-gun-YEE-kuh), and Belgium which acquired Ruanda-Urundi (roo-ahn-duh-uh-ROON-dee).

Years of Protest   In the 1900's, European policies of colonialism and imperialism had brought railroads, reading, writing, modern medicine, technology, Christianity, and commerce rapidly into Africa. Many Africans were forced into European ways of life.

Blacks Around the World Protest European Imperialism   Most Africans, however, were unconvinced of the desirability of European ways. They were joined by sympathizers from the Americas. To them, the European colonization of Africa had been accomplished at the expense of most native Africans. This became even more evident when a number of conferences were held during the early part of the twentieth century to protest European suppression of independent African voices and ambitions.

The first of these conferences met in London in 1900. It was attended mainly by delegates from the United States and the West Indies. Led by the noted Black American scholar, *W.E.B. Du Bois*, the delegates protested English treatment of non-Whites especially in South Africa and Rhodesia. Protests about the condition of Blacks in those countries focused on the continued policy of White supremacy there.

Another prominent promoter of Black African rights was *Marcus Garvey*, a native of Jamaica who had moved to the United States. He founded the Universal Negro Improvement Association and African Communities League. Garvey called upon all Africans and Black Americans to take pride in their ancient heritage. In the 1930's, W.E.B. Du Bois and Marcus Garvey were among the most prominent spokespeople for African rights. Both urged Africans to follow the lead of Liberia (which had become an independent nation in 1847) and free themselves of European domination.

SECTION REVIEW

1. Mapping: Using the map of Africa in the Atlas, describe the physical geography of South Africa. Why do you think many Europeans settled there?

2. In your own words, identify: Berlin Conference, Afrikaners, Great Trek, Cecil Rhodes, W.E.B. Du Bois, Marcus Garvey.

3. What is apartheid? How has it affected the lives of Black Africans living in South Africa and Rhodesia?

▷ What would happen in your community if a law were passed stating that all left-handed people would have to attend schools separate from those attended by right-handed people?

This sign illustrates one of the many apartheid laws that exist in South Africa today. Do you think it will be hard for people living there to change their ways?

INDEPENDENCE AND CONTINUED STRIFE

As many African countries continued their fight for independence, the continent's population increased. In 1940 Africa had about 150 million people. In 1950 it had 200 million, and by 1980 it had 470 million. By the year 2000 it could have 850 million.

Ethiopian Independence Ethiopia (ee-thee-OE-pee-uh) was one of the first African nations to become completely free of European domination. With the aid of Great Britain, Ethiopia recovered its independence during World War II by defeating Mussolini's (moo-suh-LEE-nee's) occupation forces. Its leader, Emperor *Haile Selassie* (HIE-lee suh-LASS-ee), ruled until he was overthrown in 1974 by the army. The military take-over was led by Ethiopian nationalists who were dissatisfied with Selassie's rule. The military put Haile Selassie under house arrest until he died in 1975. General *Teferi Benti* (tuh-FER-ee BEN-tee) became head of state. He devoted much of 1975 and 1976 to the nationalization of Ethiopia's major industries. Benti ruled until he died in 1977 when the provisional government separated into two factions.

The Eritreans Revolt When Benti came to power he had to face a revolt by Eritrean (ar-uh-TRAY-un) nationalists. (See the map on page 588.) The Eritreans had been part of an Italian colony until 1941 when Britain took control. In 1952, Eritrea became an autonomous, or self-ruling, state within Ethiopia. Eritrea lost its autonomous standing in 1962 when it fell completely under the rule of Ethiopia. This led many Eritreans, who are mostly Arab Muslims, to protest by engaging in guerrilla warfare against the

Muammar el-Quaddafi came to power in Libya in 1969. What are some possible causes for Libya's hostility towards its neighbor Egypt?

Ethiopian government. By the 1970's, the Eritreans received support and training from the Palestine Liberation Organization (PLO) and from Libya in their attempt to become an independent nation. Ethiopia has had the backing of the Soviet Union and Cuba. Fighting continued between Eritrea and Ethiopia into the 1980's. In August of 1982 Ethiopia also began a Soviet-backed war with Socialist Somalia in an attempt to gain control of the Horn of Africa.

Libya Libya, like Eritrea, is a mainly Arab state. It obtained its independence from Italy in 1943. Until receiving full national status in 1951, it

HORN OF AFRICA

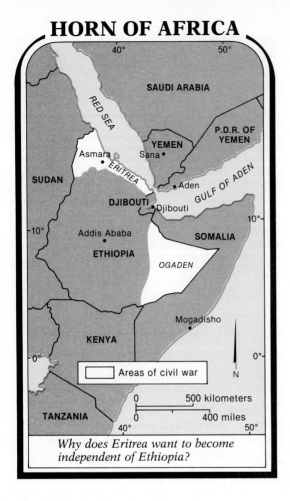

Why does Eritrea want to become independent of Ethiopia?

Areas of civil war

500 kilometers

400 miles

N

ample, the government used this new-found wealth to develop irrigation systems, to electrify power works, to import needed goods, and improve transportation and communication systems.

Other North African Nations Win Independence Tunisia and Morocco became free of French rule in 1956. Trouble between Morocco, Mauritania (mor-uh-TANE-ee-uh), Algeria (see page 590), and Spanish Sahara erupted in the latter part of 1975. In February 1976, Juan Carlos (WAHN KAHR-lose) of Spain ceded the province of Spanish Sahara to Morocco and Mauritania. The area became known as Western Sahara, which is bordered by Morocco, Mauritania, and Algeria. The southern part was claimed by Mauritania and the northern part by Morocco. Algeria and some of the people living in Western Sahara opposed this partition. They wanted to decide their own destiny. Conflicts in the region erupted and continued during the 1970's and 1980's. An Algerian-backed group of guerrillas, called the *Polisario* (pol-ih-SAHR-ee-oe) *Front*, continued to attack the forces of Mauritania and Morocco. Mauritania withdrew from the fighting in 1979 and gave up its claim to the territory. Morocco continued to fight in the 1980's.

Egypt Efforts by Egypt to achieve independence proved to be more complicated. In 1914, Egypt had become a protectorate of Great Britain. Pressure by the Egyptian nationalists forced Britain to declare Egypt a partially free state in 1922. But the British reserved the right to protect the Suez Canal and provide for the defense of Egypt. In 1936, Britain and Egypt agreed to an alliance. All British troops and officials were to withdraw from Egypt except those in the Suez Canal zone. After World War II, Egypt canceled the 1936

was under Allied and United Nation's control. In 1951, Muhammad Idris (ID-ris) became king. He ruled until 1969 when he was overthrown by military officers led by *Muammar el-Quaddafi* (MOO-uh-mar el kah-DAH-fee). Quaddafi supported various terrorist activities in other countries and was in conflict with the foreign policy of the United States. He also launched attacks against Egypt and Chad.

Until oil was discovered in 1959, Libya was a poor country. Today it is one of the largest oil producing nations. This unexpected wealth was used to improve the Libyan way of life. For ex-

agreement with Britain. When Nasser became head of the Egyptian government in 1954, he seized control of the Suez Canal, thereby eliminating the last remnant of British control in Egypt. (See page 545.) Two years later, Sudan, Egypt's neighbor to the south, also became a free and independent state with England's agreement.

Ghana During the twentieth century, Ghana (GHAH-nuh) was the first of the predominantly Black African states south of the Sahara to achieve independence. *Kwame Nkrumah* (KWAH-may n'KROO-mah), its first president, studied in the United States during the 1930's and 1940's. While in the United States, he was influenced by the writings and teaching of Marcus Garvey. Once Ghana became independent of British colonialism in 1957, Nkrumah began a policy of support for all Black African nations still seeking freedom from foreign domination. He organized the *Conference of Independent African States* (CIAS) in 1958. Its original membership included Ethiopia, Liberia, Libya, Morocco, Sudan, Tunisia, and Egypt. Like later, similar organizations of African countries, the CIAS sought ways to achieve total African independence in politics, trade, and government. Its counterpart today is the *Organization of African Unity* (OAU).

In 1958, Kwame Nkrumah organized the Conference of Independent African States. This photo shows a member of the Conference addressing the rest of the organization. What has this group achieved since its formation?

Nkrumah did much to better his country. He introduced health and welfare programs, improved living and economic conditions, and expanded the educational system. Nkrumah's efforts failed because of corruption in his government, large national debts, and his own self-importance. In 1966, he was overthrown by a nationalist military coup. Several other military governments have ruled Ghana since then.

Algeria　France gained control of Algeria in 1848. Algeria was regarded as a part of France, not as a colony. The French citizens living in Algeria, however, felt they were not given the same rights as those living in France. For reasons similar to those the British colonists in America had given in 1776, many Algerians began to call for independence from France. Some of the Algerian nationalists resorted to acts of terrorism. They called themselves the *Front de Libération Nationale* (National Liberation Front). This caused political upheaval in France over the issue of independence for Algeria. After attempts to satisfy the Algerian nationalists failed, President de Gaulle of France had to let Algeria become an independent state in 1962. A large majority of the French people approved of de Gaulle's decision. *Ahmed Ben Bella*, Algeria's first head of state, was overthrown in a military coup in 1965. After that, the country came under the leadership of *Houari Boumedienne* (hoo-AHR-ee boo-med-YEN). Boumedienne's political party continued to rule following his death in 1979.

Comoro Islands Gain Independence　France lost part of its eastern African holdings when three of the four main Comoro (KAHM-uh-roe) Islands declared their independence in July 1975. Three of the islands, Grand Comoro, Anjouan (ahn-ZHWAHN), and Mohéli (moe-AY-lee), had a predominantly Muslim population. A fourth island, Mayotte (muh-YOT), composed mainly of Christians, voted to remain under French rule and protection.

Kenya Achieves Independence　While West and North Africans were occupied with freeing themselves of European rule, other Africans were also heeding the advice given by Du Bois and Garvey. One of them was *Jomo Kenyatta* (JOE-moe ken-YAH-tuh). He was a member of the **Kikuyu** (kee-KOO-yoo) people of Kenya.

Since 1922, the British had been allowing White settlers to take most of the fertile lands belonging to the Kikuyu. When Kenyatta's protests about this policy were ignored by the British, he is believed to have organized a terrorist organization called the *Mau Mau*. During the early 1950's, the Mau Mau threatened the lives of many White settlers. However, they killed many more Blacks who supported British colonialism than they did Whites. Kenyatta was captured by the British in 1959 and charged with leading the terrorist group. He was imprisoned until 1961. When Britain withdrew from Kenya in 1963, Kenyatta became Kenya's first prime minister. In 1964, he became president and served until his death in 1978. Daniel T. arap Moi (MOY) became president in 1978.

Other British Colonies Achieve Independence　During the 1960's the British also withdrew from the southern part of Africa. Malawi (mah-LAH-wee) and Zambia (ZAHM-bee-uh), which had been part of Nyasaland (nie-AH-suh-land) and Northern Rhodesia, became independent in 1964. Botswana (bote-SWAH-nuh), formerly Bechuanaland (beck-WAH-nuh-land), achieved its statehood in 1966. Tanganyika (tan-guh-NYEE-kuh) became free in 1961 and Zanzibar (ZAN-zih-bar) in 1963. In 1964, these two nations merged and became Tanzania (tan-ZAY-nee-uh). Swaziland (SWAH-zee-land), at one time under the joint rule of South Africa and Britain, became a new country in 1968.

Uganda   In the eastern part of Africa, the British granted Uganda (oo-GAHN-duh) independence in 1962. *Apollo Milton Obote* (oe-BOTE-ee) became prime minister, and in 1967 Uganda became a republic. Obote was overthrown by the Ugandan Army in 1971. Major General *Idi Amin Dada* (EE-dee AH-min DAH-duh) became the new head of government. Soon afterward, Amin imposed numerous restrictions on most of the non-Black Africans living there. The group most affected by this action were the 40,000 Asian-Africans whose ancestors had immigrated to Uganda during the 1800's. Amin also ordered all Israeli economic and military advisers to leave the country.

Uganda Under Amin   As leader of Uganda, Amin abolished the legislature and did away with all political opposition in the country. To do this, Amin's troops killed anyone who stood in his way. As a result, over 100,000 unarmed and defenseless Ugandans—men, women, and children—were killed, including 50,000 who belonged to the same ethnic group as his enemy, former Prime Minister Obote.

In 1972 and 1973, Amin received financial aid from the United States. At the same time, Amin expelled visitors from the United States, jailed Peace Corps volunteers, and wrote insulting letters to then President Richard Nixon. Later, he helped some PLO

Idi Amin Dada ruled Uganda from 1971 to 1979. He committed many atrocities during this time. Why do you think he was able to rule for so long?

members seize and hold hostage a number of Israelis when the PLO highjacked an airplane. The hostages were rescued by the Israelis in a daring raid on the Entebbe (en-TEB-bee) airport. The United States severed its ties with Uganda because of Amin's actions.

Idi Amin, however, was not stopped by any of this. In 1978, he provoked a war with neighboring Tanzania. That country fought back. During early 1979, Tanzania invaded Uganda and, with the aid of Ugandans opposed to Amin's rule, drove him from power and into exile.

591

When Amin was overthrown, the people of Uganda celebrated in the streets. How do you think their lives were changed by his overthrow?

After Amin fled in exile to Saudi Arabia, people learned what atrocities had occurred during his rule. Torture chambers were discovered filled with hundreds of corpses. The main place where the tortures, mutilations, and murders occurred was right below the presidential mansion. Amin had justified his actions by forming the *State Research Bureau*. The purpose of this organization was to protect the state from its suspected enemies by any means necessary.

After Amin had gone into exile, the party in power was the *Uganda National Liberation Front*. The leader was former Prime Minister Milton Obote. The new ruling group favored a mixed socialist-capitalist economy. Democratic elections were promised by 1981, but those elections did not take place right away. **Conflict in the Congo** Other countries began to follow Britain's lead in the decolonization of Africa during the early 1960's. Guinea (GIH-nee) became independent of French rule and

Somalia (soe-MAHL-yuh) of Italian domination in 1960. In the same year, Belgium also granted the Congo its freedom.

Congolese (KONG-goe-leze) independence touched off a civil war that was to last for five years. One of the main reasons for the civil war was that during the years Belgium ruled the Congo, it had given the Congolese almost no training in Western forms of government. As a result, most Congolese felt more loyalty to their ethnic groups than to the nation. The various ethnic groups of the Congo had long been hostile to each other and violence soon broke out on a large scale. The province of *Katanga* (kuh-TANG-guh), an area rich in copper mines, withdrew from the Congo under the leadership of *Moise Tshombe* (MWAHZ SHOM-bay) in 1960. United Nations troops were sent to restore order and to put down the Katanga revolt. Finally in 1963, UN troops put an end to the Katanga secession. The UN troops stayed for another year at the cost of almost half a billion dollars. When the UN troops left in 1964, violence erupted again. The United States sided with the government of the Congo. The Soviet Union and the People's Republic of China sided with the government of Katanga. At one point, the Katanga rebels seized some Europeans and a few Americans as hostages and killed them. The United States then supplied planes to Belgian paratroopers in order to rescue others trapped in Katanga. Order was finally restored in 1965, when General *Joseph Mobutu Sese Seko* (moe-BOO-too SAY-say SAY-koe) staged a military coup. In 1971, Mobutu proclaimed that the Democratic Republic of the Congo would be known as the *Republic of Zaire* (zie-IR). (See the Atlas.)

President Mobutu Sese Seko's problems continued throughout the 1970's. Rebels from the Lunda (LOON-duh) group in the Shaba (SHAH-buh) province, calling themselves the *National Front for the Liberation of the Congo* (FNLC), used bases in Angola to attack places in Zaire. President Carter charged that the FNLC had Cuban-trained soldiers. With help from France, Belgium, and Morocco, the forces of Zaire succeeded in pushing the guerrillas back to Angola. Yet the FNLC continued to seek the overthrow of President Mobutu Sese Seko's government.

Civil War in Nigeria   Even more terrible than the Congolese conflict was the tragedy that struck Nigeria in the early 1960's. Nigeria has the largest population of all the nations in Africa. Soon after Nigeria became independent of British rule in 1960, it was faced with the problem of unifying a country with over 250 different ethnic groups. Two of the largest of these groups were the **Hausa,** in the northern part of the country, and the **Ibos,** in the east. The Ibos were the better educated of the two. After independence, many Ibos went north where they moved into most of the better government jobs. The Hausa, fearful of too much rule by the Ibos, staged a military take-over of the government. Bloody riots resulted, and most of the Ibos retreated to the eastern part of the country.

In the civil war that resulted, the Hausa massacred thousands of the Ibos. The Ibos separated from Nigeria and formed the *Republic of Biafra.* In January 1970, after months of bloody civil war, Biafra surrendered to the Nigerian government leaving about one million persons, mostly Ibos, homeless and starving. After Biafra sur-

The civil war in Nigeria left many homeless and starving. These Biafran children are shown waiting for food at a distribution center. Should foreign countries send supplies to war-torn countries?

rendered many Ibos were allowed to participate in military-run Nigerian politics. But most of those who held government jobs were later dismissed from service. Even in the mid-1970's, the ruling Hausa people and the Ibos continued to harbor ill feelings toward one another. In 1976, Nigeria had another military coup. This coup failed but the head of state, General *Mohammed*, was killed. General *Olusegun Obasanjo* (oe-LOO-say-goon oe-BAH-sahn-joe) then took control of the government. President Obasanjo, however, did allow the election of a national assembly in 1977 to draft a new constitution for the country. In 1979, after thirteen years of military rule, Alhaji Shehu Shagari (ahl-HAH-jee SHAY-hoo shuh-GAHR-ee) became president.

Portuguese Pull Out of Africa   Black nationalism and guerrilla warfare had spread to the Portuguese colonies of Angola in 1961, Guinea in 1962, and Mozambique in 1964. Antonio de Spinola (speen-OE-luh), the new president of Portugal, began making his country's African colonies independent. Guinea-Bissau (GIH-nee bis-OW) became a free nation in 1974. Angola and Mozambique received the right to rule themselves in 1975, and the Cape Verde Islands were given independence in that same year.

Mozambique, and especially Angola, had to adjust to a new life after achieving independence. Mozambique became a Marxist state. Angola ended years of guerrilla warfare with a broader conflict, between two regular armies, to decide which of two opposing groups would rule the new nation. That issue was settled in 1976 when Soviet-backed Cuban troops gained control of that country. A Marxist government was established

with *Agostinho Neto* (ahg-os-TEEN-oe NET-oe) as president. By 1982, *Jose Dos Santos* (hoe-ZAY dose SAHN-tose) was president of Angola. However, the guerrilla attacks continued and were led by *Jonas Savimbi* (JOE-nas sah-VIM-bee), head of the *National Union for the Total Independence of Angola* (UNITA).

South Africa   By the mid-1970's, the number of White-dominated countries in southern Africa had been reduced to Rhodesia (which had been called Southern Rhodesia) and South Africa. After years of unrest, White nationalists succeeded in creating the independent Republic of South Africa in 1961. Their new government continued the policy of apartheid (see page 584) in a country with a population of over 18 million Blacks, 4 million Whites, and 2 million people of mixed backgrounds. The latter, called Cape Coloreds, are a mixture of German, French, Malaysian, and Black. South Africa also contains about 650,000 Asian-Africans. Protests against apartheid were quickly suppressed, often by violent means. Numerous dissenters were also placed in prison. In 1974, for example, the South African government had an estimated 800 political prisoners in its jails. Most were Black nationalists.

The UN Fights Apartheid   Because of apartheid, the United Nations approved an arms **embargo** against South Africa. An embargo is said to exist when a government forbids its citizens to engage in commerce with another nation or nations. The embargo had little effect. The United Nations also attempted to free Namibia (formerly South-West Africa) from South African rule. The UN wanted to place Namibia under its trusteeship until its independence could be brought about in an orderly manner. Yet South

UNIVERSAL DECLARATION OF HUMAN RIGHTS

The United Nations adopted the Universal Declaration of Human Rights in December, 1948. The declaration outlines the basic civil, political, social, and economic rights and freedoms that every person on earth should have. The purpose of the declaration is to serve "as a common standard of achievement for all peoples and all nations." As you read the following excerpts from the declaration, see how many are familiar to you.

All human beings are born free and equal in dignity and rights.

Everyone is entitled to all the rights and freedoms set forth in this Declaration, without distinction of any kind, such as race, color, sex, language, religion, political or other opinion, national or social origin, property, birth or other status.

No one shall be held in slavery or servitude; slavery and the slave trade shall be prohibited in all their forms.

Everyone has the right to an effective remedy by the competent national tribunals for acts violating the fundamental rights granted him by the constitution or by law.

Everyone has the right to freedom of movement and residence within the borders of each state.

Everyone has the right to seek and to enjoy in other countries asylum from persecution.

No one shall be arbitrarily deprived of his nationality nor denied the right to change his nationality.

Men and women of full age, without any limitation due to race, nationality or religion, have the right to marry and to found a family.

Everyone has the right to freedom of thought, conscience and religion; this right includes freedom to change his religion or belief, and freedom, either alone or in community with others and in public or private, to manifest his religion or belief in teaching, practice, worship and observance.

Everyone has the right to take part in the government of his country, directly or through freely chosen representatives.

Everyone has the right to rest and leisure, including reasonable limitation of working hours and periodic holidays with pay.

Everyone has the right to education. Education shall be free, at least in the elementary and fundamental stages.

1. What is the purpose of the Declaration of Human Rights?
2. What rights guaranteed in the declaration above do we have in the United States?
3. Do you think all people have these rights? Explain, using two examples.
4. What other rights do you think should be added to this list? Why?

Africa, despite a UN resolution, continued to control the affairs of Namibia. South Africa's Prime Minister, *John Vorster* (VORS-ter), rejected the UN proposal. He argued that it favored the *South-West African People's Organization* (SWAPO), an Angola-backed, Black nationalist movement fighting South African rule in Namibia. In 1978, elections were held in Namibia. The results gave a victory to a coalition of Whites and moderate Blacks, all backed by South Africa. Due to poor health and increased rumors of political scandal, Vorster resigned his office in 1978 and was succeeded by *Pieter W. Botha* (BOTHE-uh), who also supported apartheid. Botha ordered raids by South African troops into Angola. The raids were designed to eliminate SWAPO guerrilla strongholds along the Namibia border.

Rhodesia   Rhodesia, the only other White dominated country in southern Africa, successfully rebelled against British rule in 1965. Rhodesia followed the White-supremacy policy of neighboring South Africa. The British, however, refused to accept their independence and proposed a United Nations economic boycott on Rhodesia. The boycott, to which many countries including the United States agreed, was to end only when a majority of the Rhodesian population—of which seven million are Black and only 260,000 are White—is given the right to vote and hold public office. This boycott was lifted late in 1979 when Britain and Rhodesia reached a settlement.

Efforts to end all-White rule in Rhodesia resulted in a series of agreements reached in 1978 between Rhodesia's Prime Minister *Ian P.*

To end the all-White rule in Rhodesia several meetings occurred between a representative of Britain, Rhodesia's Prime Minister Ian P. Smith, and Rhodesia's Black leaders. How else could Rhodesia's problems have been solved?

Smith, a White, and three Black leaders: *Abel Muzorewa* (moo-zuh-RAY-wuh), a bishop of the United Methodist Church, *Ndabaningi Sithole* (n'duh-BAH-nin-gee sit-OLE-ee), and Chief *Jeremiah Chirau* (CHIR-ow). Their agreement, which went into effect in 1979, allowed parliamentary elections in which all Rhodesians eighteen years and older could vote, job security for White civil servants, adequate repayment for any seizure of private property by the new government, and 28 percent of the seats in the new parliament reserved for Whites. The latter allowed the Whites in the new parliament to be able to veto constitutional amendments or laws that sought to overturn such safeguards. The new country became known as *Zimbabwe* (zim-BAHB-wee) *Rhodesia.* Bishop Muzorewa became Prime Minister of its government.

The Patriotic Front   Opposition to the new government continued from many Black guerrillas. Their leaders were Joshua Nkomo (n'KOE-moe) and Robert Mugabe (moo-GAHB-ee). Both led groups of about 50,000 guerrilla fighters generally called the *Patriotic Front* (Zimbabwe African National Union or ZANU, and Zimbabwe African People's Union or ZAPU) with bases in neighboring Mozambique and Zambia. The United States, the United Nations Security Council, and nearly all the other African countries also opposed the new government. This opposition focused mainly on the fact that the Patriotic Front had not been included in the agreement. The United States

government also pointed out that in the election Whites could vote twice and Blacks only once. However, about 65 percent of the nearly 3,000,000 people eligible to vote did participate in the election. Then, late in 1979, Britain decided that Zimbabwe would again become a British colony. It remained so until elections for a new government were held in February 1980. Robert Mugabe won this election with a large majority.

SECTION REVIEW

1. Mapping: Using the map of Africa in the Atlas, locate those nations that follow a policy of apartheid. Do you think their location has had an influence on their policy of apartheid?

2. In your own words, identify and state the significance of: Kwame Nkrumah, Jomo Kenyatta, National Liberation Front, Idi Amin, Moise Tshombe, Joseph Mobutu Sese Seko, Ian Smith, John Vorster, Hausas, Ibos, Kikuyu.

3. What was especially tragic about the independence movements in the Congo and Nigeria?

4. What serious problems did South Africa and Zimbabwe continue to face in the 1980's?

▷ What problems would be faced by the region in which you live if it declared its independence from the nation of which it is now a part? Would independence bring any benefits to your region? Explain.

Reviewing the Unit

Unit Summary

After you have read the selection below, answer the questions that follow it. Much of what occurred during the early twentieth century in the United States was related to the severe financial depression of 1929–1937. The depression ended when World War II began.

During World War II and well into the 1960's, the United States experienced astonishing social change and rapid economic growth. After 1945, civil rights became a national issue and many minority groups began to gain additional rights and legal guarantees.

In the 1970's, the Watergate Affair resulted in the resignation of President Richard Nixon. Watergate uncovered political corruption, but it also demonstrated that our political system works to correct itself. Other problems such as rising unemployment and federal budget deficits remained in the 1980's.

During the post-World War II era, the United States continued to be active in foreign affairs. The United States aided war-torn Europe and became involved in conflicts in Korea (1950–1953) and Vietnam (1960–1975). By the 1980's, the United States was tenuously maintaining "peaceful co-existence" with the Soviet Union and Communist China.

During the mid-twentieth century, United States' involvement in the Middle East focused mainly on achieving a peaceful settlement between Israel and its neighbors. Israel was involved in numerous conflicts with its Arab neighbors.

Elsewhere in the world, Latin American countries during the 1930's were forced to seek greater economic self-sufficiency. Many did, but in the process many turned to rule by military dictators. Cuba, for example, became communist when Fidel Castro gained power in 1959.

India, on achieving independence in 1947, experienced great religious turmoil between Muslims and Hindus. Indira Gandhi, who ruled most of the years from 1966 to the present, was criticized for the methods she used to try to modernize India. The social and economic struggles continue.

Of all the continents, Africa experienced the greatest change during the mid-twentieth century. Once colonial rule ended, dozens of new nations emerged. South Africa continued its White segregationist policies, and many African nations were ruled by dictators.

Developing Your Reading Skills

1. What do you think are four main points stressed in this reading? List those points.

2. In what ways is the twentieth century better than the nineteenth century? Explain.

Developing a Sense of Time

Examine the time line below and answer the questions that follow it.

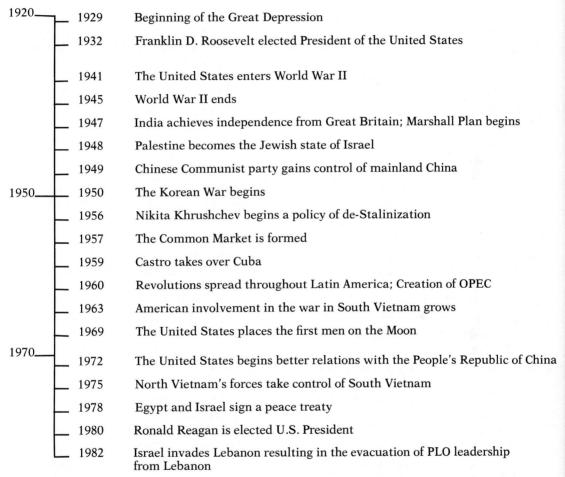

1920		
	1929	Beginning of the Great Depression
	1932	Franklin D. Roosevelt elected President of the United States
	1941	The United States enters World War II
	1945	World War II ends
	1947	India achieves independence from Great Britain; Marshall Plan begins
	1948	Palestine becomes the Jewish state of Israel
	1949	Chinese Communist party gains control of mainland China
1950	1950	The Korean War begins
	1956	Nikita Khrushchev begins a policy of de-Stalinization
	1957	The Common Market is formed
	1959	Castro takes over Cuba
	1960	Revolutions spread throughout Latin America; Creation of OPEC
	1963	American involvement in the war in South Vietnam grows
	1969	The United States places the first men on the Moon
1970	1972	The United States begins better relations with the People's Republic of China
	1975	North Vietnam's forces take control of South Vietnam
	1978	Egypt and Israel sign a peace treaty
	1980	Ronald Reagan is elected U.S. President
	1982	Israel invades Lebanon resulting in the evacuation of PLO leadership from Lebanon

1. How many years after the Great Depression began did the United States enter World War II?
2. Which events on this time line are directly related to Asia? to Africa? to Latin America?
3. List three other key events from Unit 10 that could be added to this time line and give a reason for selecting each.
4. List two conclusions that you can form about America's foreign policy from the information on your time line.

Recalling the Facts

1. List and explain three important social and economic developments that happened in the United States during the twentieth century.
2. Describe United States involvement in Asia after World War II.
3. Briefly describe the Arab-Israeli conflicts. Why did they occur?
4. Briefly describe relations between the United States and the Soviet Union, the United States and China, and China and the Soviet Union during the second half of the twentieth century.
5. Briefly describe the problems of three Latin American countries in the twentieth century.
6. Explain how India gained its independence.
7. How was Pakistan created?
8. What was the Great Leap Forward? Was it successful? Explain.
9. What do you think has been the most important development in Africa during the twentieth century?

Using Your Vocabulary

1. Define the following: inflation, OPEC, Good Neighbor Policy, Peace Corps, peaceful coexistence, de-Stalinization, ERA, Common Market, apartheid, NATO, Boers, embargo.
2. What does PLO stand for? What is its purpose?
3. Who are the boat people?
4. What do the words *foreclosure* and *mortgage* have to do with the Great Depression?
5. What does detente mean? What is the relationship between detente and the SALT treaties? Explain.
6. How can the term *imperialism* apply to an event discussed in Unit 10? Cite the event and tell how the term applies to it.
7. How can the term *nationalism* apply to an event noted in Unit 10? Explain using an example.
8. How would you define the word *history*? What examples would you use to illustrate your definition.

Using Your Geography Skills

1. Using the map on page 533 and the information on pages 566–568, tell what area of the world came under the U.S.S.R.'s domination by 1958.
2. Using the maps on pages 536 and 540 and the information on pages 535–542, describe the areas of Asia that were at war during the period 1950–1980.
3. Using the map on page 544 and the information on pages 543–548, describe the areas of controversy from 1948 to 1982 between Israel and its neighbors.
4. Using the map of Africa in the Atlas and the information on pages 587–597, tell which countries of Africa had become independent of colonial rule by 1980.
5. Our physical world has not shrunk in size. What then do you suppose is meant by the saying, "In modern times our world has become smaller."

Developing Your Writing Skills

Someone once wrote that "history is concerned not only with the past but also with the relation between past and present." Think about that as you consider the following.

FORMING AN OPINION

1. Is history only concerned with the past?
2. Should history be concerned with other things?

SUPPORTING AN OPINION

3. Do you think history should concern itself only with the past or with the relationship between the past and present? Answer in a paragraph or essay, beginning with the completion of the following topic sentence:

History should concern itself with _____

Why Study the Past?

Choose two of the ten worlds of human history you have studied in this book and tell how you think someone living in each of these historical worlds would have defined the word *history*. What examples would they have given to illustrate these definitions? Do you think the people living in the two historical worlds you chose have agreed with your definition of history? Explain. What do you think of the words, "history can have different meanings for people living at the same time or at different times in history"? Answer these questions in a brief paragraph.

Your History Bookshelf

For current information about your world, consult your local newspapers; television and radio news programs; national news magazines such as *Time, Newsweek,* and *U.S. News and World Report;* the *Hammond Medallion World Atlas* and the *Oxford World Atlas;* the *People's Almanac; National Geographic Magazine; Natural History Magazine;* the *Information Please Almanac.* You may want to ask your teacher to write to the following companies for catalogs of audio-visual materials that can be shown in your classroom:

BFA
Division of Phoenix Films, Inc.
468 Park Avenue S.
New York, New York 10016

Hartley Film Foundation, Inc.
Cat Rock Road
Cos Cob, Connecticut 06807

International Film Foundation
475 Fifth Avenue
New York, New York 10017

National Geographic Society
Washington, D.C. 20036

Time Line

	1000 B.C.	100 A.D.	1000	1100	1200	1300	1400	1500
		500	1050	1150	1250	1350	1450	1550

Unit 6

- Cushites seize control of the area from the Nile to Palestine
- Iron working begins in West Africa
- Aksum opens largest ivory market in northeastern Africa
- Bantu migration begins
- Ghanaian people master the art of ironworking
- Muslims conquer Africa, north of Sahara
- Ghana declines
- Mali becomes the most powerful state in West Africa
- Songhai controls the western Sudan
- Kongo Kingdom flouris
- Christopher Columb sails to the New Worl
- Vasco da Gama ma voyage around the Ca of Good Hope

Unit 7

- Mayas begin to move north into the Yucatan peninsula
- Post-Classic period of Mayan civilization begins
- Incas establish Cuzco
- Papal Line of Dema is declared
- Cortes sails fo
- Cortes defeats
- Council of the Indies establish
- Verrazano ex coast of North

Unit 8

Unit 9

Unit 10

602

- Portuguese begin importing African slaves into Brazil
- Slave trade is outlawed by most European and American governments

- Spanish settle St. Augustine, Florida
- Portuguese slave trade flourishes
- Jamestown, Virginia settled by the British
- Quebec settled by the French
- Dutch driven out of Brazil by the Portuguese
- French lose their colonies in the Americas

- American Declaration of Independence written
- Storming of the Bastille in France
- Louis XVI executed and the Reign of Terror begins in France
- Napoleon crowns himself emperor
- Battle of Waterloo in Belgium
- Mexico becomes independent
- Monroe Doctrine issued by President James Monroe
- Decembrist Revolt occurs in Russia
- Revolution in France
- Crimean War begins in the Balkans
- Civil War begins in America; Alexander II frees the serfs in Russia
- Revolt in Russia; Duma established
- Nicholas II abdicates the throne in Russia; Bolsheviks overthrow the Provisional Government

- China goes to war against Britain and France
- Victor Emmanuel II becomes king of Italy; French troops invade Mexico
- New German nation proclaimed at ceremonies held at Versailles
- Russo-Japanese War begins
- Revolution in China
- Munich Conference held
- World War I begins
- Nazi-Soviet alliance formed; Germany invades Poland
- Pearl Harbor attacked
- United Nations established
- World War II ends

- Beginning of the Great Depression
- North Vietnam forces take control of South Vietnam
- New Deal program begins
- India gains independence; Marshall Plan begins
- Palestine becomes the Jewish state of Israel
- Chinese Communist party gains control of mainland China
- Egypt/Israel sign peace treaty
- President Sadat of Egypt is assassinated
- Korean War begins
- Nikita Khrusnchev begins de-Stalinization in the USSR
- Castro takes over Cuba
- Yuri Andropov becomes Secretary of the Communist party in the USSR
- Revolutions spread throughout Latin America; OPEC created
- United States begins better relations with People's Republic of China

BOOK of READINGS

chapter 1 Early Peoples of the Middle East

LAW IN THE ANCIENT MIDDLE EAST

The period between 3000 B.C. and 300 B.C. was a time of development and change in the Middle East. Religions and governments became more organized. As life grew more complicated, rulers and their subjects found it necessary to write down the laws of their society. Many of these laws are now part of our present-day legal system. As you read, see how many of these ancient laws are similar to those we have today. How can you account for the differences?

1. Code of Hammurabi

Hammurabi was the most famous of the Amorite kings of Babylon. During his rule, laws were set down in a uniform way. Such a uniform set of laws is called a code. The Code of Hammurabi, and others like it, later formed the basis for our own government by law. Selections from Hammurabi's Code follow.

If a man accuse a man, and charge him with murder, but cannot convict him, the accuser shall be put to death.

If a man robs and be captured, that man shall be put to death.

If there were a loss of life, the city and governor shall pay silver to [the dead person's] heirs.

If a man neglect to strengthen his dike, and a break be made in his dike, and he let the water carry away farmland, the man in whose dike the break has been made shall restore the grain which he has damaged.

If he be unable to restore the grain, they shall send him into slavery and sell his goods, and the farmers whose grain the water has carried away shall divide the results of the sale.

If a man take a wife and do not draw up a marriage contract with her, that woman is not a wife.

If a man make his wife a present of field, garden, house, and goods, and deliver to her a sealed deed, after the death of her husband her children may not make any claim against her. The mother after her death may give them to her child whom she loves, but she cannot give them to a brother.

If a man strike his father, they shall cut off his hand.

If a man destroy the eye of another man, they shall destroy his eye.

If he break a man's bone, they shall break his bone. Adapted from: J. M. Powis Smith. *The Origin and History of Hebrew Law*. trans. D. D. Luckenbill. Chicago: The University of Chicago Press, 1931.

1. Which two of the following do you think are the main points of these selections from Hammurabi's Code? Explain your choices.
   a. Amorite laws stressed the importance of contracts.
   b. Amorite laws usually called for payment of some kind from those convicted of unlawful acts.

c. Amorite laws dealt only with accused murderers and robbers.

2. Which one of these laws do you regard as the most harsh? Which one of these laws do you regard as the most fair?

3. What do these laws tell you about Hammurabi and the people he ruled? Explain.

4. Is it important to have a written set of laws? Explain your answer.

5. List any laws in our society that are similar to those in Hammurabi's Code.

2. Hebrew Laws

Like most other peoples of the ancient Middle East, the Hebrews had their own laws. Most of those laws can be found in the Old Testament of the Bible. Some examples of the Hebrew laws follow.

I am Jehovah your God who rescued you from slavery in Egypt

Never worship any god but me.

Never make idols: don't worship images, whether of birds, animals, or fish.

Honor your father and mother (remember, this is a commandment of the Lord your God); if you do so, you shall have a long, prosperous life in the land he is giving you.

You must not murder.

You must not commit adultery.

You must not steal.

You must not burn with desire for another man's wife, nor envy him for his home, land, servants, oxen, donkeys, nor anything else he owns.

Adapted from: "Deuteronomy 5," *The Living Bible Paraphrased*. Wheaton, Ill.: Tyndale House, 1971.

1. Which two of the following do you think are the main points of these selections?

a. Hebrew law did not stress religious beliefs.

b. Hebrew law placed great importance on the family and property rights.

c. Hebrew law stressed absolute obedience to the worship of its God.

2. Which one of these laws do you regard as the most important? Why?

3. Do you think these laws can tell us something about what the ancient Hebrews valued? Explain.

4. Which of these laws are similar to those we have today? How can you explain the similarity?

607

Think about the two sets of laws you have read: those of Hammurabi and those of the Hebrews. Then explain why you do or do not believe that a society must have laws in order to survive. Give examples from the laws you have read to support your answer. You may also wish to look up other laws, either ancient or modern, to support your response.

chapter 2 The Egyptians

LIFE IN ANCIENT EGYPT

Have you ever thought how we know so much about the Egyptian past or the past of any people for that matter? Or have you ever stopped to think how such knowledge relates to our lives today?

You have been reading descriptions of life in ancient Egypt written by the authors of this book, two modern historians. Now you will examine writings by the ancient Egyptians themselves. These writings have been translated into modern English. They will give you a closer look at Egyptian life. Historians have used such evidence to form their interpretations of ancient Egyptian life.

3. A Vizier's Autobiography

Accounts people have written of their lives are a source of evidence about the past. The following selection is taken from the autobiography of a vizier who lived during the New Kingdom. Read the selection, and then answer the questions which follow.

I came to the pharaoh's place in colorful clothing. My household rejoiced over me. Eventually, I was summoned into the presence of the good god, Pharaoh Thutmose III. May he live forever.

Then His Majesty spoke these words before me: "I know that decisions are many and there is no end to them and the judgment of cases never ceases. Act as I say. Arm yourself. Be strong in action. Do not weary. Accuse evil."

I acted as he had ordered. He gave me a court of justice under my authority. And none could overrule me. I judged poor and rich alike. I rescued the weak from the strong. I opposed the rage of the angry. I defended the husbandless widow. I gave bread to the hungry, water to the thirsty, meat and oil and clothes to those who had nothing. I relieved the old man, giving him my staff, causing the old women to say, "What a good action!" I was innocent before God. No one who knew me said, "What has he done?" I judged great matters. I caused both parties to leave my court in peace. I did not use justice for a reward. I was not deaf to the empty-handed. I never accepted anyone's bribe. I was clever in all matters, deliberate in counsel, ready to listen. I was skilled in past cases. And what had happened yesterday helped me to know tomorrow.   Adapted from: Norman de Garis Davies. *The Tomb of Rekh-mi-Re at Thebes*. New York: Metropolitan Museum of Art Egyptian Expedition Publications, Metropolitan Museum of Art, 1943.

1. Which two of the following do you think were the main things expected of a vizier in ancient Egypt? Explain your selections.
   a. Honesty
   b. Greed
   c. Fairness
2. Did the vizier think of himself as a just man? How do you know?
3. Why would the vizier's autobiography be useful to historians?
4. How could your autobiography be used by a historian? Explain.

4. Egyptian Medicine
Scholars have learned a great deal about Egyptian life through information found written on papyrus or clay tablets. The following selection on Egyptian medicine was written by a doctor who may have lived 4,000 years ago. It is the earliest known scientific document.

If you examine a man with a wound in his head which penetrates to his skull bone but does not have a gash, you should clean the wound. If you find that the skull is not injured and does not have a crack in it, you should say: "I will treat someone who has a wound in his head with a gash in it."

You should bind the wound with fresh meat the first day. Then treat it with grease, honey, and lint every day until the man recovers.

If you examine a man with a break in his collarbone and you find his collarbone short and separated, you should say: "I will treat a man with a break in his collarbone."

You should place the man flat on his back with something folded between his two shoulder blades. You should spread out his shoulders in order to stretch apart his collarbone until the break falls into place. You should make him two wooden splints. You should put one of them on the inside of his upper arm and the other on the under side of his upper arm. You should bind it and treat it with honey every day until the man recovers.   Adapted from: James Henry Breasted. *The Edwin Smith Papyrus*. Chicago: The University of Chicago Press, 1930.

1. Which two of the following do you think best describe the instruction to physicians in ancient Egypt? Explain your answers.
   a. Vague
   b. Detailed
   c. Indifferent
   d. Kind
2. What could this medical document tell historians about life in ancient Egypt?
3. Could medical records be used as evidence by someone writing a history of the period in which you live? Explain.

5. Egyptian Proverbs
Proverbs are another source of information about life in ancient Egypt. They too have been found written on papyrus or clay tablets, or carved on the walls of temples and tombs. The following selection contains examples of ancient Egyptian proverbs believed to date back as far as 1700 B.C.

Beware of robbing a poor woman.

Do not let yourself be involved in a wicked deed, and do not seek the company of one who has done it.

Sleep a night before speaking.

If you are not greedy, you will find riches beyond your expectations.

Do not cover a foot of another's land, nor destroy the boundaries of your defenseless neighbor's land.

Do not trample the plowed fields of another.

Cultivate the fields so that you may find what you need, and receive the bread of your own threshing floor.

A bushel that [a] god gives you is better than five thousand obtained by force or theft.

If stolen riches are brought to you, do not spend the night with them.

Do not rejoice over stolen riches, nor groan over poverty.

The boat of the greedy is left in the mud, while the boat of those who are satisfied sails with the breeze.

The strong arm is not softened by using it to frighten someone.

The back is not broken by bending it.

Do not curse one older than you, for he has seen much more than you. Adapted from: F. L. Griffin, ed. "The Teaching of Amenophis," *Journal of Egyptian Archaeology* (XII, 1926).

1. Which two of the following do you think would best characterize the purpose of such proverbs? Explain your selections.
   a. Seek to be law-abiding.
   b. Seek to be greedy.
   c. Seek to be content with what one has.
2. Which of these proverbs seems sensible to you? Why?
3. What do you think a historian could learn about life in ancient Egypt by studying these proverbs?
4. "Easy come; easy go," and "Do unto others as you would have them do unto you," are two proverbs commonly heard today. Can you think of any others? List them. How could these short bits of wit and wisdom be used as evidence by someone writing a history of you and your way of life?

REVIEWING READINGS 3–5

1. List the ways in which these writings show what the ancient Egyptians believed and what they thought was important.
2. Why do you think it is important to study writings like these from the ancient Egyptians? Why do you think historians are interested in what a people believed and thought was important?
3. What other writings can you think of which future historians might examine to find out what you believed or what your daily life was like?

Did you know that in 3000 B.C. the world population was 100 million? That is less than half the population of the United States today!

chapter
3 The Early Indians

WOMEN IN THE ANCIENT FAR EAST

You have studied the ancient Far Eastern civilizations—the empires, the cultures, and the contributions of each. In your study, you probably discovered that with the exception of the empresses in early Japan and Empress Wu in early China, men played the key roles in ruling the empires. What, then, was the position of women in these societies? How were they expected to act? And what was the attitude toward them? Think of these questions as you read the following selections on the daily life of women in ancient India, China, and Japan.

6. A Guide for Married Women

Like most information about life in ancient India, knowledge of the daily lives of women was passed down through the ages in the form of epic tales or in religious books. The following is a selection from a volume of literature sacred to the Hindus. Its age is uncertain, but parts of it may be 2,000 years old. The selection instructs Hindu women on proper conduct for a married woman.

A woman has no other god on earth than her husband. The most excellent of all good works she can perform is to gratify him with the strictest obedience. Her husband may be crooked, aged, sick or offensive in his manners. Let him be a drunkard or a gambler. Let him live without honor. Let him be deaf or blind. His crimes and his sickness may weigh him down but his wife shall never regard him as anything but her god. She shall serve him with all her might, obey him in all things, see no defects in his character, nor give him any cause for concern.

A woman is created to obey. First she yields obedience to her father and mother. When married, she obeys her husband, father-in-law, and mother-in-law. In old age she must be ruled by her children. During her life she can never be under her own control.

She must be careful in her domestic work, watchful over her temper, and

she must never envy what belongs to another. She must always be serene.

If her husband laughs, she ought to laugh. If he weeps, she will weep also. If he is disposed to speak, she will join in conversation. When her husband sings, she must be in ecstasy. If he dances, she must view him with delight. When in his presence, she must always be gay. There must be no gloom or discontent. Thus is the goodness of woman's nature displayed.

She never notices whether any other man is young or handsome. Nor does she hold conversation with him.

If her husband goes away and bids her go with him, she shall follow. If he bids her to stay, she shall stir nowhere during his absence. There shall be no bathing. She shall not clean her teeth, nor cut her nails, nor eat more often than once a day. She shall not wear new attire until his return.

Her husband may threaten her. He may use harsh language. He may unjustly beat her. But under no circum-stance shall she speak any but meek and soothing words. Laying hold to her husband's hand, she should beg his forgiveness. There shall be no thoughts of deserting her home. Adapted from: J. A. Dubois. *Description of the Character, Manners, and Customs of the People of India.* London: Longman, Herst, Rees, Orme, and Brown, 1817.

1. Which three of the following do you think reflect the main points in this reading? Defend your selections.
   a. The husband was head of the household.
   b. Education of children was the mother's responsibility.
   c. Men and women in early India were not considered equals.
   d. Married women were supposed to be homemakers.
2. Do these instructions seem fair and just to women? Cite specific examples to explain your answer.
3. How do your own views on the conduct of married women compare with those expressed in this selection?

chapter

4 The Early Chinese

7. A Parting
If the theory that many of the anonymous poems of early China were written by women is true, then poetry is indeed a very valuable resource. Through poetry we can understand how early Chinese women viewed their role in society. The following poem was taken from a long poem written anonymously between 200 and 300 A.D. According to the poet, the story told actually took place.

"At thirteen I knew how to weave silk.
At fourteen I learned how to sew.
At fifteen I could play the small lute.
And at sixteen I knew how to sing well.
At seventeen I was made your wife and moved into your parents' house.
From care and sorrow my heart was never free thereafter,
For you cared for nothing but your work.
I was left alone.

It was not often that we two were together.
From dawn till night I toiled and got no rest.
And yet the Great One, my mother-in-law, scolded me for being lazy.
Husband, I find it hard to be your wife in your parents' house.
For it is not in my power to do all the tasks I am given!
Go then, quickly, speak to your mother
Or let me go back to my home!"
Her husband listened to her words,
Then went to his mother's room.
"Mother," he said,
"Luck was with me when I took this girl for my wife.
We have lived here and served you for two years or three.
In nothing has the girl offended you or done you wrong.
What has happened to bring trouble between you?"
Then spoke his mother:
"Come, my son, such love is foolish.
Your wife neglects all rules of behavior
And in all her ways follows only her own whim.
I have long been displeased with her.
Send her away quickly, Do not let her stay."
Her son knelt down before her and pleaded:
"Bowing before you, Mother, I make a promise.
If you send her away
I will live single all the days of my life.
I shall take no other wife!"
When his mother heard these words
She flew into a rage.
"Little son, are you not afraid
To dare answer me by praising your wife?
You have forfeited all my love and kindness.
Do not dream that I will let you have

your way."
He did not speak;
Twice he bowed and went back to his room.
He lifted up his voice to speak with his young bride.
But the words would scarcely come.
"It is not I that would send you away.
It is my mother."
The young wife spoke:
"Give me no more of this talk.
Long ago, when it was Spring,
I came to your grand home.
I obeyed my mother-in-law in every task.
Day and night I hurried on with my work,
Caught in endless toil.
Never in word or deed was I at fault.
I waited on madam's every need.
Yet now she seeks to send me away.
It is no use to talk of anything else.
These things are my possessions:
A bed canopy of red gauze
And many wooden boxes, so many that none is like another.
And in the boxes, many things.
If I am vile, my things must be vile, I am sure.
They will not be worth keeping for your next wife.
Yet I leave them here. They may come in handy
As presents for your next wedding.
Husband, we shall not meet again.
Once in a while let me have news of you,
And let us never forget one another."
Adapted from: William H. McNeill and Jean W. Sedlar, eds. "A Peacock Flew," *Classical China.* New York: Oxford University Press, 1970.

1. **Which of the following expresses the main point? Defend your answer.**
   a. The husband was head of the household in early China.

b. One's elders were greatly respected.

c. It was considered a disgrace to be unmarried.

d. Parents could not interfere with their children's marriage.

2. Why did the wife leave her husband? How did the husband react to her leaving?

3. What role do parents play today in their children's lives after they are married?

chapter

5 The Early Japanese

8. The Diary of Lady Murasaki

Wouldn't it be exciting to be able to delve into the secret thoughts of someone who lived centuries ago! The following is a selection from the diary of Lady Murasaki (moohr-uh-SAHK-ee), the famous Japanese novelist who was a lady in the court of Japan around 1000 A.D. Read what she felt about the behavior of the women in the court and about her lonely life as a young widow.

Among the younger ladies at court I think Dodayu and Genshikibu are beautiful. Each has some good points and few entirely bad. It is very difficult for anyone to possess qualities like prudence, charm, wit, and rightmindedness all at once! As to many ladies at court, the question is whether they excel most in charms of mind or of person! It is hard to decide. It is wicked, indeed, to write so much of others.

Our lovely queen, of perfect mind, is reserved. She believes that persons who are forward cannot avoid social blunders. When very young, our queen was much annoyed to hear people saying vulgar things with conceit. So she always favored modest ladies who made no mistakes. Childlike persons pleased her very well. This is why the ladies of the court have become so reserved.

Having no excellence within myself, I have passed my days without making any special impression on anyone. The fact that I have no husband who will look out for my future makes me sad.

My room is ugly. I stand my musical instrument against the wall between the cabinet and the door. On either side of the instrument, a pair of bookcases have in them all the books of my dead husband. When I am bored, I take out one or two of his books. Then my maids gather round and say, "You will not live to old age if you do such a thing as read! Why do you read? Reading is not encouraged for good women." They rebuke [criticize] me behind my back. I have heard them and I have wished to say, "It is far from certain that one who avoids forbidden things enjoys a long life!" But it would be undignified to speak thus to the maids.

Adapted from: William H. McNeill and Jean W. Sedlar, eds. "The Diary of Lady Murasaki," *China, India, and Japan.* New York: Oxford University Press, 1971.

1. Which one of the following do you think was the main point Lady Murasaki tried to make when she wrote this in her diary? Defend your selection.
   a. Humility and modesty are important for women.
   b. Women should be well educated.
   c. Women should have equal rights with men.
   d. There is no need for women to be educated.
2. How important do you think Lady Murasaki's husband was in her life? Explain your answer.
3. In what respects might Lady Murasaki be considered a modern woman? Cite examples to explain your answer.
4. Why might your diary be useful to a historian studying twentieth-century society years from now? Explain.

REVIEWING READINGS 6–8

1. What do these selections tell us about the role of women in the ancient Far East?
2. What possible reason can you give for the similarities in attitude toward women in early India, China, and Japan?
3. Why do you think a society may find a need to establish an unwritten code of behavior for people? Are there any examples of such an unwritten code for women in your society? Why or why not?

Did you know that in 400 B.C. there were 30 million people in China, 30 million in India, and 30,000 in Japan? This is only slightly more than half the population of present-day Japan alone!

chapter 6 The Ancient Greeks

LIFE OF THE ANCIENT GREEKS

Ancient Greek civilization blossomed between 800 and 300 B.C. During these years, new developments emerged in art, religion, science, literature, philosophy, and government. After the conquests of Alexander the Great, Greek influence spread throughout western Europe, the Near East, and over time to the rest of the world. As you read the following selections, see if you can recognize the Greek ideas and beliefs that have affected your society's way of life.

9. The Athenian Way of Life

It was the Greek custom to have an important person make a speech at public funerals. When the citizens of Athens gave a public funeral for the first men who died in the Peloponnesian War, Pericles (PER-uh-kleez), the leader of the government of Athens during that time, was chosen to speak. In the following excerpt from his speech, Pericles expresses pride in the Athenian way of life and compares it to that of the Spartans.

I shall begin with our ancestors. It is both just and proper that they should be mentioned first on this occasion. They lived in this country without break from generation to generation, and handed it down free to the present time by their bravery. And if our more distant ancestors deserve praise, much more do our own fathers, who added to their inheritance the empire that we now possess. Our country has furnished us with everything that can enable it to depend on its own resources, whether for war or for peace. But what was the road by which we reached our position of empire? What was the form of government under which our greatness grew? These are the questions which I shall try to answer before I proceed to my thoughts about these dead men.

Our government favors the many instead of the few. This is why it is called a democracy. If we look to the laws, they afford equal justice to all in their differences. Poverty does not bar the way. If a man is able to serve the state, he is not prevented from doing so by how poor he is. The freedom which we enjoy in our government extends also to our ordinary life. There we do not feel called upon to be angry with our neighbor for doing what he likes. But all this ease in our private relations does not make us lawless as citizens. Against this fear is our chief safeguard, teaching us to obey the judges and the laws, particularly such as regard the protection of the injured.

Further, we provide plenty of means for the mind to refresh itself from business. We celebrate athletic games and sacrifices to the gods all year round.

If we turn to our military policy, there also we differ from our enemies. We throw open our city to the world. And never exclude foreigners from any opportunity of learning or observing. In education, where the Spartans from their very cradles seek manliness by painful discipline, at Athens we live exactly as we please. And yet are just as ready to meet every danger. In proof of this it may be noticed that the Spartans do not invade our country alone, but bring with them all their friends. We Athenians advance unsupported into the territory of an enemy, and fighting upon a foreign soil, usually defeat with ease men who are defending their homes.

We place the real disgrace of poverty in the failure to struggle against it. Our public men have their private affairs to attend to. Our ordinary citizens, though occupied with business and farming, are still fair judges of public matters. We Athenians are able to judge all events and think of discussion as a necessary introduction to any wise action at all.   Adapted from: Zeph Steward, ed. *The Ancient World: Justice, Heroism and Responsibility.* Englewood Cliffs, N.J.: Prentice-Hall, 1966.

1. Which two of the following would best describe how Pericles felt about the Athenian way of life? Defend your selections.
   a. It was dictatorial.
   b. It was democratic.
   c. It allowed people to better themselves.
   d. It was military-dominated.
2. According to Pericles, what is the definition of democracy? Cite an example from the selection.
3. If people in the future were to study the government of your society, what opinions would they probably form of your way of life?

10. Another Opinion About Life in Athens

Pericles died in 429 B.C., only a few years after the beginning of the Peloponnesian War. An undisciplined and uneducated rabble-rouser named Cleon succeeded him as political leader of Athens. The following selection on democracy was written by an unknown Athenian during Cleon's rule. What do you think may have influenced this person's views of the Athenian way of life?

First of all I shall say that in Athens the poor and the common people seem to have the advantage over the well-born and the wealthy. It is the common people who provide sailors for the fleet and who have brought Athens to her power rather than the infantry and the well-born and wealthy citizens.

Some folks are surprised that everywhere the government allows the rascals and the poor rather than the good, well-born citizens to rule.

In every land the well-born and the wealthy are opposed to democracy. Among the wealthy and well-born there is very little injustice and very great thought as to what is worthy. While among the common people there is very great ignorance and disorder. For poverty tends to lead them to what is disgraceful, as does lack of education and the ignorance which befalls some men as a result of lack of wealth.

It may be said that the common people ought not be allowed to make speeches or sit on the Council, but only those of the highest capability and quality. As it is, anyone who wants to, a rascally fellow perhaps, gets up and makes a speech.

For it is the wish of the common people that they should have freedom and be in control. They don't care about disorder. From what you consider lack of order come the strength and liberty of the common people itself. If on the other hand you investigate good order, first of all you will see that good laws come from the well-born and wealthy. The well-born and wealthy will keep the rascals in check, refusing to allow madmen to sit on the Council or make speeches or attend the general assemblies. This indeed would very soon throw the common people into complete slavery. Adapted from: *The Old Oligarch, Being the Constitution of the Athenians Ascribed to Xenophon.* trans. James A. Petch. New York: Oxford University Press, 1926.

1. Which two of the following statements agree with this writer's opinion of democracy in Athens? Defend your selections.
   a. It was supported by the ignorant.
   b. It was favored by the well-born and the wealthy.
   c. It was disorderly.
   d. It was used by the well-informed common people.
2. Who do you think the author of this selection felt should rule Athens? Why do you think this person felt this way?
3. How does this description of democracy in Athens differ from the description of Athens given in Pericles' speech? (See Reading 9.)
4. How do you think Athenian democracy worked? Which view do you believe is more accurate? Explain your answer.

11. The Spartan Way of Life

The following description is of Sparta in the period 600–100 B.C. It was written by a Greek author who lived during the years 246–220 B.C. He tells how Lycurgus (lie-KUR-gus), a ninth-century ruler of Sparta, molded the Spartan way of life by regulating the education of young boys and girls.

Because he considered education to be the noblest work of a ruler, Lycurgus began by regulating marriages and the birth of children. He encouraged girls to strengthen their bodies by exercise in running, wrestling, and hurling javelins, in order that their children might spring from a healthy source, be healthy, and grow up strong. Lycurgus did not view children as belonging to their parents, but above all to the state. Therefore he wished his citizens to be born of the best possible parents.

A father did not have the right to bring up his child, but had to carry it to a certain place where the elders of the tribe judged the child. If they thought it well built and strong, they ordered the father to bring it up. But if it was misshapen, they sent it away to be exposed on the side of a nearby mountain. They considered that if a child did not start with health and strength, it was better both for itself and for the state that it should not live at all.

Nor was each man allowed to bring up and educate his son as he chose. As soon as a boy was seven years of age, he was taken away from his parents and put into an army company. Here a superintendent of the boys was appointed. He was one of the bravest and best-born men of the state. The boys looked to him for orders, obeyed his commands, and endured his punishments, so that even in childhood they learned to obey.

They learned to read and write, but all the rest of their education was meant to teach them to obey with cheerfulness, to endure labors, and to win battles. As they grew older, their training became more severe. They received one garment for all year round. They were dirty, as they had no warm baths except as a luxury on certain days. They slept together on beds made of straw that they themselves gathered.

Lycurgus did not allow citizens to leave the country at will and wander in foreign lands, where they would be put into contact with foreign habits and learn to imitate the untrained lives found in other countries. Neither did he allow strangers in Sparta who were not there for a useful purpose. He feared that they might teach the people some mischief. Lycurgus thought that strangers introduced strange ideas. He believed it was important to keep evil habits from coming into the city.

Adapted from: Nels M. Bailkey. *Readings in Ancient History from Gilgamesh to Diocletian*. Boston: D. C. Heath, 1969.

1. According to this account, which three of the following best describe Spartan method of education? Defend your selections.
   a. It was very democratic.
   b. It was athletic-oriented.
   c. The government had a great role in raising children.
   d. It was military-oriented.
2. Would Aristotle have agreed with the Spartan method of educating their youth?
3. If you were to form a school of your own, what subjects would you require students to study? Give reasons for your selection.

REVIEWING READINGS 9–11

1. Based on your examination of these selections and the information in your textbook, choose four words that describe ancient Greek society. Defend your choice.
2. What Greek ideas have been adopted by our society? Give examples.
3. Why do you think such ideas have lasted for such a long time without much change?

chapter
7 The Roman Empire

LIFE IN ANCIENT ROME

The Romans through years of trade, colonization, and other contacts were strongly influenced by the rich Greek intellectual and artistic culture. Although most of their ideas were based on Greek philosophy, the Romans did have a unique contribution of their own to give to the world. Their administrative and organizational ability and legal knowledge alone have been unequalled. As you read the following selections, compare the Greek and Roman way of life.

12. The Roman Way of Life

About 65 A.D., a Roman named Petronius (puh-TROE-nee-us) wrote a novel on how wealthy Romans lived during his time. Petronius was appointed to some official positions during his lifetime, including "director of elegance" in the court of the emperor Nero. Some historians believe that it was Nero's wasteful habits that inspired Petronius' vivid descriptions of the vulgar rich man in the following excerpt from his book.

At last we took our places. Immediately slaves from Alexandria came in and poured ice water over our hands. These were followed by other slaves who knelt at our feet and with extraordinary skill manicured our toenails. Not for an instant, moreover, during the whole of this job, did one of them stop singing. In fact, anything you asked for was served with a snatch of song, so that you would have thought you were eating in a concert hall.

We were nibbling at the splendid appetizers when suddenly the trumpets blew and our host was carried in. He was propped up on piles of tiny pillows in such a comic way that we couldn't help smiling. He wore a cloak of blazing scarlet. His neck, heavily wrapped already in bundles of clothing, was draped with a large napkin bounded by purple and with little tassels dangling down here and there.

On the little finger of his left hand he wore a huge ring. The ring on the last joint of his fourth finger looked to be solid gold of the kind the lesser nobility wear, but was actually, I think, an imitation. Nor does this exhaust the inventory of his trinkets. He bared his arm to show us a large gold bracelet and an ivory circlet with a shiny metal plate.

He was picking his teeth with a silver toothpick when he first addressed us. "My friends," he said, "I wasn't anxious to eat just yet, but I've ignored my own wishes so as not to keep you waiting. Still, perhaps you won't mind if I finish my game." At these words a slave jumped forward with a board of wood and a pair of crystal dice. I noticed one other elegant novelty as well. In place of the usual black and white coins, our host had substituted gold and silver ones.

Then he promptly sent for some of the same dishes we had already eaten and with a great roaring voice offered a second cup of wine to anyone who wanted it.

Then the orchestra suddenly began to play and the trays were snatched away from the tables by a group of singing waiters. But in the confusion a silver dish fell to the floor. A slave quickly stooped to pick it up. The host, however, gave orders that the boy's ears should be boxed and the dish tossed back on the floor. Immediately the servant in charge of the dishware came pattering up with a broom and swept the silver dish out the door with the rest of the rubbish. Two slaves followed him as he swept and poured wine over our hands. No one was offered water.

Carefully sealed glass jars were now brought in. While we were reading the labels on the jars, drinking the host's beverages, and admiring a skeleton cast in solid silver, the orchestra suddenly began to play again. Four slaves came dancing in with a huge tray covered with biscuits and rare kinds of meats. Spicy hot gravy dripped over it all and several large fish swam about in the pool made by the gravy. The slaves burst out clapping when they saw this, and we clapped too. The host, enormously pleased with the success of his little dinner, roared for a slave to come and carve. The carver appeared instantly and went to work, cutting with his knife like a gladiator practicing to the accompaniment of an orchestra.

Later, one guest commented, "As for our host, the man's got more farms than a kite could flap over. As for slaves, so help me, I'll bet not one in ten has ever even seen his master. Your or-

dinary rich man is just peanuts compared to him. And he raises everything right here on his own estate. Wool, pepper, you name it. Attic honey he raises at home; ordered the bees especially from Athens. And you know, just the other day he sent off to India for some mushrooms. That boy's really loaded!'' Adapted from: Petronius Arbiter. *Satyricon & Fragments.* trans. John Sullivan. Penguin Books, 1968.

1. Which of the following does Petronius seem to characterize some wealthy Romans as?
   a. wasteful
   b. kind to all people
   c. extravagant
   d. hardworking

2. Cite examples from the selection to support your answer to question 1.
3. How does the way of life described here compare with the way people lived in Athens and in Sparta? See Readings 9–11. Cite one comparison.
4. Would a novel about how the people in your community live give future historians an accurate impression of your way of life? Explain.

13. Roman Law
An important source of information about life in ancient Rome has survived in the form of written laws. The following selection contains examples of some of those laws, which date back to about 450 B.C.

Every person shall mend the roadway in front of his land. If he keeps it not laid with stones, anyone may drive beasts where he wishes across the land.

Should a tree on a neighbor's farm be bent crooked by the wind and lean over your farm, you may take action for removal of that tree.

A man might gather up fruit that has fallen on to another man's farm.

If a person has harmed another's arm or leg, let him be punished by having the same done to him, unless payment is made for harming the limb.

For pasturing on or cutting secretly by night another's crop, the guilty person shall be hanged and put to death. In the case of a person under the age of fourteen, he should be whipped, or for the harm done, he should be made to pay double damages.

Any person who destroys by burning any building or heap corn deposited alongside a house shall be bound, whipped, and put to death by burning at the stake, provided he deliberately committed the deed. But if it was an accident, that is by neglect, he shall repair the damage. If he is too poor to pay, he shall receive a lighter punishment.

Any person who cuts down another person's trees with harmful intent should pay 25 pieces of silver for every tree cut down.   Adapted from: E. H. Warmington, ed. *Remains of Old Latin*, Vol. 3. Cambridge: Harvard University Press, 1938.

1. Which two of the following do you think best describe these Roman laws? Defend your selections.
    a. Roman laws were easy on the accused.
    b. Roman laws stressed the importance of protection of property rights.
    c. Roman laws usually called for payment of some kind from those who committed unlawful acts.
    d. Roman laws did much to protect the equal rights of women.
2. Do you think these laws are fair or just? Explain by using examples.
3. How do these laws compare to Hammurabi's Code (see Reading 1) and to the Spartan rules for living (see Reading 11)?
4. Which of these laws are similar to the ones followed in your community?

14. Cicero's Observations on Roman Rule

Cicero lived between 106 and 43 B.C., when mighty Roman leaders conquered lands for the wealth and power that victory would bring them. In the following selection, Cicero not only advises statesmen on the purpose of war. He also reminds them that in battle they should not lose sight of the responsibility for themselves and for those they conquer.

Most people think that the achievements of war are more important than the achievements of peace. But this opinion needs to be corrected. Many men have wanted war because of ambition for fame. This is especially the case with men of great spirit and natural ability. But if we face the facts, we shall find that there have been many instances of achievement in peace more important and no less famous than in war.

War, however, should be undertaken in such a way as to make it evident that there is no other object than to secure peace. To mix rashly in the battle and to fight hand to hand with the enemy is a barbaric and brutal kind of business. Yet when the stress of circumstances demands it, we must put on the sword and prefer death to slavery and disgrace.

It is, therefore, only a madman who in a calm would pray for a storm. A wise man's way is, when the storm does come, to withstand it with the means at his command, and especially when the advantages to be expected in case of holding back a war are greater than the hazards of a struggle.

Adapted from: William C. McDermott and Wallace E. Caldwell. *Readings in the History of the Ancient World.* New York: Holt, Rinehart and Winston, 1951.

1. Which two of the following would best characterize Cicero's views on war? Defend your selection.
   a. Achievements of war are of the greatest importance.
   b. Achievements of peace are most important.
   c. War is easy to justify when seeking to settle a conflict.
   d. War should be a last resort to settling a dispute.
2. What were two ways Cicero wanted soldiers to behave? Why?
3. Do you agree with Cicero's view of war?
4. Do you think a society's attitudes toward war and peace tell something about the kind of life its people would like to live? Explain.

REVIEWING READINGS 12–14

1. Do these selections on Roman culture tell us anything about what Romans thought to be most important in their life?
2. If you had to describe Roman culture in four words, which words would you choose? Defend your selection.
3. Of the words you chose to describe Roman culture in Question 2 were any similar to those you used to describe Greek culture? Why or why not?
4. Are there any Roman ideas or beliefs that we have adopted in our culture? If so, which ones do you feel have been the most important? Explain.

Did you know that in 500 B.C. the population of the city of Athens was about 30,000, less than half the population of Portland, Maine? And in 300 A.D. the population of Rome was about one million, nearly twice the size of the population of Denver, Colorado.

chapter

8 Western Europe in the Middle Ages

LIFE AND LAW IN MEDIEVAL EUROPE

Constant barbarian invasions from the north and east soon eliminated almost any physical trace of what was Roman civilization. Cities that were once the center of culture and economic life were destroyed. Industry and commerce were almost completely gone. What remained were clusters of Germanic tribes, who were ruled by custom and not by an organized system of government. However, from this "Dark Age" developed another civilization, characterized by a brand-new economic, political, and social order. As you read the following selections on medieval life, keep in mind that it is from this civilization that modern western Europe grew.

15. The Law of the Franks

Clovis, one of the first rulers of the early Franks, issued a code of law which was based on Germanic customs. This set of laws was passed down from one generation of rulers to the next. Eventually, it became the basis of Frankish law during the reign of Charlemagne. As you read some of these early laws, see how many are similar to those we have today. How do they compare with the laws of the ancient world? (See Readings 1, 2, and 13.)

If a person steals something worth 2 denars from outside a house, he shall be fined 600 denars. If the value of what he steals is 40 denars, the fine shall be 1,400 denars. But if he has broken a lock on the house, or has tampered with a lock, and has entered a house and stolen anything from inside it, he shall be fined 1,800 denars plus the value of what he has stolen. And if he has taken nothing or has escaped by fleeing, he shall, for the housebreaking alone, be fined 1,200 denars.

If a serf steals from outside a house something worth 2 denars, he shall repay the worth of the object and besides receive twenty blows.

If anyone attacks or robs a Frank, and it is proved, the fine shall be 2,500 denars. If a foreigner attacks a Frank, the fine shall be the same (2,500 denars). But if a Frank attacks a foreigner, the fine shall be 1,400 denars.

If anyone kills a Frank, the fine shall be 800 denars. But if the body of the Frank shall have been thrown into a well or into water or shall have been covered with branches or anything else to conceal it, the fine shall be 24,000 denars. If anyone slays a foreigner who has permission to eat in the king's palace, the fine shall be 12,000 denars. But if the foreigner shall have owned no land, the fine shall be 4,000 denars. Adapted from: Richard J. Burke, Jr. *The Ancient World.* Vol I, Western Society: Institutions and Ideals. New York: McGraw-Hill, 1967.

1. Which of these early Frankish laws do you consider the most harsh? Explain your answer.

2. Which of these laws do you consider the most fair? Explain your answer.
3. How do these laws tell you about what was important to the early Franks and their rulers? Cite examples to support your answer.
4. Do we have any laws similar to those of the early Franks? List them.

16. A Certificate to Freedom

Although serfs were said to be the life property of the lord whose land they worked, freedom was not always an impossibility. A serf could legally become free if he or she saved enough money to buy freedom or if the king or feudal lord granted that freedom. The following selection is a document which served as legal proof that a serf had been freed.

In the name of Henry, king by divine permission, let all our faithful subjects both now and in the future know that at the request of Arnulf, my faithful and beloved duke, I have freed a certain serf named Baldmut. I freed him by striking a penny out of his hand in the presence of witnesses, according to an ancient custom, and I have thereby released him entirely from serfdom and I desire that he remain free forever. I order that Baldmut shall enjoy the same freedom and have such rights as all those who up to this time have been set free in this way by kings or emperors of the Franks.   Adapted from: Oliver J. Thatcher and Edgar H. McNeal, eds. *A Source Book for Medieval History*. New York: AMS Press, 1905.

1. Why was the serf Baldmut set free?
2. How was the ceremony carried out?
3. What need might Baldmut have had for a document like this one?
4. What legal proof must a young person have today before he or she is permit-

ted to be hired to work? Do you think such a procedure is necessary? Explain your answer.

17. A Medieval Ballad

Around 1200 in France, musician-poets called troubadours (TROO-buh-dores) began to set their poetry to music. The following ballad might have been sung by a minstrel (MIN-strul), who was a person of the lower classes hired by the troubadours to sing their songs. The ballad expresses the strong feeling of pride that knights had in the work they did.

Peace delights me not!
War, you are not my lot!
I do not know any lass except a good sword.
I prize neither meat nor drink,
But only the cry "On! On!" from throats that crack
And I prize the neighs when frightened horses run wild as
A riderless and frantic pack.
I prize the cries "Help! Help!" and the warriors lying
Beside the moat with faces that fade into the grass,
And bodies
Pierced with broken spears or swords.

Come knights, hurry, bring
Your vassals for some daring
    attack.
Risk everything and let the game of
    battle be played.
Sound the call to battle, play the
    fife,
Proclaim to all the world
That one hour of glorious battle
Is worth old age without a famous
    name.

Adapted from: William Stearns Davis. *Life on a Medieval Barony*. New York: Harper & Row, 1951; and Philip Warner. *The Medieval Castle*. New York: Taplinger, 1971.

1. How would the phrase "Might makes right" apply to this ballad?
2. Which lines of the ballad indicate what knights found most interesting about their job?
3. Do popular songs today reflect the life and feelings of people in your society? Give examples to support your answer.

18. An English Merchant

Nine of every ten people in medieval Europe depended on the land to live. But no feudal manor was completely self-sufficient. Specialized goods that were produced outside the manor were needed for survival. Merchants and craftsmen bought, sold, and made things in answer to this demand. The local trade and industry that resulted stimulated the growth of towns and urban life. By the tenth and eleventh centuries, population grew and the demand for these goods increased as well. Read the following account of a merchant's life, which was written in the eleventh century. How did this merchant become a success in business?

As a boy, he passed his childish years quietly at home [in Norfolk, England]. Then he chose not to follow the life of a farmer, but aspiring to the merchant's trade, he began to follow the peddler's way of life, first learning how to gain in small bargains and things of insignificant price. Thence he began to buy and sell and gain from things of greater expense. In his beginnings, he was wont to wander around the villages and farms of his own neighborhood with goods for sale. As time went by, he associated himself by contract to sell the goods of city merchants. At first he lived for four years as a peddler in Lincolnshire, going on foot and carrying the cheapest wares. Then he traveled abroad, first to Scotland, then to Rome. On his return, he began to launch on bolder courses by sea to foreign lands. At length his great labors and cares bore much worldly gain. He labored not only as a merchant but also as a shipman. In Denmark and Flanders [in Belgium] and Scotland he found certain goods which he carried to other parts wherein he knew the goods to be less familiar and greatly desired by the inhabitants. Hence he made great profit in all his bargains, and gathered much wealth by the sweat of his brow. He sold dear in one place the goods which he had bought elsewhere at a small price.   Adapted from: G. G. Coulton. *Social Life in Britain from the Conquest to the Reformation*. London: Cambridge University Press, 1925.

1. What did a medieval peddler do?
2. What role did "supply and demand" of goods play in this merchant's success?
3. What modern business practices do you recognize in this reading?

19. A Student Writes for Money

Universities were very different in the Middle Ages from those of today. Lectures were not held in classrooms but usually in a teacher's house. Books were rare and expensive, so students were forced to take detailed notes. But all in all a student's life and concerns were similar to your own, as you will see by reading the following letters written by a student and his parent.

This is to inform you that I am studying at Oxford [University] with the greatest diligence, but the matter of money stands greatly in the way of my studies, as it is now two months since I spent the last of what you sent me. The city is expensive. I have to rent lodgings, buy necessaries, and provide for many other things which I cannot now list for you. Wherefore, I respectfully beg you that by divine pity you may assist me, so that I may be able to complete the studies I have so well begun.

It is written, "He that neglects his work is brother to him that is a great waster of money." I have recently discovered that you live a pleasure-seeking life, preferring irresponsibility to responsibility, and play to work, and strumming a guitar while others study. Whence it happens that you have completed but one course of study while your more industrious companions have completed several. Therefore, I have decided to warn you to repent of your irresponsible and careless ways that you may no longer be called a waster and your shame may be turned into a good reputation. Adapted from: Charles Homer Haskins. *The Rise of the Universities.* New York: Holt, Rinehart and Winston, 1940.

1. Why was the student in need of money?
2. Why was the parent concerned about his son?
3. In what way is this student's life similar to or different from your own?

REVIEWING READINGS 15–19

1. You are suddenly transported back in time as a news columnist to France during the Middle Ages. Write a paragraph describing the latest castle gossip. Include as many different kinds of medieval people as you can in your column.
2. From what you have read in these selections and in your textbook about medieval life, do you think that the entire period was a "Dark Age"? Explain your answer.

chapter

⑨ Political Change in Western Europe

THE RISE OF THE FEUDAL MONARCH

Although the feudal king was legally the most powerful of all the nobility, it was the barons and nobles below him who held as much, if not, greater power. In order to gain the respect due them, most medieval kings fought endless wars throughout the Middle Ages. But then there were some who found other routes to success.

20. The Political Theory of John of Salisbury

In 1159, John of Salisbury, a noted medieval author and political adviser, wrote the *Statesman's Book*. The advice given in this book was based on John of Salisbury's knowledge of Roman law and his observations of the rulers of his day. The following selection from the *Statesman's Book* expresses in theory what some kings during the Middle Ages were trying to put into practice.

Between a tyrant and a prince there is this single or chief difference, that the prince obeys the law and rules the people according to what they say because he is their servant. It is the law that justifies his claim to the foremost and chief place in the management of the affairs of the realm, and in the bearing of its burdens. His position over others exists because, unlike private men who are only responsible for their own affairs, the prince is responsible for the burdens of the whole community . . . .

Therefore the prince stands above all and is honored and made splendid with all the great and high privileges which he sees necessary for himself. And rightly so, because nothing is more advantageous to the people than that the needs of the prince should be fully satisfied; since it is impossible that his will should be found opposed to justice. Therefore, the prince is the public power, and a kind of likeness on earth to the divine majesty. Beyond a doubt, a large share of the divine power is shown to be in princes by the fact that at their nod men bow their necks and for the most part offer up their heads to the ax to be struck off, and, as by divine impulse the prince is feared by each of those over whom he is set as an object of fear. And this I do not think could be, except as a result of the will of God. The power which the prince has is therefore from God, for the power of God is never lost, nor severed from Him. But He merely exercises it through a subordinate hand, making all things teach His mercy or justice.   Adapted from: Thomas C. Mendenhall, Basil D. Henning, and A. S. Foord, eds. *Ideas and Institutions in European History, 800–1715*. New York: Holt, Rinehart, and Winston, 1948.

1. According to John of Salisbury, what were the duties of a king to his subjects and to the community?
2. Why do you think the people of the Middle Ages accepted the statement that the prince is a "kind of likeness on earth to the divine majesty"?
3. Do you think that your society would support a leader who believed in such a theory? Why or why not?
4. Do you agree with the reasons given in this selection for why a king is all-powerful? Cite specific lines in the reading to support your opinion.

21. A Portrait of Louis XI

Through inheritance, marriage, war, and conquest, the medieval king gradually began to expand his territory and increase his power. The growing middle class was willing to pay the money for taxes, which the king used to build his armies so that he could put down the nobles. Louis XI, who ruled France from 1461 to 1483, was one of the new brand of medieval kings that emerged in the fifteenth century. The following description of Louis XI was written by his servant and adviser Philippe de Commynes, around 1498.

The king surrounded his castle with great bars of iron in the form of thick grating, and at the four corners of the house four sparrow-nests of iron, strong, massive, and thick, were built. The grates sank to the bottom. Several spikes of iron with three or four points attached to each were stuck into the wall and set as far away from each other as possible. He assigned ten men with bows and arrows to remain in the ditches, to shoot at any man that tried to approach the castle before the opening of the gates. He was sensible enough to realize that this fortification was too weak to keep out an army, but he was not afraid of such an attack. His great fear, however, was that some of the nobility of his kingdom, who have visited the castle, might try to take it over during the night, and might deprive him of his kingly authority with the excuse that he was no longer fit to govern . . . .

Some may think that other princes have been more suspicious of others . . . I will not criticize him, or say I ever saw a better prince. For though he oppressed his subjects himself, he would never see them injured by anybody else . . . .

When his body was at rest, his mind was at work. He would concern himself as much in the problems of his neighboring states as his own, putting his own officers over all the great families [of Europe], and tried to divide their authority as much as possible. When he was at war, he labored for a peace or a truce; and when he had obtained it, he was impatient for war again. He troubled himself with many insignificant matters in his government, which he should have left alone. But it was his nature to be that way. He could not help it. Besides, he had a fantastic memory, and he knew everybody, in other countries as well as in his own.   Adapted from: Charles T. Davis, ed. *Western Awakening*. Vol. II, Sources of Medieval History. New York: Appleton-Century-Crofts, 1967.

1. What special qualities did Louis XI have that early medieval kings seemed to lack? Cite examples to support your answer.
2. What concerns did Louis XI have that were similar to those of early medieval kings?
3. What do you think was Philippe Commynes' opinion of his master? Explain.
4. Do you think Louis XI was a strong and successful ruler? Why or why not?

22. Machiavelli's Advice to Rulers

Niccolo Machiavelli held several administrative and diplomatic posts in the city-state of Florence. From his position, Machiavelli observed the behavior of people and the need for them to be dominated by a strong leader. In 1532, he wrote a book based on his observations, which advised rulers how to win and hold power. His theory of rule influenced the behavior of Renaissance kings who set a model for the absolute rulers of the seventeenth and eighteenth centuries. A selection from Machiavelli's The Prince follows.

Here the question arises: whether it is better to be loved than feared or feared than loved. The answer is that it would be desirable to be both but, since that is difficult, it is much safer to be feared than to be loved, if one must choose. For all men in general this observation may be made: they are ungrateful, fickle, and deceitful, eager to avoid dangers and avid for gain, and while you are useful to them they are all with you, offering you their blood, their property, their lives, and their sons so long as danger is remote, but when it approaches they turn on you. Any prince, trusting only in their words and having no other preparations made, will fall to ruin, for friendships that are bought at a price and not by greatness and nobility of soul are paid for indeed, but they are not owned and cannot be called upon in time of need. Men have less hesitation in offending a man who is loved than one who is feared, for love is held by a bond of obligation which, as men are wicked, is broken whenever personal advantage suggests it, but fear is accompanied by the dread of punishment, which never relaxes.   Adapted from: Niccolo Machiavelli. *The Prince.* trans. and ed. Thomas G. Bergin. New York: Appleton-Century-Crofts, 1947.

1. What did Machiavelli consider the most important personality trait of a successful ruler?
2. What was Machiavelli's view of human nature? Based on the material in your textbook, what aspect of the Italian city-states in the late fifteenth century might have influenced Machiavelli's view of human nature?
3. Do you think this was the kind of ruler needed in Europe at this time? Explain.
4. Would you favor modern rulers adopting Machiavelli's advice? Why or why not? Explain.

REVIEWING READINGS 20–22

1. From what you have read in these readings and your textbook, what are some of the ways a king could increase his power during the Middle Ages?
2. Historians have defined Philippe Commynes, the adviser of Louis XI, as an early Machiavellian. Do you think this is an accurate description of him, based on what you have read in Reading 21? Why or why not?
3. If you were to write a handbook for kings on how to rule, what would you advise? Explain your answer.

---

chapter
10 Culture and Religious Change in Western Europe

THE RENAISSANCE VIEW OF THE INDIVIDUAL

With the increase in trade and commerce during the late Middle Ages, western Europe began to turn away from a concern for the spiritual and move toward an interest in the natural world. A renewed interest in man and his capacity to control his world characterized the period known as the Renaissance. This new view sparked a rebirth of the values and culture of ancient Greece and Rome. To study classical literature, to be well educated, to be a precise thinker, to be eloquent and virtuous, to develop many talents, and to have a physically fit body was the ultimate perfection—

the "universal man." Read the following selections and see how this new attitude influenced education, art, literature, and most of all, people's view of themselves and others.

23. The Ideal of Perfection

The Renaissance idea of the universal man greatly influenced the well-to-do and upper classes of Europe. They had the resources needed to cultivate their minds and perfect their bodies. In 1528, an Italian diplomat, Count Baldassare Castiglione, wrote a handbook that gave instruction on how to develop a well-rounded personality. The Courtier, as this guide was called, became the model for the proper conduct of the Renaissance gentleman.

I would have our courtier sometimes take part in quiet and peaceful exercises. If he is to escape envy and appear agreeable to everyone, the courtier should join others in what they are doing. Yet he must use good judgment to see that he never appears foolish. And in whatever he does or says, let him do it with grace.

I would have the courtier know literature, in particular those studies known as the humanities. He should be able to speak not only Latin but Greek as well. Let him read and know the Roman and Greek poets, orators, and historians. Let him be proficient in writing verse and prose, particularly in our own language. Even if he does not become perfect in the art of writing verse and prose, he should still practice it so that he will at least be able to judge the work of others.

My lords, you must know that I am not content with the courtier unless he is also a musician. Besides being able to read and understand music, he must be able to play the different instruments. Music is the best relaxation or medicine for a troubled man. Moreover, it is a most becoming and praiseworthy pastime during leisure hours, especially in the court, where it relieves the boredom and pleases the ladies.

Our courtier should know how to draw and paint. Do not be surprised that I believe the courtier should know this art, which today seems to be practiced only by artisans and not by gentlemen. I remember having read that the ancients, especially in Greece, had the boys of noble birth study painting in school. They believed it was an honorable and necessary thing and it was recognized as the first of the liberal arts. At the same time they forbade slaves to practice art. Among the

Romans, too, it was held in highest honor. Adapted from: Baldassare Castiglione. *The Book of the Courtier.* trans. Leonard E. Opdycke. New York: Charles Scribner's Sons, 1903, as adapted for Edwin Fenton. *The Shaping of Western Society.* New York: Holt, Rinehart and Winston, 1974.

1. According to Castiglione, what things must one do to become a well-rounded personality?
2. Name two famous people in the Renaissance who you think Castiglione might have admired the most. Explain your answer by citing references from the above selection.
3. Do you know any famous person today who you feel is the ideal person? What personal characteristics make this man or woman in your opinion "perfect"?

24. A Renaissance Scholar Discusses the Meaning of Education

Juan Luis Vives was a Spanish humanist and Renaissance scholar. He was a tutor to the daughter of Henry VIII of England and also lectured at Oxford University. In 1531, Vives wrote a book on the purpose of education. The selection that follows represents the typical Renaissance attitude toward learning.

We must not always be studying so that we do nothing but study. Nor must the mind, bound by no useful aim, delight itself in any pointless contemplation of pointless knowledge. . . . The fruit of studies is not to be estimated by their return in money. Such an opinion has been held only by debased persons, who are far removed from any true idea of studies. Nothing is so distant from learning as the desire for money. When this desire settles in a person of studies, it drives away the zeal for intellectual growth, because study does not commit itself fully to any persons except those free from that disease. People say: "First get rich; then become educated." Nay, rather it should be said: "We must first study, and afterwards get rich." For if we first get rich, we shall soon no longer wish to busy ourselves with learning. Made anxious by possession of wealth, and lacking true learning, we shall be ignorant of the true use of riches. But if once we become philosophers, then it will be easy, afterwards, to get as rich as it is at all necessary to be. Adapted from: Foster Watson, ed. *Vives: On Education: a Translation of the* De Tradendis Disciplinis *of Juan Luis Vives.* London: Cambridge University Press, 1913.

1. Which is more important to Vives—education or money? Explain.
2. How does the Renaissance view of education compare to that of ancient Greece? Explain.
3. Do you think Vives' advice could apply to students today? Explain.

REVIEWING READINGS 23–24

1. How did the cultures and values of ancient Greece and Rome affect the Renaissance view of the ideal individual? Cite examples from the readings in Chapter 10.
2. Compare the ideal medieval person with the ideal Renaissance person. Which of the two is closer to what we think are admirable personal characteristics today? Explain the similarities and the differences.
3. Do you know of a "movement" in your society or community that caused a change in people's lifestyle or attitudes (for example, the women's rights movement of the 1970's)? What evidence can you give to show that changes did occur?

11   A Time of Conflict

THE DEVELOPMENT OF PARLIAMENTARY GOVERNMENT IN ENGLAND

Important political developments took place in seventeenth-century England. The Stuart kings claimed their divine right to rule, but did not find it as easy to put into action as did the French monarchs. Parliament challenged royal authority and demanded a share in governing England. The struggle between kings and Parliament included a civil war and a bloodless revolution and ended in victory for Parliament.

Some of the key developments of English parliamentary government in theory and in practice are illustrated by the following selections. As you read, keep in mind this question: How much does American representative government owe to the political developments in England?

25. The Petition of Right, 1628

Almost immediately upon ascending the throne, Charles I, like his father James, tried to impose absolute rule over his subjects. But in the third year of King Charles I's reign, Parliament decided to stop the king before things got out of hand. They presented him with the Petition of Right. This petition was a statement of political grievances against the king and a list of demands, which follow.

The Lords and Commons in Parliament do humbly ask your Most Excellent Majesty, that no subject hereafter be compelled to make any gift, loan, tax, or such like charge, without common consent by Parliament; and that none be called upon to take such an oath, or be confined, or otherwise molested or disquieted for refusal thereof; and that no subject, in any such manner as is before mentioned, be imprisoned or detained; and that your Majesty will be pleased to remove the soldiers who have been quartered in private homes and that your people may not be so burdened in time to come; and that the forsaid royal orders for proceeding by martial law, may be revoked; and that hereafter no royal orders of like nature may issue forth to any person or persons whatsoever, lest any of your Majesty's subjects be destroyed or put to death, contrary to the laws of the land.

All which we most humbly pray of your Most Excellent Majesty, as our rights and liberties according to the laws and statutes of this realm.

Adapted from: Samuel R. Gardiner, ed. *The Constitutional Documents of the Puritan Revolution, 1625–1660*. New York: Oxford University Press, 1906.

1. What actions taken by the king were protested by Parliament in this document?
2. What would Charles I have to do to satisfy the demands of Parliament?
3. Have you or any members of your family ever been asked to sign a petition against an issue at school or in your community? If so, what did the petition demand? Was there a successful outcome? If not, why?

26. The End of Absolute Monarchy in England

The execution of Charles I in 1649 was quickly followed by a number of official acts that put an end to absolute monarchy in England. Oliver Cromwell, together with Parliament, pledged to govern for the common good of the people. As you read the following documents, note the reasons given for doing away with the monarchy and establishing the first commonwealth, or national republic, in the history of the world.

And whereas it is and has been found by experience, that the Office of a King in this Nation and Ireland, or to have such power in one single person, is unnecessary, burdensome and Dangerous to the liberty, safety and public interest of the people. The Regal power and prerogative has been used to oppress, and impoverish and enslave the people. Usually and naturally any one person in such power makes it his interest to impose upon the just freedom and liberty of the people, and to promote the setting up of their own will and power above the Laws. . . . Be it therefore Enacted and Ordained by this present Parliament, and by Authority of the same, that the Office of a King in this Nation, shall not henceforth reside in, or be exercised by any one single person; and that no one person whatsoever, shall or may have, or hold the Office, Style, Dignity, Power or Authority of King of the said Kingdoms and Dominions. . . .   Adapted from: Halton Webster, ed. *Historical Selections*. Boston: D. C. Heath, 1929.

1. What were the reasons for abolishing the monarchy in England?
2. List the word or words used in these documents that describe the effects of rule by a king. Which word or phrase is repeated?
3. According to these documents, how was England to be governed without a king as leader? Cite specific lines from these documents to support your answer.
4. If you were a citizen of England during the 1650's, would you have agreed with these actions? Why or why not?

27. John Locke and the Glorious Revolution

John Locke was a seventeenth-century English political philosopher. In 1690, he published his *Two Treatises of Government*, in which he tried to justify the Glorious Revolution and England's new form of government. It was partly Locke's ideas that provided philosophical support for the American and French revolutions of the eighteenth century.

To understand political power, we must consider the condition in which nature puts all men. It is a state of perfect freedom to do as they wish and dispose of themselves and their possessions as they think fit, within the bounds of the law of nature. They need not ask permission or the consent of any other man.

The state of nature is also a state of equality. No one has more power or authority than another. Since all human beings have the same advantages and the use of the same skills, they should be equal to each other. The state of nature has a law of nature to govern it. Reason is that law. It teaches that all men are equal and independent, and that no one ought to harm another in his life, health, liberty, or possessions.

If man in the state of nature is free, if he is absolute lord of his own person

634

and possessions, why will he give up his freedom? Why will he put himself under the control of any person or institution? The obvious answer is that rights in the state of nature are constantly exposed to the attacks of others. Hence each man joins in society with others to preserve his life, liberty, and property.

Since men hope to preserve their property by establishing a government, they will not want that government to destroy this objective. When legislators try to destroy or take away the property of the people, or try to reduce them to slavery, they put themselves into a state of war with the people, who can then refuse to obey the laws. When legislators try to gain or give someone else absolute power over the lives, liberties, and property of the people, they abuse the power which the people had put into their hands. It is then the privilege of the people to establish a new legislature to provide for their safety and security. These principles also hold true for the executive [leader] who helps to make laws and carry them out. . . .

However, it will be said that this philosophy may lead to frequent rebellion. To which I answer, such revolutions are not caused by every little mismanagement in public affairs. But if a long train of abuses, lies, and tricks make a government's bad intentions visible to the people, they cannot help seeing where they are going. It is no wonder that they will then rouse themselves, and try to put the rule into hands which will secure to them the purpose for which government was originally organized.   Adapted from: John Locke. *Two Treatises of Government*. London, 1690, as adapted for Edwin Fenton. *The Shaping of Western Society*. New York: Holt, Rinehart, and Winston, 1974.

1. What philosophical reasons did Locke give to support the Glorious Revolution or any change in government? In your opinion, did he succeed?
2. If a man is to be free, why is government necessary, according to Locke?
3. Turn back to the words or phrases you listed in Reading 26. Do you think Cromwell and Parliament would have accepted Locke's reasons for England's new government? Why or why not?
4. What specific ideas from Locke's philosophy have influenced your society's system of government? Give examples to support your answer.

REVIEWING READINGS 25–27

1. From what you have read in these selections and in your textbook, how did Parliament curb the powers of the king in seventeenth-century England?
2. Why did Parliament and the people think this was necessary?
3. Suppose you were assigned to write a contract between your local government and your community. What would you insist that the government agree to do for the community? What do you think the people should do for the government in return?

Did you know that in 1185 A.D. Constantinople, Cordova in Spain, and Kyoto in Japan were the largest cities in the world with more than 500,000 people? Today, New York, Tokyo, and Shanghai are among the largest cities, with over 10 million people—twenty times greater than in 1185!

chapter 12 The Land and the Peoples of Eastern Europe

THE DECLINE OF THE BYZANTINE EMPIRE

The Byzantine Empire came to an end in 1453 with the Turkish conquest of Constantinople. However, historians have identified many other reasons for the empire's collapse that existed long before 1453. For example, the Byzantine rulers often spent more money than the empire could afford, and nobles constantly vied for more wealth and power. Internal difficulties like these helped to weaken the empire and cause its eventual downfall. The following selections are some contemporary accounts. What evidence do you think they provide about the causes of the fall of the Byzantine Empire?

28. Weak Rulers

Michael Psellus (SEL-us), an eleventh-century Byzantine philosopher, often critically described the way of life and the administration of the Byzantine Empire. He was particularly concerned with the wasteful spending habits of emperors of the empire. One of the emperors he wrote about was Constantine VIII. Unlike his brother Basil II, Constantine VIII was not very responsible and not as skilled a statesman. His short reign (1025–1028) was typified by the following Psellus description.

Constantine was not capable of waging war. The barbarians encircling our borders had only to lift a finger against us and Constantine would hold them in check by granting them titles and giving them bribes. But if his own subjects rebelled, it was different. They were punished savagely. Suspicion of revolutionary plots resulted in vengeance. Suspects were condemned without trial. No man was ever more quick-tempered. His anger was uncontrolled and he was ready to listen to any rumor. On victims suspected of treachery awful tortures were inflicted. The Byzantine people became Constantine's slaves, not won over by acts of kindness but subdued by all manner of cruel punishments. Adapted from: E. R. A. Sweter, ed. *Fourteen Byzantine Rulers: The Chronographia of Michael Psellus.* Baltimore: Penguin Books, 1966.

1. What were some key characteristics of Emperor Constantine VIII?
2. How would you evaluate Constantine VIII's performance as emperor? Explain your answer.
3. Do you think rulers like Constantine VIII helped to strengthen or weaken the empire? Explain.

29. The Barbarian Threat to the Empire

As you have read in your textbook, the Byzantine rulers faced frequent threats from barbarian invaders from Central Asia seeking to capture parts of the empire. These emperors often fought desperately without much aid from the West because they had increasingly isolated themselves from Western Europe since the fall of the

Roman Empire. In the following account, Michael Psellus gives us a vivid description of what fighting against these brutal and unpredictable attackers was really like.

More than other nations, the barbarians are difficult to fight and hard to defeat. They are neither strong in body nor brave in spirit. They carry no shields nor do they gird on swords. The only weapon they carry is the spear. They have no military organization and when they go to war they have no strategic plan to guide them. In one mass, close-packed, they yell loud war cries, and so fall on their enemies. If they succeed in pushing them back, they dash against them in solid blocks, pursuing and slaying without mercy. On the other hand, if the opposing force withstands their assault, the barbarians turn about and seek safety in flight. But there is no order in their retreat. Later, in some strange fashion, they all meet again, all from different hiding places. When they are thirsty, if there is no water, each man dismounts from his horse, opens its veins with a knife, and drinks the blood. So they quench their thirst by substituting blood for water. After that they cut up the fattest horse, build a fire, and having slightly warmed the chopped limbs there on the spot, they gorge themselves on the meat, blood and all.

Taken in a mass, this is a nation to be feared, and a treacherous one. Treaties of friendship have no influence over these barbarians. No oaths are respected. If they win a battle, they massacre some of their captives and hold the rest for ransom. If no ransom is forthcoming, they kill their prisoners. Adapted from: E. R. A. Sweter, ed. *Fourteen Byzantine Rulers: The Chronographia of Michael Psellus.* Baltimore: Penguin Books, 1966.

1. Why were the barbarians a difficult enemy to fight?
2. Why do you think such attacks contributed to the decline of the Byzantine Empire?

30. A Western European View of the Byzantines

As the western Europeans marched eastward in hopes of saving Christian lands from Muslim takeover, many came in contact with the Byzantines for the first time. Odo de Deuil (oe-DOE duh DOY), a Frenchman who participated in the Second Crusade in 1147, left a description of the Byzantines and their city of Constantinople. What do you think might explain Odo of Deuil's harsh view of this eastern empire and its people?

The Byzantines are now very weak. They quickly swore anything they thought would please us, but they neither kept their word nor maintained any respect for themselves. In general, they really have the opinion that anything which is done for the empire cannot be considered wrong. When the Byzantines are afraid, they become despicable in their excessive humiliation, and when they have the upper hand, they are arrogant.

Constantinople is squalid and filthy. People live lawlessly in this city, which has as many lords as rich men, and almost as many thieves as poor people. In every respect Constantinople ignores moderation. For just as it surpasses other cities in wealth, so too, it surpasses them in vice. Adapted from: Odo de Deuil. *De Profectione Ludovici VII in Orientem.* trans. V. G. Berry. New York: Columbia University Press, 1948, as adapted for Strayer et al. *The Mainstream of Civilization.* New York: Harcourt Brace Jovanovich, 1969.

1. What does this writer consider the chief characteristics of the Byzantines to be?
2. How does the writer describe Constantinople?
3. How do you think this description of Constantinople might compare with one by a native of that city? What circumstances explain the differences?
4. Does this reading provide us with any clues as to why the Byzantine Empire eventually fell apart? Explain.

REVIEWING READINGS 28–30

1. Based on these readings and the information in your textbook, what are some possible reasons for the collapse of the Byzantine Empire?
2. Which of the possible causes mentioned in the answer to Question 1 do you think is the most significant? Why?
3. If you were a historian studying the Byzantine Empire, which of these selections would you consider the most valuable source of information? Why?
4. What countries do you think are the most powerful in the world today? Why? List at least five reasons why you think these countries have been able to keep their power. What do you think would cause them to lose power?

---

chapter
13 The Muslim Peoples

THE MUSLIM VIEW

We have often been frightened by the thought of being invaded by "creatures" from outer space. What would these creatures look like? How would they treat us? What would they do to us? But have you ever wondered what such "creatures" might think of you or how you live?

To the western Europeans of the Middle Ages, the Muslim invaders were strange and frightening. They particularly mistrusted the Muslims because of differences in Christian and Muslim beliefs. Interestingly enough, however, as you read the following selections you will see that the Muslims thought the same about westerners.

31. The Muslim View of the Crusaders
The following selection was written around 1175 by a Muslim warrior who fought against the Europeans in Jerusalem during the Crusades. Although he became friends with some, the Muslim soldier was still not very impressed with most of the Europeans he met. Read this excerpt from his autobiography and find out why he felt the way he did.

Mysterious are the works of the Creator, the author of all things! When one comes to recount cases regarding the Europeans, he cannot but glorify Allah (exalted is he!) and sanctify him, for he sees them as animals possessing the virtues of courage and fighting, but nothing else. They are just animals, who have only the virtues of strength. I shall now give some instances of the

Europeans' doings and their peculiar way of thinking. . . .

The lord of al-Munaytirah wrote to my uncle asking him to send for a doctor to treat certain sick persons among his people. My uncle sent him a Christian doctor named Thabit. When Thabit returned, he told us how his patient had been treated. He said: "They brought before me a knight with a pus sore on his leg. I applied a small dressing until the wound had opened and became well. Then a European doctor came and said, 'This man knows nothing about treating [him].' He then said to the knight, 'Which would you prefer, living with one leg or dying with two?' The knight replied, 'Living with one leg.' The European doctor said, 'Bring me a strong knight and a sharp ax.' A knight came with the ax. Then the doctor laid the leg of the patient on a block of wood and commanded the knight to strike his leg with the ax and chop it off at one blow. Accordingly, he struck it — while I was looking on — one blow, but the leg was not severed. He dealt another blow, upon which the marrow of the leg flowed out and the patient died on the spot. . . .

I once went with another to Jerusalem and met a blind man, a Muslim. I inquired about this man and was told that he used to practice tricks on the European crusaders and cooperate with his mother in assassinating them. They finally brought charges against him and tried his case according to European way of procedure.

They installed a huge tub and filled it with water. Across it they placed a board of wood. They then bound the arms of the man charged with the act, tied a rope around his shoulders, and dropped him into the tub. The Europeans believed that if the man was innocent, he would sink in the water; they would then lift him up with a rope. If he was guilty, he would not sink in the water. This Muslim did his best to sink when they dropped him into the water, but he could not do it. So he had to submit to their sentence against him — may Allah's curse be upon them!

. . . . . Adapted from: Charles T. Davis, ed. *Western Awakening*. Vol II, Sources of Medieval History. New York: Appleton-Century-Crofts, 1967.

1. How did this Muslim describe the European crusaders? Which characteristics did he admire? Which did he not?
2. Compare this Muslim description of the western European to the Byzantine description of the Muslim invaders in Reading 27. How can you explain the similarities and the differences?
3. Do you have any friends or relatives who were born outside of this country? How is their home life different from yours? How is it the same? Why?

32. The Koran

When Muhammad died in 632 A.D., the chief task of his followers was to spread the word of Allah, as revealed in the Koran. The Koran guided the Muslim people's lives and was the basis for their law. The defense of these Islamic principles justified to the Muslims their widespread conquests, especially in the seventh and eighth centuries. An excerpt from the Koran follows.

All that is in the heavens and the earth glorifies Allah; and He is the Mighty, the Wise.

He it is Who created the heavens and the earth in six days; then He mounted the Throne. He knows all that enters the earth and all that emerges from it. . . . He is with you wherever you may be. And Allah sees all that you do.

Believe in Allah and His messenger, and those who spread the word and believe in it will have a great reward.

Is it not time for those who believe in Allah to submit to the truth that has been revealed in order that they not become as those who believe in other Scripture and are evil-doers?

Lo! those who give for charity, both men and women, and lend Allah a good deed, it will be doubled for them, and theirs will be a rich reward.

And those who believe in Allah and His messenger, they are the loyal ones and will be rewarded. While those who do not believe and deny Our revelations, they are owners of hell-fire.

Do not be unhappy for what you have lost, nor rejoice over things that have been given to you. Allah does not love proud boasters.

O ye who believe! Be mindful of your duty to Allah and put faith in His messenger. He will give you twice His mercy and will give you a' light in which to walk and will forgive you. Allah is forgiving and merciful. . . .

Adapted from: Charles T. Davis, ed. *The Eagle, the Crescent, and the Cross.* Vol. 1, Sources of Medieval History. New York: Appleton-Century-Crofts, 1967.

1. How do the Muslims describe Allah?
2. What principles stated in this passage might have been used by Muslims to support their movement to expand and conquer?
3. Are any of the principles stated here similar to those of other religions? Which ones? Explain why such similarities exist, based on what you have read in your textbook.

REVIEWING READINGS 31–32

1. The Crusades were the Christian Church's attempt to save the Holy Land from the Muslims. How are the Crusades similar in purpose to the Muslim expansion and conquest? How are they different?
2. Both the Muslims and western Europeans referred to each other as "barbaric." Do you agree with either group's opinion of the other? Why or why not?

14 The Early Kingdoms of Eastern Europe

THE PLACE OF PETER THE GREAT IN RUSSIAN HISTORY

Even a century after his death, there was little agreement among Russians as to whether Peter I truly deserved the title "Great." Some Russians praised the western reforms imposed by Peter. Others denounced them, standing firm on the merits of Russian civilization. In the following selections, two nineteenth-century historians debate the importance of Peter I and his place in Russian history.

33. Nickolai M. Karamzin Writes Against Peter I

Nikolai Karamzin (NIK-uh-lie kah-rahm-ZEEN) was a widely read Russian historian and writer of the nineteenth century. He believed in a strong monarchy, but he criticized the rulers of the eighteenth century, including Peter the Great. In 1811 he wrote a Memoir on Ancient and Modern Russia, which he sent to Tsar Alexander I, under whose reign the western or European ways prevailed. The following is an exercpt from Karamzin's book on the merits of Peter the Great.

Shall we Russians agree with ignorant foreigners who claim that Peter was the founder of our greatness? How can we forget the princes of Moscow who built a powerful state out of nothing? Peter found the means to achieve greatness because the foundation for greatness had been laid by the Moscow princes before Peter.

While extolling the glory of this monarch, Peter, should we overlook the evil side of his brilliant reign? Let us not go into his personal vices. However, his admiration for foreign customs surely exceeded the bounds of reason. Peter was unable to realize that the national spirit was the moral strength of a state, and indispensable to stability.

Our ancestors, while taking advantage of the usefulness to be found in foreign customs, never lost the conviction that a Russian was the most perfect citizen and that Russia was the foremost state in the world. Let their belief be called a delusion. Yet how much it did to strengthen patriotism and the moral fiber of our country! Adapted from: Nikolai Mikhailovich Karamzin. *Memoir on Ancient and Modern Russia.* Richard Pipes, ed. Cambridge: Harvard University Press, 1959.

1. What did Karamzin think of Peter the Great? Cite references to the reading to support your answer.
2. How did Karamzin compare Peter's reign to that of the earlier Russian rulers? Whose ideas did he praise? Why?
3. What message do you think Karamzin tried to relay to Alexander I by sending him this book? Explain your answer.

34. Peter Chaadayev Praises Peter the Great

Peter Y. Chaadayev (chah-DAH-yev) was a Russian philosopher of the nineteenth century. In 1836, in an essay published in a

Moscow newspaper, Chaadayev attacked Russian institutions, including the Russian church and serfdom. Chaadayev's views caused an uproar, but also clarified the growing rift that was developing between Russians who defended the traditional way of life and those who supported the westernization of it. Do you think Chaadayev's views may have influenced his opinion of Peter the Great?

Peter dug an abyss between our past and our present, and into it he threw all our traditions. He saw that we Russians lacked a history upon which to build our future. Thus, he freed us from our previous history, which would have prevented our progress. Peter the Great found only a blank page when he came to power, and with a strong hand he wrote upon it the words: "Europe and the West." From that time on, we Russians were part of Europe and the West.

Russian traditions did not have the power to create the future. I do not believe in that smug patriotism, that lazy patriotism, which manages to make everything beautiful and with which unfortunately many of our good citizens are afflicted today.

One hundred and fifty years ago the greatest of our rulers, Peter, the one ruler who supposedly began a new era, was able to turn his back on old Russia. He swept aside all our institutions with his powerful breath.   Adapted from: Peter Y. Chaadayev, "Apology of a Madman," in Hans Kohn, ed. *The Mind of Modern Russia*. New York: Harper & Row, 1962.

1. Why does Chaadayev consider Peter to be a great ruler?
2. Do you think Chaadayev and Karamzin differed in their meaning of patriotism? Why or why not?
3. Do you think Chaadayev's political views of nineteenth-century Russia may have influenced his opinion of Peter the Great? Explain.

REVIEWING READINGS 33–34

1. How does Karamzin's opinion of Peter the Great differ from that of Chaadayev? Give possible reasons for the difference.
2. From what you have read in your textbook, which opinion of Peter the Great do you support? Why?
3. At the start of a new school year, did you ever form an opinion of a teacher based on what another friend said about that teacher? How can you prove that your opinion is fair? Explain your answer.

Did you know that the Black Death, the epidemic disease that spread throughout the world between 1330 and 1350, reduced the population of Europe from 80 million in 1300 to 60 million in 1400? More people died than there are living today in the cities of New York, Los Angeles, and Chicago combined!

chapter 15

The Early Peoples of Africa and Their Empires

LIFE IN THE EARLY AFRICAN EMPIRES

Perhaps no other continent has inspired more myths or false notions than Africa. For years, "knowledge" of Africa consisted more of popular fictions about the continent than of established facts. These misconceptions about Africa originated with the people who traveled there rather than with the native Africans. For example, in the 1700's, the Scottish philosopher David Hume wrote that only white people had ever built civilized nations. And in the early 1800's, Georg Hegel, a German philosopher, declared that Africa south of the Sahara Desert had no history at all. Points of view similar to those of Hume and Hegel persisted well into the twentieth century. It was not until sources on early Africa became available that such myths were proved wrong. Read the following excerpts from the writings of native Africans, Arab travelers, and European explorers.

35. The Empire of Ghana

Al-Bakri (ahl-BAHK-ree) was a Muslim scholar and geographer who lived in Spain during the eleventh century. He wrote a famous medieval geography book called The Book of Roads and Kingdoms. The author probably never left Spain, but received much of his information from Arab travelers and traders. Only a part of his book is still in existence, a portion of which follows.

The city of Ghana consists of two towns lying in a plain. One of these towns is inhabited by Muslims. It is large and has twelve mosques, in one of which the people assemble for prayer. Around the town are wells of sweet water from which people drink and near which they grow vegetables. The town in which the king lives is 6 miles from the Muslim one. The land between the two towns is covered with houses. The houses of the inhabitants are made of stone and wood.

The king has a palace and a number of dome-shaped dwellings. They are surrounded by an enclosure like the defensive wall of a city. In the town where the king lives, and not far from the hall where he holds his court of justice, is a mosque where the Muslims who come on visiting diplomatic missions pray. Around the king's town are domed buildings and woods, which contain the tombs of the dead kings. These woods are guarded and no unauthorized person can enter them.

Of the people who follow the king's religion, only he and his heir, who is the son of his sister, may wear sewed clothes. All other people wear clothes of cotton, silk, or brocade, according to their means. All men shave their beards, and women shave their heads. The king adorns himself with necklaces and bracelets. When he sits before the people, he puts on a high cap decorated

643

with gold and wrapped in turbans of fine cotton.

The court of appeal is held in a domed pavilion around which stand ten horses with gold-embroidered trappings. Behind the king stand ten pages holding shields and swords decorated with gold, and on his right are sons of the lesser kings of his country, all wearing splendid garments. The mayor of the city sits on the ground before the king, and around him are ministers seated likewise. At the door of the pavilion are pedigreed dogs, which guard the king. They wear collars of gold and silver on their necks, studded with a number of balls of the same metals. The audience is announced by the beating of a drum made from a long hollow log. When the people who profess the same religion as the king approach him, they fall on their knees and sprinkle their heads with dust, for this is their way of showing him their respect. As for the Muslims, they greet him only by clapping their hands.

When the king dies, the people build an enormous dome of wood over the place where his tomb will be. Then they carry him on a bed covered with a few carpets and cushions and put him inside the dome. At his side they place ornaments, his weapons, and the dishes from which he used to eat and drink, filled with various kinds of food and drink. They also place there the men who have served his meals. They close the door of the dome and cover it with mats and materials. Then they assemble the people, who heap earth upon it until it becomes like a large mound. They dig a ditch around the mound so that it can be reached only at one place.

For every donkey loaded with salt that enters the country, the king takes a tax of about $1/8$ of an ounce of gold,

and he takes $1/4$ of an ounce from every one that leaves. From a load of copper, the tax due to the king is $5/8$ of an ounce of gold, and from a load of merchandise over 1 ounce of gold. The best gold found in this land comes from a town which is eighteen days travel south from the city of the king, over a country inhabited by blacks. The nuggets found in all the mines of this country are reserved for the king. The nuggets may be of any weight from an ounce to a pound. It is said that the king owns a nugget as large as a big stone.
Adapted from: Al-Bakri. *The Book of Roads and Kingdoms.* Unpublished.

1. What do you think is the main point stressed in this reading about each of the following?
    a. The city of Ghana
    b. The king of Ghana
    c. The king's followers
    d. Taxes for the king of Ghana
2. Explain why Al-Bakri's account of Ghana might differ from an account written by a native of Ghana. Cite specific sections that might have been described differently by a native.
3. How accurately would a visitor from another country be able to describe the way of life in your community? Explain your answer.

36. The Empire of Mali
In 1325, at the age of twenty-one, Ibn Battuta (IB-'n buh-TOO-tuh) left his home in Tangier in North Africa and traveled widely throughout Asia, Africa, and Europe for the next twenty-four years. He returned home in 1349, only to leave again in 1352 on a tour of the black empires of West Africa. It was during this last journey across the Sahara that Ibn Battuta spent a year in the Empire of Mali, then at the height of its

power. The following account is one of the few surviving descriptions of Mali.

Among the admirable qualities of these people of Mali are the following. The small number of acts of crime that one finds there. The blacks hate injustice. The king pardons no one who is guilty of it.

One enjoys complete and general safety throughout the land. The traveler has no more reason than the person who stays at home to fear thieves.

The blacks do not steal the goods of whites who die in their country, not even when these consist of big treasures. On the contrary, they deposit them with someone they can trust among the whites, until those who have a right to the goods present themselves and take possession.

They make their Muslim prayers punctually; they attend the meetings of the faithful, and they punish their children if they should fail to do this. On Fridays, anyone who is late at the mosque will find nowhere to pray, the crowd is so great.

The blacks wear fine white garments on Fridays. If by chance a man has no more than one shirt or a soiled robe, at least he washes it before putting it on to go to public prayer.

They zealously learn the Koran, a collection of Muslim religious teachings, by heart. Those children who are neglectful in this are put in chains until they have memorized the Koran.

One day I was passing by a young black, a handsome lad and very well dressed, who had a heavy chain on his feet. I said to my companion: "What's happened to the boy? Has he murdered someone?" The young black heard what I had said and began laughing. "They have chained him," I was told, "simply to make him memorize the Koran."

The blacks throw dust and cinders on their heads as a sign of good manners and respect. Adapted from: *Ibn Battuta. Travels in Asia and Africa 1325–1354*, trans. Sir Hamilton Gibb. London: British Book Center, 1929.

1. What four aspects of life in Mali did Ibn Battuta choose to write about?
2. What characteristics of life in Mali did Ibn Battuta admire? Explain.
3. If you had visited Mali about the time this piece was written, do you think

you might have admired the same things? Why or why not?

37. Kanem-Bornu

Al-Maqrizi (ahl-mahk-REE-zee) was a Muslim scholar and historian who taught in many of the mosques in Cairo during the late fourteenth and early fifteenth centuries. He wrote the following account of Kanem-Bornu around 1400.

The inhabitants of Kanem-Bornu are a great people, and for the most part Muslims. Their king is a nomad. When he sits on his throne, his people fall on their faces. His army of horsemen and foot soldiers numbers 100,000. The king has five lesser kings subject to him.

The inhabitants of Kanem-Bornu cover their heads with a veil. The king does not show himself except at the time of the two religious festivals; the rest of the year he is not seen, and those who talk to him are placed behind a screen. The principal food of these people is rice, which grows wild in the country. They also have cheese, corn, figs, limes, melons, pumpkins, and fresh dates. As regards money, they use a kind of cloth which they make and which is called *wendy*. Other substances, such as different kinds of shells and pieces of copper or gold, are equally used in business. In this country the pumpkins are so big that they are used as boats to cross the Nile. Adapted from: Roland Oliver and J. D. Fage. *A Short History of Africa*. Baltimore: Penguin Books, 1970.

1. What clues does al-Maqrizi give that show he was impressed with the people of Kanem-Bornu? Cite specific lines from the reading.

2. Could this account be of value in studying the geography and natural resources of this region? Explain your answer.

3. What physical aspects of your city or town might give an outside observer an idea of how your community lives?

38. The Kongo Kingdom

Abbé Proyart (proe-YAHR), a French missionary, lived near the mouth of the Zaire River in central Africa during the eighteenth century. Read what he found to be amazing about life in the Kongo Kingdom.

These ministers have no offices or houses as ours have. They do not even know how to read or write our language. Their clerks are diligent servants, who they send into the towns and provinces to signify to the people the king's intentions.

In all the provinces and in all the towns, there is a governor for the king. The chiefs of the villages are also king's officers. They administer justice in his name. When anyone is accused of a crime for which there is no proof of guilt, they permit this person to defend himself or herself by drinking the *kassa*. The *kassa* is prepared by mixing a bit of wood with water. This potion is a true poison to weak stomachs. Anyone who does not die from this is declared innocent, and the accuser is condemned as a slanderer. If the drinker appears to be dying from the *kassa*, an antidote is given, provided the crime does not deserve death. But the chiefs sentence the accused, as a culprit, to the penalty fixed by law.

The inhabitants of the country have the greatest faith in this ritual. The princes and lords sometimes cause *kassa* to be taken in order to satisfy their suspicions. But they must first obtain the king's permission to do so, which is not difficult when their suspicions are strong.   Adapted from: Abbé Proyart, *History of Loango, Kakonga, etc.* Paris, 1776.

1. What aspects of the early Kongo system of justice and law affected the Abbé Proyart?
2. What might David Hume have thought of the kassa ritual the French missionary observed?
3. How do you think a foreigner might view your society's system of justice? Explain your answer.

39.   An East African Kingdom

John H. Speke (SPEEK) was the English explorer who discovered Lake Victoria and solved the mystery of the sources of the Nile River. In 1862, he was the first European to visit Uganda in East Africa. The following is an account of the welcome he received upon his arrival.

To do royal honors to the king of this charming land, I ordered my people to put down their loads and fire a volley of shots. This was no sooner done than we received an invitation to come in at once, for the king wished to see us before attending to anything else. We entered the king's quarters and, walking through extensive enclosures with huts of kingly dimensions, were escorted to a porch. The Arabs had built this porch as a sort of government office, where the king might conduct his state affairs.

Here, as we entered, we saw sitting on the ground Rumanika, the king, and his brother Nnanaji, both of them men of noble appearance and size. The king was plainly dressed in an Arab's black robe and wore for an ornament rich colored beads and neatly worked wristlets of copper. Nnanaji, being a doctor, in addition to a checked cloth wrapped round him, was covered with charms. At their sides lay huge pipes of black clay. Behind them, squatting quiet as mice, were all the king's sons, some six or seven lads, who wore leather clothing and little dream charms tied under their chins.

The first greetings of the king were warm and affectionate. The king and his people had fine, oval faces, large eyes, and high noses. Having shaken hands in English style, which is the custom of the people of this country, the every-smiling Rumanika begged us to be seated on the ground opposite to him. At once he wished to know what we thought of his mountains, for it had struck him they were the finest in the world; and the lake too—did we not admire it?

Time flew like magic, the king's mind was so quick and inquiring. But as the day was wasting away, he generously gave us our option to choose a place for our residence in or out of his palace, and allowed us time to select one. We found the view overlooking the lake to be so charming that we preferred camping outside. Our group began to work at once, cutting sticks and long grass to erect sheds.

I then put in a word for myself. Since we had entered this land, we never could get one drop of milk either for love or money, and I wished to know what motive the people had for withholding it. We had heard they held superstitious dreads. For example, if anyone ate the flesh of pigs, fish, or fowl, and then tasted the products of their cows, their cattle would be destroyed. I told the king that I hoped he did not labor under any such absurd delusions. To which he replied it was only the poor who thought so. And as he now saw we were in want, he would set apart one of his cows expressly for our use. On bidding goodbye, the usual formalities of hand-shaking were gone through. On entering camp, I found the good thoughtful king had sent us some more of his excellent beer.   Adapted from: John Hanning Speke. *Journal of the Discovery of the Source of the Nile.* Reprint of 1863 ed., Westport, Conn.: Greenwood, 1968.

1. How would you describe Speke's opinion of the beliefs and customs of these people? Cite specific lines from the reading to support your answer.
2. In what terms did Speke describe the East African king? Why do you think he liked him?
3. Think of a person you would want to be like. What about this person do you admire the most? Why do you think you chose these qualities to imitate?

40. A Chinese View of Somalia

By the 1400's, the Chinese had developed extensive trade with cities and villages along the coast of East Africa. As you have read, Admiral Cheng Ho was especially active in promoting trade with the East African city-states. Although his own reports on his naval expeditions have long since vanished, a Chinese scholar and officer who traveled with Cheng Ho has left us a description of fifteenth-century Somalia.

In the country of Somalia, the people live in solitary and separate villages. The walls of houses are made of piled-up bricks, and the houses are built in high blocks. The customs are very simple. They grow neither herbs nor trees. Men and women wear their hair in rolls. When they go out, they wear a linen hood.

The mountains are uncultivated and the land wide. It rains very rarely. Fish are caught in the sea with nets. The animals of this country include lions, gold-spotted leopards, and camels which are 6 or 7 feet tall. For merchandise they have colored silks, gold, silver, porcelains, pepper, colored stains, rice, and other cereals.   Adapted from: J. Desmond Clark, *et al.*, eds. *The Horizon History of Africa.* New York: American Heritage, 1971.

1. What aspects of Somalian life did the Chinese scholar choose to describe?
2. Do you think this description of Somalia could also be a source of information on how fifteenth-century Chinese lived? Explain.
3. Why do you think an account from a Chinese explorer would be as important for a historian studying early African empires as would an account from a European or Arab explorer?
4. Would an account of your way of life written by a person from another country be important for people who wished to learn more about you? Would it be the best source of information? Explain.

REVIEWING READINGS 35–40

1. Neither Hume nor Hegel had access to the information about Africa you have just examined. Do you think they would have changed their minds about Africa had they been able to read these selections? Explain.
2. How do your impressions of early African life differ from the impressions of Africa you had before reading these selections? What is the importance of this difference?

648

16 Village Life and Slave Trade

THE EFFECTS OF THE SLAVE TRADE ON AFRICAN VILLAGE LIFE

When Europeans landed in Africa in the fifteenth century, they found a people unlike themselves. The Africans did not worship their God, practiced seemingly tortuous rituals, and lived a day-to-day life which differed markedly from their own. Their observations seemed to support the stories heard by contemporary Europeans: Africans were not a civilized people. How do you think the European attitude, and the later slave trade, affected the traditional village life of the African people?

41. Village Life in West Africa

The following account of West African village life was written just before 1789 by Olaudah Equiano (EK-wee-an-oh). He had been captured as a slave near the capital city of Benin. He was sent to the United States and later obtained his freedom. While living in England, he wrote about his early life in a West African forest kingdom west of the Niger River delta.

The kingdom where I lived was divided into many provinces. I was born in one of the most remote and fertile provinces, in the year 1745. It was situated in a charming, fruitful valley. The distance of this province from the capital of Benin and the sea coast must have been very great. For I had never heard of whites or Europeans, nor of the sea. Our subjection to the king of Benin was very little. Every transaction of the government, as far as I observed, was conducted by the chiefs or elders of the village. The manners and government of a people who have little commerce with other countries are generally very simple. The history of what passes in one family or village may serve as an example of the whole nation. My father was one of those elders or chiefs I have spoken of.

We are a nation of dancers, musicians, and poets. Thus every great event, such as a triumphant return from battle or other cause of public rejoicing, is celebrated in public dances. These dances are accompanied with songs and music suited to the occasion. The assembly is separated into four age groups, which dance either apart or in succession, and each with a character peculiar to itself.

The first division contains the married men, who in their dances exhibit feats of arms and the representation of a battle. Next are the married women, who dance in the second division. The young men occupy the third, and the unmarried women the fourth. Each represents some interesting scene of real life, such as a great achievement, home life, a sad story, or some sport. This gives our dances a spirit and a variety which I have scarcely seen elsewhere. We have many musical instruments, particularly drums of different kinds, another which resembles a guitar, and another much like a xylophone.

As our manners are simple, our luxuries are few. The dress of all the people is nearly the same. It generally consists of a long piece of calico or muslin wrapped loosely round the body. This cloth is usually dyed blue, which is our favorite color. The dye is extracted from a berry, and the color is brighter and richer than any I have seen in Europe.

Our manner of living is entirely plain. Goats and poultry supply the greatest part of our food. These are likewise the main wealth of the country and the chief articles of its trade. The meat is usually stewed in a pan. To make it savory, we sometimes also use pepper and other spices. Our vegetables are mostly yams, beans, and Indian corn.

Before we taste food, we always wash our hands—indeed, our cleanliness on all occasions is extreme. Our principal luxury is perfume. [We make it from] a wood of delicious fragrance. [We make another from] a kind of earth, a small portion of which thrown into the first diffuses a most powerful scent like a rose. We beat this wood into powder and mix it with palm oil, with which both men and women perfume themselves.

Each master of a family has a large square piece of ground, surrounded by a moat or fence or enclosed with a wall made of tempered red earth, which when dry is as hard as brick. Within this are houses to accommodate the family and slaves, who, if numerous, often present the appearance of a village. In the middle stands the main building, for the sole use of the master. It consists of two apartments. He uses one of them in the daytime to sit in with his family. The other is left apart for the reception of his friends. He has besides these a separate apartment in which he sleeps, together with his male children. On each side are the apartments of his

wives, who have also their separate day and night houses. The living quarters of the slaves and their families are distributed throughout the rest of the enclosure.

These houses never exceed one story in height. They are always built of wooden stakes driven into the ground and crossed with branches, and they are neatly plastered within and without. The roofs are thatched with reeds. Our day houses are left open at the sides. But those in which we sleep are always covered, and plastered on the inside to keep off the different insects which annoy us during the night. The walls and floors are generally covered with mats. Our beds consist of a platform, raised 3 or 4 feet from the ground, on which are laid skins and different parts of a spongy tree. Our covering is calico or muslin, the same as our dress. The usual seats are a few logs of wood. But we have benches, which are generally perfumed, to accommodate strangers.

We have markets, at which I have been often with my mother. These are sometimes visited by stout, mahogany-colored men from the southwest of us. We call them Oye-Eboe, which means "red men living at a distance." They generally bring us firearms, gunpowder, hats, beads, and dried fish. The last we regard as a great rarity, since our waters are only brooks and springs. They always carry slaves through our land. Sometimes, indeed, we have sold slaves to them, but they were only prisoners of war, or such among us as had been convicted of kidnapping or some other crime we regard as horrible.

Our land is uncommonly rich and fruitful, and produces all kinds of vegetables in great abundance. We have plenty of Indian corn and vast quantities of cotton and tobacco. Our pineapples grow wild. We have also spices of different kinds, particularly pepper, and a variety of delicious fruits which I have never seen in Europe, and honey in abundance. Agriculture is our chief employment. Everyone works at it. And, as we are unacquainted with idleness, we have no beggars.

As to religion, the natives believe that there is one creator of all things, and that he lives in the sun, and is girded round with a belt, that he may never eat or drink. But according to some, he smokes a pipe, which is our own favorite luxury. They believe he governs events, especially our deaths or captivity.

I have remarked before that the natives of this part of Africa are extremely clean. This necessary habit of decency was a part of our religion, and therefore we had many purifications and washings. Those who touched the dead at any time were obliged to wash and purify themselves before they could enter a dwelling house.   Adapted from: Olandah Equiano. *The Interesting Narrative of Olandah Equiano.* New York: E. P. Dutton, 1970.

1. What do you think is the main point stressed in this reading about each of the following? Explain your answers.
    a. The provinces and government
    b. Dancing and music
    c. Way of life
    d. Family life
    e. Religion
    f. Slavery
2. Compare the tone of this account with that of the English explorer John Speke in Reading 39. How do you explain the differences?
3. Do you think Equiano's account is a worthwhile piece of evidence about African village life? Explain.

42. A Kanem-Bornu Slave Song

The European slave trade disrupted African village life and also brought personal hardship to those who were abruptly torn away from their families and familiar daily routine. The following song was sung by women who were taken captive by Arab traders. Read how they felt as they made the fateful journey from their homeland of Kanem-Bornu northward across the Sahara to the European ships awaiting them in the Mediterranean.

Where are we going? Where are we going?
Where are we going, Rubee?[1]
Hear us, save us, make us free;
Send our Atka[2] down from thee!

Strange and large the world is growing!
Tell us, Rubee, where are we going?
Where are we going, Rubee?

Bornu! Bornu! Where is Bornu?
Where are we going, Rubee?
Bornu-land was rich and good,
Wells of water, fields of food;
Bornu-land we see no longer,
Here we thirst, and here we hunger,
Here the Moor man[3] smites in anger;
Where are we going, Rubee?

Where are we going? Where are we going?
Hear us, save us, Rubee!
Moons of marches from our eyes,
Bornu-land behind us lies;

1. *Rubee* means gold.
2. *Atka* was the old Kanem-Bornu belief in human freedom.
3. *Moor man* refers to the Arab slave trader.

651

Hot the desert wind is blowing,
Wild the waves of sand are flowing!
Hear us! Tell us, Where are we
    going?
Where are we going, Rubee?

Adapted from: J. Desmond Clark, *et al.*, eds.
"Song of the Slaves in the Desert," *The Horizon
History of Africa*. New York: American Heritage,
1971.

1. How did these women seem to feel
   about being slaves? Cite specific lines
   from the reading, to support your
   answer.
2. Do you think this song could be used
   as historical evidence about part of
   the African slave trade? Explain your
   answer.
3. Do you know of any popular songs
   that protest against injustices in your
   society? Give examples. Could these
   songs be used by historians 200 years
   from now to learn about your culture?
   Why or why not?

REVIEWING READINGS 41–42

1. From the selections you have just read
   and the information in your textbook,
   how do you think the slave trade affected African lives?
2. Do you think these selections would
   be useful to a historian studying early
   African history? Why or why not?
3. Why do you think myths about the
   early African people developed? Do
   you think they were justified? Explain.
4. What might you do the next time you
   encounter a suspected myth?

Did you know that the population of
Africa grew from 6.5 million in 1000 B.C.
to 46 million by 1500 A.D., an increase
nearly equal to the current populations
of California, Michigan and Pennsylvania
combined!

chapter 17 The Earliest Americans

THE AZTEC VIEW OF LIFE

A very important part of Aztec education was learning to keep records of significant events. Though the Aztecs did not have an alphabet as we know it, they recorded their history in the form of pictures and symbolic characters. The few surviving pieces of Aztec history have been translated into Spanish or Nahuatl (NAH-wat'l), the Aztec language. It is through these translations that the following selections on Aztec life have become available to us.

43. Aztec Justice

Joaquin Garcia Icazbalceta (wah-KEEN gahr-SEE-ah ee-KAHS-bahl-SAY-tah) was a Mexican historian who lived between 1824 and 1894. He wrote, edited, and translated several works on early Mexican history. He also put together the Mexican Bibliography of the Sixteenth Century, which includes information on the Aztecs. The following is a selection on the Aztec system of justice.

At dawn the judges would be seated on their mats, and soon people would begin to arrive with their quarrels. Somewhat early, food would be brought from the palace. After eating, the judges would rest a while, and then they would continue to listen until two hours before the sun set.

Every twelve days the ruler would meet with all of the judges to consider all of the difficult cases. Everything that was taken before him was to have been already carefully examined and discussed. The people who testified would tell the truth because of an oath which they took, but also because of their fear of the judges, who were very skilled at arguing and had a great skill for examination and cross-examination. And they would punish those who did not tell the truth.

The judges received no gifts in large or small quantities. They made no distinction between people, important or common, rich or poor, and in their judgments they exercised the utmost honesty with all.

If it were found that one of them had accepted a gift or misbehaved because of drinking, or if it were felt that he was negligent, the other judges themselves would reprehend him harshly. And if he did not correct his ways, after the third time they would have his head shaved. And with great publicity and shame for him they would remove him from office. This was to them a great disgrace. And because one judge showed favoritism in a dispute toward an important Indian against a common man and gave a false account, it was ordered that he be strangled and that the trial begin anew. And thus it was done, and the verdict was in favor of the common man. Adapted from: Miguel Leon-Portilla. "Aztec Democracy: In Favor of the Common Man," in Aztec Thought and Culture: A Study of the Ancient Nahuatl Mind. trans. Jack E. Davis. Norman, Okla.: University of Oklahoma Press, 1971.

1. What were three things Icazbalceta noted about Aztec justice?
2. Do you believe this selection illustrates the Aztecs' concern for preserving human dignity? Explain why or why not.

44. The Aztec Way of Life

The typical Aztec family probably lived a routine life based on agriculture. While men and their sons worked in the fields, women taught their daughters how to grind corn and make clothes. But, as we all do, the Aztecs at times found life difficult. Read the following account of an Aztec father's advice to his daughter on how to cope with the everyday ups and downs.

Must We Live Weeping?
A Father's Advice to His Daughter

Here you are, my little girl, my necklace of precious stone, my human creation, born of me. You are my blood, my color, my image.

Now listen, understand, You are alive, you have been born; Our Lord, the maker of people, the inventor of men, has sent you to earth.

Now that you begin to look around you, be aware. Here it is like this: there is no happiness, no pleasure. There is heartache, worry, fatigue. Here spring up and grow suffering and distress.

Here on earth is the place of much wailing, the place where our strength is worn out, where we are well acquainted with bitterness and discouragement.

They say truly that we are burned by the force of the sun and the wind. This is the place where one almost perishes of thirst and hunger. This is the way it is here on earth.

Listen well, my child, my little girl. There is no place of well-being on the earth, there is no happiness, no pleasure. They say that the earth is the place of painful pleasure, of grievous happiness.

The elders have always said: "So that we should not go round always moaning, that we should not be filled with sadness, and God has given us laughter, sleep, food, our strength, and finally the act of love."

All this sweetens life on earth so that we are not always moaning. But even though it be true that there is only suffering and this is the way things are on earth, even so, should we always be fearful? Must we live weeping?

But, little one, there is on the earth, there are the lords; there is authority, there is nobility, there are eagles and knights. And who is always saying that so it is on earth? Who goes about trying to put an end to his life? There is ambition, there is struggle, work.

Adapted from Miguel Leon-Portilla. "Must We Live Weeping?" in *Pre-Columbian Literature of Mexico.* trans. Grace Lobanov. Norman, Okla.: University of Oklahoma Press, 1969.

1. What viewpoints of life did the little girl learn from her father? Have you ever received similar advice from your parents or relatives? How does it compare to the Aztec father's advice to his daughter? Explain the similarities and differences.
2. Could this reading be used as evidence to show how Aztec society and government worked? If so, explain how by citing examples from the reading.

45. Aztec Poetry

Aztec children also learned about their culture and traditions at school. Priests, who were some of the most educated people in society, often taught the children in school about life through poetry. Examples of Aztec poetry follow.

One Day We Must Go

One day we must go,
One night we will descend into the region of mystery.
Here, we only come to know ourselves;
Only in passing are we here on earth.
In peace and pleasure let us spend our lives; come, let us enjoy ourselves.
Let not the angry do so; the earth is vast indeed!
Would that one lived forever;
Would that one were not to die!

Who Am I?

Who am I?
As a bird I fly about,
I sing of flowers;
I compose songs, butterflies of song,
Let them burst forth from my soul!
Let my heart be delighted with them!

He Is Whole

The feather artist
He is whole; he has a face and a heart.
The good feather artist is skillful, is master of himself;
It is his duty to humanize the desires of the people.
He works with feathers, chooses them and arranges them, paints them with different colors,
joins them together.
The bad feather artist is careless; he ignores the look of things, he is greedy, he scorns other people.
He is like a turkey with a shrouded heart, sluggish, coarse, weak.
The things that he makes are not good.
He ruins everything he touches.

Adapted from: Miguel Leon-Portilla. *Aztec Thought and Culture: A Study of the Ancient Nahuatl Mind.* Norman, Okla.: University of Oklahoma, 1963.

1. What do you think is the main point of: (a) One Day We Must Go (b) Who Am I? (c) He Is Whole?
2. Do you think a people's poetry should be considered when evaluating their culture? Explain by using Aztec poetry as an example.

46. Aztec Songs

As you have read in Chapter 17 of the textbook, death had special meanings for the Aztecs. What meaning did the following song about death have for the Aztec warrior who sung it when going off to battle?

There is nothing like death in war,
nothing like the flowery death
so precious to Him who gives life:
far off I see it: my heart
yearns for it!

Adapted from: Peter Farb. *Man's Rise to Civilization, As Shown by the Indians of North America from Primeval Times to the Coming of the Industrial State.* New York: E. P. Dutton, 1968.

1. Why do you think an Aztec warrior would have sung such a battle song?
2. Do you think this song may have had anything to do with the Aztec belief in human sacrifice? Explain.

1. What picture do these readings give us of what Aztec Indians believed to be important in their lives?
2. How does the Aztec view of life compare to your own? Explain the similarities and the differences.
3. What kinds of documents or evidence would you assemble that might give another culture an idea of what your life is like? Explain your choice.

<table>
<tr><td>chapter</td></tr>
<tr><td>18</td><td>Europe Explores and Colonizes the New World</td></tr>
</table>

COLONIZATION AND THE AMERICAN INDIAN

The Europeans who explored and colonized the Americas believed they had good reason to conquer the natives of North and South America. The Spaniards, for example, felt that by imposing their culture and their religion on the Indian, they would "civilize" what seemed to them like a barbaric way of life. Yet some were conscious of the disruptive effect the Spaniards had on the lives of the Indians of the New World.

47. Justifying War Against the Indians

Juan de Sepúlveda (say-POOL-vay-dah) was a sixteenth-century Spanish historian and theologian who believed that the conqueror's treatment of the Indians in the Americas was justified. Other European colonial powers held views similar to Sepúlveda's. As you read the following argument, note how Sepúlveda refers to the Indians as "barbarians" and to the Roman Catholic faith as the "true religion."

In warfare it is proper that hostilities first be declared, so that barbarians may be asked to accept the great benefits provided by the victor, to learn his best laws and customs, to familiarize themselves with the true religion, and to admit the sovereignty of the king of Spain. If they reject this sovereignty, they may then be treated as enemies of the Spaniards, Spaniards who were sent by the king for the purpose of dominating them. If the barbarians request time to think this over, they should be granted as much time as they need to summon a public meeting and make their decision.

If, after being instructed in this, they obey our orders, they are then to be admitted into the faith. But if they do not heed the warning, then on being defeated both they and their goods should fall to the hands of the victorious leader to dispose of as he sees fit. To be sure, the cause of peace and of the public good should govern the victor's decision, for these are considerations that we should always apply in punishing the enemy after the victory. Above all, we should avoid anything underhanded. For in talent and every kind of virtue and human sentiment the Indians are as inferior to the Spaniards as children are to adults, or women to men, or the cruel and inhumane to the very gentle.

Consider the nature of those people in one single example, that of the Aztecs, who are regarded as the most courageous. Their king was Montezuma, whose empire extended the length and breadth of those regions. He inhabited the city of Mexico, a city situated in a vast lake, and a very well defended city both on account of the nature of its location and on account of its fortifications. Informed of the arrival of Cortes and his victories, and his intention to go to Mexico under the supposed reason of a conference, Montezuma sought all possible means to keep him from his plan. Failing in this, terrorized and filled with fear, he received him in the city with about 300 Spaniards. Cortes, for his part, after taking possession of the city, forced the king and his subjects through terror to receive the yoke and rule of the king of Spain, but also imprisoned King Montezuma himself because of his suspicion that a plot was on foot to kill some Spaniards. This he could do because of the stupidity of the people. And thus Cortes, though aided by so small a number of Spaniards and so few natives, was able to hold them, oppressed and fearful at the beginning, for many days. Could there be a better or clearer testimony of the superiority that some men have over others in talent, skill, strength of spirit, and virtue? Is it not proof that the Indians are slaves by nature?

I have made reference to the customs and character of the barbarians. What shall I say now of the unholy religion and wicked sacrifices of such people, who believed that the best sacrifices to offer were hair and human hearts?   Adapted from: Juan Gines de Sepúlveda. *Second Democracy, or The Just Causes of the War Against the Indians.* Angel Losada, ed. Madrid: Franciscan Institute of International Law, 1951.

1. What reasons did Sepúlveda use to justify war against the Indians?
2. What view of human dignity do you think Sepúlveda seemed to have? How does it compare with that of the Aztecs you read about in Chapter 17? Explain.
3. What is meant by the term "barbarian"? What other people have you studied that have been called barbarians? Did you think this name was justified? What circumstances usually existed that caused people to refer to another group as barbaric?

48. A Dissenting Voice

Bartolomé de las Casas (lahs KAH-sahs), a Spanish Dominican priest, devoted much of his life to improving conditions for Indians living under Spanish rule. In 1564, he voiced the following concerns about the Spanish treatment of the Indians. As you read this selection, notice how Bartolomé de las Casas reveals his own thoughts on the European quest for empire in the Americas.

All the wars called conquests were and are most unjust and truly tyrannical.

We have taken over all the kingdoms of New Spain.

Our king, with all the power God gave him, cannot justify the wars and robberies against the Indians.

All the gold and silver, pearls and other riches, brought to Spain and traded among Spaniards in the New World—all is stolen, save perhaps a very little that came from the islands and places we have already depopulated.

Those who stole it and today steal it by conquests cannot be saved unless they restore it.

The natives in any or all the areas we have invaded in the New World have acquired the right to make just war upon us and erase us from the face of the earth, and this right will last until the Day of Judgment.

By all reasoning, the Indians—who never harmed nor were subject to Christians—freely possess and rule their own lands, and no one can make just war upon them.

From the beginning until now, Spain's entire invasion of the New World has been wrong and tyrannical. And from 1510 on, no Spaniard there can claim good faith as an excuse for wars, discoveries, or the slave trade.   Adapted from: Henry R. Wagner and Helen R. Parish. *The Life and Writings of Bartolomé de las Casas.* Albuquerque, N.M.: University of New Mexico Press, 1967.

1. What reasons did Bartholomé de las Casas give for opposing the European method of acquiring colonies in the New World? Cite references in the reading to support your answer.
2. How do you think Sepúlveda would have answered him?
3. Do you think that all "wars called conquests" are "unjust and truly tyrannical"? Why or why not?

REVIEWING READINGS 47–48

1. List the arguments that the Spaniards used to justify their conquest of the Indians in the New World. Which argument do you think was used more often than another? Explain your answer by using information from the textbook.
2. What do these arguments reveal about the values that were held by some Europeans during the age of exploration and colonization—particularly their views on human dignity? Explain by citing specific references to the readings.
3. Would you regard the Spaniards as "civilized" in their attitude and actions toward the Indians during the period of colonization? Explain why or why not.

Did you know that because of economic upheaval, exploitation, and new diseases, the native population of the New World fell from 11 million in 1518 to 6 million in 1547—a loss equal to nearly half the population of Texas!

chapter
19 The American Revolution

49. Common Sense and American Independence

Many of the ideas that sparked the revolution of the late eighteenth and early nineteenth centuries in the Americas and Europe had their roots in the American war for independence. Thomas Paine was one political writer who captured the imagination of American colonists with his fiery arguments for permanent separation from Great Britain. Read the following excerpt from Paine's Common Sense, a pamphlet published in January 1776. Why do you think Paine's writings were so successful in arousing the American colonists' feelings against Great Britain?

In the following pages I offer nothing more than simple facts, plain arguments, and common sense. . . .

I have heard it asserted by some, that as America has flourished under her former connection with Great Britain, the same connection is necessary toward her future happiness, and will always be so. Nothing can be more false than this kind of argument. . . .

I am not driven by motives of pride, party, or resentment to support the doctrine of separation and independence [from England]; I am clearly, positively, and conscientiously persuaded that it is the true interest of this continent to be so. . . .

But where, say some, is the King of America? I'll tell you, friend, He reigns above, and does not bring ruin to mankind like the royal brute of Great Britain [King George III] . . . in America the *law is king*.

For as in absolute governments the king is law, so in free countries the law ought to be king; and there ought to be no other. But in case any ill use should afterwards arise, let the Crown at the conclusion of the ceremony be demolished, and scattered among the people whose right it is.

A government of our own is our natural right: and when a man seriously reflects on the delicate nature of human affairs, he will become convinced, that it is infinitely wiser and safer, to form a constitution of our own. . . .

O! ye that love mankind! Ye that dare oppose not only the tyranny but the tyrant, stand forth! Every spot of the old world is overrun with oppression. Freedom has been hunted round the globe. Asia and Africa have long expelled it, Europe regards [freedom] like a stranger, and England has given [freedom] warning to depart. O! receive the fugitive, and prepare in time an asylum [a safe place] for mankind.   Adapted from: Thomas Paine. "Common Sense," in *Life and Writings of Thomas Paine*, Vol II. D. E. Wheeler, ed., New York, 1908, as adapted for The Shaping of Western Civilization, Vol. 2. Hinsdale, Ill.: Dryden Press, 1970.

1. What reasons does Paine give to justify American independence from Great Britain?

2. According to Paine, who is the "King of America"? How does this "King" compare to the king of England?

3. Would John Locke (see Chapter 11, Reading 28) have agreed with Paine's solution to America's problems? Why or why not?
4. How does Paine describe the eighteenth-century world? Based on what you have read in your textbook, do you agree with his evaluation of the world up until his time? Explain your answer.

chapter 20

The French Revolution and Napoleon

HOW MUCH OF THE PAST MUST BE DESTROYED?

On the eve of the French Revolution, there was no social class that suffered more than the common people. They not only were forced to pay the greatest burden of royal taxes but also faced a growing scarcity of food, high prices, low wages, and unemployment. Finally, in the summer of 1789, widespread peasant uprisings gave voice to these grievances. The action of the National Assembly in 1789, and of the other legislative bodies that were founded in defiance of king and privilege, put an end to absolute monarchy and the Old Regime in France, and claimed social justice for the people. Read the following selections, which give a sampling of how revolutionary changes came about.

50. The Great Fear of 1789

The Great Fear was the name given to the series of peasant uprisings that swept the French countryside during the summer of 1789. The following eyewitness account of that summer was written by a nobleman who was a deputy (or member) in the Estates-General. Do you think this nobleman believed the peasants' actions were justified or not?

One hundred and fifty chateaux were already burned! The fire threatened to take over all the estates. . . . Shall I speak of murders, of atrocities committed against the nobles? . . . Monsieur de Baras was cut into pieces in front of his wife. . . . Another's feet were burned to make him give up his title deeds! Madame de Berthilac was forced, the ax over her head, to give up her land! Madame la Princesse de Listenois was forced to the same sacrifice, with a knife at her neck, and her two daughters fainting at her feet! The marquis de Tremand, a sickly old man, was chased at night from his chateau and hunted from city to city, arriving at Basel [Switzerland], almost dying, with his broken-hearted daughters! . . . To justify these bloody atrocities, deputies of the commons wrote to the peasants that the nobles wished to blow up the hall of the [National] Assembly . . . They told the peasants that the nobles were against the king; they sent supposed orders to burn the chateaux and to massacre the nobles. . . . These horrible ways prepared the session of August 4 [abolition of feudalism, see Reading 51]. It was while surrounded by the bodies of nobles who were massacred in the light of the flames that devoured their chateaux, that the [National] Assembly pronounced the decrees violating the sacred rights of legitimate property! Adapted from: E. L. Higgins, ed. *The French Revolution as Told by Contemporaries* as adapted for The Shaping of Western Civilization, Vol. 2. Hinsdale, Ill.: Dryden Press, 1970.

1. Who created the "Great Fear"? Who were the victims of this destruction? Who does the nobleman believe was really to blame?
2. Rewrite a short version of this account as a peasant would have described it. How does it differ from the nobleman's description? Explain the similarities or differences.
3. Describe a demonstration that has taken place in your school, community, or city that caused damage to property. What was the reason for this demonstration? Was it successful? Why or why not? Could the same things have been achieved without the damage to property? Explain your answer.

51. The Decree to Abolish Feudalism

In August 1789, the National Assembly took action to put an end to the peasant violence. A proclamation was drafted in attempt to abolish the feudal system of privilege in France. The decree issued by the Assembly read in part as follows:

The National Assembly completely abolishes the feudal system. It decrees that among the rights that are feudal, those which derive from personal servitude shall be abolished without compensation.

The exclusive right of hunting is likewise abolished, and every landowner has the right to destroy or to have destroyed on his own land all

kinds of game. All royal hunting preserves are likewise abolished.

All courts on former feudal manors are suppressed.

Tithes [feudal taxes paid to the church] are abolished, on condition, however, that some other provision be made to pay for the expenses of religious worship, for assistance to the poor, and for the support of all institutions—schools, colleges, hospitals, etc. Until such provision is made, the same tithes shall continue.

The sale of government offices is hereby suspended.

Special privileges in matters of taxation are abolished forever. Taxes shall be collected from all citizens in the same manner and form. Adapted from: Raymond Phineas Stearns. *Pageant of Europe.* New York: Harcourt, Brace & World, 1961.

1. What privileges held by the French nobles under the Old Regime were abolished by the National Assembly in its decree?
2. Why were tithes not immediately abolished by the National Assembly?
3. How did this action by the National Assembly affect the common people? Refer to the reading to support your answer.

52. The Proclamation of the Jacobins, 1792

The Jacobins were the radical revolutionaries who successfully overthrew the monarchy in France. Fearful of foreign takeover and the return of a strong monarch, the Jacobins had united before the Legislative Assembly in 1792 and filed the following petition demanding the removal of Louis XVI and the establishment of a new constitutional convention. Soon after this proclamation was issued, the National Convention replaced the Legislative Assembly and Louis XVI was beheaded.

Legislators! The city government of Paris sends us to you; it is with grief that Paris denounces to you the head of the executive power [the king]. Without doubt, the people have the right to be angry with him.

We shall not retrace for you the entire conduct of Louis XVI since the first days of the Revolution and his bloody projects against the city of Paris. We shall not retrace for you the oaths so many times violated.

However, legislators, it is our duty to remind you of the ingratitude of that prince, the public finances entirely ruined by Louis XVI, and the eternal enemies of France becoming its allies. The despot of an enslaved land has not become the king of a free people. After having attempted to flee from France in order to reign from a foreign city, he has been restored to the throne, perhaps contrary to the wishes of the nation, which ought to have been consulted.

Abroad, armed enemies threaten our territory; it is to avenge Louis XVI that Austria adds a new chapter to the history of its cruelties; it is to avenge Louis XVI that the tyrants wish to destroy at a single blow all the citizens of France!

The enemy advances with rapid steps, while aristocrats command the armies of our republic.

The head of the executive power is the first link in the anti-revolutionary chain. He seems to participate in conspiracies; his name contends each day against that of the nation; his conduct is a formal and permanent act of disobedience to the constitution. As long as we have such a king, liberty cannot strengthen itself. We invoke the constitution, and ask for his deposition.

It is very doubtful whether the nation can have confidence in the present royal family. We ask that ministers selected by the Assembly may exercise the executive power waiting for the will of the people to be pronounced legally in a National Convention.   Adapted from: J. H. Hexter, *The Traditions of the Western World*, Chicago, Ill.: Rand McNally, 1968.

1. With what offenses did the Jacobins charge Louis XVI?
2. What are the immediate reasons given by the Jacobins for the overthrow of the king?
3. How do the Jacobin demands compare to those of Thomas Paine in *Common Sense* (see Reading 49)? Explain the similarities and differences.

1. What were some revolutionary steps that were taken to improve social conditions in France between 1789 and 1792?

2. Based on what you have read in the textbook and the readings, what seem to you to be the necessary ingredients for a successful political revolution? Use the French Revolution as an example.

chapter 21 Other American Revolutions and Growth of the Americas

53. The Spanish Colonists Fight for Independence

Revolutionary fever spread quickly across the Atlantic from North America to France, and then to South America. Spanish colonists also believed their mother country had committed grave social, political, and economic wrongs against them. American and French ideas of freedom gave these people the purpose and the reason to declare themselves independent from Spanish rule. Evidence of this influence is in the following excerpt from an address given on May 25, 1826, by Simon Bolivar to the Congress of Bolivia. Note that these people did not want a strong president because, like the American colonists, they too feared he might rule as king.

The president of Bolivia is deprived of all patronage [appointment to office for political favors]. He can appoint neither governors, nor judges, nor church dignitaries of any kind. This limitation of powers has never before been imposed in any government. One check after another has thus been placed upon the authority of the head of the government, who will in every way find that the people are ruled directly by those who exercise the significant functions of the nation. The church leaders will rule in matters of conscience; the judges in matters involving property, honor, and life; and the government's officials will rule in all major public acts. As all these individuals owe their position, their distinction, and their fortune to the people alone, the president cannot hope to entangle them in his personal ambitions. If to this is added the natural growth of political opposition which a democratic government experiences throughout the course of its administration, there is reason to believe that under this form of government, an overthrow of popular sovereignty [rule or authority] is less likely to occur than under any other form of government. Adapted from: *Selected Writings of Bolívar*, Vol. 2. Harold A. Bierck, Jr., ed. New York: Colonial Press, 1951.

1. Describe how the powers of the new president of Bolivia were limited. What reason is given for this limitation?

2. What particular statements made by Bolívar in this address illustrate influence from American and French revolutionary ideas? Explain.
3. What are some limitations on the power of the American President today? What do you think might happen if the President's powers were not limited? Give an example of a recent incident to support your conclusion.

22 The Industrial Revolution in the West

URBAN LIFE IN NINETEENTH-CENTURY EUROPE

Vast improvements in industrial and agricultural production reached a peak in Europe during the late eighteenth and nineteenth centuries. But the effects of this "revolution" were mixed, as is evident from the following selections, which describe urban life in nineteenth-century Germany and Austria.

54. Middle-Class Life

Some people who were not born aristocrats took advantage of the growing opportunities made available by the Industrial Revolution. The new middle class that emerged created a set of values which measured a person's worth by the quantity of goods he or she possessed. The selection that follows is a short excerpt from the novel Buddenbrooks, written in 1901 by Thomas Mann, a noted German author. In the scene described, a middle-class family is entertaining guests for dinner. What characteristics of the middle-class life does Mann seem to emphasize?

The maid-servant passed the cabbage soup and toast, assisted by the maid from upstairs. The guests began to use their soup-spoons.

"Such plenty, such elegance! I must say, you know how to do things!—I must say—" Herr Koppen had never visited the house. He did not come of a patrician [wealthy from birth] family, and had only lately become a man of means. He could never quite get rid of certain vulgar tricks of speech—like the repetition of "I must say"; and he said "respecks" for "respects."

An enormous brick-red boiled ham appeared, strewn with crumbs and served with a sour brown onion sauce, and so many vegetables that the company could have satisfied their appetites from that one vegetable dish. . . . With the ham went the Frau Konsul's celebrated "Russian jam," a pungent fruit preserve flavored with spirits. . . .

There they all sat, on heavy, high-backed chairs, consuming good heavy food from good heavy silver plates, drinking full-bodied wines and expressing their views freely on all subjects. When they began to talk shop, they slipped unconsciously more and more into dialect, and used the clumsy but

664

comfortable idioms that seemed to embody the business efficiency and the easy well-being of their community. Sometimes they even used an overdrawn pronunciation by way of making fun of themselves and each other, and relished their clipped phrases and exaggerated vowels with the same heartiness as they did their food. . . .

But all the various conversations around the table flowed together in one stream when Jean Jacques Hoffstede embarked upon his favorite theme, and began to describe the Italian journey which he had taken fifteen years before with a rich Hamburg relative. He told of Venice, Rome, and Vesuvius; . . . he was enthusiastic over the beautiful Renaissance fountains that spread coolness upon the warm Italian air, and the formal gardens through the avenues of which it was so enchanting to stroll. . . .

"Krishan, don't eat too much," the old man suddenly called out in dialect. . . .

And truly it was amazing, the prowess of this scraggy child . . . Asked if she wanted more soup, she answered in a meek drawling voice: "Ye-es, please." She had two large helpings both of fish and ham, with piles of vegetables; and she bent short-sightedly over her plate, completely absorbed in the food, which she chewed in large mouthfuls. Adapted from: Thomas Mann. *Buddenbrooks.* New York: Alfred A. Knopf, 1954.

1. What middle-class characteristics is Mann ridiculing in this piece? Cite specific lines to support your answer.
2. From what you have read, do you think Thomas Mann was a middle-class person? Why or why not? Check an encyclopedia or biography of Mann to see if your conclusions are correct.
3. If you were to write a novel about people living in your town or community, which personal characteristics would you criticize? Which would you praise? Do you think your work would be an accurate source for a person studying the values of your community years from now? Why or why not?

55. The Working Woman
Autobiography is an important source of historical evidence. It not only gives information about a person but also about the time and place in which it was written. The following selection was taken from the autobiography of Adelheid Popp, an unskilled laborer who started working in factories when she was only ten years old. Popp's description of her life also allows us a glimpse of how the Industrial Revolution affected lower-class urban life in nineteenth-century Austria.

I found work again in a large factory which had a good reputation. Three hundred girls and about fifty men were employed there. I was put in a big room where sixty women and girls were at work. Against the windows stood twelve tables, and at each sat four girls. We had to sort the goods which had been manufactured, others had to count them, and a third set had to brand on them the mark of the firm. We worked from 7:00 AM to 7:00 PM with an hour rest at noon and half an hour in the afternoon.

I [had] never yet been paid so much. I felt that I was almost rich and I reckoned how much money I could save in the course of a year. I built castles in the air. I considered it extravagant to spend more now on my food since I was used to doing with very little. I only wanted to be well dressed so that if I went to church on Sunday no one should guess that I was a factory worker. I was ashamed of my work. Working in a factory had always seemed to me to be degrading. I had always heard it said that factory girls were bad, disorderly, and depraved. They were always talked about in the most scornful manner.

The girls at the factory were very kind to me. They helped me to learn my job in the friendliest manner. All the girls and women were badly nourished. Those who stayed at the factory for dinner would buy a sausage or cheese. Many a time they ate bread and butter and cheap fruit. Some drank a glass of beer, and sopped bread in it. Sometimes we fetched a meal from a restaurant, either soup or vegetables. But it was seldom well prepared and the smell of fat was horrible. We often threw it away and ate only dry bread. After eating a scanty meal, stockings were knitted, crocheted, or embroidered. In spite of diligence and thrift, everyone was poor. Each trembled at the thought of losing her job. Each humbled herself and suffered the worst injustices from the foreman to avoid losing her job and being without food.

Adapted from: Adelheid Popp. *The Autobiography of a Working Woman*. trans. E. C. Harvey. London: T. Fisher Unwin, 1912.

1. What were working conditions like for women in nineteenth-century Europe? Did they differ much from conditions faced by men? Explain.

2. How did Adelheid Popp feel about being a woman who worked in a factory? Why did she feel this way? Do you think her feelings were justified? Why or why not?

3. How do working conditions for women today compare to those of nineteenth-century Europe? What developments in recent years might explain similarities and differences?

REVIEWING READINGS 54–55

1. How do you evaluate the effects of the Industrial Revolution after reading these two selections? Give examples from the readings to support your opinion.

2. Interview a relative or friend who is fifty or older. Ask him or her the following questions: (a) How does your family's life when you were younger compare to your life today? (b) What new inventions or developments account for any differences? (c) Is there anything that these inventions might have changed in your life which you regret? Compare your results with those of your classmates.

chapter 23 The Beginnings of Revolution in Russia

ANARCHISTS, POPULISTS, AND TERRORISTS

A variety of revolutionary movements were organized in Russia in the second half of the nineteenth century. Although each had its own ideas, tactics, and leaders, all revolutionaries shared a common goal—the overthrow of the tsar. Despite government attempts to suppress it, the revolutionary fervor could not be stamped out. And in 1917, a successful revolution finally put an end to the tsarist regime. In the readings that follow, revolutionaries of the 1860's, 1870's, and 1880's tell of their goals and how they plan to improve Russia. Some of the young revolutionaries behind the movements organized during this period would become the political leaders of Russia after 1917.

56. The Anarchists

Mikhail Bakunin (mik-HILE bah-KOO-nin) was the founder of Russian anarchism, a revolutionary movement of the mid-nineteenth century that demanded total freedom for Russia by complete overthrow of its institutions. Bakunin published a newspaper in which he proclaimed his doctrine of anarchism. Part of what he wrote is presented in the first reading below.

Bakunin's followers, called anarchists, organized small, secret groups dedicated to carrying out their leader's goals. Sergei Nechaev (ser-GAY neh-CHIE-yev), one of Bakunin's followers, described the movement's plan for achieving its founder's goals in the second selection that follows.

We want full intellectual, social, economic, and political freedom for the people. Freedom consists of liberation from belief in God, the life of the human soul, and in general freedom from all kinds of idealism. The true and complete freedom of the people also means liberation from the family, church, marriage, government, educational and economic as well as financial institutions.

We have only one plan—general destruction. We want a national revolution of the peasants. We refuse to take any part in the working out of schemes to better the conditions of life; we regard as fruitless solely theoretical work. We consider destruction to be such an enormous and difficult task that we must devote all our powers to it, and we do not wish to deceive ourselves with the dream that we will have enough strength and knowledge for creation.   Adapted from: Sergei Pushkarev, *The Emergence of Modern Russia, 1801–1917.* New York: Holt, Rinehart & Winston, 1963.

1. What was the anarchist doctrine as described by Mikhail Bakunin? How did Sergei Nechaev and other followers decide to achieve Bakunin's plan for Russia?

2. How did the Russian anarchist definition of freedom differ from the American and French revolutionary definitions (see readings for Chapter 19 and Chapter 20)? Explain.

3. Do you think you would want to live in an anarchist society? Why or why not?

667

57. The Populists

In the late 1860's and early 1870's, young people of wealthy Russian families banded together to form the populist movement. Their goals, represented by the slogan "Go to the people," was to establish an egalitarian peasant society in Russia. According to these revolutionaries, the peasants were Russia's only hope, since they were the only members of society not affected by the evils of the tsarist regime. Prince Peter Kropotkin (kroe-POT-kin) was one young aristocrat who abandoned his royal title for the populist cause. In the following selection, Kropotkin describes how the populist movement developed in Russia. How do the tactics of these revolutionaries differ from those of the anarchists?

All Russia read with astonishment of the indictment which was produced at the trial of Karakozov and his friends, that these young men used to live three or four in the same room. They never spent more than five dollars apiece a month for all their needs, and at the same time gave their fortunes for the poor. Five years later, thousands and thousands of the Russian youth— the best part of it—were doing the same. Their password was "V Narod!" ["Go to the people" or "Be the people"].

During the years 1860–65, in nearly every wealthy family a bitter struggle was going on between the fathers, who wanted to maintain the old traditions, and the sons and daughters, who defended their right to do with their lives according to their own ideals. Young men left the military service, the counter and the shop, and flocked to the university towns. Girls, bred in the most aristocratic families, rushed penniless to St. Petersburg, Moscow, and Kiev, eager to learn a profession which would free them from their parents, and some day, perhaps, also from the possible yoke of a husband. After hard and bitter struggles, many of them won that personal freedom. Now they wanted to utilize it, not for their own personal enjoyment, but for carrying to the peasants the knowledge that had emancipated them. . . .

The aim of all reading and discussion was to solve the great question which rose before them. In what way could they be useful to the masses? Gradually, they came to the idea that the only way was to settle amongst the peasants, and to live the peasant's life. Young men went into the villages as doctors, doctors' helpers, teachers, village scribes, even as agricultural laborers, blacksmiths, woodcutters, and so on, and tried to live there in close contact with the peasants. Girls passed teachers' examinations, learned nursing, and went by the hundreds into the villages, devoting themselves entirely to the poorest part of the population. . . .

These people wanted to teach the mass of the peasants to read, to instruct them in other things, to give them medical help, and in any way to aid in raising them from their darkness and misery, and to learn at the same time what were their popular ideals of a better social life.   Adapted from: Peter Kropotkin. *Memoirs of a Revolutionist.* James Allen Rogers, ed. New York: Doubleday, 1962.

1. According to Kropotkin, what were the ways by which the populists planned to change Russia? How do these revolutionaries' tactics differ from those of the anarchists in Reading 56?
2. Describe the personal and family background of the young people who be-

came populists. Why do you think they were attracted to this revolutionary movement?

3. Do you know of any young people in your society who have left their families and changed their way of life for a particular cause? What do you think may have caused them to do this? Do you agree or disagree with their actions? Explain.

58. The Terrorists

The failure of the populist movement led some revolutionaries to organize a secret party whose aim was to attack the tsar directly by using violence and terror. In 1879, the terrorists made several attempts to murder Tsar Alexander II. And in 1881, they succeeded. The tsar was assassinated on the same day he gave final approval to a series of new reforms.

The following is an account of what happened on the day of the tsar's assassination. It was written by Alexander the Grand Duke, the son of the tsar's brother Michael, who was a young boy at the time.

The tremendous territory occupied by St. Petersburg made it impossible for the police to guarantee the safety of the members of the imperial family outside the walls of their palaces. But the easy-going Alexander II had fully inherited the personal courage of his stern father, Nicholas I. . . . He insisted on following the usual routine, which included his walks in the public park and the Sunday review of the troops of the Guard. Nothing made our mother more nervous than the fact that our father [Alexander II's brother, Michael] was obliged to escort the tsar to this weekly parade. He laughed at her fears, pointing out that the loyalty of the army could not be questioned, but her unerring female instinct was stronger than logic.

"I am not afraid of the officers or the soldiers," she used to say. "But I have no faith in the local police, particularly on a Sunday. It is a long drive to the parade field and every revolutionist in town can see you passing through the streets."

On [Sunday, March 13, 1881] . . . at three o'clock sharp we heard the sound of a strong explosion.

"That was a bomb all right," said my brother George, "no mistake about that sound."

At this moment a still stronger explosion shattered the windows in our room. Just then a servant rushed in, all out of breath.

"The Emperor has been killed," he screamed.

Mother heard his words and ran out of her apartment. We took her to the waiting carriage and started a mad race toward the Winter Palace. . . .

Thousands of people were already surrounding the palace. The women cried hysterically. We entered by the side door. There was no need to ask questions: large drops of blood showed us the way up the marble steps and then along a corridor into the study of the Emperor.

The Emperor lay on the couch near the desk. He was unconscious. Three doctors were fussing around but science was obviously helpless. . . . It was a question of minutes. He presented a terrific sight, his right leg torn off, his left leg shattered, innumerable wounds all over his head and face. One eye shut, the other expressionless. . . .

The agony lasted forty-five minutes. Not a detail of this scene could ever be forgotten by those who witnessed it. . . .

The chief of police arrived with a complete report of the tragedy. The first bomb killed two passers-by and wounded a Cossack officer who was mistaken for my father on account of the similarity of their uniforms. The Emperor, unhurt, got out of the carriage. The coachmen begged him to get off the sidewalk and proceed to the palace but he insisted on personally aiding the wounded. Then a man standing on the corner threw the second and fatal bomb, less than a minute before my father reached this spot.

"Silence, please," said a hoarse voice, "the end is near." . . .

The chief court surgeon, who was feeling the tsar's pulse, nodded and let the blood-covered hand drop.

"The Emperor is dead," he announced loudly. Adapted from: Alexander, Grand Duke of Russia. *Once a Grand Duke.* New York: Crop, Farrar & Rinehart, 1932.

1. What reason does the writer give for the success of the terrorists' final attempt to assassinate Alexander II?
2. From what you have read in your textbook, did the terrorists' action improve conditions in Russia? Why or why not?
3. Cite several examples of terroism that have occurred somewhere in the world within the last decade. What was the cause behind these terrorist attacks? Do you think such acts of terrorism could be prevented? If so, how? If not, why?

REVIEWING READINGS 56–58

1. Compare the three revolutionary movements that developed in the 1860's and 1870's in Russia. What were the similarities and differences in each movement's leaders, goals, and tactics for achieving those goals?
2. Of all the revolutionary movements that were organized in Russia during the late nineteenth century, which one or ones do you think could have been the most effective in improving conditions in Russia? Explain your choice.

Did you know that by 1650 the world's population was about 500 million and grew to one billion by the mid-nineteenth century? Today's world population is four times this amount!

chapter 24 Modern Nationalism

THE MEANING OF NINETEENTH-CENTURY NATIONALISM

Scholars have found it difficult to form a precise definition of the term "nationalism." The reason for this confusion is that nationalistic feelings existed and took various forms in many countries and periods throughout history. And in each case, nationalism has been defined according to the political, cultural, economic, or social conditions of that place and time. The following selections present two views of nationalism in the nineteenth century. How do you think the events of the nineteenth century affected these definitions of nationalism?

59. Italian Definition of Nationalism, 1858

Giuseppe Mazzini (juh-SEP-ee maht-SEE-nee) was among the early leaders in the struggle for Italian unification. In the 1830's, Mazzini organized a secret society called "Young Italy" and began a movement to which he devoted much of his life. In 1858, Mazzini inspired Italians with the following view of what a country should be.

A country is not merely a geographic territory. A country is also the idea given birth by the geographic territory. A country is the sense of love which unites as one all the sons and daughters of that geographic territory.

So long as a single person amongst you has no vote to represent him in the development of the national life; so long as there is one person left to vegetate in ignorance while others are educated; so long as a single person that is able and willing to work languishes in poverty through lack of a job, you have no country in the sense in which a country ought to exist. The right to vote, education, and employment are the three main pillars of a nation.

Let it be your task to evolve the life of your country in loveliness and strength, free from all servile fears and maintaining as the basis of the country, its people. The life of your country will be immortal so long as you are ready to die for your fellow men and women.

Adapted from: E. A. Venturi. *Giuseppe Mazzini: A Memoir.* London: Alexander and Shepheard, 1875.

1. How does Mazzini define the term "country"? What should be the duties of its citizens?
2. What did Mazzini believe were the "three main pillars" of a nation? Do you agree? Why or why not?
3. After reading Mazzini's account, how would you define nationalism?

60. German Definition of Nationalism, 1808

Johann Gottlieb Fichte (YOE-hahn GAHT-leep FIHK-tuh) was a Prussian patriot and philosopher who lived between 1762 and 1814. During the years 1807–08, Fichte gave "Addresses to the German Nation" in Berlin when the city was occupied by Napoleon's troops. An excerpt follows.

671

The noble-minded man will be active and effective, and will sacrifice himself for his people. . . . In order to save his nation he must be ready even to die that it may live, and that he may live in it the only life for which he has ever wished. . . .

In this belief our earliest common forefathers . . . the Germans, as the Romans called them, bravely resisted the oncoming world domination of the Romans. . . . Freedom to them meant just this: remaining Germans and continuing to settle their own affairs independently and in accordance with the original spirit of their race, going on with their development in the same spirit, and passing on this independence to their descendants. All those blessings which the Romans offered them meant slavery to them because they would have to become something that was not German, they would have to become half Roman. They assumed as a matter of course that every man would rather die than become half Roman, and that a true German could only want to live in order to be, and to remain, just a German and to bring up his children as Germans. . . .

It is they whom we must thank— we the immediate heirs of their soil, their language, and their way of thinking. . . .

The present problem, the first task . . . is simply to preserve the existence and continuance of what is German. All other differences vanish. Adapted from: J. G. Fichte. *Addresses to the German Nation*. trans. R. F. Jones and G. H. Trumball. LaSalle, Ill.; The Open Court Publishing Co., 1922, as adapted for *The Shaping of Western Civilization*, Vol. 2. Hinsdale, Ill.: The Dryden Press, 1970.

1. What did Fichte believe to be the most important task facing the Germans?
2. What was happening in Europe in the early nineteenth century that you think might have influenced Fichte's view? Cite evidence from the selection to support your answer.
3. How do you think Fichte would have defined the term "nationalism"?

REVIEWING READINGS 59–60

1. How does Mazzini's view of nationalism differ from Fichte's view? What historical developments might explain similarities and differences?
2. Based on these selections and what you have read in your textbook, how would you define the term "nationalism"? What about your society might have influenced your definition?

chapter 25 The Rise of Imperialism

IMPERIALISM: TWO VIEWS

Imperialism was a tremendous source of profit, power, and prestige to those countries that took part in the race for colonies in the nineteenth century. In addition, these imperialist countries felt their presence was beneficial to the less developed parts of the world that they colonized. But to the people who lived in these conquered areas, imperialism meant an entirely different thing.

61. The Imperialist's View

In the 1890's, the United States joined the Europeans in the race for colonies abroad. After the Spanish-American War, the United States annexed the Philippines, which had belonged to Spain. The following statement, by President McKinley explaining why his country had taken the islands, is representative of the nineteenth-century imperialist view.

I have been criticized a good deal about the Philippines, but I don't deserve it. The truth is, I didn't want the Philippines, and when they came to us, like a gift from the gods, I did not know what to do with them . . . . I walked the floor of the White House night after night until midnight; and I am not ashamed to tell you, gentlemen, that I went down on my knees and prayed for light and guidance. And one night late it came to me this way—I don't know how it was, but it came: (1) That we could not give the Philippines back to Spain—that would be cowardly and dishonorable; (2) that we could not turn them over to France or Germany—that would be bad business and discreditable; (3) that we could not leave them to govern themselves—they were unfit for self-government . . . and (4) that there was nothing left for us to do but to take them all, and to educate the Philippines, and uplift and civilize and Christianize them, and by God's grace, do the very best we could by them as our fellow men. . . . . And then I went to bed, and went to sleep, and slept soundly, and the next morning I sent for the chief engineer of the War Department (our map-maker), and told him to put the Philippines on the map of the United States. Adapted from: G. A. Malcolm and M. M. Kalaw. *Philippine Government.* Manila: Associate Publishers, 1923.

1. What reasons did President McKinley give for the U.S. annexation of the Philippines? According to McKinley, what was his country's duty toward the annexed islands?
2. Why did President McKinley believe the Philippines should not be turned over to another imperialist power?
3. Did the nineteenth-century imperialist view of conquered peoples differ very much from the sixteenth-century view of them as described in Reading 47, Chapter 18? Why or why not?

62. The Conquered Peoples' View

China remained technically independent during the nineteenth century. Its rulers, however, held little power over territory that was divided into various European spheres of influence. The following was circulated throughout the Chinese province of Kwantung in 1841. It expresses the widespread Chinese opinion of the imperialists' race for colonies.

We loyal and patriotic people of Kwantung Province note that you English barbarians have developed the nature of wolves, plundering and seizing things by force. In trade relations, you come to our country seeking only

profit, which resembles an animal's greed for food. You are ignorant of our laws and institutions. You have no gratitude for the favors given you by our royal court. You bring opium into our country to injure our people, cheating them of silver and cash.

Except for your solid ships, your fierce gunfire, and your other powerful weapons, what knowledge or other abilities have you?

You have killed and injured our common people in many villages. You have disturbed the peace. You have failed to pay proper respect to our religious beliefs and practices. This is a time when Heaven is angered and mankind is resentful. Even the ghosts and spirits will not tolerate you beasts.

We really ought to use refined expressions, but since you beasts do not understand our refined language, we use rough, vulgar words to instruct you in simple terms.   Adapted from: Ssu-yu Teng and J. L. Fairbank. *China's Response to the West—A Documentary Survey.* Cambridge, Mass. Harvard University Press, 1954.

1. What things had the British done in Kwantung Province to provoke Chinese resentment?
2. Why were the British more powerful than the Chinese?
3. What can you learn about the Chinese attitude toward foreigners from this document? What can you learn about the imperialist attitude toward the Chinese? Explain your answer by citing references to the reading.

REVIEWING READINGS 61–62

1. What were the reasons generally given by the nineteenth-century imperialists to explain their quest for colonies? How do the reasons reflect the imperialist attitude toward the people they conquered? Do you agree with their opinion? Why or why not?
2. What did the conquered people think of the imperialists' view of themselves?
3. Based on what you have read in these selections and in the textbook, how would you evaluate the effects of imperialism? Cite specific examples.

---

chapter 26 The Rise of Nation-States

LIFE IN EASTERN EUROPE ON THE EVE OF REVOLUTION

Throughout much of its early history, eastern Europe was in a constant state of disruption. Wars between different kingdoms for political or religious reasons resulted in the destruction of thousands of lives and much property. Whole villages in the Balkans and throughout Hungary were wiped out in the wake of Turkish invasion, and people were often forced to live under unjust foreign rule. The following selections describe what political and social conditions drove the people of eastern Europe to revolt in the mid-nineteenth century.

63. Peasant Life in Eastern Europe

The following selection, written in the 1800's, describes the life of a peasant in eastern Europe. As you read, keep in mind that in eastern Europe the nobility owned the land and everything on it until the twentieth century. And the peasants' lives were largely confined to the rules and regulations of serfdom. The conditions described in this reading were probably typical for much of the European territory still under Turkish control in the nineteenth century.

No worse punishment could be found for men and women than serfdom. People were treated worse than cattle are today. They were beaten both at work and at home for the smallest things. Every peasant had to do his work at the manor house. Only then could he work his own land, sowing and reaping at night. If one did not appear at work as ordered, the overseer would come to the serf's home. If he found the wife busy cooking, he would throw a pail of water on the fire, or in the winter he could carry off the windows or the doors. . . . The overseer would come with his men and throw the peasant out of his home. . . . Running away would have done no good, for elsewhere it was no better—rather, it was worse.

The number of houses in our village was something like seventy, each like the other—as two peas. . . . The cottage of the peasant was made up of a single living room, alongside which was a large shed and storeroom. The peasant had, besides this, a stable for horses, cattle, and pigs and storage space for grain. All such buildings were built of round logs. . . .

Of old, we used for cooking only the open hearth, on which the pots with food were set either close to or on the fire, depending upon whether we were in a hurry or not. In addition, there was in every house a bake oven, big enough so that one could bake at one time the bread from half a sack of flour. . . . The ovens were built of raw brick, and they took up a lot of room. The top surface of the oven was big enough so that four people could sleep on it. Right through the winter, the children and the hired girl slept there all the time, and anyone of the family who felt miserable or got a chill crawled up on the oven to stretch out and toast himself. Between the oven and the wall was a space which was called the oven corner, where the children would also sleep.

The house furnishings were of the simplest. For furniture we had tables and a couple of benches, a chest that took the place of drawers, and beds or bunks. . . . There were no floors except in the manor house. When the cow was to calve in winter, they would bring her into the house so that she would be warmer. . . . Adapted from: Alfred J. Bannan and Achilles Edelenyi. *A Documentary History of Eastern Europe.* Boston: Twayne Publishers, 1970.

1. Why does this writer tell us that there was no worse punishment than serfdom? Do you agree with him? Explain.
2. Describe a peasant home. What was everyday life like for the peasants?
3. Do you think these peasant serfs would be affected by the nationalistic fever of the nineteenth century? Why or why not?

64. Life under the Phanariots

You have learned that the Turks did not always directly govern the conquered peoples of eastern Europe. They sent Greek governors known as Phanariots (fuh-NAR-ee-AHTS) to rule in their place. Phanariot rulers subjected the peoples of eastern Europe to poor conditions and forced the peasants to pay high taxes just to fill their own pockets. The following selection, which was written by a nineteenth-century visitor to Romania, gives one person's behind-the-scene view of what life under the Phanariots was like.

The education of the Phanariots is not very much better in its practical use than that of the common people. Their children are taught in the houses of their parents and are surrounded by tutors who corrupt them by granting their every whim. Formed by such tutors, they pass into a world of dishonesty and vice, without one just principle to regulate their conduct, without one generous purpose, or one honorable feeling. . . .

The Phanariots have a taste for magnificent dress and splendid equipment. They love dances and public entertainments, but their gatherings are rude and noisy. Their tables are open to every person of their acquaintance, but are not elegantly served. In the cities they are forbidden to form acquaintances with strangers. But I have occasionally visited their country estates and always received a plain but decent hospitality.

Phanariots sleep after dinner on their sofas while a female servant fans away the flies and refreshes the air that they breathe. They demand from their attendants the respect which they have seen paid to the Turkish nobles. But because they have no sense of their own importance, they cannot give commands to their own servants with the same dignity as the Turks. Their vanity is shown in the insulting behavior with which they treat their inferiors.

On the death or removal of a governor, other Phanariot officials assemble immediately and take over the administration of public affairs. All the people appointed by the governor are removed from office, and other persons are appointed. If alive, the fallen ruler is immediately deserted by his followers, is always treated with neglect, and sometimes with insult and abuse. He returns privately, without ceremony, to Constantinople, where he retires. . . . Adapted from: Alfred J. Bannan and Achilles Edelenyi. *A Documentary History of Eastern Europe*. Boston: Tayne Publishers, 1970.

1. What were some characteristics of the Phanariots that the writer criticizes? Cite specific references in the reading to support your answer.
2. Which of these Phanariot traits do you think Romanians might have resented? Explain your answer.
3. Based on what you have read about the Turkish rule in your textbook in this selection, why do you think a successful revolt by Romanians was possible?

REVIEWING READINGS 63–64

1. What political and social conditions existed under Turkish rule that caused eastern European people to revolt in the nineteenth century?
2. Why would these living conditions have sparked nationalistic feelings among the eastern European people?
3. Do you think that every person who supports a political cause does so for the same reason? Why or why not? How does your answer apply to the effect of nationalism on the countries of nineteenth-century Europe?

65. The Horror of War

After the Germans made their initial invasion of France through Belgium in the early stages of World War I, they encountered considerable resistance from their enemy along the Western Front. This 960-kilometer line of battle witnessed millions of lives being maimed or lost forever. In 1929, Erich Maria Remarque, an ex-German soldier, wrote *All Quiet on the Western Front*. The following excerpt from this historical novel is a moving description of soldiers experiencing the horrors of war.

The trucks halt. We have arrived at the artillery lines. Now we must go on duty and string barbed wire. . . . Our faces change. In every face it can be read: This is the front. . . .

After a few hours we are finished with the barbed wire. But there is still some time before the trucks return for us. Most of us lie down to sleep. . . .

Then it begins in earnest. Bombardment. . . . Green rockets shoot up the sky line. Barrage. The mud flies high, fragments whizz past. The crack of the guns is heard long after the roar of the explosions.

Besides us lies a fair-haired recruit in utter terror. He has buried his face in his hands, his helmet has fallen off. I try to put it back on his head. He looks up, pushes the helmet off and like a child creeps next to me.

Finally, I sit up and shake the recruit by the shoulder. "It's all over, kid! Let's go back."

We march back toward the trucks. . . . A little wood appears. We know every foot of the ground here. There's the cemetery with the mounds and black crosses.

That moment it breaks out behind us, swells, roars and thunders. We duck down. . . .

Not a moment too soon. The dark goes mad. The flames of the explosions light up the graveyard. There is no escape anywhere. . . .

The earth bursts before us. It rains clods. My sleeve is torn away by a splinter. Now a crack on the skull. A splinter slashes into my helmet. I wipe the mud out of my eyes. A hole is torn up in front

I WANT YOU
FOR U.S. ARMY
NEAREST RECRUITING STATION

of me. Shells hardly ever land in the same hole twice so I'll get into it. I feel something on the left, shove in beside it, it gives way. I creep under the yielding thing, cover myself with it. . . .

I open my eyes. My fingers grasp a sleeve, an arm. A wounded man? I yell to him—no answer. A dead man. Now I remember that we are lying in a graveyard. But the shelling is stronger than any other thought so I merely crawl deeper into the coffin. It should protect me.

The dull thud of the gas shells mingles with the crashes of the high explosives. . . .

I wipe the goggles of my mask. Those first minutes with the mask decide between life and death. Will it keep out the gas?. . .

Cautiously, I breathe through the gas mask. The gas still creeps over the ground and sinks into all hollows. . . .

When the shelling ceases, I drag myself to the crater and tell the others. The graveyard is a mass of wreckage. Coffins and corpses lie strewn about but each of them that was flung up saved one of us.

Someone lies in front of us. We stop. The man on the ground is a recruit. His hip is covered with blood. We lay the hip bare . . . The joint has been hit. This lad won't walk anymore. . . .

I say, "We're going to a stretcher."

The youngster will hardly survive the carrying. At the most he will last only a few days. What he has gone through so far is nothing to what he's in for till he dies. Now he is numb and feels nothing. In an hour he will become one screaming bundle of intolerable pain. Every day that he can live will be a howling torture. And to whom does his suffering matter?

Kat shakes his head. "Such a kid." Adapted from: Erich Maria Remarque. *All Quiet on the Western Front.* New York: Fawcett World Library, 1958.

1. What picture of war is given in this passage from All Quiet on the Western Front? Cite specific passages to support your answer.

2. How did men on the battlefield express their concern for one another in this selection? Cite specific references from the reading.

3. "And to whom does his suffering matter?" What does this statement indicate about the author's attitude toward war? Do you agree or disagree with the intent of this statement? Why or why not?

---

chapter
28 Creating World War II

THE HOLOCAUST IN NAZI GERMANY
Adolf Hitler came to power proclaiming the ultimate superiority of the German race and denouncing the Jews as people less than human. Hitler blamed the Jews for every ill that beset war-torn Germany—from its defeat in World War I to the miserable economic setback that followed. It was Hitler's principal goal to drive the Jews out of Germany by whatever means possi-

ble. The selections below illustrate, in part, the physical and psychological suffering endured by German Jews from 1933 to the beginning of World War II.

66. An Interview with Adolf Hitler

The following excerpt is taken from an American correspondent's interview with Adolf Hitler on February 15, 1933, soon after he came to power. How does Hitler explain the Nazi policy toward Jews?

His greeting, when I was introduced to him, was perfunctory [routine], suggesting latent hostility, and my first question brought this forth into full flame. I had asked him whether his anti-Semitism concerned Jews everywhere or whether he had something specific against German-Jews as such.

"In America, you exclude any immigrants you do not care to admit," he said emphatically. "You regulate their number. Not content with that, you prescribe their physical condition. Not content with that, you insist on the conformity of their political opinions. We demand the same right in Germany. We have no concern with the Jews of other lands, but we are very much concerned about anti-German elements within our country. We demand the right to deal with these elements as we see fit. Jews have been the intellectual proponents of subversive anti-German movements, and as such they must be dealt with." Adapted from: *The New Republic*, February 15, 1933, as printed in *The Record: The Holocaust in History 1933–1945*, New York: Anti-Defamation League of B'nai Brith in cooperation with the National Council of Social Studies, 1978.

1. How did Hitler use nationalism to justify his hostility toward Jews?

2. Do you think Hitler's comparison of his anti-Semitism campaign to America's treatment of immigrants was a valid one? Explain your answer.

67. Goebbels Warns the Jews

Joseph Goebbels was in charge of Nazi propaganda and was one of Hitler's closest advisers. Goebbels included the following warning to Jews in a speech he delivered in May 1934.

We have been very lenient with the Jews. But if they think that therefore they can still be allowed on German stages, offering art to the German people; if they think that they can still sneak into editorial offices, writing for German newspapers; if they still strut along the streets of Berlin as though nothing had happened, they might take these words as a final warning. Jews can rest assured that we will leave them alone as long as they retire quietly and modestly behind their four walls, as long as they are not provocative, and do not affront the German people with the claim to be treated as equals. If the Jews do not listen to this warning, they will have themselves to blame for anything that happens to them.   Adapted from: *The Record: The Holocaust in History 1933–1945*. New York: Anti-Defamation League of B'nai Brith in cooperation with the National Council of Social Studies, 1978.

1. What things did the Nazis forbid Jews to do?
2. How do you think frequent warnings like this affected the personal lives of Jews in Germany?
3. Does your country have laws that protect you from this kind of injustice? Explain.

68. Kristallnacht—The Night of Broken Glass (Germany, 1938)

In November of 1938, a German diplomat in Paris was murdered by a Polish citizen who was Jewish. To revenge this murder, the Nazis organized a campaign of destruction aimed directly at all Jews—their homes, places of worship, and businesses. The following newspaper account, which appeared in The New York Times on November 10, 1938, describes that one night of terror.

A wave of destruction, looting and incendiarism [burning] . . . swept over Germany today as National Socialists took vengeance on Jewish shops, offices and synagogues for the murder by a young Polish Jew of Ernst von Rath, third secretary of the German Embassy in Paris.

Beginning systematically in the early morning hours in almost every town and city in the country, the wrecking, looting, and burning continued all day. Huge but mostly silent crowds looked on and the police confined themselves to regulating traffic and making wholesale arrests of Jews "for their own protection."

All day the main shopping districts as well as the side streets of Berlin and innumerable other places resounded to the shattering of shop windows falling to the pavement, the dull thuds of furniture being pounded to pieces and the clamor of fire brigades rushing to burning shops and synagogues. . . .

As far as could be ascertained, the violence was mainly confined to property. Although individuals were beaten, reports so far tell of the death of only two persons. . . .

In extent, intensity, and total damage, however, the day's outbreaks exceeded even those of the 1918 revolution, and by nightfall there was scarcely a Jewish shop, café, office or synagogue in the country that was not either wrecked, burned severely or damaged. . . .

It is known, however, that measures for the extensive expulsion of foreign Jews are already being prepared in the Interior Ministry, and some towns, like Munich, have ordered all Jews to leave within forty-eight hours. . . . It is assumed that the Jews, who have now lost most of their possessions and livelihood, will either be thrown into the streets or put into ghettos and concentration camps, or impressed into labor brigades and put to work for the Third Reich, as the children of Israel were once before for the Pharaohs.

In any case, all day in Berlin, as throughout the country, thousands of Jews, mostly men, were being taken from their homes and arrested—in particular, prominent Jewish leaders, who in some cases, it is understood, were told they were being held as hostages for the good behavior of Jews outside Germany. . . .

Grave doubt prevails whether insurance companies will honor [the Jews'] policies. Some are reported to have flatly refused to be reimbursed for the damage because of its extent, and, considering the standing the Jew enjoys in German courts today, there is little likelihood of his collecting by suing.   Adapted from: The New York Times, November 10, 1938, as printed in The Record: The Holocaust in History 1933–1945. New York: Anti-Defamation League of B'nai Brith in cooperation with the National Council of Social Studies, 1978.

1. **What were the immediate effects of** Kristallnacht **on the lives of Jews in Germany?**

2. What was the reason given by German officals for this night of violence? Based on what you have read in the readings for Chapter 28 and in the textbook, what do you think might have been the purpose of Kristallnacht? Explain.

3. What seems to be the writer's opinion of the future of German Jews after 1938? Cite specific references to support your answer.

REVIEWING READINGS 66–68

1. What were some of the means used by the Nazi regime to drive the Jews out of Germany in the 1930's? What were the reasons given for such actions?

2. Have a group of your friends ever tried to keep a person or persons from joining your group? If so, how? What were your reasons for doing this? Do you think such actions could be justified? Why or why not?

chapter 29 World War II

THE WAR AND THE CIVILIAN

An excerpt from All Quiet on the Western Front gave you a glimpse of the horors faced by soldiers during World War I. But the new defense methods used in World War II caused even more death and destruction. The civilian population was not spared the horrors of the battlefield in this war. A new military concept known as "total war" took countless civilian lives through bombing raids, artillery gun shelling, or through starvation and cold. The readings that follow present a vivid description of the effects of "total war" on civilians during World War II.

69. The Siege of Leningrad

Germany had invaded Soviet Russia in June 1941. By August, it had surrounded and blockaded Leningrad, cutting off the flow of vital oil supplies to Russia. The siege of Leningrad lasted seventeen months. But the city did not surrender, despite the thousands of civilians who died from starvation. The following is a bitter account of the long siege.

In December they began to appear—the sleds of the children, painted bright red or yellow. They had been intended as presents for sliding down hills or racing around icy curves.

Now suddenly they were everywhere—the children's sleds—on the broad boulevards, moving toward hospitals. The squeak, squeak, squeak of the runners sounded louder than the shelling of the enemy's guns. The squeak deafened the ears. On the sleds were the ill, the dying, the dead.

There were no automobiles in the city. Only the people, pulling their burdens, the dead in coffins of unpainted wood, large and small, the ill clinging to the runners of the sleds, and pails of

water and bundles of wood dangerously balanced.

On December 29, Mr. Luknitsky noted in his diary that ten days earlier he had been told that six thousand people a day were dying of starvation.

"To take someone who has died to the cemetery," Luknitsky said, "is an affair of so much labor that it exhausts the last strength in the survivors. The living, fulfilling their duty to the dead, are brought to the brink of death themselves." Adapted from: Harrison E. Salisbury. *The 900 Days*. New York: Harper & Row, 1969.

1. According to this account, how many civilians died each day during the worst period of the siege?

2. How does the last sentence summarize the effect of "total war" on the civilian population during World War II?

70. The Bombing Raids on Hamburg
As part of their military strategy against Germany, the Allied forces conducted bombing raids over German cities. In the following selection, a German official recounts the effects such bombings had on the people of the city of Hamburg.

The horror of the air raids on Hamburg is revealed in the howling and raging of the fires, the noise of exploding bombs and the death cries of human beings as well as in the big silence after the raids. Speech cannot describe the measure of the horror, which shook the people for ten days and nights.

And each of these nights of flames was followed by a day which displayed the horror in the dim and unreal light of a sky hidden in smoke. Summer heat was intensified by the flow of the fires to an unbearable degree. Dust from the torn earth and ruins penetrated everywhere. There were showers of soot and ashes, more dust and heat.

The days were followed by more nights of more horror, death and destruction. People had no time to rest or save their property or to search for their families. Ours was a city rapidly decaying, without gas, water, light and traffic connections, with stony deserts which had once been flourishing residential districts.   Adapted from: Charles K. Webster and Noble Frankland. *The Strategic Air Offensive Against Germany, 1939–1945.* Vol. IV. London: Her Majesty's Stationery Office, 1961.

1. How do you think these night bombing raids affected the future lives of the people of Hamburg?

2. Do you think these air raids were an effective form of military strategy? Why or why not?

REVIEWING READINGS 69–70

1. What was meant by "total war"? How did it affect the civilian population during World War II?

2. How is the experience of war pictured in these selections different from Erich Maria Remarque's description of World War I in All Quiet on the Western Front (see Reading 65)? How are they similar? Explain.

Did you know that between 1918 and 1945 the world lost 64.8 million people in two world wars—a total equal to three times the populations of North Carolina, South Carolina, Virginia, Georgia, and Mississippi combined?

Your World

Readings for Chapters 30–35 are in the form of biographical sketches. Each presents the life of a prominent person who helped to shape the world you live in. As you examine these sketches in turn, continue to consider the value of using biographies in your study of periods of history and the events that shape them.

71. Eleanor Roosevelt

Eleanor Roosevelt was born in New York City on October 11, 1884, into a wealthy but troubled family. Her mother was always preoccupied with the family's image in upper class society and embarrassed by Eleanor's homeliness. Eleanor's father entered a sanitarium for alcoholics when she was a child. When Eleanor was eight years old, her mother died, and she and two younger brothers went to live with their maternal grandmother in New York. Her grandmother sheltered her from all outside contacts except for family acquaintances.

At fifteen, Eleanor Roosevelt began discovering a world beyond the family at a finishing school in England. The headmistress, Mademoiselle Souvestre, taught a sense of social service and responsibility, which Eleanor began to act upon after her return to New York. Plain, gangly, and convinced that she would never marry, she plunged into social work. But soon her tall, handsome distant cousin, Franklin Delano Roosevelt, began courting her. They were married in March 1905.

A major turning point in Eleanor Roosevelt's life came in 1921, when Franklin contracted polio and permanently lost the use of his legs. Finally asserting her will, Eleanor Roosevelt nursed him back to activity. Within a few years he had regained his strength and political ambitions. Meanwhile, she entered more fully into public life. She acted as Franklin's "legs and ears," and began to acquire a certain notoriety of her own. During Franklin's New York governorship, she kept busy inspecting state hospitals, homes, and prisons for her husband.

Roosevelt's election to the presidency in 1932 meant, as Mrs. Roosevelt later wrote, "the end of any personal life of my own." She quickly became the best-known (and also the most criticized) First Lady in American history.

Besides undertaking a syndicated newspaper column and a series of radio broadcasts, Mrs. Roosevelt traveled back and forth across the country on fact-finding trips for Franklin. She assumed the special role of advocate for working women, Blacks, youth, and tenant farmers. Holding no official position, she felt she could speak more freely on issues than could her husband and she also became a key contact within the administration for officials seeking the President's support.

Much more than her husband, Mrs. Roosevelt denounced racial oppression and tried to aid the struggle of Black Americans toward full citizenship. Largely because of her efforts, Blacks, for the first time since the Reconstruction years, had reason to feel that the national government was interested in their plight.

After Franklin Roosevelt's death in April 1945, President Harry S. Truman appointed Mrs. Roosevelt American delegate to the United Nations Commission on Human Rights. As chairman of the Commission, she worked the other delegates overtime to complete the Universal Declaration of Human Rights, adopted by the U.N. General Assembly in 1948. After the election of Republican Dwight D. Eisenhower in 1952, she gave up her U.N. post, but continued to work for international understanding and cooperation.

By the early 1960's, she had accepted three new government appointments from President John F. Kennedy, but her strength was waning. She died in New York City on November 6, 1962. Adapted from: Charles Alexander. "Eleanor Roosevelt," *The McGraw-Hill Encyclopedia of World Biography*, Vol. 9. New York: McGraw-Hill, 1973.

1. How did Eleanor Roosevelt feel about herself as a young person? How did she overcome these feelings later on in life?

2. What role did Eleanor Roosevelt play in her husband's life after he became handicapped? Did she continue to work after his death? Explain.

3. What do you think should be the duties of a First Lady? How would you evaluate Eleanor Roosevelt's performance as First Lady? Do you admire Eleanor Roosevelt as a woman? Why or why not?

Golda Meir (MIE-ir) was born Golda Mabovitch (MOB-uh-vich) on May 3, 1898, in Kiev, in the Russian Empire. Her first memory was of her father nailing boards over the front door to protect the family from the raids of anti-Semitic Russian peasants. "I have a pogrom* complex," she was later to admit when speaking of her "desire and . . . determination to save Jewish children from a similar scene and from a similar experience."

Life in Russia was little more than survival. In 1906, Golda's family emigrated to Milwaukee to join her father, a carpenter, who had arrived three years earlier. At age eleven, she gave her first public speech to raise money for school textbooks; but her mother soon forced her to give up the idea of high school and spend her days working in the family grocery. At fourteen, she ran away from home to live with her sister in Denver where she later met and married Morris Myerson, a sign painter and fellow Russian emigré.

In the meantime, she returned to Milwaukee and became enthusiastically involved in teaching and public speaking. The democratic socialist ideas of Eugene Debs and the Zionist beliefs of David Ben-Gurion had led to her conviction that her destiny lay in the Jewish homeland. In 1921, she and her husband set sail for Palestine where there were only 80,000 Jews living there. "Since I believed in Zionism, the building of a Jewish homeland, I couldn't imagine myself staying in Milwaukee," she was later to explain. In 1929, she was elected a delegate to

*A pogrom is an organized massacre of helpless people.

the World Zionist Congress and went on several trips to the United States and many European countries on behalf of the World Zionist Organization. By that time, her marriage was breaking up. Mrs. Myerson moved with her children to a tiny apartment in Tel Aviv where she was to live for many years.

At the close of World War II, Golda Myerson fasted for 101 hours to protest British restrictions on the immigration of Jewish refugees to Palestine. She also toured the United States and collected 50 million dollars for Israel. When Israel's independence was almost a fact, she disguised herself as an Arab woman and secretly entered Jordan, where she unsuccessfully tried to get King Abdullah (AB-duh-lah) not to join other Arab leaders in attacking the Jews. He asked her not to hurry the proclamation of an Israeli state. "We have been waiting for 2,000 years," she answered. "Is that hurrying?"

On May 14, 1948, she became one of the twenty-five signers of Israel's independence declaration and the only woman member of its first legislature. That same year, she became Israel's first ambassador to the Soviet Union. She was Minister of Labor from 1949 to 1956, which were years of severe economic difficulty for Israel. Under Prime Minister David Ben-Gurion, she became Foreign Minister in 1956. It was he who convinced her to change her name to Meir, a Hebrew version of Myerson that means "illumination."

After many illnesses, she resigned from the Cabinet in 1965 with a sense of exhaustion. Four years later, the Labor Party selected her as its candidate for Prime Minister. She was sworn into office on March 17, 1969.

As Prime Minister, Mrs. Meir's emphasis on foreign policy did nothing to solve certain domestic problems in Israel. Many Oriental Jews who lived there complained that they were being treated as second-class citizens. She was also publicly criticized for praising Nixon's efforts in Southeast Asia. Nevertheless, most of her five years as Prime Minister established her as the unquestioned leader of her country. She had opened the way for some Soviet Jews to emigrate to Israel, strengthened the country's ties with the United States, and set up contacts with Jewish communities around the world.

At the end of her life, she explained her preference for public life over the duties of the home. "There is a type of woman who cannot remain at home," she wrote, ". . . her nature demands something more; she cannot divorce herself from the larger social life. . . . For such a woman there is no rest."

Mrs. Meir died on December 8, 1978. At that time, it was finally disclosed that she had been suffering from leukemia for twelve years, including the years 1969 to 1974 when she served as Prime Minister.

1. What early experiences in Golda Meir's life might have influenced her in deciding her life goals? What events in adulthood helped her achieve these goals?

2. What did she accomplish for her country during her term in office? What were some of the things she was criticized for? What personal qualities did she possess that might have contributed to her success as a leader?

3. What is the one thing you would want to change more than anything else to make your community a better place to live? How would you achieve this? What have you learned from Golda Meir's experience that would help you reach your goal?

73. José Lopez Portillo

José Lopez Portillo (hoe-SAY LOE-pes por-TEE-yoe) was born on June 16, 1920, the son of a Mexico City school teacher. He grew up in what he calls a "typically middle-class family" and attended the National University where he became friends with Luis Echeveria Alvarez (loo-EES ay-chay-vay-REE-ah AHL-vah-res). Echeverria went into politics while Lopez pursued a career in law. After serving as a professor at the National University for thirteen years, Lopez Portillo began accepting government posts and soon earned a reputation as a skilled administrator and fiscal specialist. Nevertheless, he was virtually unknown to most Mexicans in 1970 when he was appointed Finance Minister by his friend and ex-schoolmate Echeverria, who was serving as President of Mexico.

After his six-year term as president, Echeverria exercised the traditional right to select his own successor as presidential candidate of the Institutional Revolutionary party, which has won every presidential election since 1929. He chose José Lopez Portillo.

At first no one thought it likely that Lopez Portillo would try to undo Echeverria's policies. Echeverria had been a firm crusader for the "third world" and lower classes. But, according to many, he had only succeeded in losing the support of Mexican and foreign business investors, while disappointing the hopes of the masses. His endorsements of anti-Israeli countries had had a weakening effect on the Mexican tourist industry, one of the country's largest sources of income.

Although Lopez Portillo's victory was assured by the lack of any opposition, he began an exhaustive nine-month campaign to get acquainted with Mexican voters. When it was over, he had covered 64,960 kilometers (40,600 miles) and visited almost a thousand communities. Calling for "more administration, less politics," Lopez Portillo began to establish himself as more moderate, more practical, and less dependent on revolutionary slogans than Echeverria.

He took office in December, 1976, to face overwhelming internal problems, such as overpopulation, corruption, and poverty. The rate of inflation was increasing by leaps and bounds; 30 percent of the population was unemployed. There was growing internal discontent leading to student unrest, terrorist threats, and an increase in the flow of illegal emigrants to the United States. There was also evidence that Echeverria planned to maintain his control over Lopez by influencing his choice of political appointees.

In his inaugural address, Lopez asked for sacrifice and patience during the two years he felt were needed to put the economy on its feet again. He dramatically limited government spending, as well as the wages of workers organized in labor unions. His independence from Echeverria was strikingly demonstrated when some of Echeverria's cabinet ministers and several lesser officials were arrested and charged with corrupt practices. There were criticisms of Lopez's harsh methods of dealing with strikes and riots in the country.

Since then, legal dissent has been somewhat encouraged. More political parties, such as the Mexican Communist party and the conservative Mexican Democratic party, have been given official recognition for the first time in years. Portillo pledged to deal with inefficiency and corruption in government. He instituted measures for restructuring the Mexican bureaucracy that were designed to rid the system of intrigue and self-enrichment.

Petroleum has become the focus of much speculation in Mexico. Lopez Portillo guaranteed it as a solution to many problems in the country. But he himself took full responsibility for the future of Mexico during the years of his administration. In his annual report to Congress, he stated, "I alone was elected to the presidency, and I alone have the responsibility of this great office." Most Mexicans agreed that the responsibility was an awesome and imposing one.

However, Portillo was unable to solve most of the problems of his country. The value of the Mexican peso had greatly declined, the rate of inflation and government debts continued to rise, and high unemployment still existed. Such problems were left to the new president, Miguel de la Madrid Hurtado (mee-GEL day lah mah-DREED ur-TAH-thoe), to attempt to solve.

1. What sort of person is José Lopez Portillo? Describe him briefly.
2. What problems did Lopez Portillo face upon becoming president in 1976? de la Madrid Hurtado in 1982?

3. What characteristics should any good President possess? Do you think José Lopez Portillo had these traits? If so, why? If not, name a President who does or did. Explain your choice.

Born in a village in Hunan (HOONAN) Province on December 26, 1893, Mao Tse-Tung (MOW DZY-DOONG) did not leave his home province until he was twenty-five, when he visited Peking in 1918. On his return to Hunan the following year, Mao was already committed to communism. While making a living as a primary schoolteacher, he edited radical magazines, organized trade unions, and set up politically oriented schools of his own. With the inauguration of the Chinese Communist party (CCP) in 1921, of which Mao was one of the fifty founder members, these activities were pursued with added energy and to a greater depth.

Meanwhile, the major political party, the Kuomintang (KMT) or Nationalist party, was reorganized. A coalition was formed between the Communist and Nationalist parties. Mao's principal task was to coordinate the policies of both parties. In 1925, when the coalition ran into problems, Mao was sent back to Hunan.

A result of his return to Hunan was that he discovered the revolutionary potential of the peasants, who had been displaced in such great numbers and made hopelessly poor. By 1927, Mao proposed that the poor peasants fill the role of revolutionary leaders.

Shortly afterward, the Communist and Nationalist party coalition broke up and the Communists were persecuted everywhere in the country. Some survivors of the party went underground in the cities. The rest took up arms to defy the government and eventually to set up rural soviets* in central and northern China. One of these soviets was Mao's base area between the provinces of Kiangsi (jee-AHNG-SEE) and Hunan, where he had to rely chiefly on the support of the poor peasants.

During those years, Chiang Kai-shek (jee-AHNG KIE-SHEK) [leader of the Nationalist party after 1925] had success in his anti-communist campaigns. Eventually Chiang was able to drive the Communists out of their base area on what was called the "Long March." But in 1935 Mao was elected as chairman of the Politburo (puh-LIT-byoor-oe), [the chief policymaking committee of the Chinese Communist party], which was still influenced by Russia.

Events in the early 1940's helped the Chinese Communist party in its search for independence. Russia, preoccupied with its war against Hitler, was unable to influence the CCP effectively. Mao seized this opportunity to nationalize the Communist movement in China between 1942 and 1944. Under Mao's leadership, the party fought from one victory to another until it came to power in 1949. The Nationalist party then withdrew to Taiwan.

Mao's thought now guided the Chinese Communists in their way of thinking, their organization, and their action. But Mao's thought had very little to say on the modernization and industrialization of China. Therefore, af-

*A soviet is an elected government body of a communist country.

ter 1949 the party was left to follow the example of Russia, with Russian aid in the years of the cold war [1950's]. The importance of Mao declined steadily while China introduced its first Five-Year Plan and socialist constitution. Once more the pro-Russian wing of the CCP was on the rise, though still unable to challenge the strength of support for Mao's principles and ideas. This support enabled Mao to fight back by launching the "Socialist Upsurge in the Countryside of 1955" and the "Great Leap Forward" in 1958. The essential feature of these movements was to expand China's agricultural and industrial production.

The groundwork had been laid through the Communist education movement early in the 1960's. When this had been accomplished, Mao, with the help of the army and young students, waged a fierce struggle against the pro-Russian members in power in his own party. This was the famous cultural revolution of 1966–1969. By this Mao hoped to whip up the unbounded enthusiasm of the Chinese masses to work harder while enduring a simple life.

Yet Mao, before his death in 1976, had not achieved power without causing much bloodshed. Although at times people found him sensitive and very dedicated to what he regarded as unfairness, he was also capable of many injustices. During the time he managed to conquer most of mainland China, some experts on the subject claimed he had killed as many as a million Chinese whom he regarded as unnecessary or unfit to be ruled by him. His rule did not permit opposition from political parties or a free press. It did allow au-

thorities to jail political prisoners without benefit of protection of law as enjoyed in the United States.   Adapted from: Jerome Ch'en, "Mao," *The McGraw-Hill Encyclopedia of World Biography*, Vol. 7. New York: McGraw-Hill, 1973.

1. What group of people did Mao look to for most of his support? Explain.
2. How did Mao manage to stay in power? Do you agree with his method? Why or why not?
3. What do you think allows someone like Mao to gain and maintain such political power?

691

75. Jomo Kenyatta

Jomo Kenyatta (JOE-moe ken-YAH-tah) was born in Kenya, the son of a Kikuyu (kih-KOO-yoo) farmer. Little is known of the early years of his life. He served as an interpreter to the Kenya Supreme Court, and then was employed by the water department of the Nairobi Town Council. It is said that his name, Kenyatta, is derived from the Kikuyu word for the beaded belt he wore while at work.

A particularly vital problem to the Kikuyu was the question of land ownership within the colony. They held that the British had unjustly seized much Kikuyu land. Various political organizations were formed to advance their case. Kenyatta, as one of the few educated Kikuyu, naturally participated in their work.

In 1927, Kenyatta was asked to become the general secretary of the Kikuyu Central Association, a position which he accepted in early 1928. In 1929, the Kikuyu Central Association decided to send Kenyatta to London to present their claims on the land problem and other issues to the British government. He had little success, but the European experience was valuable.

Jomo Kenyatta asserted the right of Africans to speak for themselves, and not only through the foreign anthropologists or missionaries. More important, he declared that Africans should be proud of their own cultural heritage.

When World War II began, Kenyatta worked in England on a farm in Surrey and lectured to the British army on Africa. He helped the Pan African Federation and organized the fifth Pan African Congress at Manchester in March 1945.

Thus when Kenyatta returned to Kenya in 1946, he was generally recognized by many Africans as the most effective leader for their new moves toward greater freedom. In June 1947, he became president of the most influential African political movement to that time, the Kenya African Union. But despite his considerable success, many Africans became increasingly frustrated by their lack of progress, and extremist groups began to prepare for a direct challenge to European domination.

Kenyatta was unable to control the extremists. By 1952 the violence had risen to such a level, particularly in the so-called Mau Mau movement,* that the British reacted by declaring a state of emergency. Kenyatta was arrested on October 20.

A world-famous trial for Kenyatta was held in November 1952. The government aimed to prove that Mau Mau was a part of the Kenya African Union. The judgment of the court in April 1953 gave Kenyatta and five other defendants the maximum sentence of seven years at hard labor. Nevertheless, the Mau Mau crisis had forced the British government to realize the uselessness of continuing the development of Kenya through existing colonial government.

Kenyatta was freed in 1961. He assumed the presidency of the Kenya African National Union. In the 1963 elections, Kenyatta led his party to victory. He presided over Kenya's birth as an independent nation in December 1963.

*Mau Mau was a secret terrorist organization, composed of mainly Kikuyu tribesmen, who were bound by oath to drive the white leaders from Kenya.

692

When the country became a republic in 1964, he was its first President.

After independence, Kenyatta led his people on a relatively conservative course for Africa. He worked closely with the Western nations and gave private capital a large role in internal development plans. The European settler problem disappeared, since most of those against African rule left the country. He remained President until his death in 1978, making Kenya one of the most stable countries in Africa. Adapted from: Norman Bennett. "Jomo Kenyatta," *The McGraw-Hill Encyclopedia of World Biography*, Vol. 6. New York: McGraw-Hill, 1973.

1. About how long did Jomo Kenyatta work for Kenya's independence?
2. What was his attitude toward the African past, its culture, and how modern Africans should speak out?
3. How long was Kenyatta president of Kenya?
4. What characteristics did you admire in Kenyatta? Which did you not? Explain. Do you think he was the sort of person who should be the first president of a new nation? Why or why not?

them, what characteristics do you think are important for good leadership? Explain.
3. Do you think the use of biographies in a study of history is worthwhile? Explain why or why not by citing one of the selections as an example.

REVIEWING READINGS 71–75

1. Which people described in Readings 71–75 experienced problems when young or later on in life? Explain your choice. Were these problems overcome? If so, how?
2. All the personalities described in these readings were in some way leaders. Based on what you have read about

The population of your world in 1980 was estimated to be close to 4.5 billion, an increase of over 4 billion people since 3000 B.C.

Pinyin
The New Chinese System of Romanization

As of January 1, 1979, the State Council of China has decided that the Chinese phonetic alphabet, Pinyin, will be used exclusively in China to standardize the romanization of Chinese names and places. The United States government also adopted Pinyin on January 1, 1979. However, because Pinyin respellings have not yet replaced the more familiar spellings of Chinese names under the Wade-Giles system in the media and elsewhere, the Chinese names in this book are spelled according to the Wade-Giles system. Below is a list of the major people and place names used in this book with their new Pinyin spellings. Not all Chinese names have changed, and the State Council has maintained that the traditional spelling of certain historical places and person's names need not be changed. For example, the name *China* will not be changed to the Pinyin version—*Zhongguo*.

WADE-GILES	PINYIN	WADE-GILES	PINYIN
Canton	Guangzhou	*Meng-tzu (Mencius)*	Mengzi
Chao K'uang-yin	Zhao Kuangwin	*Nanking*	Nanjing
Ch'in	Qin	*Pan Chao*	Ban Zhao
Chou	Zhou	*Peking*	Beijing
Chungking	Chongqing	*Shen Nung*	Shen Nong
Chu Yuan-chang	Zhu Yuanzhang	*Shih-huang-ti*	Shihuangdi
Fu Hsi	Fu Xi	*Sian*	Xian
Hangchow	Hanjzhou	*Si River*	Xi Hi
Hsia	Xia	*Sung*	Song
Hsien-yang	Xian yang	*T'ai Tsung*	Taizong
Huang Ti	Huang Di	*Teng Hsiao-p'ing*	Deng Xiaoping
K'ang-hsi	Kangxi	*Tientsin*	Tianjin
K'ung Fu-tzu (Confucius)	Kongzi	*Ts'ai Yen*	Cai Yan
Lao-tzu	Laozi	*Tsu-Hsi*	Zi Xi
Li Ch'ing Chao	Quinjzhau	*Tz'u Hsi*	Tzi Xi
Li Po	Li Bo	*Wei River*	Wei He
Li Yüan	Li Yuan	*Wu Ti*	Wudi
Loyang	Luoyang	*Yang Chien*	Yang Chian
Manchu	Chinjquing	*Yangtze River*	Chang Jiang
Mao Tse-tung	Mao Zedong	*Yellow River*	Huang He

Glossary

A

Abu Bakr (AH-boo BAH-kur) chosen as the first caliph or supreme ruler of the Islamic Empire after Muhammad's death.

acropolis (uh-KRAHP-uh-lus) means *high city* in Greek.

Akhenaton (ah-keh-NAH-ton) means *he who serves the Aton.* Amenhotep IV, pharaoh of Egypt, took this name.

Alexander the Great in twelve years he created the largest empire known in the ancient world. It extended from Greece and Egypt east to Afghanistan.

Alfonso the king of the African country the Kongo. In 1540, he urged the Portuguese not to involve the Kongo in the slave trade.

Al-Khwarizmi (ahl-kwah-RIZ-mee) a Muslim scholar of the ninth century who organized the Arabic system of numbers and helped lay a foundation for modern algebra.

Allied Powers the name given to Great Britain, France, Serbia, Russia, and later Italy, the United States and thirty other nations as allies during World War I.

alphabet a system of signs that represent sounds of speech.

American Revolution the war for independence between the American colonies and Great Britain during the years 1775 to 1783.

anti-Semitism (an-tie SEM-uh-tiz-um) prejudice against Jews.

apartheid (uh-PAHR-tide) in South Africa, the policy of White supremacy resulting in restriction of Black liberty.

archipelago (ahr-kuh-PEL-uh-goe) a group or chain of islands.

aristocrats the upper class of European societies.

Aristotle (AR-uh-staht-'l) a famous Greek philosopher and a student of Plato.

Astia Muhammad (AHS-tee-uh moo-HAHM-ud) took the throne of Songhai after Sunni Ali's death.

Atlantic Charter a statement of goals agreed upon by President Roosevelt and Prime Minister Churchill on August 14, 1941.

Attila (AT-'l-uh) king of the Huns who attacked France in 451 and Italy in 452.

Augustus (aw-GUS-tus) the name meaning *imperial majesty* that Octavian adopted when he gained sole power of Rome in 27 B.C.

Avicenna (av-uh-SEN-uh)   famous Muslim philosopher and medical doctor from Persia.

Axis Powers   the military alliance during World War II formed by Germany, Italy, and Japan.

B

balance of power   an arrangement of nations in alliances so that one side or nation does not overpower the other.

barter   to exchange goods for other items of equal value rather than for money.

Basil II (BAZ-ul)   emperor of the Byzantine Empire from 976 to 1025.

Berlin Wall   the wall built on the border of East and West Berlin in 1961 by the East German government.

Bill of Rights   a statement guaranteeing certain rights and freedoms and prohibiting the ruler or government from certain practices.

Bismarck, Otto von (BIZ-mahrk)   became Prime Minister of Prussia in 1862.

Bolívar, Simón (buh-LEE-vahr)   Venezuelan leader in the early 1800's who came to be known as the Liberator in South America.

Bolsheviks (BOLE-shuh-viks)   members of the Russian revolutionary Marxist party headed by Lenin.

Book of the Dead   the book containing Egyptian beliefs about death and the hereafter.

Brezhnev, Leonid I. (BREZH-nef)   First Secretary of the Communist party in the Soviet Union.

Bronze Age   the name given to the period from about 3500 B.C. to 1000 B.C. when people learned to mix copper and tin to make bronze.

Buddhism (BOOD-izm)   a religion that teaches that desires are the root of all human suffering.

buffer zone   an area that separates the territory of rival powers.

Byzantine (BIZ-'n-teen) **Empire**   the name of the eastern Roman empire that had its capital in Constantinople.

C

Caesar, Julius (JOOL-yus SEE-zur)   famous Roman general who conquered most of what is now France and Belgium. Caesar was assassinated in 44 B.C. by Roman patricians who feared he wanted absolute power.

Calvinism   the form of Protestantism taught by John Calvin whose message included the doctrine of predestination and stressed hard work.

capital   money invested in land, machines, and other things necessary in starting a new industry.

Carlos, Juan   king of Spain since 1975.

caste system   an Indian system for dividing society. Caste dictated rules for marriage, dress, and work.

Catherine II   tsarina of Russia from 1762 to 1796, known as "the Great."

Catholic Reformation   the effort in the mid-1500's by Catholics to reform the abuses of the Catholic church from within.

Central Powers   the name given to Germany, Austria, Turkey, and Bulgaria who fought together as allies during World War I.

Charlemagne (SHAHR-luh-mane)   French name meaning *Charles the Great*. Charlemagne ruled from 768 to 814 over an empire that included what is now France, Germany, lands east of Germany, and parts of Spain and Italy.

Chiang Kai-shek (jee-AHNG-KIE-SHEK)   leader of the Nationalist party after Sun-Yat-sen's death. He became the leader of Nationalist China (Taiwan) after the Chinese civil war.

Chin Dynasty   established in China by foreign invaders called the Jurchens.

Ch'in (CHIN) **Dynasty**   the dynasty that united China and created the first Chinese empire. Their rule lasted from 256 to 210 B.C.

Chou (JOE) **Dynasty**   the longest dynasty in Chinese history, lasting from 1028 to 256 B.C.

Christianity (kris-chee-AN-uh-tee) the religion founded by Jesus of Nazareth.

Church of England the Christian church in England, created by Henry VIII in order to establish his independence from the pope.

Churchill, Winston prime minister of Great Britain from 1940 to 1945 and 1951 to 1955.

city-state an autonomous state consisting of a city and surrounding territory.

Civil War the war fought between Northern and Southern states of the United States during the years 1861 to 1865.

Classical Age a period of great achievement in Greek culture, peaking around the fifth century B.C.

Cleisthenes (KLIES-thuh-neez) Athenian noble who was one of the leaders of the rebellion against the oligarchy. He restored democracy to Athens.

Clemenceau, Georges (klem-un-SOE) French prime minister who represented France at the Paris Peace Conference at the close of World War I.

Code of Hammurabi the organized record of the laws of King Hammurabi who ruled the Amorites about 1750 B.C. This code is believed to be one of the earliest written records of law.

Code of Justinian the laws of the Roman Empire that were organized at the request of the emperor Justinian in 528. This system of laws preserved the legal advances made by the Romans.

codification (KOD-uh-fuh-KAY-shun) the process of organizing and writing down the laws of a society.

Coercive (koe-UR-siv) **Acts** Four laws that restricted the freedom of the American colonies, passed in 1774 by the British Parliament.

Columbus, Christopher Italian explorer who sailed for Spain. In 1492, he discovered the New World, thinking he had reached Asia.

Common Market the European Economic Community formed in 1957 by France, West Germany, Italy, Belgium, Luxembourg, and The Netherlands. Great Britain, Denmark, and Ireland joined in 1973, and Greece joined in 1981.

communism a system in which all property and goods are owned by the government; goods are shared equally by all the people.

Confucianism (kun-FYOO-shu-niz-um) the way of life developed by the Chinese philosopher Confucius.

Congress of Vienna 1815 meeting in which the European powers decided what to do with defeated France and how to rearrange the map of Europe among the victors.

Constantine (KAHN-stun-teen) Roman emperor who founded the capital, Constantinople (today Istanbul, Turkey).

consuls (KAHN-sulz) chief executives of the ancient Roman government.

Cortés, Hernando (kore-TEZ) Spanish explorer who destroyed the Aztec empire and conquered Mexico in 1521.

Cro-Magnon (kroe-MAG-nun) prehistoric people who are believed to have lived about 35,000 years ago.

Crusades a series of wars fought between the eleventh and the thirteenth centuries by European Christians seeking to recapture Palestine from Muslim control.

culture the art, science, economic activity, religions, beliefs, and government of a society.

cuneiform (kyoo-NEE-uh-form) the writing system invented by the Sumerians.

Cyrillic (suh-RIL-ik) **alphabet** the alphabet used by all Slavic peoples, including those in the Soviet Union.

Cyrus (SIE-rus) a famous Persian prince and conqueror.

D

da Gama, Vasco (VAHS-coe duh-GAH-muh) Portuguese explorer who sailed to India around the Cape of Good Hope.

Dark Ages the period of European history dating from 500 to 1000 A.D.

David king of the Hebrews from 1004 to 965 B.C.

Declaration of Independence the statement of grievances published by the American Second Continental Congress on July 4, 1776.

Declaration of the Rights of Man the document written by the French National Assembly in 1789 ending the special privileges held by the nobility and the clergy and granting equality to all citizens.

De Gaulle, General Charles (duh-GOLE) leader of the Free French army during World War II and President of France from 1959 to 1969.

Delian (DEE-lee-un) **League** the alliance of Greek city-states led by Athens.

democracy (dih-MAHK-ruh-see) a form of government in which the supreme power is held by the people or by the representatives they have elected.

demographers scientists who study population patterns.

despots (DES-puts) rulers who ignore the rights and interests of their subjects.

detente (day-TAHNT) a policy in the 1970's between the Soviet Union and the United States by which both nations tried to improve relations.

di Cavour, Count Camillo (kuh-MEE-loe dee kuh-VOOR) Prime Minister of the Kingdom of Sardinia and a leader in the Italian unification movement.

Diocletian (die-uh-KLEE-shun) Roman emperor from 284 to 305 A.D. who divided the empire into two areas of power, each ruled by an emperor.

Directory the name of the French government from 1795 to 1799.

dynasty (DIE-nuh-stee) a family of rulers in which power is passed from one generation to the next within the family.

E

Elizabeth I Tudor Queen of England who ruled from 1558 to 1603.

embargo a government action barring its citizens from trading with another nation or nations.

empire a large territory or group of territories held by a nation.

enclosure movement the process whereby English public or common farm and pasture lands were sold to large landowners and fenced (enclosed).

Enlightenment an intellectual movement in the 1700's based on reform and reason.

ephors (EF-urs) the holders of real power in ancient Sparta. The five ephors were elected by the Assembly.

equator the largest circle that is equally distant from the two poles and divides the earth into two parts, the northern and southern hemispheres.

estates the term used to define the three social classes in France before the French Revolution.

Estates-General the name of the French parliament under the king before the French Revolution.

ethical monotheism a belief that combines the worship of only one God and ethics.

ethics (ETH-iks) the principles of proper conduct, or of right and wrong.

F

fascism (FASH-iz-um) a political idea that glorifies one race and nation and government by dictatorship.

federal republic under this form of government, individual states or provinces govern their internal matters and delegate other powers and responsibilities to a central government.

federation (fed-uh-RAY-shun) a form of government in which power is divided between a central government and local governments.

Fertile Crescent the arc of rich, well-watered land stretching from the Mediterranean Sea to the mouth of the Tigris and Euphrates rivers on the Persian Gulf.

feudalism a system of exchanging land for military service.

First Triumvirate (trie-UM-vahr-it) the informal alliance of Caesar, Pompey, and Crassus that ruled the Roman Empire from 60 to 43 B.C.

Fourteen Points proposals presented by President Woodrow Wilson in January 1918 as a basis for keeping the peace after World War I.

free enterprise an economic system based on the belief that businesses will thrive when they are allowed to operate with a minimum of government interference or assistance.

French and Indian War the war between France and England fought in North America between 1756 and 1763.

Fujiwara (FOO-JEE-WAH-RAH) a noble clan who wielded the real power in Japanese government from about 800 to 1100.

G

Gallic (GAL-ik) **Wars** the campaigns of the Romans led by Julius Caesar into what are now France and Belgium.

Gandhi, Indira (in-DIR-uh GAHN-dee) was Prime Minister of India from 1966 to 1978 and again re-elected in 1980.

Gandhi, Mahatma (muh-HAHT-muh GAHN-dee) (also known as Mohandas) Indian leader who fought for Indian independence from Great Britain through the use of nonviolent resistance. He tried to unite Hindus and Muslims in India.

Genghis Khan (GENG-guh-SKAHN) the warrior-leader who united the Mongols and built a great empire.

geographers people who study the surface of the earth.

George, David Lloyd British prime minister and representative to the Paris Peace Conference after World War I.

Glorious Revolution the bloodless English revolution in 1688. This revolution established that English monarchs ruled by the consent of the governed, not by divine right.

Good Neighbor Policy U.S. foreign policy developed by President Franklin Roosevelt toward Latin America.

Great Leap Forward the name given to Mao Tse-tung's plan to industrialize China rapidly during the 1950's.

Gupta (GOOP-tuh) **Empire** an empire in northern India lasting from about 320 to 500 A.D.

H

Han Dynasty ruled China from 202 B.C. to 220 A.D.

Hatshepsut (hat-SHEP-soot) pharaoh of Egypt from 1500 to 1480 B.C.

Hausa one of the largest ethnic groups of Nigeria.

Hellenistic (hel-uh-NISS-tik) **Age** the period from 323 to 133 B.C. in which Greek culture spread and mixed with eastern cultures.

helots (HEL-utz) in Sparta, the laboring class of people who did most of the work.

hieratic (hie-RAT-ik) a simpler form of writing that evolved from hieroglyphics. This writing was used by Egyptians for record keeping and legal papers.

hieroglyphic (hie-ruh-GLIF-ik) the earliest form of Egyptian writing that dates back to 3000 B.C.

Hinduism (HIN-doo-iz-um) a religion that teaches that the human soul never dies but is born again and again in different bodies. Hindus believe in many gods.

historic the period of time when people began to write and keep records.

Hitler, Adolf Nazi leader who was dictator of Germany from 1933 to 1945.

Holocaust means a great destruction of life. It is the word used by Jews to refer to Hitler's extermination of about 6 million European Jews in concentration camps during World War II.

Holy Roman Empire the domain of Otto I, who ruled from 936 to 973. Otto added the word *Holy* to show the lands were Christian.

Homer Greek poet who around 750–700 B.C. wrote the *Iliad* and the *Odyssey* based on the legends about the Trojan War.

Hsia (SHYAH) **Dynasty** believed to be the first dynasty in China. Legends date the dynasty from 2200 to 1500 B.C.

I

Ibos large, well-educated ethnic group in Nigeria.

imperialism a policy involving the expansion of a country's borders, the spread of its culture, and the economic or political domination of people in other areas.

Industrial Revolution the name given to the changes in manufacturing, trade, and economic life that began in England during the 1700's and spread to Europe and North and South America in the 1800's.

inflation an economic condition that exists when the value of money declines or the prices of goods increase.

Iron Age the period after 1000 B.C. during which iron replaced bronze as the primary metal used in tools and weapons.

Iron Curtain the name of the invisible boundary between western European nations favoring U.S. policies and eastern European nations favoring those of the Soviet Union.

Isabella Queen of Spain who, with her husband King Ferdinand, defeated the last of the Muslims in Spain and united the country. She financed the voyages of Christopher Columbus.

Islam (ISS-lahm) Arabic word meaning *submission to God.* It is the name of the religion based on the teachings of the prophet Muhammad as written in the Koran.

Ivan III Tsar of Russia, also known as Ivan the Great, who ruled from 1462 to 1505 and expanded Russian territory.

Ivan IV Tsar of Russia from 1533 to 1584, known as "the Terrible."

J

Jacobin (JAK-uh-buhn) the French revolutionary group whose goal was to overthrow the monarchy and provide greater justice and opportunity to the common people.

Jesuits (JEZH-uh-wutz) priests of the Society of Jesus, an organization founded by Ignatius Loyola.

Jesus (JEE-zus) founder of the Christian religion. He lived in Palestine from about 4 B.C. to 30 A.D.

Joan of Arc French peasant girl who claimed she was divinely inspired to lead French soldiers to victory in their struggle with England.

Judeo-Christian tradition the combination of Hebrew and Christian teachings and philosophies.

K

Khrushchev, Nikita (KROOSH-choff) Premier of the Soviet Union from 1958 to 1964.

Kikuyu (kee-KOO-yoo) a people of the African country Kenya.

Koran (kuh-RAN) the holy scriptures of the Islamic faith.

Kublai Khan (koo-blie-KAHN) grandson of Genghis Khan. He founded the Mongol Dynasty in 1271.

L

League of Nations the association of nations proposed by Woodrow Wilson and established in Geneva, Switzerland after World War I.

Legislative Assembly the name of the representative law-making body created in the new French constitution written by the National Assembly in 1791.

Lenin (LEN-un) the name used by Vladimir Ilich Ulyanov, 1870–1924, Russian revolutionary leader who was the chief leader of the 1917 Revolution and head of the new Soviet government from 1917 to 1924.

Leo III emperor of the Byzantine Empire from 717 to 714.

Louis XIV the "Sun King" of France who reigned from 1643 to 1715.

M

Machiavellianism (mak-ee-uh-VEL-ee-un-izm) political behavior based on the ideas of Machiavelli in *The Prince.*

Magna Carta also known as the Great Charter, this was first document signed in England limiting the power of the king and guaranteeing certain rights to the people.

Manchu or Ching Dynasty a dynasty founded by invaders from Manchuria. It lasted from 1674 to 1912.

Mansa Musa ruler of the vast West African empire of Mali from 1312 to 1337.

Mao Tse-tung (MOW-DZU-DOONG) Chairman of the People's Republic of China from 1949 until his death in 1976.

Marx, Karl (MAHRKS) nineteenth century socialist whose theories became the basis for communism today. He wrote *Das Kapital* and the *Communist Manifesto.*

Maurya (MOW-ree-uh) **Empire** the first empire in India ruled by Indians rather than by foreign invaders. The empire lasted from about 322 to 185 B.C.

medieval (meed-ee-EE-vul) meaning *middle.* The term used to describe the period of European history dating from 500 to 1500 A.D.

Mensheviks (MEN-shuh-viks) members of a Russian revolutionary Marxist party. Though the name means minority party, the Mensheviks had more followers than Lenin's competing Bolshevik faction.

mercantilism an economic policy developed by European colonial powers in the fifteenth century, the goal of which was a self-sufficient system in which the colony supplied raw materials and the colonizing nation completed finished goods.

meridians lines drawn on the globe from the North Pole to the South Pole.

meridians of longitude distances east and west of the prime meridian.

Mesopotamia (mes-oe-poe-TAY-mee-uh) the Greek name given to the fertile valley that lies between the Tigris and Euphrates rivers.

Metternich (MET-ur-nik) Austrian foreign minister at the Congress of Vienna in 1815 who wanted to restore rulers overthrown by Napoleon to their thrones and to prevent other popular revolutions.

Middle Ages the period of European history falling between the ancient and modern periods. Also referred to as the medieval period. It lasted from 500 to 1500 A.D.

Middle Kingdom the period of ancient Egyptian history dating from 2050 to 1792 B.C.

Ming Dynasty the last native Chinese dynasty, which lasted from 1368 to 1644.

Mogul (MOE-gul) **Empire** an empire in India that lasted from the 1500's to the 1700's.

monarchy (MAHN-ur-kee) a country that is ruled by a king or a queen.

Mongol Dynasty also known as the Yüan Dynasty, lasted from 1271 to 1368.

monotheism (MAHN-uh-thee-iz-um) the belief that there is only one God.

Monroe Doctrine statement of U.S. foreign policy issued by President James Monroe in 1823 that warned European nations against attempts at colonization or interference in the Western Hemisphere.

Montezuma (mahn-tuh-ZOOM-uh) ruler of the Aztec Indians when Cortés invaded Mexico.

Mosaic law (moe-ZAH-ik) consists of the Ten Commandments and other ancient Hebrew laws attributed to Moses.

mosque (MAHSK) a Muslim place of worship and prayer.

Muhammad the prophet who taught he was God's messenger spreading the religion, Islam.

Muslims (MUZ-lums) believers in the religion Islam.

Mussolini, Benito (moo-suh-LEE-nee) leader of the Fascist party and dictator of Italy from 1922 to 1943.

N

Napoleon Bonaparte (BOE-nuh-pahrt) Corsican-born, French General who in 1978 seized control of France and in 1804 declared himself emperor.

Napoleon III the name taken by Louis Napoleon, nephew of Napoleon I, when he changed the French Second Republic into the Second Empire in 1852.

National Assembly the name of the French parliament formed during the French Revolution.

National Convention the French assembly that replaced the Legislative Assembly in September 1792.

nationalism the sense of unity felt by people who share the same history, language, and culture.

Nazis the National Socialist German Workers party.

Neanderthal (nee-AN-dur-thal) early people believed to have lived about 120,000–75,000 years ago in the Neanderthal Valley in Germany.

Nebuchadnezzar (neb-uh-kud-NEZ-ur) a ruler of the Chaldeans around 600 B.C.

Nehru, Jawaharlal (jah-wuh-HAHR-lal NAY-roo) India's first prime minister, from 1950 until 1964.

Nelson, Admiral Horatio Commander of the British fleet who defeated Napoleon twice in important naval battles and assured Britian's undisputed control of the seas.

Neolithic (nee-uh-LITH-ik) **Age** see New Stone Age.

New Kingdom the period of ancient Egyptian history dating from 1570 to 1090 B.C.

New Stone Age also called the Neolithic Age. Era in which people began to farm and improve their tools.

nomads (NOE-mads) wanderers who lived by hunting animals and gathering wild plants.

North Atlantic Treaty Organization (NATO) alliance system formed in 1949 composed of the United States, Canada, and the nations of Western Europe.

O

Old Kingdom the period of ancient Egyptian history dating from 2850 to 2200 B.C.

Old Regime a term used to describe the French government, society, and life in the 1700's before the French Revolution and the rule of Napoleon.

oligarchy (OHL-uh-gahr-kee) a small group of people, usually wealthy landowners, who ruled Greek city-states sometime between 800 and 600 B.C.

Organization of American States (OAS) formed in 1948, all countries in North and South America except Canada and Cuba are members of this organization.

Orlando, Vittorio (or-LAN-doe) Italian prime minister who represented Italy at the Paris Peace Conference following World War I.

ostracism (AHS-truh-siz-um) a practice of forced exile developed by the Athenians as a way of keeping any one person from becoming too powerful.

Owen, Robert Welsh utopian socialist, who felt that an economic system based on joint ownership and cooperation would allow people's better nature to emerge.

P

Pan-Slavism a feeling among Eastern European Slavic peoples that all Slavic peoples should help each other.

parallels of latitude lines drawn east to west that are parallel to the equator.

parliament (PAHR-luh-ment) representative assemblies or councils.

patriarchs (PAY-tree-ahrks) the important archbishops of the Eastern Christian church.

patricians (puh-TRISH-unz) the name given to the class of wealthy nobles in ancient Rome.

pax Romana (PAKS roe-MAH-nah) means *the peace of Rome*. The phrase is used to describe the two hundred year period of peace and prosperity within the Roman Empire.

peaceful coexistence a policy of economic competition rather than military confrontation between the Soviet Union and the United States.

Peloponnesian (pel-uh-puh-NEE-zhun) **League** the military alliance of Greek city-states lead by Sparta.

Pericles (PER-uh-kleez) leader of Athens at the height of its power in the mid-400's B.C.

periocei (PER-ee-oe-sie) non-Dorian people of neighboring areas who handled the economic matters of the Spartans.

Peter the Great Peter I, tsar of Russia from 1682 to 1725.

pharaoh (FEHR-oe) the term used for the supreme ruler-god of ancient Egypt.

Philip of Macedonia (mass-uh-DOE-nee-uh) king from 359 to 336 B.C. who came to control all important Greek city-states except Sparta and thus helped prepare the way for the expansion of Greek culture.

Pilgrims a group of Puritans who left England to find religious freedom.

Pizarro, Francisco (pee-ZAHR-oe) Spanish explorer who defeated the Incas.

Plato (PLAY-toe) pupil of Socrates who wrote a series of dialogues. His most famous work, the *Republic*, describes the ideal society.

plebeians (plih-BEE-yunz) the second class of ancient Rome. Members of this large class included farmers, artisans, and merchants.

prehistoric relating to the time before written history.

prime meridian the meridian of 0° longitude that runs through Greenwich, England.

prime minister chief minister to the king.

Proclamation of 1763 law prohibiting colonists from moving west of the Appalachian mountains.

prophets (PRAHF-uts) a term among the ancient Hebrews meaning a great religious thinker and teacher.

Protestants the name given to supporters of Martin Luther who protested against abuses of the Catholic church.

province (PRAHV-untz) a governmental unit.

Pueblo Revolt the 1680 rebellion by Pueblo Indians against Spanish colonial rule.

Punic (PYOO-nik) **Wars** the three wars fought by Rome and Carthage during the period 264–146 B.C.

Puritanism a form of Protestantism that developed in the sixteenth century.

Q

Quebec Act law that placed the land north of the Ohio River under the control of Quebec and restored French civil law in that region.

R

rabbi (RAB-ie) a teacher of the Hebrew holy writings.

Rameses II (RAM-seez) a king of ancient Egypt who died about 1212 B.C.

Reformation the movement started by Martin Luther in the early 1500's that sought to reform certain abuses in the Catholic church.

reincarnation (REE-in-kahr-NAY-shun) the belief that the human soul will be reborn in another body.

Renaissance (ren-uh-SAHNTS) rebirth or renewal of interest in learning, the arts, and culture.

republic (ree-PUB-lik) a government in which power rests with all the citizens who are entitled to vote.

Revolution of 1830 the French revolution in which Charles X was overthrown and a limited monarchy headed by Louis Philippe was created.

Richelieu, Cardinal (RISH-uh-loo) chief minister of France during the reign of Louis XIII.

Roosevelt, Franklin D. President of the United States from 1933 to 1945.

S

samurai (SAM-UH-RIE) Japanese warriors who eventually became a separate class in Japanese society.

San Martín, Jose Francisco de South American leader who helped Chile become independent in 1818 and Peru in 1821.

Sanskrit the name of the written language of the Aryans.

satrap (SAY-trap) a government official who was responsible for ruling a province of the Persian Empire.

Saul (SAWL) leader of the Hebrews from 1020 to 1004 B.C.

Schmidt, Helmut (HEL-mut SHMIT) chancellor of West Germany, 1974–1982.

scribes highly valued secretaries of ancient Egypt who kept records.

Second Republic the government of France formed in 1848 after the king, Louis Philippe, was forced from power.

Second Triumvirate an alliance formed in 43 B.C., after Caesar's death, by Mark Antony, Octavian, and Lepidus.

self-determination the right of a people with a common background to form their own nation and to select their own government.

Shakespeare, William one of the world's most famous playwrights who lived during the reign of Elizabeth I.

Shang (SHAHNG) **Dynasty** ruled China from about 1500 to 1028 B.C.

shogun (SHOE-GUN) a title granted by the Japanese emperor meaning *chief general*. The position later became a hereditary one.

shogunate (SHOE-gun-ate) the form of Japanese government in which the shogun had the actual power and the emperor was a figurehead.

socialism a political and economic system in which the government represents the people, owns and operates the land and companies, and handles the distribution of goods.

Socrates (SAWK-ruh-teez) the famous Greek philosopher who lived from 469 to 399 B.C. His method of constantly questioning beliefs in order to discover truth and knowledge is called the Socratic method of inquiry.

Solomon (SAHL-uh-mun) king of the Hebrews from 965 to 933 B.C., known for his wisdom.

Solon (SOE-lun) Athenian merchant who ruled Athens from 594 to 561 B.C.

Spanish Armada (AHR-MAHD-uh) the fleet of ships sent by Spain to invade England in the 1580's.

sphere of influence an area dominated by a foreign power and treated like a colony without being annexed officially.

Stalin, Josef (STAHL-un) ruthless Soviet leader who held absolute power over the U.S.S.R. from 1927 to 1953.

Stamp Act law passed by the British Parliament in 1765 requiring that a tax be paid and a special stamp be placed on all legal documents in the American colonies.

staple crop a food that is used widely and continually. Wheat, barley, and rice are examples of staple crops.

Sui (SWAY) **Dynasty** reunited northern and southern China in 589 A.D.

sultan (SULL-t'n) the title taken by the Muslim rulers of India.

Sung (SOONG) **Dynasty** a Chinese dynasty that lasted from 960 to 1279 A.D.

Sunni Ali (SOON-ee AH-lee) Muslim ruler of the West African empire of Songhai around 1464.

Sun Yat-sen (SOON YAHT-SEN) Chinese revolutionary who is known as the father of Chinese nationalism.

synagogue (SIN-ih-gahg) a meeting place for Hebrew worship and learning.

T

T'ang (TAHNG) **Dynasty** Chinese dynasty from 618 to 906 A.D.

Taoism (DOW-iz-um) a school of philosophy founded by the Chinese philosopher Lao-tzu.

Teng Hsiao-p'ing (DAHNG SHOW-PING) Vice-premier of the People's Republic of China.

Thatcher, Margaret Britain's first woman prime minister, elected in 1979.

theocracy (thee-AHK-ruh-see) a government in which leaders of the church are also the officials of the government.

Thirty Years' War fought between 1618 and 1648 for religious and political reasons.

Thutmose III (TOOT-mose) ruled Egypt from 1480 to 1448 B.C.

Tokugawa (TOE-KUH-GAH-WAH) the clan that reunited Japan in 1603 after the country had been divided by civil wars for 200 years.

Trafalgar, Battle of (truh-FAL-gur) naval battle in 1805 that ended Napoleon's ideas of invading England.

Triple Alliance military alliance of Germany, Austria, and Italy.

Triple Entente (ahn-TAHNT) military alliance made up of Great Britain, France, and Russia.

Tutankhamun (too-tang-KAHM-un) the boy-king of ancient Egypt who ruled from 1361 to 1352 B.C. The discovery of his tomb in 1922 has made him famous.

tyrants (TIE-runtz) rulers who use their power unjustly or oppressively.

U

United Nations the association of nations formed after World War II, replacing the League of Nations.

V

vassals in a feudal system, people who, in return for land, provide military service for their superiors.

Vedas (VAY-duhz) the earliest religious books of the Aryans.

Vergil (VUR-jul) famous Roman poet who lived from 70 to 19 B.C.

veto (VEET-oe) the right of one branch of government to say no or to stop another branch of government from taking a particular action.

vizier (vuh-ZIR) second in command after the pharaoh in ancient Egypt.

W

Warsaw Pact the alliance system formed in 1955 composed of the Soviet Union and most East European nations.

Watergate Affair the 1972 attempted burglary of Democratic party campaign headquarters ordered by members of the Republican reelection committee, and the subsequent coverup of this and other illegal activities that implicated President Richard Nixon.

Waterloo the Belgian village where English and Prussian armies defeated Napoleon in 1815.

welfare state a term applied when a government actively intervenes in the social and economic affairs of its citizens in order to maintain a certain standard of living.

Wilson, Woodrow President of the United States from 1913 to 1921.

writ of habeas corpus a document protecting an individual from illegal imprisonment.

Wu, Empress the first woman ruler in Chinese history. She ruled China from 690 to 705 A.D. after her husband's death.

Y

Yahweh (YAH-way) the Hebrew name for the God they worshipped.

Yalta Conference the meeting held in Russia in February 1945 at which Roosevelt, Churchill, and Stalin committed the U.S., Great Britain, and the Soviet Union to help European nations after World War II.

Yamato (YAH-MAH-TOE) **State** the Japanese government founded by the Yamato clan around 400 to 500 A.D.

Yüan (YOOAHN) **Dynasty** the Chinese name taken by Kublai Khan for the dynasty he founded, which is also known as the Mongol Dynasty.

Z

ziggurats (ZIG-uh-ratz) Sumerian temples built of sun-dried mud that stood several stories tall.

Zoroastrianism (zore-uh-WASS-tree-uh-niz-um) a religion that was started by an ancient Persian prophet named Zoroaster in the seventh century.

Zoser (ZOE-sir) the pharaoh of ancient Egypt for whom the first pyramid was built around 2600 B.C.

Index

709

Art and Photo Credits

277—HRW collection. 278—The Bettmann Archive.

Unit 6: Unit Opener—287—Lee Boltin, Museum of Primitive Art. 291—Norman Myers. 293—Document Mission of Henri Lhote. 295—George Rodger/Magnum. 298—Trustees of the British Museum. 300—Brooklyn Museum. 303—Marc and Evelyn Bernheim/Woodfin Camp. 305—Rhodesian National Tourist Office. 306—Marc and Evelyn Bernheim/Woodfin Camp. 307—After a drawing by Dr. Repin, 1856; first appearing in J. A. Skertchly's *Dahomey As It Is.* 309—New York Public Library. 311—New York Public Library. 312—Williams, John, *Africa Her History, Landscape and People.* 314—New York Public Library. 315—Liberian Consulate.

Unit 7: Unit Opener—323—National Maritime Museum, Greenwich. 327—HRW photo by Richard Weiss. 331—Museum of the American Indian. 333—American Museum of Natural History. 335—HRW photo by Richard Weiss. 337—HRW photo by Richard Weiss. 338—American Museum of Natural History. 345—American Museum of Natural History. 353—State Capitol, Bismarck, N.D. 358—Woolaroc Museum, Bartesville, Okla.

Unit 8: Unit Opener—363—Musée Carnavalet, Giraudon. 367—The Bettmann Archive. 373—New York Public Library. 377—Segelat, Paris. 378—Museum of Fine Arts, Brussels, EPA/Scala. 379—Museé de la Legion d'Honneur. 381—Louvre, EPA/Scala. 383—Giraudon. 388—Giraudon. 391—New York Public Library, Schoemberg Collection. 392—HRW Collection. 398—HRW Collection. 404—*Harper's Monthly,* 1858. 405—Albany Institute of History and Art. 406—HRW Collection. 408—Doré, G., *London, A Pilgrimage,* 1872. 409—George Eastman House. 415—Library of Congress. 414—The Bettmann Archive. 419—New York Public Library Picture Collection. 422—Russian Museum, Sovfoto. 423—The Bettmann Archive.

424—Sovfoto. 426—A la Vielle Russie. 427—Sovfoto.

Unit 9: Unit Opener—433—Library of Congress. 438—HRW Collection. 439—Museo Nazionale del Risorgimento, EPA/Scala. 440—Culver Pictures. 442—George Eastman House. 443—History Museum, Chapultepec, Mexico. 445—Peabody Museum of Salem. 447—The Bettmann Archive. 448—Jack Willis, *Life,* 1957, Time Inc. 450—The Bettmann Archive. 453—New York Public Library. 455—The Bettmann Archives. 457—Peabody Museum of Salem. 465—Museum of the City of New York. 466—Culver Pictures. 468—Frank Darmsteader, Jewish Theological Seminary of America. 469—The Bettmann Archive. 471—Culver Pictures. 474—Imperial War Museum. 476—United Press International. 479—Imperial War Museum. 485—The Bettmann Archive. 486—Margaret Bourke-White, *Life,* 1960, Time Inc. 490—United Press International. 494—Wide World. 495—National Archives. 497—Black Star. 499—Library of Congress. 505—U.S. Air Force. 506—F.D.R. Library. 508—Wide World.

Unit 10: Unit Opener—515—Shelley Katz, Black Star. 517—Map reprinted from *The Japanese,* by Edwin O. Reischauer. Cambridge, Mass: The Belknap Press of Harvard University Press, 1977. 519—The Bettmann Archive. 520—United Press International. 522—HRW Collection. 523—United Press International. 525—David Burnett/CONTACT Stock Images; NASA. 527—John Ficara/Woodfin Camp. 534—Black Star. 537—United Press International. 539—P. J. Griffiths/Magnum. 541—Chuck Fishman/Contact Stock Images. 543—Sygma. 546—Sygma. 547—Sygma. 548—Wide World. 549—Sygma. 551—Dennis Brack/Black Star. 553—Wide World. 556—Philip Teuscher. 560—Henri Bureau/Sygma. 561—J. P. Lafont/Sygma. 563—Wide World. 564—Don Goode, Sygma. 565—Peace Corps. 567—Sygma.

568—Sipa/Black Star. 570—Wide World. 571—Argles-Sipa/Black Star. 573—Wide World. 576—Black Star. 577—United Press International. 578—Wide World. 581—Max Scheler/Black Star. 583—New York Public Library. 585—The Bettmann Archive. 586—Black Star. 587—United Press International. 589—W. Campbell/ Sygma. 591—W. Campbell/Sygma. 592— W. Campbell/Sygma. 593—United Press International. 596—Arthur Grace/Sygma.

Book of Readings: 607—The Granger Collection. 611—Private Collection. 615— Freer Gallery of Art. 621—Museo Nazionale, Naples, EPA/Scala. 625—Communal Library, Forli, Italy, EPA/Scala. 631— Vatican, EPA/Scala. 639—Edinburgh University Library. 645—Trustees of the British Museum. 657—American Museum of Natural History. 661—Musee Carnavalet, Giraudon. 665—Royal Holloway College. 669—Sovfoto. 673—Peabody Museum of Salem. 677—Library of Congress. 682—Herbert Orth, Life Picture Service. 685—Wide World. 687—Simon Pietri/Sygma. 689—Larry Downing/ Woodfin Camp. 691—Sygma. 693—Sygma.

Maps: *General Cartography, Inc.*

Front cover: top row, left to right: *Neil Armstrong*, NASA; *Alexander the Great in the Battle of Issus* mosaic, Alinari; *Ginevra Bentivoglio* by Ercole Roberti, National Gallery of Art, Washington, D.C., Samuel H. Kress Collection; *Edward VI as a Child* by Hans Holbein, National Gallery of Art, Washington, D.C., Andrew W. Mellon Collection; bottom row, left to right: *Napoleon as First Consul*, Musee de Legion d'Honneur, Paris; *Ife Bronze Head*, Nigeria, Africa, British Museum; *Portrait of the Chinese Emperor K'ang Hsi*, Metropolitan Museum of Art, Rogers Fund, 1942; *Queen Hat-shepsut*, Metropolitan Museum of Art, Rogers Fund.

Back cover: top row, left to right: *Caroline Remy* by August Renoir. National Gallery of Art, Washington, D.C., Chester Dale Collection; *Oh nee Yeath Ton no Rion*, American Indian chief, British Museum; *Portrait of a Lady* by Roger van der Weyden, National Gallery of Art, Washington, D.C., Andrew W. Mellon Collection; second row, left to right: *Jomo Kenyatta*, photo by William Campbell, Sygma; Indian miniature of *The Love of Krishna*, Victoria and Albert Museum: *Reliquary Bust of Charlemagne* from Aachen photo by R. J. Segalat; *Portrait of a Couple from Pompeii*, Alinari; bottom row, left to right: *World War I poster*, Library of Congress; *Golda Meir*, photo by Simon Pietri, Sygma: *Mosaic of Justinian* from the Church of San Vitale, Ravenna, photo courtesty of the Italian Cultural Institute; *Japanese Woman*, Freer Gallery of Art, Washington, D.C.

S